Basic Airman to General: The Secret War & Other Conflicts

Basic Airman to General: The Secret War & Other Conflicts

Lessons in Leadership & Life

General "Pete" Piotrowski

To order additional copies of this book, contact:
Xlibris LLC
1-888-795-4274
www.Xlibris.com
Orders@Xlibris.com
540465

CONTENTS

DEDICATION

I dedicate this book to my lovely and wonderful wife, Sheila, who agreed to marry this wild-eyed and underpaid captain assigned to a clandestine Air Commando unit with an uncertain future. As the result of a one-day notification of a classified assignment to Southeast Asia that ruined our wedding plans, we were married over the telephone. Sheila excelled as a mother and air force wife, raising three children through nineteen moves while supporting me as a gracious hostess. Moreover, our youngest child, Jon, was born with tuberous sclerosis (TS). TS is a regressive disease that causes severe retardation and seizures as a person ages. She carried this burden selflessly while I was away on three combat tours in Vietnam. While caring for our children, she still managed to excel in supporting air force families under my command, while their spouses were deployed to numerous trouble spots throughout the world. Moreover, it seemed like I was on temporary duty (TDY) more than I was at home to assist her in raising our family. Like the words in the song, Sheila was the "wind beneath my wings"! After fifty-two years, she is, as always, the love of my life and my dearest friend.

ACKNOWLEDGMENTS

Many individuals who were successful were very influential in motivating me and helping me along the way as I pursued my air force career. I take this opportunity to identify the most influential and thank them for their help.

One of the most important was Sergeant Sams, the drill instructor who shaped my life during the twelve weeks of basic training and taught me that honor, integrity, and hard work were the keys to succeed in the air force.

Brig. Gen. Ben King, the first commander of Jungle Jim and subsequently the First Air Commando Group, demonstrated superb hands on inspirational leadership of this all-volunteer combat unit and led us in everything we did, including flying across the Western Pacific Ocean in single-engine propeller aircraft. He also led us in combat in Vietnam, his third war. He was an inspiration and role model for the remainder of my career.

Maj. Edwin W. Robertson II, then commander of the 36th TFW, Bitburg, Germany, who struggled hard to teach me to be a good deputy commander for operations, was another example of an outstanding wing commander.

Gen. William V. McBride, then USAFE vice commander, interviewed me for my first command and recommended me for command of the Fortieth Tactical Group at Aviano, Italy. Following my assignment at Aviano, General McBride followed up with a couple of visits to Aviano to provide on-scene guidance that was extremely helpful.

Maj. Gen. Edwin A. McGough III, commander of Sixteenth Air Force, Torrejon, Spain, while I was commanding the Fortieth Tactical Group, was my immediate commander and made several visits to Aviano to mentor me. Most importantly, he taught me how to listen and that listening was the most important part of communication.

Gen. Robert J. Dixon, commander TAC, selected me to be the initial commander of the 552nd AWAC Wing being equipped with the revolutionary E-3A aircraft. Building the wing from scratch to combat status with global span was an enormous challenge.

Gen. Wilbur L. Creech was influential in providing insightful guidance on leadership and for selecting me for a number of command assignments, including ADTAC (now First Air Force), TAC director of operations, TAC vice commander with a promotion to lieutenant general, and Ninth Air Force.

Gen. David C. Jones, Air Force chief of staff and chairman of the Joint Chiefs of Staff, for selecting me to accompany him on a critical visit to several PACAF air bases and then to be his troubleshooter to many air force bases experiencing problems stemming from racial unrest.

Gen. Charles C. Gabriel for selecting me to be his vice chief of staff, promoting me to the rank of general, and allowing me to assist him in running the United States Air Force, as well as subbing for him in JCS sessions.

Further, I'm indebted to all the officers and enlisted personnel I served with and had the pleasure of commanding throughout my thirty-eight-year-long air force career. My success rests on the shoulders of dedicated hardworking professionals who were making all the right things happen no matter how difficult the task or formidable the environment. Many of their names are mentioned throughout this odyssey from airman basic to four-star general.

CHAPTER 1

The Early Years

It was 1941 when my mother passed away; I don't remember the day or the month. I was only seven at the time and spent more time missing her than on temporal things. Shortly thereafter, the Japanese struck Pearl Harbor, the naval base just outside Honolulu, Oahu. The war came and my father, a police officer in Detroit, Michigan, and formerly a sailor serving on a destroyer in WW I, quickly became very busy. In addition to his police duties, he supported the war effort by delivering army trucks from production lines to railheads or army camps in the tristate area. He tried to reenlist but was disqualified for his age and his police-officer duties. My older sister and I didn't see very much of him during the war years. He barely had enough off-duty time to remarry and start a second family. By the time I left home for military service during the Korean War, there were nine children; four girls, including my older sister, and five boys. I delivered papers, worked as a stock boy in one of the early chain grocery stores at night and on weekends, and babysat for my younger siblings. There wasn't much time for play or getting in trouble.

We lived in a Polish and Italian neighborhood; Polish families outnumbered Italian families about three to one, so most of my playmates were immigrants and second-generation Polish Americans like me. Mom and Dad both spoke Polish fluently but did not speak it to their children. They didn't want us to grow up with a Slavic accent. Most of my friends who spoke the native tongue had difficulty pronouncing words starting with *th*. The words "them" and "these" came out as "dem" and "dees." My best friend and surrogate older brother was Eugene (Gene) Niedzwicki.

From my earliest memories, Gene was always in my life. He was two-plus years older than me and therefore a role model and mentor.

Some of my fondest childhood memories came from time spent at the lakeside cottage that my father and uncle purchased in partnership. There was never a conflict sharing the cottage, as no one had that much leisure time during the war years. Following the war, there was a huge economic boom resulting from the pent-up demand for cars and appliances that were out of production during the war. Everyone in Detroit was working long hours and earning a lot of money—making up for the lean years during the Depression. We spent a couple of weeks and a few weekends at the cottage by the lake every year. Most of that time was spent working on the cottage and repairing the water well to keep them in good order, but there were always a few hours fishing for bass, perch, bluegill, and crappie. The latter could be caught around the dock, whereas bass and perch required rowing one of the two wooden boats out to weed beds and other haunts for the more desirable fish. There was nothing like fresh-caught fried fish for dinner. The work, rowing, and swimming in the fresh air provided good exercise to build up an appetite.

One year, Dad thought my two closest friends and I were old enough to spend two weeks at the cottage by ourselves. Gene, the oldest, was fourteen, and I just turned twelve. We caught a lot of fish, swam nearly every day, ate our own cooking, and occasionally walked two miles along an old dirt road to the nearest store for food and ice for the icebox. The ice was always packed in straw to reduce the loss of melting in the forty-minute walk back. One day, I decided to swim across the lake—a distance of about a mile. The other two boys rowed and fished, following me in an old row boat because they didn't think I could make it and didn't want to have to explain to my father why I drowned. To everyone's surprise, I made it! However, my legs were rubbery, and I couldn't stand when I reached the opposite shore—they had to drag me into the boat.

I remember clearly that from the day my first half brother arrived, there was never a day that the clothesline was not full of diapers drying on the line in the yard. Winter cold didn't matter, but if it was raining or snowing, the diapers hung on clotheslines in the basement. It was my job to put them up and take them down. I don't know when the diapers finally stopped because I left home while there were still babies in the house.

My father was a superb craftsman! Woodworking was his specialty— he could make anything, and it was always a thing of precision and beauty. He constantly admonished me to always do my very best in anything I did. His creed, passed down to me, was in large part key to my success in the military and life in general. While in eighth grade at middle school,

I was selected by the shop teacher to represent the school in a citywide woodworking competition. Each competitor would be judged on his precision in shaping a block of white pine to precise dimensions as well as the location of a three-fourths-inch hole to be drilled in the block. The work would involve the use of a saw, wood plane, drill bit, and hand drill. I spent the best part of a weekend sharpening the blade of Dad's wood plane to a razor-sharp edge, as well as hand-sharpening our crosscut saw. I also took with me a wood square that was true and a rather new twelve-inch steel ruler to make sure the measurements were correct. Upon arriving at the competition, I asked the judges to verify that my ruler was consistent with theirs. Each contestant was provided a large block of wood that had to be planed to the correct thickness and cut to the stipulated length and width. The last step was to correctly locate and drill the proper-size hole with a hand drill. Points were lost if the edges of the hole were chipped or jagged. I was surprised when I won the first-place cup and mechanical screwdriver—my father was absolutely amazed.

It was about this time, while I was in the seventh grade, that my closest friend, Gene, enrolled in the Henry Ford Trade School (HFTS), a technical school, because they paid a small scholarship fee every two weeks and his family needed the money. The major benefit is that you learned marketable toolmaker skills and were placed in a very good-paying skilled job at the Ford Motor Company upon graduation. In the summer of 1948, I took the admission test for HFTS. Enrollment was competitive for obvious reasons, and testing was extensive and comprehensive. I was accepted and began school in late summer. HFTS was, in a word, unique. The academic curriculum was designed to prepare a student for university admission. Apprenticeship training ran the gamut of metal machinist skills: foundry, welding, pattern making, sheet metal, tool repair, and the entire suite of precision tool-making machines (lathes, shapers, grinders, and milling machines). Apprenticeship training at Ford's Rouge plant ran for two consecutive weeks, followed by a week of academics at a facility on one of the Ford estates. There was a week off for Christmas and two weeks off in July. Both academics and technical training were very demanding. It was a good education. HFTS was an all-male school, and both academics and shop work ran eight hours a day plus transportation time, so there wasn't much socializing or dating during those years. In June 1951, I graduated as the class valedictorian and continued my apprenticeship as a draftsman and toolmaker, as I was too young to be hired into the regular Ford workforce.

The Korean War had been raging for a year, but because of my age, it didn't have much of an impact on me except to create a plethora of opportunities for higher-paying jobs as factories ramped up production to meet military demands. Machinists and draftsmen were in high demand. Soon I was making over $420 a week ($21,420 a year) with pay raises coming on a regular basis. To put this in perspective, in 1950, a skilled machinist earned $5,000 to $6,000 a year. One of the tasks I was given in 1952 was to design the assembly jigs for the horizontal airfoils of the B-52 vertical stabilizer. In 2013, the B-52 is still an operational bomber in the air force inventory sixty years after its maiden flight.

The Air Force Takes Over

On my eighteenth birthday, February 17, 1952, I registered for the draft and started considering my options. Close friend Gene, who was the pathfinder for HFTS, had enlisted in the air force immediately after the Korean War broke out and repeatedly extolled the virtues of air force technical training and follow-on job opportunities. I wanted to shop around for myself, so I visited all the recruiting stations nearby. It was clear that the army would make a man out of me, the marines would *really* make a man out of me, and the navy would provide a tour of the world from a ship's fantail. On the other hand, the air force said they would give me all the education I could absorb, a warm room to sleep in, and clean sheets every week. Education was what I was after, so the air force was my choice. Still, I thought I could get a better education at the Naval Academy, but after failing to secure a congressional appointment, I applied to the Coast Guard Academy. The latter accepted me, but a couple of weeks prior to class start at New London, Connecticut, I received a letter suggesting that I take some additional math courses in summer school and reapply. That was a real downer, as math was my best subject, and I could feel the Selective Service bearing down on me.

The Korean War was ebbing back and forth and had just taken a turn for the worse. Accordingly, on September 2, 1952, I enlisted in the air force. At that time, with the rapid buildup and sustainment for the war effort, there were three air force bases for basic training, one each in northern California, New York, and Texas. For no good reason, Texas seemed like the romantic place to go—but that was a role of the dice held by the air force. Besides, with winter approaching, the other two states could get cold and miserable. Of course, before being sworn in, there was a qualification test to be taken to determine your mental category and if indeed you were acceptable to the air force. As I recall, the tests were comprehensive and challenging, but not intimidating. After the tests had been scored, a master sergeant called me aside and told me

I scored 100 percent on the test and that no one in the history of that recruiting station had ever achieved a perfect score. I not only was pleased with that to start my my military record, but also was surprised, as at least one-fourth of my fellow recruits had college degrees and apparently had not aced the test.

The next day, we recruits boarded a train for San Antonio, Texas, home of Lackland Air Force Base and twelve weeks of basic training. I should note that while Detroit was not hailed as a center of racial harmony in the early 1950s, schools were integrated; restaurants, stores, nightclubs, and public transportation did not discriminate. There were a number of black guys in my class at HFTS, and we helped each other learn the trades. We all worked together harmoniously to succeed and graduate. So it was a shock to me when the train stopped briefly in St. Louis, and I discovered that water fountains as well as toilet facilities were labeled Colored and White! About a fourth of the recruits were black, and they were forewarned either by their parents or by the recruiters because they didn't blink an eye or raise a fuss but used the facilities designated for them. I had entered the South, crossed the Mason-Dixon Line, and realized things would be different in Southern cities and towns.

In San Antonio, the train troop cars were met by air force buses, and all the new recruits were moved to Lackland AFB, Texas, and introduced to the military way of doing things. I quickly learned what the phrase "hurry up and wait" meant. Seventy-one other recruits and I were assigned to the care and leadership of one Sergeant Sams. Sergeant Sams, our tactical instructor, or TI, was an imposing figure. He was an intimidating six feet four inches tall and weighed roughly 230 pounds, if an ounce, and sported a head covered in bright-red hair. No question about who was in charge. As I learned throughout the twelve weeks of basic training, he was a fine and honorable man; and fifty-six years later, I can still remember his name and picture him in my mind's eye. He also changed my life in an odd way. Sergeant Sams had trouble pronouncing my last name. Everyone in the military goes by his or her last name, and during basic training, everything with our last name on it came through Sergeant Sams. When mail call came, I was "Pint-a-Whiskey." That moniker brought laughs from my barracks mates, but I didn't think it would be a good idea to go through my four-year enlistment known as a bottle of booze. So one day, I bravely told Sergeant Sams that my name meant Peterson, and he could just call me Pete. I've been Airman Pete, Lieutenant Pete, and so on ever since—and for good reason.

At first, everything was a blur. Clothing issue was humorous at best. The supply clerks sized us up in one quick glance and started throwing military clothing at us. It came at us real fast, along with an olive drab duffel bag to pack it in. Everything you needed was issued; good thing too because the next day, we were directed to pack all the civilian clothes we wore to Lackland AFB or brought along for the trip. Those items were sent to our homes, never to be seen again. As you may know, the air force became a separate service shortly before the Korean War erupted. It was no longer the Air Corps or Air Service of the US Army as a result of the National Defense Act (October 1947). Still five years later, some of the things we were issued were army green or brown instead of air force blue. Surprisingly, all of the clothing items I was issued, from dress blues to fatigues, fit properly. A word about the fatigues: they were a one-piece jumpsuit with a sewn-in belt—absolutely the worst possible design. I later learned that the jumpsuit fatigues were left over from army tank crews. I hope the tank crews were issued something better.

The physical was daunting as well. I can't remember seeing more than two doctors in my eighteen years as a civilian. We were both poor and healthy. When a child in the neighborhood contracted the measles, parents took all the unaffected kids from a few surrounding blocks to the home of the sick child, and we all came down with the measles, and that was the end of that sickness. I guess that was the frontier form of inoculation. My fellow recruits and I were about to be overwhelmed with doctors. Stripped naked and in single file, we snaked through a maze of test stations and medical personnel. Most feared was the immunization gauntlet. At least five technicians per side, armed with needle-tipped syringes, zapped us in the arms as we walked by. Some fainted in the process! This was back in the days before disposable needles. At that time, medical technicians sharpened, sterilized, and reused the needles. Often, the resharpened needles had barbs on the end. As such, it was not uncommon to see the man in front of you have the skin on his arm pulled out an inch or so before the barb let go.

With clothing issue and medical examinations behind us, we marched and we marched, and we *marched*! And we marched everywhere we were required to go. There was the rifle range, where we attempted to qualify with the M-1 carbine and perhaps earn an air force marksmanship ribbon. The gas chamber, where we learned all about gas masks, how to don them in a hurry, the chemical agents that could kill you in a New York minute, and those that could just make you wish you were never born. In the gas chamber, we donned our gas masks and were exposed to CS or tear gas—with mask on, it was not a problem. Then we were ordered to take the masks off—it was a problem! When it was obvious we were all incapacitated and nearly blind, Sergeant Sams, who kept his mask on, opened the door and let us out in the fresh air of wintertime Texas. Last, there was the obstacle course—the kind where we belly-crawled with our M-1 carbine held out of the mud under hundreds of yards of barbed wire obstacles while someone fired machine gun bullets with tracer rounds over our heads. It was at night, so we could see the tracers and know the bullets were real.

Soon a month passed by, and it was payday—the old-fashioned kind, where we lined up by rank and alphabetically in front of a small wooden table stacked with twenty-, ten-, and one-dollar bills, and coins too. The squadron commander counted out the money stipulated on the pay list after we dutifully saluted and said, "Sir, Airman Piotrowski reporting for pay," and the captain returned the salute.

He then loudly counted out, "Twenty, forty, sixty, seventy, seventy-five dollars." We took the money, signed our payroll signature in a very small space, saluted, did an about-face, and got out of the way. Once out of sight, the money was recounted to make sure there was no mistake. Things may have changed recently, but sailors aboard ship still get paid the old-fashioned way because they need cash aboard ship, or in a foreign port, personal checks or cashier's checks wouldn't work. (Fast forward to 2011, I just learned from an admiral friend that sailors are now issued government credit cards aboard ship that can be used on the ship or any port in the world). The monthly pay for each man in the unit was recorded on a thick yellow sheet of paper (almost cardboard) approximately eighteen inches by eighteen inches. There was no other record of pay except this yellow sheet. If it was lost, stolen, or somehow destroyed a person's pay could be held up for two or three months while personnel in the orderly room tried to recall when you were paid last. This large yellow sheet was carried from base to base by the individual and turned into the squadron orderly room or finance, depending on who paid you and how. It is hard to imagine such an archaic system with the computers of today, but it worked for millions of servicemen for decades. Payday always reminded me that I had been earning twenty-two times as much as a civilian before becoming patriotic.

When the weather was too lousy for marching, we stayed in the barracks for schooling on the air force. The barracks was a WW II wooden facility with paint on the outside, asphalt shingles on the roof, and bare wood on the inside. So it was hot inside when it was hot outside, and likewise when it was cold. It was a two-story rectangular building with a large latrine and private room for Sergeant Sams on the bottom floor. Each floor held thirty-six trainees in double metal bunks, metal springs, and four-inch thick mattresses. We recruits were as diverse as the land we came from. New Yorkers and Red Necks, cowboys and Native Americans, farmers, factory workers, miners, and eastern shore fisherman-Americans and patriots all. But there was something in our past that divided us. As previously noted, it was 1952; the Civil War, or War of Northern Aggression as some of the barracks mates referred to it, ended on April 9, 1865, some eighty-seven years earlier. In my Detroit grade school civics classes, the Civil War was covered in one or two days. The war was deadly and ended in 1865, but not so in the former Confederate states. The war raged on between the recruits of Yankee and rebel heritage. The discussions were heated, loud, and long. The black recruits, perhaps ten or twelve of the total, largely stayed mute during these rancorous debates. And wisely so, as there was no end to the burning passion of the rebels even though from reveille to the sound of retreat, we were the best of friends and pulled together as a team. As an aside, the Civil War was the deadliest war on record for the United States because Americans were killing Americans.

In the barracks, schooling on the young air force was necessary and instructive then and for years to come. We were informed on the *Universal Code of Military Justice (UCMJ)*, or the military law book. What the offenses were and what the range of punishments could be—from a letter of reprimand to a general court-martial and execution by firing squad. Sergeant Sams encouraged us to be good law-abiding airmen by working hard and following the directions of our superior noncommissioned and commissioned officers. He also noted that every unit we would serve in would have an officer with an additional duty as the inspector general (IG), whose job was to hear and act upon complaints. He also noted that we had the right to write to our congressman and lodge a complaint. He opined that anyone seen talking to the IG was a marked person, the same for a congressional complaint. I believed him, and it wasn't until I reached the rank of colonel that I realized that the IG system was fair and those lodging a complaint were protected from retaliation. There may have been exceptions to this in some units, but if so, it was rare and usually resulted in harsh treatment of those tolerating or perpetuating retaliation.

As an aside, there were women recruits as well, and it was rumored that there were some at Lackland AFB. Sergeant Sams was asked about women in the air force, or WAFs, and he responded that there were WAF recruits at Lackland; but for their safety, they were housed way on the other side of the base and were protected by a double fence of barbed wire. Our society and the air force have changed a great deal since those days.

Some of the training sessions were more mundane—subjects such as history of the air force and Army Air Corps, memorizing the chain of command from air force chief of staff on down. None of us worried too much about meeting any of these luminaries, as it was extremely rare to see a second lieutenant even from a great distance. Enemy and friendly aircraft recognition was also taught and was somewhat of a reminder of the Cold War and the hot war raging in Korea.

It was amazing when the moment came that you realized that seventy-two men thrown together could march in unison and look good. Actually, there were only seventy, as one was discharged because of epileptic seizures, and the other for a social behavior disorder. Soon, the twelve weeks had passed; we were issued a single stripe and were airmen third class and on our way to various technical schools. In this regard, we were all tested for our skill aptitude to determine what technical training was in store for us. With my HFTS toolmaker apprenticeship behind me, as well as two years of commercial drafting experience, I expected I would be going direct to an operational unit in one of those vocations. Surprise! The needs of the air force come first, and I was destined for basic electronics and then ground radar repair school at Keesler AFB, Mississippi.

Before leaving Lackland, we barracks rats got together to decide what to do with the seventy-dollar Hallicrafters short-wave radio we collectively purchased to hear news about the Korean War and the latest popular songs. The most popular were "Why Don't You Believe Me," by Joni James, and anything by Hank Williams. It was decided the radio would be given to Sergeant Sams as a small token of our appreciation. When presented with the radio, he refused, saying it was against regulations. Instead, he initiated an on-the-spot raffle, with everyone putting their name in his helmet. I remember the big redheaded TI very well; he was a good man and a hard taskmaster.

With great efficiency, the air force provided me a bus ticket to Biloxi, Mississippi, and a ride to the bus stop along with several other GIs.

It was early December 1952 when I arrived at Keesler AFB on the Gulf Coast and assigned to a training squadron. Unfortunately, the Electronic Fundamentals course I was assigned to didn't start for ninety days. As a result, I was assigned to various and sundry duties, such as kitchen police (KP), painting barracks, cutting grass, raking sand, and the most demanding of all, putting the final touches on the rebuilt officers' club. Except for the HFTS prom held at Ford's Posh Dearborn Inn in Dearborn, Michigan, it was the nicest facility I'd ever seen the inside of. It was a marathon to get the place ready for the officers' wives' club Christmas ball gala that was only a few days off by the time the powers to be decided to bring in the captive labor force. The crew I was part of worked thirty hours straight, mostly picking up, sweeping up, and carting out the construction debris. At first, it was nice to be inside, as it was biting cold on the Gulf of Mexico in December; on the other hand, I wasn't really happy to get back to the routine of painting and such.

In a few days, the squadron first sergeant told us we could go home for Christmas on leave but that those who remained would be given various details over the holidays. Most, including me, decided it was better to go home. While checking the barracks and finding out for the first sergeant who was leaving and who was staying, I came across a young airman, a one-striper like me, sewing master sergeant stripes on his dress blue uniform. When I inquired if he had lost his mind, he responded that he had been telling his folks, in letters to home, that he had received several promotions in the few short months he'd been in the air force and was now a master sergeant (M.Sgt.). Therefore, he had to arrive home with master sergeant stripes on his uniform plus some ribbons that he collected. I suggested he couldn't possibly get away with this ruse and that anyone familiar with the military would realize he couldn't possibly have achieved the highest-enlisted rank (at that time) in less than six months. He replied that he was from a village of fifty people in northern Maine and that no one there knew anything about the military. When he returned from leave, he said the ruse worked, and his folks and relatives were really proud of him.

Details awaited those of us who hadn't yet started school upon returning from holiday leave. One of the nastiest jobs I was given was removing paint that had been splashed on several barracks floors when the walls were painted. The floors were made of pine and about twenty years old. The first sergeant took about a dozen of us "casuals" (as those waiting for classes to start were referred to) to one of the barracks in need of cleanup. On the floor were a pile of beach sand and some bricks. Our job was to rub out the paint by grinding the sand on the paint spots with a brick. A few hours later, the first shirt came back and said he needed three volunteers for another detail. My hand went up with lightning speed—nothing could be worse than what I was currently doing! I had just volunteered for ninety days of KP. KP started at 4:00 a.m. and ended when everything was cleaned to the mess sergeant's satisfaction after the evening meal. Mess sergeants are not easy to please when it comes to cleanliness! The duty was two days on followed by one day off, so there was time to recover from the sixteen-hour days. Years later, 1975 to be exact, I learned that the slack time between arrival at Keesler AFB and start of formal training was contrived by the course commanders and instructors to ensure there was a large labor force to take care of all the work details—so they wouldn't have to.

Sometime in March, my forced labor duties at KP ended with the start of formal training. Electronics turned out to be fascinating. I was a good student and relished the fact that I was learning an entirely new discipline instead of practicing an old one. My success at learning involved a four-step process: listening to the instructor, taking copious notes, reading the assigned text while underlining what the instructor emphasized, and then reviewing all my notes and underlines before a test. For this process to succeed, the proper materials were needed. On a day away from KP, I walked into Biloxi (it was only a mile or so into town) and found a Notions store. It didn't take long to find what I needed: good-quality bound notebooks, mechanical pencils, extra lead, and good erasers. The cashier was a beautiful reddish blonde, about my age. When I politely said to her, "I'd like to purchase these items"; she replied, "Well, I declare, you're a god-damn Yankee, aren't you?" I hadn't realized, till then, that those words ran together and were hyphenated!

There was a war going on, so school went eighteen hours a day in three shifts, 6:00 a.m. till noon, noon until 6:00 p.m., and 6:00 p.m. till midnight. The first and the last were the desired shifts because it gave the student plenty of time for daytime activities. Of course, I was assigned the middle shift. The first and second shift gave the Keesler Technical Training Center Commander an opportunity to observe two-thirds of the students march to and from class at the noon formation. This is where "hurry up and wait" really reared its ugly head. We marched in a large formation, six abreast, from the barracks past the reviewing stand and then onto the schoolhouses, which were three-story concrete block, windowless, air-conditioned buildings. "Hurry up and wait" went something like this: the squadron commander told the first sergeant, "Have the students in formation by eleven thirty." The first sergeant told the barracks chiefs to have the students in formation for roll call and inspection by ten thirty. To make sure we were there on time, the barracks chiefs told us students to be in formation by ten o'clock to go through "dress right, dress" and some other arcane drill stuff. So there we were all polished and shined in our khaki (army issue) uniforms waiting for at least one hour and forty-five minutes for the martial music and the order "forward march." There was the obligatory "eyes right" at the reviewing stand and then on to class. Marching was graded, and it was not a good thing to receive a poor grade. If so, weekends were filled with marching practice. We marched in heavy downpour, but could straggle to class during hurricane warnings. Our classrooms were supposedly hurricane proof—hurricane Katrina proved otherwise. Usually, the vice commander, a colonel, was on the reviewing stand if it was raining, cold, or very hot.

All was fine until it warmed up and open collar replaced the blue air force tie worn with the army khaki uniform. Word came down that the general's wife saw an airman with his white T-shirt showing and didn't think it was proper for underwear to show. The issue T-shirts came with a crew collar. Thereafter, formation started fifteen minutes earlier so we could reach up through the trouser fly and pull down on the T-shirt until the collar could no longer be seen. Soon, the T-shirts were stretched so far out of shape, they couldn't be used for anything but a rag. However, it was not long before word came down that the general's wife spotted an airman with a hairy sweaty chest and was offended. We were then told to wear our distorted T-shirts backward so that no chest hair could be seen. By this time, T-shirts were so pulled out of shape that the only option left was to buy new ones with tight crew necks.

Soon, the gulf waters were warm enough to go to the beaches nearby. The water was murky because the barrier islands about twelve miles from shore kept the normal wave action from bringing in clean gulf water. However, the tides moved the sand under the waves from one place to another, changing the depth of the water up to several feet. There were signs on all the piers warning people not to dive off of the pier. This was because the water depth varied from ten feet one day to four the next. Still nonlocals, like airmen from the base, didn't understand the purpose of the signs and dived in anyway—several died every year from broken necks. As noted earlier, I came from an integrated city and school system and was ignorant of how things were in the segregated South, especially Mississippi. Often I would say to my barracks mates of all colors, "Let's go to the beach for a swim." The black airmen always had other things they wanted to do and never accepted my offer. It was years later before I realized they were too polite to tell me they weren't allowed on the segregated "whites only" beaches of Biloxi.

Electronic Fundamentals ended, and I was assigned to the Ground Radar Technicians course. This course had some classroom learning but was mostly hands-on with a real operational radar. The first radar we were trained on carried the nomenclature AN/TPY-1B and was called the Tipsy-1B. The nomenclature was an arcane art devised by mad scientists at the dawn of US Military Services and agreed to by the army and the navy. *AN* denoted is was under the army/navy nomenclature; *T* meant it was transportable; *P* meant that it was a radar (*R* was already taken for radio, which historically came first); *Y* stood for search, and *1B* meant that it was the second instantiation of this radar. The AN/TPY-1B came apart in six major pieces so that six airmen could pack it up to the top of a hill or mountain, put it together, and operate it. There was a lot of practical learning in the Ground Radar course. Once system operation was mastered, the instructors would create malfunctions by opening or shorting a circuit, removing a vacuum tube (this was 1953; transistors hadn't been invented yet), or loosening a connector. It was challenging, but there was a simple logic to follow—and if done correctly, it didn't take long to put a complex radar system back in operation. Next came much larger and more complex search and height-finder radars. Somewhere along the way, a second chevron was awarded, primarily because of my academic achievements in Electronic Fundamentals and Ground Radar Systems. I was now an airman second class earning eighty-two dollars month. What to do with all that *extra* money?

Somewhere in the middle of learning to be a radar technician, there was a dramatic life change. While checking the weekend duty roster, KP, grass cutting, painting, etc., I noticed a letter calling for volunteers for flying training. Basically, the letter stated any airman that could pass a college equivalency exam, a stanine (standard nine) psychomotor test, and graduate from flying school would be commissioned as a second lieutenant in the United States Air Force and be authorized to wear the silver wings of a pilot or navigator. Allegedly, the tests administered to prospective aviation cadets measured judgment, mathematical ability, mechanical ability, comprehension, and leadership skills. Another section measured reflexes, hand-eye coordination, and ability to perform under pressure. In addition, there were spatial awareness and visual acuity tests. It would not be a stretch to say that Henry Ford Trade School training went a long way in preparing me to excel in these tests.

Air Corps and Air Force Headquarters adjusted the Aviation Cadet Program over the years since inception in 1930 to meet rising and declining demands for aviators. At the onset of the Korean War, entrance standards were reduced, from 1950 through 1953, including lowering the minimum age to nineteen. Clearly, the minimum age requirement lowered the bar enough for me to squeak in on that account. Lower test standards may have also helped; on the other hand, a "revitalized" program was introduced in 1952 that lowered the washout rate below 34 percent.

A keen observer, I had already noticed that officers dated prettier women, lived in better quarters, and were paid a lot more money; how much more, I wasn't sure—but it had to be a lot. I told the first sergeant that I was a volunteer for the test and waited, hoping I would at least get an opportunity to compete.

After a couple of anxious weeks, I received temporary duty (TDY) orders to Moody AFB, Georgia, where the testing was being administered. There were a large number of airmen who were selected from the volunteer pool, and the competition appeared tough—many of those on the bus had a year of college under their belt before the Korean War drove them to enlist in the air force. The trip took the better part of a day, and the college equivalency exam took the better part of a day, because it was given in sections, math, geometric and spatial relationships, reading comprehension, and English. The next day was filled with psychomotor tests. They were simple to comprehend but hard to execute. They were tests developed for selecting personnel for pilot training in WW II. One example was a double bank of red and green lightbulbs in both the vertical and horizontal planes. The vertical lights were controlled by a simulated aircraft flight control stick, while simulated rudder pedals controlled the horizontal lights. When two lights came on, it was necessary to move the stick and rudders to a position that would turn the lights off. The faster this could be accomplished correctly improved the score. There were hundreds of lights to douse. The most insidious test required the applicant to keep a very flexible wand in contact with a metal disk that could move from the center to the edge of a revolving platter. The platter was the size of a 78 rpm phonograph record, and the disk was about three-eighths inch in diameter. For those readers not old enough to remember 78 rpm records, they were about twelve inches in diameter. The platter rotational speed varied, as did the movement of the disk from the center to the edge. If one tried to keep the wand in contact with the disk with downward pressure, the wand would bend, and contact would be lost. As you may have surmised, all the psychomotor devices were designed to test hand-eye coordination. Good athletes would have an edge. My skill in the game of ping-pong honed at the Biloxi USO may have helped me somewhat.

The following day, those who passed both the academic college equivalency tests and the psychomotor tests were notified that we would have an interview with an officer to determine what programs we had qualified for and obtain a class opening. To say that I was elated when notified of passing all the tests is a whopping big understatement! Getting in the door was the hard part, given the chance I knew hard work and commitment would get me through.

My interview was with an air force major—I had never met one or been that close to an officer before. He informed me that I had qualified for any flight program that was available, pilot, navigator, bombardier, weapon system officer, electronic warfare officer, or aircraft performance engineer. I responded quickly that I wanted to go to pilot training. His response was "Good. We can get you into a class in two years. In the meantime, you will continue in the career field you're presently in." My mind raced through the timelines. A year had almost past since I enlisted, two years from now plus some slippage in getting into pilot training, my four-year enlistment would almost be up. Besides, it would be two years more at eighty-two dollars a month versus the big money officers and fliers were paid. I must have looked crestfallen because the major said that he could get me into a navigator class in just a couple of weeks.

I was quick to say, "Sir, you got yourself a navigator." On the bus back to Keesler, my mind was jumping between the elation of opportunity and doubt that I had what it would take to succeed. While on the bus, I learned that my cubicle mate, Oscar Knight, a fine young man from northern Louisiana, had also passed the tests and asked for navigator training. I was really excited about the possibility that I would have a good friend at my side as we together faced the trials and challenges ahead.

Back at Keesler, everything moved in slow motion, but I had to excel because there was always the chance I would fail in navigator training and find myself finishing the Ground Radar Technician course. Then the setback hit! The squadron commander, a captain I had never been within a hundred yards of, except on payday, summoned me to his office. I reported smartly, saluted, and said, "Airman Second Class Piotrowski reporting as ordered!"

He looked me over carefully and said, "Piotrowski, you are out of uniform."

I knew I was properly dressed, shoes shined, and brass polished, so I responded bravely, "No, sir!"

Then he dropped the hammer. "I'm taking a stripe and busting you back to airman third class. You won't need it, so I'm giving it to another deserving airman."

I pleaded, "But, sir, if I wash out, I'll have to start from the bottom again!"

His response was "All the more incentive for you to succeed. Dismissed!" The bust cost me seven dollars month and the time and money it took to remove all the chevrons from my uniforms and get new ones sewed on. In those days, a commander was given a number of stripes to award to his best people, the ones he could count on. He rightly didn't want to let that stripe he had earlier given me to get away and lose the opportunity to reward another deserving individual. I was disappointed, but he did the right thing!

Soon it was time to leave. Oscar and I were assigned to the same class in preflight training at Lackland AFB, Texas. It was Class 54-11C, which indicated our class would graduate in mid-1954 and be commissioned shortly thereafter. Oscar invited me to stop at this home in the country near the small town of Jena in northern Louisiana. I learned that the closest town to Jena was Opp, but that didn't help much in understanding where his home was. Oscar's father was a retired naval officer who fought in WW II and achieved the rank of captain, equal to a colonel in the air force. His mother was a typical sweet and charming Southern lady, and he had a younger sister. I had to listen very carefully with my Yankee ears to understand what they were saying in their Southern speak. Their home was large, but not quite an antebellum mansion. There was one thing that immediately caught my attention—a large hole in the roof above the formal living room that served more as a family room in the tradition of today. Large in this case was about a six-foot diameter ragged hole. Oscar explained that the hole brought in fresh air on a good day, and they just avoided that area when the rain came pouring in. It was somewhat of a concern to me, as I was sleeping on a temporary cot in that room. Fortunately, as he pointed out, "The hole doesn't matter on a good day."

One day, Oscar asked me if I liked to hunt, to which I replied, "Yes, but I don't get to hunt much these days." Shortly thereafter, he handed me a well-worn pump action .22-caliber rifle and suggested I try my luck with the squirrels that thrived in the woods surrounding his home. This was really a subterfuge on his part to keep me occupied while he visited the very lovely young lady he was dating prior to enlisting in the air force. It had not been long since they'd been together, since Oscar had been able to hitchhike home a few weekends while we were stationed at Keesler AFB. I reminded Oscar that aviation cadets had to be single when they entered the flying training program and until they graduated. It made sense if you had to live in a barracks, were otherwise occupied eighteen hours a day, and didn't earn enough money to support yourself, let alone a family.

Soon I was deep into the woods looking for some chatty squirrels to harvest for dinner. Unfortunately for me, but good for the squirrels, a herd of wild boars found me first. Up into a tree I went, and there I stayed for several hours while the hogs rooted up the ground nearby. I stayed in the tree for a couple of hours even after they left arriving back at the house late for dinner with some explaining to do. They all laughed at the picture of a Yankee treed by some pesky wild hogs.

Our orders required we report to the 3700th Air Force Indoctrination Wing not later than 1600 hours on July 17, 1953. Just ten days later, the Korean War ended in an armistice on July 27, 1953. I was back at Lackland AFB, Texas, at a more remote part of the base, assigned to the 3744th Preflight Squadron and in for some more marching. Only this time, there was a full-fledged parade every Saturday with about twenty-four squadrons of preflight cadets marching and passing in review. Room inspections came daily, and discrepancy reports or "gigs" received above an acceptable number were marched off on Saturday afternoons and all day Sunday, if necessary. Just to make it interesting, this marching required the individual to wear a parachute and shoulder an M-1 rifle. I wasn't the worst offender in the room on uniform discrepancies, but I did my share of weekend tours, as they called them. One excessive gig was worked off with an hour of marching between two posts on a parade field.

Once I got my head above water, so to speak, and found out who was in the preflight program, I learned that many of the airmen who passed the testing at Moody AFB and held out for pilot training were already in training. As it turned out, the two-year delay story was just a ruse to encourage people like me to opt for navigator training. I swore that if I ever ran across that major who tricked me, he would regret duping me. As you'll find, it all worked out in the end, but it certainly wasn't obvious to me at the time.

In addition to marching, parades, and daily inspections, preflight training entailed a lot of intense individual and group harassment by upperclassmen. The program was twelve weeks long, so you were a maggot (the lowest form of life with the prospect of one day flying) for four weeks, then a second classman for four weeks, and finally an upperclassman the last four weeks. In the latter two instantiations, your role was to make the newly arrived maggots miserable. There was a real purpose to this harassment, and that was to drive out those who were not totally committed to complete the flying training program and achieve the goal of gold bars and silver wings. The earlier the faint of heart left, the better it was for them and for the air force. As for me, I knew they couldn't kill me (murder was punishable under the UCMJ), and I was determined to graduate. I can remember telling one of my classmates, "I can stand on my head and march on my hands if that is what it takes." Well, it never came to that, and the screaming in your face was replaced by normal conversation once you got past the first four weeks.

Class status was depicted by the shoulder boards attached to shirt and jacket epaulets. Maggot shoulder boards were bare, second classmen had one-color stripe, and upperclassmen had the color stripe plus one to four white stripes depicting cadet rank. Cadets also were paid at the rank of staff sergeant or about $145 a month, nearly double my pay as an airman third class. Cadets' lives were very controlled—sixteen hours a day, leaving little time for recreation, so the savings piled up.

Three months is a long time to just march, so our upperclassmen had to find other diversions to ensure that we maggots were suitably committed and had little time to think. There were the obligatory lectures on the history of the air force, now six years old, and its predecessor, the Army Air Corps. Plus there were motivational movies like *Air Victory*, filmed in the European Theater, which entailed several hours of aerial gunnery film from P-47s and P-51s engaged in dogfights with Luftwaffe Me 109s and Fw 190s; as well as film of strafing trains, airfields, military convoys, and supply dumps. In addition, there were lectures on air force major commands and their missions. We learned about the Strategic Air Command (it ceased to exist in the early 1990s) and its nuclear deterrent mission with B-50 and B-36 bombers. Next was the Tactical Air Command (it also ceased to exist in the early 1990s; replaced by the Air Combat Command) with its missions of air superiority, interdiction, and close air support to army units engaged with enemy forces. Last, there was the military airlift command (MAC) that provided global air transportation for military personnel, equipment, and supplies. The C-124, a radial engine-powered propeller aircraft, was the mainstay of the airlift units at the time. The C-124 was affectionately known as "Old Shaky."

Still there was time left over, so the ever-creative upperclassmen came up with the idea to create a monumental tiger made of rocks covered with cement and painted to resemble a Bengal tiger. I suspect this idea sprang from the motto popular in the air force during and after the Korean War, "Every man a tiger." We carried rocks for days, maybe weeks. Local rocks resembling river rock, round, hard, and anywhere from three to eight inches in diameter—they were ubiquitous in south central Texas. Soon there was an enormous pile of rocks laid out in the form of a gigantic tiger, larger than life with a disproportionally large open mouth that would serve as a birdbath for a few days after it rained. When the tiger was complete, we were ordered to growl at it when we marched by. One day, a high-level civilian group was visiting the preflight training program and observed formations of cadets growling as they passed the prostrate tiger. They found it degrading and, I suspect, suggested to the commander that the practice be stopped immediately. As underclassmen, my fellow classmates and I built the tiger. As second classmen, we were obliged to supervise the new maggot classmen in the destruction of the tiger and the scattering of his remains back to the sands of Lackland AFB.

When we achieved upperclassmen status, we were allowed off of the base for a weekend. One or more of my classmates had access to cars, and we were off to Bandera, a fabled town in the west Texas Hill Country. It was rumored that there were saloons and dance halls where young ladies were known to be. The rumors were grossly misleading—Bandera was more like a Super Bowl party. The saloons and dance halls were more barns than finished buildings. They were wide open with a bar at either end, bandstand against one of the long walls, and tables along the edges. There was one woman who seemed to want to dance with all the guys. When I took my turn "towing" her around the floor, she informed me she owned a string of bordellos around Texas and suggested I visit one of them when I had the chance. When the dance ended, she handed me her business card, which backed up her boast. Fortunately, the air force owned my time and absolutely controlled where I went, so I never had the opportunity or the interest for that matter.

On October 6, 1953, I woke up, and it was over and time to move on. Preflight was successfully behind me, and the 3610th Observer Training Wing at Harlingen AFB, at the far southeastern tip of Texas, was the next stop in the quest for gold bars and silver wings.

For reasons that escaped me, the cadets bound for Harlingen AFB were given seven days travel time to get there. Four of us teamed up with a cadet that had a car and headed for Mexico, that exotic land south of the Rio Grande River. There wasn't much traffic into Mexico in the early 1950s, so in no time, we were across the bridge and through the border checkpoint on the Mexican side. With total ignorance of Mexican laws, we sped down the highway to Monterey. About fifty miles from the border, we were stopped at a federali checkpoint by a man in uniform holding a machine gun. We spoke no Spanish, and he no English. Immediately, we collected ten dollars each and handed it to him. Satisfied with the bribe, he motioned for us to head back to the border. Fifty dollars was a lot of money in those days, and worth a lot more in Mexico. Back at the south side of the Rio Grande, Mexican border control officers informed us that we could visit the local border town without any paperwork. However, if Monterrey was our destination, each of us would have to fill out some paperwork that would enable us to proceed past the checkpoints into the interior. Several hours after our initial start, we were once again speeding down the highway. When we reached the point where we had been stopped earlier, there was no barrier or armed federali. On we went wondering if a bandit had taken us for fifty dollars.

Monterrey was worth the trip! It was a beautiful city nestled in the hills. We visited shrines, cathedrals, and the Carta Blanca brewery. The brewery provided tours of their brew facility and furnished free beer in their garden patio. As I recall, it was good-tasting beer and refreshing in the heat of the day. We slept in the car and headed back to the border the following day. We had entered Mexico through Nuevo Laredo but returned on a more easterly route that led to McAllen, Texas. Prior to crossing the river and entering the United States, we stopped in Reynosa. At the time Reynosa was a small village consisting of a restaurant, couple of bars, and less than fifty houses. Today, Reynosa is a high-tech industrial town with a population of over one million. We stopped for some *cabrito* (goat), which was roasted on a spit before our eyes, and some Carta Blanca beer. The food was delicious, and I went back to the village several times for more.

The training at Harlingen AFB was less pomp and ceremony and had more academics pertaining to navigation and flying. On the other hand, we went from first-class status at Lackland back to maggot class, only this time for three months. We marched, but only to classrooms or the flight line where the T-29B aircraft stood proudly, waiting for us to successfully complete classroom training and qualify for flight training.

The Basic Observer course consisted of dead reckoning ("dead," as in the seventh definition in *Webster's Second Edition Unabridged Dictionary*, i.e., unerring and unfailing, e.g., dead shot), LORAN (long range navigation), and radar navigation. The advanced course covered celestial navigation by stars and the sun, and pressure pattern navigation.

Dead reckoning (DR) was simple to understand. All that was required was knowing where you started, a compass heading corrected for several errors, the speed of the aircraft, the effect wind had on the aircraft, and an aeronautical chart of the area to be flown over. Then with a diabolical tool knows as a Weems E6B Plotter, you could deduce where the aircraft would be in any given point in time. In DR, looking out the window was allowed. Landmarks, such as roads, would confirm ground speed and direction. The only problem was there were no landmarks in southeast or southwest Texas. As I recall, Uvalde was the only town within about 250,000 square miles. It was bisected by one road running north/south and one road running east/west. If you missed Uvalde, you were lost! Further, the routes flown by the pilots, directed by our navigation instructors, often came nowhere near the town. Absent any landmarks, there was an instrument called a drift meter that enabled you to peer through the belly of the T-29B and see objects on the ground passing underneath the aircraft. These objects were mostly large cacti or stationary cattle. Drift meter optics had fine red lines inscribed on the lens that could be aligned with the objects on the ground by rotating the lines. When a fixed object on the ground moved exactly along one of the red lines, the student navigator could read the deviation between the longitudinal axis of the aircraft and the actual track it was making across the ground. This deviation was caused by the wind. Knowing this angle and the true ground speed, the navigator could calculate the real wind at flight altitude, which was almost always considerably different than the forecast wind. It occurred to me that they probably gave us the wrong winds to make navigation more challenging. It was continually impressed on us over and over again that DR was the only true method of navigation; everything else was just an aide to DR.

Next, we studied LORAN. If DR was simple and straightforward, LORAN was devious and complex. LORAN beams were propagated out over the oceans and seas from transmitters near the coast. These beams bounced off of the ionosphere for ships and aircraft to pick up and assist their navigators in deducing their position over the water. What made this difficult was the relative height of the ionosphere. It varied by time of day and often resulted in multiple plots of the same beam. For example, there could be an F-1 and an F-2. F-1 was intended to be stronger than F-2, but on many occasions, the reverse was true as a function of what the ionosphere was doing and whether the sun was throwing off weak or powerful solar storms. When plotted on a LORAN chart, the beams were curved lines intersected by other curved lines from other transmitters. In the early 1950s, the LORAN receiver display on board the T-29 was a rather small oscilloscope depicting fuzzy wiggly lines. It was the navigator's job to deduce what D, E, or F "hops" these were. DR would put the aircraft in the "ballpark" most of the time, but there was still a good chance of being convinced the incorrect "hop" line was the correct one and being off fifty or more miles. Not a good thing if you're trying to find the Azores in the mid-Atlantic on a dark and stormy night without enough fuel to go elsewhere. LORAN classroom trainers were deceptively devoid of clutter and ambiguity; finding the right solution was relatively easy. On the other hand, the aircraft equipment would have you flipping coins in short order.

Some government branches are always looking for ways to save money. For example, the Department of Defense (DOD) and the air force, while others like the Congress dole out gifts in the form of pork on a regular basis. What I'm referring to is how the 3610th Observer Training Wing (OTW) scheduled our flying training. First, the reader needs to understand how an air force flier earns hazardous duty pay for flying, otherwise known as flight pay. Back then, air force regulations required a flier to be airborne for four hours each month to receive one hundred dollars flight pay. These hours could not be banked for the future (e.g., fly eight hours in May and receive flight pay for May and June). Anything less than four hours in any given month resulted in the loss of flight pay for that month, period! Accordingly, the 3610th bunched our flight training so that we didn't fly for three months and then flew several training sorties the fourth month, perhaps logging twenty or thirty hours. This resulted in flight pay for one month and zero for the other three. They could have spread the flights out but chose not to. Thus, in nine months of training, navigator aviation cadets (ACs) would only receive flight pay for two months, or three if they were lucky. ACs in pilot training flew almost daily from the start of training; downtime of any length would result in loss of proficiency and possibly an increased accident rate. Thus, student pilots were able to earn flight pay every month of their training.

Aside from navigation training, there are three things I remember from Harlingen. First, there was the Little Creek Inn, a restaurant near the base. The inn had a bevy of attractive young waitresses, great-tasting steaks of giant proportions, and home-made apple pie like your mother used to make—cover it with a heaping scoop of vanilla ice cream, and it was divine. While the waitresses were attractive with interesting Southern drawls, they didn't date cadets because they knew we didn't make much money, couldn't marry, and would be transferred to another base to complete our training before getting those gold bars, silver wings, and the privilege of being eligible to marry. Therefore, the real attraction was the food. One of those meals consisting of steaks, baked potato, beans, and dessert, after the Saturday parade, would provide enough calories to carry you halfway through the next week. When I wasn't marching tours, a good friend, John L. Taylor, from Snow Hill, South Carolina, and I would dine there every Saturday afternoon. John had been an undertaker working at his father's funeral parlor and preparing to take over the family business prior to entering the air force. He was a character in the nicest sort of way! He was outgoing, spoke with a heavy drawl, and was cocksure of himself. He successfully completed the navigator program and went back to Snow Hill, North Carolina, when his obligation to the air force was fulfilled. Another activity that lives in my memory was the attempted eradication of a local bird known as the fan-tailed grackle. This critter, abundant in the area, was bigger than a robin, shiny black in color, and made an annoying noise. One day, while standing in inspection formation, a fan-tailed grackle flew over and dropped a load of digested dinner on my flight cap. I was written up by the inspecting officer for having bird feces on my hat, which resulted in a huge number of demerits and many tours working off the resulting gigs.

A couple of weeks later, when I had completed the tours, John E. Hughes and I went off base to a sporting goods store, where I purchased a .22-caliber rifle and several boxes of ammunition. Armed and bound for revenge, we headed for a tree-lined dry wash where thousands of grackles roosted. Over time and several trips to that dry wash, I put a serious dent in their population. They must have recognized me because my uniforms were never again soiled by one of their kind. John Hughes was another outstanding person, kind and generous to the extreme. He invited me to spend the Christmas of 1953 with him and his family in Gallup, New Mexico. John fancied himself as a cowboy growing up in what was then still the Wild, Wild West. On one long holiday, John flew from Harlingen to San Antonio with the intention of competing in a major rodeo taking place there. He purchased a set of rodeo duds, a saddle, and a rodeo-savvy quarter horse. John didn't win any events, and when it was time to return to the base, he was broke, so he sold the horse for bus fare and made it back just in time to keep from being absent without leave (AWOL). John spent much of his time planning the next great adventure—I was glad for his parents (I came to admire) that he successfully completed the cadet program prior to embarking on any future escapades. Most, if not all, of the cadets in our class were exceptionally fine individuals, and I have kept in touch with a number of them. By early spring of 1954, I had saved enough money for a down payment on a car. John L. Taylor, a self-appointed expert on cars, drove me around to the used-car lots, advising me on the best cars and the best buys. *We* settled on a 1951 green, four-door Oldsmobile sedan with Hydramatic transmission. It turned out to be a very good car.

Airborne Radar (as an aide to Navigation) was the last subject in our program. The radar in the T-29 was at least a generation old but had seen service in aircraft like the B-50. The radar antenna, housed in a radome on the aircraft nose, was designed to sweep back and forth sixty degrees on either side of the fuselage centerline radiating pulses of electromagnetic energy. These pulses bounced off the ground and man-made objects, painting a luminous green picture on a cathode ray tube. The picture continued to be redrawn as the aircraft flew along its path. Buildings in towns, lakes, grain silos, and other reflective objects were easily identified on the radar display if the set was properly tuned and you had spent most of your adult life studying Rorschach ink blots. As mentioned earlier, there was only one town in west Texas, but no lakes, and only a few large grain silos marked on the map. If the flight plan took a northerly route, San Antonio would come into view, and the radar would provide good position fixes. Randolph AFB, near San Antonio, was a navigator's best friend. When the base was laid out prior to WW II, the engineers designed a number of runways in a pentagon or hexagon shape to make it easy for student pilots to always have the opportunity to take off land into the wind. When aircraft were parked on the ramps adjacent to the runways, the radar return depicted a perfect doughnut image. Once you'd seen it, it was easily remembered and was a perfect navigation fix for a significant portion of a flight.

Cabrito roasted on a spit on an open mesquite fire was one of my favorite meals. Unfortunately, the only place I could find it was at a bar in Matamoros, Mexico. By road, Matamoros was a long drive through the crossing at McAllen, Texas, and then a considerable distance east on distressed roads. One of my fellow cadets showed me a shorter way. We drove south from Harlingen to the Rio Grande and parked in a grove of trees on the edge of the river. Nearby was a concrete structure just under the surface of the water. It wasn't a dam; perhaps it was a river flow gauging station. Whatever it was, it led right to Matamoros on the southern bank of the river. Off came our shoes and socks, and with our pants rolled up, we walked across the Rio Grande. The structure was about eighteen inches wide and easy to see where it was under the water because of the disturbance created as the water flowed over the structure. The river was about one hundred yards wide at that point, so it was a short walk. After dinner and a beer for less than three dollars, we walked back across the river and drove back to the base. The entire affair took less time than just driving to the legal border crossing at McAllen. I made that trip several times, never considering that the Federal Police of Mexico or the Border Patrol might be waiting on the other side to apprehend me on one of those many crossings.

June came rather quickly once the in-flight training started and graduation was at hand. I finished in the top five of my class as a distinguished graduate. I didn't realize at the time that this automatically qualified me for an Air Force regular commission, vice the reserve commission given to most cadets. The implications were that a regular officer was in for a full career, whereas a reserve officer was a surge resource and would likely not serve until eligible for retirement.

Electronic warfare officer training at Keesler AFB, Mississippi

Once again, the needs of the air force dictated my next assignment, and I was sent back to Keesler AFB in late June 1954 for advanced training as an electronic warfare officer (EWO). EWOs flew reconnaissance missions to collect radar emissions that would enable the intelligence community to determine the enemy electronic order of battle (EOB). The EOB included the type, emission fingerprints, location, and mission of all enemy radar. EWOs were also crew members on strategic bomber aircraft with the responsibility for jamming enemy radars and preventing those radars from determining the position of the bomber.

After completing nearly a year of Electronic Fundamentals at Keesler a year earlier and then mastering the operation and maintenance of several radar systems, this EWO course was going to be a cakewalk for me.

Technical training for cadets and officers at Keesler was a lot more relaxed than it was for enlisted personnel. We went to school in the morning and were able to drive or walk to the large windowless building where classes were held. This allowed for a lot more time for relaxing, swimming in the gulf waters, or lying on the beach. A Saturday at the beach made me thirsty, so I stopped at the White House Hotel for a cold beer before heading back to the barracks. Inside there was another EWO student, Jack Naughton, a few months ahead of me and already a commissioned officer. He was sitting at the bar between two young women who were obviously overdressed for the occasion. One of the two women took a twenty-dollar bill, one of many sticking out of his shirt pocket, and ordered a round of drinks for the bar. When Jack got up to go to the men's room, I followed him and offered to take him back to the base before the gals cleaned him out. He responded that it was their money; they just put it in his pocket to make him look like a big spender. With that, I bowed out, thinking this tour at Kessler as an officer was going to be a lot more fun than the previous one as an airman. Later I learned that Jack was engaged to one of the women and married her a few months later.

The EWO course started out with the TPY-1B radar, a typical radar that we students had to master in order to understand basic radar operation. Our instructor was a first lieutenant that didn't know much about the TPY-1B. When I caught up with him after class, I pointed out a few major flaws in his lecture. He informed me that his primary job was competing as the top singles tennis player on the base tennis team.

This was back in the days when every base had a baseball, basketball, football, and tennis team. Players were recruited in and out of college, just like in the professional ranks. The fact that the Cold War in Europe continuously threatened to become hot was a huge motivator to join a service just to play your sport. Teams from one base played teams from other bases in the Air Training Command. The same occurred in all the other commands and services. Annually, the commands formed a select team form their bases to play the other Air Force Commands. Eventually, the air force put together a select team to play against the army and navy teams. Commanders took great pride in their teams winning these competitions. Well, our instructor was not capable of teaching the course he was assigned to teach to justify drawing an air force paycheck, and he realized that he was shortchanging the students. His response to my comments was to ask me to teach the TPY-1B course so he could spend more time honing his tennis skills for the coming command tournament. The downside for players losing in these tournaments is that they could be knocked off the team and have to perform military duties. I accepted his offer and taught the class, which lasted about ten days.

Keesler AFB located on the Gulf of Mexico was a fun assignment, but the course material was old hat and boring; more importantly, flying missions were bunched in two months to save the air force from paying students flying pay for the entire ten months of the program. It was time to move on by capitalizing on my electronic skills and accelerating through the EWO training program.

Commissioning

It was a regulation that all cadets of a given class, for example 54-11C, would be commissioned on the same day. This uniform commissioning date was determined by the completion date of the shortest course. For 54-11C, it was August 11, 1954. On the day prior, August 10, I was given an honorable discharge from the USAF and told not to wear a uniform until the commissioning formation the following day. The commissioning uniform was a tan gabardine version of the army's famous pink-and-green blouse and slacks. Garrison hat (a round hat with visor) was also specified. The commissioning was short and sweet, attended by some ladies with babies who looked a lot like wives. These couples, if married previously, had to remarry to establish a post commissioning date for pay, allowance, and medical care purposes. After the ceremony, we went to the officers' club that I helped complete eighteen months earlier. It still looked impressive to me. When I left the club after dinner with my fellow second lieutenants, there was only one wheel hat left in the cloakroom. It was not the brand-new hat I wore to the ceremony; it was well worn and somewhat soiled. I took the high road, believing my new hat must have been taken by mistake.

Commissioning resulted in a third air force serial number that I would be tracked by from this day forward, AO3009097; AO designated a reserve officer. If I had been aware that my distinguished graduate status enabled me to ask for and receive a regular commission and understood what advantages that would have afforded me over time, I would have requested it.

"Washing ahead" was the term applied to skipping courses by taking and passing the end-of-course tests. I washed ahead through all the remaining courses, except the last one, which covered the currently fielded EWO equipment installed in operational aircraft. These suites of equipment were unfamiliar to me, and I needed to be an expert on them when I arrived at an operational unit. By washing ahead, I cut short the training at Keesler by about four months, graduating in late January 1955 with the award of pure silver navigator wings—initial goal accomplished! The entire class I graduated with was assigned en masse to the Sixty-Seventh Tactical Reconnaissance Wing flying RB-26s out of Kimpo (K-14), Korea. We were to report to Travis AFB, California, on March 15 for military transportation to Tachikawa AFB, Japan, and then forward to K-14. I was offered the opportunity to stay on at Keesler as an instructor in the program I had just completed—I declined! I'd been in training for two and half years and wanted to discover what the real operational air force was all about.

Many aviation cadets distinguished themselves in the service of their country. A few notables were Generals Jimmy Doolittle, George C. Kenney, Curtis LeMay, Thomas Power, Elwood Quesada, and Larry Welch. Ten of the Air Corps Top Aces in WW II were aviation cadets, and twenty-eight of thirty-eight Air Corps Medals of Honor were awarded to aviation cadets. I was in good company!

After graduation, I drove home to Detroit to spend the time remaining before reporting to Travis AFB in March. Gen. Douglas McArthur once said, "You can never go home again, the fires of yesterday will have turned to ashes." The general was right! Most of my school chums had disappeared into their own lives. My teenage sweetheart had grown tired of waiting and married. My older sister had left home, married, and was busy with her own life. The family dynamics had changed dramatically. I was anxious for time to pass and to get on with my air force life.

On to the mysterious Far East

While on leave in Detroit, I learned from a young woman I had dated in the past, Rose Lipa, now secretary to an executive VP at Ford Motor Company, that Ford had a "drive to a dealer" program. If I qualified, this program would pay me one hundred dollars plus fuel and oil expenses to drive a new 1955 Ford to a dealer in California. Soon I was set up to drive a new Ford Fairlane to Fresno, California, with a deliver date one day prior to reporting to Travis AFB, which was located in the Bay Area. Being an air force officer helped seal the deal, despite my youth and limited driving experience. What a deal! I called one of my classmates, Vaughn T. Lancaster (Lanc), to see if he was interested in sharing the driving chores and saving the airfare from Wheeling, West Virginia, where he lived. He agreed taking a bus to Detroit shortly before our planned departure.

Together, we poured over the maps, selecting a route to the South that we thought would keep us out of the way of any major spring storms. This was 1955; President Eisenhower had just started the interstate infrastructure program. Work on this high-speed continuous and divided highway was just getting under way. Accordingly, our best route was US-24, a highway, such as it was, that passed about a mile from my house and intersected the fabled Route 66 just south of Colorado Springs, Colorado. We made a pact not to stop in Las Vegas, Nevada, in order to avoid any trouble that might find us there. The new car came with radio but no antenna. Not a problem for a couple of air force trained electronic geniuses. We straightened out a wire coat hanger and attached it to the radio antenna receptacle, stuffing rags around the wire where it penetrated the fender. The car was nice, fast, and provided good gas mileage. It wasn't long before the bright lights of Las Vegas were on the horizon. As we drove down the strip, our resolve not to stop in Vegas faded to zero. We pulled into a cheap hotel, cleaned up, and changed into uniforms. We were hoping for some goodwill or sympathy.

I don't remember which one of the many gambling casinos we went into, but I recall that it had all the trappings, scantily clad waitresses, free dinner buffet, bar entertainment, and extravagant shows. We hit the free dinner buffet to get our energy level up and so as to not drink on an empty stomach. Then we hit the tables. I don't know where Lanc went, but other than pitching pennies, I had never gambled before, so I observed what was going on at the tables and roulette wheel. Finally, I settled on blackjack as the game that was relatively easy to comprehend with one simple rule: hit on sixteen and stand on seventeen. I was told that remembering the number of face cards could increase your odds by understanding how many were left in the deck. This was long before the dealers started using a "shoe" with several decks of cards in the shoe, making it nearly impossible to keep track of face cards. Moreover, the minimum bet was one dollar, so I figured I could play a long time for twenty dollars. It didn't take long for me to prove most of my assumptions wrong, and nearly one hundred dollars of my hard-earned pay had gone down the money slot next to the dealer. With the banter around the table, the dealer learned that I was on my way to Korea to fly in RB-26s.

To my surprise, he asked me if he could deal my cards up and throw me a card or cards if he thought I needed them. He suggested that I didn't seem to understand the game of blackjack very well. It seemed like a good opportunity for him to take advantage of me, but it couldn't get any worse—I was already out half a month's pay. Of course, he couldn't look at his hole card, or he would have been in big trouble with the people watching all the gaming tables through holes in the ceiling. Of all things, I started winning, and chips were piling up on my side of the table. The buildup of chips didn't come fast but rather steady with occasional setbacks. Finally, he asked me if I thought I'd won enough; his tone suggested the right answer was yes! I looked at the pile of chips and at him, and said, "Yes," took the chips, and offered him a tip as I'd seen other winners do. He declined rather loudly and wished me luck in Korea. When back at the buffet line for some desert and coffee, I counted the winnings—over $600, a gain of over $500 when subtracting my contribution. I found Lanc, and we headed for the motel to change back into our travel duds and to hit the road for Fresno. I was driving because it appeared to me that Lanc had been drinking too much to get behind the wheel.

We headed southwest out of Las Vegas toward Barstow, California. The next thing I remember was the sun was shining. The car was hot, and my mouth felt like cotton. Lanc was snoring with his head pressed up against the window. A quick look around, and everything seemed intact with the car parked about ten feet off the road next to a Joshua tree. No damage to the car. It was ten o'clock, but what day? We weren't sure how long we'd been zonked out. I took off in the direction the car was pointing, and in about two hours, a gas station appeared in the distance. In that part of the country, it was miles and miles between crossroads, let alone towns. At the gas station, we asked the attendant what day it was; he responded with the time, giving us a weird look. Again, we asked what day it was. It was a big relief to learn that we hadn't lost a day and were on track to turn the Ford in at the Fresno dealership.

The rest of the drive to Fresno was uneventful. California was still waiting to be discovered, and there wasn't much traffic on the highways, even though the freeways and interstates were still in the distant future. The manager of the Ford dealership was happy to see us, and even happier when the inspection of his new car revealed it was still in mint condition with no unexpected miles on the odometer. We removed the makeshift antenna before turning in the car, so he was unaware we had put some hours on the car radio. As promised in Detroit, the dealer paid me for the gas and the oil change. The dealership owner was kind enough to have one of the salesmen give us a ride to the Greyhound bus station. There we bought one-way tickets to Travis AFB and rode the bus to the base, arriving in midafternoon on our reporting date. At the base, a military car from the motor pool (a fleet of military vehicles used as taxis for transients) took us to Base Operations, where we learned our flight to Japan would not leave for two days. Another motor pool vehicle took us to the Visiting Officer Quarters (VOQ), where we made contact with other classmates from EWO School. CO Paul was a former staff sergeant that earned his wings and commission through the aviation cadet program and a good friend of Lanc. The three of us decided to spend the next day in San Francisco, seeing the sights and having some of the great food for which the city was famous. We had an enjoyable day and managed to return to Travis without getting in trouble.

Lessons Learned

The formal record of your life begins in kindergarten!

Upon graduation from high school, your only life record is your grades, which speak to your ability, willingness to study, and commitment!

If you're lucky enough to get a job, work hard and always do your best. Volunteer for the tough jobs and always be cheerful! Be the kind of employee you would like to have working for you!

When opportunity knocks, don't hesitate! Jump through that door with all your energy, grit, and commitment! Keep on driving until you succeed! Don't look for luck, just work hard! It is hard work that carries the day and wins the prize!

Airman Basic Piotrowski, Lackland AFB, TX

Airman 3C "Pete" Mop Detail, Keesler AFB, MS

Airman 2C Pete, ready for class, Keesler AFB, MS

Cadet "Pete", Lackland AFB, TX

Cadet "Pete" Harlingen AFB, TX, 1st Row 4th from left

CHAPTER 2

The Mysterious Far East

At the appointed time at Base Operations and Passenger Services, we learned that the air force's newly acquired C-97 Stratofreighter would be our aircraft for the Pacific crossing. The C-97 propeller aircraft was equipped with four reciprocating engines and appeared to be made from two fuselages, one upper and one lower with a distinct crease where these two halves joined. The unique design was based on seating passengers on both the upper and lower decks. However, the FAA did not certify the C-97 to carry passengers in the lower bay for safety reasons; seems like the FAA didn't believe people in the lower seating area would survive a gear-up landing. Perhaps the FAA restriction is the reason that only sixty of these aircraft were ever procured by the air force. The four power plants were Pratt and Whitney 3350 Wasp engines, the same engine that powered the B-50. The C-97 had a range of 2,672 miles at a cruising speed of 244 miles per hour (mph).

With this performance, the C-97 could make it from Travis AFB to Honolulu, Hawaii, against a very light headwind in 10.5 hours with just a little gas to spare. Getting to Tokyo, Japan, would require a stop in Hawaii and another at Wake Island for refueling, with each leg approximately ten hours long. In the 1950s, the air force had sufficient flight crews to position one or two at each refueling stop. Thus, shortly after the refueling and maintenance checks, a fresh and fully rested flight crew would be in the cockpit to fly to the next destination. The arriving crew would go into crew rest and be ready to fly the next day. Passengers had a four- or five-hour layover in the passenger terminal to snack or snooze before being rounded up for the next leg of the journey.

The stop at Wake Island brought to mind images of the fight to take this island from the Imperial Japanese Army during WW II. It was a hell of a battle, and every inch was paid for in too much American blood. But taking Wake Island as another stepping stone in the Pacific was a critical step in bringing land-based aircraft closer to the Japanese mainland islands. Looking out over the undulating hills and coral reefs, one could almost hear the sounds of rifle fire and artillery from salvaged guns taken from US Navy battleships and cruisers based on Wake Island and operated by US Marines attempted to defend Wake against Japanese invaders from December 8 through 23, 1941, before being overwhelmed. On September 4, 1945, Wake Island was retaken by a detachment of US Marines. Again, we had a handful of hours to wander around, just as we did at Honolulu, except the amenities were not nearly as plentiful or nice. The runway started near the shore on one side of the island and came close to the shore on the other end. There was a small cove that could be seen from the airfield ramp, and some people appeared to be fishing there. I learned it was likely they were fishing for sharks, which made swimming in the cove a dangerous pastime for the locals.

Soon we were back on the aircraft and, shortly thereafter, climbing into the night and winging our way toward Tachikawa AFB, Japan. I learned that we had gained a day in crossing the International Date Line into Wake Island and that Tachikawa Air Base was one of three air force bases in the Tokyo suburbs. It was also the headquarters for Far East Command (FECOM) and the point of entry into the Far East for all US military personnel. Fifth Air Force (5th AF) under FECOM also had a headquarters in Tokyo. The Sixty-Seventh Tactical Reconnaissance Wing (TRW) under command of 5th AF and Eleventh Tactical Reconnaissance Squadron (TRS) that CO, Lanc, and I were assigned to was located two hundred miles southwest of Tokyo. It all seemed like a lot of gobbledygook to someone that had spent his entire career in the Training Command.

Once on the ground and in the VOQ, it was nothing but one surprise after another. For example, the men's latrine was full of women cleaning this or that while you went about your business. At first, I decided to wait outside until they finished their cleaning chores. However, after watching several officers go in and come back out after what seemed a normal time, I came to the conclusion that in the Orient, the line between men and women was different. There was more to learn.

Sixty-Seventh Tactical Reconnaissance Wing

Two nights in the VOQ, and we were all processed in and sent down to Itami Air Base near Osaka, Japan. Itami was a pleasant surprise, as we expected to be living at K-14 Korea. We learned that the 67th TRW had recently moved from Korea to Japan but kept a detachment in Korea for operational missions tasked by Fifth Air Force to be flown out of Korea. In essence, the 11th TRS, our squadron, would be rotating aircraft and crews to K-14 to fly those missions, keeping several weather and electronic warfare crews and aircraft in Korea all the time.

The RB-26 had no heat or air-conditioning, like their counterparts designed, built, and flown during WW II. To stay warm in the winter, we were issued boots insulated with sheepskin (the wooly side against the foot). To keep the body warm, flying suits, crisscrossed with copper wire heating elements, were plugged into a rheostat that drew power from the aircraft electrical system. These heated flying suits kept you warm when they actually worked. Unfortunately, they were vintage early 1940s and were heavily used during the big war. Sometimes they would catch on fire; often they would experience a broken wire preventing current from flowing through the wires and providing warmth. Other times, when EWOs in the rear of the RB-26 moved around in performing their duties, the plug would be pulled from the rheostat. When that happened in the winter or at altitude, it only took a few minutes for the cold to sink in. The alternative was to wear several layers of wool clothing under a heavy sheepskin-lined leather jacket. Unless the temperature at altitude was extremely cold, this proved to be the best solution for staying warm. Oxygen masks were mandatory to prevent hypoxia on missions requiring flight altitudes above ten thousand feet. Masks were carried on every flight just in case weather or mission requirements forced the pilot to climb above ten thousand feet. Another item of issue was a Model 1911 .45-caliber automatic pistol. These pistols were to be worn in Korea and carried on flights flown out of K-14. The gun seemed rather large and heavy at the time. I didn't realize how famous the Model 1911 was in the annuals of warfare until years later.

Shortly after arriving at Itami AB, I received a letter from the Detroit Draft Board forwarded to me by my parents. It started with the traditional "Greetings" and ended with an admonishment to report to my local draft board for induction into the army. It seemed humorous at the time, and I penned a letter back, stating I was a second lieutenant in the USAF serving in Japan and Korea, serial number AO3009097. Two or three weeks later, I received a second letter urging me to quit evading the draft and report to my local recruiter or I would be guilty of a felony and possibly desertion. This got my attention! I took both letters to the squadron adjutant and asked for help. I never heard from the draft board after that.

I had only been at Itami for about a week. I was just getting settled in, meeting some of the old-timers who lived at K-14 before the transfer to Japan and learning the daily routine of the 67th TRW. There were actually four reconnaissance squadrons in the wing. Two squadrons, the Eleventh and the Twelfth, were based at Itami. The Eleventh Squadron's mission was electronic and weather reconnaissance. The Twelfth Squadron, another RB-26 unit, flew photo reconnaissance missions. There were two additional squadrons in the wing, the Fifteenth and the Forty-Fifth. These two squadrons were equipped with jet fighters with cameras. Cameras were installed in the aircraft nose, replacing six .50-caliber machine guns normally mounted there. The 15th TRS was based at Yokota Air Force Base near Tokyo, and the 45th TRS was based at Misawa Air Force Base in Northern Honshu. The Fifteenth, known as the Cotton Pickers, was converting from F-80s flown during the Korean War to RF-86As; and the Forty-Fifth, known as the Cats, was already equipped with RF-86As.

The 67th TRW Headquarters with all the major staff agencies was located at Itami AFB. The deputy commander for operations (DO), Col. Gerald R. Dix ("Dixie" to his colonel friends), was also located at Itami AB with his staff. Colonel Dix was a fighter pilot in WW II, and our paths would cross twice again in the years to come. The 67th TRW geographic span of control was quite large, requiring a lot of RB-26s flights to take the wing senior staff on visits to dispersed units. The wing motto was *"Lux Ex Tenebris,"* or "Light out of Darkness." The 67th TFW, like many air force wings post WW II and Korea, had some oddball aircraft for administrative and logistic support. Our oddballs were one C-47 Gooney Bird and one C-119 Flying Boxcar, both were powered by twin reciprocating engines like the RB-26.

While absorbing all of the noteworthy history and current activity of the 67th TRW, I, a lowly second lieutenant, received a letter from the commander, Col. Prescott M. Spicer (he retired years later as a major general). His letter stated that he reviewed my personnel file and noted that I lacked a college education, requesting that I reply by indorsement (RBI) as to what I was doing to rectify my educational deficiency. Well, I had never seen a colonel up close and personal before, let alone received a letter from one asking me to write back, so I sought advice from the squadron adjutant. His advice was that I should immediately enroll in one of the college courses taught on base and RBI with that information. Within an hour, I was enrolled in two college courses taught by a Japanese professor from Kansi University under the aegis of the University of Maryland. I wrote a very short letter, thanking Colonel Spicer for his interest and informing him I was enrolled in two courses with the U of M. His letter started a long journey that ended eleven years later with a bachelor of science degree from the University of Nebraska. I never heard another word from the wing commander until I flew as his navigator to Yokota Air Base so he could visit the Fifteenth Squadron located there. The aircraft had dual controls for pilot checkouts, and Colonel Spicer let me get some stick time. It was dark, and I was fighting the gauges when he asked how many college credits I had earned. What a surprise, the answer was twelve and still enrolled. I learned years later that commanders' secretaries provided the kind of information that led to that question.

It wasn't long before I was sent to K-14 to fly missions from there for an extended period of time. During the two years I was stationed in Japan, I had many tours in Korea. It was the place to go because that is where most of the operational flying took place. We lived in WW II squad tents with a wood floor and kerosene-fed potbellied stove, with a couple of bare bulbs of dubious wattage for light. There wasn't any place in Korea or Japan to buy 110 volt lightbulbs; hence we were stuck with the low-wattage bulbs provided by base civil engineers. On a sunny day during the summer, the dark-brown tent soaked up the heat and made life inside the tent unbearable. When it rained, the tents leaked, and beds moved through the night in a fruitless effort to get out from under the most recent leak. In the morning, all the cots were jammed together under the only waterproof section of the tents. In winter, the potbellied stove at the hottest setting would not provide enough heat to prevent frost from forming on our GI wool blankets. Earlier, I mentioned the M1911 .45-caliber pistols issued to all crew members. They hadn't been a problem until Lt. Herbie Dwight had his ear gnawed on by a rat and had to take the full series of rabies shots in the stomach. After that word got out, pistols were kept loaded and handy. Any noise would result in a couple of shots in the direction of the sound. Canvass tents don't stop or even slow down bullets, causing a lot of people to cower behind the stove away from the sound of the shots. Fortunately, no one was hit during these firefights.

Showers at K-14 were located about two city blocks from where the Eleventh Squadron tents were located and were only available to our squadron personnel for two hours, from 1400 to 1600 hours. During at least eight months of the year, showers were mandatory unless one was willing to sleep outside the tent. The most practical way to go to the shower facility was to wrap yourself in a towel, carry a second towel, wash cloth, and soap, and walk in flip-flops across the red dirt of South Korea. What I remember most was that every time I got lathered up, the water turned off. Believe me, it is a real mess trying to get soap off your skin without water, and the itching doesn't stop until the next time when running water is available. It was advisable to be there at 1400 hours sharp and be very quick. There were no leisurely showers taken at K-14.

The officers' club at K-14 was a large, long, heated, and watertight Quonset hut. It was where most aircrew members spent a majority of their time. Breakfast was twenty-five cents, lunch was fifty cents, and dinner cost one dollar and twenty-five cents, or roughly sixty dollars month. In those days, a bachelor officer received $47.88 for rations, so it was a near breakeven proposition if you ate all of your meals at the club. On the other hand, there wasn't another option for meals. There were three other things of note about the club; these were slot machines, occasional nurses, and nightly free movies. I've already made it clear that gambling was not something that I knew anything about, so I avoided the slots. Moreover, the large sign above the machines stating "If you think our slots are too slow, bring $100 to the cashier and she will give you $80 in return," indicating the machines were set to only return 80 percent to the players was enough to discourage a sober man. The nurses were not pursued by even the boldest lieutenant; they knew lieutenants had very little money and therefore chose the company of field grade officers, majors, through colonels. Movies were advertised to start at 1900 hours; however, in reality, they started when the base commander, a colonel, took his center seat in the front row. This seemed tolerable to the masses as long as he wasn't too inconsiderate in arriving late. One night, when he was over an hour late and the movie held for his pleasure, everyone up through the rank of major got up en masse and left the club. Surprisingly, he started being more punctual or sending a message to start the movie without him.

Electronic reconnaissance (ER) missions for RB-26s or the C-47 were tasked by fragmentary order, or frags. This slang evidently originated because a tasking order addressed all operational units on a daily basis; however, any given unit only received the fragment that applied to their unit, hence the frag order, or frag. The frag specified the route of flight, targets to be struck or information to be collected, call signs, frequencies, control agencies, and other necessary information to effectively complete a mission. The usual route of flight for RB-26 ER missions was to fly east from K-14 to the Sea of Japan and then north over international waters (at least twelve miles from the coastline of North Korea) to a latitude north of Wonsan Harbor and return along the same route. Another ER mission flew back and forth along the Demilitarized Zone (DMZ), while a third flew west to the Yellow Sea and north to Sinuiju, located just south of the Chinese border. Again, we always flew at least twelve miles from the Korean coastline and over international waters. During these flights, all enemy radars were precisely located and fingerprinted. The two EWO positions in the RB-26 bomb bay were equipped with current-generation receivers and direction-finding equipment. EWOs like me would record the precise angle and time of each event. After the flight, this information would be plotted in conjunction with the navigator's log and map plots to locate all the various enemy radar systems that illuminated the RB-26 during the flight. These would include the locations of search radar, surveillance radar, associated height-finder radar, and gun-laying radar that could point 37 mm, 57 mm, and 87 mm antiaircraft guns at aircraft with appropriate elevation and lead to hit them. The intelligence briefings received prior to these reconnaissance flights always emphasized that the North Koreans were mercurial, and even though there was an armistice between UN forces and North Korea, they could not rule out an attempt to intercept and shoot down one of our aircraft. Flights along the North Korean DMZ and coastlines were always fragged as night missions, usually three hours after nautical twilight. For this reason, our aircraft were painted black to make them more difficult to acquire visually by enemy pilots or ground gunners.

Of all the fragged electronic reconnaissance (recce) operational missions I was scheduled to fly, not one was successfully completed. There were many reasons for the aborted missions (i.e., excessive magneto drop on one or both engines, low engine oil pressure, fluctuating engine oil pressure, excessively high engine oil pressure, high cylinder head temperature, etc.) I began to think that the RB-26 was not a very reliable aircraft, but then the weather reconnaissance missions almost always flew as scheduled. There were times when it crossed my mind that the EWO pilots just didn't want to fly a few hundred miles within eyesight of North Korea's DMZ or coastline. I always pushed this thought into the background, but it lingered. Six years later, while flying B-26s as a pilot in Vietnam, I learned it was a very reliable combat aircraft (chapter 4).

Finding the electronic warfare (EW) missions nonproductive with regard to flying time and experience, I volunteered to fly as navigator on weather recce missions—as many as they would schedule me for. These recce missions were vital to understand the weather patterns moving over

North and South Korea for the two days after the mission. The RB-26 would take off from K-14, fly along the DMZ to the west, and then fly in a straight line across the Yellow Sea until the Shantung Peninsula of China was in sight, and then reverse course back to K-14. Each flight lasted about eight hours and was flown at 1,500 feet above the water. The onboard-enlisted weather observer sat in the clear acrylic nose recording barometric pressures, surface wind vectors based on ocean wave patterns, and temperatures along the route. These observations were broadcast in the clear over a high-frequency radio as the data was collected. Both China and North Korea could receive this data if they chose to. I suspect China did, and perhaps that was the reason why they didn't send fighter aircraft out to intercept our recce aircraft and shoot them down. These missions flew during the day, every day that weather permitted, and I don't recall one abort. I do recall an engine problem on one mission where the pilot was required to "feather the propeller" and shut the engine down in flight. Feathering the propeller involved pushing a large red button at the top of the instrument panel that caused the blades to turn in the propeller hub until they were parallel to the longitudinal axis of the aircraft. This greatly reduced the drag on that side of the aircraft and made it much easier to control yaw with the rudder. As I recall, the pilot in question started the engine back up just prior to entering the traffic pattern for landing. Perhaps he didn't feel comfortable landing the aircraft on one engine, although the RB-26 handled extremely well on a single engine because of the power available in a single R-2800 engine. What concerned the more experienced pilots is that a reciprocating engine that has become very cold in flight is not a reliable engine shortly after restarting, and if the reason for shutting it down was valid, then those are two good reasons for not restarting it. The more experienced and senior RB-26 pilots felt the restarted cold engine could have failed during a critical part of the landing pattern and overtaxed the pilot's ability to control it. The 67th TRW did not lose any RB-26s during the two years I was assigned there, so this incident was noteworthy, and we heard about it for some time in flight safety meetings.

Kimpo Airbase was guarded externally and internally by South Korean military. The only US Security Police were those at the entrance gates to ease the language problem and to respond to incidents on the base inside the wire. The flight line was guarded by South Korean military personnel, and they took their job very seriously. Failure to do their job properly and with enthusiasm resulted in harsh punishment and transfer to a much more demanding assignment. One extremely cold morning, when K-14 was enveloped in very dense fog, I was making my way to the flight line to assist in the preflight of the RB-26 scheduled for that day's early morning mission. I heard a shout but didn't understand it or think it was directed at me because I couldn't see anyone, therefore no one could see me. Wrong! The next sound I heard was not another "shouting" with a heavy Korean accent, but rather the mechanical sound made by the bolt of an M-1 .30-caliber carbine driving a bullet into the chamber. Once you've heard that metallic sound, it sticks in your mind. I froze until the Korean guard appeared out of the fog and spread-eagled me on the ramp. I lay there motionless until his superior arrived and checked my security badge. I've often wondered if he would have fired a warning shot or just gone for the kill if I hadn't stopped.

From a flier's standpoint, K-14 was an exciting place, and there were always a lot of F-86F flights taking off and landing. They patrolled along the DMZ, hoping, I suppose, that a MiG-15 would stray across the line, allowing one of our pilots to get a shot at a MiG. Periodically, the F-86 sorties would increase to what seemed like a wartime tempo—taking off in flights of four every fifteen minutes. This activity, I learned, was in support of RB-45 photo recce flights along the DMZ. The B-45 was supposed to be the first all-jet bomber, but production was cancelled in favor of the longer-range six-engine B-47. One or more of the B-45s were converted to the photo recce mission with a very long focal length lens that, on a clear day, could take pictures deep into North Korea. When they flew along the DMZ or up the North Korean coastlines, the MiG-15s came up in large numbers, and 4th TFW F-86s from across the runway provided protective cover for the RB-45, should the MiGs get opportunistic. I suspect the 51st TFW stationed nearby also took part in these escort flights. The F-86F had to be one of the greatest classic fighters of all time. She had beautiful sleek lines, easy to fly, and provided excellent visibility out of the cockpit. Further, the F-86F best represented an air superiority fighter that pilots craved since the dawn of aerial conflict over France and Germany in WW I.

The temporary duty (TDY) in Korea made it difficult to keep up with the college course work I had committed to and paid for. The professor was understanding and needed to keep the student numbers high enough to justify his fee. So with some extra effort to make up missed classes and assignments, it worked out, and college credits were piling up!

Itami AB was an entirely different story. It was a peacetime garrison with all the administrative trivia one could imagine. I can't recall how many EWOs were stationed at Itami in the 67th TRW. Regardless of the number, there were too many, as we had very little to do. Captain Johns was the senior EWO and our flight commander. EWOs were assigned to crews, as were pilots and navigators. A formed crew would consist of a pilot, navigator, and two EWOs. The concept was that we would usually fly as a formed crew and function more effectively because we learned to function efficiently and safely as a team. However, we didn't function as a crew, nor did we often fly as a designated formed crew. We spent most of our time at Itami in a room on the flight line allocated for EWOs. There were only two desks in the room, and these were designated for Captain Johns and 1st Lt. Harvey Ottinger, the second-ranking EWO and assistant flight commander. In addition, there were six second lieutenant EWOs that reported for duty every morning and were obligated to stand waiting for orders to do something. Most of us just leaned against the wall until lunchtime. The officers' club, where we usually ate, was next to the officers' barracks, both about a mile walk to the Eleventh Squadron's buildings on the flight line. An hour was allocated for lunch, so it was a brisk walk there and the same on return. There was no transportation for lieutenants, and tardiness was noted and not tolerated. In the morning and afternoon, fifteen-minute breaks were allowed for a base exchange (BX) run, which weren't really needed, as we had to walk by the BX going to and from the barracks every day—but it was a reason to get loose from the wall. Those were the days when everyone smoked but me, and it didn't take long for that little two-desk room filled with eight people (seven smokers) to fill it from floor to ceiling with smoke. After a few months of wall standing, an aircrew lounge was provided where we could go and play ping-pong or one of many card games, but not poker. We still had to report for duty at 0800 hours and hang around the walls until 0900 and then report back to the EWO office after lunch, just in case something came up. It was then I resolved that if I was ever in charge of something and there was nothing for the troops to do, I would release people for whatever they chose to do. It always proved to be good for morale.

In the late afternoon, 1600 hours as I recall, all aircrew members were required to attend the daily standup meeting. This was supposed to be a short meeting covering the operational accomplishments of the day, mission aborts, aircraft status, and the following day's flying schedule. Often there was a short flight safety item, and of course, the squadron commander, Lt. Col. Vigil E. Sheppard, was asked if he had any comments. This all took place in a rather large briefing room with rows and rows of benches for all officers and enlisted aircrew members, as well as a few senior maintenance officers and noncommissioned officers (NCOs) to brief the aircraft status. The squadron operations officer, a senior captain with WW II experience, was responsible for the standup and spent the better part of each afternoon collecting information and preparing view graphs for the meeting. Standup was a gross misnomer, as the only person standing was the briefer. The current-day and following-day information went quickly, and those who were scheduled to fly the next day already had received that information from their supervisor. The only new and relevant information was the aircraft tail number and readiness for flight status. Aircrew names, aircraft tail number, call sign, and takeoff times were also posted on the operations scheduling board next to the duty officer's counter, so the meeting was mostly form and very little substance. I don't recall Lieutenant Colonel Sheppard ever declining an opportunity to "say a few words" at the end of standup. He would usually regale us with stories about missions in WW II that were always interesting. Lieutenant Colonel Sheppard was a bomber pilot and claimed to have served in a unit in the Pacific Theater of Operations that was equipped with both B-17s and B-24s. It should be noted that the B-17 had a tail wheel, whereas the B-24 was the first bomber to have a nose gear, making it a sleeker and faster aircraft. Accordingly, the B-17 had its center-of-gravity aft at the main landing gear, while the B-24 center of gravity was well forward of the main landing gear. He claimed that some of his fellow pilots, current in both aircraft, would mistakenly try to make a three-point landing (all wheels touching at the same instant) with the B-24 and cause considerable damage to the aft fuselage structure. It's hard to imagine how a pilot and copilot could actually bring this about—they would have to achieve such a high angle of attack, causing the B-24 to stall. This would not be a good thing for the tail gunner or the twin vertical fins and rudders on the B-24. Nevertheless, it made an interesting story.

Mostly, Lieutenant Colonel Sheppard would digress into stories about disgusting behavior by young officers, like the time he saw a second lieutenant eating an ice cream cone in public while in uniform. It could have been me, as I was fond of ice cream and often purchased an ice cream cone at the BX to enjoy while walking back to the flight line after lunch. Once I learned how abhorrent this behavior was, I had to take a longer route, one where I wasn't likely to be seen. He also had a distracting habit of removing his wedding ring, one of those that came apart into three individual pieces but appeared to be a one-piece ring when worn. He would then roll those individual pieces around in his fingers as he spoke to the aircrews. *The Caine Mutiny* with Humphrey Bogart immediately came to mind when he did this.

Probably the biggest gaffs occurred when Lieutenant Colonel Sheppard talked about enlisted personnel as if they were a lower form of life. He often quoted a British officer who said, "Enlisted men are stupid, but cunning and bear watching." As mentioned earlier, the 11th TRS had a lot of enlisted aircrew members, mostly middle-ranking NCOs serving as weather observers. As a junior second lieutenant, I sat in the last officer row of benches right in front of the enlisted aircrew and maintenance personnel that were obligated to attend standup. The operations officer usually tried to signal our commander that there were enlisted in the room, but to no avail. One evening after repeating his favorite quote about enlisted men, a master sergeant sitting behind me stood up and said, "Sir, you're not talking about us enlisted men, are you? You must be talking about some other enlisted men!" Well, that ended Lieutenant Colonel Sheppard's diatribe, and he departed without apology or comment. As I recall, he missed the next several standups and thereafter rarely spoke at these meetings. He did not bring his wife to Japan and rotated back to the United States about a year after I arrived. I learned that not too long after returning to the CONUS (continental US), he was committed to an insane asylum in his home state of Idaho. Sad ending to a man who served his country bravely during WW II, but not surprising based on behavior I observed.

Lieutenant Colonel Sheppard was replaced by Maj. Demay H. White, also with WW II experience. He seemed to be more in touch with the mission and the men, flying more and getting involved with the various aspects of the squadron. He was also a very religious man and expected us to follow his lead in this respect. More than once, on payday, he would return my salute when I reported for pay and then say, "I didn't see you in church last Sunday."

I would usually respond with "That would not be possible, sir, I wasn't there."

Then he would ask, "What could be more important than church?"

And I would respond, "Sir, I was playing golf."

When there was enough of a murmur from those in the pay line behind me, the major would dole out my money with the final comment, "I expect to see you there next Sunday." He even went so far as to schedule an appointment for me to see the Catholic chaplain. However, motorcycle rides through the beautiful Japanese countryside and playing golf still came first. Later, I would regret not being more accommodating of Major White's requests. It was January 1956, eighteen months from my commissioning date, when Major White relayed my promotion to first lieutenant. With over two years of service behind me, this amounted to about a 30 percent increase in base pay. About this same time, a new Fifth Air Force commander, Gen. Fredrick H. Smith, arrived on the scene. After about two weeks on the job and observing some behavior held over from the Korean War, he published a directive that there would be no cohabitation with Japanese women by men under his command. Many servicemen to whom this directive applied to seemed amused but not concerned. About a month later, General Smith, evidently displeased with the impact of his initial edict, put out another and stronger directive. The latest directive stated in part, "Any man in this command living with a woman other than his wife will receive a below average officer efficiency report!" Now that conveyed a real and unambiguous threat to an officer's career! As a result, behavior changed immediately and significantly, but not necessarily for the better. Bachelors, who otherwise might have been involved in domestic bliss at some Japanese ladies' abode, were now spending a lot of time at the O'club and drinking too much. To some, the goal was to get drunk, and little was done to curb this activity. A large percentage of the captains, majors, and colonels had brought their families to Itami and hence spent little time observing what their subordinates were doing at the O'club. Excessive drinking was not a drain on the wallet. Mixed drinks sold for twenty-five cents; domestic beer was cheaper.

Despite the excessive drinking on the part of a few bachelors, flying continued without mishap. Not all sorties were flown for training or crew member proficiency; some were logistical in nature for the purposes of picking and delivering aircraft parts from one unit to another or picking up much-needed supplies. There was one logistics run I remember well for three reasons. First, and foremost, it was an unusual mission to pick up money! Itami AB had run out of change and needed a replenishment of several thousand dollars' worth of pennies. Second, I learned how some pilots could induce a magneto drop in the engine when it was to their advantage. And third, something occurred on that flight that saved my life and crew on a B-26 mission over South Vietnam six years later.

Pennies were the only US currency used in Japan and Korea and were important for making change at all the sales outlets (e.g. base exchange, officers' club, NCO club, commissary, etc.) At that time in the Far East, all cash transactions among DOD and other government agencies were in "monopoly money," or at least it looked like monopoly money, vice normal US tender. It was called script. Script came in denominations of twenty-dollar, ten dollar, five-dollar, and one-dollar bills, each in its own distinctive color. Change, half dollars, quarters, dimes, and nickels were also printed on paper but in smaller sizes than bills. Pennies were the only coins used for change. Evidently, the "real pennies" were needed so our wallets were not stuffed with one-cent paper notes. Script was evidently created to thwart black market activities. At least once while I was stationed in the Far East, all script in circulation was recalled and replaced with a different version, catching black marketers with hordes of worthless money.

On the penny mission, First Lieutenant Decker was the pilot, and I filled the right seat acting as copilot and navigator. The flight took off at twilight, landing at Yokota AFB just after dark. The pennies were waiting for us in tightly sealed wooden boxes. They were very heavy, at least eighty pounds each, so it was necessary to strap them down in the bomb bay of our ECM configured RB-26. The bomb bay was welded in the closed position, hence it was not possible to open them and lose all the pennies. However, there was a hinged access door in the bomb bay to enable the EWO working at the bomb bay console to bail out in an emergency. The penny boxes were loaded through this access door. After parking the RB-26 in the transient area, Lieutenant Decker walked over to the left engine nacelle and stuck a common straight pin, used for hemming dresses and things, into the ignition harness of the left engine. The ignition harness was nothing more than a very heavy-duty spark plug wire with a plastic insulating cover encased in a woven metal wire protective shield. The straight pin was the same color as the wire shield and difficult to see, especially if placed out of sight. Before we left the aircraft, Lieutenant Decker put an entry in the forms stating the left engine was running rough and requested a ground run-up. As we were eating dinner at the officers' club, a phone call came for Lieutenant Decker stating the left engine failed the ground check and would undergo maintenance the following day. For those not familiar with aircraft reciprocating engines, the spark plugs were fired by a magneto coil that rotated with the engine. There were two magnetos and two ignition harnesses for each engine, and two sets of spark plugs in each cylinder. The safety pin shorted out the spark to several or more cylinders. A ground check consisted of running an engine at 2,700 rpm and thirty inches of manifold pressure (ambient pressure at sea level). Under these conditions, a maintenance technician would move the magneto switch from both to the left position, back to both then to right and back to both. During this procedure, when the magneto switch was selecting the shorted harness, the engine would run extremely rough, if at all. An acceptable flight-worthy engine would have less than a 200 rpm drop when running on one magneto. When Lieutenant Decker was ready to return to Itami AB the next morning, he preflighted the aircraft, removing the pin from the left engine ignition harness, and all the pretakeoff engine checks were fine.

The weather was CAVU (clear and visibility unlimited), and takeoff was normal. However, during climb to altitude, there was a very light but noticeable vibration. As the aircraft accelerated to its cruise speed, the vibration increased and became alarming. At this point, Lieutenant Decker scanned all the switches and found that he left the landing/taxi lights extended after the night landing on arrival. The switch had three positions, off, extend, and on. The landing/taxi lights were half spheres about twelve inches in diameter located several feet outboard of the engine nacelle. When the switch was in the off position, the lights were submerged flush in the wing. If extended above normal approach and landing speeds, they caused the wings to vibrate. The faster the aircraft flew, the greater the vibration.

Lieutenant Decker was considered one of the top pilots in the Eleventh Squadron and was always hanging around the Ops Desk just in case a pilot was needed to fill in for someone who was coming down sick or for a maintenance test flight. He was infamous for one of his means to reduce boredom on a long recce flight. He would reduce power slowly on one engine while increasing power on the other to maintain speed while trimming the ailerons and rudders to maintain coordinated flight. His goal was to bring one engine to idle without the ECM or weather crewmen, who could not see the pilot, detecting the change. Once he had one engine in idle, he would reverse the process until the other engine was in idle. He would continue the process throughout a mission until his actions were discovered or until it was time to configure the aircraft for approach and landing. I was often fooled by his smooth manipulation of throttles and flight controls.

Motorcycles were not my thing, but some form of transportation was needed to get around the base expeditiously and for going places off base. Unfortunately, I failed to heed my father's wise advice about buying things. He always said, "When you buy a tool or something that you will use for any length of time, always buy the best you can afford, or you will spend a lot of money buying poor quality and will eventually end up buying the item you should have purchased in the first place." I started with a pedal bike that had a little gasoline engine with a friction wheel that could be held against the wheel rim once the bicycle was in motion. The gasoline engine would keep the bike going at reasonable speed on level ground. It worked reasonably well on base. However, it lacked the ability to carry anything and was useless off base. It was traded in on a slightly more powerful motor scooter that still was far from what was needed. Besides, most of my fellow barracks mates were into big full-fledged motorcycles. "Big" in those days meant something with 500 cubic centimeter displacement that would top out at 80 kmh, or 50 mph. That was fast enough on Japanese potholed roads of post-war Japan.

Eventually, I bought a used 350 cc Cabton. Cabton was the only manufacturer of large motorcycles in Japan at that time. Honda, Kawasaki, Yamaha, and Suzuki did not exist. This bike was big enough and powerful enough to get me back and forth to the Takarazuka Golf Course and around Osaka for shopping. Finally, I got to where I should have gone in the first place.

Post-war Japan was largely a nation of women. There were very few Japanese men between the ages of twenty and sixty—most of that age group were killed during the war, still holed up in caves on some of the Pacific Islands, or in Russian or Chinese prison camps. When there was a work party filling potholes or doing other labor-intensive tasks, it consisted of middle-aged women.

There is one flight incident that must be recorded. Lieutenant Baird and I were scheduled to fly a night ECM training mission over Japan, locating and fingerprinting US military radar. Baird and I were close friends after having climbed Mount Fuji, the famous snowcapped volcano just west of Tokyo, together in a torrential rainstorm. Poor timing on our part! On this mission, the quality and accuracy of our ECM work could be checked against the known location and type of radar. If we missed a radar that was emitting in the area during our flight, that would be known as well. These flights for EWOs were something like standardization and evaluation flight for pilots. Lieutenant Baird took the bomb bay position, leaving me the position just aft of his and through a bulkhead. If the event of an in-flight emergency required us to bail out, there was a two-foot-by-two-foot door in the bottom of the bomb bay that opened downward for us to jump out of. Pilot and navigator who were wearing backpack parachutes opened their individual acrylic canopies and jumped left and right, respectively, over the wing root. The downward bailout for the EWOs was devised for us to avoid bumping into the aircraft's elevator, which protruded from the tail, as well as having our parachutes becoming entangled with it. Going downward instead of left or right kept us out of the way of the flight crew as well.

We always wore yellow Mae West flotation vests when flying over Japan or Korea. Over that, we wore a parachute harness with snap rings for attaching a chest pack parachute, should bailout be necessary. These chest packs were never worn in flight because they would prevent EWOs from sitting at their electronic countermeasures (ECM) consoles. On this particular mission, the aircraft had been at altitude for a couple of hours when there was a rush of cold night air into my compartment. WW II aircraft were only equipped with red lights to preserve night vision when looking outside of the plane. Thus, it was difficult to see what had happened with much clarity, but it was good enough to see Lieutenant Baird slipping through the open escape hatch in the bomb bay with his chest pack lying next to his console. I struggled to get unbuckled from my seat and forward into his compartment while avoiding the open hatch, knowing full well I would be too late to help. To my amazement, there were his hands hanging on to the hatch's aft edge. Slowly, to my astonishment, he pulled himself back into the bomb bay! When he was safe, I quickly pulled the hatch in and closed and locked it. This may not have been a religious miracle, but a miracle nonetheless! The pilot aborted the mission after being told what happened. A subsequent safety investigation of all the RB-26 bomb bay hatches concluded that the door handle needed to be secured with a heavy canvas strap that would prevent the handle from being inadvertently kicked open in flight.

In early 1957, the word was out that the Eleventh and Twelfth Squadrons would transition to RB-66 aircraft and move to Yokota Air Base because the RB-66s needed a longer runway. Another rumor was that Warner Bros. Studios was going to make a film in Japan and that Itami was going to be involved. Pretty heady stuff, but not very interesting to me, as I would be returning to the United States in three months for a follow-on assignment, so it was unlikely that I would transition into the RB-66.

One Friday evening during happy hour at the O'club, Lanc slipped off of a bar stool and was comfortably lying on the floor. I was trying to coax him up and out of the club when a stranger in civilian clothes approached and asked if my friend and I would like to be in the movies. I impolitely told him to get lost. A few minutes later, he came back with the same request, only this time he said he was with Warner Bros. (WB), and they needed some air force officers to play the role of drunks in a bar scene. With this new information, I offered to see if our squadron commander would give us the time off.

The following Monday morning, I was in Major White's office with three requests. The first, a request for pilot training when I returned to CONUS; second, an application for a regular air force commission; and third, some time off or leave to play extras in the movie *Sayonara*, which was being filmed in nearby Kyoto. The first two required his endorsement and signature, the third just a head nod. At this time in my short career, it was obvious that regular officers were selected for all the schools and training that would enhance an officer's chance for promotion. Lieutenant

Colonel Sheppard, when asked why he only selected the two regular officers in the squadron for these choice temporary duty assignments, responded, "Reserve officers are a short-duration fix to a manning shortage. Only regular officers will be around for any length of time and therefore deserve the training." With this in mind, in addition to the fact that the air force was mounting a regular officer augmentation, I wanted to get elevated to regular officer status and be on the "First Team."

After hearing my requests, Major White authorized participation in the movie, noting that we would not be in the RB-66 upgrade because of our imminent departure for CONUS, and with the proviso that we not allow ourselves to be drawn into any movie participation that would discredit the air force. With regard to the other two requests, he said he would consider them. That sounded ominous, but he didn't say no or throw the paperwork in the trash can.

Filming actually started at Itami Air Base. One of the F-86F Squadrons in Japan painted up one of their aircraft to mimic the Fifty-First Tactical Fighter Wing (TFW), the unit that scored the most MiG kills during the Korean War. The aircraft was filmed landing at Itami. After engine shut down, Marlon Brando climbed into the cockpit, and Red Buttons, his crew chief, climbed up to talk to him about his latest mission and MiG kill.

Lanc and I packed our best dress blue uniforms and took the local train to Kyoto, an ancient Japanese city with numerous famous Buddhist and Shinto shrines located throughout the city. Because of its historical, religious, and cultural importance to Japan, Kyoto and its sister city, Nara, were taken off of the target list during WW II and were spared from bombing. We stayed at the same hotel as the stars, with all expenses paid for by WB, and received a stipend of twenty-five dollars a day for our work. We may have been at the same hotel, but did not have the same accommodations. It was a star-studded cast. The most famous then and now were: Marlon Brando as Maj. Lloyd Gruber, USAF, as well as F-86 pilot and ace; James Garner, as Capt. Mike Bailey, United States Marine Corps (USMC); Ricardo Montalban, as a famous Japanese kabuki performer by the name of Nakamura; Red Buttons as Sgt. Joe Kelly, USAF, and F-86 crew chief; Patricia Owens as Major Gruber's fiancée; Nancy Umeki as Katsumi, the Japanese girl who steals Major Gruber's heart.

The next day, we were on the set in uniform and ready to play the role of air force officers doing whatever the famous director, Josh Logan, wanted us to do that was creditable from an air force point of view. James Garner was the only "real person" in the cast. He regularly played catch and touch football with the enlisted extras and spoke casually with all of us.

It was January and exceptionally cold for Japan. The movie setting was springtime, and the dresses Patricia Owens wore in the outdoor scenes must have chilled her to the bone. We were dressed in winter wool gabardine and wore parkas over our uniforms when we weren't on camera and still felt the damp chill. We were told the bar scene was off in the future because Director Logan wanted to get all of the outdoor scenes done before the real spring rains made outdoor filming impossible. I must admit there was nothing glamorous about making movies. Everyone but Brando arrived on the set at 0700 and stayed until the film was in the can, sometimes as late as 2000 hours.

One day, there was a short indoor scene where two army MPs arrive to subdue and escort James Garner away from an argument he was having with an actor playing the role an army major general. It was indoors, and the MPs removed their hats when they crossed the threshold. They were real soldiers and following normal service customs and courtesies. However, MPs carrying sidearms never remove their hats when going into a building because that compromises their ability to use the gun if needed. They also were wearing ribbons for the movie that they hadn't earned and therefore didn't have them on their uniform in the proper order. We brought this to the director's attention, and in the next instant, we were no longer just extras for a bar scene; we were technical advisors. These new responsibilities, disappointingly, came without an increase in pay. Lanc and I called back to the squadron to see if we were needed for any operational duties or another stint at K-14. We were assured that we weren't needed and to make the air force look good in the movie. That was an impossible task with Brando and Buttons wearing the uniform.

After many more outdoor shoots, the day of the officers' club bar scene finally arrived. It didn't really take place in an officers' club, as there weren't any US military facilities within miles of Kyoto. The most representative facility the Warner Bros. team could find was a high-class house of prostitution. Evidently, Warner Bros. paid the madam and her charges enough for them to take a week vacation, and the ladies turned the facility over to Director Logan and his crew.

The scene in the bar was relatively simple and short. Capt. James Garner, USMC, was seated on a bar stool near the middle of the bar just left of center. All Maj. Marlon Brando, USAF, had to do was enter through the front door and walk past the table where I was seated with a bottle and glass of Asahi beer, then over to the bar and sit down on a bar stool. Once Brando sat down, there was to be a few minutes of banter between them; they would form a friendship and then depart to meet some dancers and singers at the Takarazuka Music Hall. The latter was a real place and very popular with both Japanese locals and US service personnel. Brando, evidently, was in a foul mood or determined to punish Director Logan, as it took all day and late into the night before there was enough good film to end the farce. It was embarrassing to watch. Brando did just about everything one could do to ruin the filming. He'd slam the front door when he came in, bump into tables when he walked through the room, knock over the bar stool, slide off the bar stool, mumble something to me when I spoke my line, "Good *morning*, Major Gruber," or torture his lines when speaking with Garner. When he was ready for the long day to end, he did everything flawlessly from beginning to end, and the film was in the can. All through this, Lanc slept soundly on a couch after drinking a few Asahi beers during the early missed takes.

There were a few more outdoor scenes with Lanc and me, along with other military and Japanese civilians, filling up the background. Then it was time for us to end our Hollywood careers and return to Itami Air Base. Back in the real world, I was surprised and excited to learn that I had orders to proceed to Stallings AFB, North Carolina, and join Class 58M for pilot training. I thanked Major White for his support and started the journey back to the CONUS with a big smile on my face, accompanied by a little uneasiness, wondering if I had what it took to get through pilot training. The washout rate in pilot training was a lot higher than it was in observer training, and with the Korean War over, the bar would be set a lot higher for graduation.

Lessons Learned

Never give up on your dreams!

Higher education is essential in the professions!
Getting a bachelor's degree in residence is not the only
option—avail yourself of every opportunity!

Life is a continuum of learning—recognize
this early in life rather than later!

Volunteer for jobs that need doing; supervisors
appreciate and notice volunteers!

2nd Lt. Pete, K-14 Korea, RB-26

1st Lt. Pete, Itami AB, Japan

Bar Scene in Sayonara, Kyoto, Japan

CHAPTER 3

On to Pilot Training

Somewhere over the Pacific heading east, it occurred to me that I had taken the first step toward a longer, much longer stint in the air force. Originally, I applied for flying training to better my life in the service, to improve my civilian job opportunities when it came time to leave, and to make more money. At this juncture, my service totaled four and a half years—longer than my original enlistment. Pilot training would take a year with a follow-on commitment of four years upon graduation. That came to a total of nearly ten years, halfway to retirement. This was something to consider in the future.

The air force provided commercial air transportation back to San Francisco, California. They would pay me a mileage rate to get to my next assignment at Stallings Air Base, North Carolina. That was a good deal because the trip would allow me to stop off at my boyhood home in Detroit, Michigan. I hadn't the foresight to book a follow-on flight to Detroit, where I would pick up the new 1957 blue-and-white Mercury Monterey ordered in Japan for delivery at the Ford Rouge Plant in Dearborn, Michigan. On arrival at San Francisco International Airport, I learned there were no seats left on the last flight to Detroit. I purchased a seat on the next available flight and went into town to see the sights of the city by the bay. After walking the streets and taking in the vistas and cacophony of the city, I took the elevator to the Top of the Mark hotel, a place often talked about by fellow aviators in the Orient.

Sitting at the bar, I noticed tens of bottles of booze, all of them covered with a knitted sock, each with a different squadron emblem. I recognized that all these squadron patches belonged to units in Korea and Japan—with four from the 67th TRW. I asked the bartender for the story behind these covered bottles. He said it all started with one young officer on his way home who passed through the bar with an idea for preserving some of the esprit from the Korean conflict. He paid for a bottle of good scotch, covered it with a knitted sleeve, and handed it back to the bartender. He asked that anyone in uniform (or with a military ID card) could request a drink from the bottle, and it would be free because the scotch had been paid for. In addition, the lieutenant stipulated that the person who took the last drink from the bottle had to replace it. Soon, the bartender said they had tens of covered bottles, emblazoned with unit emblems, covering that particular shelf. He reported that many drinks were taken free, and many bottles were duly and cheerfully replaced over time.

After a little calculation, I came to the conclusion that a replacement bottle of booze couldn't cost more than fifty dollars. Cocktails were five dollars! Therefore, if I had four drinks over a long evening and had to replace a bottle, the net cost would be thirty dollars, not a lot of money to perpetuate a tradition! I'd have four drinks and a couple of bowls of peanuts. I started with a drink from the Foxy Few and ended with one from the Owls of the 11th TRS. All were paid for by aviators going home from a combat tour who passed through this bar before me.

The next day, I found myself getting acquainted with young sisters that were barely born when I left home. My father had retired from the Detroit Police Force and was earning more money than ever before in his new job as a toolmaker at General Motors, using the skills he learned in the US Navy in WW I. We now had a lot in common and talked for hours about how precision machining had changed as Detroit retooled for commercial production after the Korean War.

Shortly after arriving home, there was a call from Air Force Personnel advising me that Stallings AFB was closing, and I was being diverted to another Primary Pilot Training base. I could have my choice, either Marianna AFB, Florida, or Marana AFB, Arizona. I chose Marana, thinking the weather for flying would be better in the desert than on the Gulf Coast, and I was really weary of living in very humid locals. My new reporting date meant my stay in Detroit was being cut short. I visited a number of high-school classmates, a few girlfriends that were still single, gassed the car, and headed west. Once on the road, it struck me that the air force would only reimburse me for the travel from San Francisco, California, to Marana, AB, Arizona, which was about a third of the distance from California to Stallings AB, North

Carolina, my original assignment. I was out of pocket a few hundred dollars because of the change in training bases.

It was March 1957; the weather was good. The new Mercury was fast, smooth, and comfortable. I stopped in Albuquerque, New Mexico, to visit a short while with John Hughes's aunt and uncle whom I'd met over the Christmas holidays of 1953. A few hours down the road, and I spent the night in Gallup, New Mexico, with Babe and Earl Hughes, John's parents. The whole trip was uneventful except for a speeding ticket south of Colorado Springs on what is now I-25. The trooper was just trying to run me down to find out why the car didn't have license plates. When he discovered how fast he had to go to catch up, he decided a ticket was in order.

It was late afternoon, the day after leaving Gallup. The gate of Marana was in sight, and the local radio station was handing out the news. I couldn't believe what I was hearing; the newscaster stated that the air force announced it was closing Marana Air Base. I hurried to the assigned squadron orderly room and signed in—this would ensure the air force had to reimburse me for getting there and then again, it seemed, to go yet again to another base. I was beginning to think the air force was going to shut down pilot training altogether, and I was too late. With the Cold War between NATO and the Warsaw Pact getting testier, this seemed far-fetched, but ballistic missiles were going into silos, perhaps far fewer pilots were needed.

The next day was filled with in-processing for Class 58M, as we learned that Marana AB would stay open long enough for all currently assigned pilot trainees to get thirty hours of flying time, enough to be ready for the T-28 at our next base. That was a relief!

My roommate at Marana was John "Jack" Carr. He came to pilot training directly from College ROTC in New York City. He was a very nice young man, about my age, but looked at me as a big brother because of my few years of experience in the USAF. Jack didn't have a car and asked one day if I would take him to town so he could buy something he needed. I trusted him, so I threw him the Mercury keys, saying, "Take the car, I need to study the Dash-1 (aircraft manual)."

He replied, "I don't have a driver's license, and I don't know how to drive."

My jaw dropped open, and a long conversation started along the line of "How could any red-blooded American boy pass through his teenage years without knowing how to disassemble a car and put it back together, let alone know how to drive it?"

His response was that a car is not needed in New York City, and if you had one, there is no place to park it; and the traffic is so bad, you can't get from his apartment to where you want to go.

I rejoined with "How do you take a girl out on a date?"

He responded, "Take a cab or the subway." I was astounded but drove him to town, relieved that he didn't try to learn to drive with my new car.

The T-34 Mentor was a tandem Beechcraft aircraft with tricycle landing gear, the single aspirated Continental engine producing 225 horsepower. The military version was rated at +10 and −4.5 Gs. It's inconceivable to me that a pilot could put 10 Gs on the aircraft at the speeds the T-34 could attain, even in a pullout from a very steep dive. It was a sleek little plane with a nice-sounding engine, a modification of a commercially available Beechcraft 45 Bonanza. All the instructors were civilians with thousands of hours flying time; some of that logged during WW II, and the rest logged while instructing wannabe air force officers and cadets. No doubt they were all very good pilots and excellent instructors with a passion for flying.

It was largely nonstop flying once we passed a written test on various airspeeds for takeoff and landing and emergency procedures, as well as a blindfold test on switches and levers in the cockpit. Marana was in the desert, about halfway between Phoenix and Tucson. In those days, both were small towns, and there were no distractions like girls or bars in Marana.

I soloed on the fourth flight, as did my roommate. It was a strange feeling when the instructor got out and said, "Go fly for another hour, and make a good landing when you return. Be sure and tell the tower this is your first solo when you enter the traffic pattern." That speech was longed for, but sobering. I'd flown over six hundred hours in RB-26, C-47s, and C-119s but never alone. The traditional dunking in the pool took place that afternoon with classmates doing the honors.

Flying came almost daily after that. Training us to fly well and safely was the instructor's job, but as the time for graduation neared, you could see the concern on their faces as they wondered about their future as military instructor pilots. After the first solo flight, about every other flight was on aerobatics and emergency procedures with an instructor. Making perfect landings with the main wheels touching down on a painted white line across the runway was also emphasized. There was also a contest to see which student could land the closest to that line in three consecutive attempts. This was a little more difficult than it sounds! It was stipulated that the throttle had to be set on the base leg of the traffic pattern prior to turning final. Throttle adjustments on final approach would disqualify the pilot from the competition! A pair of instructors in the mobile control unit graded the performance. One observed and scored the touchdown points, while his partner watched and listened for any indication of adjustment to the throttle setting. I scored three perfect touchdowns on the line and won the contest.

Aerobatics were challenging and rewarding when executed perfectly. The T-34 was power limited and could fall out of a loop or Immelmann (maneuver named after a French pilot in WW I) if the maneuver was not entered properly and flown smoothly. Any ham-fisted movement of the stick, and the pilot was in the recovery mode. The aerobatics repertoire also included the aileron roll, barrel roll, lazy eight, split S, and cloverleaf. Of all these maneuvers, the cloverleaf was the most demanding to do correctly. It involved starting to climb as if entering a loop while slowly blending in aileron so as to turn the aircraft ninety degrees to the left or right while coming over the top and descending inverted down the back side. This was done four times in succession until the aircraft was back on the same compass heading from which it started. It was also important to be at the same altitude and airspeed at the end of the maneuver as at the beginning. Done right, the cloverleaf was a thing of precision and beauty. Because the heading changes in a cloverleaf were exactly ninety degrees, it helped if you could start the maneuver at an intersection with the roads crossing perpendicular as in two section line roads. The roads helped immensely in getting the direction change of ninety degrees spot-on without reference to a compass. Unfortunately, there were few roads in the area, let alone two crossing at right angles.

One incident from Marana sticks in my mind. Most of the students were up for solo flights to build their confidence and practice the obligatory stalls, spins, aerobatics, and landings. On returning to the airfield, the wind was kicking up a lot of dust, and tumbleweeds were racing across the ramp and runways at great regularity. Turbulent winds down the runway can be a problem; turbulent gusty wind across the runway can be a very big problem. This day it was the latter. An instructor pilot (IP) was always on duty in mobile control, a small glass-enclosed structure on wheels that sat near the approach end of the runway in use. Except for a low metal wainscot, it was glass all around and had multiple radios to communicate with the control tower and aircraft in flight and on the ground, as well as landlines to senior officers and emergency services such as fire stations and ambulances. The IP's responsibility was to ensure safety of flight, which included changing the runway if crosswinds exceeded the T-34's limits. As I switched to tower frequency for landing instructions, I overheard the tower operator ask the mobile control (MC) instructor if he wanted to change runways because the wind gusts were exceeding the Dash-1 limits of the T-34. The MC instructor, in a laconic western drawl, responded, "No, let's leave it the way it is. If someone crashes, we will change the runways." High winds and summer thunderstorms are common in the high desert of Arizona, so it was not surprising that the airfield was one big square of concrete measuring about four thousand feet on each side. The three primary runways were laid out with thick painted stripes in a big triangle. All runways had appropriate lighting for twilight and night operations. However, because it was all paved, if a major storm came up by surprise, the instructors would drive vehicles on the concrete in a line pointing directly into the wind. Thus, a pilot could bring an aircraft in for a landing directly into the wind as long as the wind was a few knots lower than the landing speed of the aircraft.

The decision to not change the runway until someone crashed applied to me, as my aircraft was about to enter the landing pattern. With a little extra speed on final to accommodate wind gusts and the cross control needed to compensate for the direct crosswind, I flew the plane down final with the right wing down into the wind and putting in all the top rudder available. The touchdown was hard, almost scraping the low right wingtip. But the plane stayed straight along the centerline. It was a good feeling to be on the ground. I learned later that night, the landing runway was changed shortly after my landing to bring in the last few remaining pilots.

Soon, Marana was in the rearview mirror, and the Mercury was headed to Bainbridge, Georgia, where basic pilot training would continue in the T-28A, a much larger aircraft with a powerful radial engine. This time, I had a lot more confidence in my ability to succeed as a pilot. While at Marana, Jack Carr had learned to drive, purchased a car, and was headed to Bainbridge as well. We would be roommates there too.

Bainbridge was a very small town in southern Georgia, not far from the Florida line, but at least it was a town; as opposed to Marana, which was just an airfield in the middle of nowhere. After signing in to prove I had arrived and going through the obligatory in-processing, all students in blocks of four were assigned to an instructor and a flying unit. My instructor was Mr. Taggart. When he arrived at our small table, we stood stiffly at attention until he sat down. The routine was pretty much the same as at Marana, except everything was bigger. The T-28A Trojan weighed about three times as much as the T-34. It was about as big as a WW II P-47 with tricycle landing gear powered by a Wright 1300

Cyclone radial engine that developed 800 horsepower, nearly four times as much as the T-34. The Dash-1 aircraft manual was much thicker, and the number of phases in the training program included instrument flying, night flying, and cross-country navigation along with basic maneuvers and aerobatics. With my background, navigation looked like it could provide more time for learning the T-28.

Just sitting in it, the T-28 was impressive! The engine had a putty-putty sound like an idling Harley-Davidson motorcycle and was hard to start without one or two backfires. When it backfired hard and loud, it was necessary to shut it down while the crew chief checked the exhaust stacks to make sure one hadn't cracked. Mr. Taggart emphasized over and over the need to get the start procedure exactly right. It didn't come easy or quickly, but it was eventually mastered. The little T-34 didn't exhibit any torque when the throttle went forward on takeoff, but the T-28 required a lot of left rudder until the airspeed built up and the rudder became more effective. It was a skill and art form to blend in the power and rudder to keep the nose on the runway heading throughout takeoff and climb-out.

Solo time in the big bird came and slipped into history. Stall series required more attention to torque, as did aerobatics. If the pilot didn't blend in rudder during the maneuvers with large changes in speed, the aircraft nose would track as much as thirty degrees off line in a loop, unacceptable on a check ride. There were lots of section line roads and ninety-degree intersections in southern Georgia, so there was no getting away with sloppy aircraft control while doing aerobatics. Spins were a hoot. The T-28 was so honest, you had to hold it into a spin to achieve three or four turns, and it lost altitude like a rock when in a spin.

On one of the solo flights, I was waiting on the runway for permission to take off behind another T-28. He got the green light from the tower and started his takeoff roll. Shortly after getting airborne, there was a puff of smoke from the engine, and the plane settled to the ground on its belly in a shower of sparks and slithered off the runway to the right. The fire trucks raced to the spot as I heard the tower give me permission for takeoff. I was still focused on the crash when the tower operator came back in a stern voice, "Two, what are you waiting for?" The throttle went forward, and away I went. The rest of the day was uneventful. Another thing about the T-28A that could get your attention was a little red light in the center of the instrument panel. It was called the sump warning light and was connected to two prongs of a magnet that were insulated from each other. If metal shavings from the engine found their way into the oil sump and shorted the magnet, the little red light lit up, conveying the message that the engine is shedding metal and may fail eminently. The pilot's response was to get the aircraft safely on the ground immediately. While returning to Bainbridge or a closer suitable runway, the pilot needed to keep looking for farmers' fields to put the T-28 down in should the engine seize up. There were some red lights, but no engine failures in flight.

At the end of contact flying, it was time for the navigation flight—a round-robin of about 120 minutes in a triangle over the countryside to the north of Bainbridge. I would be the laughing stock of the class if I got lost on this solo check ride. We were told that usually two or three students became lost and ended up at a strange airfield once they started running low on fuel. At forty minutes per leg, the T-28 would travel about one hundred miles. It would be dead reckoning the entire route, time and distance with the aid of checkpoints on the ground. I didn't get lost, but two of my classmates did. Airplanes with two instructors in each T-28 had to go out to rescue them and pay for the fuel that had to go into the airplanes.

Instrument flying was the first new skill to master, and for me, in the beginning, it was a big and seemingly insurmountable challenge. There was a primitive device called a Link Trainer that was used to teach basic instrument flying skills on the ground before attempting them in flight. About ten of these trainers were lined up side by side in a long low building. To my surprise, the Link instructors were all rather young attractive women. The Link routines were quite simple in theory: vertical S's on a compass heading then vertical S's while turning sixty degrees to the left and then back to the right, climbing and descending at a constant speed and rate of descent for one thousand feet, then climbing and descending at a constant speed and rate while turning to a given heading. All these maneuvers were designed to bring different instruments into play, forcing the student to develop a constantly moving instrument cross-check at an increasing rate. When a student was having difficulty with these maneuvers, these attractive young ladies would pop open the Link Trainer door, throw a leg over the side, and with one hand for stick, throttle, and trim, demonstrate perfectly the maneuver being attempted by the student. Those Link Trainer instructors were attractive, but very intimidating.

Instrument flying in the T-28 was easier than in the Link Trainer because the aircraft was a more stable platform. As soon as I perfected the cross-check, instruments became a breeze and a source of pride. It wasn't long before Mr. Taggart had me flying ground-controlled approaches (GCAs) under the hood. The hood was a canvas contraption that was stowed behind the rear seat of the T-28A. It was pulled forward to mate with the top of the instrument panel when a student was flying instruments or receiving an instrument check. To fly a GCA, the student contacts Approach Control on the proper radio frequency and is then given heading vectors and altitudes to fly until handed over to the GCA radio frequency. The GCA controller sits at a radar console that displays aircraft returns on both heading and glide slope displays. The controller radios commands to the pilot to turn left or right so many degrees and when to start a descent on the glide slope. After that point, the commands included how many feet the aircraft is above or below the glide slope and instructions to climb or descend. I became so proficient at GCAs that Mr. Taggart allowed me to land under the hood and then initiate a touch-and-go and missed approach to another GCA, all on instruments under the hood. This gave me the confidence that I could make a blind GCA to an airfield that was well below weather minimums rather than bail out and lose a good aircraft. On these GCAs and missed approaches, I noticed that the control stick seemed to shake slightly from time to time. I knew the controls were cabled directly to the stick and rudders, so the shake didn't make any sense. Upon landing, I reported the occasional but slight shake to the crew chief. He started to laugh. I thought he was laughing at me until he explained that Mr. Taggart had taken a bag of pecan nuts with him on the flight and was known to crack the shells open between his gloved fist and the top of the control stick—thus the occasional jiggle. He went on to say that it was a compliment to my flying ability. There were more jiggles on future flights—a sign that I was doing well.

Recovering from unusual attitudes was always a challenge but great training. They were done with the student under the hood in the backseat. The IP would say, "Close your eyes," and I always did; otherwise, you could look good but not learn anything. Then the IP would dive, climb, and turn for several minutes to create a vertigo condition in the student. With the nose pointed steeply up or down and in about a ninety-degree roll, the IP would say, "Recover." Recovering was important, but it had to follow the correct procedure. If the nose was above the instrument horizon, the procedure is, increase power, lower the nose, and roll wings level. If the nose was below the horizon, the procedure is, decrease power, roll wings level, and pull the nose up to the horizon. The unusual altitudes created by Mr. Taggart were always extreme. All this was done with the student under the hood on instruments. There was a rearview mirror in the front cockpit that enabled the IP to see if you tried to cheat by looking out from under the hood.

Mr. Taggart added a few extra maneuvers to the syllabus but asked me not to say anything to other students or instructors. We flew inverted, and we did Snap Dragon 8s. A Snap Dragon 8 is a conventional lazy eight until the T-28 reached the low speed wing down point at ninety degrees of turn. At this point, the pilot pushes in full rudder and snatches the control stick full back! In an instant, the aircraft snaps 360 degrees around its longitudinal axis. Once back to the proper attitude, the pilot releases stick and rudder pressure and continues the lazy eight to the opposite side of the maneuver and then repeats the snap roll. We also flew rolls, loops, and Immelmanns on instruments.

About halfway through the T-28 Phase, the air force announced a change that would have a profound effect on my fellow student pilots. The change was that all student pilots would now incur a five-year obligation after graduation from pilot training versus the four-year commitment they had signed up for. No big deal, I thought, just another year of operational flying before the air force would consider letting me go. Was I wrong! My classmates with no prior service, who earned their commission through ROTC then entered directly into pilot training, viewed this as a unilateral change in their contract with the air force. They saw the air force as an untrustworthy employer who could not be relied on to honor a contract.

The air force attempted to sweeten this change in contract by allowing all students to attain eighty hours of flying time in the T-28 before they had to take a decision to continue pilot training or revert to a four-year nonflying career starting on the day they entered active duty. Immediately, there was a lot of unease among my fellow aviators, except for the other three with prior service. For two weeks, I talked to individuals and groups about what the real air force was like. I suggested that the hours of flying time they would log and experience gained in five-year commitment would be beneficial! Further, I opined that the additional year would likely result in promotion to captain and that the additional rank and experience could greatly benefit them in their chosen follow-on career, whether it was with the airlines or in the corporate world. During these conversations, it appeared there were some converts. However, when left alone, they tended to revert to believing the air force was an employer that could not be trusted.

A few days later, when Mr. Taggart arrived at our table, he started giving out assignments for the day. "Student X will fly solo." OK. "Student Y will go to the Link Trainer" brought a loud "I quit" from Y, who got up and walked out. I was scheduled to fly instruments, and the other student had that period off. That scene repeated itself day after day until there were only a handful of students left. Mr. Taggart must have had seniority over other instructor pilots because students who were continuing in pilot training were being transferred to our table.

As pilot trainees continued to quit, flight instructors started getting nicer. Instead of telling us what we were going to do for the day, they started asking us what we would like to do. Most of those who intended to quit but were hanging on to get the full eighty hours before reaching the decision point said they wanted to go solo. There were only so many authorized solo hours per student, so that tactic only worked to a point. As I saw this unfolding, I asked Mr. Taggart if we could talk privately. When we were out of hearing of other students, I told him that I was going to continue in the program and wanted him to be as tough on me as he would be under normal circumstances and that I wanted to leave Bainbridge the best pilot that he could produce. After that discussion, Mr. Taggart would arrive at the table with a bag of Dunkin' Donuts and say, "Pete, get your butt over to the Link. You'll fly instruments with me the second period!" Then he would turn to the rest of the table, saying, "Let's have some coffee and doughnuts while we discuss what is best for you."

Night flying and night navigation training were not difficult, and I overcame my concern of getting lost on the night navigation round-robin. Next, there were a couple of flights with Mr. Taggart to polish up aerobatics and instrument work, which would be tested on the final check ride. He stressed "unusual altitude recoveries," as there is very little opportunity to find yourself in one of these altitudes unless you really screw up and nearly kill yourself. An instructor pilot other than your own or a military check pilot could give check rides. The military pilots were there to ensure the government was getting pilots trained to the standards specified in the contract they had with Southern Aviation. I drew the senior military check pilot for my check ride. It was very formal, and he didn't say anything during the flight except tell me what to do next and when to get under the hood. When it was over, he had little to say with the exception of a few suggestions on how to do something a little smoother or better.

The T-28A was history, but on a sad note. On the local news, there was an announcement that the air force was closing Bainbridge AFB. I received orders sending me to Bryan AFB, Texas, for the T-33 Basic Course and the path to jet fighters. The other path was the B-25 Basic Course and then on to multiengine aircraft, primarily Strategic Air Command (SAC) flying bombers or tankers, or the Military Airlift Command (MAC) flying cargo aircraft.

Only four student pilots in Class 58M graduated from Bainbridge—our class picture was taken in the Commander's Office instead of the usual crowd on the wing or in front of a T-28A aircraft. Nearly a hundred had washed out either due to flying deficiencies or because they refused to accept the five-year obligation following training. I've often wondered if the air force leadership during that time expected and wanted the outcome produced by not "grandfathering" the commitment of those already in pilot training.

Bryan AFB, located in east central Texas, was a full-up air force base. No more civilian IPs, all our instructors would be fighter pilots, many having combat experience in Korea and maybe even some in WW II. Bryan was located near College Station, Texas, home of the Texas Aggies and about seventy-five miles northwest of Houston along the Brazos River. This was my fourth assignment in Texas with only six years of service.

The T-33 was a two-seat version of the F-80, the first US jet fighter to see combat in Korea and the first to shoot down a North Korean jet fighter. It was low and sleek compared to the T-28. Moreover, it was actually smaller than the T-28 in many respects, and it lacked a propeller. My permanent instructor was Captain Epperson, a veteran fighter pilot who flew F-86 combat missions in the recently abated Korean Conflict. At our briefing table, there were four student pilots of which I can only remember one, Joe Wheat. Joe was memorable for a couple of reasons: first, he was a superb pilot; and, second, he married a beautiful young lady famous in her own right as Miss Florida. Together, they made a very handsome couple.

Training in an altitude chamber is a mandatory requirement before flying an aircraft capable of going above twelve thousand feet mean sea level (MSL). The chamber is actually two chambers, one large enough to seat twenty-four adults, and the other much smaller, capable of seating only four adults. After several hours of lecture on hypoxia symptoms, aircraft oxygen systems, regulators, oxygen masks, and the proper way to preflight all three, we were cleared for a chamber flight. Hypoxia, for those who aren't familiar with the term, is oxygen starvation of the brain that results in unconsciousness in a matter of seconds. As altitude in flight increases, air pressure decreases. When air pressure decreases to the point where there isn't sufficient pressure to push ambient air across our lung membranes, it causes the onset of oxygen starvation and hypoxia. There is no pain or breathing difficulty associated with this form of oxygen starvation, therefore it is very insidious. Prevention or immediate recognition of one's systems is the only hope of escaping incapacitation and death. The purpose of the altitude chamber is to expose aviators to hypoxia and their symptoms.

Students are seated in the large chamber with two or more instructors whose job it is to observe the students and prevent any problems. Instructors also observe through windows from the outside in case the instructors on the inside are incapacitated. The chamber doors are closed and the air evacuated until the chamber experiences a pressure equivalent to 18,000 MSL. At that point, one-half of the students are instructed to remove their masks and write a poem on a clipboard. They are also told to redon their masks as soon as they notice symptoms of hypoxia. The other half of the students observe their partners and encourage them to replace their masks when their writing has obviously deteriorated. Most people don't recognize hypoxia and have to be ordered in a strong commanding voice to replace their masks. We were told that brain cells start dying after only a handful of seconds of reduced oxygen levels. We were required to revisit the altitude chamber every two years—I wonder how many brain cells I lost over thirty-five years of flying. With this training behind us, we could fly the T-33.

My first flight in the T-33 was both unexciting and memorable. First, there was no engine roar, just a slight whine. Further, it was a chore to get ready to fly the jet. There was the parachute one wore from the equipment room to the flight line. There were all the harness connections to get right, or ejection would be painful, if not deadly. Last, there was the helmet and oxygen mask that at best were uncomfortable but necessary. Of all the thirty-five aircraft I flew, the T-33 was the most difficult aircraft to taxi because the nose wheel would cock at ninety degrees from the desired direction of travel if one wasn't extremely careful with brake application for steering. When the nose wheel cocked, excessive power was required to break it free. If there was insufficient forward room for the brute force method, then ground crewmen had to bounce the nose and turn the wheel. Both options were embarrassing to the student and resulted in a write-up on the grade slip.

On takeoff, the T-33's thrust, acceleration, and takeoff roll were disappointing compared to the T-28 that accelerated immediately and rapidly. In the T-33, a pilot could count to three after pushing the throttle to 100 percent before the aircraft moved. However, the T-33 engine offered other significant advantages over conventional reciprocating engines. Reciprocating engines have three levers, one each for throttle, propeller rpm, and mixture. A jet engine has only a throttle. Further starting the engine could not result in a backfire. Also eliminated were levers and switches for carburetor heat and cowl flaps, which, if ignored, could ruin your day and the engine. Last, there were fewer engine gauges that required monitoring on takeoff and in flight.

On our first flight, Captain Epperson had me climb the T-33 to forty-five thousand feet altitude; you could actually see the curvature of the earth from that height. Moreover, at that altitude, the blue in the sky was definitely darker and continues to darken as one goes higher. We practiced the obligatory cabin pressure and oxygen system checks to ensure hypoxia would not overcome us. Air force regulations required a cockpit pressurization of twenty-five thousand feet or below, or descent to an altitude where that could be achieved. Landing the T-33 was easy. The only concern was the slow acceleration of the engine from idle (65 percent rpm) to sufficient power (100 percent rpm) to make a safe go-around from a bad approach to landing.

The squadron to which I was assigned had four foreign students, one from France and three from Korea. They were all assigned to the same instructor pilot, Lieutenant Gross. Lieutenant Gross had an interesting history, flying in the Luftwaffe in WW II. He was an ace (having shot down more than five enemy aircraft) and claimed all his kills were on the Eastern Front against the Russians. He flew the top German fighters of WW II, the Me 109, Fw 190, Me 262 jet known as Schwalbe (Swallow), and the Me 263 Komet (Comet) rocket-powered aircraft. Both the Me 262 and Me 263 were employed against the US daylight bombing raids against the German homeland, so Lieutenant Gross's story about all his air-to-air victories being on the Eastern Front may not have been entirely true. To say that Lieutenant Gross was an exceptional and highly skilled pilot was a gross understatement, no pun intended. He immigrated to the United States after the war and enlisted in the USAF. After basic training, he was accepted into Officer Candidate School and commissioned as a second lieutenant after graduation. I don't know the facts, but I suspect his pilot training was accelerated and that he contributed a great deal of useful information to our research and development agencies on the jet and rocket aircraft that he flew in combat.

The Me 263 combat sortie was especially unique. The aircraft had only enough fuel to take off, climb to altitude, and accelerate to top combat speed. The pilot would then zoom up through an attacking bomber formation, shooting at a bomber on the way up, then reversing and diving down through the formation, again shooting on the way down. By this time, all rocket fuel had been expended, and the Me 263 was a glider looking for an airfield to land. All propeller and jet aircraft had to clear the traffic pattern and give priority to the rocket plane, as it had only one chance to make a good landing.

Every instructor in our flight had a call sign that began with the flight letter. We were Bravo Flight or B Flight; therefore acceptable call signs for the instructors and their students were Buzzard, Beefcake, Bronco, Buffalo, Baker, etc. However, there was one notable exception. Lieutenant Gross's call sign was Rocket in recognition of his skill and experience as a rocket pilot.

As noted earlier, the T-33 was an honest aircraft. It was especially good at aerobatics. In fact, everything was easier in a jet because the pilot didn't have to fight the torque of the big radial engine in the T-28. True, the speeds were faster and the altitude gained or lost greater, but it was easier. Instrument flying was also easier because the torque didn't have to be compensated for with power changes necessary for climbing and descending, and there were two less levers to move when adjusting power. Jets made teardrop penetrations that were expedient, easy, and graceful. All the teardrop required was flying to a fix at twenty thousand feet MSL or higher, turning to an outbound heading and starting a rapid descent (250 knots) turning back to the fix at a prescribed altitude and leveling at a prescribed altitude. Usually, the inbound heading was aligned with the final approach heading, so all that was required was to configure the aircraft for landing, fly the aircraft to the minimum approach altitude, and look for the airfield.

The training syllabus required each student to successfully complete a cross-country flight to another air force base. This entailed filing a flight plan with Base Operations and getting the weather and flight clearance. Normally, an entire flight would fly to the same destination, along the same instrument flight rules (IFR) route with five-minute intervals between departures. The squadron commander would prearrange approval for all the aircraft arrivals and billeting for all the pilots. The cross-country was supervised, so additional instructor pilots from the Wing and Group Staff were recruited to fill all of the instructor seats. I drew the short straw, so to speak, and was assigned the group commander, a lieutenant colonel, for my instructor. I got to fly the front seat out to make a landing at an unfamiliar airfield and the rear seat back for an instrument check. Our destination was Maxwell AFB, near Montgomery, Alabama, which assured sufficient fuel reserve on arrival in case the aircraft in front of us experienced problems and closed the runway. There was also an Air National Guard Base on the other side of town that made for a good alternate airfield.

The flight out was uneventful. The landing pattern was tight with a touchdown near the approach end of the runway to accommodate its rather short length. Maxwell AFB is the home of air force officer professional education at three levels: Squadron Officer School, Air Command and Staff School for field grade officers, and the Air War College for officers in the grade of colonel or on the promotion list. With all those students, it was almost certain that you would run into an old friend at the officers' club bar. Not surprisingly, I ran into a navigator I served with in Korea. We filled in the gaps about where our careers had taken us and parted early, as I needed to be sharp for the return flight. Unfortunately, my instructor pilot experienced a late night and was hardly fit to fly, let alone lead or instruct. The weather was near minimums at Maxwell and about the same at our destination. An alternate was required, and Waco AFB, Texas, filled that requirement. The lieutenant colonel advised me that he was not well and that I would need to make the departure and fly back to Bryan AFB and perhaps make the landing from the backseat, depending on his condition. That was easy! All I had to do was get the plane up and down safely and would be guaranteed an excellent grade. All the training from Captain Epperson paid off. The GCA in the weather was perfect, and the lieutenant colonel took the aircraft over the approach lights and landed it. There was no debriefing, and I never saw him again.

It was at about this point in the training program that I asked the flight commander when we would make our practice parachute jump. He looked at me rather strangely and asked, "Wherever did you get that idea?"

My response was "Well, I've had a number of pilots that I've flown with tell me that would be part of our training."

He laughed and said, "Well, it used to be, but statistics showed that there were just as many injuries from practice jumps as from emergency jumps, so you're going to have to do it right the first time without practice!" That comment stuck with me, and I never looked at bailing out or ejection as anything but the absolute last option. As a result, I've nursed a lot of badly stricken aircraft to an airfield, even with two engines not running.

The Regular Officer Augmentation list was released while I was a student pilot in training at Bryan AFB, Texas. I applied for this augmentation prior to leaving the 67th TRW in Japan and had asked Major White, my squadron commander, for a strong recommendation. The list of augmentees was published in the *Air Force Times* alphabetically under each rank. I looked for my name under the first lieutenant heading, but to no avail—there wasn't any John L. Piotrowski in the list. I was disappointed but with strong resolve to improve my record academically and militarily and try again on the next augmentation—if there was one. The Air Force Academy would graduate its first class in two years, and one thousand more every year thereafter. They would all be regular officers; therefore, there might not be a future need to upgrade reserve officers to regular status. A few weeks later, one of the instructors stopped by Captain Epperson's briefing table to congratulate me on my selection for regular status. I thanked him for his good wishes but noted that I was not selected. He produced a copy of the *Air Force Times* with the list and showed me my name under the second lieutenant listing. Major White had evidently given me a good endorsement, or the Selection Board had access to my Distinguished Graduation from Observer Training and awarded what I had previously earned. The air force has two distinct and separate promotion systems, an arcane fact unknown to me at that time. One system is called temporary promotions and reflects the rank one wears on the uniform. The second is called permanent promotions and can come a few to several years later than a temporary promotion. Because I was commissioned a second lieutenant when I was only twenty years old, the clock for permanent rank did not start until my twenty-first birthday. Therefore, for augmentation purposes, I was a permanent second lieutenant but was authorized to wear the rank of a first lieutenant in carrying out my duties. Temporary rank was the rank de jure. While that sounds very complicated, it was a great relief that I had passed the augmentation hurdle and was now a regular officer, with a new serial number 49636A, my fourth serial number since joining the USAF. With this behind me, all my focus was on flying to the best of my ability—there was plenty of competition.

Formation flying was the last part of the syllabus as I recall. It was pure enjoyment! Formation flying starts with a two-ship, with the wingman taking off on the leader's wing and occasionally landing on the wing as well. As proficiency improves, a second element of two is added, often with a student pilot leading the second element. My breakthrough in formation flying came when I realized that a correction in power or position must be made instantly when relative movement from the desired formation position is noted. When one gets good at formation flying, a movement of one-fourth an inch is sufficient to change power or position. A really good formation pilot anticipates change. Because of the "spool-up" lag in the T-33 engine, the throttle was always moving when in formation. One measure of a pilot's skill in formation was the speed and control of a rejoin to close fingertip formation. Once the direct line to get back on the wing was achieved, it was elegant to just slide up that line into perfect formation without any roll or throttle adjustments.

My formation check ride came on the wing of an instructor by the name of 2nd Lt. Dick Burpee. When I met Lieutenant Burpee, I was a little dismayed, thinking I had drawn someone with little flying experience and likely not very smooth as a flight leader. All the students in the formation were getting check rides with instructors riding in the backseat. I was flying number three and element lead. Joe Wheat was on my wing as number four. His grade depended somewhat on my flying. There was no escaping bad technique or just being lucky. I was wrong about Lieutenant Burpee; he was the smoothest pilot I had flown with up to that point in my flying career—he made it easy to fly good formation. As an aside, he retired with three stars and was the Joint Chiefs of Staff (JCS) J-3 during Operation El Dorado Canyon, the punitive raid against Col. Muammar Kadafi for his sponsorship of a discotheque bombing in Germany in which several American military personnel were killed and many more wounded, along with a number of German civilians.

Now the last T-33 flight was behind me, and with no problems in any phase; it was now clear that I would graduate and be awarded those coveted silver pilot wings. In those days, graduating pilots in descending order from the top got their choice of the available assignments. Captain Epperson asked me what assignment I would ask for given that there were assignments available to a variety of aircraft. My response was "Fighters!"

His reply was "What kind of fighters, air superiority fighter or air defense fighter?"

Once again, my limited exposure to and ignorance of the air force left me without an answer. I came back with "What do you recommend?"

With a few colorful words and some expletives deleted, he opined that the all-weather air defense mission is CONUS and Alaska based and unlikely to see action if there was another war. He also noted that since the War of 1812, the United States had done a good job of carrying the fight to our enemies on their soil, instead of waiting for them to attack us at home, thus preserving our cities, culture, institutions, infrastructure, and civilian population. I thought this was a rather profound observation and that if there was another war, I wanted to participate instead of watching from the comfort of an air defense base in the USA. I would choose the Air Superiority Fighter Track if it was available.

Much to my surprise, I earned the recognition as the top pilot of Class 58M at Bryan AFB, Texas, and was awarded the Commander's Trophy, a handsome silver bowl engraved with the award and my name; 2nd Lt. Joe Wheat was the runner up. What was really important is that I had the first pick of assignments, and if there was an Air Superiority Fighter assignment, it was mine. There were several assignments to F-86F Fighter Gunnery course at Williams AFB, Arizona. I, along with a handful of my classmates, was headed there.

At that time, the F-86F Saber, even though past its prime, was a fighter pilots icon. The Saber had destroyed fourteen North Korea MiGs for every F-86 lost! Never before and not since has one model of American fighter aircraft achieved such a high exchange ratio. Some might dismiss it as the result of inferior pilot skills of North Korean pilots; however, many of the top Russian and Chinese pilots were also flying North Korean MiGs. As a final point, which many not familiar with recent conflicts may not have considered, American pilots carried the fight to the enemy, not the other way around. All engagements took place over North Korea or North Korean controlled territory. North Korean pilots had the advantage of radar warning and tracking, providing enemy pilots vectors to our fighters and bombers. They enjoyed short distances to the fight, hence more fuel to outlast American pilots, recovery airfields close to the air battle, and the knowledge that if shot down, they would be recovered as heroes not captives.

Little did I know it, but Williams AFB (WAFB) was going to have a huge impact on my life and future in the air force. When I arrived at Willy, as it was known throughout the air force, and signed in, I was informed that my F-86F class would not start for about ninety days. Further because of my experience and rank, they wanted to give me an assignment that would further my experience and benefit flight operations at WAFB while I waited for training to start.

All this sounded grand, and I was full of anticipation when I reported to the major in charge of Base Operations. He was full of compliments as he introduced me to Technical Sergeant Thome. His parting words were that Sergeant Thome would explain my duties to me. When the major was out of hearing, Sergeant turned to me and said apologetically, "I don't know what kind of bull the major laid on you, but all I do is change the pages in the letdown books. My guess is that you're supposed to help me."

Letdown books contained all the information pilots need for departures from and approaches to airfields. Each page in the book would have information that was approved by the FAA and valid from that day forward until a revision was required to accommodate local changes to taxiways, runways, radio frequencies, and altitudes or fixes to accommodate noise abatement, etc. In the 1950s, the pages were kept in a four-inch-by-seven-inch loose-leaf binder. Changes approved by the FAA arrived at every flying installation monthly where someone had to remove the obsolete pages and replace them with current pages. At Willie, that someone was Sergeant Thome and me. While it was our job to ensure all the books the pilots took with them when they flew were current and correct, it was also the pilot's responsibility to check the pages they needed for departure and landing at their destinations and alternate fields. Our goal was to ensure perfection and never get a reject or put an aircraft in jeopardy.

Sergeant Thome did a wonderful job of respecting my rank, although we both understood that he was in charge. When we arrived at the office in Base Operations each morning, Sergeant Thome would say something like "Lieutenant Pete, is it OK with you if we start working on inserting data for new airfields this morning?" Later, he would ask, "Lieutenant Pete, I'd like to take a coffee break, would that be OK with you?" We became good friends over the three months that we worked together, and I came to appreciate his dedication and work ethic. Sergeant Thome didn't need any supervision from the majors and captains that ran Base Operations, nor did anyone ever check on him the entire ninety days that I was there. He worked hard and efficiently, and his work was always 100 percent correct because it needed to be just that. Many have said that NCOs are the backbone of the air force, and Sergeant Thome was clearly one of them. As an aside, a few years later, it became cheaper to print and bind new letdown books in their entirety on a monthly basis and distribute sufficient copies to each flying installation. The Sergeant Thomes of the air force were then able to move on to more challenging and rewarding assignments.

F-86F Gunnery School was getting ready to start; I reported to the squadron commanded by Major Lipscomb and was assigned to E Flight and Captain Edward Duzan. Captain Duzan had F-86 combat experience in Korea. Unlike Captain Epperson, who was hyper, Captain Duzan was laid back and easygoing with the call sign Easy. I was pleased to learn that Lieutenants Joe Wheat and Dick Wakefield from my class at Bryan were also in my class at Willie. In addition, the F-86F Gunnery Course had a navy flier joining our class as an exchange officer and then going on to a FJ-4 Fury assignment. He was navy lieutenant (equivalent to an air force captain) and an experienced fighter pilot. He would be our toughest competition for the Top Gun Award.

The F-86 was unusual, in one respect, from all other fighter aircraft that I've flown over the years. The cockpit canopy slides back on rails rather than opening from a hinge in the back of the canopy like a clam shell. The front of the canopy had thick aluminum reinforcement called a canopy bow that mated with the "windscreen" to enclose the pilot in flight. The canopy rails were about waist height when a pilot was seated in the ejection seat, providing excellent visibility around and below the fuselage—important in a dogfight. There was, however, a downside to this! When the canopy was blown back in the "ejection sequence," the canopy bow would take off the top of a pilot's head if he didn't duck prior to pulling the ejection handles. Therefore, we had some pretty lengthy training in the ejection trainer to get the duck in prior to pulling the handles. The training was accomplished without a helmet, and a pair of flexible plastic paddles replaced the thick rigid aluminum canopy bow. If you didn't duck prior to initiating the ejection sequence, the paddles gave you a painful smack on the forehead. After two or three painful smacks, all of us learned to duck. As I recall, every one of us practiced this about twenty times to satisfy the instructor that we had the procedure down pat and would not forget in an emergency ejection.

We were given ground training on aircraft systems and aircraft performance and a blindfold cockpit check on the important switches and knobs in the cockpit. Then while Captain Duzan was still standing on the wing, we started the engine and did a radio check with the tower. Captain Duzan moved to the aircraft next to the one I was in, started it, and called for a radio check and taxi instructions. We were on our way. Never before had I flown a new aircraft without an instructor in the backseat. This first flight in the F-86F was alone. One aircraft, one engine, and one pilot—neat! I had the lead with Duzan taking off on my wing. We flew to a restricted airspace over the famous Superstition Mountains and did some maneuvers, including clean and landing configuration stall series, hard turns, and some aerobatics. When it was time to land, I led the flight back to the airfield and through the pitchout and landing, with Duzan on the wing, so he could make sure the airspeeds were correct. With a smooth touchdown, my checkout was over! I was an F-86F pilot! All I had left to do was learn how to fully employ the F-86F in combat in all the various missions it could perform. The remainder of the syllabus would take us through air combat tactics, conventional air-to-ground weapons delivery, aerial gunnery, and then finishing up with tactical nuclear weapons delivery. All live bombs including the nukes were simulated with twenty-five-pound practice bombs of which there were two varieties, slick to emulate the ballistics of conventional and nuclear shapes, and blunt to emulate napalm. There were .50-caliber bullets that were real, and the 2.75-inch Folding Fin Rockets were tipped with solid steel inert warheads.

All the ordnance dropped or fired was scored by a range officer observing from a tower at one of the many gunnery ranges supporting

Willie in the desert southwest. The .50-caliber bullets fired in aerial gunnery had painted noses that would leave color smears on the towed banner target as they passed through a plastic mesh. It was each pilot's responsibility to check/verify the color of the paint on his bullets and confirm that no other aircraft had the same color. For air-to-ground strafing, each pilot had an assigned target, with two sets of four targets on each range. Shoot at the wrong target, and you were helping a classmate but hurting yourself. Practice bombs had white smoke charges about the size of a 12-gauge shotgun shell that would mark where they hit relative to the bull's-eye. Rockets hit the ground at over three thousand feet per second, kicking up enough dirt that there was no need for a smoke charge to mark the point of impact. Scoring was necessary because all pilots had to meet the qualifying scores for combat-ready pilots in all gunnery events. For conventional weapons, these were high and medium dive angle bombing, skip bombing, medium angle rocket delivery, strafing, and aerial gunnery. For nuclear weapons, qualification in toss and over-the-shoulder weapons delivery was mandatory. On a typical air-to-ground gunnery mission, a pilot would drop four high-angle delivery bombs, four medium-angle delivery bombs, shoot four rockets, drop two skip bombs, and make five strafing passes shooting about twenty rounds per pass. A gunnery mission was fast paced; everything counted, and the bomb and rocket impact distances were averaged for scoring purposes. You couldn't afford a bad pass, or qualification would be impossible. There were something like six air-to-ground gunnery missions for qualification, so learning how to hit the targets while in a steep dive at 400 knots had to be learned on the first one or two sorties and honed to a real skill on the rest.

To illustrate how a gunnery mission should look from the cockpit, Capt. Charlie Carr, a Korean ace, took some gunnery film on the same ranges we would be flying on. Captain Carr made it look extraordinarily easy. Rolling in on the target, allowing the pipper (aiming dot) to slide toward the target as airspeed built up and the correct release angle and altitude was achieved, then releasing the bomb while compensating for wind speed and angle that would affect the bomb's movement as it fell through the air to the target. It looked so easy, but not for me. While I qualified, it took years of practice to even come close to the skill level of Captain Carr.

Air-to-air combat came first because the maneuvers and dogfights quickly built up great confidence and pilot skills in flying the aircraft at its limits. The first flights were done in two-ship elements and then four-ship elements with elements going against each other—and they were paying me to have this much fun! I recall one mission where I was the element lead with Dick Wakefield on my wing. Captain Duzan was leading the other flight, with Joe Wheat on his wing. The entry to a fair fight always started out head-on, and the fight was on the instant you passed abreast of each other. In one of the several engagements that day, I went up to use the vertical to our advantage but got overaggressive and put the F-86 into a spin. I recovered in about two turns, and when I looked for Dick, he was tucked in tight in a fighting wing position. He never admitted how he was able to stay with me in the spin—I think he just lucked out. A spin maneuver is not recommended as a tactic, but it did throw off Captain Duzan. In addition to just learning how to fight the F-86F in this phase, we also got to take it through the Sound Barrier. Yes, the F-86F would go supersonic in a dive, although we weren't allowed to talk about it. Captain Duzan took our flight up to forty-five thousand feet MSL and bunted the aircraft over with about three-fourths of a negative G until a forty-five-degree dive was achieved. It wasn't long before the Mach needle pushed through the Mach 1 indicator, and the aircraft did a slight roll as it went through the speed of sound. Not a lot to write home about.

Officially, Capt. Chuck Yeager flying the Bell X-1 Experimental Rocket Plane broke the speed of sound in level flight on October 14, 1947, just a few days after the air force was recognized as a separate service. However, George Welch broke the sound barrier in an XP-F86 twice in a dive much like described above before Captain Yeager officially broke the barrier. George Welch's sonic booms were directed at the Happy Bottom Riding Club near Edwards Air Force Base and recorded by a waitress working there.

Air-to-ground gunnery was hard work but fun! Soon we were about to enter the aerial gunnery phase. There were the lectures on how the APG-30 radar in the F-86F nose provided range and range rate to the MA1A Fire Control System that positioned the pipper for a perfect lead pursuit curve toward the target and computed a perfect firing solution. All the pilot had to do was fly the aircraft smoothly with the needle and ball centered, indicating perfectly coordinated flight controls. Then there was Capt. Charlie Carr's aerial gunnery film, where you could actually see the bullets tearing the target to shreds. The aerial target was a plastic mesh banner six feet high and thirty feet long attached to a pole with a lead weight that kept the pole and banner vertical. The pole was attached to a 1,500-foot steel cable that came off a spool hanging on the belly of a T-33 aircraft that towed the target. When the T-33 took off, the target was rolled up tightly and stowed longitudinally under its belly. When the T-33 arrived over the aerial gunnery range close to the California and Mexican borders, it released the target, which automatically deployed to the full length of the cable. A flight of four F-86s would join up on the T-33 and then climb five thousand feet above and the same distance out to the right, maintaining line abreast. When cleared in "hot," each F-86 pilot would turn in and down toward the T-33. The F-86 pilot was supposed to maintain a minimum of fifteen degrees angle off and point slightly down at the banner target, placing the pipper on the first third of the banner and firing at about one thousand feet but no closer than eight hundred feet. If these minimums were not observed in the opinion of the tow pilot, he would wave off the pilot on the shooting pass; otherwise, the tow plane was likely to take a .50-caliber hit. After the firing pass, the F-86 would climb back to the "perch" high and wide and cycle back in on another pass. If all went smoothly, a flight could get between five to seven passes for each pilot. Only two of the F-86F's six guns were loaded with fifty rounds of painted ammo in each gun's ammo can. The tow aircraft had enough fuel to accommodate two flights, which meant eight colors, black, brown, red, orange, yellow, green, blue, and purple, could be used on a single target. The number of strands of mesh cut by the bullets was a reasonable measure of the angle off the firing pass. Anything over twelve strands was a violation of the fifteen-degree rule, and the shooter was due for a serious butt chewing. If there were no problems with the tow plane, it would drop the target adjacent to the Willie runway, where it could be recovered and delivered to the appropriate squadron. Students got to score the target under their instructors' supervision. Seventeen percent was required to qualify, and despite Charlie Carr's 90 percent score on his demonstration movie, it was more difficult than it looked. I scored 21 percent on my last mission. A couple of my classmates never qualified in this event and received waivers.

Last were the nuclear delivery events. At that time, there were two ways a fighter could deliver a nuclear bomb and hopefully survive the blast from it. First, there was the toss maneuver. In the toss maneuver, a pilot would fly toward the target at 420 knots and very low altitude to escape radar detection for as long as possible. When he reached a preplanned easily recognizable navigation point, he would start a timer to arrive with some precision at a point where he would start a wings level pull up at four Gs. The g-force would be maintained until the pilot felt the bomb release at a preset angle, approximately forty-five degrees nose up. The bomb would be flung toward the target in a maximum range loft. The pilot would continue the loop until the aircraft was about forty-five degrees nose down going the opposite direction, then roll upright and continue descending until the escape route altitude was reached. This placed considerable distance from the bomb blast with the aircraft escaping almost as fast as the blast wave coming toward the tail of the aircraft. The second maneuver, called over-the-shoulder (OTS), provided a little more delivery accuracy because the pilot would fly directly over the target before initiating the wings level pull-up. In the OTS delivery, the bomb was also released by a preset gyro setting, just slightly past the vertical, throwing the bomb well above twenty thousand feet and back toward the target before gravity stopped its ascent and pulled it back to earth. The pilot continued the loop until upright and escaped the blast of the weapon just as in the toss method, but with a little less separation. The F-86F was slow compared to Century Series aircraft that could achieve 480 to 520 knots in level flight at low altitude and thus could throw nuclear bombs further or higher, gaining greater safe separation from the ensuing blast.

To allow sufficient time for the lofted bombs to find their way back to earth without hitting the next aircraft coming in to pull up over the target, students were sequenced in on the nuclear range about ten minutes apart. On one training day, I was the aircraft just ahead of Dick Wakefield. I pulled off of the range on the route back and then orbited to pounce on him when he was exiting the range. It wasn't long before he came along, and I dove into his six o'clock position and shouted, "Check Six," over the radio. It wasn't a fair fight, but who wants a fair fight in combat? We went round and round as he tried to gain an advantage, but before that could happen, I realized I was very low on fuel. I immediately climbed to forty thousand feet and pulled the throttle back as far as I could while still maintaining level flight. While doing this, it occurred to me that I might have to bail out before I could get back to Willie. I was down to six hundred pounds of JP-4 fuel, the minimum required on the initial approach for landing, and Willie was over one hundred miles in the distance. It didn't look good, but the distance kept shrinking, and there was hope as long as the engine kept running. It wasn't long before the Superstition Mountains came into view, and I could start judging the distance for a fuel-saving letdown. The best tactic would be to arrive over the center of the base at five thousand feet then reduce power and spiral down onto initial. Hopefully, another aircraft wouldn't enter the pattern and force me to declare a fuel emergency for priority spacing. I didn't want to call attention to my plight. It worked! Now if there was enough JP-4 in the fuel tanks to make it to the ramp before flaming out and having to be towed in. I made it, but one more turn on the Gila

Bend Range at full throttle, and I would have had to walk home. Later, Captain Duzan came up to me with the bomb scores, congratulating me on qualifying. He then turned serious and said the crew chief on my plane reported that the fuel tanks were nearly bone dry when he serviced the aircraft. I told him what happened and waited for the outburst. All he said was "I hope you've learned that there is no acceptable excuse for running out of fuel and ejecting from an otherwise good airplane," and walked away. It was a lesson well learned and remembered for the next thirty-two years of flying.

We were just about finished with F-86F gunnery training and acting like real fighter pilots. One of the students, Frank Soare, was the nephew of Sen. Mike Mansfield, a powerful chairman of the Armed Services Committee. Frank called his uncle and suggested that the senator request a flight of four F-86s to perform at the Billings, Montana, air show scheduled to take place in two weeks. Billings was the home of both the senator and Frank. The Korean War had ended just a few years earlier, and the F-86F Saber was the superstar of that air war. Evidently, the senator liked the idea and requested the air force to send a four-ship of F-86s to Billings, Montana; the flight to be led by 2nd Lt. Frank Soare.

The air force caved on the request, but added an instructor pilot, Hank, to the flight to keep us out of trouble. In fact, it turned out to be it was the three students that had to keep Hank between the white lines.

Echo Flight arrived at Billings without incident, and the red carpet had been rolled out for their "native son" Frank Soare, with an eye to pleasing the senator as well. Serendipity was on our side that day, because as we swaggered into Base Operations to close out our flight plan, three Frontier Airlines flight attendants walked in from their plane and were scheduled to spend the night. It was a party atmosphere, and after a year of intense training where failure wasn't an option, we fell right in.

The next day, the F-86s were expected to put on an aerial demonstration, but "Hank" kept us on the ground on static display in the hot sun. The four F-86s were the hit of the show, and I enjoyed talking to the youngsters about the air force and places I had been. That night, there were more festivities, and we were right in the middle of them. The original flight attendants were gone, but another plane came in with replacements—another enjoyable evening.

We were scheduled for a morning departure the next day, but we slept in and slipped takeoff a couple of hours to swill more coffee and orange juice in order to get the blood sugar up, and to time our departure with the end of the air show. Preflight, taxi, formation takeoff, and join up in four-ship fingertip were normal. The four-ship fingertip looked good and tight as I recall; maybe there is something about how a couple of cocktails the night before makes for smoother formation flying. Hank led the flight in a low sweeping turn over Billings with a pass down the runway then off to Hill Air Force Base, Utah (near Salt Lake City), for a refueling stop and then on to Williams AFB, Arizona.

We all must have been sucking on 100 percent oxygen during the flight because all four aircraft were lower on oxygen than jet fuel on arrival at Hill AFB. Coffee and a Coke, and we were ready to roll once again. I had led a two-ship from Billings, so it was my turn to play wingman and was number four taking off on Frank Soare's wing. Takeoff seemed normal as I hung onto Frank's wing. Lead normally runs his engine up to 98 percent of full power, so the wingman has a little power to play with. I was at max power and dropping back. Frank backed up to me, waved, and then took off like a rocket. Then it dawned on me: my engine was suffering from a big loss of power. Two-thirds of the runway was behind me, and the options flashed through my head: try to stop, not a good idea, as the aircraft was heavily loaded with fuel; eject on the runway, not a good idea, as the ejection seat was primitive, the parachute canopy wouldn't open before I hit the ground. The only option was to stick with the jet and hope it reached flying speed on the sick engine. Then I remembered there was a sheer cliff at the end of the runway in the direction of our takeoff. After clearing the end of the runway, I could drop the nose and hope to pick up flying speed before hitting the canyon floor. If the aircraft didn't reach flying speed, I would have enough time and altitude to eject at about five hundred feet above the canyon floor. Takeoff speed for the Saber fully loaded was 150 knots, about three miles a minute. All these options flashed through my mind in about ten seconds. The end of the runway slipped by, I pushed the nose over slightly and had flying speed. Looking up for the three other aircraft, I found them circling over top of me, waiting to see what would happen. We joined up and flew home to Williams AFB, with me wondering what had happened to my aircraft.

After landing, we all gathered at my F-86F trying to discover what went wrong with the J-47 engine. The crew chief exclaimed, "Where did all the mice go?"

"What mice?" I asked.

Then he explained that little rectangular blocks of steel, about the size of a mouse, were placed around the inside of the tailpipe to force the exhaust gasses into a tighter cone, increasing temperature and thrust. All the mice from my aircraft were missing. Did they become souvenirs?

One particularly good thing resulted from the Billings trip: Frank married the flight attendant he met there, and they are still happily married, and we are still good friends. All's well that ends well!

I graduated third in the class. The navy lieutenant was understandably first, Joe Wheat was second by a handful of points, and I took third out of twenty or so.

We were all scheduled to attend survival school at Stead Air Force Base near Reno, Nevada. It was early December 1958. I had already completed the Far East Survival School on the island of Eta Jima off the coast of Kyushu in southern Japan. This training would be much different, as it would be very cold, and we would most likely be up to our waists in snow. I was right on both counts.

Stead AFB held the record for being the highest air force base, altitude wise, in the Continental United States. Many a pilot had misjudged how that altitude affected final airspeed as it translated to ground speed and braking and how the thin air affected jet engine thrust for a go-around. As a result, there were a lot of aircraft that went off the end of the Stead runway.

Survival school exposes students to interrogation; what it feels like to be treated badly and made very, very uncomfortable. Exposure to food depravation and being fed the kind of slop a POW could expect in captivity was also part of the course. Last, they drummed home that a POW should only give name, rank, and serial number to their captors as required by the Geneva Convention. After three days in a stockade with numerous interrogations and routine punishments, we moved on to evasion and survival training. This entailed navigating through the Sierra Nevada mountains to a series of "friendly" contacts and finally a pickup point. This was to take seven days! For food, we were issued one rather small potato, one WW II issue pemmican bar, and one live rabbit for each two survivors. It was no surprise that some could not bring themselves to kill and eat the rabbit. Some just carried it along with them for the entire seven days. Others turned the rabbit loose out of kindness, only for it to be eaten by a lynx, bobcat, coyote, or fox. A few, like me, who had hunted and eaten rabbit to augment the dinner table while growing up, killed, cooked, and ate the rabbit with their partner on the second day out on the trail.

The snow was deep that year, making snow shoes necessary most of the time. Breaking trail is hard work, so we were always changing the lead to even the workload. A survival instructor stayed with us for three days, training us on making lean-tos for shelter and other survival skills. We were always on the move, so setting snares to catch small animals was something we learned but didn't apply on that outing. The last four days, we were on our own, but generally moved at night in pairs just in case someone got hurt and needed on-the-spot assistance. Navigation from contact point to contact point was by compass and the stars. The object was to find a trusted agent at a checkpoint and pick up a hand-drawn map that would lead to the next trusted agent. On the fourth night, we had completed our evasion training upon reaching the last trusted agent. I had been out of food for at least three days, but water was not a problem given all the snow. They had steaks back at the chow hall, but stomachs had shrunk for lack of food, and no one could eat much even though it was very tasty. The next day, we were heading back to our bases.

When we arrived back to Willie, we learned our entire class of F-86F fighter pilots had a block assignment to the Strategic Air Command (SAC) as B-47 copilots. That was a real downer, and to say I was disappointed was the world's greatest understatement.

I decided that there was nothing to lose by talking to the Willie wing commander. In a few words, he told me the needs of the air force come first, and SAC needed B-47 copilots. However, he said that if I was willing to switch from flying to maintenance, there was an opening at Willie for a lieutenant-grade electronics maintenance officer. Without thinking, I said, "Sir, you just found the maintenance officer you're looking for!" I didn't have an electrical engineering degree, but I had over two years of air force electronics training and figured I could learn the rest on the job. In a few days, I had orders to the Armament and Electronics Squadron as an armament and electronics (A&E) maintenance officer. The wing was getting F-100C/D aircraft to replace the F-86Fs for USAF pilots. The F-86Fs would be around for a few more years training Indian, Pakistani, and South American pilots. So F-86F and F-100C/D fire control, weapons delivery, and communication systems would be my responsibility. I reported to the A&E Squadron and met the commander, Maj. Fred Saunders, and the chief maintenance officer, Capt. Don Rathgeber. Both had served in the Army Air Corps during WW II. Both fought in the Pacific Theater and really knew the business of bombs, bullets, and fire control systems. I don't think they expected much of me and didn't have much use for pilots in the maintenance field—both of them were nonrated. There were two other officers in the squadron, both on the armament side. One was a senior-grade warrant officer, a real expert in aircraft guns and release systems. The other was a first lieutenant and a pilot, also responsible for pylons, release systems, aircraft machine guns, and cannons.

I would share an office with Master Sergeant Shanklin, a big bear of a man and a real expert in avionics and supervising a large number of enlisted personnel. I learned a lot from him about avionics and leadership. He quickly explained the scope of our responsibilities and took me around to meet the next level of NCO supervisors and the troops. Essentially, we were responsible for correcting all pilot discrepancies entered in the aircraft 781 forms. The work involved troubleshooting the equipment on the aircraft, replacing equipment that didn't meet standards, and finally repairing that equipment back at the squadron's high-tech repair facility. I learned that the electronic side of A&E did not have a good reputation among the majority of the instructor pilots in both the F-86 and F-100 training units, so I set about to correct that. In addition, I learned from one of our best in-shop technicians that Lowery AFB, Colorado, the technical center for airborne electronics, had a Correspondence Course for the APG-30 radar and MA1A fire control system. I enrolled in the course and was soon learning more than I wanted to know but, on the other hand, just about as much as I needed to know to stay abreast of the enlisted technicians working for me.

To work the reputation issue with the instructor pilots in the training squadrons, I started attending mission debriefings to find out what worked to their satisfaction and what didn't. One of their biggest gripes across all training squadrons was that the aircraft radar (F-86 & F-100 APG-30) that provided range and range rate to the fire control system broke lock on the tow target long before the aircraft was in effective firing range. While working a solution to this problem with the chief radar technician, we discovered that the circuit determining break-lock range had the right components, but the air force bought them from the lowest price bidder. The two components, one a resistor and the other a capacitor, were both within specification but always on the high side of acceptable tolerance. We calculated that with the installed "high side" components that "break lock" would happen at 1,100 feet to 1,200 feet vice the 800 feet desired for effective air-to-air gunnery. The solution was relatively simple! Instead of using air force issued parts, these components were purchased out of pocket from a local electronics supplier with a 5 percent variance instead of the 20 percent allowed. Problem solved; the pilots being supported were happy!

Once I was comfortable with my maintenance responsibilities, it was time to enroll in college courses at Arizona State University in Tempe, Arizona. Lt. Jay Bayer also took some courses at ASU on the same evenings, so we shared the drive, giving us an opportunity to talk about work in the A&E Squadron. I was still on the quest for a degree, a journey that started in Japan four years earlier.

By this time, it was obvious that the enlisted troops working in the Fire Control Section became embarrassed when they butchered the pronunciation of "Piotrowski." It didn't offend me, as it happened most of my life. Nonetheless, the pronunciation problem had to be put to rest to achieve effective communication with the troops. At the next all-hands meeting, I mentioned that instead of Lieutenant Piotrowski, I would prefer to be addressed as Lieutenant Pete, or Lieutenant P if that was easier to remember. From that day forward, I was Lieutenant P, and no one had the slightest reservation with coming to me about a problem or suggesting a better way to accomplish our mission.

In one of those all-hands sessions, I learned that some of the tools needed to do the job were not authorized by Air Force Supply Regulations. There weren't many tools we lacked. However, there was need for a specific open-end and box-end wrench, and an Allen wrench. It didn't seem like much, but without these tools, certain electronic boxes could not be accessed. I asked the squadron supply sergeant, a much-respected taciturn individual, if he would issue the needed tools to the electronics repairmen. His answer was "No, even though we carry them in supply, they are not authorized in the Unit Equipment List (UEL)!" Evidently, some wise men in Air Force Logistics Command (AFLC) decided what tools were needed by maintenance personnel in the field, and that was that. The supply sergeant said we could submit justification and request a change to the UEL, but he doubted it would be approved. I'd read *Catch-22* while lounging in my tent in Korea and understood what we were up against. I submitted the request with pages of justification, including pictures of the bolts and nuts that needed to be removed for access to fire control black boxes. All electronic equipment was painted black, ergo the term "black box." As predicted, the request for a UEL change was disapproved.

The solution was also easy, but expensive! The needed tools, one for each flight line and shop technician, were purchased from the local Sears store out of pocket. When these tools were handed out to the troops, Chief Master Sergeant Shanklin informed me that we would have to collect them all back if higher headquarters ever inspected us. Apparently needed, but unauthorized tools, in a maintenance person's toolbox would result in a failed inspection. He opined that this would not please Major Saunders or Captain Rathgeber. So much for simple logic and just trying to get the job done! The chief and I made a list of the men with the "illegal" tools and agreed we would get them back before the inspectors came. It was also decided that we would make the lack of these needed tools an issue for the inspectors to consider.

There was a side benefit to visiting the training squadrons and talking to the instructor pilots. My former squadron commander, Major Lipscomb, asked me if I would like to continue flying the F-86F with the squadron. The only possible answer was "Yes, sir, when can I start?"

His response was "How about tomorrow?" I was back flying fighters! In the 1950s and into the 1960s, all that was required to maintain proficiency was a flight every ninety days. Night proficiency had the same provision. Often pilots would take off in the daytime, fly for a couple of hours, and land five minutes after sunset, which qualified for a night landing even though it wasn't really dark. It had only been about forty-five days since I last flew the F-86F, so by all regulations, I was current and eligible to fly without any reservation. It wasn't long before I was flying the F-86F once or twice a week as the fourth ship of a gunnery formation, or sometimes as the element lead. Once in a while, I would get invited to participate in a Turkey Shoot, where instructors had the opportunity to hone their skills without the distraction of training students and have a friendly competition at something like a quarter a bomb and a dime a hole on strafing. One could easily lose five dollars on a really bad day at the gunnery range.

One day, while I was in Major Lipscomb's squadron getting pilot feedback on aircraft systems performance, we passed in the hall, and he asked if I was getting enough flying time. Again, the only correct answer was "No, sir!"

To which he responded, "We can always free up an aircraft for an evening or weekend. Just let the dispatcher know when you'd like to fly." That comment let the genie out of the bottle. From that day forward, I was flying at least twice as much as the average operational pilot, logging nearly one hundred hours a month. One day, I was notified that Air Force Regulations stipulated that a pilot of a single cockpit fighter aircraft could only fly eighty hours in a single month without a waiver. Seventy-nine hours became the self-imposed monthly maximum after that.

As payback for all the F-86F flying, Major Lipscomb asked me if I would tow the banner target during the air-to-air training phase. "Yes, sir" was the right answer. Capt. Bob Touchette was given the task of checking me out in towing the target, all the visual checkpoints on the range to keep from straying into Mexico or spraying bullets on one of the very small settlements adjacent to the range. There were emergency fields to land at and procedures for dropping the target on the range or back at Willie, depending on the "fuel state" when the mission was completed. When we landed at Willie after dropping the banner along the runway, I filled out the forms and handed them to Captain Touchette, who was sitting in the front seat so that he could enter his name and serial number. He threw the forms back at me, saying that he didn't want any straight-wing jet-flying time on his record. He had at least one combat tour in Korea and lots of flying time logged in the F-86F. We were at opposite ends of the experience spectrum.

Another surprise package got dropped in my lap. The chief functional test pilot called and asked if I was interested in becoming a T-33 functional check flight (FCF) pilot. I was a maintenance officer, and this was a maintenance function, so it seemed like the right thing to do. WAFB had T-33s modified to perform the air-to-ground gunnery mission as a lead in to the F-86F for foreign students. The T-33 was only slightly easier to fly but was an aircraft they were already proficient in, so gunnery skills became just another T-33 training phase. Once proficient in gunnery, the transition to the F-86 was much easier and accomplished in a much shorter period of time. As a result, the entire training package cost less for the United States and the nation we were helping.

Functional check flights were required anytime certain critical maintenance actions were performed on an aircraft. These included engine changes, flight control changes or adjustments, and serious anomalies discovered in flight that could not be duplicated on the ground. The latter was referred to in the Aircraft Form 781 as CND (could not duplicate). The concept was that the FCF pilot was better equipped and skilled to handle an in-flight emergency than the run-of-the-mill operational pilot. In my mind, that meant we were more expendable. Soon I was flying two or three T-33 FCFs a week and enjoying every second of it. All FCFs carried a light fuel load, only fuselage fuel and fifty gallons in each tip tank. The purpose of this was to make it possible to land the aircraft immediately after takeoff if a dire emergency was encountered. It was possible to land a fully loaded T-33 immediately after takeoff, but it was not recommended without jettisoning the fully loaded tip tanks.

Normally, an FCF was simply a matter of going through the flight profile and recording the data collected during the obligatory maneuvers and noting any abnormalities, such as falling off to one side in a stall series, failure to recover from a spin with normal recovery procedures, etc. Engine data recording and acceleration times were also important data necessary for releasing the aircraft for routine operations following the FCF. If the pilot developed a smooth routine of maneuvers that led from one check to another, the entire FCF took less than thirty minutes.

This left a lot of fuel remaining and an opportunity to practice landings and simulated flameout patterns (SFOs). SFOs replicated landing a T-33 or any other jet, for that matter, with a flamed out engine. This procedure enabled the pilot of a stricken aircraft with enough altitude to glide to an airfield, make a turn over the runway, and safely land the aircraft with a desired touchdown point about one-third down the runway. The more you practiced this procedure, the higher the probability you could do it correctly if fate made it necessary, so I practiced at least one SFO on every FCF. Moreover, if the traffic pattern at Willie was not crowded with students, I would shoot touch-and-gos (T&G) until the minimum fuel light came on. A T&G was the application of power, resetting the flaps from full down to one-half flap setting and adjusting trim settings to take off again as an extension of the landing. T&Gs are no longer authorized, being deemed unsafe by later generations of air force leadership. I would usually accomplish ten or more T&Gs at the end of an FCF. Flying time and proficiency were building exponentially.

It was about this time that I had a meeting with the enlisted maintenance crews that were responsible for working the postflight pilot write-ups in the Form 781. These maintenance crews were finding far too many discrepancies that they could not duplicate on the ground but which would be written up again by the next pilot that flew the aircraft. I asked if they had any suggestions as to what we might do differently that would enable us to find and fix these equipment problems. After some discussion, one sergeant pointed out that the aircraft was electrically powered with a ground power cart during maintenance activities that essentially delivered perfect 400-cycle power to the F-86 equipment they were troubleshooting. He opined that it was possible that the aircraft generator could be the root cause of a problem, but that they had no way of checking that. I leaped on that thought and told the maintainers that when they ran into the next CND, call me and I would start the aircraft engine, and they could troubleshoot the write-up while it was running on aircraft power. A check with safety personnel, and they deemed the procedure we developed safe.

It wasn't long before I received a phone call from the flight line maintenance team, stating they could not duplicate a malfunction written up by a pilot and asked if I would come to the ramp and run the F-86F engine to power the malfunctioning system for them. I donned a flight suit and drove to the aircraft on the flight line. The maintenance crew was waiting with their test gear, wondering if this would identify the real problem. In no time, the aircraft systems were running on internal power; and as the sergeant had suggested, it was aircraft generator and alternator power fluctuations that were causing the fire control system to malfunction. About that time, I noticed a number of flashing lights surrounding the aircraft, and an air policeman (AP) was climbing up the aircraft ladder to the cockpit. Over the engine noise, he informed me I was under arrest. I shut the engine down, and he hauled me off to the military jail on base.

From behind bars, I learned that a recent joyride by an F-86F crew chief resulted in a directive that mandated anyone intending to start an aircraft engine had to request and receive permission from the control tower before starting the engine. This directive did not get to the enlisted personnel who worked for me because they did not normally start aircraft engines in the course of their maintenance duties. It never got passed to Willie pilots, as we normally filed a flight clearance that was sent to the control tower. When the tower spotted an aircraft starting up without the necessary approval, they alerted the air police, who dutifully arrested me. The air police were just about as embarrassed as I was once they checked my identification card and interviewed a number of the enlisted personnel participating in the troubleshooting maintenance procedure. The APs offered to call my commander to verify that I was who I said I was. I gave them Captain Rathgeber's and Major Saunder's names, but neither one was home. They offered to go higher up the chain of command, but I was reluctant to give them the maintenance group commander's name because Colonel Kellogg was prone to violent outbursts. He spent a couple of years in a Japanese prison camp during WW II and didn't tolerate fools or incompetence. But considering a night behind bars versus a chewing out, I reluctantly gave the APs his name. I was released from jail by midnight.

The usual weekly maintenance staff meeting chaired by Colonel Kellogg (nicknamed Cornflakes behind his back) or his deputy was scheduled for the next morning. Normally, I accompanied Captain Rathgeber to these sessions to hear firsthand the direction given by our Maintenance Leadership. I was hoping for the deputy, but Colonel Kellogg presided. After the colonel told us to be seated, he roared, "Where the hell is Piotrowski?" I stood up, expecting the worst. Colonel Kellogg then said, "Take a look at him. He's the only damn officer working around the clock, and they put him in jail. Some more of you need to get arrested for working after five o'clock!" I suspect Colonel Kellogg thought there was the scintilla of a chance that I could be molded into a good maintenance officer, as he occasionally asked me questions about the reliability of A&E systems at staff meetings. I was always armed with the availability and reliability and spare part status of all the fire control and weapons delivery systems of the F-86 and more importantly the F-100C/D. In response to a question, I noted that the Auto Low Altitude Bombing System (Auto-LABS) was extremely reliable, as there hadn't been a pilot discrepancy on it for the last ninety days. To this, he responded, "You idiot! The only way that could happen is that the pilots are afraid to use it! Find out what's going on!" There was merit to what the colonel said. The Auto-LABS was engaged by the pilot to deliver a nuclear bomb in the Toss mode. With the aircraft flying at 520 knots, two hundred feet above the ground, the pilot was supposed to depress the bomb release button with Auto-LABS selected. At the instant the bomb release button was depressed, the F-100 would automatically pull 4 positive Gs. If it didn't work perfectly, the aircraft could crash before the pilot could recovery from an erroneous input to the flight control system.

On my following visits to the F-100 Squadrons, I asked the instructor pilots how they liked the Auto-LABS. The responses would burn your ears. They didn't trust it. They told their students not to use it because they considered it unsafe. F-100 IPs and students were required to qualify on Auto-LABS to maintain combat currency and for the students to graduate. Essentially, they were using a manual release and getting good enough scores to qualify. I asked them if they, the instructors, would engage the system at ten thousand feet above ground level (AGL) and write it up if it didn't work properly. I also asked the F-100C/D FCF pilots if they would do the same. My argument was that the air force needed data on these systems to have the spare parts and spare systems on hand or to get the contractor to modify them to work properly. They agreed, and we started getting malfunction write-ups in the Form-1.

Performance of fire control systems improved across the wing for several weeks, and I took that as the result of some of the changes I had implemented. Then complaints started to come in again about systems' performance.

Some of them coincided with maintenance that had been performed the evening prior to the flight in question and signed off by our night-shift flight line supervisor. Chief Master Sergeant Shanklin (he had been promoted twice), however, sensed that our night shift was goofing off. Together, we went out to an aircraft that finished flying for the day and was scheduled for preventative maintenance that night. Shanklin opened up a panel that provided access to fire control electronics and removed a fuse. Early the next morning, we went back to the aircraft to check the aircraft forms. There was a write-up indicating the fire control systems had been calibrated and checked OK. We then removed the panel and found the fuse had not been replaced. The write-up in the aircraft forms was a lie! No work could have been accomplished with the fuse missing. It was time for the chief and me to have a meeting with the night-shift supervisor and then the troops. The supervisor received an Article 15 (nonjudicial punishment), which demoted him one rank. We put another staff sergeant in charge and followed up his team's performance with random spot checks during the night.

Aside from flying a lot and learning the ins and outs of maintenance, my social life improved. Major Saunders and Captain Rathgeber each had a civilian secretary who shared a common office. It was not often that Chief Master Sergeant Shanklin and I needed something typed, but occasionally, a new procedure or revision to a regulation needed to be typed for publication. That's how I happened to meet Ms. Sheila Fredrickson, whom I started dating on the sly. There was no prohibition from dating civilians, nor did I supervise her work in any way, so there was no authoritative relationship over her. There will be more discussion about Ms. Fredrickson later.

Once the electronics of the fire control systems were in good repair, there was time to work on harmonization. Harmonization is a fancy word that means aligning the guns to shoot through the pipper at the desired distance. Pipper is fighter pilot jargon for the aiming dot displayed on the windscreen glass by the fire control system. For the F-86F and the F-100C/D, that would be one thousand feet at 400 knots for the F-86F, and at 450 knots for the F-100C/D. The airspeed mattered because airspeed changes the aircraft angle of attack, which in turn changes the angle of the gun barrels relative to the airflow, causing bullets to "jump" or otherwise be influenced by the airflow. All the guns, six .50-caliber M2 machine guns on the F-86 and four 20 mm M39 Cannons on the F-100 were fired into a dirt-filled concrete-backed firing butt at one thousand feet. The aircraft were jacked so that the fuselage alignment fixture could be aligned with a cross on a large cloth target. Once aligned, aircraft were tied down so they wouldn't jump off of the jacks due to recoil from the guns. Ten round bursts were fired from each gun, and the points where the bullets went through the target were marked with black paint. Eighty percent of the bullets (eight of ten from each barrel) had to fall into the bull's-eye. If they didn't, the gun was adjusted until it passed. Usually, this was done one gun at a time, but I instituted a procedure where once each individual gun passed, we fired the guns in pairs to ensure vibration from one gun didn't disturb the other. Harmonization was usually done at night, and I liked to be in the firing butt (backstop) area to make sure the troops were not faking the bullet impacts on the target to shorten the process. Both the

.50-caliber and 20 mm projectiles traveled above three thousand feet per second, or roughly three times the speed of sound. The first thing heard in the butt was thump, thump, ten times as the projectiles slammed into the dirt. After a few seconds of delay, you heard the sound of the guns firing. This proved the WW I saying that you never heard the bullet that killed you! This was because the projectile arrived well ahead of the sound. Once the guns were harmonized in pairs, strafing and banner average scores improved.

I was flying a number of T-33 FCFs each week and enjoying getting in the air so often. I must have been doing something right, as I was asked to check out as an F-86 FCF pilot. There would be no dual ride to show me the procedures, as there were no two-seat F-86Fs. I was briefed on the FCF procedures and given the check sheet with all of the parameters. One procedure caught my attention in a big way. It specified slowing the aircraft to below 175 knots, opening the canopy, and rolling inverted, and then maintaining inverted flight for at least ten seconds. What was this about opening the canopy in flight? Was this a joke? Were they pulling my leg? No one opens a canopy in flight! The captain briefing me very patiently explained to me that below 175 knots indicated airspeed, the angle of attack was so high that the airflow over the nose would not enter the open cockpit and tear off the canopy. He further explained that this procedure was specifically designed to pull all the loose debris out of the cockpit. The sky was a vacuum cleaner. You can believe I entered this procedure very carefully and made sure the airspeed stayed below 170 for the entire time the plane was inverted. It worked; you could see all kinds of dirt and trash being sucked out of the cockpit.

The visit of Gen. O. P. Weyland, commander, Tactical Air Command, in the summer of 1959 is worth recounting. General Weyland was one of the great Army Air Corps leaders of WW II and a respected fighter pilot. His XIX Tactical Air Force supported General Patton's Third Army on their drive through France. General Patton praised Major General Weyland for his air support, stating, "Opie"—as he was known—"was the best damn general in the Air Corps." During the Korean War, he commanded the Far Eastern Air Forces and the United States Air Forces. He was promoted to the rank of general on July 5, 1952.

General Weyland was on a farewell tour of his far-flung Tactical Air Command Bases, and Willie was one of his stops. I'd been in the air force seven years and had seen one major general from a distance at Keesler when I was an airman marching to class. General Weyland was an air force icon, commanding the largest Fighter Command in the world. I was looking forward to seeing this man, even if from a distance. A wing parade was held in his honor on the parade field adjacent to the base entrance and the flagpole. Most of the base participated including me, passing in review with General Weyland doing the honors on the reviewing stand. Fortunately, it was held early in the morning before the temperatures reached one hundred-plus degrees. It was very well done for a bunch of amateurs who hadn't marched in a parade for several years. However, we had two very lengthy parade practices to make sure everything went smoothly.

After the parade, all those in the parade marched to the flight line, about two miles distant, where there would be something of an air show for General Weyland. By direction of our wing commander, the bleachers on the flight line were packed with those participating in the parade. The first event was an F-86F flight demonstration by Maj. Mike Encinnies. He had practiced the routine for several days without any problems. It started with an aileron roll on takeoff and was to go on from there with aerobatic maneuvers. The rest of the routine will remain a secret because the major crashed on takeoff. Fortunately, Mike got the wings level prior to hitting the desert off the end of the runway. His luck continued, as the base fire chief, wanting a good vantage point for the show, had driven a fire truck outside the fence just about one hundred yards from where the stricken F-86 came to rest. Also in Mike's favor, the aircraft carried very little fuel, so he could get airborne and accelerate quickly, thus there was no fire at the crash site. Remember what I said about the F-86F canopy and canopy bow? Well, in the major's hurry to get out of the aircraft, he forgot to duck when he jettisoned the canopy. Normally, that would have killed him, but the fuselage was deformed sufficiently to slow the canopy's rearward motion, so all it did was crease his helmet, badly bruise his forehead, and knock him dizzy. The fire chief busted out the canopy and pulled him free of the airplane and took him to the base hospital. We were all relieved when it was announced over the base public address system that the pilot was OK.

I wasn't sitting very close to the distinguished visitor stand, where General Weyland and our wing commander were seated, when the crash happened, but I could hear the general bellow, "Who authorized that?" The crowd turned quiet, but I didn't hear the answer.

With that behind us, the next airshow event was test pilot Mr. Bob Hoover flying an F-100C and repeating the show he had performed the previous year in an F-86F. Mr. Hoover was in the stands wearing a business suit and seated close to an F-100C parked nearby for his use. When his name was announced, Mr. Hoover came over to the DV stand, saluted General Weyland, and then walked to the aircraft in his business suit. In just a few short minutes, he was taxiing to the runway. His performance started with a role on takeoff, which was crisp and perfect. He then executed a number of difficult aerobatics and various maneuvers at low level near show center. It was a solo performance that I still remember and will likely never forget. It was superb flying in an aircraft often referred to as a widow maker. More on that subject later! As of 2012, Mr. Hoover is still flying, putting on aerobatics shows and thrilling crowds with his remarkable skills.

Gen. Otto P. Weyland retired from the United States Air Force on August 1, 1959. Gen. Frank F. Everest, experienced in both fighter and bomber aircraft, as well as the commander of Fifth Air Force in the Far East during the opening years of the Koran War, assumed command of the Tactical Air Command headquartered at Langley AFB, Virginia. There was no noticeable change in day-to-day operations at the wing level due to the leadership change. It was still a very loosely controlled operation.

As you might expect, I was getting some pushback from Captain Rathgeber for my flying activities, which continued to expand. I had checked out in the C-47. Willie had two in their stable and one C-45. Both were tail draggers (used a tail wheel instead of a nose wheel) and of WW II vintage. I enjoyed flying these old crates and logging the time. Normally, wing or group headquarters scheduled these aircraft for parts pickups. When tasked to fly these missions, you had to have a good reason in order to decline. Captain Rathgeber couldn't complain about the FCFs, as they were a maintenance function. On the other hand, the F-86F flights could hardly be justified. However, I convinced him that these flights enabled me to check on the quality of maintenance our squadron provided, and the goodwill gained from the operational squadrons was well-worth short absences. He grudgingly backed off but let me know there was a limit. As a result, I started flying the F-86F more at night and on the weekends, taking advantage of Major Lipscomb's generous offer to provide an aircraft whenever I wanted to fly.

I would call the squadron dispatcher around noon and ask if it was possible to have an aircraft ready for a night flight by 6:00 p.m. with a return by 2:00 a.m. the next morning. I don't ever recall being denied an aircraft. The flight plan would usually take me to Northern California, landing at Hamilton AFB in the Bay Area. Hamilton, closed in the 1970s, supported a squadron of air defense fighters. From Hamilton, I would fly north to Klamath Falls, Oregon, or south to Oxnard AFB fifty miles north of Los Angeles, CA. Both bases also supported air defense missions. Each flight was about ninety minutes long and would have me landing back at Willie by the agreed-upon time. It made for a short night's rest, but it was worth it. It's noteworthy that there wasn't any crew rest regulation at that time. Pilots were expected to exercise good judgment.

I thought my movie career ended in Japan, but to my surprise, 20th Century Fox Studio convinced the air force to support flying scenes for the movie *The Hunters*, starring Robert Mitchum as Maj. Cleve Saville, a MiG destroying ace, and Robert Wagner as Lt. Ed Pell, an ace wannabe. The setting was the Korean War, and our heroes were flying F-86Fs. Willie had the only F-86Fs flying, and Luke AFB had F-84Fs with a high horizontal stabilator that made it look a lot like a MiG-15 when painted blue with a red star on the fuselage. A couple of the real Korean War heroes at Willie flew the combat scenes. But when they needed a bunch of aircraft filling the sky, they called on the guys who hung around the Operations Desk, guys like me. I flew wing in several scenes that showed about forty MiG-15s (F-84Fs) and forty F-86Fs in echelon formation. These formations were filmed separately and smashed together through the magic of Hollywood. The schedulers must have considered me the best formation flier of the lot because they put me on the end of those other thirty-nine aircraft. Turning that formation around threw me about 150 feet up and then down because we were flying show formation and maintained the same plane as our leader. A very persnickety photographer did the filming from the backseat of a T-33. He must have been persnickety because he had us fly past the T-33 over and over again. We flew by level; we flew by low and high. Finally, aircraft in the formation became extremely low on fuel, and the flight leader called it off. When lead checked us in on tower frequency, we all discovered a sandstorm had closed Willie. Instead of returning in an orderly formation, it was every man for himself. We were south over the gunnery ranges, so I landed near Tucson at Davis-Monthan, a SAC base at the time. A number of other pilots in the formation made the same decision. We waited out the storm and flew back to Willie in flights of four when the field reopened.

The word must have been out that if a pilot was needed, call Piotrowski; he was always ready, willing, and able to fly anything anywhere. Accordingly, I got a lot of calls to fly officers and airmen on emergency leave. It was customary that when Red Cross confirmed the parent of a service member was unexpectedly determined to be near death, the air force would allow the service member to be flown to an airbase nearby before death occurred. The return travel would be the member's responsibility. I always felt good about helping someone out in these circumstances, and some proved downright exciting. The T-33 was the aircraft of choice for these flights, and one mercy flight sticks vividly in my memory.

A sergeant's mother, living in Wisconsin, was reported to be near death by the family doctor and verified by the Red Cross. The sergeant asked for emergency leave and was supported by his commander. The commander asked the operations group commander to approve a T-33 flight. I was called and asked if I would fly the sergeant home. I agreed and went to Base Operations to locate the nearest military field and file a flight plan. The weather was down to minimums, and the NOTAMs (notices to airmen) listed the field as closing at midnight local time. The T-33 could not hold enough fuel to fly to our destination then make a missed approach with enough fuel to reach an alternate airfield and land as required by FAA regulations. Hence, I planned for an intermediate stop at McConnell AFB, Kansas, where we would take on a full fuel load and then fly to the base near the sergeant's home. The pilot was required to provide all the required ejection briefings and emphasize, "Do not touch or move any switches in the rear cockpit." With all this done, we took off and landed in good time at McConnell. Just for added insurance, I called the control tower operators at our destination and explained the situation to them—basically, that I was filing a flight plan to their base and expected to arrive shortly before midnight. Last, I asked them to keep the tower open just in case FAA delays caused me to be a little later than planned. The tower operators would receive the flight plan and expected arrival time as soon as we got airborne at McConnell. When we reached the letdown fix and called the control tower for landing instructions, no one answered—repeated calls did not produce a response. The tower operators had gone home for the night despite my best efforts to appeal to their humanitarian side.

It was time to fly to the alternate airport, which was Chicago's O'Hare International Airport. I wasn't looking forward to landing at O'Hare, considering the weather, traffic, and the time—it was late. Flight Service cleared me to a fix serving O'Hare and told me to descend and hold at twenty thousand feet. After thirty minutes of turns around the holding pattern, I was cleared by approach to descend under radar vectors to a back-side ILS Approach to one of their runways. After descending and remembering how to do a back-side ILS, Approach Control told me I was cleared to land! I responded that I was still in the weather and did not have the field in sight. That is when they informed me they could see my landing lights and to execute a missed approach. With that bit of news, I realized the canopy had iced up real bad while I was in the holding pattern, and the deicing windshield heat was not hot enough to break it loose. Just as I started a reluctant go-around on the gauges, a small piece of ice broke off of the lower left corner of the windscreen. If I lowered the ejection seat to the bottom and scrunched way down, I had about a two-inch opening I could see through, enabling me to see the runway. I was high and fast, but the runway was long, so I put the iced-up T-33 down. The added speed probably saved us from a stall due to the increased weight from the ice. Ground Control provided taxi instructions to the KC-135 Air Force Reserve Aerial Refueling Unit across the field. It was after 1:00 a.m., and Reserve personnel were long gone for the day. I taxied as close as reason would allow to their operations building and parked the jet, using anything I could find for chocks and closed the canopy for the night. The sergeant and I found a window that wasn't locked and broke into the building. A phone connected him with a taxi, and he was on the way to the hospital to see his dying mother. Mission accomplished! I piled some loose cushions from lounge chairs on the pool table used for a bed and fell into a troubled sleep. Later that morning, air reserve personnel arrived for work and woke me up. Suffice it to say, they weren't happy to see me, but their maintenance personnel refueled the T-33 and towed it far enough from their operations building for me to safely start the jet and head for home. That adventure reminded me that flexibility is one of the attributes of air power.

Another flight that almost ended in disaster for me took me to Waco, Texas, headquarters for FlyTAF, which I believe stood for Flying Training Air Force. This was the next higher level headquarters for Willie, and evidently, they needed something from our wing faster than the speed of USPS mail. FedEx and UPS did not exist at the time. Operations called and asked me to fly a package to Waco; it was a place I'd never been to, so why not? It wasn't long before I was headed for a T-33 on the flight line with the weather report and a flight clearance. The only problem was the possibility of weather at Waco. It was scheduled to be above minimums by the time I arrived, but just in case, there was a good alternate airfield at Dyess AFB, Abilene, Texas.

When I arrived at the fix serving Waco, I was informed by Approach Control that the field was still closed and to hold in a racetrack pattern at twenty thousand feet. After several orbits, fuel was approaching decision time: land here or head for the alternate. While turning in the holding pattern, I was in the clear, but a low overcast had Waco closed.

I spotted a hole in the overcast and saw a C-47 sitting on the end of a runway. I called Approach Control and asked if there was a C-47 on the runway at Waco—the answer was yes. Soon I saw another hole and more of the base; based on what I could see, I cancelled my IFR clearance and did a split S down to pattern altitude, keeping the runway in sight the entire time. There were a few puffy clouds at 1,500 feet AGL, the altitude for initial to an overhead pattern for landing. I dropped down to one thousand feet above ground level (AGL) and was in the clear. One thousand feet (AGL) was the standard landing pattern altitude before Century Series fighters, like the F-100, entered the operational inventory. Because of their pattern and landing speeds, they required a little more altitude to have a good flight path on final. In a few minutes, I was on the ground and taxiing up to Base Operations, which was standard procedure for transient aircraft.

I was handing the forms to the transient alert crew chief when a bird colonel burst out of Base Operations and started chewing my butt for landing at a closed airfield and threatening dire punishment. I was standing at a very rigid attention, looking at him when I noticed the sky behind the colonel was absolutely clear. When he paused for a breath, I asked, "Colonel, have you looked at the sky?" He seemed shocked at the comment but looked up! In a split second, he spun around and darted back into Base Operations. So much for people who look at weather forecasts but never look out their windows to see what is really happening. I may have jumped the gun by a minute or two, but I was VFR from twenty thousand feet to the runway, while the folks in the weather station were probably still drinking coffee and eating doughnuts. I departed as soon as I was relieved of that very important package. "Seagull" is a disparaging term applied to senior officers who stay on the ground and make a lot of unpleasant noises. The colonel I encountered at Waco might have qualified as a seagull—someone with wings that makes a lot of noise but doesn't fly. I was hoping he could not remember my rather difficult name.

Flying time was building up quickly in the four different aircraft in which I was simultaneously current. These were the F-86F, T-33, C-47, and C-45. Flying often builds confidence—in fact, overconfidence—and it was likely that something would come along to give me a dose of reality, and it did.

I was asked to take Air Force Academy cadets for orientation rides in the T-33, a plane that was more like "putting it on" than "getting into it" for me. I was one "hot rock" first lieutenant fighter pilot and would show these young cadets what a single engine jet could do—hoping they wouldn't get sick. Unfortunately, on the day of the cadet flights, the sky was gray and overcast—not the best for flying and certainly not good for aerobatics. The drill went like this: a cadet was strapped in the backseat by the crew chief, engine start, communications check, and taxi to the runway for takeoff. The first flight was always tame because of a full fuel load, both internally and in the tip tanks. So I took the first cadet on a low-level jet ride, buzzing cows and antelope in Southern Arizona near Yuma. On returning from the first flight, the crew chief yanked out the first cadet passenger and stuffed in another one for a second flight. The plane was now light and nimble—good for aerobatics, but the weather was still low and overcast. The second cadet pleaded for some aerobatics, and I was in the mood to show my stuff. First, an aileron roll then a barrel roll. Nothing to it with about three thousand feet ground to cloud. This cadet wasn't satisfied; he wanted to do a loop, which is a perfect circle in the vertical. Well, I thought, I do loops in clouds and I do loops at night on instruments, so why not in these clouds?

Being a little cautious, I decided to do an Immelmann instead, a half loop with a half roll on top to level flight. I'd be in the soup but didn't see a problem in picking my way down as long as I stayed away from the nearby mountains. Setting a course away from the mountains, I took the jet at full throttle up to the bottom of the cloud deck and dived down to get sufficient airspeed to complete the half loop with energy to spare. Pulling four Gs, we arced up into the gloom with eyes on the attitude indicator, watching the attitude indicator for an indication that we were on our back and it was time to roll to canopy up.

In the process, I forgot something important: the instrument picture of being upside down. When the attitude indicator flipped, as it is supposed to when you are going perfectly straight up or straight down, I rolled the plane 180 degrees, but we were still going straight up! The airspeed went to *zero,* and the jet started to slip back on its tail—not good. The air being forced up the tailpipe would put out the flame, and the engine would quit. I didn't need to add an air start to an already rapidly deteriorating situation, so I kicked the rudder hard, and the jet flopped over nose down and started gaining airspeed. I rolled to a heading away from the mountains (this is all taking place in the clouds) and started gently blending in some Gs to bring the nose up to level flight from the vertical dive we were in. Just as we approached level flight, the jet broke out of the clouds; and at that moment, I knew we were going to *live.* I had said nothing to the cadet during the recovery because the whole process took less than two minutes, and I was very busy and very intent. As the ground came into view, I calmly asked the cadet how he enjoyed the Immelmann. He said, "That was great. Can we do another one?" Now that I knew what I was doing, we did another Immelmann correctly and returned to the base and landed to refuel and pick up another cadet.

There was another emergency leave flight that comes to mind. This one was to take a lieutenant colonel of WW II vintage who had flown a lot of combat missions in Europe. The takeoff was in the late afternoon with a lot of daylight left heading for McChord AFB, Washington, near his parents' home. As we flew along after reaching an altitude of thirty-five thousand feet, he started asking me what I would do if the engine quit. My answer was straightforward and by the book: inform Air Traffic Control of our emergency and request a heading toward the nearest suitable airfield with a long-enough runway; next, attempt air starts while looking for the airfield and setting up for a flamed-out landing pattern. I remember telling him that I was an expert at the latter, practicing several every week. Then it got dark when he asked me what I would do if the engine quit now. By this time, we were over Northern California with fewer airfields. Again, a straightforward by-the-book answer: contact Air Traffic Control, advise them of our emergency, ask for a heading to a suitable bail-out area, and attempt air starts until we glided down to roughly ten thousand feet above the terrain and initiate the ejection sequence. This upset him big time as he proceeded to tell me that he had a bad back that could not stand the force of ejection or of a parachute landing. I sympathized with him but related that the odds of a successful engine-out landing in the dark was very low—much lower than his odds of recovering from another injury to his back. "On the other hand, think positive," I said. As I reminded him that the J-33 engine was running fine, all the instruments were in the green, and McChord AFB was only about forty-five minutes away. He was in a near panic but held on until we touched down at McChord in uncharacteristically good weather for coastal Washington.

It seemed that 3525th Pilot Training Wing (single-engine jet) at Willie was losing a lot of aircraft due to accidents, approximately one every week. Most of the losses were F-100s, which was a treacherous aircraft to fly. Unlike previous aircraft that turned with an application of aileron by moving the control stick in the direction of desired turn, the F-100 was turned mostly, if not totally, with rudder. It was the first operational aircraft that had a violent "adverse yaw" characteristic. Adverse yaw occurs when an aileron goes down into the airflow under the wing of a swept wing aircraft. The impact of the air against the down aileron causes the aircraft to yaw violently in the opposite direction of the intended turn. This happens because instead of lifting the wing and causing the aircraft to turn in the opposite direction, the down aileron causes excessive drag that snaps to aircraft in the direction of the down aileron. In addition, the wing was losing about a pilot a month from the aforementioned accidents. Those were huge losses of aircraft and pilots, but they did not result in the firing of the wing commander or the operations group commander. Based on these loss rates, I calculated that I would be smoking hole in the ground before reaching my thirty-fifth birthday. I accepted that outcome and went about my business as a maintenance officer and fighter pilot without a second thought about the future. I'm reminded of a line from one of *The Godfather* movies where a mafia hit man tells Don Corleone's son, "This is the business we chose."

Pilots should not be too self-confident, but it's the nature of the breed! I couldn't get enough time in the air and was always applying for cross-country flights on the weekend. One such application of mine resulted in a call from the operations group commander, with a conditional approval: if I would agree to take a brigadier general's son, a cadet at the Air Force Academy, from Colorado Springs to Andrews AFB, the request would be approved. I agreed, it was a done deal. It was June; the academy was allowing cadets go on leave for the summer, and I was getting to fly. I landed at Peterson AFB, Colorado Springs, Colorado, on Friday night. Saturday morning I was hanging around Base Operations waiting for the cadet to show up. Unfortunately, he was late, and the outside temperature was rising fast. Underpowered jets, high altitude, and hot air make for a dangerous situation, but I didn't think it would be a problem. I filled out the clearance and handed it to the gray-headed captain behind the Ops Desk, He scrutinized it carefully and handed it back, saying he didn't believe the go/no go distance written on the clearance and asked me to double-check it. Back to the planning room and run the numbers in the Dash One. He still didn't accept the numbers and sent me back to get the Dash One so we could do the calculations together. I was beginning to think this guy had singled me out as a troublemaker or was anal about numbers. We went over the nomograms in the Dash One together and came out with a number that was about one hundred feet longer—big deal! I should note that at that juncture, pilots needed 1,500 hours of flying time and a senior pilot rating with a star affixed to the top of their wings to have their own clearance authority. I had the hours but not the seven years of rated time. I was still a slick wing pilot and required the Base Operations officer to approve and sign my clearance. In this instance, that requirement played an important role.

With the paperwork approved and the clearance signed, I loaded the cadet in the backseat, gave him the obligatory briefing about the ejection seat and ejection procedures, and asked him not to move any switches or turn any knobs. The T-33 had a hot mike so we could talk to each other without having to actuate any switches. Everything was normal with the start and systems checks, and a few minutes later, we were ready to roll. The captain at the Ops Desk had impressed upon me that at 6,200 feet of runway altitude on a hot day, I would need every foot of runway to abort and stop safely! So I taxied into the paved overrun and hung the tailpipe over the grass. Hold the brakes, 80 percent gauge check, release brakes, and full throttle. Acceleration was slow due to the altitude and ambient temperature. We rolled and rolled! The end of the runway was drawing near, and we were still a couple of knots short of takeoff speed, but it was too late for anything other than to pull gently back on the stick and hopefully fly. It did, and slowly, the plane accelerated while skimming the empty high desert prior to initiating a shallow climb with the gear down. I called the tower and asked if they would check the boundary barbwire fence with their glasses. I didn't want to attempt raising the gear if I was dragging fence wire and jam the gear in the up position. The tower operator called back to report that the fence was undamaged. With this good news, I headed for Barksdale AFB, Louisiana, to refuel and continue on to Andrews AFB, Maryland. Barksdale was a SAC bomber base and had a very long runway. The rest of the trip was uniquely uneventful, landing at Andrews AFB under a clear sky. It was a big relief for me to turn the cadet safely over to the brigadier general he called dad.

As you can appreciate, cross-county flights can build up flying hours and experience, and they can also provide some unexpected surprises that those with little imagination would never anticipate. For no other reason than to fly, Captain Smirnoff, a T-33 instructor pilot and I decided to take a cross-country with an overnight on Saturday at an air force base near his hometown so he could visit with his parents and siblings. We filed a clearance to land and refuel at Dyess AFB, Texas, flying a long way around to add time to the flight. When the aircraft was shut down in front of Base Operations, which is typical for transient aircraft, security police vehicles immediately surrounded it. We were arrested at gunpoint, taken to the base jail, and locked up without explanation. Hours passed before we were released; no explanation was given for the arrest and lockup.

At Base Operations, while filing a clearance for the next leg of our journey, we learned the reason for the bizarre treatment. The SAC bomber wing at Dyess AFB was undergoing an operational readiness inspection (ORI). A wing commander's future depends on whether or not the wing passes or fails, and if it passes, how well it did. When our flight plan was transmitted to Dyess Base Operations a few minutes after it was approved at Williams AFB, the Dyess Base Operations officer saw Smirnoff and Piotrowski on the form. His immediately thought it was a test by the inspector leading the ORI to see if they were alert to sabotage. The fact that it was an air force aircraft on a legal flight plan did not cause him to question or pause; he had us arrested. Perhaps the commander received kudos for the alertness of his staff to the possibility of sabotage. Never again did I fly with someone with an obvious Polish or Russian name.

While at Willie, I had the opportunity to lunch one afternoon with more than a dozen instructor pilots from the F-86 and F-100 Squadrons. They were all captains, some of them with fourteen or more years' service and flew combat in both WW II and Korea. Promotions did not come easily to fighter pilots because the current emphasis was on strategic bombers, the underpinning of the Nation's Nuclear Deterrence Strategy. Strategic Air Command owned all the bombers and had a number of programs for rapid promotion of their aircrews during most of the Cold War. There were lead crews that could earn accelerated promotions, and spot promotions were given to the best of their best. A spot promotion was temporary in nature, but the pay was real, and the time served in a spot rank counted as real time-in grade for the next promotion. Nonetheless, it was clear to me that none of the fighter pilots at the table would switch to bombers if given the chance. My hope was that I would earn the rank of major before I had twenty years of service and then could elect to retire. I remember making that statement to Sheila Fredrickson, the woman I was dating.

There is one more flying episode worth recounting. Jay Bayer and I had flown off on a weekend cross-country in a T-33 to build some flying time. This was mostly for Jay, as he had only recently checked out in the jet. His previous aircraft was the SA-16, a twin-engine amphibious aircraft that was used primarily for overwater rescue. There was a detachment of them at Itami AFB, Japan, because of all the overwater flying there and in Korea. Jay's flying career had been curtailed by an accident that resulted from a search and rescue mission. The pilot in command of the SA-16 aircraft on that rescue mission flew up a canyon looking for wreckage and survivors instead of down the canyon. The plane stalled and crashed. It was standard procedure with an underpowered aircraft like the SA-16 to climb to the highest altitude for a search mission in the clear then conduct the search flying from the top of the canyon downhill to eliminate the possibility of being unable to climb at a greater rate than the terrain. Jay was badly injured and off of flying status for an extended time.

Jay had just returned to flying status and had only a few hours in the T-33. Our last stop on the way home was McConnell AFB, Kansas, about two hours flying time from Willie. To make sure we had enough fuel to get some touch-and-go landings for Jay, we climbed to forty-five thousand feet to escape jet stream headwinds. After about an hour of flight, we noticed the hydraulic pressure was just above zero instead of one thousand pounds. Normally, speed brakes that extended from the T-33 belly would provide sufficient drag to descend at a reasonable rate without pushing the aircraft up to its Mach limit, which was only .82 Mach. Speed brakes weren't an option now, as they were hydraulically operated, and there wasn't any hydraulic pressure to make them extend. Moreover, if there was any residual hydraulic pressure, we wanted to use that for lowering the landing gear. What to do? I suggested to Jay, who was in the front seat, that we spin the aircraft down to a reasonable altitude, say twenty thousand feet. A spin is just an aggravated stall and easily recovered from. Jay wasn't an FCF pilot, and all he knew was that spinning the T-33 was prohibited. The T-33 flight manual also said spinning was prohibited. I finally convinced him it was something we did on every FCF, and it was the best option to get down from forty-five thousand feet. When we arrived over restricted airspace near Willie, I put the T-33 into a spin, and down we went. It isn't a comfortable feeling, but I held it in the spin until we reached twenty thousand feet and then recovered. When the tower was informed that the hydraulic system had failed, they called out the fire trucks, which made quite a show. Fortunately, the gear came down normally. Jay made a perfect low-speed landing, touching down in the first five hundred feet of the runway, and the emergency brakes worked as advertised.

Out of the blue, TAC announced that they were closing Willie and that the F-100, F-86, and Lead-In T-33 training would move to other bases. The F-86 and T-33 were scheduled to move across the Phoenix Valley to Luke Air Force Base near Glendale, Arizona. Major Saunders informed me that I was moving with the A&E Squadron to Luke AFB along with him and Captain Rathgeber. That was a relief, and I would still be flying fighters—I hoped. The Air Training Command would find Willie a desirable flying training location with hardly any training days lost to weather. Sheila, a civil services employee, was hired to be the secretary to a commander of a Student Training Squadron and stayed at Willie. That made for long-range dating. Just before moving to Luke, I was notified that I had been promoted to captain after serving six and a half years as a lieutenant.

When I left Williams AFB, it occurred to me that every base that I was assigned to for pilot training had been shut down by the air force. These were Stallings AFB, North Carolina; Marana AFB, Arizona; Bainbridge AFB, Georgia; and Bryan AFB, Texas. Only Williams AFB was saved by being taken over by Air Training Command. The air force had also switched to all Jet Trainers for Primary and Basic Flight Training, the T-37 and the T-38 replacing the T-34, T-28, and T-33 that I trained in.

At Luke, there were about five hundred enlisted and civilian personnel working for me, as there were a lot more aircraft to maintain, including the F-84F, a swept wing fighter made by Republic Aviation. There was no commonality between Willie and Luke! The flying was a lot more regimented, maintenance procedures were different, and what worked well at the base across town wasn't accepted at Luke. I wasn't going to be successful changing the institutional thinking, so I had to adopt and yet achieve the same results and rapport with the operational units as well as the team working for me. It was a good thing that Chief Master Sergeant Shanklin had been such a good and patient teacher over the two years we worked together because he retired instead of transferring to Luke with the rest of the A&E team. To get my arms around the maintenance practices and get to know all the people, I spent about twelve hours a day on the flight line and in the repair shops. It was amazing to me how different two bases could be yet in the same command structure and operating in exactly the same environment.

Soon, I was flying both the T-33 and F-86F again, mostly FCF flights, as Luke did not have these aircraft in their inventory before they were transferred over from Willie. Immediately, I was put up for a proficiency check ride in the F-86F. The check pilot was someone I didn't know and only had a few hours in the F-86F himself. Check rides in jet fighter aircraft that don't have two seats are done on the wing. That is to say that the instructor pilot would brief the flight and then take off on my wing and grade me through all of the instrument procedures from that position. The weather went from about 500 AGL to well above twenty thousand feet, so all the instrument procedures would be for real, with the IP hanging on the wing. The F-86F was equipped with a very crude, if not primitive, navigation system called a "bird dog" receiver because all it could do is point at the station selected. There was also a draconian procedure called an "aural null" in case the needle-pointing feature failed. Over every VHF navigation transmitter on the ground, there is a cone of silence getting larger as altitude increases. You determine where you are in the sky by figuring out which quadrant you are in by the Morse code letters *A* (dot dash) or *N* (dash dot). When an aircraft is on a quadrant leg, the tones overlap, creating a solid tone. Once you are on a leg, the sound increases as the station gets closer and decreases outbound. Station passage is determined when the sound gets loud and then stops. After flying around the sky to locate the "cone of silence," a descent to the final approach is initiated. If everything has been done correctly, there will be a runway out in front when descending out of the clouds. All these maneuvers have to be done smoothly with a wingman, especially if he is an IP and you are on a check ride. After the low approach, we climbed out to above the weather, and he took the lead. There was aerobatics on the wing, one dogfight and then a radar approach, with me landing on his wing. A hard day's work done well, and I was accepted in to the Luke fighter community.

Mayday, Mayday

It was a routine F-86F FCF. The engine had been replaced, and all the ground engine run-ups and checks had been OK as written in the forms. The aircraft had been washed to remove all of the grease, grim, and dirt that resulted from the heavy maintenance of removing and replacing the aft section, which was required to expose the engine mounts. In this process, everything from mechanical flight controls to the rudder, stabilator, and fuel lines were disconnected and reconnected. Hence, the purpose of the FCF was to validate that the engine and flight controls were in accordance with specifications and safe for flight.

It was a beautiful day. The aircraft looked pristine and ready for flight. Recognizing the plane had been torn apart and put back together, I performed a thorough preflight with emphasis on the aft section. Everything appeared to be in good order. There were no leaks or telltale stains of oil or hydraulic fluid from taxiing to and from the engine run area and running the new engine at full power for several minutes. Start, taxi, and all system checks at the end of the runway were normal—it was time to fly. Luke AFB had long runways to accommodate the F-84F and F-100C/D aircraft in the occasional 115-degree Fahrenheit days during July and August. This was comforting on a FCF with an F-86F because the runway was long enough for this bird to accelerate to takeoff speed and abort safely.

Acceleration to takeoff speed at 140 knots indicated airspeed was normal, and I was airborne, heading for the FCF working area. A glance at the airspeed showed that I was stuck at 175 knots with the engine gauges indicating 100 percent rpm and normal temperatures. I decreased the climb angle so as not to stall and called the control tower. "Mayday, Mayday, Bronco has engine failure! If I can keep the bird flying, I'll set up for an engine-out pattern."

Tower responded, "Roger, Bronco, we have an F-86 in the pattern. Head for the green spot and orbit. Tower will vector him to join on your wing." The green spot was a small agricultural spot in an otherwise light-brown desert landscape. It must have covered about ten acres because it could be seen for at least fifty miles from ten thousand feet AGL. I reached the green spot and started to orbit, still at 100 percent rpm and 175 knots, with some slight excursions above and below that number. Soon came the call, "Bronco, I have you in sight, say altitude?"

Response was "Fifteen thousand feet, in a left-hand orbit."

A minute or two later came the call, "I can't catch you, pull off some power!" Well, maybe the engine was OK, but the instruments were screwed up. I gingerly pulled back the power to about 80 percent, and the airspeed stayed at 175 knots. It wasn't long before the other F-86F was on my wing, claiming we were doing about 350 knots. After checking both sides of my aircraft for damage or anomalies, he offered to lead me back for a landing on his wing. We switched places and headed for Luke AFB and a straight-in pattern. All I had to do was fly good formation, no matter what the gauges said! If his aircraft was flying, my aircraft should also be flying. In formation, everything was done with hand signals and head nods for execution. Speed brake signal and head nod, gear down signal and head nod, flaps down signal and head nod. As the runway comes into view in peripheral vision, the wingman flies a little wider and a little higher than tight fingertip formation to make sure wings don't touch and to ensure that the wingman touches down after lead. When lead touches down, he adds a little power and delays application of brakes so the wingman has safe spacing behind and to the side.

Back on the ramp, the crew chief was going over the aircraft and found the problem causing erroneous airspeed readings. When the aircraft was washed, the wash crew covered the static air pressure ports with clear Scotch tape to make sure water didn't get into the static pressure system. Airspeed instruments rely on two inputs: dynamic pressure measuring air pressure coming in the Pitot tube and static pressure from the static ports. This comparison between the two pressure sources is necessary to ensure correct airspeed indications at all altitudes. Because the static ports (one located on each side of the fuselage) were blocked, the indication was erroneous. The clear Scotch tape fooled me on the preflight. Not only did I look at the static ports, but I also ran my gloved hand across them and did not detect the tape visually or tactically.

Maintenance gave me one more chance to get it right. The second flight was uneventful!

College credits were building with courses primarily in math and sciences at Phoenix College in downtown Phoenix. It was a much longer drive from Luke to Phoenix College than it was from Willie to ASU, but again, I found another officer (Capt. "Hoppie" Hopkins) doing the same thing, so we rode together and talked about the important things of life, like flying and sweethearts, as we drove back and forth.

The word was out that a general was coming to Luke to interview pilots for a special assignment. That was the extent of what we were allowed to know. A couple of weeks later, I was directed to wait outside a specific briefing room in one of the fighter squadron buildings at 5:00 p.m. I was there early and waited as instructed. At 5:00 p.m., on the dot, the door opened, and a voice said, "Come in!" The briefing room had been transformed to look like an interrogation setting at Survival School. There was someone seated in a chair behind the desk, but he was in darkness. The only light in the room was a bright, tightly focused lamp over the only other chair in the room. The voice said, "Sit down!" and I did. Then the voice said, "You are Capt. John L. Piotrowski, is that correct?" When I responded in the affirmative, the voice said, "I will ask you three questions. If you answer the first one correctly, you will be asked the second one, and so on. Do you understand?"

"Yes, sir!" was the immediate response. In the dim light, the Silver Stars on the man's collars were barely visible. Then the voice began asking questions:

"Are you willing to fly old obsolete aircraft?" was the first question.

That was an easy one; I was already flying old nearly obsolete aircraft. "Yes, sir!"

"Are you willing to fly combat?" the voice demanded.

That seemed to be a stupid question to ask an air force pilot trained for combat. "Yes, sir!"

"If sent into combat, shot down, and captured, are you willing to be disowned by your government?" pressed the general.

This required more thought! However, if captured, no one came home till the war ended, so what did it matter? "Yes, sir!" I firmly replied.

The general then said gruffly, "That completes the interview. You'll hear from us if we need you!" So I got up and left.

It was a Friday, and that night at the O'club, the place was packed more than usual, and the conversation was all about the general's visit.

Everyone who had been interviewed was expressing strong views, pro and con, about the interview and what might lie ahead. It was April 1961. John F. Kennedy was president, and the recent Bay of Pigs Invasion had failed. Most thought, as I did, that the interview was related to Cuba or perhaps other areas of unrest in South America, like Nicaragua. The general thrust of the conversation at the O'club leaned toward not wanting anything to do with combat, unless there was an all-out war with US national interests at stake. This surprised me because I thought that countering inroads of Communism would prevent its spread and keep the Soviets in their backyard. Containment was the national strategy of the day. To say the least, I was disappointed in the attitude of most of my fellow fighter pilots.

Weeks passed. I was at Sheila's apartment, on leave, and we were about to depart for Las Vegas to take in a couple of shows. It seemed like we both needed a break from the press of business. How the personnel shop found me there, I don't know, but their message was short and pithy! "You have secret orders and will have to travel to your new assignment as soon as possible! Report to wing personnel for a briefing immediately!" Las Vegas would have to wait for another day and time!

Personnel showed me the "secret orders" but couldn't give me a copy, as I had no way to secure them. They assured me that the organization at the other end would have copies and would recognize me when I reported for duty. That was little comfort as I was reporting to Project Jungle Jim at Eglin Auxiliary Field no. 9. Everyone knew about Eglin AFB, Florida, but no one had ever heard of Aux no. 9. The reporting date was May 7, 1961, and it was a long drive—there wasn't much time. The orders stated that I was shipping as a 4236 personnel code for Munitions Maintenance Officer, not as a fighter pilot personnel code. That was a disappointment, but if recent history was any indicator, I had high hopes that I could do both.

It struck me hard that I could be assigned to a unit heading into combat and that I didn't know anything about real bombs, fuzes, and bullets. All I had experience with is training ammunition. I went to Captain Rathgeber and told him what he already knew. I lacked the knowledge on combat munitions that would be critical in my new assignment. He reached into the bottom drawer of his desk and pulled out two buff-colored WW II Army Air Corps field manuals. One was titled *Bombs for Aircraft,* and the other, *Ammunition for Aircraft.* He handed them to me, saying, "I knew these would come in handy someday. These manuals contain all the information you'll ever need to know!"

While I was clearing the base (closing all accounts and turning in all equipment that I had signed for), a tragic thing happened. My good friend, Capt. Hoppie Hopkins, was killed in a freak flying accident. What happened to Hoppie was influenced by the death of another respected pilot mentioned earlier, Capt. Bob Touchette. Bob had taken an F-86F on a cross-country and was climbing out from Maxwell AFB, Alabama, when the jet's engine flamed out climbing through a severe thunderstorm. It was speculated that large hail ingested into the engine caused failure of the compressor. Bob could have bailed out but chose to try a "deadstick" flame-out landing at Maxwell. Approach Control guided him through the weather toward the end of the short runway. Bob's words when he broke out of the clouds were "Too low, too late!" He was found in the cockpit of the aircraft with the nose buried in the bank of the river flowing past the runway. His words were interpreted to mean that he did not have the glide speed to reach the end of the runway, and his aircraft was too low for him to bail out. The cloud bases were at about two hundred feet, and as I recall, minimums for a successful bailout were 250 feet at 250 knots in level or climbing flight. Bob had neither condition when he broke out of the weather. Hoppie and I had talked about the mishap that took our colleague and friend, and I learned that Hoppie was firmly committed to bail out under just about any circumstances.

A short time later, Hoppie was pulling the rag (aerial gunnery target) and after a successful mission flew back to Luke to jettison it alongside the runway. The rag cable didn't disconnect, and the banner with pole and weight was dragging on the ground, collecting debris and causing a loss of airspeed and altitude. Hoppie, spring loaded to eject, did just that. The aircraft was so low and slow that the ejection seat hit the ground with Hoppie still strapped in the seat. There was a lot of conjecture that he would have been OK if he bellied the aircraft in on the infield, as it was flat and clean for several thousand feet. As noted earlier, "It is the business we chose," and it is a dangerous one. After thinking about how these two close friends lost their lives in aircraft accidents, I found myself more aligned with Bob Touchette's approach to analyze the situation and, if possible, to try and save the aircraft rather than Hoppie's preconditioned commitment to immediate ejection.

Jungle Jim, here I come

I had dumped the Mercury sometime back, as it was too expensive to maintain and was a gas hog. The replacement was a used dark-green

Morris Minor, not exactly the color for "hot as Hades" Phoenix, Arizona, but it ran forever on a tank of gas and was so simple; even I could repair most breakdowns. The green machine would have to carry me and all my possessions to Aux no. 9, some two thousand miles away.

It was difficult to say good-bye to Sheila. We had become very close, and I was convinced she was the girl I wanted to marry; but the future was so uncertain, and there was no time. Whatever the future held for us would have to wait until I learned what the air force had in store for me. We parted with the promise that the separation was only temporary!

Every night, when I stopped to rest at a motel, I studied *Bombs for Aircraft* and *Ammunition for Aircraft*. During the next day's drive, I would go over the data in my mind—like a self-quiz. Both books were a treasure trove of information, more than just the descriptions of bombs and the fuzes that made them detonate. There was also information on explosive content, markings, recommended target sets, and appropriate fuzes to achieve desired effects. Essentially, it was a weaponeering manual. My goal was to have both manuals memorized by the time I reached Aux no. 9, and I did. Mission accomplished.

Lessons Learned

Be the very best at what you do.

Learn everything you can about the endeavors you are responsible for.

Know the business of your business—earn the respect of you subordinates.

Value the counsel of your subordinates; they best
know how to improve the process.

Go where the action is and find out firsthand what is going on.

Continue the learning process—we should never stop learning.

Volunteer for the tough and unpopular assignments.

1st Lt. Pete & T-34, Marana AB, AZ

Solo Dunk with Jack Carr, Marana AB, AZ

Class 58M, Marana AB, AZ

1st Lt. Pete & T-33, Bryan AFB, TX

T-33 Formation, Bryan AFB, TX

1ˢᵗ Lt. Pete (center) receives 58M Commander's Trophy, Bryan AFB, TX

Capt. Pete/ F-86F, Williams AFB, AZ

CHAPTER 4

Jungle Jim

Something humorous happened on the way to Florida. I was making good time travelling across the southern United States, considering there were no interstate highways at that time. However, travelling nearly coast to coast was consuming all my cash. Gas, meals, and lodging all required cash, and credit cards had not yet been thought of. Furthermore, cashing checks in east Texas or Louisiana drawn on an Arizona bank wasn't the easiest thing to do. A cash infusion was needed fast! The easiest solution was to stop at Barksdale Air Force Base, Louisiana, a hundred miles or so down the road, and visit the Finance office there. In those days, pay records accompanied service members on permanent change of station (PCS) moves, hence it would only take a few minutes for them to check my ID card against the pay sheet, give me $200, and annotate the records. Simple! When I stopped at the security checkpoint at the main gate of Barksdale AFB and asked the security policeman for directions to Finance, he politely asked me to step inside the gatehouse to look at the base map. Once out of the car, I found myself looking down the barrel of a .45-caliber military issue automatic pistol. It was then I remembered the front passenger seat of my car was covered with two pistols, two rifles, and a shotgun, used for hunting mourning dove, gamble quail, mule deer, and the occasional rattlesnake in Arizona. My father, a Detroit City policeman, had counseled me to always transport guns in cars unloaded and in plain sight; otherwise, I could be slapped with a concealed weapons charge—not a good thing. The security policeman saw the guns, and when he heard the request for directions to

Finance, where the money is kept, he suspected a robbery was part of the visit to Finance. After checking my ID, military papers, and pay records, they decided it was a real air force captain they had spread-eagled on the pavement. They had me park and lock my car and called for backup. The backup consisted of two armed security policeman who drove me to Finance and escorted me to the pay window with guns in hand. After receiving an advance in pay, they drove me back to my car and then followed me a few miles down the road toward Florida. I suppose they were making sure I wasn't coming back. In retrospect, it was a good thing the gate guard was alert, observant, and not trigger happy; otherwise, I might not have made it to Florida.

I arrived at Auxiliary Field no. 9 on Monday, May 3, along with several other officers and many enlisted personnel, mostly senior NCOs. Aux Field no. 9 was also known as Hurlburt Field, now Hurlburt AFB. A cadre of senior officers, the unit leadership, had already been formed. They consisted of

> Col. Ben King, commander, fighter pilot, WW II Ace, and Silver Star recipient;
> Col. Chester Jack, vice commander;
> Lt. Col. Bob Gleason, director of operations;
> Maj. Rocky Stillwell, director of maintenance;
> Maj. John Downing, director of logistics; and
> Capt. Warren Trent, Headquarters, squadron commander and chief of personnel.

There were a couple of B-26s and C-47s on the ramp, but nothing else. The rumor was that the unit would also be equipped with T-28B Navy Trainers modified with two-wing mounted .50-caliber machine guns and four pylons capable of carrying bombs, rockets, and napalm.

All during the week, additional aircrew and maintenance personnel arrived, swelling the Jungle Jim ranks. Soon, we learned that the unit would be named the First Air Commando Squadron. Subsequently, it became a group and later an air force wing. I was surprised to find that I was the only officer from Luke AFB that was selected for the Air Commandos. Perhaps I was the only one that responded appropriately to the three questions asked.

On Wednesday, all squadron personnel were assembled at the base theater. There were now about three hundred or more in the First Air Commando Squadron ranks. Captain Trent called the squadron to attention, and Colonel King strode out of the wings to the middle of the stage, a lot like General Patton in the movie *Patton*. While the assembled mass stood at attention, Colonel King made the following brief and poignant remarks:

"Welcome! Some of you are here because it offered an opportunity to escape your former unit. Some of you are here because you anticipate the opportunity for rapid advancement in rank and other rewards. Some of you are here for the right reason, because you heard the clarion call that your country needs you. Well, all I can promise you is long hours and hard work! If that does not suit you, come to my office, and I'll see that you are reassigned."

With those words ringing in our ears, he left the stage, and we were dismissed. I was impressed with the directness of his message and the tone in which it was delivered. A new mission, a new spirit, and an old way of warfare, "counterinsurgency," were reborn in those few moments. Within just a few months, all who remained after that day, and many who would follow, would write large on the world stage until this day and for years into the future.

For the rest of the week, I hung around the T-28 Flight (which later became a squadron) to make sure the senior captains knew of my qualifications and that I was eager to get involved in the flying program. In the B-26 Flight, I ran into an old friend from the Sixty-Seventh TRW, Capt. Wally Walvogal, who was also an RB-26 navigator in Korea and Japan. He had also been selected for pilot training upon his return to the United States and had been towing aerial targets for air defense units with the B-26 prior to volunteering for Jungle Jim.

The C-47 aircraft at Hurlburt were already flying, with the mission of checking out aircrews in this old war horse. One of their instructor pilots (IPs) was Capt. Dick Sanborn, a man I met in the parking lot when I arrived at Hurlburt. He was also a bachelor, temporarily living in the BOQ while looking for off-base quarters. We agreed to share an apartment or house as soon as we could find something suitable.

During the first week, all flying personnel were subjected to a full two days of psychological testing and then individually interviewed by two psychiatrists. The tests were mind boggling! There were at least a thousand multiple-choice questions. The first group of questions required you to select which four characteristics from a list of five that best described you. For example, the five choices might be honest, trustworthy, loyal, friendly, and hardworking.

The next group of five would include four of the above five plus one new trait. There were at least five hundred "good trait" questions to be answered. Some of the five-word groups were repeated over and over. I suppose it was to determine if you were consistent.

The next section contained undesirable traits, and you had to select four of the undesirable traits that least described you, and "none of the above" was not an option. For example, the five choices could be liar, thief, disloyal, malingerer, and murderer.

Again, the list of five traits was changed by one word for each subsequent question. Several of the lists were repeated to check for consistency.

The second day was devoted to meetings with the two psychiatrists. The first interview was all about inkblots and what you saw in them. They all looked like inkblots to me. Occasionally, I saw something that vaguely resembled a butterfly. The second interview was a series of questions about your childhood and family relationships. Years later, while strolling through Pentagon corridors, I spotted one of the psychiatrists approaching from the opposite direction. I stopped him, introduced myself, and asked him if they learned anything about the original cadre of Air Commandos that was helpful to Colonel King. His response was unexpected! He said, "You were all guinea pigs to create a database. We are still following you to see if we can correlate behavior to indicators from that battery of tests." In hindsight, I suspect the then surgeon general saw an opportunity to collect data from a bunch of pilots and navigators who volunteered for an unknown mission.

Friday night found most of the newly arrived officers in the officers' club for what came to be known as the "Friday night fights." Air Commandos proved to be feisty and combative. This particular Friday, the O'club was festive, but calm. However, the local ladies were strutting their stuff for the new guys on the block. I can vividly remember the young lovelies shinnying up the columns holding up the ceiling. It must have been a ritual to attract the male of the species, and it was somewhat revealing for 1961. The O'club was originally a winter vacation home for the infamous Chicago mobster, Al Capone. The federal government had taken his property for partial payment of back income taxes and turned it over to the Army Air Corps, which became the USAF in October 1947.

That first Friday at Hurlburt, Colonel King strolled into the O'club for what proved to be an uncharacteristic appearance. About seven officers of the initial cadre gathered around him for whatever crumbs of knowledge he might pass out regarding what lay ahead. All was right with the world until he asked the wing administrative officer, Capt. Warren Trent, if the armament officer had reported in yet. Warren, a friend to all, said, "Yes, sir, he's here, but I can't put a face with the long funny name!"

The game was up, and I was it! Gathering up all my courage, I volunteered, "Colonel King, I shipped in as an armament officer, but

I'm really a fighter pilot with a lot of flight time in T-28s, F-86Fs, and B-26s, and the squadron needs me."

His response was a crisp. "Be in my office at 0700 hours!" It was considerate of him not to dress me down in front of my peers, but the steel in his voice was a warning to all.

I arrived at the commander's door at 0630 on Saturday and waited—he didn't show up? I knocked on the door at 0700 sharp and heard, "Come in." He'd been there a long time prior to my arrival. I reported with a snappy salute, "Sir, Captain Piotrowski reporting as ordered!"

He left me at attention as he snarled, "Captain, I will fly a B-26 early Monday morning, and I expect it to be a gunnery mission—dropping bombs, firing rockets, and strafing with .50-caliber machine guns, all six or eight of them. That is all, Captain!"

If there was one thing I had learned in nine years with the air force, it was "Don't make the wing commander mad the first time you meet!" I was now in a big hole and in recovery mode.

The colonel had thrown down the gauntlet, and it was time to deliver—but how? There were no tools, no ammunition account, and no enlisted personnel to help me do the necessary work to get a B-26 ready for a gunnery mission. I ran down Captain Trent, as Saturday was an Air Commando workday, and asked if by chance an enlisted armament technician had reported in. Good news, the answer was yes. A quick check of the roster revealed the man was T.Sgt. Dennis Premeaux, from Baton Rouge, Louisiana. Great, now to find him! The first sergeant was the next call. He promised to run Premeaux down and bring him to the wing maintenance hangar. Next, a stop at the maintenance library and tool crib for technical manuals and tools—manuals, yes; tools, no. I wrote down a shopping list:

> aircraft jacks
> leveling tools
> find a firing-in butt to fire the .50-caliber bullets into to calibrate
> the gun sight and bomb sight
> .50-caliber bullets, belted for the M2 machine gun
> practice bombs
> spotting charges for the practice bombs
> rockets with inert warheads,
> and so on.

The first sergeant arrived, with Technical Sergeant Premeaux in tow. Premeaux proved to be a jewel! He had been previously assigned to a Tactical Fighter Wing at Myrtle Beach, South Carolina, and was experienced on the guns, bombs, and rockets we would be using, both training and real munitions. On the other hand, I knew the B-26 and how to do what had to be done. As I poured over B-26 technical manuals, he started calling friends that had access to the ammunition storage area at Eglin AFB, just twenty miles down the road. The task at hand was still a hopeless long shot, but now there was a small dim light at the end of the tunnel.

There were no aircraft tugs or tow bars, so it was necessary to crank up the B-26 engines and taxi the aircraft across the ramp and down the taxiway to an old dilapidated WW II firing-in butt. Fortunately, this was not a problem for an experienced reciprocating engine pilot. The firing-in butt was the same one used by Lt. Col. Jimmy Doolittle nineteen years earlier for harmonizing his B-25 machine guns while training at Hurlburt for the famous raid on Tokyo, Japan. My old beat-up Morris Minor was used to tow three aircraft jacks, one at a time, and a power cart out to the aircraft to provide electricity to the gun sight and machine guns. The jacks were required to properly position the B-26 in relation to the target we would be shooting at. More good news: Premeaux's friend at Eglin AFB would give us belted .50-caliber ammunition! We could have all we wanted because modern Century Series aircraft didn't use .50s! However, practice bombs were in short supply, as were spotting charges. Rockets were not available either. So far, we were only one out of three with regard to what Colonel King wanted.

A day's work was accomplished by lunchtime, so we headed for the closest food source to the flight line, Hurlburt Marina Snack Bar, while eating outside, because we had worked up a pretty good sweat and didn't fit in with the yacht club set inside. With a view of the boat slips, we spied something we needed very badly. Someone had devised a pulley system to keep the boats from banging into the dock sides of their slips when the wind was up. This arrangement also allowed the boats to rise and fall on the Gulf of Mexico tides. The weights tied to the ropes that held the boats centered in their slips were rusty and beat up twenty-five-pound practice bombs! Eureka! We would be back at midnight to swap out the bombs for bricks, rationalizing that we weren't stealing—just returning government property back to the air force! Metal primer and blue spray paint were added to our supply list, as practice bombs were painted blue at the time.

Next, it was time to go shopping. We needed wrenches (to adjust the M2 machine guns and change out bomb racks), paint, bedsheets, a hammer (to straighten out the fins on the bombs), bricks, a long pole, a paintbrush, nails, and some nylon rope. I won't go into detail regarding the purpose of all these items, but the purpose of the bedsheets require some explaining. Adjusting the guns so they would fire though the pipper (aiming point on the gun sight) required a large cloth hanging one thousand feet in front of the aircraft guns with an eight-foot circle and an alignment cross painted on it. The alignment cross corresponded with a leveling telescope mounted in the aircraft bomb bay and was located in perfect relationship to the eight-foot circle the bullets had to fire through to coincide with the gun sight. Sewing would take too long, so the sheets were pinned together, requiring another purchase—a large quantity of safety pins. All the harmonization calculations were made while Technical Sergeant Premeaux combined the sheets and did the preliminary aircraft jacking. When our separate tasks were done, we painted the circles and lines on the sheets and hung them in the center of the firing-in butt. Now to adjust and lubricate the machine guns so they would fire properly. No Mil-Spec oil was available, but oil is oil, so a half-full quart of motor oil in the trunk of my car was put to good use.

At first, the guns wouldn't fire when the trigger was depressed. We didn't have the right armament tools for head-spacing the M2s. Fortunately, Technical Sergeant Premeaux knew how to time them in with a dime, which just happened to be the right thickness for head spacing. Ten round bursts were fired through each gun. After each burst, we drove down to the sheet and marked the holes with paint so we could identify the next set of holes. It took until dark to align all the guns. We rewarded ourselves with big grins when we fired all eight nose guns simultaneously and found sixty-five new holes in the sheets; 80 percent in the circle was the standard, and we bettered that by one bullet. Then it struck us that more sheets needed to be sewn together to provide a target for Colonel King to shoot at on the range; I was going broke making the colonel's request come true.

Dinner, a couple of beers, then some time to kill with war stories until midnight, then back to the Marina to exchange our bricks for bombs. We had decided the colonel should be happy with eight bombs, four dive bombing runs, and four skip bomb runs, so we only bought eight bricks. With eight bombs in the Morris Minor, we retired for the night. On Sunday, just after dawn, we attacked the bombing system and were lucky to find that half of the twenty bomb racks in the bomb bay released properly. The racks in good working condition were repositioned to the lower stations in the bomb bay. Next, we refurbished and painted the bombs. Premeaux did the hammer and sandpaper work, and I, the painting. For a final check of the bombing system, we dragged the bed mattress out of my room in the bachelor officer quarters (BOQ) and laid it under the open bomb bay to protect the newly refurbished bombs from damage. I turned on the electrical power and put the gear handle up (after making sure the safety pins were installed in the landing gear struts so the gear couldn't collapse). It is necessary to have the gear handle up in most aircraft to close a switch that prevents undesirable things from happening on the ground. Dropping bombs and firing machine guns are two of those things that shouldn't happen with the gear handle down and the gear locked in place. Then I released the bombs one at a time, while Premeaux monitored the bomb rack releases for hang-ups.

Three things remained to be done; one was really hard. First, a checklist had to be typed for Colonel King so he could properly set up the switches to fire the guns and drop the bombs. Second, I needed to prepare a mission briefing on the range, along with weapon deliver parameters. These were easy; they just took time. Third, it was necessary to find an open gunnery range for the mission and talk to one of my fighter pilot buddies into playing range officer. The range officer acted as a safety observer: cleared aircraft onto the range and supervised scoring of bomb impacts and strafe targets. More importantly for this mission was to call out good bomb impacts no matter where he scattered them! There would be no smoke on impact because smoke charges were not available. Colonel King wouldn't be able to see his own bomb impacts. I planned to tell him during the mission briefing that the range was very wet, and he probably would not see any smoke from the impacts, but the range officer would.

On the chance that there would be someone at Eglin Range Control, I called, only to find it was a twenty-four-hour, seven-day-a-week operation due to all the test activity on the Eglin Range Complex. To my surprise, Colonel King had requested a gunnery range for his mission, and one had already been set aside for his use. I learned later that he had been commander of the BOMARC Test Force and was very familiar with Eglin ranges and scheduling procedures. He made sure that I didn't overlook that important detail. The sheets bought for a range target weren't needed but couldn't be returned because they were sewn together. Premeaux drove to Eglin to get a manual on the ranges, and I called the colonel at home to ask him where he wanted to receive the mission briefing. He said, "My office at 0700, you've got fifteen minutes."

Colonel King had probably never flown a B-26 before, but he was an old-school pilot that believed there wasn't an aircraft he couldn't fly. I have to admit I thought he could fly the B-26 based on his P-38 experience. He flew the gunnery mission with Captain Grob, a highly experienced B-26 driver with combat experience in Korea and perhaps WW II. It all went as planned! Technical Sergeant Premeaux and I were waiting on the ramp for his return and his mission debriefing on the armament systems. When he parked the aircraft, he was grinning—happy as could be! He walked over to me, returned our salutes, and shook my hand. Smiling, he said, "Pete, you SOB, I didn't think anyone could get the job done!"

I introduced the colonel to Technical Sergeant Premeaux, saying, "Sir, this is the man who got it done."

Premeaux and I went to unload the guns and discovered he had fired all eight hundred rounds loaded the night before. We drove to the range, only about twenty miles from the base, and took down the strafing target so no one would score it. We gave him a 26 percent hit rate, 1 percent above qualifying. The rest of the day, Premeaux and I made lists of all the things we discovered that were needed by the armament section and turned the lists over to Maj. John Downing, who was the supply officer and a War Eagle from Alabama. Based on my Catch-22 experience with supply, I made sure that every tool and piece of test equipment we would need was on our unit equipment list. At that moment, we were a month ahead of everyone else in Jungle Jim in getting ready for whatever was in store for us.

That night, Sergeant Premeaux and I had a few more beers, and from that moment, we were as close as any captain and sergeant ever were. As it turned out, he was the senior NCO in my armament shop for all the years I was in the Air Commandos—he was my go-to guy; he could make it happen and proved that time and time again.

We still had a lot more work to do in restoring the bomb storage area (bomb dump) and filling it with the bombs and ammunition needed for practice. We also ordered real bombs and fuzes in case some real world missions had to be flown from Hurlburt; in addition, practice bomb racks, practice rocket launchers, and lots of rockets. MJ-1 bomb loaders, trailers, tractors, and other loading equipment were placed on order and started arriving. Our munitions personnel started arriving as well. They were a good crew, dedicated, hardworking, and committed to getting everything done right. Air force personnel responsible for Jungle Jim made must have handpicked them. That isn't too surprising when everything you're handling is loaded with explosives and has the potential to ruin your day, and your life, in addition to everyone else's within few hundred feet. There were two staff sergeants named Ballard and Barger assigned under Technical Sergeant Premeaux, each led a team of young airmen. Ballard was responsible for the B-26s; and Barger, the AT-28s. Both were really dedicated, hardworking, and capable leaders.

My counterpart in aircraft maintenance was Capt. Jim Walls, nicknamed "Four Walls" after a then-popular country western song. Jim grew up somewhere in the west, was tall, thin, and very laconic. It was hard to get him to put more than three words together. When we had a conversation, I spoke sentences, and he responded with yes, no, or maybe. He was, however, a Cracker Jack in the business of aircraft maintenance and had the full confidence and support of his enlisted personnel. Jim and I got along extremely well and worked as a team to support the operations-driven flying schedule. We never lost an aircraft while Captain Walls was running flight line maintenance, and that is the real tribute to the man. Even more so when you consider that most aircraft being flown by Air Commandos were retrieved from the graveyard at Davis Monthan AFB, Arizona. Moreover, our planes were years out of production and maintained at the end of long and tenuous supply lines under primitive conditions.

The AT-28Bs for the Air Commando Group took a while in arriving, so we had time to focus on our B-26s and their aircrew-training program. Most of the initial B-26 pilots had no gunnery experience and were squeamish about getting too close to the ground for shallow strafing runs or too steep in dive bomb deliveries. A napalm run was usually flown at fifty feet above the ground, making it easy to hit in front of a target and cover it with the flaming gel. The B-26 crews didn't like the low-altitude runs either. Accordingly, they were releasing bombs and strafing a much greater distances and altitudes. Not surprisingly, they kept writing up B-26s for being out of harmonization and having improper sight settings. I asked Lieutenant Colonel Gleason, who was flying the B-26, if I could check out in the aircraft so I could do some quality control on the fire control and bombing systems. There was not a bombardier position on the B-26; all the munitions delivery work was done by the pilot.

Colonel Gleason agreed, and my check ride came quickly; as I recall, it required only one flight. The instructor pilot hammered home the need for quick thinking and action if an engine was lost on takeoff. "Failure to act immediately and correctly would result in a crash," he said. Of course, he was right. I pointed out that nothing I had flown as a pilot had two engines (C-45 and C-47 excluded), so I was delighted to have the second one and would make sure it was put to good use. The memory jogger for a failed engine was "dead leg, dead engine." This meant that the leg that needed a lot of pressure on the rudder pedal to keep the plane flying straight was the side with the good engine. The leg not being used was on the dead-engine side. For example, if the right engine failed, asymmetrical thrust from the left engine would pull the aircraft into a right turn unless hard left rudder was used immediately and until the aircraft was "trimmed" (all control pressures relieved). Adding power to the left engine to keep the aircraft flying in the situation described only made matters worse, requiring even more left rudder. It was important to focus on the dead engine because while the pilot was keeping the aircraft flying and under control. The next immediate step was to feather the dead engine, thus reducing significant drag on that side of the aircraft.

It wasn't a surprise when the IP pulled the right throttle to the off position on takeoff, killing the right engine. The Wright 2800 Cyclone engines had plenty of power, and the aircraft carried no ordnance, so it was light. The immediate action was heavy left rudder, add max power to the left engine, feather the right engine (dead leg), and trim, maintaining a shallow climb. My own emergency word was "MAD," for maintain control (which I did), analyze the situation (ditto), and do something (which was to accomplish the emergency procedure, feathering the dead engine). The check ride was over in two or three hours, and I was cleared to fly the B-26. My first flight on the range assured me the harmonization and sight settings were correct. On the other hand, I caved a little and had another foul line for the B-26s set at 1,500 feet in addition to the line for AT-28s at one thousand feet. Tracers, one every ten rounds, were added to B-26 ammunition belts for night missions. This enabled the crews employing laze pull-ups off a strafing run to see the .50-caliber ricochets they were flying through.

A few words about the B-26 are necessary in order to clarify which of the two different aircraft designated as a B-26 we were operating. There were two aircraft built during WW II, both twin engine and at different times both carried the moniker B-26. The Martin B-26 was a larger aircraft that carried a much heavier bomb load. Unfortunately, it was underpowered and became known as a "widow maker" and earned the slogan "One a day in Tampa Bay." Pres. John F. Kennedy's older brother, Joseph Kennedy, was killed while piloting a Martin B-26 during WWII in the European Theater. The Douglas A-26 was of a sleeker design, highly maneuverable, and was used more like a fighter than a bomber. When the Martin B-26 went out of the inventory, the Douglas A-26 was redesignated B-26. The Douglas A-26 AKA B-26 was used in WW II, Korea, and Vietnam. It was also loaned to French forces fighting to retain their hold over Indochina after WW II until their defeat at Dien Bien Phu on May 7, 1954. The aircraft flown by Air Commandos was the Douglas A-26/B-26. The B-26 story had another twist when an upgraded version was deployed to Thailand in the late 1960s. Thai law prohibited the basing of bombers in Thailand. With a convenient stroke of the pen, the B-26 reverted to its former type designation of A-26.

Coaching some of the new B-26 crews on gunnery parameters required riding in the jump seat behind the navigator. It was obvious from jump-seat rides that pilots were rolling in at well over a mile from the target on their bombing, rocket, and strafing runs. The roll-in point establishes the dive angle, hence these pilots were releasing bombs and strafing well beyond ranges that could yield any modicum of accuracy. Slowly, with coaching (and challenging their manhood), the gunnery scores improved, and their training became more productive. Another aspect of rolling in too far out was that the aircraft would remain on a predictable flight for an extended period of time. This would make them easy targets for enemy ground-to-air gunners. The B-26 gunnery issue started me thinking along the path that it was easier for a pilot trained in the fighter mission to transition to a new aircraft than it was to take pilots skilled in a particular aircraft and change their mission.

Every day in the Air Commando organization was intense and brought new challenges to personnel and equipment. Captain Eagleston, known to all as the "Gray Eagle" because of his age and hair color, became the maintenance physical training (PT) officer. Every day the entire unit fell out for calisthenics and a two-mile run in fatigues and brogans. After the run, aircrews stayed with the Gray Eagle to practice knife throwing—yes, knife throwing. He had obtained a four-foot-thick section of a log, which was about seven feet in diameter. It was set on the ground on edge, and the face of the log was painted the silhouette of a man. Individually, we would run across in front of the log at perhaps twenty feet and throw our knives at the silhouette. Over time, we learned to throw the knife so it stuck in the log and, once in a while, hit the silhouette. I had read the history of the great Zulu king, Shaka, in South Africa. His warriors only became victorious when Shaka shortened their spears to become stabbing sticks that could not be thrown with any accuracy. Thus, the warriors held on to their short spears, using them as stabbing sticks to kill many enemies, vice throwing them away and then running from the enemy. Woe be it to any Zulu warrior who returned from battle without his stabbing stick. It seemed that King Shaka had it right. It was probably much better to hold on to the knife instead of throwing it away.

It seemed to me that a knife was an important survival tool, so I researched knife makers to find the best in terms of blade strength and ability to take and hold an edge. I settled on a custom-made blade by

Randall Made Knives in Florida. The knife cost seventy-five dollars, a fortune at that time. It is unquestionably one of the best investments I've ever made. I still have it and use it regularly.

Fort Walton Beach was a great place to live. The quality of life was good, perhaps too good, and the cost of living was low, except during the tourist season. Tourists started arriving in June and stayed through August. During that three-month period, local restaurants raised all their prices. The area offered a wide variety of activities for airmen and dependents. The beaches were the best in the world, and the deep-sea fishing for king mackerel, amberjack, and grouper was unparalleled. Freshwater fishing was equally as good. The climate was humid but mild. Fresh ocean fish, shrimp, and oysters were so inexpensive in the marketplace, they were almost free. There was a sense of history there as well. On the short runway that joined the long north/south runway at Hurlburt, there was a painted white silhouette of a WW II carrier deck. More specifically, it was the silhouette of the carrier, USS *Hornet*. Allegedly, this is where Lt. Col. Doolittle and his Tokyo Raiders did their dry-land training to get their B-25s airborne in the length of the carrier USS *Hornet*. That silhouette was easily visible on every takeoff and landing. It always seemed too short to me.

Colonel King repeatedly advised us that flying regulations had been waived for Jungle Jim and that we needed to train realistically! One day, when the entire southeastern United States was covered with low ceilings and poor visibility, a couple of C-47s took off on training missions. One of the aircraft was flying a "nap of the earth" low-level navigation mission. The route took it over Barksdale AFB, Louisiana, which was below minimums, which, I'm guessing, were set at a two-hundred-foot ceiling and one-half mile visibility. The Jungle Jim C-47 flew over the field at fifty feet above the ground. The tower got their tail number and traced them through Flight Services to find their VFR clearance was filed at Hurlburt. The SAC wing commander had the tail number and called Jungle Jim at Hurlburt. Colonel King was away, and Colonel Gleason took the call. In response to the Barksdale wing commander's questions, Lieutenant Colonel Gleason responded, "The mission was directed by higher authority," with the belief that the SAC wing commander wouldn't go any higher. The ruse worked!

The T-28Bs finally arrived. For a conventionally powered prop aircraft, they were impressive as long as your adversary was not too sophisticated or flying modern jet-powered aircraft. For example, in the Bay of Pigs disaster, Cuban T-33s equipped with .50-caliber machine guns, which had escaped the initial attacks on their airfields, made short work of clearing the skies of B-26s flown by Liberating Forces. Once the B-26s were gone, the forces landing on the beaches without air support as their heavy artillery were easily defeated.

AT-28Bs proved to be a trainer on steroids. They were powered by a Wright 1820-86 engine developing 1,425 horsepower driving a three-bladed propeller. Essentially, it had P-47 performance with a nose gear that made it much easier to take off and land. The only drawback: there were only two .50-caliber machine guns slung below the wings, creating drag, vice six guns mounted in the wings of the P-47. In addition, the AT-28B had two outboard pylons on each wing that could carry bombs, napalm, or rockets. If the guns were removed and replaced by inboard pylons, those pylons could each carry 750 pounds of ordnance. Pilots preferred the guns because they offered sustained firepower. Five-hundred-pound bombs and rocket pods were readily available. However, the standard napalm tank was 750 pounds and could not be carried because of weight limitations on the outboard pylons. Napalm proved to be a weapon of choice in Korea, so the air force procured thousands of five-hundred-pound napalm tanks for Air Commando use.

Capt. John Pattee was the only current T-28 pilot coming from the USAF Air Training Command without any fighter experience. He checked us all out in the aircraft and had no trouble assimilating the fighter-bomber role the AT-28B was intended to play. We only had these aircraft for a short while, and then they were returned to North America, in Columbus, Ohio, for modifications to include ferry tanks that would enable the AT-28B to fly over 2,500 nautical miles without refueling. Perhaps Colonel King had some inkling as to what was in store for the Air Commandos.

The first Air Commando deployment came in the summer of 1961. It involved sending two C-47s, along with aircrews and a support team to Mali, Africa. Their mission must have been very sensitive because the crews never talked about what they did after they returned. Fifty years later, I learned they had been training Mali paratroopers in conjunction with US Army Special Forces.

The summer of 1961 was jam-packed with things that needed to be accomplished. One of those was another visit to Survival School at Stead AFB, Nevada. This would be my third survival training in five years; I hoped to get it right this time. Colonel King, with help from the air force, had a special course set up for aircrews and selected ground crews. This course had a heavy emphasis on interrogation. Of course, inflicting great discomfort was part and parcel of interrogation techniques, an area where Survival School instructors excelled. In comparison to the

December 1958 Survival School I attended, the boxes we were stuffed into were smaller, the duration longer, and it was much hotter. One contraption added to their chamber of horrors was a large steel box that would hold approximately fifty adults if they were packed in very tightly. There were only a few small airholes in the tank, creating a high carbon-dioxide content in the air. When they filled the tank with water to thigh level, the high summer heat raised the humidity in the tank, which came to nearly 100 percent. Some had serious breathing problems and fainted. It wasn't water boarding, but it came close. In addition, we were given a basic course in karate, not enough to earn any color of belt, but enough to quickly disable one opponent.

B-26 aircrews lamented the fact that they could not carry any external stores, just various bombs in the bomb bay, up to twenty, depending on size and weight. This limitation deprived them of delivering napalm (the thin-skinned tank could not be safely dropped out of the bomb bay) or firing rockets. I proposed to Colonel King that the B-26 wing could easily be modified to carry external stores and showed him some engineering sketches that I had drawn up. The undersides of the wings were covered with one-quarter inch steel armor plate, making it very easy to bolt or weld pylons to the steel plate. I suspect the steel plate was part of the initial design intended to protect the fuel cells imbedded in the wings from Antiaircraft Artillery (AAA) ground fire.

Colonel King was a man of action! The next day, he informed me that we were going to McClellan AFB, California, to discuss the proposed wing pylon concept with the air force engineers responsible for B-26 logistic support. He had convinced Eglin Air Force Base Operations to loan him a T-33 for the trip. The fact that he hadn't flown the T-33 for years didn't bother him in the least; it was just another airplane, and he was firmly convinced he could fly any plane ever made. Somehow, he discovered that I was still current in the T-33 by a couple of days, and that became his cover. I wasn't too concerned, thinking I could talk him through any problem we encountered. In fact, I talked him through the start, taxi, and takeoff. On climb out, I suggested the T-33 climbed better and on less fuel at 250 knots, etc. Our flight plan had us stopping at Tinker AFB, Oklahoma, a convenient refueling stop en route to the West Coast. The pitchout in the pattern was loose and very wide, and the turn to final was more suitable for an AT-28 than a T-33. I fed him the correct airspeeds around the pattern with a little fudge factor on the high side for safety. When captains fly with colonels, they are expected to take care of all the mundane details. So be it. In less than an hour, we were airborne and on our way to McClellan. With the one flight behind him, Colonel

King had everything under control. I just tuned in the navigation aids along the route. The pitchout and traffic pattern at McClellan was much improved, and I was just along for the ride and at the ready in case of an in-flight emergency.

The McClellan engineers were eager to meet the challenge Colonel King gave them and happy for the additional work. They agreed that my idea was easily doable. They promised to expedite the mechanical and electrical design for his approval and start modifying aircraft as soon as possible. Mission accomplished; now to get back to Hurlburt safely and without incident. Everything went according to plan, and I became convinced that Colonel King was one of those gifted aviators, like Charles Lindbergh, Jimmy Doolittle, John Alison, Chuck Yeager, and Bob Hoover, who became part of the airplanes they flew.

One summer day, a B-26 that didn't belong to the Air Commandos appeared on our ramp. There was no crew, just the aircraft. Major Stillwell said that the unknown B-26 appeared to have some battle damage and asked me to take a look at the plane and make a list of repairs needed. Sure enough, there were holes in the nose, forward of the cockpit and armor plate, that looked to be about .50 calibers in diameter. I asked one of our crew chiefs, as well as Staff Sergeant Ballard's armament crew, to pull off the nose panels so we could assess the damage to the aircraft. To my surprise, there was no indication that any projectiles had gone through the nose, just holes in the skin. This wasn't battle damage; instead, it appeared that someone with a half-inch steel rod had punched holes in the aircraft's skin to make it look like battle damage. The only repairs required were some skin patches. To this day, I have no idea where the mystery B-26 came from or who operated it before it was found on our ramp. It could possibly have been a holdover from the Bay of Pigs fiasco. In any case, the phantom B-26 was a welcome addition to our fleet.

Sheila Fredrickson was still in Mesa, Arizona, and we kept in touch with frequent letters and an occasional long-distance phone call. Long-distance phone calls were horribly expensive and outside our respective budgets. In one letter, I suggested she come to Fort Walton Beach for a summer vacation, and we could make some plans for our future. In her response, she indicated spending time on the beach in a resort town sounded great. She quit her job and was planning to get a civil service position at Eglin AFB. It wasn't long before she arrived with her roommate, a lovely blonde, Lou Tiberio. Lou returned to Mesa after a couple of weeks but later came back to stay for good. They met another single gal, a fetching redhead by the name of Wanda Boggs, and the three of them rented one side of a duplex house on Santa Rosa

Island, about one hundred feet from the high tide line on that beautiful white sand beach. A blonde, brunette, and redhead together in bathing suits on that white sandy beach was a sight to behold!

The Air Commando operational readiness inspection (ORI) came in late August 1961. The purpose of an ORI is to determine if a unit is combat-ready. Aircrews had to qualify in all relevant events, the ground crews had to demonstrate their proficiency in maintaining the aircraft combat ready, and the group had to demonstrate that the equipment and spare parts were in sufficient numbers to sustain operations for sixty days. In my opinion, we were still a long way from being ready for combat, but things were coming together. Maintenance manning was nearly 100 percent, aircrew manning continued to outpace the number of assigned aircraft, and proficiency was good for the amount of time the group had to prepare. The size of the ORI team overwhelmed us— they were everywhere, observing munitions movement from the bomb dump to the flight line and checking munitions loading for safety and quantity distance of explosive content. The inspectors also gave aircrews spot checks on proficiency and graded their gunnery scores against the standards set by the Tactical Air Command. To my surprise and that of a few others, the First Air Commando Group passed the ORI and was declared combat-ready. I look back on that ORI, after having experienced many more, and have to wonder if the outcome was preordained.

Years later I learned that shortly after Jungle Jim was forming up at Hurlburt, Lieutenant Colonel Gleason developed a series of scenarios that the AT-28, B-26, and C-47 aircrews trained on. He believed these scenarios were the most likely missions we would be tasked to fly in a combat environment. When representatives of the TAC IG Team visited to assess if the Air Commandos were far enough along in their training to be subjected to an ORI, Lieutenant Colonel Gleason gave them the scenarios we were training to. Lacking anything better to use as a measure of our combat readiness, similar scenarios were used in the ORI. This doesn't detract one bit from the excellent gunnery scores and precision air cargo deliveries achieved during the ORI, which resulted in the Outstanding rating.

One evening, over dinner at a favorite restaurant in early September, I proposed marriage to Sheila. Ever the doubter in how the air force could impact our future, she asked when we would get married. I responded, "Early December so we can take our honeymoon in Phoenix and visit with your family." That seemed to satisfy her, and she said yes!

A few days later, I took off on a B-26 cross-country with a very good friend, Capt. Ira "Iwo" L. Kimes. He was called Iwo because his father retired from the Marine Corps as a colonel. Iwo was also a B-26 and AT-28 pilot, and we took turns sitting in the left seat, flying the plane, while the other took care of dialing in the navigation aids. Not long after we took off, we noticed some backfires coming from the left engine. It was occasional and didn't affect the engine's performance, so we continued on. Our destination was March AFB, where we would spend the night and return to Hurlburt the following day. When Iwo lowered the flaps at the appropriate point in the traffic pattern at March, we experienced a violent roll to the right. Iwo hit the flap switch to up, and the roll stopped. Apparently, only the left flap extended when the switch was activated, causing a split-flap situation. If not for Iwo's immediate analysis and corrective actions, we would have been a smoking hole off the end of the runway. Iwo took the aircraft around and landed with flaps up from a straight in approach. We discussed our problem with Transient Alert personnel, and they passed the problem to the chief of maintenance.

The next day, our B-26 was towed into a hangar and attended to by a number of aging maintenance personnel. We learned that all of these gentlemen had worked on B-26s during WW II and the Korean War. We were in luck—we hoped? We reported our problems to both Operations and Maintenance at Hurlburt and informed our commanders we would return as soon as the aircraft was flyable. Iwo and I spent every day at the hangar working with the maintenance crew, believing we might be able to help. Five days later, the main gear would no longer retract properly, nor would the flaps extend properly, and they had yet to start working on the left engine repairs. Our commanders at Hurlburt told us to fly the broken aircraft home with the flaps locked up and the gear bolted down.

It would be a long day in the cockpit, as the maximum speed with the gear down was 150 knots, and range would be severely limited. It was my turn in the left seat flying the aircraft home, with Iwo in the right seat. Dyess AFB, Texas, provided a conveniently located long runway for the first landing after departing March AFB. We wanted to get a good check on fuel consumption with the gear-down configuration and a long runway for the flaps-up landing. Dyess had a thirteen-thousand-foot runway and was in just the right spot for our needs. The numbers on range and fuel consumption came up in our favor so that we could make Hurlburt without another fuel stop.

When we taxied to the B-26 ramp at Hurlburt, Colonel King's staff car was already there waiting. Iwo and I both thought we were in for a good butt chewing. When I climbed down the ladder and saluted, the colonel said, "Get in the car." He drove to his office without speaking—not a good sign? Once in the office, he shut the door and handed me a sealed manila envelope and said, "Take this, go to Taiwan, and find Al Westy—he'll tell you what to do."

My response was "Yes, sir!"

He then added, "Pete, you're out of the air force for the time being. Don't take any uniforms and cover your tracks. You're leaving in the morning!" With that limited information, I saluted and left.

It was already early evening, and I had some packing to do. There were a lot of unknowns in this surprise assignment, mostly how to find one man in a whole country and also how to cover my tracks. First things first: I called Sheila and asked her to join me for dinner. Over dinner, I told her about my departure early the following morning. I couldn't tell her where I was going or when I would be back because the TDY was open-ended. Last, I wasn't sure that I could write to her or her to me because of the classified nature of the assignment, but we'd work that detail out as things unfolded. It's an understatement to say that my short monologue was not well received. Her first question was "When are we going to get married?"

My answer was "When I get back!" She responded that this was the third time the air force had separated us, that if we were not married by Christmas, as promised, she would have to make other plans. Not a good note to part on! However, she agreed to drive me to the airport the following day. Capt. Warren Trent had purchased a ticket to Los Angeles for me with a layover there and then on to Honolulu. The rest was up to me.

I arrived in LA on Friday and went to a number of embassies. It was convenient that they're all located in one area. I picked up visas for Japan, Korea, Thailand, and Taiwan. The next stopover was in Hawaii, where I picked up another visa, this one for Australia. As Air Commandos, we carried official government purple passports, so getting visas was relatively easy. With all those visas, I thought my tracks were covered. I flew to Tokyo and stayed the night, then to Bangkok for one night, and then on to Taipei, capital of Taiwan. With several open visas, I thought it would look like I was still on the move.

What to do next? This was the hard part—finding Mr. Al Westy. Doing what comes naturally, I found out there was an American officers' club in downtown Taipei, a few blocks from the hotel. Sauntering into the club, I spotted a classmate from pilot training at the bar. Over I went and introduced myself, saying, "I'm out of the air force and looking for work."

He responded, "I can think of a lot better places than Taipei to be looking for work."

I bought a round of drinks and continued, "I hear a guy named Al Westy is hiring and paying good money. Do you know where I can find him?"

He said, "Everyone knows Al. He heads up the CIA operation known as Air Asia down in Tainan!" How lucky and improbable was that! The next morning, I was on an Air China flight to Tainan and before long was standing in front of Al Westy. My job assignment was to take six B-26s from the Air Asia boneyard near Tainan and get them combat-ready. These aircraft had been loaned to the French to fight the Viet Minh in Indochina and were returned to United States' control after the French were defeated at Dien Bien Phu on May 7, 1954. To save time, trouble, and expense, the loaned aircraft were flown to Taiwan and turned over to the CIA for storage near their Air Asia facility.

Al said to me, "You're in trouble, kid! The brass in the Philippines expected you to be here three days ago—they're considering you AWOL." So much for me being deceptive and covering my tracks. The package Colonel King gave me contained drawings of the wing pylon modifications made at the McClellan Air Depot. When the Air Asia engineers saw these drawings, they laughed, saying they looked like something designed for a Union Pacific railroad car. A few days later, they showed me a streamlined design they said was vastly superior to the one engineered at McClellan. I wasn't given any limits to my authority, so I approved it. In addition, engineering drawings for a B-26 camera installation for airborne reconnaissance were also included in the manila envelope. There was a lot of work to be done in order to get these aircraft modified and combat-ready.

Corrosion had to be removed, and then the aircraft had to be given a new coat of anticorrosion paint. Machine guns were removed, refurbished, test-fired, and reinstalled. Harmonization, according to Air Commando specifications, had to be accomplished on all aircraft. Engines were removed and overhauled. Test flights, including gun firing and ordnance release, were accomplished on each aircraft. I flew on every test flight to ensure the work was done correctly and that all deficiencies recorded in the forms were corrected. The B-26 crews would be pleased with these aircraft when they received them at Clark AFB in the Philippines.

I felt compelled to send messages back to Hurlburt on how the B-26 reclamation project was progressing. The only way this could be accomplished was to let the local colonel base commander in on my mission. He was reluctant but eventually agreed to grant access to his

Base Communications Center for one message (TWX) a week. The colonel introduced me to a technical sergeant in the Communications Center with the proviso that I could only work with him—good enough! When submitting the first hand written message with Top Secret on it, the technical sergeant asked me for a message site number; P-1 came to mind, which became P-2, and so on, with successive TWXs. They all went through. The originals stayed with me in a money belt until reaching Bien Hoa, SVN, where they were turned over to the classified accounts officer.

After my meeting with the base commander, he took great pleasure in throwing me out of the officers' club every time he saw me there. I guess he thought he was contributing to my cover, as a civilian not associated with the air force. I stayed in a hotel in town for a few days. It was going to be expensive, and reimbursement wouldn't come until I returned to Hurlburt at some uncertain future date. Fortuitously, there was an American civilian, a new hire into Air Asia, who was planning to bring his family over in a couple of months. He had leased a four-bedroom house in preparation for their arrival and asked me if I would like to live there and pay a portion of the rent. "Deal," I said, and the price was much lower than even the cheapest hotel. He had hired a maid, so all we had to do was eat cereal for breakfast and hang out. It was only a short walk down a gravel path to catch the bus that we rode daily to Air Asia. Even in the rain, the walk wasn't anything to complain about.

There was an APO (Armed Forces Post Office) serving the air force detachment at Tainan Air Base, who were working with Air Asia in conjunction with the depot level work they performed on USAF aircraft deployed in the Far East. The APO address was used to correspond with Sheila. Mail service in that part of the world was extremely slow. It took one week for a letter from the APO to reach Fort Walton Beach and another seven days for a response to come back. With Sheila's first letter came three documents that needed to be completed in order for us to be legally married over the phone. I was against an over-the-phone wedding but thought there was no harm in getting the documents taken care of and returned to Sheila. The blood test seemed simple enough. Because I was undercover, so to speak, and masquerading as a civilian, I went to see a Chinese doctor who drew the blood. When I returned for the results and to have the paperwork on my blood type completed, all the doctor said was "You not have VD!" Subsequently, I filled out the paperwork myself, knowing my blood type was O+ because it was stamped on my dog tags. To make the document look official, a Chinese character stamp of the word "rabbit" was purchased and stamped on the document. Another document required notarization that I was the person who agreed to be married over the telephone. Again, I ran into a Chinese brick wall, so the Chinese character stamp was put to good use again. The third paper had something to do with obtaining a marriage license back in Florida; yet again the rabbit character stamp came in handy. These papers were dutifully sent back to Sheila for possible use. We tried one phone call to see if we could actually get through. A simple phone call required a reservation for the line a week in advance. We lost that reserved line after a couple of minutes of hurried conversation.

Sheila was having problems at her end as well. There were very few ministers willing to perform a marriage over the phone. Finally, she found one both willing and helpful in preparing for the big event. When informed of the limited availability of a telephone linkup and short time connections, the minister suggested a script. Our vows would be read like lines in a play. We would all read our parts quickly in the proper sequence to minimize the time required for the ceremony and hopefully not lose the line before we were declared husband and wife. Ma Bell was not very cooperative either. The local phone company refused to install a speakerphone in Sheila's duplex so that all four participants could hear the ceremony performed. The participants were the minister, Sheila, Lou Tiberio, the maid of honor, and the best man, Capt. Dick Sanborn. Finally, the phone company relented and installed the speakerphone for one day at an exorbitant price. Sheila was so busy pulling everything together that she fell behind on getting the *marriage license!* She had filled out the application for the license, but the application had to be turned in at the county courthouse in Crestview, Florida, to obtain the actual legal marriage license. Two close friends, Wanda Boggs and Sandy Tegge, whose husband was a C-47 navigator, took the application to the courthouse, whereupon the county clerk discovered the application had not been signed. When told the troubled story of the pending wedding, the county clerk allowed Wanda to sign Sheila's name on the application. Then another problem raised its ugly head: the application had to be posted for five days prior to issuing the marriage license. The five days would expire on December 20, but the courthouse would be closed on that day for the Christmas holidays. The helpful and understanding county clerk agreed to meet Sheila at the county jail on the twentieth with the license. It must be true that love conquers all. I reported to the pay phone in the fish market at the appointed time. The phone rang; we raced through our vows, and the minister pronounced us husband and wife. As a result of being on different sides of the international date line, Sheila's anniversary is December 22, and mine is on the 23! All of the documents supporting the marriage license application were forged! There will be more about the legality of our marriage in another chapter.

Al Westy had me paged to his office one day and said he was having some problems with the air force with regard to the B-26 paint scheme. The air force wanted them painted with Vietnamese emblems, and that was not permissible in Formosa. Could I help? Al gave me the phone number of a colonel at Thirteenth Air Force headquarters in the Philippines, requesting that I call and explain the problem. I did, but with no success. The colonel was adamant about Vietnamese markings on the aircraft leaving Tainan. Al said he would handle the problem. The next day, a call came in from a general at the Pentagon, asking me "to get the CIA off my butt," and for all he cared, "they could paint the B-26 purple." Al smiled when I passed him the message. He tried to work the issue at the lowest level, and when that failed, he called in the Washington CIA heavyweights.

With the painting issue resolved, the thoroughly inspected, repaired, and modified B-26s started flowing through Clark AFB, where Air Commando pilots stationed at Bien Hoa picked them up and flew them to their jungle base north of Saigon. Soon I would follow with the last of the six refurbished aircraft.

Another call came from Mr. Westy. This time, he asked me if I would do him a favor and inspect the Air Asia bomb dump, as well as the munitions stored there. He offered me a driver and a snack pack, and said the driver would return at 5:00 p.m. to take me home. The request was unusual, but my orders from Colonel King were to take direction from Mr. Westy, so the obvious answer was "Of course." I spent the next eight hours writing up deficiencies found in the bomb dump—things like the grass is too high, causing a fire hazard; five-hundred-pound bombs in Igloo no. 7 have Composition B explosive leaking into nose and tail fuze wells and need to be properly cleaned; bombs in Igloo no. 9 show extensive corrosion and need to be sandblasted and painted; etc. The next morning, I turned in several pages of discrepancies to Mr. Westy. I wanted to ask why there was such a large inventory of bombs but thought better of it. After glancing at the list for a moment, he said, "The reason I asked you to go the bomb dump was to hide you. There was a brigadier general from Thirteenth Air Force that flew in yesterday. He was interested in talking to you, and I didn't think that was a good idea." Then he went on to say, "I have to tell you that the general was angry that you couldn't be found, but he'll get over it." I had a feeling that I was in trouble, which meant that I needed to get in and out of the Philippines without Thirteenth Air Force knowing I was ever there.

On one of my last days in Tainan, my host and I left the house early. While walking down the path to the bus stop, we saw his maid and her family crawl out a haystack. We had seen them in that vicinity before cooking over a fire pit not too far from a small house. What we didn't realize was that fire pit was their kitchen, and the haystack, their shelter and home. That brief moment in time gave both of us an even greater appreciation for our good fortune and the tremendous opportunities afforded to all American citizens. Further, we suddenly realized why the maid took a hot bath every day, using most of the hot water. We never said another word to her about the lack of hot water in the evening; we just counted the many blessings we had being born Americans! The last of the six B-26s was ready for takeoff, and I was on it, anxious to join my fellow commandos at Bien Hoe and to contribute to their efforts in support of the South Vietnamese government as they fought against the Vietcong insurgents.

Bien Hoa, January 1962

My first glimpse of Bien Hoa was from the window of a C-47 turning downwind in the landing pattern. The runway was short, very short by US standards, and appeared to be made of steel matting used during WW II called perforated steel planking (PSP). Subsequently, I learned it was 1,000 meters long, or just under 3,300 feet, and slippery as axle grease when wet. I didn't see many buildings of any size anywhere, but there was a tent city off to one side of the runway.

The C-47 stopped in front of Base Operations, such as it was, and let me out. The aircraft wasn't one of the Air Commando's birds and was returning immediately to Saigon, so the aircrew couldn't give me any directions. Inside of the old stucco building, I ran into another American, Capt. Gary Willard. Gary was an exchange officer with the Vietnamese Air Force (VNAF) flying A1 Skyraiders with the 1st VNAF Squadron located at the other end of the airfield. Gary welcomed me to Bien Hoa and told me how to find the Air Commando bivouac area. I walked in the direction he indicated and, within a half mile, stumbled onto a tent city, still half under construction. There was an American flag hanging on a pole beside a big squad tent. I rightly assumed that was the detachment headquarters where Colonel King and/or Lieutenant Colonel Gleason would be directing Air Commando operations. I reported in and was put right to work.

The AT-28, even with ferry tanks, did not have enough range to island-hop across the Pacific Ocean. I learned from my comrades that the AT-28s had their wings removed at Hurlburt and were then flown to Clark AFB in the Philippines in the belly of C-124 cargo planes. At Clark, the AT-28s were reassembled and test flown to validate they were ready for the long overwater flight to Vietnam. The C-47s flew the northern route across the Pacific to Clark AFB with Colonel King flying the lead aircraft. At Clark, Colonel King transferred to an AT-28 and led the little birds to Bien Hoa, SVN. Lieutenant Colonel Gleason then led the C-47s to Bien Hoa. The C-47 had much better navigation equipment and a navigator who could use the stars and sun for determining their position over water. The C-47 also carried rafts and survival gear that could be dropped to anyone that had to ditch or bail out over the water. I wasn't the least bit surprised that Colonel King led his troops across the Western Pacific. He was that kind of leader, one who would never ask his subordinates to take risks that he would not take himself. Clearly a single conventional engine aircraft with barely enough fuel to reach Hawaii was somewhat of a risk. During WW II, then Lieutenant King had a P-38 (twin-engine aircraft) quit on him. He bailed out and survived with some shipwrecked sailors on Mono Island until rescued.

The Air Commando detachment area at Bien Hoa was primitive, to put it mildly. Initially, the troops were sleeping on the ground but were now moving into tents with plywood floors. Shower and latrine tents were also being erected. Cobras and pythons were common in the area, so we were always on the lookout for sticks that moved. Security was a prime concern, so Colonel King had both officers and NCOs pulling perimeter guard duty. On my second night at Bien Hoa, he escorted several of us to the perimeter he had established and positioned us in foxholes, which the first arrivals had dug. Initially, I was more concerned about snakes than I was about Vietcong (VC). He swept the horizon with his hand and said, "If you see anything move out there, shoot it!" I didn't have any trouble staying alert, thinking about the snakes.

With the arrival of the first light of dawn, I saw several women laden with water buckets and some boys towing water buffalo in the kill zone, but I didn't think they were hostile, so I let them pass. I only pulled security guard duty twice; evidently, Colonel King was able to get a real security force on the scene shortly after I arrived. Nonetheless, officers always carried their sidearms, and enlisted personnel carried M1 .30-caliber carbines wherever they went, be it the mess tent, sleeping tent, or the flight line.

I also learned that combat operations had started, but at a snail's pace. Even though the Vietnamese government and VNAF were expecting us, there was very little, if any, infrastructure put in place for exploiting the newly arrived air combat and airlift capability. There was a stipulation from the US government that we had to fly with a Vietnamese person in our aircraft so that if we were shot down, the higher ups in Washington could claim that we were just training Vietnamese aircrews and not involved in combat operations.

The solution to this political directive was for the VNAF to select some very young enlisted personnel and assign them to fly on AT-28, B-26, and C-47 missions. There was no training involved, except the signal for bailout and how to safely jump from the aircraft and pull the D ring to deploy the parachute. AT-28 pilots asked the interpreter to tell these reluctant passengers, "If the cockpit canopy opens in flight, bail out!" Pilots or aircrews scheduled for alert duty were introduced to their "trainees" immediately after breakfast. After saying hello and remembering what they looked like, we went to our respective alert tents, one for Americans aircrews, the second for the Vietnamese. When the alert horn sounded, we were both supposed to run to our aircraft. However, after a few flights in the backseat of an AT-28 and being hurled at the ground, the trainees ran the other way and had to be run down, tackled, and led reluctantly to the airplane. Not a good thing to have someone in the aircraft that could really ruin your day playing with switches and levers in the rear cockpit.

There was another political directive, stating that aircrews could not log combat flying time because our mission was covert. We were required to log our flying hours as training sorties (TS), or sometimes combat support (CS), whatever that meant. This really didn't bother anyone. We were doing important work to help the South Vietnamese preserve their independence and freedom—that's what mattered.

My first combat mission came at dusk; two T-28s were scrambled to support a Special Forces (Green Berets) team embedded in an Army of Vietnam (ARVN) Company in a triangular fort protecting a nearby village. It was the VC's strategy to drive ARVN forces from the field and then terrorize the villagers into supporting them with cover, food, and shelter. The Green Berets were there to provide training and make sure the ARVN stood their ground when the fighting started. Our flight arrived at the fort as the sun was setting. The VC had started grass fires, creating dense gray smoke that significantly reduced in-flight visibility. Lead rolled in on some phosphorus smoke launched from the fort. I took spacing and followed lead into the target area, dropping one tank of napalm off of the left wing and pulling up sharply while looking over the target area for VC activity. Suddenly, I felt unusual forces in the seat of my pants and checked the gauges. The AT-28 was just about to stall with the right wing down and the nose high; the yaw ball was full left. Immediately, I applied full climb power, stomped on the left rudder while pushing the nose down, rolled wings level, and looked for lead. On the next pass, I dropped the outboard right napalm; no problem this time, as the drag and weight were off of the right wing. The remainder of the mission, as well as the recovery to Bien Hoa, was plain vanilla. We learned later that our repeated attacks had driven off the enemy. The village and fort were saved for the time being. All things considered it was a good day.

Once on the ground, I started thinking about the near disaster I had just avoided. The North American—designed weapons release panel allowed for releasing pairs of pylon stores (left and right side simultaneously), or singles one store from the left pylons (inboard or outboard). The problem I experienced was caused by the design of the weapons release panel. The rotary switch had only three choices: single, pairs, or ripple. Selecting single, releasing only one bomb or firing one rocket pod, caused the ordnance to release/fire from the left wing first. Upon pulling up from an attack, the drag and weight on the right wing were additive, causing a sever yaw because of the cumulative effects of torque, weight, and drag. Contributing factors were the lack of a single training sortie carrying and releasing a full load of ordnance back at Hurlburt, plus the darkness as well as the thick smoke, which denied visual cues when coming off of the target. I discussed my experience with Lieutenant Colonel Gleason, operations officer, and suggested a redesign of the weapons release sequence. I also recommended adding at least one fully loaded range sortie with live or inert bombs be added to the training syllabus at Hurlburt. He agreed and asked me to write a message (TWX) on these recommendations for him to send back to the Air Commando Group at Hurlburt. I firmly believe that someone with less experience would have stalled out and crashed on the mission flown the previous day. The armament panel fix was simple: six toggle switches; one representing each wing station enabled the pilot to select any combination of releases except ripple.

With the slow pace of Combat Operations, Colonel King decided to test our ability to defend ourselves if shot down and confronted by the enemy while trying to evade and escape. Colonel King escorted us down to a harmonization range where he had silhouette targets set up. Acting as range officer, he directed us to "load, lock, and blast away."

Many aircrews were using .38-caliber government-issue (GI) revolvers, while others like me were carrying automatic pistols or revolvers we had owned for a number of years. At the first firing, anyone using government-provided .38-caliber ammunition didn't hit the targets. In fact, some of the bullets could be seen hitting the ground short of the target silhouettes. I was shooting a Ruger .357 Magnum, but using GI .38-caliber rounds for this exercise to conserve my own more powerful magnum ammunition. My bullets were hitting the ground short of the targets, as were those shooting GI revolvers. Colonel King wasn't happy with the overall performance and directed me, as the armament officer, to find out what the problem was.

After collecting all the GI revolvers and other .38-caliber weapons, I measured the bore groove diameters. As you may know, the groove diameter of a .38-caliber weapon is really .357 inch. In a crude field situation like we were in, the bore measurement is accomplished by pounding lead material into the front of the bore and then measuring the outside diameter of the lead plug with a micrometer. Lead is soft; therefore, forcing it into the bore does not in any way injure the barrel. All the guns checked within a few ten thousands of an inch (.357 inch, plus or minus .0002 inch). The guns were OK! While checking diameters of over one hundred rounds of GI .38-caliber ammunition out of several different ammunition boxes, I discovered that all the bullets were five-thousandths of an inch undersized (.352 versus .357). The bullets were too small in diameter to seal the bore. Hence, the gas from the burning powder was blowing by the projectiles as they traveled down the short revolver barrel. These defective bullets were almost falling out of barrel. Problem found!

The evidence was presented to Colonel King and Lieutenant Colonel Gleason, stating that the Ogden Air Logistics Center (OALC) at Hill Air Force Base, Utah, had shipped us several cases of defective and useless ammunition. If it weren't for the colonel's insistence that we needed to practice with our weapons, we would have carried that junk into combat. In fact, some of us already had but, fortunately, didn't need to use it. To say that he was angry was a significant understatement. I had drafted a message for him to send to the OALC, informing them of the .38-caliber lot numbers that were defective, requesting serviceable ammunition, and asking for disposition of the junk on hand. It was the kind of message a captain would write to a major general OALC commander. Colonel King replaced most of my words with very strong language; only about three sentences survived in their original state. He also added a courtesy copy to the commander of Tactical Air Command to let our boss know how Air Commando Detachment 2 was being supported. The response from the OALC was really a shocker, one never to be forgotten! The small-arms item manager (IM) who was responsible for managing the air force small-arms ammunition account admitted he knew the ammunition was defective and purposely sent it to us, hoping we would use it up! The response also noted that we would receive an expedited shipment of serviceable ammunition and to destroy what we had in a fire pit. To this day, I wonder about all that defective ammunition sitting in a warehouse without the IM reporting it defective and then seeking recovery of the money paid to a contractor for it. Was this another lowest-bid procurement? Did the IM get a kickback for it? Lesson learned: Always, always do your best to support the forces in the field and in combat, and be wary of those who have never heard the sounds of combat!

Capt. Bill Dougherty, the AT-28 section commander, and I were on alert when we were scrambled to a point not too far from Bien Hoa. Bill spotted some VC in the open, crossing a river where the jungle tree canopy was very sparse. He rolled in with rockets. I followed with spacing and on a different heading. The next pass was with guns blazing. I could see the guns on the ground winking back at me. We each made several passes before the VC were no longer visible and we were Winchester (term indicating out of ammunition).

Colonel King sought permission for us to fly along the Ho Chi Minh Trail and interdict supplies being brought from the North into South Vietnam for the VC. There wasn't much of a military higher headquarters in Saigon at that time, but whoever was in charge was saying no. In addition, the very limited radar surveillance in South Vietnam was picking up low-level, slow-flying aircraft coming out of North Vietnam and disappearing from radar at various locations north of Bien Hoa. These aircraft were only detected on radar at night. It reminded me of the AN-2 Colt (NATO Aircraft Designation) for the "Bedcheck Charlie" aircraft dropping hand grenades during the Korean War. Colonel King wanted to nail one of these aircraft, and a plan was devised.

The plan called for a B-26 with a bomb bay loaded with parachute flares, providing one million candlepower apiece. The B-26, the mother ship for the operation, would fly about three thousand feet AGL followed by two AT-28s, with guns only, trailing the B-26 visually on its navigation lights. Radar would vector the B-26 over the target, where the B-26 would then jettison one or two flares to illuminate the area around the phantom aircraft. Iwo and I were chosen to fly the AT-28s because we had the most aerial gunnery experience. Radar reported a bogey (unknown aircraft) and the B-26 followed by AT-28s all launched. Upon reporting to the Command and Reporting Center (CRC), we were given a northerly vector. After about twenty minutes, the sump warning light on the instrument panel in my aircraft lit up. This light illuminates when metal in the oil sump shorts out two magnetic probes, closing the circuit to the light. The AT-28B Dash 1 stipulates landing immediately to avoid imminent engine failure. I reported the situation to Iwo, indicating I believed it was a false warning and would continue. Our commanders at Bien Hoa were monitoring our radio frequency and ordered me to return to base. I declined but was overridden by Lieutenant Colonel Gleason in a very stern tone. I hated to leave Iwo, but he still had the B-26 for company. I stayed high and flew an SFO pattern back at Bien Hoa, landing safely without further incident.

When the B-26 and AT-28 returned, I was waiting on the ramp for Iwo. He was not happy and related that when the CRC reported the B-26 was over the bogey, the pilot set the B-26 bomb release switch on salvo, instead of single, dropping all twenty flares. Twenty million candlepower lit up the sky, temporarily blinding Iwo. If there was a bogey, it wasn't spotted, probably because all eyes were suffering from overexposure. The mission was aborted. I don't believe it was ever tried again—although I thought it was a reasonable tactic and the best we could do with our equipment.

The real heroes of the initial deployment, and of many follow on deployments, were the medical technicians who visited the nearby villages and treated the South Vietnamese residents. When they found something beyond their ability to treat, Dr. Threadgill, our flight surgeon, would go back with them to provide appropriate care. They were winning the hearts and minds of the people who lived within a few tens of miles of Bien Hoa. As a result of the contact these med techs had with the nearby villages, Air Commandos adopted a local orphanage and supported it until South Vietnam fell in the summer of 1975. Our relationship with the villagers was also important for our own security because the base was located only twenty miles or so from an area deep in dense jungle known as Zone D, a VC stronghold.

Colonel King had already returned to Hurlburt AFB, Florida, to provide hands-on leadership to a rapidly growing organization, now a full-fledged wing, when Admiral Felt, commander in chief of Pacific Command (CINC PACOM), paid an unexpected visit to Bien Hoa. His plane landed and was met by Lieutenant Colonel Gleason, who provided the admiral a tour around the flight line and the tent area. The admiral was wearing navy summer whites and looked very impressive with all the stars and gold braid. But he looked very out of place among the many enlisted troops stripped down to the waist and drenched in sweat, repairing aircraft or loading them with bombs, rockets, and ammunition for the next mission. I heard him bellow out, "What are all these sailors doing with guns? Get these guns locked up in the armory before someone gets hurt." It was easy to understand why sailors aboard ship did not carry sidearms or carbines, nor would they carry them in homeport or ports of call where local police forces had jurisdiction and provided protection. The same protocol did not apply to a combat zone, where the enemy hid among the innocent and could be anywhere at any time. He also took exception to the Australian bush hat that Colonel King had adopted for Air Commando uniform wear, replacing the olive drab fatigue hat. Lieutenant Colonel Gleason wisely ignored the admiral's orders, and the rest of us decided not to take offense at being called sailors. It seemed to me that a Joint Forces commander should know the difference between the services and their uniforms.

One morning, Lieutenant Colonel Gleason and I passed at the shower tent and spoke briefly. The roar of two VNAF A1 aircraft taking off, loaded wingtip to wingtip with five-hundred-pound bombs, drowned out our conversation. We both commented that something must be up because the 1st VNAF Squadron we shared the base with did not normally fly that early and were never loaded up with so much ordnance. Shortly thereafter, the alert flights were scrambled. I was on Captain Dougherty's wing. Once airborne, we checked in with the CRC and got cryptic instructions that didn't make sense. The first instruction was "Watch out for the bad guys, they're together." That didn't make any sense! We asked for more information and got none. It wasn't long before we noticed black smoke rising from Saigon. Later, we learned that the 1st VNAF Squadron fighters seen on the uncharacteristically early morning takeoff bombed the presidential palace. Was there a widespread coup in progress? Were the pilots in cahoots with the VC? Were our comrades left on the ground back at Bien Hoa safe or fighting for survival?

The next radio call from the CRC notified us that if we spotted two A1s in formation; we were authorized to engage them. Shortly thereafter, I spotted a lone A1 closing from about four o'clock. "Taco lead, two has a single A1 closing at four o'clock." "Two, spread out and keep him in sight. Go guns hot!" We were taking no chances! The stranger kept closing but wasn't pulling lead as if to shoot at us with his 20 mm cannons. I kicked rudders, causing my aircraft to wiggle side to side, a standard formation signal to spread out. It had no effect; the stranger kept closing to wingtip formation as lead and I watched. After what seemed an eternity, the CRC called and directed us to return to Bien Hoa. Lead informed the CRC controller we had picked up a stranger but had no radio contact. The controller opined that the A1 on our wing might have been scrambled for the same reason we were—to shoot down the two A1s that attacked the presidential palace. When the base came into sight, we noticed that ARVN tanks were lined up in the center of the runway! There was no place to land. Lead called the tower for landing instructions. Tower responded that the ARVN had taken over the base and to hold nearby as long as our fuel would allow. Our alternate would be Tan Son Nhut Airport on the edge of Saigon. An hour later and low on fuel, lead and I pitched out to land at Tan Son Nhut, with the stranger following us in. Transient alert parked the three of us side by side, so Captain Dougherty and I had a chance to talk to our pickup wingman. Turned out, he had lost his leader and just wanted to join up because, like us, he didn't know what was going on. Lunch at the military mess hall at Tan Son Nhut was much better than what we were getting up north, so that was a plus. Just about dark, we received word that Bien Hoa's runway was back in operation and we could return home. I was beginning to see a pattern! Every time I flew on Captain Dougherty's wing, exciting things happened. Just another day at the office!

The flying tempo picked up, and days passed quickly. Soon, it was my turn to return to the CONUS and meet my bride of several months. The roughly forty officers and enlisted men scheduled to rotate back were flown to Tan Son Nhut Airport near Saigon, where we would connect with a commercial contract carrier. Unfortunately, when we landed at the airport, it was obvious that the only commercial carrier aircraft there was missing one of its four engines. There was also a C-124 "Old Shaky" sitting on the ramp. When we asked where the C-124 was going, we were told Travis AFB, California.

Next question: Can we get manifested on the C-124?
Answer: No, you guys are privileged passengers. You have to wait for the contract carrier to get fixed.
Next question: When will the engine for the contract carrier arrive?
Answer: It will be at least two days at the earliest.
Response: Forget the privileged passenger crap. Put us on the C-124. We're anxious to travel!

The return trip rivaled Homer's Odyssey. The initial C-124 broke down at Clark AFB in the Philippines, our first refueling stop. Forty people with tools, gear, sidearms, and souvenirs had about ten tons of cargo that had to be manually unloaded and guarded—guarded was the key word, considering the reputation for on-base thievery at Clark AFB! The daily rains meant that we had to secure tarpaulins to protect a mound of property the size of a very large haystack. There were no pallets on which to put the cargo, so the lower tier got wet regardless of what we did. Officers took a collection to pay the enlisted servicemen who volunteered to stand guard 24/7. We learned another C-124 would be arriving the next day with parts for the broken aircraft. We boarded the inbound aircraft and got all the way to Wake Island before we were marooned again. Only one day at Wake Island before another C-124 took us all the way to Hickam AFB, Hawaii, where it broke down. Hickam AFB is a major transshipment point into the Western Pacific for cargo and personnel, so we didn't expect to be there long. Wrong again! As "hitchhikers," we wanted to stay together as a unit, not wanting to leave anyone behind to fend for themselves. As a result, there were not many aircraft passing through that could accept our large number of passengers and their cargo. Days passed without any movement. One afternoon, I was sitting at a poolside bar when my name was paged. It was Sheila, wanting to know where the heck I was and when I would be home. My letter saying I was leaving Bien Hoa beat me home, which was unexpected, as mail took seven days for delivery to Fort Walton Beach. I explained the situation and said I would call her when there was news on the next leg of the journey. "How did you find me?" I asked.

She said, "Once I found out from another wife that you were at Hickam, I just started calling person to person until I found you. It didn't cost me anything if you didn't come to the phone, and I've been trying to locate you for four hours."

The next day, another C-124 landed at Hickam on its way back to CONUS. A captain was the highest-ranking officer we had in our gaggle trying to reach Hurlburt, so we didn't have much sway with the Military Airlift Command (MAC) schedulers at Hickam. A sympathetic C-124 aircraft commander agreed to take us all the way to Hurlburt and cleared it with MAC Operations at Scott AFB, Illinois. He even set up a takeoff that would get us home at noon, local time. Wives, relatives, and girlfriends back at Hurlburt were notified. There was joy in Florida's panhandle. All "refugees" from Bien Hoa were notified, and we were all aboard with all our cargo at the appointed time. It seemed like days later when we finally landed at Travis AFB, California, located near San Francisco. Once again, our travel plans were torn apart by MAC schedulers. They decided to send our aircraft on another mission. Hastily, we unloaded our cargo for about the sixth time. We would now leave that afternoon, arriving Hurlburt at 0200 hours on the eleventh day since departing Bien Hoa. Calls were made to inform everyone of the early morning arrival. Wives with children scrambled to find babysitters so they could pick up their husbands. The end was in sight. Again, we reloaded our cargo for a flight longer than Hawaii to California. The welcome Florida coastline came into view as the C-124 descended to traffic pattern altitude. We could see a stream of car lights heading from Fort Walton Beach toward Hurlburt. At 0200 hours, there had to be a caravan of wives and sweethearts heading for a long-awaited reunion. It was then we realized the aircraft commander (AC) had filed his clearance to land at Eglin Air Force Base (Eglin Main), vice Eglin Aux no. 9. Hurlburt was still not listed in the appropriate airfield information books. I ran to the cockpit to have a conversation with the AC; he wasn't in the mood to land at Hurlburt and insisted he had to land at Eglin. Dire threats were made; we had just about had enough grief, and landing at Eglin with all the families at Hurlburt was the last straw. Moreover, it would be virtually impossible to get in touch with the wives and tell them to reverse course and drive another hour to the ramp at Eglin. The AC used HF radio to call MAC Headquarters to get permission to land at Hurlburt. Approval took about an hour with the huge C-124 orbiting Hurlburt, shaking the ground below with those big WP 4350 engines. How airlifters successfully ran the Berlin Airlift suddenly became a mystery to me. Hurlburt Air Base didn't have a MAC terminal, so after the C-124 landed and parked at the ramp, it took a couple of hours for us to unload all our baggage and account for all the personnel. It was nearly dawn before I was able to give my new bride a hug and kiss. This was not exactly the romantic reunion we had been looking forward to.

Sheila was still living with her two girlfriends on the beach. A short nap on the couch in her apartment, and then she took me to see the duplex she had on hold for us at 91A Pine in Fort Walton Beach. The apartment was neat, clean, secluded, had two bedrooms, and the price was right. We lived there happily for nearly four years.

First Combat Applications Group

Sheila and I both took two weeks' leave from work and went on our long-overdue honeymoon. We drove to Detroit, where I introduced her to my stepmother and eight brothers and sisters. Then we traveled across the Belle Isle Bridge to Windsor, Canada, and east along the Queen's Highway to Niagara Falls. After viewing the impressive falls, we came back into the United States at New York State. From there, we drove to Washington DC to catch the cherry blossoms in full bloom and then back to our apartment in Fort Walton Beach, Florida.

When we returned, setting foot on Hurlburt AFB was a new experience. The place was humming with activity, training replacements for the detachment at Bien Hoa. The group had become a full-fledged Air Commando Wing, and the aircraft flights had become squadrons with full complements of aircrews and aircraft. Everyone I met thought I was a new guy and welcomed me into the organization, telling me how lucky I was to be there. A new detachment, Det 3, was being formed at Howard Air Base in Panama with the mission of training aircrews from South American countries in the AT-28 and C-47 for a counterinsurgency role.

My former roommate, Capt. Dick Sanborn, married a lovely blonde air force Nurse working at the Air Force Hospital at Eglin AFB. Dick volunteered for duty in Panama with the Air Commandos there, but there was no position for Kelly in Panama, so she continued with her assignment at the Eglin AFB Hospital in Florida.

When reporting to Major Stillwell following leave, he told me I had been reassigned to a new organization called the First Combat Applications Group (1st CAG) under the Command of Col. Ben King.

The 1st CAG was formed to expedite improvements to the air force's capability in Counterinsurgency (COIN) Warfare. The charter was broad gauged to include every facet of warfare, inter alia, aircraft, communications, armament, weapons delivery systems (fire control), command and control (C2), training, logistics, etc. Iwo Kimes and I were involved in aircraft, armament, fire control, and C2. Two aeronautical engineers were primarily involved in evaluating the cost benefits of aircraft improvements and designing a new aircraft specifically for COIN.

Among those assigned to the 1st CAG were Capt. Jerry Carlisle, an F-86F veteran of the 51st TFW during the Korean War, who was also a graduate of the Air Force Test Pilot School; Capt. Tony Scarpace was a jocular communications officer who advanced COIN communications significantly under his watch; Capt. Ira (nicknamed Iwo) Kimes was a fellow fighter pilot I served with in Vietnam; Capt. Brooks Morris was added later after earning a Silver Star flying out of Bien Hoa. We were a small group, but overall quite effective. Brooks Morris was the son of Chester Morris, who played the lead role of Boston Blackie in a series of Hollywood movies. Boston Blackie was the first of many Hollywood and TV tough-guy private detectives and a famous star of his genre. Brooks often talked of his childhood association with Elizabeth Taylor, who lived next door when they were both in their early teens.

Quite unlike the ponderous DOD Acquisition Bureaucracy of today, the commander of 1st CAG had a $10 million budget, plus immediate access to more for special projects. If a 1st CAG project officer had a good idea and could convince Colonel King the idea had high potential for improving combat effectiveness, it was funded immediately. Some ideas moved from concept to combat in less than six months. On the other hand, many died in infancy with very little expenditure of money.

Captain Carlisle came across an aircraft called Pilatus Porter powered by an aspirated inline engine. The Pilatus Porter was a short takeoff and landing (STOL) aircraft capable of taking off and landing in less than a football field with a respectable load. It was a tail wheel aircraft with unique main landing gear that could "break loose" from their normal position under side stress and swivel. Thus, pilots could intentionally ground loop the Porter and, at the 180-degree point of the ground loop, add power to stop the aircraft in a very, very short distance. In addition, the Porter could carry heavier loads at higher altitudes than helicopters of that era. It was extremely useful for delivering supplies and personnel to Special Forces where no other aircraft could operate. The Porter was flying out of Bien Hoa shortly after Jerry completed his test program. Total time from start of the test to combat duty was less than nine months.

Today, under DOD Acquisition Regulations, it takes that long to write and get approval on a Request for Proposal (RFP). It takes another nine months to solicit a response from potential commercial providers, and then about six more months to select a winner, assuming no protests from the losers. These time spans are for a very simple acquisition like a bomb guidance kit using the global positioning system (GPS) from satellites.

Jerry then had the Pilatus Porter equipped with floats and developed techniques for landing the aircraft on water during hours of darkness. I flew some of these sorties with Jerry to log the test data collected on these flights. Landing on small ponds by the light of the moon was exciting, to say the least.

About four months into my assignment to 1st CAG, my supervisor, who was a major, approached me, asking for some material so he could write my Officer Efficiency Report (OER) because I was long overdue for one. The period to be covered was about eighteen months, everything from the date I arrived in May 1961. I thanked the major, but said I wanted the people I worked for in the 1st ACW to write the OER. Capt. Barbara Owens, wife of Capt. Bob Owens, a C-47 pilot, was the new personnel officer at Hurlburt, so I took my case to her. She wasn't very happy with the request but put it in her job jar. This fell into the category of "be careful what you wish for." Years later, I had an opportunity to read that OER signed by Col. Chester Jack, formerly the vice wing commander who had moved up to the top job when Colonel King was reassigned to the 1st CAG. Colonel Jack's endorsement said, "I would rate this officer outstanding if I knew but one thing he had accomplished." What a nice kiss of death that was! I put it in the same category as "I would not breed this officer" or "I didn't know he drank until I saw him sober."

The Tactical Air Command was reorganizing to address the kind of wars that we were currently fighting versus the nuclear war our nation never wanted to fight, but prepared for under the emerging National Deterrence Strategy. TAC was creating centers of expertise, or excellence, in four areas. The first was the Special Air Warfare Center (SAWC) at Eglin AFB that became the parent command for the First Air Commando Wing and the First Combat Applications Group. SAWC was followed by the Tactical Air Warfare Center (TAWC) at Nellis AFB, Nevada; then came the Tactical Airlift Center at Pope AFB, North Carolina; and last, the Tactical Air Reconnaissance Center (TARC) at Shaw AFB, South Carolina. Each of these centers was commanded by a general officer and chartered to advance the state of the art in their warfare role. This included, inter alia, aircraft, equipment, tactics, command and control, etc. All of the centers were direct reporting units to Gen. Walter C. Sweeney, commander TAC.

During this period, air force officers were not allowed to see their Officer Efficiency Reports (OERs), so I was surprised when General Prichard's secretary, Ms. Scotty Russell, called and asked me if I'd like to see my OER. "Yes" was the answer; I was in her officer in a flash. She handed me the OER. It read as if I was the second coming of the Savior. The only problem was that it wasn't signed, so I asked politely, "Is the general going to sign this?"

Her response was a little scary for a lowly captain. She said with some firmness in her voice, "The general signs everything I write!" Wow, I got the picture and thanked her for her confidence and support. This brief encounter gave me a whole new and important perspective on the role of senior officer executive secretaries. From then on, whenever I was going to SAWC Headquarters, I had flowers or a box of chocolates for Scotty.

In the summer of 1962, the United States Army established the Howze Board to evaluate Air Force Close Air Support of engaged army forces. As implied, the board was chaired by Gen. Hamilton Howze, USA. At that time, Air Force Tactical Air Forces claimed three primary missions. These were air superiority (dominance of the air), air interdiction (cutting lines of communication and attriting enemy forces before they reached the battlefield), and close air support (providing fire support to soldiers and marines in close contact with the enemy). Brigadier General Prichard selected me as the SAWC representative to testify before the Howze Board.

Historically, when the Army Air Corps was part of the US Army, Air Corps units were assigned directly under divisions and corps, just like infantry, armor, and artillery units were assigned to divisions and corps. As a result, a resource with the attributes of speed, range, and flexibility was tied to a small frontal area along with their division. During the North African Campaign (Operation Torch) of WW II, the first battle at Kasserine Pass on February 19 was lost to German forces under the command of Field Marshal Rommel. There were many problems that disadvantaged American forces, such as a tank with a fixed turret, requiring tank movement to aim the gun; another was the lack of air support during the battle. At that moment in time, air support was lumped under the command of Air Vice Marshal Conningham, RAF, and aircraft were committed to another effort. During the second battle of the Kasserine Pass, air and ground forces were both commanded by Lieutenant General Patton, who won a decisive battle over Rommel's forces. Not only did Patton have better tanks, but he also had dedicated air support. From that moment forward, the US Army Air Corps advocated centralized control and decentralized execution. Their doctrine called for air power to be unleashed and tasked to support the forces that needed them most or sent to where concentrated firepower would carry the day, versus being tied to ground units that may not even be engaged in combat.

The Howze Board was readdressing the control of air forces, and the deck was stacked against the air force. However, there was no way the army could overturn the October 1947 Defense Act that morphed the Army Air Corps into a separate and equal service as the United States Air Force. Moreover, DOD limited the army in the type and size of fixed-wing aircraft they could own and operate, but there was no limit on helicopters. Gen. Hamilton Howze, USA, was intent on using this platform to prove that an increased number of capable helicopters were needed to support engaged army forces.

I testified before the Howze Board, with General Howze presiding, answering questions on the close air support provided to soldiers in Vietnam. When the opportunity afforded itself, I suggested that US Army aircraft and helicopters be equipped with radios that would enable cockpit-to-cockpit communication because the combat was too intense and too critical for relayed or delayed messages. The Howze Board was held at Fort Bragg, North Carolina, home of the Eighteenth Airborne Corps and the Eighty-Second Airborne Division.

The soldiers of the Eighty-Second Airborne Division were some of the finest soldiers in the world. They were lean, mean, and tough as the proverbial nails. After testifying, I stopped at the officers' club for lunch before firing up the AT-28B and returning to Eglin. At the club, I was subjected to one hell of a chewing out by an army captain. He certainly had the advantage, being one of the Eighty-Second's finest and standing about a head taller than I did. He was upset about my fatigue uniform, citing no branch insignia, ridiculous hat, improper blousing of the pants into the boots, etc. It finally occurred to me that he thought I was a soldier. When he asked what branch I was in, I was certain he had no clue that I was air force. When he stopped shouting and gave me a chance to respond, I said calmly but loudly (he had everyone in the O'club looking at us), "I'm sorry that you're color blind and can't read (pointing to the tag above my left shirt pocket). This says 'Air Force in blue.' No need to apologize!" For a moment, I thought he was going to take a swing at me, but he just spun around and left with the laughter of his peers ringing in his ears. The lunch went down in a hurry, and I left the same way. Two other army captains came up to me as I was heading out the door and apologized, saying the man who accosted me was a real hothead and troublemaker.

The report out of the Howze Board recommended new helicopters for the army and the formation of the Eleventh Air Assault Division (AAD). The 11th AAD eventually morphed into the First Calvary Division. The army seemed to be on a full court press to provide close air support with helicopter gunships; unfortunately, helicopters just don't survive well in a high-intensity conflict even in a COIN environment.

One of the test programs under my direction encompassed putting an army-developed 40 mm automatic cannon used on helicopters into a pod and mounting it on the AT-28B. The 40 mm shell had an impressive fragmenting warhead with a very sensitive fuze. This combination proved to be a very effective antipersonnel weapon in just about any environment. General Electric in Burlington, Vermont, manufactured these cannons for the army. One of their field representatives brought it to my attention. GE wanted more money than I was willing to spend on building a pod-mounted weapon from scratch. After some wrangling, they agreed to mount a loaner gun in a napalm tank, which I would provide. The amount of the contract is long forgotten, but it was probably around $50,000. A prototype

40 mm pod was available for test in less than four months. The 1st CAG aeronautical engineers blessed it as safe to fly. To evaluate the effectiveness, I had twenty three-dimensional full-size (Asian male) mannequins fabricated, which I personally located in one of the tree-covered shallow swamps on the Eglin Range Complex. A couple of markers were placed on the edge of the swamp so it could easily be found from the air. These markers essentially simulated smoke grenades or other markers that Special Forces or Forward Air Controllers would provide when supporting army units.

On test sorties, at least two passes would be made against the swamp walking the rounds through the trees. The actual mannequins were never seen from the air on those test sorties. However, if these were enemy personnel moving though the swamp, they would have been detected from the air. After each sortie, I would personally wade though the swamp, counting the fragmentation hits on the mannequins. On every test sortie, each mannequin was hit with several lethal fragments. The 40 mm warhead was an impressive projectile, evidently detonating instantly on touching the water. The 40 mm cannon operated much like an automatic revolver with the rounds linked together and pulled into firing position by an electric motor. Even though the projectiles left the barrel at a slow 800 feet per second (fps), an additional 450 fps of aircraft velocity gave the round about the same firing range as the .50-caliber M2 and was far more lethal against dispersed personnel. Only about eight rounds were fired per pass because of the slow rate of fire built into the initial helicopter design. However, each round fragmented into at least three hundred high-velocity fragments, equating to 2,400 lethal fragments per firing pass compared to perhaps forty bullets from two .50-caliber wing-mounted machine guns per pass. The 40 mm pod was at Bien Hoa about six months after the start of the project.

Another project I initiated was improving the effectiveness of proximity fuzes on conventional WW II 250- and 500-pound bombs. Proximity fuzes operated on radar. A small radar transmitter was activated in this nose fuze when released from an aircraft. The radar received a signal reflected from the ground, causing the fuze to activate, and detonated the bomb at a predetermined distance from the ground, spraying deadly fragments over an area about four hundred feet in diameter. Standard nose fuzes detonating a bomb on impact would cause most of the fragments to move upward in a cone, reducing the lethal fragmentation pattern and blast radius to about fifty feet.

There were tens of thousands of proximity fuzes left over from WW II. However, when dropped over a triple jungle tree canopy, the fuze radar would detect the thick jungle canopy and detonate the bomb, spreading fragments several hundred feet above insurgents on the ground with little or no effect except for the noise. Picatinny Arsenal, an army development house, agreed to modify some of these WW II fuzes they had designed with a delay. The delay occurred between the fuze sensing the jungle canopy and the time the fuze was activated to detonate the bomb. This delay allowed the bomb to fall through several tree canopies to about seventy-five feet above the ground before detonating. This placed the lethal fragmentation pattern and blast effects perfectly for maximum effectiveness against personnel and soft targets. Picatinny Arsenal scientists and engineers did the fuze redesign for the cost of the materials used and their salaries.

Fortunately, the Air Commando detachment in Panama had ready access to jungle environments very similar to those found in South Vietnam. I flew a B-26 loaded with 250-pound bombs and a box of fuzes to Howard AFB, Panama. A suitable and uninhabited area of the Panamanian jungle was located where the live bombs could be tested, and access into the jungle to observe and document the results would not be too difficult. One of the local Air Commando C-47s dropped weighted parachutes, hoping to get one to hang up on the jungle canopy to serve as an aiming point for bomb drops. Without the aiming point, it would have been difficult to localize the desired impact area.

Several sorties were flown; two bombs dropped on each sortie. Sorties were flown in the early morning after which we would drive to the impact area and document the results. Jungle access was extremely difficult on the first penetration because of the dense foliage at the edge of the jungle. Natives were hired to chop a path that would allow us access. I purchased a working machete with the idea that I might be of some help and would have something to do besides watch hard labor in progress. It took three hours to chop through about twenty to thirty feet of very dense vegetation. Once we were past the fringe, it was like walking in a cathedral. The jungle floor was mostly comprised of moist dirt. Tree trunks were spaced thirty to fifty feet apart, disappearing into the triple canopy 150 to 200 feet over our heads. It was nearly dark under the multiple canopies because they filtered out most of the sunlight. We walked around for a while, finding nothing. I was expecting to find trees lying on the ground. To the contrary, all the trees were still standing. We finally discovered that when the bombs detonated, they destroyed about ten to twenty feet of the tree trunks about thirty feet from the jungle floor. The canopies were so entangled that the undamaged trees prevented the trees that were cut in half from falling to the ground.

The fuzes functioned just as intended, creating deadly blast and fragmentation at the perfect height for maximum effectiveness.

Bombs dropped on the second and third days were aimed slightly off of the parachute aim point in order to collect additional data not influenced by the previous day's detonations. Access was now a walk in the park, so to speak, after the entrance path was created on the first day. All results were documented with measurements, charts, and photographs. After three days of bombing the jungle with consistently good results, the test was deemed successful. No further bomb drops were required. The unused bombs were left in Panama, and the remaining fuzes returned to Eglin. Based on the successful test results, the air force contracted with Picatinny Arsenal to modify several thousand proximity fuzes left over from WW II for use in Vietnam.

The fuze test reinforced the need for an effective way to mark the location of enemy forces hiding under a jungle canopy. For example, the standard smoke grenade or rocket cannot be seen through the canopy. This problem was the motivation for the development of "foam target markers." This concept called for an expanding "foam" grenade that would cover a twenty-square-meter area of the jungle canopy with white sticky foam. In an hour or so after dispensing, the foam would turn brown so that new target markers could be differentiated from old ones. Theoretically, the foam-making chemicals would expand in volume about fifty to seventy-five times when mixed and cover the canopy. It worked by hand, but the contractor could not develop a reliable means of mixing, dispensing, and dispersing the foam. Several mixing and dispensing concepts were prototyped, but none worked satisfactorily when dropped from an aircraft. The project cost roughly $25,000 and was a disappointing failure. Due to advances in technology, GPS coordinates and precision-guided munitions have overcome the problems Air Commandos and tactical pilots faced at that time in locating and marking targets.

Colonel King called to tell me I was being assigned on a part-time basis to SAWC as a command briefing officer under Maj. "Limpy" Limpansis. Limpy was one of the original cadre of Jungle Jim and was drawn up to SAWC Headquarters. I told Colonel King, "Thanks, but no thanks! I was an operator and not a pretty face standing behind a podium briefing Chambers of Commerce and such." The Colonel exploded, telling me that 1st CAG projects were important, but it was far more important to get the word out to the American people, to earn their support, not only for what we were doing but for the war effort as well. So I became a briefing officer telling the SAWC, Air Commando, and 1st CAG stories. In the style of Huntley and Brinkley, Limpy was Huntley, and I was Brinkley, giving a one-two punchy briefing from separate podiums. The skills learned from giving those briefings benefited me for the rest of my career, although it was not an obvious benefit at the time. Fortunately, it was only a part-time job, which allowed me to continue working on 1st CAG projects and to continue flying.

While visiting Picatinny Arsenal during the proximity fuze project, I learned about a new series of bomblets that were dispensed from tubes as the delivery aircraft flew at high speed and low altitude. One of the bomblets was designated the BLU-3, which stood for Bomb Live Unit no. 3. These bomblets were dropped from a long cylindrical dispenser filled with nineteen longitudinal tubes loaded with these bomblets. The bomblets were held in place by an explosive bolt and pushed out of the tube by air pressure aided by a spring when a release signal from the cockpit blew the bolt. The air pressure came from a hole in the streamline nose of the dispenser, allowing airflow generated by the speed of the aircraft to press against plastic obturators in front of the BLU-3s. I thought it was a concept that could be adapted to COIN aircraft like the AT-28, although the AT-28 didn't go fast enough to generate enough air pressure to dispense the bomblets; perhaps a longer spring would do the job.

The Air Logistics Center at Mobile, Alabama, just down the Beach Highway from Fort Walton Beach, Florida, was contacted about fabricating a test dispenser for the AT-28B and the B-26. The engineers there were very eager to make a contribution to the Vietnam War and, in short order, developed what I dubbed the P-2 dispenser. It had four six-foot-long 2.75-inch diameter aluminum tubes mounted on both sides of a rectangular strongback. The mounting lugs on the top of the strongback fit and would lock into a standard wing pylon. The front of the dispenser had locking metal orifices held in place by steel pins. Attached to the orifices were long springs to expel the bomblets. At the back end of the tubes were electrically activated plungers that would withdraw when an electrical impulse from the cockpit was sent to the dispenser. One of the eight tubes was emptied with each "Bomb Button" impulse. Air Commandos were denied access to the BLU-3 Bomblets, therefore an alternate effective antipersonnel grenade had to be found. With the aid of now technical sergeant Barger, a WW II explosive white phosphorus (WP) grenade was located. The WP grenade looked a lot like a smoke or tear gas canister, except that it was heavier and had rounded corners instead of the rolled corners like the ones found on soda pop cans.

Technical Sergeant Barger got his hands on a couple of these WP grenades for a test of their effectiveness. There were a lot of abandoned runways in the Eglin Range Complex. Using aerial photographs and an Eglin Range Complex manual, we located a runway that would make a good testing ground and was easily accessible from an existing road. At first, it was planned to just toss the grenade like soldiers do from a behind a barricade or out of a foxhole. Fortunately for us, none of those options were available; we couldn't locate a barricade and were too lazy to dig a foxhole. There was about fifty feet of stout cord in the trunk of my car, so we tied it to the grenade handle release pin and the grenade to a fence post. I'd read up on the WP grenade; it had a six-second delay before detonating after the pin was pulled from the handle and the grenade thrown. We pulled the pin by tugging on the fifty-foot cord and then ran away from the grenade. It was a good thing we ran because globs of burning WP landed only a few feet from where we were when the grenade exploded. Everything within the radius of the dispersed WP was set on fire. Eureka, this was a weapon that would create a smoke screen, set things on fire, and severely wound unprotected VC.

We tested the P-2 dispensers with more harmless smoke grenades, and the dispenser worked just fine. More about how the P-2s were employed later.

Colonel King called, wanting me to fly down to Howard Field, Panama, with him to visit the unit there. The idea was to elicit ideas for new 1st CAG projects and get some good pictures and data for the SAWC Briefing Team. We were going to fly down in a C-46, a WW II relic that could carry about twice as much as the C-47. I don't know why, but the C-46 never became as popular as the C-47. The trip down to Panama was uneventful. Colonel King was a fighter pilot all through WW II and the Korean Conflict, so he never had the opportunity to fly the C-46 until he flew as the copilot down to Howard Field. The team spent two days at Howard, just long enough for our pilot to get very sick and unable to stand, let alone fly. That didn't deter Colonel King one bit. He gave me a copy of the C-46-1 (pilots' handbook) the evening prior to our departure and told me to study it because I was going to be his copilot on the flight back home. Taking off is always easy; the aircraft lets you know when it's ready to fly. All you do then is pull the yoke back gently, and up you go. All the controls and gauges are basically the same and in the same location determined years ago to be the best for instrument flying in weather or at night. It is landing a strange airplane that can kill you. After several hours of boredom, Hurlburt was in sight, and Colonel King brought the C-46 around the pattern to final. I was poised for an emergency of some kind, but the landing was a smooth roll-on. I don't think he ever flew the C-46 again, and neither did I, but I have about ten hours of C-46 CP time in my logbook.

Then there was the time Colonel King asked me to fly an air force major back to the insane asylum he had been temporarily released from to brief General Prichard and a few handpicked and cleared senior officers on a covert operation the major previously led in Indochina. I said, "Yes, sir!"

There was a very pregnant pause, and then the Colonel said, "I promised him he could fly the AT-28 from the front seat." Then he quickly added, "You're the only guy that I know that can handle it." Yeah, right! It was an interesting flight, to say the least. The weather was good, and it was visual flight rules all the way to our destination in Mississippi. The major kept my nerves on edge by diving the AT-28 to look at something or rolling up in a steep bank for the same reason. I guided him through the landing pattern; though he wasn't as dangerous as some normal students I'd previously flown with. I trust that what he shared with General Prichard was worth the stress and anxiety I endured on that particular flight.

The 1st CAG was a great assignment for pilots. Most of us were able to maintain currency in several aircraft at the same time. For example, I was current in the AT-28, B-26, T-33, and the AT-37, while Jerry Carlisle was testing it. It was never clear why we were able to maintain proficiency in the T-33 because it was never involved in any of our COIN projects. One day, Capt. John Hunsucker and I were scheduled for a night T-33 proficiency flight. It had been quite a while, since either of us had flown, and we were about to lose currency in the T-33. The task of developing new weapons for the war in Vietnam had tied us to the office, and we needed to get in the air. Not many options were available; the only time we could get free was in the evening after a full day at the office. Luckily, there was a T-33 available for a night flight. An out-and-back cross-country with an o-dark-thirty return would keep us in the air for about five hours of flying time, along with an instrument approach and night landing for both of us. The planned flight would nearly fill our semiannual nighttime requirement too. It was winter in northern Florida; night came early, and it was raining lightly as we walked to the aircraft. Aircraft don't know or care if it's dark or foggy, but fighter pilots know, and they care! John was an interceptor pilot by training and operational experience, a different kind of fighter pilot. I was an F-86F jock, inclined to fly when the skies were blue and the sun was shining.

Everything was normal for the preflight, taxi, takeoff, and climb out to thirty-five thousand feet. I was in the front seat, and John in the back. We would trade places after we landed and refueled at Homestead AFB, near Miami. All was quiet except for a little chitchat about the projects we were working on. Suddenly, without warning, there was a "bump in the night" accompanied by a noticeable loss of trust from the J-33 engine. "John, what do you think?" I quickly asked as I scanned the cockpit for indications as to what might have happened, then the vibrations began. Rotating machinery doesn't usually vibrate, especially finely balanced jet engines.

John came back with "I think we just swallowed something through the engine—time to head back before we lose everything and have to punch out over the gulf." The engine continued to thump and belch, and the vibrations became more pronounced. When John and I agreed that we had reached a point from which we could glide home, I reduced the engine rpm to idle. The engine was still producing a little thrust, but an idle power setting reduced the stress on the stricken engine. We needed it to keep turning to generate the electricity that was powering our radios and flight instruments, to provide hydraulic power for lowering the landing gear, and for hydraulic braking once on a runway.

The T-33 has a straight laminar flow wing that generates a lot of lift, more than any other modern jet with the exception of the U-2 and RB-57 reconnaissance aircraft. From thirty-five thousand feet, you could glide a T-33 about 105 miles in a no-wind condition. We were about 150 miles from Eglin, so we needed the engine to push us at least thirty-five miles before we could glide all the way back to Eglin with a little altitude to spare.

During the twenty minutes of flight time back to Eglin, we tightened the ejection seat straps and rehearsed bailout procedures. The rear seat would eject first to prevent getting burned by my ejection seat rocket motor. With some optimism, we divided up the tasks for getting us back on the runway in one piece. We dialed in Eglin Approach Control on the radio and made contact, only to be informed that the field was below minimums and closed for landings. We advised approach that the engine was barely running and protesting violently with heavy vibrations. We only had one chance, and that was to attempt a landing in the fog. Failing that, we would pull up and bail out because we couldn't generate enough power for a go-around, nor could we make any suitable alternate runway. We had already passed by Panama City, and that runway was also below weather minimums. We recommended an approach from the north; if we had to bail out, the aircraft would likely end up in Choctawhatchee Bay and do no harm to anyone except a few stingrays and mullet. We also asked to be kept high on the glide slope until over the runway in case we lost the engine on final. The north/south runway was thirteen thousand feet long; being a little high would not pose a problem. Approach Control agreed to the plan and turned us over to the radar approach frequency.

John would fly the approach on instruments from the backseat. Interceptor pilots are superb on instruments because they get "scrambled" in the worst weather to intercept and identify unknown aircraft in US airspace. I would keep my hands on the controls in case I saw a need to pull up and eject. My primary responsibility was to look for the runway, take control of the aircraft, and land if the runway lights came into view. We agreed that if the approach was smooth and on glide slope, we would go down to one hundred feet, maybe even down to fifty feet, on the altimeter prior to pulling up and ejecting.

John was supersmooth coming down the glide slope. About seventy-five feet above the ground, I could just barely make out the runway lights—we were home and able to save the aircraft. Too bad it didn't know we were in the dark and fog; it might have appreciated how hard we worked to keep it from becoming an artificial reef in the bay.

After engine shutdown and with feet finally on the ground, we took out our flashlights and peered into the tailpipe. Most of the turbine blades were missing! Just enough blades remained to keep the compressor turning and blowing compressed air into the combustion chamber. We were very fortunate that one of the many turbine blades and fragments that came out through the fuselage didn't cut a control cable to the rudder or elevator, making the T-33 uncontrollable. The good news was we got preferential scheduling for another flight three nights later, as we still needed flying time.

SAWC sponsored several civic leader briefings and static displays. At General Prichard's direction, I was a briefer and then assigned to be part of the Static Display showing off SAWC aircraft, munitions used in Southeast Asia (SEA), and the many innovations of 1st CAG. The biggest hits were always the AT-28, B-26, and all the new revolutionary communications gear developed by Capt. Tony Scarpace in concert with the Electronics Industry.

One summer day, a few of Secretary McNamara's "whiz kid" advisors came to Eglin AFB for SAWC briefings and to view the equipment used in SEA. I was standing in front of the AT-28 and B-26 with numerous munitions positioned in front of them. General Prichard had the whiz kids in tow as they walked by the Air Commandos, all combat-proven, standing at parade rest in front of the aircraft and ordnance displays. It appeared they had no interest in asking questions of those who'd been in combat, as they just continued to walk on by. As they were passing by my position, General Prichard grabbed one by the arm and steered him to me, saying, "Captain Pete has been to Vietnam. Do you have any questions for him?"

The distinguished gentleman from OSD asked, "Are you married?"

My answer was "Yes, I have a wife who is expecting." There were no further questions. So much for the DOD under Secretary McNamara!

In late October 1962, I received a call from Colonel King asking that I supervise the loading of sixteen P-2 dispensers with white phosphorus (WP) explosive grenades. In a few hours, I had pulled together a team of weapons personnel who had worked for me at Hurlburt. By midnight, all sixteen P-2 dispensers were loaded and placed on a munitions trailer ready for delivery to the Hurlburt flight line. The following afternoon, Colonel King called again and asked if I would volunteer for a special highly classified mission. "Yes, sir" was the only possible answer. We were to meet at one of the Hurlburt AT-28 Squadron briefing rooms at 1600 hours on October 28. I was clueless as to what was in store for us.

I told Sheila I would be flying that night to maintain my night-landing proficiency. When I arrived at the specified briefing room, there were eight AT-28 aircrews there, counting Colonel King and me. As I recall, most of us were senior captains with recent combat experience. It was a typical combat mission briefing. First, the intelligence officer briefed the threat, Cuban MiG-21s, antiaircraft artillery (AAA), and SA-2 SAMs. Next, the targets: Soviet medium-range ballistic missile (MRBM) sites on the northern coast of Cuba. Then the operations officer said that each AT-28 crew was assigned to one or more of the missile sites—all sites were covered. Following that we were briefed on the obligatory rescue procedures—all the missile sites were close to the beach, so it was assumed any aircraft that was damaged by gunfire could make it to the water before bailing out or ditching in the Gulf of Mexico. We were told that our mission was to mark each of the missile sites with WP grenades from P-2 dispensers so that the high-performance jets that would arrive five minutes behind us could easily pick up the missile sites and minimize their time in the target area. Last, we were briefed that the entire mission would be conducted in radio silence. Engines would be started on the clock. Aircraft would taxi to the north run-up area when the tower showed a green light. Once in the run-up area, aircrews would watch the tower for a second light. A second green light from the tower was the signal to take off and proceed to our targets in radio silence. A red light signaled the mission was cancelled and to return to the ramp and shut down.

It was dark when Colonel King and I, along with the other seven aircraft, taxied into the north run-up area and set the brakes, with the aircraft pointing at the tower. Each aircraft carried two P-2 dispensers under the wings. Each dispenser was loaded with seventy-two white phosphorus grenades. There was nothing around the north run-up area except swamp and gunnery ranges. Essentially no one, except the AT-28 crew chiefs, would know we were there. Local flying had ended three hours earlier. Taking off to the south, the planes would be airborne about one-third of the way down the runway in the dark and well above the beach highway. Our plan was to over fly Key West for a last precision fix and then fly another ninety miles or so to the MRBM sites. We would be flying just above the tops of the waves to avoid radar detection, with navigation lights out to make it harder to pick us up visually.

I suspect Colonel King wanted me along as an IP because at that time, he wasn't current in the AT-28. He had flown combat in WW II in both the Pacific and European Theaters, as well as in the Korean War and in Vietnam. He was the embodiment of the warrior spirit and wasn't about to miss a Cuban Conflict if there was one. We had flown together in the AT-28 a number of times. As such, he had confidence in my ability to navigate to our target, talk him through the weapons switches to release the WP grenades, and handle any emergency situation that might arise.

We were sitting in the run-up area, waiting for a green light from the tower that would serve as our execution order. Time was running out for a negotiated settlement between the Soviet Union and United States to remove the offending Soviet missiles in Cuba. Most likely, there were hundreds of supersonic fighters fully loaded with ordnance ready to launch from other air force bases, throughout Florida, with similar missions to destroy the missile sites. In addition, it is likely that there were also aircraft poised on navy carriers within striking range of Cuba to attack the Soviet missile sites.

It was important for the strike force to get in and out of their target areas quickly in order to limit their exposure to the SA-2 surface-to-air missile sites protecting Cuba. The intelligence community rated the SA-2 as highly effective. Neither the air force nor the navy had any experience against the SA-2, but we would soon learn just how deadly they could be when the Vietnam War expanded into North Vietnam in the mid-1960s.

Time was passing slowly, and we were burning precious fuel that would be needed to get back safely to either the navy base at Key West or Homestead AFB, just south of Miami. A light from tower bathed the cockpit in red light, signaling that our mission was cancelled. We watched as the red light moved from AT-28 to AT-28 in the run-up area. When we had parked at the ramp and gotten out of the aircraft, we learned that President Kennedy and Premier Nikita Khrushchev had reached an agreement. The Soviet MRBM sites would be dismantled and removed from Cuba. I stayed on the ramp until the P-2 dispensers were made safe. I was tempted to ask Colonel King if TAC tasked us for the pathfinder and target marking mission or if he had called General Sweeney and volunteered us to do the job. I never did ask.

Another project I was involved in was the development of an infrared sensor that could detect conventional aircraft at long distances by the heat from their engine exhaust. I suspect this is a project that Colonel King sponsored so that aircraft like the AN-2 Colt could be detected and tracked from aircraft like the B-26 and AT-28. The project involved endless hours of night flying at low altitude over the Gulf of Mexico. The sensor under development was housed in an Eglin laboratory with a window overlooking the gulf. The B-26 was flown in a racetrack outbound from the beach to about twenty miles out to sea and back, over and over again, for about four hours. The same routine was flown with the T-28B. Collecting sufficient data to satisfy test team requirements for data took weeks. It was boring work, but it was flying.

I was also being drawn into more and more briefings, informing senior officers what the First Air Commando Wing (1st ACW) and First Combat Application Group (1st CAG) had accomplished, as well as projects that were currently in development. As a result, I was getting further from the task of making improvements in armament, tactics, and such. One day, Colonel King called me into his office and told me I was going back to Vietnam, only this time I would be briefing the generals there on advances being made that needed to be "pulled" into the combat arena from their end. This was because the military and political bureaucracy in Saigon had grown both ponderous and powerful, and the 1st ACW could not make things happen on their own anymore.

Just before I departed for Vietnam, an idea from a major, an aeronautical engineer at Wright-Patterson AFB, Ohio, landed on my desk. The major suggested that an aircraft making a "pylon" turn could put enormous firepower on a point target with a side-mounted machine gun. He further suggested that a .30-caliber Gatling gun mounted in the cargo door of a C-47 would provide an ideal solution. I put the suggestion in my in basket, thinking I wouldn't be long in Vietnam and would evaluate the idea when I returned. However, when the major didn't get an immediate response on his suggestion, he asked his boss to call Brig. Gen. Gil Prichard for an update on its status. General Prichard thought the idea had merit! He also liked to fly, so he had a .30-caliber M-1 machine gun mounted in a C-47 on the cargo floor with the entrance door removed and flew the aircraft over the Gulf of Mexico, shooting at raft targets. For a gun sight, he put a grease pencil mark on the pilot's side window. It worked! The general could put sustained fire on a point target while orbiting in a pylon turn at five thousand feet above the gulf waters. "Puff the Magic Dragon" gunship was born on that flight and the gunship concept has served our forces in combat in several instantiations over five decades.

In early January 1963, I was back at Bien Hoa. Sheila was about five months pregnant with our first child, and there was some hope that I would be home in time for the blessed event. In those days, dependent wives were cared for by air force doctors who fully understood the additional burdens placed on military wives left behind, as well as the concerns they had for their husbands at war. Wives also gave birth in air force hospitals, where all the staff were part of the air force team and had experienced the trials of long family separations. I was confident that Sheila, along with the many other Air Commando wives, would be well cared for in our absence. Today, military wives and dependents are no longer taken care of by military doctors in military hospitals. Instead, both wives and dependents must find civilian doctors who will provide medical services under Tricare. Unfortunately, most civilian doctors and care providers are not familiar with the long separations and the stresses endured by military dependents.

The 1st ACW detachment commander at Bien Hoa was an officer I did not know, and initially, he wasn't very supportive of shuttling me back and forth to Saigon for my "dog and pony" shows to senior officers in Military Assistance Command Vietnam (MACV). He did, however, see some benefit from the work 1st CAG was doing. They had P-2 dispensers at Bien Hoa and were using them to provide smoke screens for ARVN and Special Forces, and they also had the 40 mm cannon. It wasn't hard to convince the commander that I could relieve some of the pilots (AT-28 and B-26) by flying missions so they could get an occasional day off. The combat tempo had really picked up, and Detachment 2 was now actually training Vietnamese pilots to fly the AT-28B. There were lots more aircraft on the ramp, and more requests for air support were coming in daily from the ARVN and Special Forces detachments.

The first sorties flown were in support of the army and the navy. A USN carrier had ferried a dozen army helicopters from the United

States and would arrive the next morning about one hundred miles off the coast of Nha Trang, SVN. A flight of two AT-28s were fragged to fly to Nha Trang, spend the night there, and fly out the next morning at 1000 hours to escort the helicopters back to Nha Trang. In addition, the AT-28s were tasked to provide fire suppression if there was any hostile fire en route to the airbase. Nha Trang was a quiet and pretty little town on the seashore surrounded by former French rubber plantations. Everything went as planned. The next morning, our flight headed out to sea to find the aircraft carrier and escort the helicopters to Nha Trang. The AT-28 had no radar, just a radio and compass, but we were convinced we could spot the big ship easily from ten thousand feet altitude on a clear sunny day. We were considerably short of the hundred miles that we had expected to fly out from the coastline when a radio call came over Guard Channel (243.0 MHz). "Aircraft approaching US Ship, if you come any closer, you will be shot down!"

Lead responded with "We are US Air Force aircraft fragged to escort army helicopters to Nha Trang. We are squawking the specified 'friendly code' on IFF!"

The voice came back with "I repeat, turn around, or you will be destroyed!"

Lead obliged and started a left-hand orbit and responded, "We are in a left-hand orbit. Send the helicopters to our position!" About thirty minutes later, a dozen H-21 twin-rotor helicopters appeared on the horizon, heading toward our position. The maximum speed of the H-21 was about equal to the AT-28's landing speed, so we slowly orbited their formation as we led it to Nha Trang Air Base, SVN. With the helicopters safely on the ground, we landed, refueled, and then returned to Bien Hoa.

The Seventh Air Force ADVON had declared large work animals as VC transportation and supply animals, and therefore enemy combatants. Orders were published to shoot water buffalo and elephants anytime they were observed in jungle clearings or otherwise a long way from villages, agricultural areas, and main lines of communication. Fortunately, I never found buffalo or elephant under those conditions, so I never had the opportunity to become an airborne big game hunter.

After flying a few missions to earn credibility with the senior officers in Saigon, I went there to set up a series of briefings to army and air force general officers at Tan Son Nhut Air Base, where all the military brass lived and worked. Maj. James D. "Don" Hughes allowed me to share his office when in Saigon. Major Hughes was a West Point graduate who seemed exceptionally sharp and was the assistant operations officer and chief of the Special Operations branch of 7th ADVON commanded by

Brig. Gen. Rolin P. Anthis. Don had been in the job several months and was well connected in 7th ADVON. He was very helpful in getting me set up to brief General Anthis and several of the general's key staff officers. The briefing, approved by Brigadier General Prichard, commander, SWAC, was a scripted briefing, which I was obligated to read verbatim. With months of boring experience as a SAWC command briefer, I had learned to read briefings like a talking head on television. The briefing went well, and General Anthis set me up to brief senior US Army officers in Vietnam a couple of weeks later. Then I went back to Bien Hoa for more combat missions.

My next mission was very memorable for all the wrong reasons. It seemed rather simple: escort a number of army H-21 helicopters that were going to insert troops in a landing zone (LZ) deep in the jungle, not very far from Bien Hoa. Intelligence information indicated there might be a large force of VC operating in the area. The army helicopter unit was located on the far end and other side of the Bien Hoa runway. Our flight drove over to their operations facility to brief the mission with them so that we had a clear, from the horse's mouth, understanding of what the helicopter force expected from us. The H-21 unit and the troops they were lifting into the LZ were the primary force. We were their supporting heavy artillery. The army mission commander wanted us to prepare (prep) the LZ by dropping bombs just inside the tree lines surrounding the LZ. The bomb drop was to be done just prior to their descent into the LZ and then pull up to provide .50-caliber gunfire support, if needed.

During the briefing, I asked the army mission commander what radio frequency we could communicate on with them once we were airborne. The answer was something like 127.43 Fox Mike. I didn't understand and asked if he meant 274.3 UHF. He responded that the army had switched to frequency-modulated radios in the VHF spectrum. In that brief moment, I learned that army aircraft and air force aircraft could not communicate with each other! In just a little over a decade since the air force became a separate service, we lost our ability to communicate between "service unique" aircraft. The air force stayed with the equipment provided us by the army of 1947. Shortly thereafter, all aircraft procured by the US Army were equipped with VHF FM radios with little or no coordination with the US Air Force. What should have been a simple mission now became very difficult. If the helicopters or the personnel they were inserting into the LZ ran into trouble, we had to operate on the basis of what we could see or purely on instinct. This was a very sad state of affairs in combat with live ordinance, but unfortunately, it was the current reality.

Everything seemed to go as planned. When the LZ came into view, we pulled ahead and dropped bombs about twenty or thirty feet inside the tree line. There were no secondary explosions. No movement was observed on the ground. There was a small hut in the clearing with what appeared to be a woman and two children. We dropped our bombs well clear of the hut and the people. We had to assume the helicopter pilots also saw the hut and the people. The lead helicopter flew past the hut to the far end of the LZ and landed. The remaining helicopters followed one after another, landing perhaps fifty feet behind the whirlybird in front. After several helicopters landed, one came to rest directly opposite the hut, about two hundred feet away. As soon as the H-21 engines slowed to idle, machinegun fire erupted from the hut, killing everyone in the helicopter and setting it on fire. Gunners in the nearest forward and aft helicopters opened fire, destroying the hut and, unfortunately, killing the woman and two children. When the mission was debriefed back at Bien Hoa, we learned that every H-21 crew that passed the hut inbound to touchdown called out the people standing out in the open, noting they did not appear to be hostile. Later, soldiers on the ground discovered the woman and children were tied to stakes and could not escape from the VC hiding in the hut. We were up against very cruel adversaries who saw little value in the lives of their own people, even the very young and innocent.

After the mission debriefing, I sent a message back to Colonel King informing him of the radio disconnect between air force fighter aircraft and army helicopters. I emphasized that support for helicopter operations would likely increase exponentially as army force levels in Vietnam increased. He agreed, and to the air force's credit, our fighters, even the fast movers like the F-100, were modified with VHF FM radios and their buggy whip antennas.

As mentioned earlier, flying was getting rather intense. I was sent as an element lead in a flight of four to Soc Trang, a small strip in the southern delta region of Vietnam. Soc Trang was also shared with a US Army H-21 helicopter unit. The unit commander had a Bengal tiger for a mascot. The tiger named Tuffy roamed free inside a short white picket fence about fifty feet in length on each side with a door from the fenced-in area, which lead into the commander's office. Tuffy was restrained by a rather flimsy chain and shared the yard with a black-and-white mongrel dog named Tiger. The two animals were friends and played together well. This fenced area was on the path we took regularly from our operations tent near the flight line to the mess hall. As a result, we passed Tuffy and Tiger at least three times a day. One day, while heading to the mess hall after a couple of morning missions, one of my cohorts said, "Let's get a picture with the tiger." We'd seen several people get pictures taken with Tuffy, so why not? I went up to the fence and called, "Here, Tuffy!" The big cat bounded over and put his paws on my shoulders, licking my face with his sandpaper-rough tongue. Evidently, he liked the taste of salt from perspiration. Tuffy was full grown and towered over me. When I patted him, just as one would a pet dog, his front leg and shoulder muscles were as hard as concrete or rock. I also noticed that his canine teeth were about two inches long. I was sure glad that he was well fed and friendly. Not too long after that morning, a soldier who had too much native beer to drink decided to jump the little white picket fence and wrestle with Tuffy, probably on a dare. They rolled around, none the worse for the encounter, until the soldier decided he had enough. As he pulled away, Tuffy's claws came out to prevent the man's escape, scratching him and drawing blood. Shortly after that incident, Tuffy was shipped back to a municipal zoo in a large eastern metropolitan area of the United States.

It wasn't unusual to fly five sorties a day out of Soc Trang in support of United States or ARVN forces in close combat with the enemy. In that heat, it took a lot of water to prevent dehydration, which could lead to loss of judgment. The effects of the outside temperature in the cockpit were compounded by the heat from the big radial engine hanging just in front of the thin aluminum firewall that separated the cockpit from the engine. One of our flight surgeons taped a thermometer to the bottom of the control stick in the front cockpit. The thermometer had a memory lock to hold the low and high temperature measured in that area. When the thermometer was recovered at the end of the sortie, the high temperature recorded was 178 degrees Fahrenheit. There was no cooling system to alleviate the heat, just a three-inch hole in the canopy that allowed some heat to escape.

Back at Bien Hoa, Maj. Leroy W. "Swede" Svendsen Jr. decided it was time to give me a tactical check in the B-26. I was sitting in the alert tent with my Vietnamese rider and navigator when I was informed that Major Svendsen would take the navigator's place. The major said he expected me to perform all of the functions necessary to accomplish the flight, reminding me that he was just an observer along to grade my performance.

For those of you old enough to remember Milt Caniff and his comic strip, *Steve Canyon*, Swede was Steve Canyon in the flesh: tall, handsome, with blond hair, and at the top of his game as a fighter pilot.

In the Douglas B-26, the right-seater (navigator) doesn't play a vital role during an air-to-ground mission except keep track of a few things and charge the .50-caliber guns in the nose, so I didn't see much of a problem with not having a qualified flier in the right seat, although charging those eight .50-caliber machine guns by reaching across his lap could prove awkward. With over two thousand hours of time in single-engine, single-seat fighters, I believed I could multitask with the best of them.

Within a matter of minutes, the klaxon went off signaling a scramble for the alert aircraft, my B-26. The aircraft had been preflighted and cocked earlier that morning. She was loaded with twenty contact-fuzed one-hundred-pound bombs in the bomb bay, six napalm tanks on the wings, and a full load of .50-caliber ammo for the eight nose guns. That would be a total of 3,200 rounds of tracer and armor piercing incendiary (API), four hundred rounds for each gun with a total firing rate of 9,600 rounds per minute. This was 60 percent greater rate than the famous Gatling gun.

Once airborne, we contacted the local radar controller and were given a southern vector to the target area in the Delta, where we would be turned over to an airborne forward air controller (FAC). As we leveled off at ten thousand feet, the radar controller directed us to "go buster," requiring full military power, which doesn't mean much when the throttles are connected to a couple of PW R-2800 engines.

I added a couple of inches to the cruise power setting and replied, "Roger," and chambered a round in all eight guns.

A few minutes later, the same controller said with some authority, "Go gate," which translates to "plug in the afterburner."

Again, "Roger," but no corresponding action—I had no intention of blowing out the radial engine cylinders with sixty-two inches of manifold pressure. Swede was stoic. The only thing I could deduce is that there was some urgency for us to get to the target area, but this WW II war bird was ill equipped to do more than a high cruise at forty-two inches of mercury.

We checked in with the ALO FAC as directed and were informed that a Special Forces A team had uncovered a flotilla of VC moving up river in sampans. For those not familiar with the Far East, sampans are powered wooden boats ranging in length from forty to sixty feet. A few minutes earlier, one sampan reversed course and was moving at a higher rate of speed to separate from the rest. The FAC's logic was that this boat had important cargo or people on board, so take it out first. We rolled in broadside to the boat with two cans of napalm selected—just because I liked to clean the wings off first. Both hit the water just short of the sampan and covered it with 150 gallons of flaming jellied gasoline. For good measure, I came back around and put a one-second burst (160 bullets) into the boat. The harmonization pattern covered it from stem to stern.

Next, we went after the remaining six boats trying to escape, hitting them all with a short dose of .50-caliber armor piercing ammunition. The remaining ammo load was only good for about twelve seconds, so I had to conserve. As I brought the B-26 around for another attack, it was clear that all boats were damaged, with three attempting to hide under tree branches overhanging the shore, while the other three were still heading up the river. The boats in the river were close together, so I covered them with the four remaining cans of napalm and then strafed the three under the trees again and again, after which all appeared dead in the water and sinking. FAC reported that nothing was moving, and he had other targets that needed to be struck. He put rocket smoke on a tree line and said, "There's a VC force in the trees about two kilometers upriver from my smoke." I confirmed a landmark at about where I thought the two-kilometer point was, and he rogered. With the wings clean, bombs were next on the menu. Ten bombs rippled on the first pass with roughly one-hundred-foot spacing right into the middle of the forty-foot-wide tree line paralleling the river. With any luck, some would have detonated on tree trunks and created airbursts over the VC. The FAC liked that so much, he asked me to do it again! The bomb bay was now empty. The B-26 was now five thousand pounds of ordnance lighter, plus the fuel burned. It was a lot more nimble.

I pulled up into a five-thousand-foot AGL race track, while the FAC looked for more VC. Over my shoulder, I could still see the sampans, still on fire and burning down to the water line with some small secondary explosions—probably fuel.

Then the call came. "I've got a VC, maybe someone important, trying to sneak across a rice paddy." We spotted him and rolled in about two thousand feet, which was out of gun range. I liked to shoot from 1,500 into 1,000 feet because that is where the bullet impacts are harmonized with the gun sight. He went underwater, probably using a hollow reed to breathe. The burst went into the general vicinity where I thought he was. The FAC called, "He's up and running." After four strafe attempts to get this VC, I knew I was running out of bullets, but he was also getting closer to the paddy bank, allowing me to get a better fix on where he went under.

Bingo! He floated up to the surface, and on the next pass, I nailed him and went Winchester at the same time.

The FAC was ecstatic! He reported seven sampans destroyed and 261 VC killed in action (KIA). It was a fun mission—I couldn't miss. Swede never said a word, but he was smiling. I passed the tactical check ride.

Swede later became better known for his heroic action in evacuating the American embassy in Saigon when the Viet Cong and Viet Min overran Saigon. He retired as a major general and lives in San Antonio, Texas.

The next B-26 mission was supposed to be a milk run. I was fragged to drop a bomb bay full of one-hundred-pound general purpose bombs of WW II vintage into a vegetable garden growing in a small opening in the vast jungle north of Bien Hoa. Four of the bombs were fuzed to go off on impact. The remainder had twelve-hour-delay fuzes installed. The assumption by the intelligence team down in Saigon was that this was a VC vegetable garden and that when I blew it up, they would return to salvage what edible food was left and get blown to smithereens when the delay-fuzed bombs exploded around midnight. All went as planned. It took some time to find the opening where the garden was located because the trees were so tall, you had to be right over it in a steep bank angle to see it. The dive angle on the bombing run also had to be fairly steep to pick up the opening. The plan was to ripple ten bombs on each of two passes. We were in about a forty-degree dive at over 350 mph approaching release altitude when the plane started coming apart due to extreme vibration. A quick glance out the side window revealed that screws and rivets were popping out of the wings. My right hand swept the cockpit, jettison bombs, gear handle checked up, flaps checked up, landing light switch up! That was it! The Vietnamese rider in the jump seat behind the navigator had placed his left hand on the upper center switch console as he leaned forward to see the target. His hand must have pushed the landing light switch forward to the down position. If it hadn't been for that experience in Japan with Lieutenant Decker when he inadvertently left the landing light switch down on takeoff and climb out, I would have not reached for that switch, and the sever vibration would likely have caused structural failure in flight.

I pulled the throttles back, easing out of the dive as gently and smoothly as I could with just enough g-force to clear the jungle canopy. The bomb bay doors were left open to more rapidly slow the aircraft down to gear lowering speed, reducing the air loads to the minimum. I declared an emergency and requested a long, straight-in, no flap GCA from Approach Control. Looking out at the left wing, I could see screws and rivet sticking up out of the wing; the navigator confirmed it was the same on the right wing. I had no clue as to the integrity of the airframe. I was just hoping to get it on the ground in one piece. The landing was smooth, and I used the entire 3,300 feet to get the plane stopped to reduce stress. When the bird was parked, there was a crowd of maintenance people looking at it and shaking their heads. As I mentioned earlier, the Vietnamese riders we had to carry as political cover for covert operations were eventually going to get someone killed, and this time, he almost did. It was a long time with a lot of maintenance hours before that aircraft flew again.

Changes at Bien Hoa continued. A new ten-thousand-foot concrete runway was almost complete; the last piece of concrete had been poured and was in the cure phase. Looking at that long wide slab of concrete while landing on 3,300 feet of pierced steel planking (PSP) was almost immoral. If I didn't already say it, landing on PSP during the monsoon rains, or any visible moisture for that matter, was like trying to stop on an ice-skating rink, only worse. A heavily loaded C-124 landed at Bien Hoa one day and, while trying to stop, pushed all the PSP up in front of the main wheel trucks like they were bellows on an accordion. With three front loaders holding the folded PSP firm at one end, it took three bulldozers line abreast to pull it back out to its full length of 3,300 feet.

Air Commandos were no longer in charge of the area we operated out of at Bien Hoa. Thirteenth Air Force owned, operated, and commanded the air base. The Air Commando detachment was now a tenant. Tenancy is hardly ever a good arrangement for an operational unit, let alone an operational unit flying high-tempo combat operations around the clock, or in current vernacular, 24/7. There were some improvements: tents had wooden floors, and each occupant had a metal locker. In addition, there was a small base exchange, and both an officers' club and enlisted club. The base commander kept trying to impose more and more control over aircrews and maintenance personnel, but he really had no clout. Still he kept trying to exert more control, until one day, he went way over the top. Keep in mind, we are in high-tempo combat operations, supporting both United States and ARVN soldiers and Special Forces engaged in continuous combat operations with a brutal and determined enemy. The base commander frowned on us wearing flight suits or fatigues in the club, so he posted a directive stating that a tie must be worn at the O'club after 1700 hours. Heck, no one had even brought a tie to our little snake-infested hole.

You can see it coming, can't you? The first six men to go to the O'club after the directive was posted wore makeshift ties around bare necks and not another stitch of clothing covering their bodies. When asked to leave, they held up a copy of the directive stating "ties were required." The directive failed to list any other required items of attire. One of the O'club employees must have called the base commander because air police came to evict us. The O'club went without patrons for several days. All aircrew officers ate at the mess hall with the troops, which was a good thing in of itself. After a few days, the dress requirement was rescinded for fear the O'club would go broke! Subsequently, but slowly, the aircrew patrons returned.

Because the B-26 had the range to reach targets just about anywhere in the country, most B-26 missions were flown out of Bien Hoa. However, one day, the frag writers in Saigon directed us to fly three B-26s loaded with bombs and ammo to Play Cu in the Central Highlands and stage out of there for a few days. Perhaps intelligence gathered from Special Forces units in the field indicated a buildup of VC and North Vietnamese forces in that area and wanted responsive close air support when needed. Pilots who had experience flying out of Play Cu airfield emphasized that although the runway was the same length as the one at Bien Hoa, the altitude was much higher. Thus, the correct indicated airspeed (IAS) on final would result in a higher true airspeed (TAS) and resultant ground speed because of lower air density. They further emphasized that the runway was not at all level but had a high point in the center and sloped down from the high center to either end. Final had to be flown slightly below "on speed," and touchdown had to be at the approach end, considering that we were heavily loaded with bombs. The Play Cu runway was in sight; lead and two landed. I was last on a slow dragged-in final. Touchdown was perfect, and brakes were applied immediately. In a heartbeat, the end of the runway was coming up, and I pushed hard on the brakes. Both main tires blew out as the aircraft skidded to a stop at the high point in the middle. I now see another 1,700 feet of runway that was not visible until reaching the center point! Fortunately, there were spare wheels and tires propositioned at Play Cu because my mistake was all too common for first-timers landing there. This was one runway where you couldn't believe your eyes. I recommended the base put a small sandwich board sign alongside the runway at the high point so pilots would know there was runway beyond what they could see. A B-26 pilot's eyes are roughly thirteen feet above ground when sitting in the cockpit. Not being able to see that last half of the runway from that height indicates the slope was pretty steep. The close support missions subsequently flown out of Play Cu went well.

Back at Saigon, it was time for another series of briefings. An army major general, his staff, and some field commanders hosted the first one. They provided a nice podium with a reading light powered by a car battery. About a third of the way through the briefing, the light started growing dimmer. The car battery must have been running low on power. In a few minutes, my head was about a foot from the script. It was no use! I gave up and started talking to the charts. After the briefing, the hosting army general came up to the podium and said, "The last part of your briefing was fantastic. My recommendation to you is that you never read another briefing. Just talk to your charts—you know your stuff!" That was good advice, and I followed his guidance whenever I could get away with it. The army general made arrangements for me to brief a Joint Service Session with senior members of all services attending. This briefing was expected to get the high-level operational pull for the new equipment and capability being developed by 1st CAG for combat operations. Toward the end of the briefing, I had three or four charts on the P-2 dispenser and some of the munitions it could dispense. One of those was the BLU-3, a preformed fragmenting grenade that had proved extremely effective against simulated personnel and light vehicles back in the CONUS. When I spoke to the BLU-3 slide, an army brigadier general stood up and addressed the crowd, saying, "The captain has just violated security by discussing the BLU-3. Its classification is highly protected, and I strongly suggest you forget everything you've heard here today!" There was dead silence. Everyone got up and walked out. I caught up with the army brigadier general and told him I had documents signed by the Picatinny Arsenal commander that the BLU-3 and its operation were completely unclassified. He acknowledged that was true but stated he personally didn't agree with that position and opposed bringing the BLU-3 bomblet into Vietnam.

I spoke to the army general who hosted the meeting, informing him of what had just transpired. His only response was "Unfortunately, the damage has been done, and I don't have the time to try and undo it." It wasn't until after President Johnson expanded the war that F-100 aircraft came to Vietnam with the BLU-3 in CBU-2 dispensers.

There was always flying to take your mind off of service rivalries and higher headquarters politics. When I returned to Bien Hoa, a supposedly good deal was dropped into my lap. A B-26 needed to go to the Philippines for extensive depot level maintenance, and Major Svendsen had picked me for the flight. Actually, I suspected the B-26 was going back to Air Asia in Tainan. When I went out to preflight the aircraft, the crew chief told me that the right drop tank didn't feed the last time they put fuel in it, and the left engine caught fire on the previous flight, but he was fairly certain it was OK now. I went back to operations and discovered that all the other B-26 crews declined the flight even though it meant a night or two at Clark AFB, which was only a few miles from Manila. A thorough review of the aircraft forms gave me some confidence that maintenance personnel had worked the problems about as hard as they could. The B-26 navigator I usually flew with agreed to go on the flight because he wanted to do some shopping in Manila.

I didn't think there was anything that could go wrong on the flight that couldn't be coped with. If the engine caught on fire, we'd shut it down and feather the propeller. The B-26 flew reasonably well on one engine, and we could turn back or proceed to Clark AFB, depending on our position at the time. The fuel system on the B-26 was rather primitive, just some rotating valves to select tanks that would provide avgas to the engines. It would be a good sign if, as the fuel burned down, the lateral trim wheel stayed neutral, indicating both wings tanks were feeding normally. Checking lateral trim on climb-out when the tanks were reasonably balanced would provide an indication on how the tanks were feeding. Increasingly greater trim to hold the right wing level would indicate the right drop tank was feeding slowly or not at all. This would mean we would be short of fuel getting to Clark AFB. If we did make it to a runway, a lot of cross control would be required to hold up the heavy right wing. Considering all the maintenance-related problems, the best option was to take a slightly longer route via Da Nang at the northern tip of South Vietnam and then head east to Manila. If problems occurred early, there were several airfields that could accommodate the B-26, including Play Cu. The flight was uneventful. Dinner that night at Clark AFB was enjoyable with the band playing the latest Chubby Checker songs that were popular back in the CONUS.

Some things are remembered because they were so far out of place and time. I was leading a flight of two AT-28s scrambled from alert. I checked in with the CRC and was given a flight vector that would take us to the target area. When we reached cruise altitude, normal cruise power was set, resulting in airspeed of 180 knots with the load of bombs and ammunition normally loaded on aircraft placed on alert. After about ten minutes, the controller called and directed to flight to go "buster," which meant "full military power." It's important to note that the AT-28B engine was turbine boosted and could pull fifty-two inches of manifold pressure at 2,700 rpm, with the fuel mixture rich for takeoff power. With gear and flaps up, power was normally reduced to forty-five inches at 2,400 rpm for climb to altitude. The AT-28 wasn't pressurized; therefore, maximum altitude was normally ten thousand feet. It took about ten minutes to reach that altitude from sea level. Maximum power in routine cruise was about thirty-five inches at 1,800 rpm, with a lean fuel mixture. Jet engines in fighter aircraft could run at 100 percent rpm and with full afterburner until they reached minimum fuel. Reciprocating radial engines could run at cruise power until they ran out of fuel, but the times at climb power and takeoff power were much more limited.

In response to the CRC controller's call for full military power, the throttle was pushed up to thirty-seven inches, resulting in a negligible increase in airspeed. Soon, the controller called and directed the flight to go "gate," indicating afterburners. "Roger," I said and advised him that our equipment did not have afterburners. We were going as fast as we could without incurring significant risk of losing an engine. In another thirty minutes or so, the flight was turned over to an airborne FAC. We sent some VC to their final resting place.

As is customary when returning from a mission, the detachment intelligence officer was waiting to debrief the mission and gather data for a report to higher headquarters. For those who followed the Vietnam War, there were several phases of reporting mission effectiveness. There was the sortie phase, where increasing numbers of sorties flown were used as a measure of effectiveness (MOE). This was followed by the body count phase, where the number of VC and things destroyed were used for MOE. We were in this phase. Next, there was the tonnage phase, where tons of ordnance dropped was used as the MOE. And sometimes, the number of medals awarded was used as an additional MOE. The airborne FAC gave us a body count, and we passed it to the intel officer, along with anything else that might be of interest, such as number of antiaircraft artillery (AAA) we saw firing at us, battle damage sustained, and the like. When the debriefing was finished, the intel officer poured us a shot of "mission whiskey." I declined mine, as I expected to fly more sorties that day and didn't want to have any of my senses dulled by alcohol. I had repeatedly suggested to the detachment commander that one shot per day was plenty and should be reserved for the last sortie of the day, certainly not the first. As expected, it wasn't long before I was airborne again on another mission.

Probably my most disappointing mission was also the longest. The navigator and I were sitting B-26 alert when the klaxon went off at about 2200 hours. We rounded up our Vietnamese rider and headed for the aircraft we had preflighted and cocked earlier that afternoon. It was only a few minutes before we were airborne and climbing into a dark but relatively clear sky. The CRC controller gave us a vector to a triangular fort and village under VC attack. It wasn't too long before the fort was in sight. The VC had set fire to the grass. The resulting smoke was making it hard to find the "fire arrow" that pointed in the direction from which the attack was coming. Fire arrows were a Special Forces concept to communicate with an aircraft. They had a long, wide board on a pivot, and on the board were several flare pots in the shape of an arrowhead. When the pots were lit at night, the point of the arrow indicated the direction of attack. It usually helped the pilot get ordnance on target quickly, but tonight was the exception.

Even with the smoke masking the triangular fort, we finally could determine that the fire arrow pointed to the nearby village. But without radio communications, we couldn't know if the VC were in the village or just between the village and the fort. The large number of unknowns made it nearly impossible for me to determine where to put the ordnance, except between the village and the fort. Moreover, precise bombing and strafing was required to make sure we didn't cause fratricide on our friends in the village and forces on the ground. If only we had Fox Mike (FM) radios and could talk to the Special Forces inside the fort. I made several low passes without dropping napalm or firing a shot. We could see the winking of automatic weapons coming from inside the fort but no return fire from the outside to indicate where the VC were located. I climbed up above the smoke to get a better view looking down through the smoke and haze. The fire arrow was still pointing in the direction of the village. I even tried slowing down to landing speed and turning on the powerful landing lights, but the result was like driving a car in the fog with high beams on. The landing lights just bloomed on the smoke and made matters worse.

Finally, I made a pass with a better view. The guns chattered, and hopefully some VC died and more withdrew. Those clear vision passes were few and far between that night. When we started running low on gas, after six hours, over the fort, it was time to head for Bien Hoa. We landed after 0400 hours, tired and red eyed from staring hard into the murk and smoke. Later that morning, we learned that the fort held, and they gave us credit for the save. It was Special Forces' opinion that the repeated passes by the B-26 caused the VC to hesitate, not wanting to expose themselves to guns, bombs, and napalm. We chalked up that success to good luck and the B-26's reputation for causing enormous pain.

The following night, there was a similar mission with a different B-26 crew. The pilot, Maj. "Skinny" Ennis, had B-26 combat time in Korea.

He didn't have a nearby village to contend with and thus no ordnance restrictions except for the triangular fort itself. Halfway through expending their ordinance load, one of the engines quit, but Major Ennis made the decision to stay on target until they were Winchester. As mentioned before, the B-26 flies good on one engine, except you always have to turn in the direction of the good engine to make sure the drag of the dead engine doesn't lull you into a steeper turn and more trouble than you can handle. You've also increased the chances that you'll lose the second engine because you're putting a greater load on just one engine. It had to be an interesting second half to the mission. When they returned and debriefed, they put the commander on the spot. Should he court-martial them for stupidity or recommend them for a Distinguished Flying Cross (DFC) for valor? He chose the latter after talking to the Special Forces that were successfully defended as a result of the major's decision to stay and fight on one engine.

Air Commandos were developing a great reputation with the army units we supported. One of the things they really appreciated was our role as the "good humor man." A couple of our pilots visited Special Forces camps to find out how we could improve our support and do a better job. Their answer was "Figure out a way to drop ice cream into our triangular forts." Well, it wasn't long before some of the jump qualified pilots at Bien Hoa had rigged makeshift parachutes to five-gallon ice cream tubs that were available in the mess hall. An AT-28 with an American in the backseat would fly to a fort, role inverted with the cockpit canopy open approaching the fort at low altitude, and drop the ice cream cargo just as the plane crossed the fort boundary. Air-delivered ice cream was enjoyed by all. There was no way to keep the ice cream cold in these very primitive forts, so all five gallons had to be eaten as soon as it landed.

I mentioned that the Helio Courier was evaluated for use in Vietnam by Capt. Jerry Carlisle. A few had been delivered to Bien Hoa and were being used for special missions where runways were not available. One day, I was asked to fly as copilot on a mission to visit Fr. Wa, a Chinese Catholic priest, who led a large group of South Vietnamese in the fight against the VC in the Delta Region. He had proven very effective in denying the VC any local support and was winning, at that time, on all fronts. His operation was down in the southern rice fields of Vietnam. Our mission was to take a CIA agent from the US embassy in Saigon down to Fr. Wa's headquarters and then return him to Saigon. The Helio Courier was the perfect aircraft for the mission because it could land and take off on a dry rice paddy just slightly larger than a postage stamp. When we deplaned next to the small village, I learned that our passenger was carrying a briefcase full of gold bars and coins for Fr. Wa for recruiting and paying his anti-VC soldiers. I noticed that all adult male villagers carried .45-caliber Thompson submachine guns. The .45-caliber bullet doesn't have much range, but it sure is lethal when it hits something. There was a ceremonial lunch with Fr. Wa comprised of many pots of unknown food. Rice was the only recognizable dish! No one in the party got sick or shot, so overall, it was a successful mission!

The next day, the Air Commando detachment commander said he was going to send me along with a Special Forces team supporting an ARVN Battalion in a major effort to dislodge the VC from an area known as the Parrots Beak in northwest South Vietnam. He wanted me to accompany them in the role of forward air controller (FAC) because I was qualified in both the B-26 and AT-28 that would be flying close air support missions for this major push against the VC. I checked out an M-16, lots of ammunition and the necessary radios to communicate with the aircraft. I also suggested to the detachment commander that he should base most of the AT-28s at Da Lat to reduce the flying time, thus getting more sorties on target in a given day, and to keep at least one B-26 airborne continuously to ensure air support was responsive if the ARVN ran into trouble. For this operation, aircraft were taking the place of Division Artillery because of the difficult and precipitous terrain.

Two days before I was to join up with the Special Forces team, a message came from Colonel King informing me that Sheila had given birth to a baby girl, and I was to return home immediately, as my briefing mission had long since been completed. The detachment commander took exception to my returning and replied to Colonel King's message that I was needed at Bien Hoa. Colonel King's reply insisted on my immediate return, noting that I was assigned to the 1st CAG, and ordered me home. That was the end of my opportunity to work directly with the Special Forces.

On my way back to the CONUS, I was directed to stop by Thirteenth Air Force Headquarters at Clark Air Base in the Philippines and give the 1st CAG innovation briefing to Maj. Gen. T. Ross Milton, commander, 13th AF. Evidently, one of the senior officers who received the briefing in Saigon SVN called General Milton and said it was worth his time. I suspect it was Brig. Gen. Rollin P. Anthis that made the suggestion. General Milton was tall and very gracious and spent considerable time going over the various projects, making suggestions, and pontificating about the future of SOF Operations. His officer aide was a very outgoing first lieutenant, William Harvey Low Mullins, with the nickname "Moon" after the cartoon character *Moon Mullins*. Moon was easy to like and a

1957 graduate of West Point. In 1974, Moon and I shared an office during our year as members of the six-man group. Subsequently, Gen. T. Ross Milton earned his fourth star and was assigned as the US senior military representative to NATO. Moon and I had the pleasure of meeting with General Milton in 1974 as members of the six-man group on our swing through Europe and NATO.

I arrived home when my first child, Denise Lynn, turned eleven days old. I also learned that the birth was by an emergency caesarian operation, with Sheila needing help. That was the reason Colonel King was so adamant about my immediate return.

Two weeks' leave was enough to get me acquainted with my daughter and for Sheila to regain her strength. The tempo at both the First Air Commando Wing and the 1st CAG had increased exponentially. Capt. Iwo Kimes had convinced SAWC to get an A-1E bailed to 1st CAG for a COIN evaluation. If truth be told, no evaluation was needed. The A-1E was a combat proven workhorse in Korea and with the 1st VNAF Squadron in Vietnam. On the other hand, the USAF had been bragging about being an all-jet air force for several years, and the A-1E would be another step backward for that slogan and policy. Iwo believed the justification resulting from a thorough evaluation might help convince the staff at TAC and air force that the A-1E was the right way to go. Iwo convinced me that my help was needed on this project, so I lent my support to his all-out effort. While not immediately apparent, the air force eventually embraced the A-1E for a number of missions in Southeast Asia—most notably was the role protecting rescue helicopters going into harm's way to pick up downed aircrew. They were known by their Sandy call sign.

Capt. Dan Grob, supported by all the line B-26 crews, convinced SAWC that the B-26 needed to be upgraded. Their goal was to incorporate some of the features already developed by On Mark Aviation and FAA certified for the civilian market. These refurbished B-26 war birds were already being sold in the commercial marketplace for transporting executives. On Mark, based in California, replaced the original propellers with more-efficient square-bladed propellers with reverse pitch to shorten the landing roll and save tires, incorporated KC-135 wheels and antiskid brakes for safety, modernized the cockpit with improved instrumentation and standardized locations for every switch and lever in the cockpit, and installed modern navigation systems. The On Mark B-26 also provided cockpit air-conditioning for aircrew comfort. I thought the latter was a little too much, but all the commercially available features were approved. After all these modifications were completed, the overall performance was about the same. The improvements in engine/propeller performance were somewhat cancelled out by the additional weight. On the other hand, braking and stopping were vastly improved. I never did get to fly the upgraded aircraft, but those who did swore by it.

There was a period of time when I primarily flew the B-26 in a number of test projects, including a Lazy Dog test. It had been eighty-nine days since I'd flown the AT-28. The operations section at Hurlburt noticed that and scheduled me to fly an AT-28 from Hurlburt to Eglin about thirty miles as the crow flies. I hated those delivery flights because my car would be at Hurlburt and I would be at Eglin, requiring my wife to pick me up there and drive me to Hurlburt to recover my car, a waste of about two hours for the both of us. Nevertheless, I drove to Hurlburt found the plane and checked the weather. The ceiling was holding right at two hundred feet; the minimums for an instrument approach and the visibility was about a half mile. The weather forecaster suggested I wait an hour or so, as he expected the ceiling and visibility to improve a little. After a boring hour or two in Base Ops, the cloud ceiling was still holding steady at two hundred feet. The weather at Eglin AFB was the same and forecast to stay there for the next hour. The nearest alternate airfield, in the event the weather went below minimums, was somewhere in east Texas, so the fuel tanks were full. As Maj. Gen. "Boots" Blesse, Korean War double ace, would say, "No guts, no glory," so I filed the clearance, cranked, and taxied to the end of the runway. Air Traffic Control cleared me for takeoff and to hold at nine thousand feet off of a fix near Crestview, Florida, to await further clearance. That meant a lot of other aircraft had higher priority for landing at Eglin, and I would be hanging in the sky for a long time, waiting for clearance to a ground-controlled approach (GCA). Not a happy thought. Fighter pilots dislike night flying and hate weather, although I've been told the aircraft doesn't know it's dark and wet.

I took off to the south over the gulf with a mild case of vertigo building because I was hanging on the gauges and slow to neutralize the takeoff trim set to compensate for the initial torque of the big radial engine. Think manual trim wheels, not the handy little trim button on the top of the stick of modern jet aircraft. While turning and climbing in the soup toward the holding fix, the red engine failure light blinked and then came on steady. The cobwebs were gone, and all the senses were on full alert! The light's illumination indicated that there were enough steel particles in the engine oil to short out across two poles of a magnet in the oil sump (or oil pan if you relate better to cars).

This didn't necessarily mean the engine was going to fail, just that you needed to get the bird on the ground quickly. Good deal for me. I called ATC, declared an emergency, and requested priority landing at Eglin. They vectored me from my present position (somewhere on the wet side of the beach south of Fort Walton Beach) to a position north of Eglin for a tight turn to final on the north/south runway—just what I was hoping for.

A few minutes later, the engine quit; it had stopped running altogether! By my calculation, I was over the center of Fort Walton Beach. Abandoning the aircraft at that point would likely result in lots of damage on the ground below, and perhaps some people being killed. At 8,000 feet altitude, it didn't bode well for me either, as the AT-28 didn't have an ejection seat, and a manual bailout at that altitude was not the best of alternatives. You know the drill: open the canopy, raise the seat, and lower the flaps to get them out of the way, then unstrap from the seat and dive between the flaps and the elevator, hoping to miss the latter! Pull the D ring quickly because of the downward vector, as well as not knowing your body's orientation because it's very dark at night in the clouds. The plane and I were going down as I attempted air start after air start. I had already called ATC, told them my engine quit in addition to declaring a couple of Maydays. I had asked for a vector to the center of the north/south runway, hoping I would find the clear area around the runway when I broke through the overcast. They gave me the vector and cleared me down to five hundred feet. My response was "Idiots, the engine isn't running, I'm coming all the way to the ground! Advise the tower to get the fire trucks ready." All the AT-28 fuel tanks were fully loaded because of the distance to the alternate airfield. Throttle off, props low, fuel off; then props full, fuel rich, throttle idle to full, over and over—no luck with the air starts. I busted through the overcast at the reported two hundred feet AGL right over the top of a B-52 vertical tail fin. What luck, I was over the SAC Victor Alert area near the north end of the runway. A quick right descending turn, and I landed on the parallel taxiway; the engine sputtered and started to run, so I taxied in.

As Paul Harvey, famous newscaster, would say, "Now for the rest of the story!" The next morning, maintenance personnel checked the engine, replaced the contaminated oil, installed new spark plugs, and did some engine run-ups. They couldn't find anything wrong with the engine! Don't you just love the maintenance response—CND (could not duplicate). Maintenance personnel called me and asked lots of questions. They seemed convinced that I used the red engine failure light to get preferential landing (I did) and faked the engine out (I did not). Being a little cautious, in spite of their suspicions, they scheduled the aircraft for a functional check flight. The functional check pilot called me to review what had really happened. Half believing me, he used all thirteen thousand feet of runway for takeoff. Good thing he did; the engine blew up at full power (fifty-two inches of manifold pressure) on takeoff. It literally came apart in pieces. He still had plenty of runway ahead of him, so he was able to put the aircraft back down safely. End of story!

The word came down from TAC through SAWC that counterinsurgency and the acronym COIN were no longer appropriate. The new politically correct words were "Special Operations" and "Special Operations Forces" (SOF), and so it was. All our briefing charts were out of date and had to be redone. I tried to push back a little with the argument that COIN was specifically the support of an allied government against a forceful internally led effort to overthrow a government. Internally led could also indicate the insurrectionists were receiving support from outside forces hostile to the allied government. Special Operations was an overarching theme that covered everything except conventional forces used in conventional ways. As always, our political masters won the argument. With the benefit of having lived long enough, COIN is once again receiving traction as the word of the realm.

The Lazy Dog test had its interesting moments. Lazy Dogs were essentially the steel core of a .50-caliber bullet with tiny fins spot welded to the blunt end. Allegedly, Lazy Dogs were used in WW II. The concept was to drop these free-falling projectiles from a dispenser as an antipersonnel weapon. The speed of the aircraft in a dive plus the pull of gravity would accelerate these tiny inert bombs to about the speed of a .45-caliber bullet. These steel projectiles were about twice the weight of a pistol or rifle bullet with a sharp point and would easily penetrate any protective clothing or helmet an enemy combatant might be wearing. The dispenser looked like a wedge of cheese with a hinged opening at the back of the wedge. My assignment was to test dispenser operation, and Lazy Dog dispersion and performance from a B-26, while working with the Eglin range personnel to determine the dispersion pattern and projectile effectiveness. For these measurements, range personnel placed several four-by-eight-foot plywood witness panels on the ground in a large oval pattern. My job was to release the Lazy Dogs in a thirty-degree dive at 350 knots IAS so that they would impact the witness panels. Effectiveness against personnel would be based on the Lazy Dog penetration of the plywood panels.

The test was scheduled in the early morning with the 1st ACW providing a navigator to fly the right seat and record all the mission parameters. Two Lazy Dog dispensers were loaded, one on each wing. Everything went as planned. We checked in with Range Control and received permission to make a dry pass over the target and then as many hot Lazy Dog releases as needed. I used the dry pass to practice the procedures developed with the navigator. I was responsible for the dive angle, airspeed, and aiming. His job was to tap me once on the shoulder at five hundred feet above the release altitude, and twice when we reached the release altitude. The early tap gave me a few seconds to correct any aiming errors prior to release. We practiced this procedure three times to make sure we had this relatively simple routine down pat.

On the first live Lazy Dog drop, range personnel said we had released well above the specified release altitude, and the projectiles had impacted short of the witness panels. If anything, the release should have been low because there is a lag in a normal ambient pressure altimeter. The only thing I could think of that would cause a short impact was erroneous ballistic data for the Lazy Dog projectiles. I asked the range personnel if they could measure aircraft altitude with their instrumentation. They responded affirmatively, commenting that the range we were using was equipped with a harp, and they could use the harp to measure altitude. Basically, a harp is a bunch of wires that align with aircraft dive angles. We made two more practice passes, with range personnel calling out release altitude. In all cases, they had us high, while the navigator sitting next to me reading the altimeter said we were low. I thought we were low as well. The next pass was live with the second dispenser, and I was determined to meet the test parameters. The turn onto final was crisp, and down we went. I felt the tap, indicating five hundred feet to go, then two sharp taps, indicating release altitude, but I was waiting for the harp release. More taps on the shoulder with greater intensity. I was just about to pull out to avoid hitting the ground when the harp called release; I did and pulled hard. We probably only cleared the ground by fifty feet, way too close for comfort.

The results from the Lazy Dog test were less than satisfactory from a weapon-effectiveness standpoint. Evidently, the projectiles did not disperse satisfactorily and impacted the ground in a very dense pattern. Further testing was cancelled, and the program scrapped for lack of effectiveness.

Another test that almost did me in was on the .30-caliber gun pod. The .50-caliber pods that were standard equipment on the AT-28 only carried about 150 rounds of ammunition, hardly enough for close air support missions. Someone came up with the idea of replacing the .50-caliber M1 machine gun with a .30-caliber version of the same WW II machine gun. The targets were largely VC personnel, and a .30-caliber projectile would be sufficient for lethality. The smaller gun would take up less room, and the .30-06 cartridges were significantly smaller and lighter; and when belted for feeding a machine gun would bend in a much smaller radius. All of these factors would allow at least 1,500 rounds of .30-caliber ammunition to be loaded in the gun pod under the wing.

The M1 machine gun fired about eight hundred rounds per minute, or thirteen rounds per second. A typical firing burst would be two to three seconds. Most of the missions in Vietnam, up to that point, were flying top cover for our soldiers and coming to their rescue when they were outnumbered and outgunned by the Viet Cong. In these support missions, it was desirable to have the ammunition last as long as fuel would allow the plane to stay over the troops. These M1 machine gun pods would help significantly in that regard.

As the armament and gun expert, it was my job to test the new gun pods. It would be a boring mission, as it takes a lot of gunnery passes to fire out 1,500 rounds at thirteen to twenty-six rounds per pass. I calculated that somewhere between fifty and one hundred climbs and dives would be needed to complete the required testing. To make it worse, the mission was scheduled against one of the raft targets about one hundred miles south of Hurlburt in the Gulf of Mexico. Flying at ten thousand feet above the gulf, the AT-28 would, on a really good day, glide twenty miles if the engine were to quit. Most of the time, the aircraft would be flying well below ten thousand feet. The test aircraft carried two gun pods, so it would not likely glide very far if there were engine problems. The thought of spending several hours in the water with big sharks and hungry barracudas was not pleasant, so I tried not to think about it as I searched the Gulf of Mexico for the assigned raft target.

There it was, about twenty feet by twenty feet with markings to identify it as the correct target. I set up a pattern and started firing short bursts as the AT-28 descended in a shallow dive to about five thousand feet above the waves. Subsequently, the firing passes descended to 2,500-3,000 in a thirty-degree dive, so I could see the bullets impacting on or near the target. It didn't help my mood any to find thin clouds slowly moving into the area, making it more difficult to tell the sky from the water. Up and down, up and down, to be followed by more ups and downs. Soon I was firing two bursts on each pass with enough time for the gun to cool between each firing burst. After what seemed to be a very long time, the guns stopped firing. Either they broke or ran out of ammunition. In either case, it was reason enough to head home and evaluate the condition of both guns—especially the barrels.

After landing and parking the bird, I noticed the crew chief running his hands over the leading edges of the wings and shaking his head. Once out of the cockpit, I walked over and asked what he was looking at. "Captain Pete," he said, "this airplane is shot full of bullet holes—were you low enough to pick up ricochets off the water?"

"No," I replied. "I never went below 2,500 feet." But sure enough, there were at least fifty .30-caliber bullet holes in the wings and engine cowling. Most were key holed, indicating the bullets were tumbling through the air when the aircraft ran into them. Damn, I almost shot myself down! I surely would have if one of the bullets had hit a vital part of the engine like the oil cooler. It is somewhat disturbing, if not humorous, when you realize you've been hit with more bullets in one test mission out of Florida than in two combat tours in Vietnam.

An investigation of the guns showed that the barrels had eroded badly, allowing the burning gasses from the cartridges to blow by the bullets in the barrels, causing the bullets to tumble as they left the end of the barrel. Further analysis suggested that the pod was poorly designed and did not allow sufficient air to flow into the pod and over the gun barrel to help cool it down. Just another day in the office!

A project that I really had my heart in was the development and testing of a survival weapon that could be put into a parachute survival pack that aircrews sit on in the cockpit. The survival pack is connected to the bottom of a backpack parachute and is available to a pilot and crew who had either bailed out or crash-landed. Two contractors responded to phone calls, stating they would provide weapons for the proposed test. Winchester provided a four-barrel shotgun with very short barrels, and Mr. Stoner, inventor of the AR-15, a .223-caliber automatic rifle (AR), provided a short-barreled version of his military rifle. The shotgun, rifle, and appropriate ammunition were provided at no cost by their manufacturers and were returned to them when the test was completed.

Winchester believed the four-barrel 16-gauge shotgun with a folding stock was the best all-around weapon for killing wild game (up to the size of tigers), as well as enemy combatants at a distance of up to seventy-five yards. Winchester came up with four barrels because just about any mechanical or automatic loading action would not yield a weapon that would be short enough to fit into the parachute pack. The AR-15 folks believed their short barrel weapon, already in production except for the shorter barrel and folding wire stock, would best meet our requirements.

The criteria for the survival weapon were simple! It was to enable a downed aircrew to dispatch a squad of six VC or other enemy combatants that were between the survivor and a helicopter pickup. It was no more sophisticated than that, except for the lethality at seventy-five yards. Lethal in the test criteria was that the enemy, when hit, would no longer be able to fight or interfere with the rescue attempt. Field data to confirm the Winchester lethality claim was needed, so two cases of Winchester shotgun shells were sent to Special Forces in Vietnam, asking them to use the shells wherever appropriate and provide documented results. Effectiveness of the AR-15 .223 (5.56 mm) cartridge was well established and documented. Therefore, it was accepted that one 5.56 mm hit in the torso, neck, or head would be considered lethal for the test.

Air Commandos, both officer and enlisted, volunteered to participate in the test. Eight pop-up-on-demand standard target silhouettes were positioned at seventy-five yards from the firing line. Volunteers were asked to shoot both the four-barrel shotgun and the short-barrel AR-15 in the order of their choice. They were required to engage six pop-up targets with each weapon. The time to engage all six targets and the number of lethal hits were scored and recorded, along with the shooter's name and organization. The shooter's weapon preference was also recorded. Engaging six targets required the shooter to break open the shotgun to reload, which was included in the elapsed time. Reloading was not normally required with the AR-15 because its detachable magazine carried enough ammunition to be effective against six targets. The second and follow-on targets were popped up singly while the shooter was engaging the previous target. One disadvantage to the shooter in this test is that he or she received no feedback from the target. A more realistic test would have had the target fall if hit or provide a sound or flashing light, indicating a lethal hit.

There were about two hundred shooters in the first part of the test. In general, shooters preferred the shotgun because they didn't have to aim—just point, and the pattern compensated for minor aiming errors. Time required for engaging all six targets, as well as achieving lethal hits on targets, also favored the shotgun.

The second portion of the test required a shooter to engage a silhouette target through thick brush to determine if this might be a factor that favored one survival weapon over the other. For this test, a single silhouette was placed behind twenty feet of thick scrub and vines. It was difficult to see the target, so an aiming point was placed at the front of the scrub and about twenty feet in front of the shooter in a small clearing. The AR-15 would be fired first, followed by the shotgun. Then the target and aim point would be moved to ensure the brush didn't get shot out, thus giving an advantage to one weapon over the other. After each shot in this phase, the target was scored, and each hit was marked and labeled. A series of fifty firings of one AR-15 round and one shotgun shell were fired in this phase of the test. The brush test also favored the four-barrel shotgun because a number of the AR-15 rounds never reached the target. It was assumed that this was as a result of the lightweight and pointy 55-grain 5.56 mm projectiles being deflected as they passed through the heavy brush. Shotgun pellets may have also been deflected, but there were enough pellets in a shell for at least two to find the target. I did all the brush phase testing to ensure range unfamiliarity did not skew the test results.

While the range tests were being conducted, documentation from Special Forces in Vietnam supported the lethality claims by Winchester for the 00 buckshot at seventy-five yards and greater distances. Polishing up the final report was all there was left to do. The rest was up to the air force.

The air force approved my Bootstrap application with the University of Omaha (now the University of Nebraska at Omaha). Bootstrap was an air force program offering officers and enlisted personnel who were thirty credits shy of a degree a six-month sabbatical to earn a bachelor's degree in residence. I had been going to night school and taking correspondence courses for nine years and had finally reached the point where an application for Bootstrap was credible. The University of Nebraska accepted me and honored enough of my credits so that only thirty more were needed to earn a degree. If the air force didn't have the bad habit of reassigning me in the middle of night-school courses, the degree opportunity would have come much earlier. The summer semester started on July 5, and plans were made for Sheila and daughter Denise to stay with her parents in Mesa, Arizona, until the fall semester began in September.

Out of the blue, higher headquarters announced that it was permissible to log combat time for Air Commando combat missions flown in South Vietnam. The written directive went even further, stating that anyone that thought they had flown a mission that would be worthy of a Distinguished Flying Cross (DFC) could submit a nomination for the DFC, and it would be favorably considered. Many ran for paper and pencil to submit themselves for the DFC. I had strong reservations about saying that I deserved such a coveted decoration. Awards and Decorations Regulations required a supervisor or commander to submit individuals or groups of individuals for medals. I couldn't muster the chutzpah to submit myself for a DFC and never did.

The Survival Weapon Test Report was in rough draft, and I was on the rifle range collecting data on the short-barrel AR-15 accuracy at one hundred and two hundred yards to fill in a report table when the call came. Mississippi senator, John Stennis, chairman of the Senate Armed Services Subcommittee on Preparedness, was holding hearings on the serviceability, reliability, and utility of COIN aircraft. It wasn't clear whether he had selected four Air Commandos by name or if Brigadier General Prichard had nominated us to testify before the Senate Subcommittee. The 1st CAG found me at the rifle range and told me I had one hour to pack and report to the flight line to board an aircraft taking us to Washington DC. Sheila and I were to depart for Arizona and Bootstrap in two days, and she was not exactly thrilled with my departure, leaving her to do most, if not all, of the packing.

It was rumored that Senator Stennis was concerned about information on COIN aircraft contained in a letter written by Capt. Jerry Shank to his wife. Jerry was killed flying an AT-28B mission in Vietnam. I had met Jerry but really didn't know him. He received his training while I was at 1st CAG, and he arrived at Bien Hoa after my second tour ended. Apparently, he crashed while attacking a sampan. Data from the accident report indicated he had fired rockets against a sampan and then reattacked with .50-caliber machine guns against the same or another sampan. Another AT-28B pilot on the same mission said he saw the machine gun bullets initially impact past the sampan and then come back into the target. To me, this indicated that he forgot to change the gun sight depression angle from the rocket setting to a gun setting. Gun sights were always harmonized to a setting of zero mill radians. All other aircraft-delivered ordnance required a setting greater than zero because of gravity and the typically higher altitudes and ranges for rockets and bombs. If Jerry fired rockets first, he would have a sight depression of approximately seventeen mill radians. Leaving this sight depression in for a strafing attack would cause bullets to impact past the target. The only way to walk the bullets back to the target would be to "bunt" by pushing the nose over, significantly increasing the dive angle, which would cause a greater loss of altitude, making it almost impossible to pull out of the dive without hitting the ground. This latter scenario seems to explain what may have happened in the fog and urgency of combat.

U.S. News & World Report obtained copies of Jerry's letters to his wife and published the following excerpts, with "bird" referring to the AT-28B.

"The bird is great it takes a beating."

"The bird is great everyone is feeling good."

Subsequently, *Time Magazine* published considerably more of the same letter, including a number of emotional passages typical of a man in combat who is separated from his family for an extended period. Moreover, *Time* editors took the liberty of changing the wording in Jerry's handwriting as follows:

"The bird is great if it takes the beating." (*Time* editors inserted the word "if" in Jerry's handwriting.)

"Morale is great everyone is feeling good." (*Time* editors substituted "moral" for "bird," again in Jerry's handwriting.)

When I read those magazines' articles, I was shocked at the differences in the wording. Perhaps we would learn the truth about what Capt. Jerry Shank really wrote at Senator Stennis's hearing?

Our gang of four arrived at the Pentagon early the next morning and was escorted to Gen. Curt LeMay's office. He was the air force chief of staff at that time and had a reputation for being a demanding leader and inveterate cigar smoker. When we walked in and saluted, he had his feet on his huge desk and was smoking a large cigar. He seemed somewhat gruff when he said, "When you go over to the Senate tomorrow, all I want you to do is tell the truth!" That was a big relief, and I immediately gained an enormous respect for the man. Then he said, "Let me instruct you on what the truth is!"

My thought then was, *Here it comes!*

General LeMay went on to explain, "The truth is hardly ever a simple yes or no! You have to make sure you qualify your answers with how many missions you flew and how many times something happened. For example, if you're asked if you ever had an engine failure, and you did, the answer must go something like this: 'I flew 125 missions and had one engine failure but managed to make it back to Bien Hoa' or whatever really happened!" I felt good again about our chief and about the air force.

General LeMay got up from behind his desk and said, "Secretary Zuckert wants to meet you boys!" The secretary's office was just one door down the hall. General LeMay knocked on the door and walked in, introducing us by name to Mr. Eugene M. Zuckert. What happened in the chief's office was repeated here. The secretary emphasized that we were to tell the truth and that the air force welcomed the opportunity to let the Congress know what we were doing and how the equipment was holding up. "We have nothing to hide," he said in closing. Again, I was proud of my air force and its top leaders! As General LeMay walked us out to the E-ring hallway, he mentioned that he was sending his judge advocate general (JAG), a major general and the senior air force lawyer, to accompany us to Senator Stennis's hearing, just in case some of the senators tried to intimidate us. As it turned out, this was not a good move.

The next morning, our gang of four was standing outside the hearing room, with the JAG mothering over us and telling us not to worry. When we were called into the hearing room, Senator Stennis zeroed in on the judge advocate general, asking what he was doing at the hearing. Not being satisfied with anything the JAG had to say, the senator had the JAG escorted out, protesting all the way. As it turned out, he wasn't needed; all the members of the subcommittee treated us with the utmost courtesy and respect.

Senator Stennis called me to the witness chair first and said his subcommittee wanted to ask a few questions to get to the bottom of the allegations made by the magazines *Time* and *U.S. News & World Report*. I boldly asked if I was allowed a question. In his folksy Southern drawl, he allowed that a question would be just fine. I asked which of the two versions of Captain Shank's letters, published in *U.S. News & World Report* and then *Time*, were a faithful reproduction of his actual letters. The senator responded as he held up some papers, "We subpoenaed the letters, and I have them right here. The *U.S. News & World Report* got it right!"

I quickly threw out a second question, "How could *Time* change the letters in Jerry's handwriting?"

Senator Stennis responded with "I asked them that same question, and they said that's what Jerry meant to say." So much for truth in reporting! The liberal media was starting to turn against the war as combat operations were beginning to grow and expand. Nearly all forms of media were fanning antiwar sentiment.

The questions for me lasted about four hours. They were honest questions dealing with equipment and equipment shortages, moral, leadership, and living conditions at Bien Hoa. I was happy they didn't ask me about the quality of pistol ammunition.

Our testimony before the committee was over in two days. We returned to Hurlburt that night just in time for me to pack a trailer full of our belongings for school. Our days at 91A Pine had come to an end.

Off to the University of Nebraska

Interstate 10 was only partially completed at that time, so it was a hard drive through the southern states to Mesa, Arizona, where Sheila's parents, as well as her brother and sister, lived with their spouses. With only a day to get Sheila and Denise settled, it was off to Omaha and the University of Nebraska at Omaha.

There I met a number of Bootstrappers cramming thirty-plus semester hours into one summer and one fall semester. A number of core courses were common for many of us, and we became good friends. First Lieutenant Joe Moore, an F-86F instructor in my squadron at Williams AFB, Arizona, was there as well. At that time, he was stationed in the United Kingdom flying the F-101 Voodoo in a tactical nuclear NATO mission. Because the school was only temporary duty (TDY), he left his family behind in England. Some of my fellow Bootstrappers had already located apartments and were able to steer me to a large house with many bedrooms owned by a travelling salesman who hawked envelopes and stationary. He rented rooms to college students to keep the house occupied while he was on the road and to pay the bills. The price was right, and there were plenty of tables throughout the house that were perfect for studying and doing homework. To my surprise, Omaha was hotter and more humid than Fort Walton Beach, Florida, and the house was not air-conditioned.

I cannot think of an easier time in my life than being a university student in residence. I could have worked two jobs and still carried a full load. I hadn't realized that a three-credit course required only three hours of lecture each week. Twenty-one credit hours only required twenty-one classroom hours, but a classroom hour was only forty-five minutes long for a total of sixteen actual hours a week. At the Air Commandos and 1st CAG, an eighty-hour week was routine. In combat, it's 24/7 and sleep when you can. I wanted to graduate with honors and a perfect 4.0 grade point average. I studied hard, which made the tests seem all too easy, and 4.0 was never a challenge.

During the break between semesters, I picked up Sheila and Denise, and we settled into a nice affordable apartment I had rented in advance. The headquarters for several large insurance companies were located in Omaha. Because of this, two or three young single women occupied all but two of the twenty-four apartments in our apartment building. It was a good thing I didn't live there before Sheila arrived, or there would have been some explaining to do. The apartment was air-conditioned, and with Sheila there, life only got simpler and easier. Shortly after the Christmas holidays, the semester ended, and it was time to drive back to Eglin AFB and reality. A bad storm was forecast to hit Omaha the day after graduation, so I skipped the walk across the stage, and we headed home a day early with diploma in hand. The storm finally caught up with us in northern Alabama, and cars were strewn all over the interstate median. The only thing that kept us on the highway was the heavily loaded trailer with all of our possessions, putting lots of tongue weight on the trailer hitch and thus the rear wheels. It was February 1965 and good to be back in Fort Walton Beach, Florida.

Back to the First Air Commando Wing

I found temporary quarters on Eglin AFB and reported to the 1st CAG. There I learned that, while gone, I had been transferred back to the Air Commando Wing as an AT-28B/C/D instructor pilot. I suspected that Colonel Kruge (who replaced Colonel King as commander before I departed for school) didn't really care much for me and engineered the transfer. I also learned that Capt. Brooks Morris polished up the Survival Gun Test Report and had it published in his name, without even a mention that I had conducted the entire test and drafted the report. When asked about taking credit for my work, Brooks said Colonel Kruge wanted to get the report out, and putting his name on it seemed like the thing to do. I was really disappointed in Brooks for "stealing" my work, but it was water under the bridge and time to move on. Years later, after my retirement, I discovered a letter in my files written by Colonel Kruge to Air Force Personnel. In his letter, Colonel Kruge persuasively requested that I be allowed to continue in 1st CAG and that he would personally ensure that I would get plenty of flying time testing combat systems. Air Force Personnel denied his request, stating that I needed to spend more time flying in operational units.

Most of the faces had changed. Col. Harry "Hiene" Aderholt had replaced Col. Chester Jack. Hiene came from the same mold as Ben King, who had been promoted to brigadier general and had taken command of the Air Force Safety Center at Norton AFB, California. This platform gave General King plenty of opportunity to visit South Vietnam to check on "flying safety issues" and, while there, fly combat missions.

My only job was to be a line instructor pilot; no more armament maintenance, no more development, just fly. Because I hadn't flown in six months, I received a recurrency check ride, which was passed with flying colors. There was something new under General Sweeney, commander of TAC. Pilots were required to know, by rote memory, all the important emergency procedures and to be able to write them down verbatim. These were called "boldface" procedures because they were written in bold capital letters in the emergency portion of the pilot's checklist. The instructor who gave me the recurrency check handed me a sheet with the emergency procedure titles and a numbered line for each step in each procedure. I put some words down on each line and failed the test. After a quick study of the Dash-1, I retested and passed. It's easy when the rules of the game are known. However, there was still the TAC Regulation that stipulated an instructor pilot (IP) must have ten recent hours in the aircraft prior to being placed on orders as an IP. The squadron commander said, "I need you as an instructor right now—go get nine more hours tonight!"

My first call was to Sheila to tell her I wouldn't be home until after midnight. Then I filed a flight plan for MacDill AFB, Florida, near Tampa. The Transient Alert at MAFB provided quick turnarounds and was a favorite cross-country destination for the 1st ACW. They knew a lot about AT-28s. The weather officer advised me there was a squall line just east of Panama City, but he thought I could pick my way through the thunderstorms imbedded in the front. Takeoff was just before dark with clear skies. It wasn't long before I could see lightning bolts illuminating towering cumulus clouds ahead. That was one of the few good things about night flying! You could easily spot the storms that could hurt you. I had filed an IFR clearance because of the weather to be penetrated. I called Flight Service on the UHF radio and requested permission to deviate from course and altitude to avoid thunderstorms. My request was granted with the comment there were no other aircraft within miles of my flight plan, implying there were no other stupid pilots aloft. In just a few minutes, I was in the heart of the squall line, being tossed about like a feather. My eyes were glued to the gauges, noting that up and down drafts were throwing the AT-28 1,500 feet above and below the assigned altitude. Trying to hold a fixed altitude was not possible, so I just kept a level attitude and let it happen. Helmets were not an issue item in those days, and my ball cap protected head was bouncing off the canopy left and right, so I lowered the seat to prevent serious injury by getting a little more separation between my head and the canopy. It wasn't long before a serious case of vertigo was building in my head from all the turbulence. "Just hang on to the gauges," I kept telling myself over the pounding of the hail on the fuselage! The squall line and I were moving in the same direction, so it was going to take a lot longer to penetrate. I thought about reversing course but ditched that idea. A level attitude on the attitude indicator was about all I could handle! With a heavy dose of vertigo, a thirty-degree bank 180-degree turn was out of the question. Altitude was now varying plus and minus two thousand feet. Thoughts of bailing out before I succumbed to the vertigo and became a smoking hole in the ground were starting to creep into my thought process when at last the plane squirted out of the storm into a clear and starry night. I got back on course and altitude and reported to Flight Service that I was clear of the storm and back on the assigned flight plan. His "roger" seemed more surprised than professional. An hour or so later, I landed at MacDill and taxied to the ramp in front of Base Operations. I sauntered into Base Operations with all the bravado that I could have mustered under the circumstances, remembering the line, "Don't let them see you sweat."

The officer on duty in Base Operations turned out to be a gray-haired master sergeant wearing Command pilot wings, which signified that he had over three thousand hours of flying time and fifteen years of rated service. I immediately pegged him as one of our WW II heroes who was separated by the Army Air Corps when they deeply cut personnel at the end of the war. Most likely, he accepted enlisted status in lieu of separation so he could reach retirement at twenty or more years of service. He could have also been recalled for Korea and then reverted to enlisted rank to reach retirement. I politely asked what he flew. "Fighters" was the crisp reply! He then asked if he could provide transportation to the VOQ.

"Negative," I said. "All I need is a Hershey bar and a Coke, and I'll be heading back to Hurlburt."

I found some nourishment, filled out a flight plan, and handed it to the sergeant for approval. I was still a few months shy of earning my own clearance authority, so I couldn't legally sign the flight plan myself. The weather officer had put bizarre comments all over the flight plan, but I'd already been there; there was nothing new he could offer. Besides, storms normally lose energy the longer they go without sunshine.

Start, taxi, complete engine checks, call for clearance, and take off. The tower said there was a weather update from Base Operations and patched them in. Base Operations advised that Hurlburt weather, for the time of my arrival, was deteriorating and was forecast to be below minimums with the closest alternate at England AFB, Louisiana, and asked, "What are your intentions?"

After a short deliberation, I responded, "Cancel my flight plan, I'll spend the night." I checked with the weather officer for the next day's weather and discovered Hurlburt was in the clear and expected to stay that way for the next couple of days. I asked the master sergeant with Command pilot wings what the hell he was up to, giving me that phony forecast for Hurlburt. He looked me in the eye and calmly replied, "When I saw the look on your face as you walked in, there was no way I was going to let you fly back through that storm! I also checked your aircraft and saw the hail damage. You're lucky to be alive!" I thanked him and spent the night. Instructor pilot status for me would have to wait another day.

Teaching experienced pilots how to fly the AT-28 was not very stressful. Air Commando student pilots all knew how to fly; our task was just a matter of getting them familiar with the critical airspeeds and limits of a new but very forgiving airplane. However, you always had to be alert for danger. One of our student pilots was having trouble in formation, especially night and weather formation. He had failed a check ride, failed the recheck, and was up for elimination from the AT-28B. In such cases, pilots with limitations were sent to another aircraft, usually a transport aircraft that required two pilots. This meant that a new pilot could fly as a copilot for an extended period of time. The student pilot in question was a West Point graduate; hence the squadron commander was hesitant to wash him out and wanted another opinion, so I was scheduled to fly with him on a night weather formation flight.

The pilot's problem was somewhat simple but very dangerous. When a flight or element leader turns toward a wingman, the wingman maintains the same position on the wing and stays in the same plane with his leader. When a leader turns away from a wingman, the wingman remains level and slightly back of the leader while matching fuselage and wing planes. When the leader rolls out of the turn-away, the wingman slides away to maintain wingtip clearance and returns back into fingertip formation. The only deviation from these standard procedures is called "show formation," when wingmen always fly in fingertip no matter what maneuvers the leader performs. When a wingman stays beneath the leader after the leader returns to level flight, there is a serious danger to both the leader and the opposite-side wingman. This was our pilot's problem. He continued to match lead's fuselage by flying beneath his leader after the turn-away was completed.

Night weather is worse than either night or weather alone. On our elimination recheck flight, the student stayed under lead's aircraft on the first turn-away and return to level flight. In a turn in our direction, the student started to slide into the opposite-side wingman. I took control of the aircraft and flew it back into the proper position. The same thing happened again and again. After landing and debriefing, I wrote my report, recommending the pilot be reassigned out of the 1st ACW and to an aircraft with both a pilot and copilot. The next day, the squadron commander grilled me on the pilot's performance, asking me to change my recommendation. I held my ground, responding, "Sir, he is going to kill someone sooner or later, and I don't want that blood on my hands. He should not be allowed to continue flying the AT-28B!" Good intentions saved his career but ultimately cost him and his Vietnamese passenger their lives. He crashed three months later on a combat mission in Vietnam. I learned a valuable lesson from that experience: be fair but tough on standards and have the courage to do and stand for what is right!

Colonel Aderholt decided to elevate me to the position of wing weapons officer (WWO). A WWO is responsible for keeping up with all that is new in ordnance, fuzes, and tactics for every assigned type of aircraft and ensuring that this information is passed on to all pilots in the First Air Commando Wing. It was a surprise to me, and I was honored to be selected. As soon as the training for WWO was completed, I would be replacing a good friend, Capt. Glen Frick, who was doing a great job but lacked the in-depth knowledge that I had assimilated over the years as 1st ACW armament and electronics officer and at 1st CAG. Glen had just returned from training at the Fighter Weapons School and had initiated a project to develop a Dash 34 manual for the AT-28 and B-26 aircraft. The air force directed prime contractors to develop Dash 34 manuals for all modern fighter and bomber aircraft; however, the obsolescent AT-28 and B-26 were not included in this effort. A Dash 34 manual described all the weapons' release and firing modes and associated switchology for each aircraft. In addition, it included detailed descriptions of all the weapons and munitions approved for delivery by a specific aircraft.

Modern aircraft went through a rigorous process called Seek Eagle that analyzed weapons release parameters and then tested those parameters in flight. During these flight tests, a second aircraft flying loose formation filmed the actual weapons releases to ensure dropped munitions and forward firing ordnance would operate properly and would not damage the aircraft employing the ordnance. In the 1st CAG and 1st ACW, we just hung stuff on the pylons and tried it out. Most of the time, everything worked as expected.

Aside from IP duties, Glen and I put considerable effort into building Dash 34s for the AT-28 and B-26. The pilots were happy to have a consolidated source for all this important information. Flying became the way we relaxed. One memorable flight consisted of four AT-28s to MacDill AFB, with an overnight, and returning the next morning. As I recall, it was with four students and four instructors. The students were in the front seat both ways. On the return, Capt. Glen Frick was the IP in the lead aircraft, Capt. Dick Secord was the student in another aircraft, and I was in the fourth aircraft with my student, Capt. "Charlie" Brown, in the front seat. The flight broke into two elements for a little air combat maneuvering as we entered the eastern end of Tyndall AFB, Florida, airspace. Tyndall is located just outside Panama City and surrounded by nothing but swamp and pine trees to the north and gulf water looking south. After pulling some Gs and getting the heart rate up, the flight resumed its homeward journey. We were in tight formation for student training. As such, a wingman always has his eyes glued on the leader. Captain Secord was our element lead when, all of a sudden, his aircraft started descending and falling behind. Then came the "Mayday, Mayday, my engine's quit" radio transmission! The formation was right over the beach when the engine failure occurred. The rest of us circled overhead as we watched Captain Secord put his aircraft down gently on the sand just a few dozen feet from the gulf water's edge. He and his IP exited the stricken aircraft and waved, indicating they were OK! Lead reported the aircraft's position to Air Traffic Control and the Tyndall Tower. Dick retired as a major general, and our paths crossed several times over the coming years.

Colonel Aderholt decided that I needed the education offered by the Fighter Weapons School (FWS), at Nellis AFB, Nevada. I was scheduled to attend the next class. Upon arriving at Nellis, I was informed that the first phase test of the course was in three days and would cover the F-100 fire control system, the APG-30 radar, the M39 20 mm cannon, and harmonization procedures. I would be held responsible for all the course material covered in the first phase, even though the three days attended prior to the exam would only cover harmonization. That seemed unfair! I asked for all the course materials and burned the midnight oil studying the subject matter to be tested. I didn't want to get a bad grade or to look like a dunce. Fortunately, not much had changed on the F-100 fire control systems from the time when I maintained them at Willie, and Luke and I felt comfortable going into the test.

Immediately after the test, I was called into Mr. Vern Spradling's office. Mr. Spradling was the dean of the FWS and served as a fighter pilot in the air defense role during WW II. He was assigned to defend, of all places, Hoover Dam near Las Vegas. In the office with Mr. Spradling were the chief of Academics and the chief instructor for the first phase. They wasted no time in getting to the point, accusing me of cheating! They wanted to know where I got a copy of the exam. How else could I score 100 percent on the test without attending the first seven days of the course, not to mention never having flown the F-100! This was quite a shock to me and put me off balance for a few seconds. I fought back, asserting that I did not have a copy of the exam and invited an oral quiz on the phase from all three of my accusers. They invited in a couple of more instructors and fired away with a barrage of questions. I initially gave them the easy answer to each question and then went into as much technical depth as I could remember, well beyond their knowledge, just to add to my credibility. After about an hour of questions and answers, they gave up and admitted I was an expert on the F-100 fire control and radar systems. Nonetheless, I was fighting mad and vowed to myself to score 100 percent on all the remaining phases. This I accomplished, plus spending some time in the base hobby shop, making training aides to replace the ones the school used, which incorrectly demonstrated the concepts being taught. To be fair, I should mention that I traveled to and from Nellis by commercial air and didn't have a rental car to drive. Hence, I wasn't distracted by all the temptations in Las Vegas just a few miles down the road from Nellis. When the FWS course ended, I turned out to be the second student to score 100 percent on all academic tests. The first was Capt. Ron Catton, a student in an earlier class, now flying with the Thunderbirds. Oddly enough, Ron Catton was forbidden to drive his Corvette while attending the FWS after speeding on the base and trying to elude the security police. So we both had to walk everywhere we went on base. Later, Ron and I became friends and met again in Vietnam.

After returning to Hurlburt, Sheila, Denise, and I settled into a new house that we purchased while it was under construction. It was a lovely three-bedroom, two-bath bungalow on a quiet street across from Black Bayou with access rights to the water. It was a really big step for us, but before committing to buy the house, I had asked Brigadier General Prichard if I would be in the 1st ACW for another two or three years. He laughed and said, "Pete, you're not going anywhere, buy the house!"

Shortly after moving into our new home, I received a one-year assignment to Waterpump, a covert operation in Thailand based not too far from the Laotian border. Waterpump involved AT-28B/C/Ds and had two primary missions: the overt mission was training Thai pilots to fly the AT-28 and to employ all the various weapons it could carry up to US standards, and the covert mission was interdicting the infamous Ho Chi Minh trail where it wound through Laos. It had been over two years since my last combat tour, and I was getting stale. It was time to get back into the fight. Here I was, instructing pilots on how to be effective and survive in combat, while I was woefully out of date.

Prior to deployment, I flew a number of range missions with other pilots who were also scheduled for deployment to Waterpump. It was really good training, and if you didn't score above 90 percent in strafing, you lost money.

Colonel Aderholt was promoting a plan for Air Force SOF on a global scale. Capt. Jim Auman was doing most of the writing, and I was drawn into the project as a critical editor and "Napoleon's corporal" as an additional job until I departed for Thailand. In other words, if I didn't understand the plan, I had to rewrite it. The concept for the plan was well thought out, but it reached too far. Moreover, the Vietnam War had escalated well beyond WW II aircraft capabilities. While that plan was not aircraft specific, WW II workhorses like the C-47 and B-26 were the cheapest to give to third-world nations and easiest for them to maintain. Perhaps, if such a plan was in place in the late fifties, many of the Cold War insurgencies could have been snuffed out in their infancy.

Late one Friday night in mid-May, while at home, relaxing on the couch and watching TV, Sheila called me to the phone. The command post (CP) was calling. The CP duty officer informed me that I had orders directing me to report immediately to the FWS, Nellis AFB. It was a TDY assignment pending permanent change of station (PCS) orders effective July 1, 1965. The latter meant that TAC didn't have enough money to pay the moving costs until the start of the new fiscal year, on July 1. Congress did not move the start of the fiscal year to October 1 until many years later. The reporting date was Tuesday, barely enough time to pack our belongings and drive to Las Vegas.

I went back to the couch, with Sheila following closely behind, asking me what the CP wanted. She had learned that late-night calls from the CP usually meant I was being sent somewhere on very short notice. I relayed to her what I had been told. Her surprising comment was "You're drunk!"

My response to her was "You may be right about me being drunk, but that's what the duty officer said!" It was not a good night; Sheila had really come to like our new home and wasn't happy about the thought of pulling up and moving again. She insisted that I call the CP back to confirm what I had been told. The duty officer was a little annoyed at my request but confirmed the assignment to the FWS. I, or we, would be leaving in two days.

Saturday was supposed to be a relaxing day, working with Glen Frick on our draft Dash 34s for the AT-28 and B-26. General Prichard's Secretary, Scotty Russell, called, informing me that the general wanted me in his office pronto. When I reported to General Prichard, he informed me that he was going to stop the move to Nellis and the FWS. I mustered up enough courage to ask the General not to intervene, adding that I had spent five years with SAWC and its subordinate commands and this was an unexpected opportunity to get back into the real air force. More importantly, modern fighters were being introduced into the Vietnam War at an increasingly faster pace, and it would be helpful if they had someone with SOF combat experience to help them understand the nature of the enemy and the conflict. The general wasn't pleased, but he agreed not to kill the assignment.

Back at the house, Sheila was packing, while Glen and I finished our work on the draft Dash 34 for AT-28 and B-26 aircraft. He asked if he could buy our house. Deal! The house was sold that morning, and we were free and clear of the debt without ever making a payment. In hindsight, we were foolish to sell the house. In less than ten years, it was worth more than five times the original cost and would have had lease tenants continuously due to the growth of the 1st ACW and missions at Eglin AFB. Monday morning, we put all our furniture in storage and pulled out of our dream home driveway. My Morris Minor was in the shop for repairs and would have to wait until there was time to come back and drive it to Nellis.

I had deeply mixed emotions leaving 1st ACW, 1st CAG, and SAWC. In those organizations, captains were given enormous responsibility and expected to perform and deliver. Captains in COIN, by and large, had more responsibility and authority than lieutenant colonels in standard air force squadrons and wings. On the other hand, the air force had at least thirty-six fighter wings based in Europe, the Pacific, and the United States, compared to a single SOF Wing of three squadrons. SOF was important, but merely a sideshow compared to the forces deterring the Soviet Union.

Years later, the 1st ACW would install me in the Air Commando Hall of Fame, a great honor, considering others who served and had also received the honor!

Lessons Learned

Challenges are to be met, not avoided.

Most people have more ability than they realize, until challenged!

Challenge after challenge in the crucible of life,
and combat will temper our steel.

Know your job better than anyone else! Understand the
critical activities and monitor those above all others!

Willingly volunteer for the tough, demanding jobs!

When you are handed a challenge, grab it and
make the right things happen!

Never compromise your integrity or the truth!

Always have the courage to do and stand up for what is right.

Higher education is important! Avail yourself
of night and correspondence courses.

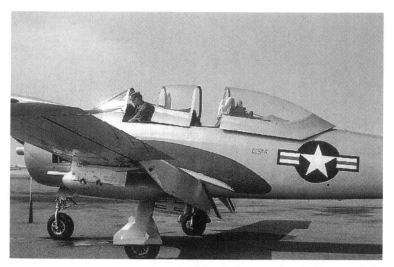

Capt. Pete & AT-28, Hurlburt AFB, FL

Capt. Pete & Sheila enroute to Airport, Departing for Far East

Lt. Col. Gleason awards Capt. Pete Commendation Medal, Bien Hoa, SVN

Air Commando Pete, Bien Hoa, SVN

AT-28 & armament, Bien Hoa, SVN

B-26 & armament, Bien Hoa, SVN

AT-28 P-2 Test, WP Grenades, Hurlburt AFB, FL

Capt. Pete 2nd Combat Tour, Bien Hoa, SVN

Flying AT-28, Soc Trang, SVN, Tuffy the Tiger

October 13, 1961

NATIONAL SECURITY ACTION MEMORAANDUM No.104

TO: THE SECRETARY OF STATE
            THE SECRETARY OF DEFENSE
            THE DIRECTOR OF CENTRAL INTELLIGENCE

SUBJECT: Southeast Asia

The President on October 11, 1961, directed the following actions be taken:

1. Make preparation for the publication of the white paper on North Vietnamese aggression against South Viet Nam which is now being drafted in the Department of State.

2. Develop plans for possible action in the Viet Nam ICC based upon the white paper, preliminary to possible action under paragraph 3 below.

3. Develop plans for presentation of the Viet Nam case in the United Nations.

4. Subject to agreement with the Government of Viet Nam which is now being sought, introduce the Air Force "Jungle Jim" Squadron into Viet Nam for the initial purpose of training Vietnamese forces.

5. Initiate guerrilla ground action, including use of U.S. advisors if necessary, against Communist aerial resupply missions in the Tchepone area.

6. General Taylor should undertake a mission to Saigon to explore ways in which assistance of all types might be more effective.

CHAPTER 5

Fighter Weapons School

We'd only been on the road for one day, when after checking her calendar, Sheila exclaimed, "They want you there Thursday evening for a Friday morning meeting, and Monday is a holiday—Memorial Day!" She went on to say, "I'll bet you don't do anything until Tuesday. Why don't you call them and see if you can report in Monday evening?" There was no point in arguing, so at the next stop for gas, I placed a long-distance call to Las Vegas from somewhere in the middle of Texas. After many handoffs, I finally had Maj. Richard Merkling on the phone and asked about the possibility of reporting on Monday due to the holiday weekend. After checking with the project officer, he said, "That is not possible. We need everyone here for the kickoff meeting on Friday!" As an aside, Maj. Richard Merkling retired as a lieutenant general in July 1983.

The 1961 Chevy Impala was pushed hard to deliver Sheila and Denise to her parents' home in Mesa. I spent a little time there and then drove to Nellis for the 0800 meeting on Friday. Major Merkling, who was heading up the FWS Test Organization, was there, but he wasn't in charge. A tall self-assured major, resembling *Sky King* from WW II comic strips, was leading the meeting. Evidently, the air force deputy chief of staff for operations (DCSOPS) office symbol AF/XOO had concluded that a training program was required to reorient air force general officers heading for Vietnam from nuclear to conventional operations. This was understandable because after nuclear bombs were used to end WW II in the Pacific, nuclear weapons were at the forefront of air force operational thinking, planning, and training. Knowledge of conventional weapons, tactics, and employment was a lost art and largely forgotten. The responsibility for conducting this one-week training program on conventional operations was levied on the FWS.

Two new guys were brought in to augment the FWS cadre, Capt. Ray McNally, and me. Ray was also a FWS graduate and an expert in tactical nuclear weapons designed to be delivered by tactical fighters—the course wasn't going to be totally conventional. I was assigned the responsibility for teaching conventional weapons, weapon's effects, weaponeering, and targeting. It would take a full day of lectures to cover all this subject material. Hundreds of 35 mm slides would be required to adequately cover and convey the necessary information.

After reviewing the syllabus and noting there was nothing about night close air support (CAS) and night interdiction, I asked when these subjects would be covered. Maj. Sky King running the meeting responded with, "We ran a test several months ago that proved night CAS and night interdiction are not possible with century series jets."

The fight was on, and it was time for pushback. I responded with "The VC attack at night, reposition at night, move at night, and resupply under cover of darkness. Further, I suspect you day fighter guys were not really motivated to find a way to support soldiers and marines at night. If you're not willing to fly and fight at night, you might as well stay at home."

Maj. Sky King said, "Our test report was published and well received throughout PACAF, TAC, and USAFE (the three regional fighter commands)."

My response was "If you can have an open mind, I'll show you how to conduct night operations. Moreover, if you don't teach night operations, I suspect this course will be short lived. We simply cannot let the Viet Cong own the night!" There were no other opinions expressed about night operations by the rest of the FWS cadre identified to lecture in the proposed senior officers' course.

To their credit, a few months later, the FWS ran another night close support test using parachute suspended flares, the same way it was being done by Air Commandos, and found that high performance jet aircraft could operate effectively and safely at night.

The next hand grenade from Maj. Sky King was that the GO course was going to be presented as a play. The play would be in three acts. Mission tasking, intelligence briefing on the target set, and enemy defenses would constitute the first act. The second act would cover mission planning, weapons selection, and weapons effects with a back and forth between planners and the mission commander. The third act would consist of a formal briefing to a hypothetical wing commander.

Again, it was time for pushback! I noted that the entire air force operated on a lecture/briefing format. It had proven to be the best way to inculcate students with knowledge and convey ideas. Air force senior officers and generals had grown up in this environment and understand it. They will also expect to receive comprehensive and in-depth material, which they can take away with them to their new responsibilities in Vietnam. They won't be happy with a script from a play. Finally, I noted, "I'm an instructor, not an actor." I went on record but failed to carry the day on this issue.

As the meeting was drawing to a close, I asked where we were working for the rest of the day and on the weekend. I was told that it was a holiday weekend and that no one was planning to work on this project over the weekend. That was the last straw for me; strong language followed about dragging Ray and I there for a two-hour meeting and then three days of watching television in the VOQ. I insisted that someone be there on Saturday, Sunday, and Monday to open the Academic Building, open the safes, and provide the necessary materials to get moving on the project. The first class was expected to arrive in six weeks to review and approve the course. What Ray and I got were the keys to the Academic Building, keys to the supply cabinets, and combinations to all the safes holding classified material. The latter was a gross breach of security, as the FWS didn't hold any evidence of the level of our security clearances. Nuclear weapons information was then and still is very closely held. The nuclear document logo "Formerly Restricted Data" is very strictly enforced to this day.

Ray and I became close friends. He was quiet, and I was vocal, but he tolerated me. We worked twelve to fourteen hours each of those three days over the holiday weekend and accomplished a lot. My entire course of instruction was roughly outlined and perhaps as many as one hundred slides laid out in detail. We were driving the train! Mr. Vern Spradling took responsibility for graphics design of all course material and slides and standardized colors to harmonize the presentations across all subjects. He also published a directive on preparation of course material for the GO course. Because of the head start over the Memorial Day weekend, Ray and I were soon getting finished slides back from the graphics shop and were fleshing out and polishing our presentations.

Weeks went by quickly as we drove toward the finish line and our first presentation to a Pentagon "murder board" consisting of one- and two-star generals from the Operations and Plans Directorates. There were a couple of practices of the "play" scenario. I would rate them as absolute disasters. Still we moved ahead, building on and practicing our play under the tutelage of Maj. Sky King. Our play had to last eight hours a day for four and a half days! Even the hits on Broadway only run three hours. Moreover, we didn't have the benefit of a real stage where the players could enter from stage left or stage right. I didn't have a good feeling for the outcome and really didn't want any part of it but gave it my best effort.

The Pentagon murder board arrived on schedule, and as they say on Broadway, "The show must go on." It did, and it flopped badly! Our general officer students were patient but, in the end, suggested a standard format of lectures with texts the real students could take with them to their assignments in Vietnam, especially in the areas of weapons, fuzes, weapons effects, weaponeering, and tactics. They also suggested a block on the SA-2 to include tactics that could be employed against this surface-to-air missile (SAM) system. Their recommendation did not set us back but rather made the job easier for all the FWS instructors. All of which had years of experience in the lecture mode and were very good at what they did. I don't know what happened to Maj. Sky King; he just faded back into the test side of the weapons school, and I continued on the FWS academic and flight instruction side.

With the "murder board" behind us, the Senior Officer School was scheduled for one course every six weeks, or as necessary. All the classes were filled with general officers and an occasional colonel. I often wondered if the course was that good or was the Las Vegas strip really the draw, along with the chance to get away from the Pentagon for a week. With very minor changes, I was ready for the next course and started to think about flying. The FWS instructor course was expanding from one to three aircraft. The F-100 course would continue along with the addition of the F-105 and the F-4. The conventional thinking was to upgrade me into the F-100. My thoughts were that the F-4C is the newest fighter in the inventory and the best we have—why take an intermediate step and then have to upgrade again in the future? I presented my case to Lt. Col. Grady Morris, Fighter Weapons School commandant, a crusty WW II and Korean War veteran flying P-51s. He agreed I could check out in the F-4C. This meant going to a formal F-4C Ground School conducted at Davis Monthan AFB, Arizona, near Tucson. Up to this point, I had flown aircraft with relatively simple flight control, fuel, electrical, and hydraulic systems. The F-4C systems were redundant and complex. You had to know and understand them to survive even a relatively benign emergency. F-4C Ground School was two weeks long with tough exams at the end of every phase.

Back at Nellis, I was scheduled for an F-4 "dollar" ride with Capt. Lee Kriner. Lee worked on the FWS test side but was a former instructor with a few hours in the F-4C. I was in the backseat, carefully monitoring every switch action and check that Lee performed. On the runway, hold brakes, throttles 80 percent, check gauges, release brakes, throttles 100 percent, then around the "gate" and advance them smoothly through four stages of afterburner. You could feel each stage of afterburner kick in and push you forcefully in the back! Approaching 140 knots, pull the control stick full aft against the stop. When the nose came up to a ten-degree, nose high attitude, stick forward to hold that attitude and let the aircraft fly off the runway, which took just a couple of seconds. Gear up, flaps up, and gone! The official nickname for the F-4C was Phantom II. The unofficial nickname was Rhino because the aircraft was somewhat ugly, hard, and tough. It was easier for me to relate to the latter name. At about one thousand feet AGL, Lee allowed me to take control of the aircraft and climb out to twenty thousand, heading for some restricted airspace, where we could do some stalls and maximum performance maneuvers. I found the aircraft to be extremely sensitive in pitch control, as I was constantly trimming the elevator to find the neutral spot. Lee had his oxygen mask off and had lit up a cigarette, a very bad practice, to say the least, but he had the nicotine habit real bad. Lee was puffing and kibitzing at the same time, "These modern jets are a lot tougher to fly than those WW II jobs you've been flying," etc., etc.

After a few minutes of struggling with pitch control, I decided to check the aircraft's dynamic stability. Dynamic stability implies that if the aircraft is trimmed to level flight and the control stick is moved to lower the nose, the aircraft will gain speed, increasing elevator authority and raise the nose back up through the level position. These oscillations will continue getting smaller each time until the aircraft stabilizes at level flight. I didn't even perturb the stick; just let go and the nose went down, then up, and repeated this with increasingly larger oscillations. I grabbed the stick, while Lee opined, "Don't worry, you'll get the hang of it."

Then I asked, "Is the F-4 dynamically unstable?"

His response was "No, why?"

"Well, this one is. Try it yourself," I said.

He took the stick and went through the same control experiment, only letting it go longer until the nose was rising and diving forty-five degrees and getting more violent each time. "Mayday, Mayday" was the call from the front seat. I gave Lee directions to the approved bailout area, but he went in another direction—more on this later.

The Nellis Tower connected us with the FWS Operations Desk, and they in turn patched us to McDonald Flight Test in St. Louis. After describing the problem, the advice was, turn the stab augmentation off, burn down fuel to two thousand pounds, and perform a landing configuration stability check. If the aircraft is controllable, land; if not, execute a controlled bailout. Simple! The stability augmentation system of yaw, roll, and pitch was turned off, and we started orbiting at ten thousand feet at 300 knots, which would be a good bailout speed if we needed to do that. As we orbited, I noticed a rather luxurious-looking set of buildings, a large swimming pool, and a small runway below us. I asked Lee what that was on the ground below us and why we weren't orbiting over the approved bailout area. Lee responded that the area with swimming pool and bungalows was known as Mustang Ranch, the finest little whorehouse in Nevada, and if we had to bail out, this was a heck of a lot better than a barren spot in the desert. His logic seemed impeccable at the time!

It took about forty minutes to turn ten thousand pounds of JP-4 into smoke! More importantly, it reduced the aircraft weight sufficiently to enable Lee to perform the controllability check at our projected landing speed. Normal final airspeed for the F-4C was 140 knots; to be safe, Lee flew the final configuration at 150 knots. Control and stability seemed OK, and we landed without incident.

My next checkout flights were scheduled with Capt. Don Calvert, an FWS IP. He was a taciturn, hard-as-nails instructor, my kind of guy. The F-4C had very bad adverse yaw characteristics that could put the aircraft in a departure and spin in a heartbeat if aileron was induced at high angles of attack—similar to the F-100. Rudders were used to turn the aircraft when maneuvering at high angles, or else you went for a wild ride with little chance of recovery. McDonald-Douglas connected the rudder to the ailerons when the flaps were extended so that rudder was blended in when the control stick was moved left or right in the landing pattern. The automatic application of rudder most likely saved a lot of pilots from entering a spin on the turn from the base leg to final approach. There was another quirk to the F-4C that I personally didn't like: the gear handle was a large switch with a red plastic wheel on the end. Moving the handle up raised the gear, and down lowered the gear—pretty standard stuff. However, a slight pull on the red wheel activated the air-pressurized emergency gear lowering system while, at the same time, failed the hydraulic system, including the wheel brakes, due to the air introduced into the aircraft's hydraulic system. The old heads said not to worry, just slap the handle up and down with an open hand, and you won't activate the emergency gear lowering system.

Don and I were going through high angle of attack maneuvers, with me trying to keep the stick centered. If the stick was centered, the

Rhino would shudder like a wet dog, and the nose would fall through for an easy recovery from a stall. Induce just the slightest aileron, and the bird would snap violently in the opposite direction from the adverse yaw caused by the down aileron. Immediate stick forward of neutral, ailerons and rudders neutral, and power up would stop the gyrations. I was getting the hang of the big bird. You had to love the immediate response of those two J-79 engines. Landing was something radically different from anything I had encountered in eight years as a pilot. Don demonstrated a landing from the backseat; I thought he was going to destroy the landing gear as he flew the F-4C into the ground. This was a navy aircraft forced on the air force by Secretary of Defense Robert McNamara. It was designed to crash onto an aircraft carrier flight deck and hook a wire. F-4C landing gear struts were designed to absorb the shock of this kind of landing and make it feel like a "grease job," but the optics was horrible. I aborted three approaches in a row, not being able to fly the aircraft into the ground without rounding out and gliding onto the runway. With Don screaming in my ears, I was determined to make a navy crash landing on the next attempt: on speed at 140 knots, on angle of attack with the visual doughnut, and on glide slope with the VASI lights. The landing gears struts absorbed all the force of impact; it felt like one of the best landings I ever made. This was a touch-and-go; the next one would be a full stop because of low fuel. Everything was fine until the gear handle was moved down for the final landing—red lights came on, indicating hydraulic system failure. I had inadvertently moved the gear handle out ever so slightly, causing activation of the emergency gear lowering system and failing the hydraulic system. Don talked me through the emergency braking system as we turned off of the main runway and waited for the tow truck to pull us back to the ramp—embarrassing, to say the least!

All that was required was another training sortie followed by a check ride, which I passed. Same story: "We need you as an IP, but you don't have ten hours. Take an aircraft on a cross-country and come back with more than ten hours."

It was legal then to strap down the backseat of an F-4 and fly it solo from the front seat. The backseat was primarily for a weapon systems officer (WSO), often referred to as the guy in back (GIB). Some F-4 pilots that had converted from the F-100 (one aircraft, one engine, and one pilot) just told their GIB to go cold mike (microphone) and don't touch any switches. I spent a lot of time in that mind-set, flying the F-86 and AT-28, but after some combat experience, believed chances for survival in your enemy's backyard were greatly enhanced if you used all the capability at your disposal. Said another way, I demanded a lot from the GIB, expecting him to be an expert on the F-4 air-to-air and air-to-ground radar, keeping his head on a swivel looking for bandits, and operating all the other electronics. However, this was just a cross-country. All I had to do was find Eglin AFB, Florida, my former home base, and land. Landing an F-4 was so easy after you got past the feeling the aircraft was going to break into pieces on impact with the runway. Eglin also hosted an F-4C Wing, so I expected good service from transient alert.

The F-4 was peculiar in a couple of ways! To start the J79 engine, a very powerful air cart was required to rotate the engine fast enough to provide sufficient air from the axial compressor section to light a fire in the combustion chamber. The F-4C could also be started with an explosive charge the size of a two-pound coffee can. Igniting this charge created hot gasses that performed the same function as the air cart. The air cart was preferred over the explosive cartridge because of problems with "hang fires," meaning a very slow burn that accomplished nothing but heating the can and engine. The F-4C also used a "drag chute" to reduce wear on the brakes and tires, and to allow the F-4 to operate from shorter runways. While it was expected a pilot would deploy a drag chute on every full-stop landing, it was almost never deployed on cross-countries for fear that you would have to pack it and reinstall it yourself. Pilots and GIBs were trained to pack drag chutes, just in case we had to do it.

The flight to Eglin was routine. The state-of-the-art Inertial Navigation System (INS) pinpointed Eglin from a thousand miles away, taking all the angst out of navigation. Land, refuel, file a clearance, and go. I had just been awarded senior pilots wings (seven years and 1,500 hours). I could sign my own clearance. Upon landing back at Nellis, I had logged over the obligatory ten hours. IP orders were published, and I was immediately one of the elite FWS instructors. Capt. Ron Catton (Thunderbird demonstration pilot, former FWS IP, and legendary fighter pilot) took me under his wing, instructing me on how to intimidate incoming students. Enough said.

It should be noted that all FWS students were exceptionally well qualified in the F-4C and were handpicked by their wing commanders to attend. At the FWS, they would improve their flying skills and gain esoteric technical knowledge on weapons, weaponeering, and tactics that they would then pass on to their fellow squadron pilots. The goal of the Tactical Commands PACAF, TAC, and USAFE was to have an FWS graduate in every flying squadron.

Another rather notable FWS graduate and instructor, Maj. John Boyd, had just finished graduate school (Georgia Tech, I believe) and was hanging around the Academic Section working on his energy maneuverability (EM) theory. The EM theory enabled a scientific comparison of dissimilar aircraft pitted against each other at various airspeeds and altitudes. The computed energy curves would reveal which aircraft had a maneuvering advantage. It also indicated what regime F-4 or F-100 pilots should avoid if they wanted to have an advantage over MiG-21s they encountered. Essentially, it put on paper what pilots instinctively knew when they studied the wing area, thrust, and weight of an adversary aircraft. Maj. John Boyd's other discovery was the infinity maneuver, which revealed that a fighter pilot could easily defeat an SA-2 missile guiding on his aircraft if two things were in his favor. First, the pilot had to know that the SA-2 was launched at his aircraft; and second, that he must be able to see the SA-2 in flight. The RHAW (radar homing and warning) receiver satisfied the first condition. The second required good weather so the SA-2 could be acquired visually, although I personally would execute the infinity maneuver in the weather if there was no other alternative. To execute the infinity maneuver, the pilot simply turned down and toward the SA-2. When he saw the missile try to turn down to reacquire a lead pursuit curve, the pilot pulled up sharply and back away from the missile. Once the SA-2 pointed downward, it did not have enough lift to pull vertical lead on its intended target and stalled. I personally thought this was more important to pilots than EM, which was primarily for aircraft designers. John and I became friends, but after he left the Weapons School for his follow-on assignment, our paths rarely crossed.

A number of the students that came through the FWS F-4C course while I was instructing there went on to stardom and fame. Capt. Bill Kirk retired as a four-star general, commanding air forces in Europe. Bill was also credited with two MiG kills in Vietnam. Capt. Mike Loh later became the air force vice chief of staff and subsequently commander TAC. Capt. Tom McInerney retired with three stars as the assistant vice chief, and 1st Lt. John Corder later became the air operations officer of Desert Storm, retiring as a major general. John was largely responsible for the outstanding Interdiction Campaign and Close Support of Army Forces in Desert Storm. Capt. Joe Moore, Bootstrap buddy, retired as a major general, commanding Chanute Technical Training Center. Capt. Bill MacAdoo was one of the best fighter pilots I ever flew with and was a natural combat leader. Capt. Les Prichard became the deputy director of operations at Aviano Air Base, Italy, when I served there. Many of these men I would fly with in combat. I apologize to all those not mentioned here; they were all great warriors and exceptional combat leaders.

Once the senior officers' course (SOC) was approved by the Pentagon, I was appointed as the chief of FWS Academics, a lofty sounding title, but with all the prima donna FWS instructors, it was like herding tigers. In addition, platform instruction on weapons and weapons systems, instructing students in the air, and the senior officers' course filled the job jar.

The senior officers' course (SOC) was also a learning experience because the generals of that time had earned their spurs in World War II and Korea. They all had experiences to share that made us better instructors and more aware of our limited grasp of aerial warfare. For example, Capt. Duke Johnson instructed air-to-air combat in the F-4 FWS and the senior officers' course. Duke was an exceptionally good instructor and very adroit at gaining and maintaining the advantage in mock dogfights. One of the SOCs had the air force vice chief of staff, Gen. John C. Meyer, as a student. All the instructors attended every class to learn from this outstanding aviator. General Meyer was not an ordinary general; he was the air force's all-time eighth scoring ace. In WW II, he flew the P-40, P-47, and P-51, with aerial victories in both the P-47 and P-51 against the Luftwaffe, including shooting down one of their jet fighters with a P-51. Deployed to Korea in 1950, he shot down two MiG-15s while flying the F-86A. His aerial victories totaled twenty-four, plus fifteen more aircraft destroyed on the ground. Gen. J. C. Meyer was a legend in his own time.

Captain Johnson was good but had no combat experience and was challenged to tell one of the air force's greatest living aces how to engage an enemy in aerial combat. Duke waxed eloquently, using model aircraft to demonstrate various maneuvers that were proven effective against modern high-performance jet aircraft. Throughout Duke's lectures, General Meyer remained silent but listening intently while chewing and smoking a very large cigar. When Duke concluded, he asked for questions or comments. All the lesser generals declined to speak. There was a long pause before General Meyer spoke pithily. He said, "Captain, that's all a bunch of BS! To kill the enemy, you fly right up his ass and blow him to bits!" No one challenged this bit of wisdom from the air force's eighth leading ace of all time.

It was about this time that a new model of the F-4 series was put into production. The FWS received some of the early production F-4Ds to replace the older F-4Cs and keep the school equipped with the leading edge of air force combat capability. The F-4D had improved avionics and weapons delivery modes.

There was a lot to like about the F-4! It carried one hell of a bomb load, had a powerful radar to locate enemy aircraft before they could find you, carried excellent short and long range air-to-air missiles, and would accelerate at the mere thought of speed and go fast. On the downside, it lacked a gun and suffered from high wing loading—the latter meant it turned like a waterlogged hippo compared to the MiG-17 and 21, our adversaries over North Vietnam. Teaching pilots how to exploit the F-4 strengths against MiG weaknesses was our job. To do this, instructors were always probing to gain better understanding how F-4D systems really worked, as well as what could be done before flight and in the cockpit to improve performance. FWS instructors frequently went to the McDonald Douglas Plant in St. Louis, Missouri, to extract esoteric information from the design engineers. Often, it was the other way around, with us educating them because they really didn't understand how F-4C/D systems worked when installed in the aircraft. FWS instructors were always innovating and finding ways to better exploit the F-4's capabilities. One day, while talking about adverse yaw and ways to help pilots anticipate its onset, someone suggested a yaw string, like the ones on the T-33 and F-86, to help the pilot detect yaw without looking at the needle-and-ball gauge in the cockpit. At first, it was thought the yaw string would not survive supersonic flight at Mach 1.4 or higher. Others opined that the boundary layer air over the nose would not put heavy loads on the string. It was decided to tape a "yaw string" on an F-4D nose with duct tape and fly it to find out what would actually happen. It worked fine just being held in place with duct tape. Yaw strings became standard on the F-4, enabling the pilot to detect the slightest onset of adverse yaw and/or eliminate yaw during weapons deliveries.

It is important to make clear the difference between the Air Force Fighter Weapons School and the Navy Top Gun School. The difference was intentional, and I make no suggestion that either concept was better than the other. The FWS was designed to polish a good pilot's skills in all fighter pilot disciplines and train them to be instructors back at their parent wings. All current fighter aircraft were included in the FWS curriculum. The A-7 was the one exception because there were so few in the air force inventory. The FWS published a quarterly newsletter mailed to FWS graduates to keep them abreast of the latest techniques and tactics to be passed on to their squadron mates. The goal was to have an FWS graduate in every air force fighter squadron. On the other hand, the Navy Top Gun School was aptly named and focused only on aerial combat with its top of the line fighter, the F-14 Tomcat. The intent was to graduate pilots and WSOs who could prevail against an enemy in air-to-air combat. They learned and honed air-to-air combat skills, not instructional skills. The movie *Top Gun*, starring Tom Cruise, highlighted this focus. There was no intent that Top Gun graduates teach when they returned to their operational squadrons; however, I'm sure they passed on what they learned to their fellow aviators.

A fighter pilot never gets enough flying time. Accordingly, I volunteered for every static display at every air show or airbase that wanted to put an F-4 on display. Some were not very distant as the crow flies, but with full internal fuel and two bags of gas, the F-4 could fly for three plus hours—nearly seven hours in a round trip to an airfield less than one hundred miles from Nellis AFB.

One day, when I was the operations duty officer, the fighter weapons wing commander, Col. "Buckshot" White, walked in escorting our new vice wing commander, Col. Don Hughes. He immediately recognized me from the time we had shared an office at Seventh Air Force Advanced in Saigon and walked over to the duty desk to shake my hand. "How are you doing, Pete?" he asked.

My response was a little awkward. "Sir, I thought I was doing great till I saw you! The last time we were together, you were a major and I was a captain. Now you're a colonel and I'm still a captain—double congratulations!" He laughed! In case, I forgot to mention it, in a previous assignment, then Major Hughes was the military assistant to Vice Pres. Richard Nixon and took action to protect the vice president's life during a trip to South America. Apparently, his heroic efforts on behalf of the vice president didn't go unnoticed by Air Force Promotion Boards. In my book, Colonel Hughes richly deserved the promotions. He retired as a lieutenant general commanding PACAF.

Sheila finally came to join me in Las Vegas. There was no base housing available for captains, so we decided to buy a house and found two we really liked in different developments. Unfortunately, the bait-and-switch sales representatives offended me to the point that I wouldn't buy from either of them. We rented a suitable bungalow, a short and easy drive from Nellis. The different bait-and-switch techniques were instructive. At the first development, Sheila picked out a model house she liked and a vacant lot that suited her, and we proceeded to seal the deal. When the paperwork was being filled out, the salesperson quoted a price $5,000 above the $27,000 listing in the brochure we'd been given on arrival. When I questioned the price, the salesperson asked to see my brochure. Upon inspection, she said, "You have an outdated brochure!" I responded that it was the one we'd been given from the pile on the front table that same morning. Without hesitation, the salesperson said it was outdated. I offered to meet the price if she would allow me to trash all the remaining "outdated" brochures. She wouldn't allow the trashing of her so-called outdated brochures, so we left.

At the next development, the process of purchasing a house went much better. Sheila picked out a lovely modern-looking model home and a large corner lot. I was surprised the lot hadn't been previously sold, as it was very large and somewhat sheltered. We signed the papers and shook hands—it was a done deal. Early the next morning, the salesman called, apologizing that the house we chose would not fit on the corner lot; however, there was still one lot left in the development that the house we chose would fit on. We raced down to the sales office only to find that the "acceptable" lot was considerably smaller than the original lot we selected and were surprised to learn that it carried a price tag $7,000 higher because it required a brick privacy fence to shield it from a perimeter road. When asked how the house could easily fit on a smaller but much more expensive lot but not on a much larger lot, the salesman said, "The setback requirements were very complex." The big unsold lot was part of the "bait and switch," and I wasn't buying the ruse.

Sheila and I both enjoyed the FWS assignment. The flying was great, and once a month, we took an evening out on the town for dinner and a show, which, at that time, was very affordable. Neither one of us gambled, so there was no gaming addiction straining our budget. However, one day, I came home from a hard day in the sky to find Sheila crying. She wasn't eager to tell me what was causing her distress but finally blurted out that the wing commander's wife told her that if she didn't come to all wives' club functions, it would "ruin my career." That came as a shock to me! I thought my career advancement largely depended on my performance. Out of curiosity, I asked what wives' club activities she participated in and learned that she attended all the morning coffees but not the afternoon teas. When asked why coffees and not teas, she said, "The coffees are short, and it's easy to get a babysitter for Denise. The teas are much longer and drift into the afternoon cocktail hour, and I believe I need to spend that time with our daughter."

It all made good sense to me, so I told Sheila, "If the wing commander's wife says that to you again, just tell her that I won't let you attend the teas because I want you to spend that time with our daughter! If she (wing commander's wife) controls my career, I don't want to be part of this organization anyway." That threat to Sheila was a very important lesson to me about how some senior officer air force wives improperly wore their husband's rank.

In the fall of 1965, I was promoted to major, below the zone. Mrs. Scotty Russell's OER must have been signed by the general and influenced the Promotion Board. It would be two years before the promotion became effective. However, as some sage officer once said, it is much easier to wait for your number on the list to be called than to wait to get on the list.

A secret opportunity to fly a MiG-21 had the FWS all stirred up. Evidently, Egypt wanted to curry favor with the United States, and the "chief of mission" in the US embassy there had passed the word through intelligence channels that a MiG-21 was available for US pilots to fly. I suspect the FWS was chosen to provide these pilots because there were graduates of the Air Force Test Pilot School in the FWS Test Section. Three pilots were chosen for this mission, Capt. Robert Chastain, Capt. Lee Kriner, and me. What a surprise! However, it seemed that my being on the team was more than likely because of my weapons and munitions background. There was a flurry of activity to get ready for the trip; study manuals on the MiG-21, bone up on Soviet weaponry, and make decals in English to superimpose over the Cyrillic and Arabic words and numbers. Last, we had to look like Eastern Europeans by letting our hair grow long, wearing tweedy clothing, and sporting beards. After much preparation, we learned that the team would fly into Egypt in an unmarked C-141 cargo aircraft. This ploy really smelled horrible and had bad optics! The United States was the only country in the world that operated C-141s. No one in Egypt was going to be fooled by long hair and cheap suits if we arrived in an unmarked C-141. We soon learned that the plan briefed up the chain was disapproved. I was looking forward to flying a MiG-21 and was deeply disappointed that the opportunity was lost because of poor planning.

On the heels of the cancelled clandestine trip to Egypt, I was teamed up with now major Lee Kriner to develop techniques and tactics for delivering the navy-developed Walleye antiship weapon from an Air Force F-4D. My F4D IP duties were curtailed, but not the academic lectures. I was loaned to the FWS test flight to assist Maj. Lee Kriner in developing tactics, techniques, and procedures for employment of the navy's Walleye electro-optical (EO) guided glide weapon from the F-4D. When the development work was done, we would deploy with Walleyes to Ubon Air Base, Thailand, as part of the 435th TFS from Eglin AFB, Florida. The Walleye was one of a series of Eye weapons developed in the laboratories of Naval Weapons Center at China Lake, California, in the vast desert area west of the Nellis ranges. Another impressively effective weapon developed at China Lake was the AIM-9 Sidewinder Heat-Seeking Infrared Air-to-Air missile, which was developed at the end of the Korean

War. It is still a prized frontline weapon in its nth instantiation as the AIM-9M. Other China Lake naval munitions developments were the Sparrow AIM-7, Shrike, and Snake Eye.

The Walleye Weapon System was comprised of a six-foot long linear-shaped charge with eight individual linear-shape charges surrounding a cylindrical core. When the weapon detonated on impact, eight copper slugs formed by the shaped explosive, each six feet long, traveled at thirty thousand meters per second with enormous destructive power. Guidance for the Walleye was provided by an edge-tracking electro-optical (EO) seeker. This EO seeker was designed to be locked on to a target by the pilot prior to release and then, after release, guide autonomously on the target until impact. Unfortunately, edge trackers can run along the edge they are locked on to. For example, if the edge is the deck of a bridge, the tracker could run left or right until it found another edge to stop it, such as a shoreline or a pylon supporting the bridge. We found that when planning a mission, it was important to know each Walleye's proclivity to run left or right, up or down. The Walleye was equipped with large wings in a swept back cruciform configuration, rotated forty-five degrees from the suspension lugs. While not a powered munition, these large wings gave the Walleye considerable glide range from ten thousand feet AGL at 480 knots.

The navy developed the Walleye to employ against enemy ships, but employed it from A-4s against North Vietnamese fixed hard targets like bridges. The A-4 was a single-seat aircraft. Pilot loading must have been very demanding on the final run to the target when the aircraft would be most vulnerable to AAA and SAMs. Using F-4Ds as the launch platform allowed splitting the tasking between weapons system officer (WSO) and pilot. Sharing the Walleye lock-on workload only required the aircraft to be stable, not jinking (rapid jerky movements to avoid AAA) on the final attack heading for less than five seconds. The F-4D radar display in both cockpits was not capable of displaying the video picture captured by the Walleye EO tracker. Therefore, a replacement for the radar tube that could handle both radar and EO inputs had to be developed. The development was marginally successful with regard to the EO display, however, with adequate target study, the display was marginally acceptable, and flight testing could begin.

Lee and I flew tens of captive flights on Nellis ranges developing procedures and tactics, and learning to exploit the video image of the target in both cockpits. The Walleye image processor superimposed a two-mil square over the target scene. If the desired target impact point fell in this square, the tracking system could be engaged and the weapon released from several miles away with reasonable certainty that the Walleye would impact the target. Two mils or mill radians subtends two feet for every one thousand feet of range. Therefore, at six nautical miles (thirty-six thousand feet) from a target, the two-mil box would cover seventy-two feet in both the vertical and horizontal dimensions. This allowed a lot of extraneous objects to appear in the target box that could have greater influence on the tracker logic and cause the tracker to move off of the actual target. One recommendation we had for spiral development of the Walleye was to automatically shrink the tracker "square" to one mil or less at lock-on, thus reducing the number of extraneous objects in the track window.

We interrupted our work long enough to fly to Navy China Lake and visit with the scientists and engineers there who had conceived, designed, and nurtured the Walleye through its initial production and testing. What we learned from those gentlemen would accelerate our work and help us in mission planning once we arrived at our operational base in Thailand.

One lasting memory from China Lake was of a car coming down a deserted desert road as we were driving toward it. It was a government-licensed car moving slowly in our direction. Both front doors of the other car were open, with the wind blowing the car, engine off, down the road at a pretty good pace. The look on the driver's face left me with the impression he was mentally calculating the drag in the wheels based on wind velocity, door area, car weight, and the speed of the car. Perhaps these kinds of ad hoc experiments happen when you are working one hundred miles from nowhere and working on stuff you can't talk to anyone about.

Lee and I also developed ways to harmonize the Walleye tracking index with the F-4D gun sight. With these two harmonized, it was easy for the pilot to maneuver the aircraft to place the aiming dot, pipper, on the desired point of the target and call out "on target." The WSO would view the scene on his scope and, if the four-mil window was on the desired target, engage the Walleye tracker with a trigger squeeze and call "locked on." The pilot then glanced at his scope, verifying the desired target was captured in the tracker box, squeezed his trigger to take control of the Walleye, and then released the Walleye by depressing the bomb release button. These aircrew procedures were accomplished in five seconds or less of nonmaneuvering flight.

When the pilot felt the jolt of the 850-pound Walleye being released from the pylon shackles, he knew he was free to maneuver. The Walleye EO video was recorded on VHS tape up to the release point for after action analysis. No tracker images were transmitted from the weapon to the aircraft after release; however, there was sufficient scene information in the last frame prior to release to understand why a Walleye might have tracked off of the initial aim point. As noted, the roll-in, lock-on, and release steps required less than five seconds and took place eight to ten miles from the target, depending on the release altitude and airspeed. The Walleye had big fins acting as wings. It was truly a precision-guided glide bomb. It worked best when target shadows were short, requiring that missions be planned for the Walleye to impact at local noon for the target's longitude to achieve the highest probability of success. This would prove to our disadvantage in NVN, as all the rest of the fighters took off at 10:00 a.m. and 2:00 p.m. in big attack packages and were coming home from the early "go" when our four-ship Walleye-loaded F-4Ds were entering North Vietnam.

Lee and I flew many sorties scouring the Nellis Range Complex for suitable targets to test the Walleye against. There were no bridges to be found in the desert, but there were other things we could test the EO tracker and Warhead against. A cave would be a useful target, in that the North Vietnamese stored munitions in caves along their clandestine routes into South Vietnam. We found many caves that would have made superb targets and were easily accessible by vehicle to assess damage. To our disappointment, almost all of them had been lived in by earlier civilizations and were covered with archeological treasures being analyzed by scientific organizations and universities. These caves were protected for good reason and off limits as potential targets. One cave that wasn't protected looked promising, and we flew captive sorties against it, studying how the tracker responded to various light and shadow conditions. We had two live warheads for test and used one of them on the cave used in captive runs. The mission was planned with a sun/shadow contrast well inside the cave mouth. The results were spectacular! The cave was collapsed internally almost twenty feet from the mouth, with rock debris blocking the remainder of the cave. The next live shot was against an intact mint condition WW II Sherman tank. This tank was routinely used as a target for close air support missions flown with twenty-five-pound practice bombs with no evidence of any direct hits. There was a good sun/shadow line below the top of the upper tracks. With the sun at local noon, the Walleye must have hit the center of the tank at that exact point, cutting a line through the hull armor, and blowing the turret with its cannon completely off of the body and landing about twenty feet away. It was time to try our Walleye tactics on real targets in NVN!

The 435th TFS of the 33rd TFW at Eglin AFB, Florida, was deploying to Ubon AFB, Thailand, just prior to Lee and I departing for Thailand to run the in-theater Walleye testing. Our preparations called for a trip to Eglin to brief the squadron aircrews and to participate in a training flight to fire an AIM-4D against an airborne drone target.

The briefings on Walleye tactics, techniques, and procedures took about four hours, with Lt. Col. Grady Morris running interference for Lee and me. The next day, Lee and I flew against the BQM-47 Drone, each firing one AIM-4D. I flew with Lt. Col. Dick Collins, 435th operations officer, and a dead ringer for Audie Murphy in looks, speech, and mannerisms. Years later, he retired as Brigadier General Collins with numerous decorations for valor in combat.

The AIM-4D was designed to be launched from the internal bay of an F-102 or F-106 to engage Soviet bombers in the air defense mission. Its IR seeker was supercooled from a nitrogen bottle in the missile itself. Unfortunately, the bottle only held two minutes of liquid nitrogen, sufficient for an air defense engagement, with the ground controller telling the pilot when to cool the AIM-4D (cool down took two minutes) and then when to fire. The ability to exercise this tight control came from having both the target and fighter tracked by a ground or airborne radar. This level of control does not normally exist against fighter aircraft over enemy airspace, so the nitrogen cooling was extended to four minutes for Tactical Fighter Air Superiority Missions—still way too short in my view. Frankly, it was a terrible idea to convert an air defense missile system with a two- or four-minute supercooled IR seeker to the air superiority Mission. It is virtually impossible for a fighter pilot to know two minutes ahead of time when the AIM-4D would be needed and then get into position to fire it against a highly maneuverable enemy aircraft before the nitrogen coolant runs out in four minutes.

AIM-4Ds were referred to as "hitiles" because they guided so accurately on an IR source they routinely flew right to the heat source. These missiles were equipped with contact fuzes that detonated a few milliseconds after hitting the fuselage or engine of an aircraft. The slight delay enabled the warhead to penetrate inside an aircraft or engine nacelle and then explode. The AIM-4D warhead, with only four pounds of explosive, was miniscule compared to the AIM-9. Typical air-to-air missiles designed for the air superiority role had proximity fuzes that would detonate the warhead if it passed close enough to a highly maneuvering enemy aircraft to cause damage with a twenty-five pound, or larger, controlled fragmentation warhead. Normally, in a tactical engagement, both aircraft are maneuvering at maximum available g-forces. In these maneuvering engagements, the AIM-9, for example, may only be able to guide close to an enemy aircraft; the proximity fuze makes up for misses up to several feet.

Nonetheless, the AIM-4D worked very well in the strategic defense mission it was designed for. On my training mission, the target was a ground-controlled BQM-34 target drone with infrared (IR) flares attached to replaceable wing extensions. I turned on the AIM-4D coolant and called, "In range," alerting the ground controller to maneuver the drone, which immediately began a four G turn. While maneuvering to keep a lead pursuit approach to the drone and remain in the AIM-4D field of regard, the "locked-on" tone sounded in my headset, and I squeezed the trigger. The missile leaped off of the pylon rails and sped to the target, knocking the IR source from the BQM-34 drone wingtip, leaving the drone unharmed so it could be recovered by an internally carried parachute and fly again. Unfortunately, that degree of control is not possible in a tactical environment deep in enemy territory.

An air force colonel, who accompanied Lee and me to Saigon, assured us that the AIM-4D had to work, or the navy would get the nod to develop all future air-to-air missiles. He was wrong on both counts. I politely advised him the air force should use the most effective weapons available for combat, so be it if they were navy designed and developed. Pilot's lives and the outcome of combat should not be put in jeopardy because of service rivalries in weapons development!

On the way to Ubon, we stopped off in Saigon to brief Seventh Air Force on the Walleye Weapon System and our employment procedures on the F-4D. We also emphasized the differences between Navy A-4 Walleye delivery procedures and air force delivery procedures on an F-4D with pilot and WSO. Upon arrival at Ubon, we checked to see if all our tools, test equipment, and alignment fixtures had arrived. F-4Ds dedicated to the Walleye mission were offered to us to calibrate a number of Walleyes being held in the munitions storage area. It took several missions over Thailand to calibrate enough Walleyes for the anticipated missions and to identify those that held the target in the "tracking box" best. It wasn't long before the Walleye and I were ready for priority targets in North Vietnam.

Shortly after Lee and I reported into the 435th TFS at Ubon, Col. Robin Olds, wing commander, paid a visit to welcome the unit to the 8th TFW. He jumped up on a table with ease in order to gain a commanding position for his remarks. He was quite the athletic figure, about six feet two and 220 pounds of lean muscle. Evidently, Colonel Olds didn't like the appearance of the 435th squadron commander, Lt. Col. "Bull Moose" Tietro, who was a little portly, so he referred to the 435th as the "Four-Thirty Fats," not a good sign. I never did get to shake Colonel Olds's hand but often saw him around the base and at the officers' club at dinnertime.

Primary targets for the Walleye were bridges, especially bridges that had escaped hits from conventional bombing attacks. I planned and flew all of the missions until called back to the Weapons School. The first mission was against a pier in Route Pack 2. The pier was destroyed along with a few sampans tied up to it! Our second Walleye tasking was against a bridge across the Red River, northwest of Hanoi. Two Walleyes were employed against this target. The one released by Element Lead slipped off of the target and flew long. The Walleye from lead tracked at the top of a pier, where two spans rested. These two spans fell at Walleye impact, with the span on the left hitting the adjacent pier, causing a third span to fall into the river. Up to this point, Walleye flights accompanied the strike packages or were provided MiG cap when flying alone up north. Strike packages were comprised of forty to eighty, or more, fighter aircraft going against targets near Hanoi. MiG cap consisted of a flight of four F-4Ds loaded only with air-to-air missiles. Their purpose was to engage any MiGs that came up to engage the Walleye flight. With two destroyed targets, to Walleye's credit, our future flights would be unescorted. The targets got more important and thus were in more highly defended areas. However, the requirement to strike targets when shadows were short and more favorable to the Walleye tracker resulted in Walleye flights being the only four USAF aircraft in North Vietnam when the time over target (TOT) was local noon.

Walleye missions were briefly interrupted when Lee and I were ordered to fly to Vientiane, Laos, and meet with some very important people. In the meeting room was my old Air Commando friend, Maj. Dick Secord, now masquerading as a civilian and working for the chief of mission at the US embassy. I understood how those things worked, as I'd been there myself. We briefed the assembled group on the Walleye, its capabilities, and our success in theater to date. The chief of mission had some targets that he wanted struck with Walleye, but he didn't describe the targets or say where they were located. In response, we advised our hosts that we were assigned to the 8th TFW and had no authority to freelance. Perhaps they could use their channels to insert their targets into Seventh Air Force tasking in which case we would be obliged to strike their targets. Dick Secord spent most, if not all the rest, of his illustrious career working outside the air force. The next time I saw him was in the aftermath of the failed Iran Desert One rescue attempt.

At least two more successful Walleye missions were flown before Maj. Tippy Tyler, a former student at the Fighter Weapons School, asked me to be his GIB flying escort for a strike package going against targets in and around Hanoi. There were no Walleye missions on the horizon, so why not see how the 8th TFW normally executed their missions? Prior to heading for his squadron's planning room to plan the next day's mission, I was having dinner at the O'club with Tippy when Col. J. J. Burns, 8th TFW DO, stopped by our table. He came right to the point, saying, "Pete, Seventh Air Force has sent us a very high priority Walleye tasking! Plan it ASAP and brief me in the morning!" I asked Colonel Burns if it could wait until the afternoon because I was committed to fly a Route Pack Six mission with Tippy on the 1000 hours launch. The answer was "No!" so Tippy had to leave to find another pilot or WSO for his backseat. I immediately headed for the wing mission planning room and then to the wing tactics cell to talk with the expert tacticians. There were F-4D pilots in this cell that I knew and respected, such as Lt. Col. Richard Collins, Maj. Bill Kirk, Maj. Bill McAdoo, Capt. Joe Moore, and Capt. John Corder.

The next day, while I was briefing Colonel Burns, word came in that the entire flight of four F-4s led by Captain Tyler were shot down near Thud Ridge by a flight of MiG-21s making a high-speed attack from the rear and out of visual range of the F-4 flight. It was also learned that Red Crown, an EC-121 early warning radar aircraft, had not picked up the MiG-21 flight on their radar and thus was not able to provide a "bandit" warning to the many tens of fighters on the morning mission. That day, August 26, 1967, was from then on known as Black Friday at the 8th TFW. I don't know the fate of all the eight men in the flight, but Tippy spent the next five and a half years of his life in the Hanoi Hilton prison camp. If it hadn't been for that priority tasking and Colonel Burn's insistence that planning for it be started immediately, I would have joined Tippy in Hanoi, assuming I survived the ATOL missile impact. The fact that North Vietnamese fighter airfields were off the target list for the entire seven-year war is bizarre, to say the least. The North Vietnamese three primary fighter bases from 1965 through 1972, Phu Cat, Hoa Lac, and Kep were never bombed or strafed. On several missions going north, I could see as many as thirty aircraft lined up in two neat rows on just one of those airfields. A major tenant of airpower since WW I, espoused first by Italian general Guilio Douhet in Command of the Air, was to destroy your enemy's aircraft when they were helpless and concentrated on an airfield. His theories on air power were studied in all Air Force Staff and Leadership schools. I have to believe that Seventh Air Force commanders and Air Force chiefs of staff continued to recommend that these and other North Vietnamese airfields be destroyed. However, they remained untouched throughout the entire war. That flawed and wrong-headed policy had to come from the highest levels of our government.

The priority tasking from Seventh Air Force that Colonel Burns directed me to work on was bizarre! The ATO tasked us to destroy the Lang Son Bridge, north of Haiphong, located on a major highway coming out of China, just five kilometers from the border—well inside the "keep out" buffer zone. It was a nice and relatively long bridge. The tasking was very specific. The route to the target was direct to Dien Bien Phu, then to a point north of Hanoi, then directly to the target, and finally to reverse course and return the same way. The tasking also included a ridiculous statement that "the primary mission was to avoid combat with Chinese MiGs from a base thirty kilometers inside China." I prepared a pithy message for Colonel Burns, noting, "If the primary mission was to avoid combat with Chinese MiGs, then that could be easily accomplish by canceling the mission. However, if destroying the bridge was the mission's primary purpose, we would do that, but if Chinese MiGs entered North Vietnam to intercept our flight, we would engage as necessary and then go 'feet wet' to Da Nang, SVN." "Feet wet" was slang for flying over water. With regard to our mission, it meant exiting North Vietnam by flying southeast from the target, passing north of the port city of Haiphong to the Gulf of Tonkin. Once over international water, it was a direct flight to Da Nang Air Base just south of the DMZ.

Seventh Air Force acknowledged both that the primary purpose of our mission was to destroy the Lang Son bridge and that the target was to be destroyed ASAP. We offered two alternative routings to 7th AF. First, to fly to Da Nang Air Base, refuel there, go "feet wet" to the target, and return the same way. The second routing was to fly the route as originally tasked but then go "feet wet" after destroying the bridge and recover at Da Nang AB. Either option reduced aerial refueling requirements, putting a tanker up twice for just four F-4s, and reduced the flight's exposure to MiGs, AAA, and SAMs. Both options were rejected by Seventh Air Force. We were ordered to take the long route to the target and return to Ubon by the same route. To quote a line from *Forrest Gump*, "Stupid is as stupid does."

The weather was unusually clear, not a cloud in sight. Takeoff was timed to put Walleyes on target at local noon. Col. J. J. Burns (who later retired as a lieutenant general) led the flight with me as his WSO because he had no training with Walleyes. As the 8th TFW chief of tactics, Lt. Col. Richard Collins flew element lead. Flight to the target area was uneventful and quiet; we were the only US aircraft over North Vietnam. Not even Red Crown, the EC-121 that provided "bandit calls," was airborne. When the target came into view, I noted that several spans were carrying traffic coming out of China. With the sun high and slightly at our backs, lead rolled in from the south on the right span as planned, with the element taking short spacing on the left center span. I called out "locked on," and Colonel Burns did his thing—problem was he didn't set up switches properly, so his trigger squeeze fired an AIM-7, and depressing the bomb button released the Walleye. Someone in the flight saw the AIM-7 but thought it was from a MiG shooting at our flight and called "break left." Flight discipline was solid, and the element released their Walleye before making a hard break. Both Walleyes hit the bridge, bringing down three spans—some Chicom (Chinese Communist) trucks crashed into the river. The flight cleared the target area and reversed course, passing just north of the SA-2 sites around Hanoi.

We expected MiGs, and they didn't disappoint us. Just as we approached a point north of Hanoi, four MiG-21s passed about eight thousand feet above us, going in the opposite direction. The shadow of a MiG-21 darkened my cockpit for a split second. There were no radar contacts, and no one had a visual until they were inside AIM-7 minimum range. Fuel was expected to be a problem, and it was. We were lower on fuel at this point than planned because of high-energy maneuvers exiting the target. Colonel Burns pushed the throttles up slightly and started a gentle weave to give us a better look to our six o'clock. On our minds was the flight of four F-4Ds shot down four days earlier by ATOLs fired from MiG-21s in high-speed descending attacks. We were doing about 520 knots TAS (true airspeed), and I suspect the MiGs that flew over us were doing about the same, if not faster. This meant the two flights were separating at nearly 18 knots per minute—said another way, 18 nautical miles per minute. We had about enough gas to make one "burner" turn, and we'd go tanks empty over North Vietnam, but we never saw the MiGs again. With the F-4s telltale exhaust trail and ground radar supporting them, it's hard to believe they couldn't find us. Perhaps they just couldn't catch up if they had hesitated too long before turning back to attack us from the rear.

We rendezvoused with our tanker over Laos, refueled, and landed uneventfully at Ubon. When the flight parked on the ramp, Colonel Olds was there to greet Col. J. J. Burns, his director of operations. Evidently, armament personnel who met the flight to make safe our remaining munitions after we turned off the runway noticed that an AIM-7 missile was missing from flight lead's aircraft and informed Maintenance Control that we had a MiG engagement. Shooting down MiGs was Colonel Olds's passion. He must have met our aircraft to hear the story—only to be disappointed. Colonel Burns and Lt. Col. Collins were awarded Silver Stars for the mission. I vowed that if I ever had had an operational command, I would pay attention to pilots in the field when they suggested there was a better way to employ aircraft in combat—and I did!

Later, we learned that the US Intelligence Community knew the North Vietnamese Air Force had been practicing a high-speed rear engagement for a couple of weeks prior to four F-4s being shot down on Black Friday, August 26, 1967. I started wondering if the route our flight was directed to fly on the Lang Son Mission was dictated by the intelligence community to excite North Vietnamese Air Defense Systems in an uncluttered electronic environment. Perhaps if your own life is not a risk, you can afford to direct others to take unnecessary risks. Beware of people giving suspect orders when their own lives are not at risk.

Long before our team was scheduled to depart Ubon, all the AIM-4Ds were back in the munitions storage areas, never to be used again. It only took one lost opportunity to shoot down a MiG because of a flawed concept, and wing commanders were having nothing more to do with this very limited air-to-air missile. The air force would have to work hard to earn its way back into the air-to-air missile business, and it eventually did with the AIM-120 advanced medium-range air-to-air missile (AMRAAM).

I was looking forward to flying more Walleye missions to collect data and to gain more experience flying missions up north to enhance my knowledge and credibility as a FWS instructor. However, shortly after the Lang Son Bridge Mission, Lee and I were called upon to brief Gen. Jack Ryan, commander, Pacific Air Forces (PACAF), on the Walleye missions we'd flown. PACAF was located at Hickam AFB, Hawaii, three-fourths of the way back to Nellis AFB. Prior to our departure from Ubon Air Base, we loaded up with before and after target photos and viewgraphs of the various ingress and egress routes. General Ryan was a good audience. He penetrated deep into all aspects of mission planning and the missions we'd flown. At one point, he jumped out of his chair and ran to the poststrike bridge picture projected on the screen, asking about the aim point and how many Walleyes it took to fell the spans. We cautioned General Ryan that the Walleye was a very effective and economical weapon when employed appropriately, but that it was not a silver bullet that would bring the war to an early close.

One of the things that puzzled me about the many missions over North Vietnam was the apparent failure of the intelligence community to understand the disposition of North Vietnamese AAA gun locations. The North Vietnamese had 37 mm, 57 mm, and 85 mm AAA weapons for point defense of targets, and SA-2s surface-to-air missiles (SAMs) for area defense. Under Secretary McNamara, our adversaries were able to prepare SA-2 sites, put the equipment in place, train operators, and become fully operational without the OSD (Office of the Secretary of Defense) ever approving a strike against these deadly weapons. This absolute stupidity allowed the enemy to field a number of SA-2 sites with overlapping coverage. When these SA-2s became operational, they took a heavy toll on American fighters going to targets along the Red River in Route Package 6. All of North Vietnam was divided into geographical areas numbered from one to six, with Route Package 1 being the most benign, and 6 the most heavily defended. Route Pac 6 was further subdivided into alpha and bravo. Route Pac 6A covered the area around Hanoi and to the west. Route Pac 6B covered the area around Haiphong and westward to the edge of Route Pac 6A. Most targets struck by the air force were in Route Pac 6A, whereas most of the targets assigned to carrier based naval aircraft were in Route Pacs 1, 2, 5, and 6B because of their proximity to the Gulf of Tonkin. Back to the AAA, the Intelligence briefing would usually start by briefing the target and end with enemy defenses. The briefer would say something like "The NVN have thirty thousand AAA weapons dispersed throughout the country. You can expect your target to be defended by a few tens of 37 mm, twenty 57 mm, and ten 85 mm batteries. However, when approaching the target, the sky would turn black with bursting flak. It seemed that all the AAA in the NVN Inventory was protecting your specific target on any given day."

Nearly twenty years later, I saw former secretary of state Dean Rusk being interviewed by Peter Arnett on a CBS Documentary called *The Ten Thousand Day War*. Mr. Arnett asked, "It has been rumored that the United States provided the North Vietnamese government the names of the targets that would be bombed the following day. Is there any truth to that allegation?"

To my astonishment and absolute disgust, the former secretary responded, "Yes. We didn't want to harm the North Vietnamese people, so we passed the targets to the Swiss embassy in Washington with instructions to pass them to the NVN government through their embassy in Hanoi." As I watched in horror, Secretary Rusk went on to say, "All we wanted to do is demonstrate to the North Vietnamese leadership that we could strike targets at will, but we didn't want to kill innocent people. By giving the North Vietnamese advanced warning of the targets to be attacked, we thought they would tell the workers to stay home." No wonder all the targets were so heavily defended day after day! The NVN obviously moved as many guns as they could overnight to better defend each target they knew was going to be attacked. Clearly, many brave American Air Force and Navy fliers died or spent years in NVN prison camps as a direct result of being intentionally betrayed by Secretary Rusk and Secretary McNamara, and perhaps, President Johnson himself. I cannot think of a more duplicitous and treacherous act of American government officials. Dean Rusk served as secretary of state from January 21, 1961, through to January 20, 1969, under Pres. John F. Kennedy and Lyndon B. Johnson. Perhaps Sen. John McCain, POW for five years and presidential candidate in 2008, was one of the many victims of this utter stupidity and flawed policy flowing from Pres. Lyndon B. Johnson. Mr. Peter Arnett opined that this would be a treasonous act by anyone else.

With an idle afternoon in Hawaii prior to returning to Nellis, there was time to learn to ride a surfboard—it looked so easy. I was thirty-three at the time. Donning a bathing suit and renting a surfboard at Waikiki Beach, I paddled out to where all the "big kahunas, moondoggies, and gidgets" (surfer talk) were bobbing up and down on their surfboards. Initially, there were about fifty in the surfboard flotilla.

It looked fairly easy. All you had to do is paddle like hell when a wave was coming up from behind, and the board would be lifted up on the front slope of the wave, trying to slide down as the wave continued to push it up and forward. Either I wasn't getting the board going fast enough or there was some subtle trick that I hadn't mastered because I didn't catch a wave on the first three, four, or five attempts. It didn't seem to matter. All the surfers paddled back out to join me after their thrilling rides into the shore. Then after missing a wave again, with all my newfound friends going shoreward on the wave, it struck me after a while that they didn't come back. I was alone at sea! Worse, I now realized that the wind or currents had been slowly pulling me out to sea. I could barely see the palm trees on the beach in the distance. Oh well, I said to myself, it's a long paddle back to Waikiki, so I better get started. Soon it became apparent that the day was about over. I would soon be dark. Fortunately, the lights on the beach hotels would guide me in the right direction. I was getting a little tired, so I put a little more effort into the paddling without paying much attention to the waves. By the way, when you miss a wave, the wave just runs under you and you slide down the back side. So there I am paddling hard when along comes a wave, and miracle of miracles, I caught it and am now riding the front side. I decided to stay low on the board so as not to fall off and lose the wave (smart thinking for the first time that day). That wave took me all the way to the beach, dumping me, rather unceremoniously, on the sand about two hundred yards from the stand where I rented the board. The guy at the stand was a little put out that I stayed out so long, preventing him from closing the stand at the usual time. I made some smart remark like I was having so much fun, I didn't want to come in! That was the first and last time I ever ventured out on a surfboard.

We took all that we learned from flying missions in Route Packages 1 and 6A & B back to Nellis and plowed it into the student courses and the senior officers' course. The FWS Leadership immediately recognized this was the only way these courses could remain relevant. Accordingly, instructor pilots from the F-100, F-105, and F-4 FWS courses and FWS test pilots were rotating to units in Thailand and South Vietnam to bring back the latest tactics innovated in combat.

Back at Nellis, changes at the helm had taken place. Brig. Gen. Frank "Speedy" Pete Everest, a.k.a. "the Fastest Man Alive" (for the record he set in the Bell X-2 reaching Mach 2.9), had taken over as the Tactical Fighter Weapons Center commander. General Everest was a fighter pilot in WW II, downing two German aircraft in Africa and four Japanese aircraft over China, making him an ace. Subsequently, he was shot down in a P-51 over Hankou, China, and taken prisoner by the Japanese.

General Everest was also the chief air force test pilot for the F-100, the first Century Series aircraft in the USAF inventory. He was just a name and a picture in the chain of command until fate took an odd twist one late summer night.

Word came down from on high that General Everest wanted the carbon blown out of his staff car engine so it would run better. This was a little bit out of the ordinary, asking junior officers to drive a military vehicle at high speed. The conclusion was that night range officers driving to and from the Indian Springs Range Complex, about seventy-five lonely road miles northwest of Nellis AFB, were in the best position to satisfy the general's request when he wasn't using the car himself. Night range duty came my way, and motor pool delivered the general's staff car to the FWS with instructions for me to call them to pick up, wash, and refuel the general's car when I returned from the range at about midnight. It was immediately apparent why the general wanted the carbon blown out. The car was initially a real dog, barely able to accelerate to highway speed. But after nearly an hour at 80 mph, it ran fine. One flight scheduled for the range aborted; as a result, I was back at the FWS Academic Section where my car was parked about 2300 hours. I looked in the base phone book and called Motor Pool Dispatch, and when a voice answered, I said, "I've got the general's car at Building 300 on the flight line. Keys are on the seat. Pick it up."

The voice replied sternly, "Who the hell are you?"

"Major Pete. Pick up the car so I can go home!"

The stern voice then said, "This is General Everest. Bring the #%*^& car to my office!"

The late night cobwebs disappeared, and the brain was alert! What kind of trouble was I in now? I parked the general's car in his reserved parking spot close to the front door of TAWC headquarters. I didn't dare leave the keys in the car, so I went inside and knocked on his office door. "Come in," said the stern voice. Once I was in the door, the general was very gracious offering me a cup of coffee and asking how the FWS students did on the range.

"Good," I said, "all qualified in every event!" He went silent, giving me the ball, so I asked, "Was the F-100 prototype you tested the same as the C&D Model we're flying today?"

"No," he responded. "It was a real widow maker with a lot of other wicked tendencies that were just as bad as the adverse yaw problem!" He went on to explain that he strongly recommended that the F-100 not be procured, considering it an unsafe aircraft. However, he opined, the air force was embarrassed that the Soviets had fielded the MiG-21, a supersonic aircraft, and we had nothing that came close to it, so against his recommendation, the air force put the F-100 into production. He said that the F-100C/D was a vast improvement over the A/B Models but still far short of an honest aircraft. His comments helped me understand why so many F-100s turned into "lawn darts" in the hands of students and inexperienced operators at Williams and Luke AFBs. As I drove home, I realized that I had a very rare opportunity to have that conversation with a true legend and one of the truly great airmen of the twentieth century.

The next morning, during normal duty hours, I called the motor pool dispatcher telephone number listed in the current/official base phone book. A pleasant female voice answered, "General Everest's Office. How may I help you?" I explained to the general's secretary that I was trying to call the motor pool. She laughed, saying the misprint in the phone book was causing her a lot of grief and that the *Daily Bulletin* was going to carry a correction every day for the next two weeks with the hopes that most people would correct their phone books. Her comments on the phone number screw-up made me feel a lot better, knowing it wasn't my fault—and more importantly, the general knew that as well.

General Everest moved on to command the Air Force Air Rescue and Recovery Service; his replacement was Maj. Gen. Zack Taylor. General Taylor attended different sessions of every senior officers' course and got to know the instructors and their qualifications—somewhat of a hands-on leader. He also asked a lot of questions with regard to my course. He was always probing me on targeting and weaponeering. Both those subjects were based largely on the laws of probability and the circular error probable (CEP) assumed for pilot performance in combat. One day, I was in General Taylor's office, answering his questions on probability of hit when his secretary paged him to the phone. He motioned me to remain while he took the call. I could tell it wasn't a pleasant conversation and started to leave. Again, he motioned for me to stay. When he put the phone back in the cradle, he paused and turned to me with the following comment: "That was the Lieutenant Governor! He is visiting friends at the Mustang Ranch, not too far from here. He is outraged that one of our F-4s flew over the ranch and toilet-papered the ranch, plugging up their swimming pool water pumps." He then looked at me and said, "Pete, I want you to take a small team out there to investigate the allegations." Perhaps General Taylor did not know the Mustang Ranch was a high-end house of prostitution. I thought he needed to know that before the issue went any further. He was incredulous when I told him the Mustang Ranch was a fly-in high-class house of prostitution, arguing that the lieutenant governor would not be there if that were true. I suggested he check with the local Office of Special Investigation (OSI) and his staff judge advocate before taking any action.

Two phone calls later, he was reconsidering his options and wanted to know how an F-4 could drop toilet paper (TP). I explained how the F-4 speed brakes worked and that someone could load the speed brake wells with TP then close the speed brakes. If the speed brakes were then first opened when the area to be toilet-papered was off the nose at low altitude, as many as twenty rolls of TP would be sucked out of the speed brake wells by the airflow over and under the wings. I also noted that George AFB had F-4s and that it was very unlikely that a FWS aircraft was involved because few of our aircraft were flown solo, and if it were, the aircraft could be identified by the time of the incident. The general thanked me for my thoughts and said the matter raised by the lieutenant governor was probably better attended to by his TAWC legal staff. I would have liked to get a peek inside the Mustang Ranch, but I was really glad to be off the hook for conducting an investigation.

Each senior officer's course, dedicated to generals heading for staff jobs in South Vietnam, had its own individual character, which was driven by the particular interest and personalities of the students. A class that I will long remember had a colonel from the Pentagon as one of its students. He was tasked with calculating the number of air-delivered munitions required to be stockpiled by the air force in case of simultaneous wars in Europe between NATO and the Warsaw Pact, and in Asia between the divided Koreas, with China intervening. He wasn't going to Vietnam but rather inserted himself into the class to learn firsthand what was being said about munitions employment. The student was Col. Sam Almon from AF/XOXFCM. One day, he stood up during one of my lectures on weaponeering and said in a very loud and commanding voice, "Major, you are full of #%*^&!" His assertion caught me off guard but not without a response.

I spoke in what I thought was a respectful but firm voice, saying, "Colonel, you are probably right about me being full of #%*^&. However, what I said to the class is exactly right, and I can prove it if you would like to discuss it during the break!"

During the next coffee break, he was on me like a chicken on a june bug, spouting his job title and responsibilities. Undaunted, I pulled out a green-covered legal-size document titled PC 550. It was about three hundred pages thick and full of equations, nomograms, and charts, showing how probabilities were derived and used for calculating the number of weapons required to destroy a given type and size target. My briefing charts were taken right from PC 550, a military treasure trove on the subject. He backed off, saying my next assignment would be to work for him in the Pentagon. That would be my worst nightmare, but I blew it off, thinking he couldn't make it happen.

The FWS commandant called me up to his office to inform me that several congressmen were coming to visit the FWS to receive briefings on our air-to-air training program in the F-4D. In particular, they were concerned that the ratio of MiG to US aircraft lost in aerial combat was the lowest in any recent conflict and wanted to know why. The commandant finished by telling me that he wanted me to host and brief the congressional delegation when they arrived in a couple of weeks. I thanked the commandant for considering me but suggested that our expert in air-to-air combat was Maj. Dick Meyer and that he would do a much better job than me. His answer caught me by surprise when he said, "Yes, Dick is the expert in air-to-air, but you'll do a much better job because you will become the expert in two weeks, and you're the best briefer in the Weapons School and the air force, so get on with it!" I had no idea that I had that kind of reputation among our leadership, but the challenge to be the "expert" in two weeks was daunting! Ten days later, the commandant called and said the congressmen had cancelled their visit, and I was off the hook. I sure learned a lot in those ten days but was happy to get back to my normal duties.

Once the FWS commander and staff were convinced that night close air support and night interdiction were essential if the air force was to have a favorable impact on limited wars like the counterinsurgency in Vietnam, these night missions became a big part of the flying syllabus. As such, when night range missions were scheduled, someone had to drop the parachute-suspended flares that were used to light up the target complex. One particular dark night in the fall, that was my responsibility. The F-4D was loaded with two multiple ejector racks (MERs). A MER could carry up to six stores each. One on each wing brought the total number of one million candlepower parachute flares we were carrying to twelve, enough to light up the target area brightly for a several tens of minutes.

The illuminator aircraft orbited the target complex in a lazy racetrack pattern about three thousand feet above the highest altitude that the flight of four attackers would be climbing to as they come off of their individual attacks on various targets in the complex. The first pair of flares was dropped when the flight leader calls "two minutes out." Getting over the target one orbit early enabled the illuminator aircraft pilot to get a reading on the wind from the INS and drop the flares about two-thirds of the drift time upwind of the targets. The flare light covers more area from a higher altitude with the illuminated area shrinking as the flares slowly descend by parachute.

The students were just about Winchester (out of munitions), and I was turning in to drop the remaining two flares when I felt a thump. The right engine lights came on, and the right engine rolled back to 0 rpm. It was an engine failure! Run boldface checklist, which was committed to memory and tested every week. Maintain control, dead engine throttle off, dead engine electrical power switch off, and check for fire. There was no immediate requirement to head for Nellis. After dropping the last pair of flares, I asked the flight leader to come up and check us over for external damage. One more orbit, and he was on my wing, then sliding under to check the bottom and the other side, he said we looked OK with no indication of fire.

The nice thing about the F-4 is that it has two engines and flies just about as well on one as it does on two, and if you need more power, there is always one good afterburner available. I never tried it, but I believe a clean and lightweight F-4 would go supersonic with one engine in afterburner. A lot of pilots converting to the F-4 from single-engine/single-crew aircraft like the F-100, F-102, and F-105 criticized the two-engine concept. They didn't like the second engine because it upped the cost by $5-10 million; added weight, increasing wing loading; increased frontal area, adding drag; and increased fuel consumption by a significant factor, reducing range. These allegations were all true. If combat pilots never had to fly over the ocean or over enemy territory where they were subject to attack, one engine would probably be the best design. However, the F-4 was a navy aircraft issued to the air force by Secretary of Defense McNamara, and two engines suited me just fine, especially in the situation I found myself in that night. Bailing out over precipitous mountains full of rattlesnakes was not my idea of the best way to spend the night.

After the flight leader gave us a clean bill of health with regard to airframe and fire, it was time to head the horse we were riding for the barn. Nellis was about seventy-five miles, as the crow flies, from our position or about fifteen minutes on one engine. I climbed to twenty thousand feet just in case something else bad happened and paralleled the highway to Nellis in the event we had to bail out. It's a lot easier to walk a couple of miles to a highway full of cars than thirty or forty miles through nasty mountains. Nellis tower was alerted that I would fly a simulated flame out (SFO) pattern as a precautionary measure. The flight leader and I agreed that he should land his flight of students ahead of me, just in case I closed the runway, even though the probability of that happening was very remote.

When cleared to land, I spiraled the jet on down from fifteen thousand feet, normal SFO entry at Nellis with an F-4, and landed "on speed" just slightly long. All the gauges except the right engine looked good, so we taxied to the ramp and shut down in the spot we left about two hours earlier. On the ground, several airmen were looking into the right engine with flashlights; one shouted, "Hey, Major, you swallowed a goose or two!" Sure enough, there were blood and feathers splattered on the inside of the right engine intake. An adult goose weighs about fifteen pounds and will bust up the compressor blades; some of which will go through the combustion chamber and take out the turbine section. We were lucky that none of the turbine blades cut fuel lines, causing a fire in the aft fuselage section. An inspection of the left side revealed that a couple of geese had also hit that wing just outboard of the engine intake.

Again, we were fortunate that we didn't take a goose in both engines, forcing us to bail out over the gunnery range. It was also comforting to have the flight of F-4s we were supporting right there when the engine quit. They would have been able to tell rescue where we were, shortening the time it would have taken to find us in the mountains at night.

In my spare time, I was taking a career enhancing program called Command and Staff by correspondence, not so much because the learning was essential but rather in an attempt to ensure I wouldn't have to spend nine nonflying months taking the course in residence at Maxwell AFB, Alabama. Going to an Air Force School in residence meant you were going to be reassigned at the end of the school and not likely back to the organization from which you came. I really enjoyed my work at the FWS and wanted stay there as long as air force-rated assignment personnel would allow me. Staying out of Air Force Professional Schools would increase the likelihood of staying put longer.

It was the fall of 1967, and I had already served fifteen very fast years in the air force and had only recently pinned on the gold leaves of a major. I was a realist and didn't expect that my trade school education and night school/Bootstrap degree stood me very high in the competition for advanced rank. I expected to retire as a major in five years, and my desire was to stay at Nellis, instructing at the FWS and rotating back to the Vietnam War as necessary to stay current in my profession.

I finished Command and Staff by correspondence and thought I was bulletproof! Wrong again—orders arrived, directing me to attend Armed Forces Staff College, a Joint Service School, in residence at Norfolk, Virginia. The only advantage it offered was it was shorter, only five months, vice nine for the air force course at Maxwell AFB, Alabama. Our son, Scott, was born in Las Vegas in 1966, and Sheila was now with child, expecting in June 1968. It was a tough decision, but together we decided it was best for her to stay with her parents in Mesa, Arizona, with doctors that could attend to her through the entire pregnancy and birth. I would take a couple of weekend trips home, schoolwork permitting. My reporting date was early February, and the FWS would graduate a class about mid-December and wouldn't start up again until mid-January. This break gave FWS instructors time to update their course material, which was never static, with a war on and new innovations coming at a fast pace. More importantly, the break allowed me to fit in a number of proficiency F-4 flights and spend time with the family prior to leaving for school.

The only lasting marks I left at the Weapons School were the yaw string, the night attack, and an equation that Capt. Vern Kula and I derived to provide pilots the optimum angle for attacking a bridge. Bridges are almost always long thin targets. Attacking along the length of the span compensates for the long and short bomb delivery errors, but the left/right errors are usually larger due to wind and jinking on final to avoid being hit by AAA. Attacking across the narrow width introduces problems with impacting long and short. After-action reports on bridge attacks in North Vietnam almost always included the following phrase: "Approaches to the bridge were cratered, hampering vehicle movement." This is code for not hitting the bridge with a bomb! The ideal attack axis for any bridge proved to be approximately a thirty-degree angle off the long axis of the span, providing the bomb spacing could be set equal to or less than the new apparent width of the bridge. Essentially, if the stick of bombs fell across the bridge, at least one hit was guaranteed.

Lessons Learned

Have the courage to stand your ground on the
important issues and do what is right!

Always try to do your best at everything you
do, and be the best in your field!

Be flexible, volunteer for the tough jobs!

Set high standards for yourself!

Long hours never hurt anyone, but rather helped them advance!

Know the business of your business better than
the competition or the enemy!

If your purpose in life is to "fly, fight, and win," then go where the fight is!

Be true to your moral compass!

F-4D Loaded with Walleye for Tactics Development

Majors Pete & Kriner with Crew Chief
checking F-4D forms prior to flight.

CHAPTER 6

Armed Forces Staff College and the Pentagon

The Armed Forces Staff College offered three advantages compared to other military field grade staff courses. It was short; it was triservice (Joint), so I would learn a great deal about concepts and doctrine of the army, navy, and Marine Corps; and last, if I needed to do research for the course, it was close to Headquarters TAC at Langley AFB, Virginia. Classes were conducted in a seminar format with a faculty member as the facilitator. The facilitator of the seminar I was assigned to for the duration of the five-month course was an air force colonel. The air force wasn't big on doctrine, neither was the colonel, which meant most of the discussions in seminar were civil, and learning was accomplished. I don't recall exactly, but the seminar accommodated about twenty students. All services were equally represented except the Marine Corps—there was only one marine in our seminar. Perhaps one marine was all that was needed.

The chief of staff of each service was scheduled to present a lecture during the course. These four-star lectures were the highlight of the year, and the students of each service were hoping their chief would make a good impression. They all did, except for one. The air force vice chief was a last-minute substitute because the chief was at a White House meeting as a member of the JCS. All the other service chiefs spoke powerfully and extemporaneously to a handful of viewgraphs. The air force vice, a very successful fighter pilot during WW II, read his speech in a monotone. At one point, when he bravely broke away from the script for emphasis, he got lost and read the whole page over again. Air force students took a lot of heat over that for the rest of the course. It was a lesson relearned for me—never read a speech! Know your subject well enough to speak extemporaneously.

Without a family to go home to every night, I needed something to keep me busy. I had previously hunted unsuccessfully with a bow and arrow, and this unexpected time on my hands was an opportunity for me to perfect my archery skills. I joined a local archery club and spent most of my weekends competing in tournaments—I eventually became very good. An archery tournament is much like a golf tournament and highly competitive. It consists of twenty-eight targets spread over a few hundred acres with four arrows shot at each target. That's 112 arrows shot in competition, plus practice arrows shot beforehand added up to a number similar to many of my golf scores for eighteen holes. I also enjoyed woodworking, and the navy base at Norfolk had an excellent shop with a master craftsman in charge. Evenings were spent at the hobby shop making a stereo cabinet and a dining room table out of walnut. I'm not sure how the navy did it, but they brought wood back from their cruises to South America. The best walnut I've ever worked with could be purchased for about twenty-five cents per board foot. I kept busy, saved money, and had something to show for the time Sheila and I were apart.

About a month prior to graduation, assignments were posted. Mine read Headquarters Air Force XOXFCM. Col. Sam Almon, who said I was full of #%*^&, was a very patient man, and I was going to be working for him.

I took leave after completing Armed Forces Staff College and went to Mesa, Arizona, where Sheila was staying with her parents. Prior to my arrival, she rented an apartment where we could have some privacy. She was just a week or so from giving birth to our third child and second son, Jon. He was born shortly after I arrived in Mesa, leaving me plenty of time to help Sheila recover from surgery. These uninterrupted days with Sheila and our children were really good days. Before I left for the Pentagon, Sheila and the family moved back in with her parents with the understanding she would fly to Washington DC in about six weeks as soon as little Jon was old enough to travel. The Chevy Impala headed north into Wyoming to connect with I-80 and then east to DC and a whole new world of higher headquarters staff work waiting.

The Pentagon AF/XOXFCM

Travel to and arrival in Washington DC was uneventful, and I settled into a room at the Bolling AFB, VOQ. The VOQ manager couldn't promise me a room for six weeks but agreed to try, even if it required lots of moves from room to room. I had Saturday and Sunday to practice driving to the Pentagon, which seemed easy on the weekend, but I hadn't counted on Monday morning rush-hour traffic. I couldn't out fake those Washington pros and found myself locked into a middle lane when it came to the Pentagon turnoff. The next familiar exit sign I saw was Arlington Cemetery. I exited but couldn't find a way back to the Pentagon visitor parking lot. The heck with it! I parked the car at the cemetery and walked to the Pentagon, which I could easily see through the trees. I arrived at the office address at 10:00 a.m. looking a little haggard, wearing a business suit! I'd been told that military uniforms weren't allowed in the Pentagon because the secretary of defense didn't want the public to see a big military presence in the city. This was the summer of 1968, and the antiwar movement was ugly and on the rise.

I met the officers I would be working with for the next four years—I hadn't remained in any one assignment for four years, and looking forward, it seemed like an eternity. My immediate chain of command from the top down were

> Gen. John P. McConnell, AF/CC (Air Force Chief of Staff)
> Lt. Gen. Glenn Martin, AF/XO (DCS/Operations)
> Maj. Gen. Richard Ellis, AF/XOX (Plans)
> Brig. Gen. Charles W. Lenfest, AF/XOXF (Forces Planes)
> Colonel Nolkamper, AF/XOXFC (Force Computations)
> Col. Sam Almon, AF/XOXFCM (Munitions Force
> Computations)

General Lenfest was a gruff guy! As a former member of the Idaho National Guard, he applied for West Point and graduated from the US Military Academy in January 1943. Typical of the time, he completed pilot training while a cadet and then returned to West Point to complete his education. In July 1943, he was sent to the European Theater where he flew eighty-one missions in P-47s and P-51s with the 345th Fighter Group. He was credited with nine aerial victories, nearly a double ace. After being shot down he was a POW from October 1944 to April 1945. He also flew jet fighters in the Pacific Theater and served in the Pentagon on the Joint Staff in the J-5 (Plans shop).

Under Colonel Almon were several clutches of officers assigned to Conventional Munitions and Nuclear Weapons. I was assigned to the conventional group. The nuclear guys were locked in a big vault behind us. The place was a forest of safes containing classified material that was needed to do our job. Immediately, it became clear that the most important thing in the Pentagon was to avoid having a security violation. A security violation led to immediate and harsh punishment—one had occurred a month before I arrived, and the check-the-checker system had been redoubled to ensure it didn't happen again. The check-the-checker system went like this: A Pentagon staff officer was responsible for making sure his/her desk contained nothing but pencils and pens. Except for writing implements, nothing, absolutely nothing, was to be kept in any of the drawers or on top of a desk. Each individual was responsible for certifying their desk was cleared and their safes locked. Then a second person in the office was responsible for checking to determine that all desks were properly cleaned out and safes locked. The new procedure added a third person to follow up and check that desks were empty and safes were locked. Thus, every desk and safe had three initials on the security log sheet along with the time these checks were accomplished. In my experience, adding checkers didn't improve the quality of the job but rather reduced it. The first person got sloppy because he/she knew two more were going to check it, and those two got sloppy because they knew it was already checked. It was not uncommon to work late; as a result, two additional people also had to stay after-duty hours to accomplish security checks for the one person actually working.

Lt. Col. John Budner headed up the group of officers that I worked with. He was solid, patient, and knew the ropes in the Pentagon. Under Colonel Budner, there was Maj. Al Hamblin, West Point graduate class of 1957. Al's first priority was to pass any work assigned to him off to someone else. His motto was, an action passed is an action completed. Next was John Clayton, a solid guy who was building an apple orchard business in Wenatchee, Washington, near the Columbia River. Maj. Ed Stelleni held a master's degree in math and was the man Colonel Almon told me who was giving him bad advice. Last, there was a civil servant who helped with the raw calculations that fed a gigantic computer program that produced the total numbers of conventional munitions and air-to-air missiles the air force should put in their budget request that went to the Office of the Secretary of Defense (OSD) then to the Office of Management and Budget (OMB) and finally to the Congress.

I met with Major Stelleni on my second day in the Pentagon, and we sat down to discuss the problem of calculating bomb requirements with Colonel Almon and how we should approach Colonel Almon on the subject. As it turned out, Major Stelleni's calculations were absolutely correct from my perspective—the problem was how to handle multiple ejector bomb racks (MERs) and triple ejector bomb racks (TERs).

These racks enabled a fighter pilot to drop a string of six to twelve bombs, depending on the rack and the load out. The string of bombs compensated for the pilots long and short errors and improved the probability that one or more bombs in the stick would hit the target on a single pass. Colonel Almon insisted that the only thing dropping six to twelve bombs did was waste bombs. He wanted the basic calculations for each target multiplied by six, eight, or twelve, depending on the actual load out used. Major Stelleni was leaving for an assignment to Air Force Studies and Analysis, so he volunteered to tell the colonel that he now saw his mistake and that I was right. Colonel Almon wanted nothing more than to hear the major apologize, thus exonerating him. After that, the calculations were done exactly as both Ed and I believed to be correct, and Colonel Almon was content with the results. Without this change, the colonel was telling the air force to buy far more weapons than were needed and far more than could be afforded. I learned there was another problem with the valid munitions stockpile requirements: the calculated numbers were doubled when they were inserted into the budget submission. When I questioned this logic up to the next level, I was told it was absolutely necessary to double the requirement because Congress or OMB always funded only half what the air force asked for. When I suggested that if our munitions requirement calculations were unassailable, we could win that fight; I was told that I just didn't understand how Washington worked. In that regard, Colonel Nolkamper was right. The only problem standing in the way of getting it right this time was explaining the big dip in the procurement list to OSD, OMB, and Congress. That fight would come on another day.

My next integrity test came when the Air Force Research and Development (R&D) community wanted the Air Staff to approve funding to develop an electro-optical guided bomb, something like the Walleye, but with an air force label and pedigree. Someone discovered that I had successfully introduced the Walleye into the Vietnam War for the air force and decided I was the ideal person to convince Generals Ellis and Clay (the new DCSOPS) that this was the right approach. The "buff" paper came to my inbox to work. Basically, the task was to research the topic of precision-guided weapons, prepare a briefing to the generals with a recommended air force position, and draft a letter for the generals to send forward for the chief to sign. At that time, the chief was Gen. John P. McConnell.

Papers staffed in the Pentagon were different colors, so one could tell at a glance the level of staffing that the paper was in. For example, a "buff" paper was at the lowest level, just starting up the approval chain. A green-colored paper had received approval at the service level. Last, a green-and-red striped paper had been approved at the JCS level. After doing research on the number of Paveway EO bombs the air force should procure based on the number of targets and the optimum bomb for each target, the Paveway concept emerged as the best option for the air force. This was true in both cost and effectiveness. The air force needed bombs that would penetrate steel-reinforced concrete without deforming or breaking up before they penetrated to the desired depth. Moreover, the air force design called for adapting guidance and control kits to MK 84 two-thousand-pound bomb of which there were thousands already paid for and in the inventory. There was some poetic justice here because the MK 84 was a navy-designed low-drag general-purpose bomb.

It all made sense, but there was one stumble along the way: Brigadier General Bray was in charge of all green papers being briefed up the chain of command. He approved my briefing, which was on bond paper, asking where the viewgraphs were. I told him I had only been in the Pentagon a couple of days and hadn't learned where viewgraphs were made and could he please point me in the right direction. He glowered at me like I was an insect and said, "Get out of here!" It was ten minutes before the briefing. As I passed his secretary, she said, "I'll make the charts for you—this is where it's done." I briefed how effective EO bombs were, essentially one target one bomb, showing them some before and after photos from Walleye missions in Vietnam, and explained that the MK 84 Paveway would cover a wide spectrum of targets in existing plans supporting regional commanders. They approved the package going to the chief, but I had to coordinate it with all the other two-star generals and deputy chiefs of staff (DCSs) on the Air Staff.

This is when I found out how the "system" worked. There was a network of "make it happen" majors and lieutenant colonels that worked as an ad hoc team to get papers coordinated. All that was required was to convince these field grade officers that the paper supported a good idea that the air force needed to pursue. Once they had bought into the paper, they would get coordination accomplished up through their three-star DCS. Once all the DCSs had approved the paper, it went to the chief for his approval and signature. I've often used the expression that "I didn't like majors, even was I was one." The reason being that I quickly realized majors like me were assigned one action at a time. We had plenty of energy and plenty of time to accomplish one thing at a time, and very seldom did we have to attend meetings. Action officers had it easy; on the other hand, the higher the rank, the more crowded and complex their day. I remembered the inverse allocation of youth, energy, and time to responsibility as I moved up in rank. Nothing put me on alert quicker and raised the hair on the back of my neck faster than a major action officer handing me a fully coordinated paper with the words, "Nothing important here, sir, just a routine action, sign it, and I'll get it off your desk!"

In the fall of 1968, the lieutenant colonel promotion list came out, and my name was on it. This was a really big surprise because I was a deep select from below the zone. This doesn't usually happen when you've been away at school and don't have a current OER in your present job. I had to believe it was the three combat tours and the Walleye introduction into Vietnam that influenced the Promotion Board. I expected to retire as a major and now had exceeded my expectations. I didn't need to go out and purchase a fancy hat and new rank, as I would still be a major for a long time. Services were limited in the number of personnel in each grade; therefore, vacancies had to open up by means of a lieutenant colonel being promoted to colonel or separating by retirement. All I had to do to realize that promotion was to keep from having a security violation.

It was a pleasant surprise to find that rated officers were given the opportunity to fly while they were assigned to the Pentagon. There were two aircraft types available to fly, the T-33 and the C-131. Obviously, my first choice was the T-33 to stay current in jets. The C-131 was a later version of the T-29 used for navigation training. It was powered with the same engines used on the B-26 but had a modern four-bladed square-tipped propeller with reverse pitch and brakes with antiskid. Andrews AFB, Maryland, Flight Operations had more T-33 pilots than they could handle but needed C-131 pilots to transport generals to various meetings they had to attend. The C-131 was so much like the B-26 that the required checkout and standardization and evaluation ride were rolled into one. Something like riding a bicycle, you never forget. The nice thing about flying the C-131 is they were real missions and necessary. The one thing that was strongly emphasized was that generals should arrive at their destination exactly on time. Dropping off a general at Base Operations early or late was an unpardonable offense. In addition, it was strongly recommended that turbulence be avoided and landings be smooth; otherwise, a pilot might be taken off of the list. Accordingly, when a general officer passenger said he wanted to arrive at Shaw AFB, South Carolina, at 10:00 a.m., that is when the door should open in front of Base Operations. This required a little fudging of the time en route—you could always spend a few extra minutes taxiing to Base Operations, but you couldn't get back lost time. I became an expert at opening the aircraft door within ten seconds of the appointed time.

Once a month or so, there was a requirement to take a gaggle of navigators on a navigation training flight. There was no navigation equipment on the C-131, so it was merely a means for them to log four hours in flight and collect flight pay. Eight to twelve hours of flying was even better because in those days, you could stockpile up to three months' flying time for pay purposes. It also pleased the navigators if the flight went somewhere useful—Bermuda, for instance, where you could stock up on cheap booze and have a good lunch at the British officers' mess. However, when checking out in the C-131, I was told that before one could be pilot in command (PIC) of a plane going to Bermuda, one had to go there as a copilot to be certified as "Bermuda qualified."

Then it happened: my name appeared on the schedule to fly one of these training missions to Bermuda as the copilot. I arrived early for the necessary briefings (weather, safety, customs, etc.). After the briefings, I asked the other pilot how many times he had been to Bermuda. His response was none, zilch, nada! He thought I was the experienced pilot; besides, he was only copilot qualified—I was the PIC on this flight. Dutifully, we went to the lieutenant colonel, Base Operations officer, and informed him that there had been some sort of screw-up in the scheduling process and that neither of the pilots (us) scheduled for the flight had flown to Bermuda and therefore could not fly to Bermuda! Another catch-22!

He explained that there were no other pilots available that morning, and there were several senior-ranking navigators on the flight who expected to go to Bermuda, so he would make an exception because of our impeccable qualifications. So much for rules and the *guts* to enforce them! Off we went. I was the ranking and most experienced pilot, so I became the pilot signing the flight clearance and the responsible officer. It was a good thing that I had a lot of B-26 experience behind me that I could call upon if we ran into trouble.

The flight to Bermuda was unusually boring, roughly six hours over the Atlantic to find a big rock flying a British flag. We did it all, lunch at the club and a trip to the liquor store. Then customs, weather briefing, preflight, taxi, and takeoff. The weather briefing was interesting. A significant cold had followed us out into the Atlantic and was in our path on the return home. Light rime icing was expected at our flight altitude of eighteen thousand feet, but nothing more. Rime icing is the least threatening to aviators because it is full of air pockets, soft, and the easiest ice to knock off the wings or other surfaces of an aircraft. Ice is bad for two reasons: it spoils the airflow across wings and control surfaces, reducing the wing's ability to generate enough lift to keep the airplane in the sky, while at the same time adding tons of additional weight to the aircraft. Jets fly above the weather and only collect ice on the way up and the way down through the icing layer. Propeller aircraft are relegated to fly in the worst icing conditions and therefore have flexible boots or heated leading edges on the wings, as well as deicing fluid that can be released on the propellers.

No problem for us, though; we were going home, only light rime icing to be expected. Soon it was dark, and we were in the clouds. If there is anything a fighter pilot doesn't like, it's flying at night in the weather. Only one thing is deemed worse: an emergency at night in weather over the cold, cold Atlantic Ocean. Things were going as planned until the airspeed started to decay. Add more power and look out the window at the wings only to be greeted by the unmistakable shine of a sheet of glare ice—the worst kind. Soon we heard the sound of chunks of ice being thrown off of the propellers into the fuselage. The navigators were beginning to wake up. In order to maintain safe separation from other aircraft that we couldn't see in the weather, I foolishly tried to maintain our assigned altitude. Ha, what other idiots would be out in this mess. We were too far out to sea to reach any FAA control stations and outside of radar coverage as well, so we were on our own. If we had to ditch or bail out, no one would have a clue as to where we were in that vast expanse of ocean. I made the decision to preserve the engines; we were now running well over maximum climb power and still not holding altitude. There was one chance for survival of the aircraft and crew: we would descend to just above the wave tops, hoping for warmer air that would melt the ice. Bang, bang, bang went the ice chunks slamming against the fuselage. Soon we were at five hundred feet mean sea level on the altimeter. But what did that mean? Over the ocean, fliers adhered to an International Convention to set their altimeters at 29.92 inches of mercury. This setting ensured that all airplanes had the same reference for safe separation when outside radio and radar coverage. While this over-the-ocean setting provides safe separation from other aircraft, it is relatively useless with regard to how high above the waves you are, and we were still in clouds or fog and couldn't see. For the non-flier, when 29.92 is set in the altimeter and the aircraft is being flown toward a low-pressure area (the big red *L* on the TV weather map), the aircraft will be lower than indicated on the altimeter! With this in mind, I knew we were closer to the ocean than five hundred feet; how close was unknown, ten feet? The outside air gauge read three degrees Celsius (thirty-seven degrees Fahrenheit), and no more ice chunks were flying into the fuselage. We inched the plane up to 1,500 feet on the altimeter and stayed there until we could see stars and realized we had passed through the front and were in the clear—the danger had passed. The laws of physics suggested it would be about two degrees Celsius at 1,500 feet, still above freezing. We climbed back to eighteen thousand feet, where we were supposed to be, and relaxed. Soon we had radio contact and made a casual comment about running into some severe icing conditions about an hour back, and by the way, the glare icing we encountered wasn't forecast when we filed our flight clearance in Bermuda, ho-hum! Smooth landing, taxi to the ramp, shut down the engines, and fill out the forms; navigators are happy to be home. It was just another day at the office.

The only sign of the drama over the Atlantic that night was the huge dents in the sides of the forward fuselage caused by the chunks of ice slung off of the props. The sheet metal panels were never replaced, so the dents were a constant reminder whenever I flew that aircraft.

Ever heard of the Bermuda Triangle, graveyard of lost ships and planes? There are a few survivors and just about as many believers! I no longer think it's a mystery, just storm fronts and hurricanes that frequent that area.

One day, Colonel Nolkamper walked into the office where Lieutenant Colonel Budner and his action officers had their desks. This was a break with tradition and quite a surprise. He nodded to Budner and asked, "Who's running the Bare Base Program?"

No one spoke; it was a very pregnant silence until Budner said, "Pete's got that action, sir!"

· Colonel Nolkamper tossed over a piece of paper and said, "Draft a letter inviting the president to the Bare Base demonstration!" I had no idea what the Bare Base Program was, but it was mine from now on. The silence of my fellow action officers indicated the Bare Base Program was in big trouble, or they would have spoken up. Like it or not, I had some real work to do. I learned Maj. Dick Toner was the Air Force Systems Command project officer and made arrangements to meet with him the next day. I immediately liked him; he was bright and articulate and wasted no time in telling me straight out that Bare Base was in big trouble—almost none of the equipment worked, and the things that did work were in short supply. Essentially, the Bare Base Program was intended to provide all the equipment necessary for a fighter wing to deploy to an isolated runway and ramp with a source of water nearby that could be made potable. Everything else was provided in the Bare Base Program. Some of the items included in the program are listed below:

- turbine-driven electrical generators for prime power
- ERDLators to convert available water to potable water for up to four thousand people
- air-conditioned tents for personnel
- a dining facility in a shelter that folded up with all the kitchen equipment attached to the walls and when folded fit into a C-141 or C-130
- maintenance facilities equipped with all the necessary tools and equipment to repair an F-4 component, engine, radar, communications, INS, etc. Each shelter performed one of the necessary maintenance functions.
- shower and latrine facilities. The latrine was ultramodern with an electronic human waste burner.
- fold-up shelters for squadron briefing rooms, maintenance control, etc.
- special trailers designed to haul all the shelters from the airlift aircraft to their site on the airfield

The Bare Base program provided a complete airbase ready to operate at combat tempo in less than three days after the first airlift aircraft landed on the bare runway.

Major Toner made it very clear that the program was in trouble and that it was unlikely the Bare Base demonstration could take place on schedule. Items of the Bare Base Program that were working well and in large numbers were the maintenance shelters. The dining hall was also performing very well. Some of the items in trouble were the latrine, trailers to haul the shelters, and the insulated tents. Without working trailers in large numbers, the demo would surely fail. Engineering changes on the failing items were in work; however, the schedule for getting these changes into production would not support the Bare Base demonstration dates.

Two days after the initial meeting, I was in Colonel Nolkamper's office with a draft invitation to the president, as directed, and a strong argument to cancel the Bare Base demonstration because the equipment was woefully behind schedule and some critical pieces were not working properly. The colonel asked me if I was familiar with the 4th TFW, the unit tasked to participate in the demo. "No," I responded. With a few strong words, he told me to get myself to Seymour Johnson AFB, North Caroline, home of the 4th TFW, and get to know the people and the equipment. It turned out they had a couple of maintenance shelters to work with and had practiced setting them up and using them for actual maintenance procedures.

A few days later, I was sitting in a tent next to Colonel Boswell, commander 4th TFW, being briefed by his staff on their preparation for the demonstration. Col. Marion L. Boswell was a hands-on, make-it-happen kind of commander, a lot like Colonel King. He had flown a combat tour flying B-17s in Europe during WW II and F-4Ds out of Da Nang during the Vietnam War. He had only been commander of the Fourth Wing for a short time and was doing his best to make the Bare Base demo a success.

After an hour or so of briefings, I toured all the sites where enlisted personnel were training on the various maintenance shelters. I watched a couple of shelters being opened up and set up for maintenance work. Each shelter had its own built-in air conditioner, power strips, and lighting. One of the two shelters set up that morning was to be used for repairing an F-4D radar that morning. When asked how they liked the shelters, the universal response was "Have you ever worked out of a tent? Moving from tents to air-conditioned boxes is great!" I thought of my own experiences in Korea and Vietnam and had to agree that a rainproof box with integral heat and cooling was a very good thing. When asked if they could pull off a successful demonstration, their answer was a resounding "yes!" After two days spent with the enlisted maintenance and civil engineering personnel who were primary users and installers of the equipment, and I was convinced that they were committed to success. Moreover, that they would make it happen if given enough of the radically new shelters and temper tents.

Back at the Pentagon, I briefed Colonel Nolkamper on my findings and stood firm on a recommendation to slip the demonstration from the fall of 1968 to October 1969 and to not invite the president. My next assignment was to get the Tactical Air Command (TAC) to agree to slip the Bare Base demonstration. That required a letter from the chief or vice chief of the air force to Gen. William Momyer, commander TAC, requesting his support in rescheduling the demonstration. Much to everyone's surprise, General Momyer's reply stated the Bare Base demo was too important to slip and that he wanted it to go on as scheduled. However, the following day, Gen. "Spike" Momyer put on his AFREDCOM hat and wrote a letter to the commander of Readiness Command, which was a Unified Command. This letter advised CINCREDCOM that the Bare Base demo would require an enormous amount of airlift to transport a fighter wing's worth of shelters and equipment to North Field, South Carolina, and therefore jeopardized an important REDCOM exercise. He further advised CINCREDCOM to request that the JCS direct the air force to deconflict the Bare Base demo by moving it forward. It was a Machiavellian move to get a Unified commander to ask that the demo be moved, vice the air force having to ask. As an aside, at that time, the TAC, commander was the air component to three Unified Commands. These were Readiness Command (REDCOM), Atlantic Command (LANTCOM), and Southern Command (SOUTHCOM). CINCREDCOM wrote the chairman JCS, requesting the Bare Base demo be slipped so as not to conflict with his exercise. In turn, the CJCS directed the air force to slip the demo, and we were happy to comply. The breathing room we received made a significant difference in the projected availability of Bare Base equipment. With light at the end of the tunnel, as far as the equipment was concerned, Air Force Systems Command put pressure on the contractors, and they delivered.

When the day came to deploy, most of the equipment was available, and hundreds of airlift sorties began hauling cargo and personnel from Seymour AFB, North Carolina, to North Field, South Carolina. First to arrive were Red Horse civil engineers to lay out the base and put in place the utilities, including electrical power and a potable water system that drew water from a nearby river. Once base utilities were operational, personnel support and maintenance facilities streamed into North Field. It was a beehive of activity but well orchestrated like a ballet. I was there to observe and comment on the buildup and operational phases. Maj. John Lowery from TAC Safety was there to provide an extra set of eyes with regard to maintaining high safety standards in the air and on the ground. John was an old and dear friend with whom I'd flown F-86s at Williams AFB a decade earlier. In addition, an Air Force Audiovisual Team was there to film the operation for historical purposes and to provide documentation that could be used in congressional testimony to support air force budget requests. Quarters (tents) on base were limited to base support and operational personnel. All the observers, like Major Lowery and me, were living in a motel away from North Field.

Base buildup was another superbly executed effort by maintenance and civil engineering personnel. The 4th TFW Squadron arrived on schedule with a full complement of twenty-four F-4D aircraft. Aircraft landing with pilot discrepancies were either immediately repaired on the flight line, or components were replaced and then repaired in the appropriate component shelter. The squadron deployed with its authorized war readiness spares kit (WRSK). Think of WRSK as boxes of spare parts set aside and packaged to go to war. Failed electronic boxes are removed from the aircraft and replaced with a like part from the WRSK. The failed part is then repaired in the appropriate repair shelter and returned to the WRSK. The WRSK also contained nonrepairable items such as wheels, brakes, tires, etc.

Maj. John Lowery suggested that he and I go over the audiovisual film for the day and put together a thirty-minute story of the day's activities with narration to send to our bosses, General Momyer at TAC and Major General Ellis at AF/XOX. XOX, which had responsibility for plans, would not normally be in charge of a flying exercise; but in this case, it was the Bare Base plan that was being evaluated, not the flying. The F-4Ds were there primarily to ensure the equipment could realistically support intense operations for ten days. Because it was a plan's show and I was the plan's program manager, it was also my show.

John and I used the Huntley/Brinkley format for the narration. He would write and narrate a portion of the film, and I would follow sequentially until the entire thirty minutes of film was covered. We labored long into the night to get the narration polished without stutters, slurs, and such. My training and experience as a SAWC briefing officer paid great dividends in this endeavor. Major Lowery was a narrator for the Air Force Sky Blazers aerial demonstration team in Europe and was very smooth. The videos arrived at TAC and the Pentagon in time for General Momyer's and General Ryan's morning staff meetings. Gen. Jack Ryan, formerly commander PACAF, replaced Gen. John McConnell on August 1, 1969. Apparently, the video was a big hit because we received requests to put more events on film. These requests were passed to the audiovisual team. Every day for twelve days, films taken of the Bare Base demonstration were edited, clipped, and narrated. The only screen credits were of the audiovisual team; John and I wanted to remain anonymous for reasons of survival. We both wanted to fly, not make movies or give briefings.

It was a joy to watch the exercise unfold. Not one of the sorties flown was ineffective because of an aircraft malfunction. The Bare Base equipment was the future of air force contingency operations. All that was needed to support soldiers in combat was a suitable runway and a source of water that could be made potable—there was hardly a place in the Northern Hemisphere that didn't meet these requirements, and most of the Southern Hemisphere was covered as well.

The exercise was going too well; the sortie rate being achieved was too high and threatened to undercut the air force policy of 1.5 sorties per day per aircraft. This number was the basis for calculating the number of aircrews required per squadron, as well as fuel, munitions, spare parts, and maintenance personnel. Major General Ellis, the director of plans on the Air Staff, intervened with a message to cut back on the flying at North Field. The deployed squadron from the 4th TFW had to slow down the sortie rate! I carried the message to Colonel Boswell, who was there just as an observer, while the squadron commander and his teams ran the show. Colonel Boswell understood all the implications and curtailed half of the last day's sorties to make the sortie rate come out exactly on the number advertised by the air force. There was one abort on the last day. There was a hard TAC requirement that the attitude indicator in both cockpits be functional at takeoff. This requirement was based on a belief that if the pilot became disoriented in weather, the GIB would recognize the problem and call it to the attention of the pilot. On the day in question, there was not a cloud in the sky, but the GIB's altitude indicator was malfunctioning. Regulations are to be adhered to, and the pilot aborted as he should have.

There was much joy back at the Pentagon. The Bare Base equipment worked as advertised, although the human waste burner put out quite an offensive odor and needed rework. Clearly, the 4th TFW maintenance and civil engineering personnel were true to their word when they told me that if they got the Bare Base equipment needed for the demo they would make it work! Without question, they did an exceptional job learning to operate and maintain complex aircraft out of Bare Base shelters under a rigorous test. There was no question in my mind that Colonel Boswell, 4th TFW commander, provided the leadership and hands-on involvement that motivated his wing's personnel to excel in this difficult task. It was apparent that he convinced them that the future of the air force's ability to go to war, in large part, rested on their shoulders in the Bare Base demo. Soldiers were clearly the big winners because the air force had developed a way to get to the fight in a hurry, no matter where it was. The air force was no longer tied to large operational airbases. It was no surprise that Bare Base equipment played a large role in Operation Desert Storm twenty-one years later.

It was not supposed to happen, but it did: Colonel Nolkamper's office was written up for a security violation. There weren't many people in his office, just the colonel, his executive, and a secretary, but they had a roomful of safes that contained very sensitive material, including a lot of operational plans. After the principal closed a safe, a second and third person checked the safe. The procedure for the checkers was to spin the dial and then try to open the safe. If the safe would not open, it was considered locked. In addition to the three office personnel who checked their own safes, there were people from Air Force Security who rechecked safes at about 2:00 a.m. on a random basis. It was one of these early morning random checkers that found a safe that they could open! In fact, what they found was a safe that was broken and could not be locked even though it passed the simple spin-the-dial test.

There was no indication that anything was missing or that anyone had access to the material in the defective safe. Nonetheless, senior officers had said that "heads would role" if there was another security violation. Colonel Nolkamper paid the price and was forced to retire in two months. Those who worked for him down in the various branches were sad to see him go. He provided strong leadership and astute guidance on the JCS papers his action officers were given to work. It was sad to see this dedicated officer leaving under a cloud, so we decided to take him out for dinner at one of the high-end restaurants. After dinner, he went around the table, giving each of us his assessment of our performance and potential.

"John Budner, you're a strong effective leader, you'll make general."

John retired as a brigadier general and is currently living in Virginia.

"Al Hamblin, you're lazy, but as a West Point graduate, you'll make colonel."

Al retired as a colonel and is currently living in Florida.

"John Clayton, your apples consume you, you'll peak as a lieutenant colonel."

John retired as a lieutenant colonel and made a small fortune on his orchards.

"Pete Piotrowski, you're too abrasive to go any higher."

I respected him and believed him! I thought I was just honest and direct?

Prior to Colonel Nolkamper leaving, the branch chief gave me the task of writing a paper on a particular topic that was hot at the time. He also told me what the conclusion should be, which riled me. However, after doing all the research on the subject, I came to the same conclusion and wrote the paper for Colonel Nolkamper's signature with a coordination sheet from the branch chief. At that time, signature blocks and dates were done with stamps because just who would finally sign the paper was never clear. The branch chief came by to tell me he really liked the paper and that he sent it to the division chief for signature.

Time passed, and the branch chief who had asked for the paper moved up to replace Colonel Nolkamper when he retired. A week later, the paper in question came back to me with big Xs across the pages. There wasn't any memo providing guidance, so I made an appointment to see the colonel who originally gave me the task, liked the paper, and then by an act of fate, forwarded it to himself. Standing in front of his desk, I asked, "What is wrong with the paper, sir?"

"Nothing" was the response, "but I have a different perspective from where I now sit—put it in the burn bag!" That was an interesting lesson!

A tasking to work a JCS paper came direct from Brigadier General Lenfest to me. There was a cover memo from the general providing some guidance, but it was absolutely illegible. I passed it around the office to see if anyone could decipher it—no luck. I took it to the branch chief. He couldn't make any sense out of it either. I then called General Lenfest's secretary and made an appointment to see the general. At the appointed moment, the secretary opened the door to the general's office and shoved me in. The general looked up at me, looked around, and then said, "Where is your branch chief, where is your division chief, what the hell do you want?"

I showed him his memo and said, "Sir, I came for clarification on your memo so I could get the job done right and not waste any of your valuable time with an inappropriate response."

To that, he responded, "How dare you come to see me without your branch chief and division chief, get out of my office!"

Not exactly what I expected, but it was a valuable lesson. I made myself a promise that if I sent someone a memo and they needed clarification, they could come directly to me. This would ensure that after some discussion, we both would be wiser for having talked about the matter before us, and I would advise them to be sure and back-brief the chain of command on what had transpired so no one would be out of the loop. I did back-brief my two bosses about the butt chewing from General Lenfest and worked the paper as best I could. It never came back for rework. I was learning that Higher Headquarters worked differently than operational units, where getting the job done right was what mattered. There were numerous times at the Commando Wing, at SAWC, and at the FWS where general officers would call me up to their offices. However, dragging along supervisors was never required, nor would the response be timely if you had to round everyone up. The key was always the back brief so everyone would be on the same page, and supervisors could add value or make corrections if they felt it was needed.

I was working late on another JCS paper when a call came, someone claiming to be General Ryan's executive officer, saying that he had to talk with me immediately. I informed the voice on the phone that I was working on a JCS paper with a tight suspense in the morning and asked if I could meet with him at his convenience the following morning. The voice said, "No, what I need from you can't wait!" I ran across to the opposite E-ring and down to General Ryan's office, all the time thinking it was a spoof being played on me by a fellow action officer. At that time, General Ryan was the air force chief of staff. When I reported in to his exec's office, sure enough there was a brigadier general sitting behind the desk. He informed me that I was being considered to be his assistant and the assistant executive officer to General Ryan. He went on to say, "The hours are long, and on occasion, I would be working directly with General Ryan. Do you want to be considered for the job?" I replied that the long hours didn't bother me, but I was an action officer and took pride in working tough problems and making good things happen and didn't think I would be a good assistant executive officer. With that comment, I was excused. As I walked back to my office, I started having second thoughts about turning down the position. When I reached my office, I called Brig. Gen. Ben King, now chief of the Air Force Safety Center at Norton AFB, California. I told him about the job offer that I just turned down and asked for some advice. After about five minutes of expletives and comments about insanity, General King urged me to go back and tell General Ryan's exec that after a few minutes' thought, I realized what a privilege it would be to directly serve General Ryan and that I would very much appreciate being considered for the position. I retraced my steps to chief's exec's office and repeated what General King urged me to say. The exec graciously accepted my request. It should not surprise the reader that I didn't get the job. Lt. Col. Charles R. Hamm was selected for the assistant executive officer position. He retired in June 1991 as a lieutenant general serving as the superintendent of the Air Force Academy. At that time, congressional law prohibited a follow-on assignment for Military Academy superintendents to ensure their independence from the service chiefs.

That was the last time I spoke with Brigadier General King until he was nominated to the Oklahoma Aviation Hall of Fame. He was born in Add Lee, Oklahoma, on December 9, 1919, and was honored for his many signal achievements in the Army Air Corps and the United States Air Force over twenty-nine years when he retired on February 1, 1971. I was asked to introduce him to the Oklahoma Hall of Fame in 1989 while serving as CINCNORAD and CINCUSSPACECOM. It was a distinct pleasure and personal honor to extol his leadership and combat exploits, including seven aerial victories in WW II (three Zeros while flying a P-38, and two FW-190s and two ME-109s flying a P-51).

I had a degree, but it wasn't as impressive as those earned in residence at a respected university. The Pentagon was host to a University of Southern California degree program in Technical Management. On top of the normal MBA courses, it included Rocket Propulsion, Aerodynamics, and Advanced Physics. After a year as an action officer, I enrolled in this program. The course required three hours, two nights a week, which I thought I could fit into the normal workload. Sheila was supportive. The Bare Base exercise took me out of the classroom for two weeks, but the instructors understood the absence and allowed me to make up the assignments that were missed. The Pentagon was a directed four-year assignment, so there was plenty of time to acquire the thirty-plus semester hours required for the MBA degree. This four-year assignment would end in 1972, twenty years since my enlistment. The degree was needed to help find decent and hopefully financially rewarding follow-on employment.

During the Vietnam War, most, if not all, Pentagon offices were manned on Saturday until released. Munitions were no exception, and the duty came around monthly. I can understand the generals not wanting to be called on an issue and not have the answer and no one to call to get the answer. Besides, it was a quiet time to get caught up on the paperwork and get some typing done without having to wait in the priority queue. On one of these boring Saturday mornings, a memo came in, requesting that officers who were interested in an MBA to put their name on the memo. It further stated that Howard University had openings, and the air force would pay the tuition in residence. Manna from heaven! Howard was an all-black university, but an MBA was an MBA. I put my name on the list, thinking there was an outside chance that I would be accepted; but if I didn't put my name on the list, it was a guaranteed lost opportunity! Time passed, and I started receiving brochures from Harvard University about some of their programs, including the cost. These all went into the "round file" under my desk. More brochures, more trash. Then one day, the DCS/Personnel called, wanting to know why I had not returned the applications to Harvard. My answer was "I can't afford Harvard."

To which he replied, "You put your name on the memo, and you've been selected to attend the Harvard program for Management Development next year. If you don't fill out the forms in my office, you've lost your chance." It doesn't take long to circle the Pentagon on the E-ring if you're in a hurry. The forms were executed and sent to Harvard. I was amazed how a typo on a memo could alter your future. I believe the words "Howard University" didn't attract any names but mine, and I was selected by default. How I was selected for this rare opportunity didn't matter; I was going to Harvard. My plans for USC went on hold after completing the current semester, but I still had two years left in the Pentagon.

The Program for Management Development (PMD) at Harvard was different, interesting, and, in some ways, a disappointment. There were 151 students in the class. One hundred were American, and the remaining fifty-one were from the world at large. The largest contingents came from England and Europe in that order. South America was perhaps the third-largest foreign student body, with a few from Africa. All were in middle-management positions from companies large and small. Two were ministers. We all attended the same classes together. Learning was based on case studies and the Socratic method of discussion.

Essentially, we were issued a number of case studies to read after class. These case studies covered accounting, marketing, management, labor union negotiations, business failures, etc. The following day, in the round room laid out much like an amphitheater, a professor who was an expert on the subject matter would ask students for the solution to the problem illuminated in a specific case study we had read. For 151 students, there were at least 149 solutions offered. I might have heard something that sounded a little akin to my own view, but not often. I left these discussions wondering what the professor believed the solution to the problem or issue was.

It was also a little disconcerting to me that over half our professors had never held a job or met a payroll—they were theorists without any practical experience to draw upon. These professors started their academic life in preschool and went all the way through school to earn a doctorate degree and then were selected to a position at Harvard without ever holding a job that produced something. There were two professors who had my respect because they earned their spurs in the toil and sweat of running an enterprise. One had built and/or run several successful companies—his forte was organization structure and management. The other was a union negotiator who had represented the large auto unions in negotiations with Detroit's Big Three. He'd been in the ring and was full of good advice for managers when it came to labor relations. The academic year was from February through May 1970, the height of the Vietnam antiwar fever and demonstrations. Flower children were in vogue, and the "pig people" thrown off federal land they were squatting on in a "free love" commune came to Harvard. The purpose of their visit was to raise money through charitable donations at the Harvard field house made available to them at no cost by Harvard's leadership.

I could see the field house from my "coop" window. Coop was the name given to the very, very small room two PMD classmates shared. Four coops shared a common latrine—it was close quarters but still a lot better than I enjoyed during most of my bachelor military assignments. Students were not allowed to live off campus, so all 151 were in this dormitory building. The building also contained a nice dining facility and some recreational equipment. There were pool and ping-pong tables, where I was able to best most of my classmates, except a British student named Brian Bevan who was my equal. As I mentioned, I could see people streaming into the field house on Saturday afternoon. I'd read all the case studies assigned, so why not see what the "pig people" were up to?

It was a bizarre scene! Several people were playing various musical instruments, all to their own tune and somewhat oblivious of the other musicians. There were many young women in various states of dress, all carrying young babies. When I asked one if her husband was there, she looked at me with dull eyes and said she didn't know who the father was; their commune was a free-love society. The place was hazy with cigarette smoke down to about waist level. The field house was also full of police officers; I suppose to keep the free loaders and students from physical disagreements. I asked a police officer if the field house had been fumigated to eliminate the smell of sweaty athletic clothes for the visitors. He said, "Son, what you smell is a lethal dose of marijuana. If you didn't know that, I suggest you leave before you're overcome with it!" His advice had a truthful ring to it, so I left, but I never forgot that odor, and that was very helpful in years to come.

During an amphitheater session on organizational principles, the professor who had started and run a number of successful businesses was leading the class through a case study on General Motors (GM). The case study was about Chairman Roger Smith, who managed GM to the point of squandering away about 15 percent of their market share during his tenure. It was clear to me that Roger thought the business of General Motors was building cars when in fact their real business was selling cars because that is where the money was made and returned to the corporation. My fellow students danced all around the issue with fancy theories, and once again, 151 students came up with at least 150 remedies for fixing the problem at General Motors.

During a brief lull in the discussion, I asked the professor point-blank, "What is the school solution for the basic principle on which enterprises should be organized?"

His immediate reply was "At Harvard, we do not provide school solutions. It is up to the student to deduce this from the discussions."

To this I replied, "Sir, I am in the air force, and organization is everything in the military. Surely there is a guiding principle for building an organization, and if I leave Harvard with nothing else, I would like to know that principle!"

With a great sigh and a lot of reluctance, he said, "You should always organize around the *strategic purpose* of the enterprise!" The light came on! General Motors' "strategic purpose" was selling cars—that's how they made money. Roger Smith's goal was to streamline manufacturing to cut cost. This resulted in Cadillacs that were built on Chevy frames, with Chevy engines, and Chevy transmissions. Buicks and Oldsmobiles suffered the same fate. They were cheaper on the margin that is true, but that is not what their customers wanted. Roger Smith's background was financial; however, at that juncture, General Motors needed someone who understood market dynamics and the customer base. This was an enormously valuable lesson for me and played a big role in how the E-3A AWAC Wing was organized.

The tragedy at Kent State University had a big impact on college campuses all over America, and Harvard was no exception. The Business School student president scheduled a rally to decide whether or not they should go "on strike" to demonstrate solidarity with other student bodies across the United States that had opted out of school en masse. The rally was held on the lush green common at Harvard near the banks of the Charles River. Speeches were made both pro and con prior to the vote; following the speeches, each student in attendance was given a simple ballot to mark. Ballots were numbered, so no signature was required. When the vote was tallied, a very slim majority was *against the strike*. A load roar rolled across the common when the results were announced, and then there were speeches against the PMD and AMD (Advanced Management Program) students who allegedly swayed the vote against the strike. What surprised me most was that the more radical students honored the vote and stayed in school. I really believe they wanted to stay in school, graduate on time, and get the big-paying jobs on Wall Street; they just needed someone to drag them from what was popular to what was right. The *courage to do what is right* is hardly ever popular but is just as important in business as it is in government and war.

Many of my Harvard student associates returned to promotions and heady successes in the business world; two were fired. The school was just a nice way of saying good-bye and giving them an edge in the job market. I returned to the Pentagon having enjoyed the sabbatical but wondering how it would make me a better action officer.

Not much had changed at the Pentagon; however, there were a few new faces in the hierarchy. Lieutenant Colonel Budner was promoted and moved to an operational assignment, and there was a new branch chief in XOXFCM. His primary motivation was to avoid work. I didn't think it was the work itself that he feared because branch chiefs didn't do work; they just reviewed what action officers did prior to sending it up the chain, perhaps all the way to the chief of staff to be used in a session of the JCS. He feared that something he forwarded might be viewed as shallow, sophomoric, or worse, just plain wrong. The way to protect against this fear was to go to great lengths to convince another branch an action really belonged to them.

This manifested itself in a branch directive that we would all work until midnight each day to ensure that our desk logs and safe logs showed that we were working roughly seventeen hours per day. This directive was motivated by a rumor that someone at the two-star level in XO was checking the logs to see who was working overtime and who wasn't. The rumor also carried the threat that the JCS paper workload would be spread around to the branches working the least number of hours. The plain truth was he wanted us to stay late to avoid the slight chance that we would be assigned to work JCS papers because our branch wasn't working as much overtime as other branches. We met with the boss to explain that we were willing to work late if there was a reason, but his plan was just plain stupid. He was the boss, and we stayed at our desks until midnight for a couple of months. While the branch was never tasked to do anything outside the normal routine, we all caught up on our reading. I don't know if it ever ended because I left while mandatory overtime was still in effect. I can still hear the colonel saying, as he departed for his home at 6:00 p.m., "We're working late tonight. Call me if you need any help."

It really didn't matter to me, as I was working late on purpose. In preparation for the 1971 air force budget submission on munitions procurement, I was doing all the manual calculations for free-fall bombs on targets set in Europe and North Korea. The air force had some IBM computers that could crunch the numbers, but they weren't facile like the computers of today. At that time, it took an experienced pilot and weaponeer to calculate the aim point or points on a given target with various types of ordnance that would yield the number of bombs required for the desired level of damage. Normally, I wouldn't have had to work late to meet the deadline; however, the air force had selected me for promotion to colonel in the fall of 1970, and following that bit of good news, I was selected to attend the Royal Air Force College of Air Warfare at Manby Royal Air Force Station near Louth, England. Even though I had an escape from the colonel's madness, I was committed to get the job done, which I was there to do. Further, there was no capable replacement on the horizon that could be expected to do the work correctly.

Just a week or so before my last day at the Pentagon, I was tasked to present the air force recommended munitions procurement numbers to the Office of Management and Budget. I wasn't familiar with the process, but armed with operational experience and a stack of computer printouts, I didn't expect any problems. There were two air force officers ahead of me on the schedule, which was a good thing. I expected to learn from the questions they were asked by OMB, as well as how they responded. What transpired was a shock to the mind and logic in general.

The first officer was trying to defend the recommended procurement of aluminum pallets used by C-130, C-141, and C-5 aircraft. Cargo was strapped down on these pallets, and the pallets were then loaded into the aircraft on a system of rollers built into the floor of these aircraft. Without the aluminum pallets, loading cargo would have been a manually intensive operation, as would be unloading the same cargo and moving it to its follow-on destination. The whiz kids of OMB looked very young, like they had just graduated from college, and by their words and actions had no concept of military air operations. The OMB representatives expressed great displeasure with the large numbers of pallets the air force proposed to buy. The reason was the air force could not account for every pallet they had in the previous year's inventory. The officer on the hot seat explained that the conflict in Vietnam required the air force to air-drop thousands of tons of supplies to soldiers and marines engaged in combat operations and that there was no way for the aircraft to receive a receipt for these air-dropped pallets. Further, he explained that the enemy overran some of the locations where these pallets were dropped, and in some cases, American fighting men were evacuated under emergency conditions, and the pallets could not be recovered. The officer went on to explain that pallets were also used for the low-altitude parachute extraction system (LAPES) in combat operations. When these pallets were parachute extracted at twenty-five feet altitude and 100 mph, the pallets were often damaged beyond use, but it was the only way to get food and ammunition to soldiers in fierce combat; and again, there was no way to either get a hand receipt for the delivery or to recover the pallets. The wise men of OMB were unmoved and cut the pallet request in half, with the admonition, if you don't come up with a way to get hand receipts from the army and recover the cost from them, you will get no funding next year.

The next officer was defending the air force procurement of aircrew helmets. At this time, the air force had gone to an expanding foam material to fill the void between a person's head and the inside of the helmet shell. Helmets were purchased in a variety of sizes, based on historical data, to serve the newly recruited aircrews and replace helmets that were damaged beyond repair. Again, the whiz kids railed against the officer, asserting the buy was at least four times larger than their computations suggested. They went on to point out that there were only so many hat sizes between 6 3/4s and 7 3/4s, which they believed covered the range of male heads (there were few, if any, female pilots at that time). According to the OMB whiz kids' view, it was simply a matter of aircrews sharing helmets of the same size. The defender of helmet procurement explained that a flying schedule was based on operational and training needs and would not likely be amenable to add another scheduling criterion for hat size. He also pointed out that even though a hat size was the same, the shapes varied from round to oval and that size was not the only variable that needed to be taken into account. Again, the wise men of OMB were unmoved, telling the officer it was simply a scheduling problem. In desperation, the officer made one last attempt. He pointed out those helmets and the oxygen masks attached to them were full of sweat, spit, and sometimes vomit. Thus, putting someone else's helmet on was like putting a stranger's tennis shoe over your face. To my surprise, this point carried the day, and OMB approved the helmet buy.

Now it was my turn, and I expected the worst, as there were few compelling arguments for the munitions stockpile for a hypothetical future war. To my surprise, they were so pleased to see the numbers reduced from the previous year's erroneous calculations under Colonel Almon's edict that all they wanted to know was why. I explained that some numbers in one of the calculations had been transposed when converted to machine language, and the error wasn't caught until just recently when a rigorous scrub was made between selected computer solutions and hand calculations. There was only a scintilla of truth in my statement, but all they wanted to hear was the air force had a reduced requirement. It was approved without further debate.

My work at the Pentagon being finished, I closed out the log on my desk and went home to Sheila. The movers were scheduled to arrive the following day.

Lessons Learned

Work is normally a team effort, be a team player.

Leaders support their teams.

Always be willing to meet with people subordinate
to you to clarify tasking you have sent them.

Never force people to be present when there is no work to be done.

When supporting a field unit, visit the unit and get
their inputs face-to-face at every level.

A well-led wing/organization can produce miracles.

When you observe behaviors that demotivate
people, avoid doing these things.

Your view of issues may change when your responsibilities change! Keep
this in mind when tilting with windmills!

Sheila and Lt. Col. Pete at Harvard PMD Graduation

CHAPTER 7

England and Europe

It seemed incredible that a pilot who had served in Korea, Japan, Vietnam, and Thailand would be assigned to Europe. With an Asia expertise portfolio, I believed the air force would never allow me to experience how the United States had postured itself against the Soviet Union and the Warsaw Pact. Yet it was happening. Sheila and I were making decisions on what to take to Europe and what to store. The senior air force officer on the faculty at RAF College of Air Warfare, Col. Robert Lines, assured us in his welcome letter that the house we would live in at RAF Manby was fully furnished. Thus, all we had to bring were clothing and special kitchen utensils that Sheila might favor. The rest of our furniture, recreational equipment, etc. went into storage while we were overseas. Cars were sold, as it didn't make sense to take a three-year-old Chevy to England for driving on the wrong side of the road at roughly four dollars per gallon at their prices. The car I drove to the Pentagon was a dilapidated Ford Falcon that we let go for fifty dollars.

Our departure for England was scheduled out of Dover AFB, Delaware, on a contract carrier at 10:00 p.m., a difficult time for three small children unless they could sleep during the flight over. The first important observation when arriving at Dover AFB was that the B707 Tiger Airliner was missing an engine on the right wing. Hanging engines and checking their operation is not a trivial series of events and could take hours or days if the replacement engine was not handy. It didn't look good for a smooth departure and crossing. On the other hand, it was necessary to convince Sheila that the aircraft would be safe; after all, the pilots don't want to take unnecessary risks.

Time passed slowly with about two hundred military personnel of all services and their families scheduled for the flight. Of all the passengers, I was the senior officer, so I started looking for a more pleasant place for mothers with young children. There was a large VIP lounge visible from the passenger lounge; it was worth a try. The door was open, and a senior NCO was busy doing some paperwork behind the bar. He looked up, and when the silver leaves on my shoulders came into focus, he said, "Only colonels and generals are allowed in here."

Ignoring his remark, I made my case, "Sergeant, there are a number of dependent wives with very young children trying to make do in the passenger lounge, and there is no estimated departure time for our broken aircraft. Would you allow the wives and children to stay in here where it is quiet and much warmer?"

"No!" was the terse response, "it's against regulations, and we might have a general coming in!"

I asked, "Do you have a VIP scheduled to land here at this late hour?"

Again, "No, but one could come in unexpectedly."

I wasn't going to accept defeat so easily. I called the base commander and asked for his understanding and permission to let the wives with young children into the VIP lounge at the passenger terminal. Another turndown! I always held some disdain for Military Airlift Command (MAC) pilots who carried plastic spoons in the pencil pockets of their flight suits. My disdain was reinforced. They carried plastic spoons to eat their flight lunches while flying and sitting in the cockpit. It left me with the opinion that eating was their highest priority. These could not be the same breed of pilots and leaders who prevented an encircled West Berlin from being starved by the Soviets with a yearlong around-the-clock airlift of food and coal.

At 2:00 a.m., the situation only got worse. A senior NCO running the passenger terminal ordered everyone outside so a contract cleaning crew could clean the terminal. I asked the NCO if we could move to one side and then the other for the cleaning operation. "No!" came the standard response, "their contract specifies that the terminal will be empty and their work will be free from interference—you must all go outside!" It was now 2:00 a.m. on December 21 and below freezing outside. More than two hundred people were herded out in the cold for about an hour. The image of Gen. George Washington and his men at Valley Forge getting ready to cross the Delaware River came to mind. It was almost that bleak for the dependents huddled in the snow. At that moment, it was impossible for me to have a lower opinion of MAC, and there was little I witnessed during the rest of my air force career to raise that opinion.

The Flying Tiger Airline aircraft finally boarded at 4:00 a.m. and got airborne about an hour later. I was dubious about the engine replacement and checkout but believed the pilots liked themselves and weren't going to do anything really stupid. We arrived at Mildenhall AFB in the United Kingdom at 8:00 p.m. local time. There was a car and driver from Manby waiting to take us north to our destination. It was about a three-hour drive in a packed car on snow-covered roads. Everyone was exhausted from the ordeal. Upon arrival, we were astonished to find all the American faculty and students at RAF Manby assembled at our house, with a decorated Christmas tree, a hot dinner on the table, and fires in all the fireplaces. It was heartwarming to the Piotrowski family, especially after the brutal treatment experienced at Dover AFB. After introductions all around and many best wishes for the holidays, our fellow American families went to their homes nearby, and we trundled off to bed with the fires properly banked.

Late the next morning, all five of us woke up somewhat in a daze. It was bitter cold with considerable snow on the ground. I tried starting fires in the several room fireplaces. There was a convenient coal bucket next to each fireplace, but more importantly, the resident Americans had left a small can of charcoal lighter fluid where I could find it. There was a note that said the hot water heater in the kitchen was the most important fire to light. Without it lit, there would be no hot water, period! With heat attended to, we looked around for the refrigerator and couldn't find it. It was supposed to be there. We were told all household appliances came with the house. After hours of searching every room over and over without finding the refrigerator, Sheila asked me to go next door and ask the neighbors where the refrigerator might be lurking.

Our house was at the end of a row of houses; there was only one next-door neighbor, and he was an RAF group captain (equivalent to a US colonel) permanently assigned to RAF Manby. His wife answered the door, the perfect person to answer my question. She assured me the "cold cupboard" could be found on the north side of the kitchen. All I needed to do to find it was open the cupboard doors on the north side, and the one with bricks missing and the hole covered with fine mesh wire was the cold cupboard. This didn't sound like a refrigerator to me, but I thanked her profusely and went back to our house. Before saying anything to Sheila I found the cold cupboard. It was just as described.

Cold air from the outside was coming into the cupboard enclosure, and in late December, it was cold! I called my sweet wife and showed her what I had found. She looked at me and said in a hushed voice so the children wouldn't hear, "We're all going to die!" I believe she meant what she said, thinking about bacteria growing in unrefrigerated food.

The overkind resident Americans brought over some hot lunch that was also enough for dinner. I learned that there were two permanent Americans at Manby RAF station. The one in charge, Col. Bob Lines, had very few lecture responsibilities. The other American officer was a lieutenant colonel who taught courses in the Staff College Electronic Warfare Course. Sheila pumped the wives for information about grocery shopping and the dreaded cold cupboard. To her utter amazement, she learned that six days a week, Monday through Saturday, the green grocer (vegetables), the meatmonger (fresh meat), and the fishmonger (fresh-caught fish) came around house to house and provided whatever was needed for the meals that day. Milk and butter were delivered early every morning. The only reason to go to the small store in Manby Village was for canned goods and staples, such as sugar, flour, salt, and spices. And yes, the cold cupboard would do just fine. With good planning, there should be very few leftovers, and they would keep just fine for a day or so. All this good news was met with a bit of skepticism. However, when the mobile grocers came to the door, taking orders, all became well with the world.

For history buffs, the area around Manby was cereal grain farming and sheep herding. Manby was also located not far from the North Sea and the fishing port of Grimsby from where many of the pilgrims had sailed to Plymouth, England, where they then embarked on bigger ships to sail across the Atlantic to settle in the New World colonies. The local stone church was built in 1490, two years prior to Columbus's discovery of the Americas. The nearby city of Louth, Lincolnshire, was home to a beautiful cathedral built in the year AD 1,000. The thatched huts surrounding the cathedral were established in the years around AD 900 for the workman who toiled for nearly one hundred years to complete this elegant structure.

I learned from Col. Bob Lines that there was another air force officer attending the College of Air Warfare course, a navigator, and one of us would be kept on after graduation to take his place. I immediately wished that Lieutenant Colonel Bishop would enjoy the good fortune of an extended tour at RAF Manby. The course was technically excellent and covered topics not normally covered in a staff course. Examples of these are Principals of Radar and Electronics Countermeasure against Radar and Surface-to-Air Missiles (SAMs). The latter was a serious concern of NATO because the Soviets were continuously developing and deploying increasingly more capable SAMs throughout the Warsaw Pact. These new systems, like the SA-6, were very capable against low-flying aircraft and were highly mobile so they could accompany ground forces and be operational with very little setup time.

The main thrust of the RAF Air War College was, however, the utility of their new and revolutionary fighter aircraft, the Harrier jump jet. It was studied in great detail, and there was a mandatory requirement for each student to write an end-of-course thesis on the Harrier. While the Harrier represented a breakthrough in aerodynamics, flight control, and thrust vectoring, I did not find it a very practical war-fighting machine. While the RAF contended this vertical takeoff and landing aircraft could operate from "postage stamp" sites and immediately scoot into and hide very close to forward edge of the battle area (FEBA) without detection, there were serious drawbacks to this concept that the RAF chose to ignore.

A fighter-size aircraft can easily be hidden under trees and/or camouflage netting that was not the issue. On the other hand, a fighter that flies three or more sorties per day consumes enormous quantities of fuel, ordnance, ammunition, and spare parts, requiring support personnel at the hide site. Moving the fuel, ordnance, and other supplies from the rear area to the front has a significant signature and more than likely would alert the enemy to the location of the Harrier hides. Even under combat conditions, bombs are kept a safe distance away from aircraft to ensure that if you lose one, you don't lose the other. Bombs are not light and generally require some sort of tug and trailer to move them to the aircraft and a gasoline-powered lifting device to load them onto the aircraft. Personnel required to service a single aircraft would number between five and seven. If several aircraft were hidden in close proximity to each other, it might lessen the total requirement. All these requirements create a fairly large footprint and signature not far from a fluid front line that could be penetrated. Last, enemy SAM surveillance radar could track the Harriers back to their hides and provide locations to their own rocket and fighter forces.

One of the reasons it was desirable to locate Harrier aircraft closer to the enemy was that the engine technology at the time limited the Harrier's range and payload. Even when located forward, it was limited to two five-hundred-pound bombs. When operating from the rear off a runway, the range and payload were still very limited when compared to more conventional aircraft of that period, such as the F-105 and F-4.

The Harrier did enable the British to operate from low-cost aircraft carriers without the need for canted decks and costly steam catapults. This allowed them to defeat the Argentine forces in the Falklands several thousand miles from England in Argentina's backyard. However, this concept was not at the forefront in 1971 when the Harrier was conceived to do battle against Warsaw Pact forces in Central Europe. My thoughts were not warmly received by the RAF College of Air Warfare staff, but pleasing them was not a requirement for graduation.

One great benefit of the British Air War College was the travel and opportunity to learn about NATO and our British Allies. We traveled on RAF Military transport to a German air force fighter base flying American built F-104 aircraft in an air defense role. There I met two senior German air force officers who flew against the Allied forces in WW II. They each had scored a high number of aerial victories and flew in constant combat for over six years. They both had been shot down by Allied aircraft more than once. However, being shot down over Germany allowed them to avoid capture and continue to fly and fight against the Allies. I still have a small bottle of brandy given to me as a memento from the Red Baron Squadron.

We also visited a Canadian fighter squadron based as Baden-Soellingen, Germany (GER). This squadron had a nuclear strike mission, with the nuclear weapons under the control of the United States Air Forces in Europe (USAFE). The nuclear bombs stored at Baden-Soellingen Air Base would only be turned over to Canadian Forces if a coded message was received and authenticated over what was called the Cemetery Communications Network, or Cemetery Net for short. They had a unique way of using the F-104 radar to navigate to their targets. The technique involved filming a high-precision terrain model of their respective target areas and producing ninety-degree wedge pictures of the shadows caused by the terrain. Hills, valleys, and mountains all cause the same kind of returns from light and radar waves. The pictures taken over the terrain model looked exactly the same as what the F-104 radar would portray along the same route over the actual terrain. Running the camera over terrain models of the unit's training routes and then flying the same route using the F-104 radar and matching it with pictures made on the model board tested this concept. The accuracy obtained with this method was remarkable but required significant variations in terrain and a very precise model of the actual terrain. It would not work over the featureless terrain of the north German plain, or for that matter, Kansas.

It was immediately apparent that there was a friendly rivalry between the RAF and the Royal Canadian Air Force (RCAF), much more so than with American forces—perhaps because the British and Americans were allies, whereas the British felt the Canadians were still under the Crown and therefore a colony. That evening, our Canadian hosts, our Manby instructors, and we students assembled at the officers' mess for dinner. During predinner conversation, the Canadians challenged the Brits to a beer-drinking contest. This would entail a relay of five officers each drinking a pint of ale, placing the empty mug upside down over their head as a signal for the next person in the relay to start drinking. The Brits tried to get me to join their team, but I was smart enough to decline. Chugalugging beer was not something I did, and I certainly did not want to be the cause of the RAF losing their pride and honor. When the Brits had chosen their team and were lined up at the bar, in walked the Canadian team. Much to our surprise, the RCAF team consisted of five schoolteachers, none taller than five feet three, and all rather petite. Once the drinking bout started, it was immediately apparent that it was a slam dunk for the ladies. When the five of them had finished, only three Brits had their mug overturned on their heads with a lot of beer streaming down their faces because they hadn't completely emptied the pint. The schoolteachers took a few moments to enjoy the victory and then marched smartly out the way they came. They must have been able to open the throat valve and pour the ale down without a single gulp or swallow.

Our next stop was the Island of Cyprus, where the British had an airbase. From a historic point, it was fantastic. There were Roman ruins toppled over in the fields without any protection from random visitors like us, or professional looters of historic treasure. Most interesting to me was the precision work on the fallen marble pillars, where you could view and touch the stone from top to bottom, as well as the intricacies and color of the tiles in the Roman Baths throughout the island. The only restraint from picking up these ancient treasures was a law that prohibited the removal and export of antiquities. I wonder if there is anything left after the past forty years of looting.

Cyprus was an interesting study in ancient history and modern politics. The island was officially divided into Turkish and Greek enclaves. Clearly, the Turks could have swept Cyprus clean of the Greek settlers but chose not to do so because of NATO or perhaps the economics of commerce on the island itself. The British interest was their air base on the eastern tip of Cyprus and the powerful long-range radar located there. This radar could sweep the skies of the entire eastern Mediterranean and well into the interior of southern Soviet territory at medium to high altitudes. The air base was a very strategic asset in the soft underbelly of Europe.

The College of Air Warfare also involved a number of visits to RAF installations around England and Scotland. Of primary interest to me was the phased array radar at Fylingdales Moor just south of the border with Scotland, Headquarters Strike Command, and the radar research establishment on the southeastern coast of England. The latter was where the first radar of WW II detected the incoming raids of Nazi Germany's fighter and bomber aircraft, enabling the RAF to effectively employ their very limited fighter force to soundly defeat the Luftwaffe in the Battle of Britain. Since then, both ground and airborne radar have played a very important role in every armed conflict.

The last trip during my time at the College of Air Warfare was to the USAF 81st TFW at Royal Air Force Station Bentwaters. At that time, the Eighty-First was equipped with F-4Ds under Third Air Force at Mildenhall Royal Air Force Station and USAFE at Ramstein AB, Germany. The 81st TFW hosted us for a cocktail hour and dinner at their officers' club. At the social, our host was Col. Richard (Dick) G. Collins, whom I knew from both Eglin AFB, Florida, and Ubon AB, Thailand, where I flew combat missions with him against bridges in North Vietnam. As we shook hands, he asked, "Why aren't you wearing your Silver Star, Distinguished Flying Cross, and Bronze Star that you were awarded for the combat missions you flew at Ubon?"

His question took me by surprise, but I was able to get the answer out: "I was never awarded those medals or any others for the time I was demonstrating the Walleye in Thailand."

He came back with, "Col. J. J. Burns and I wrote the award recommendations for you, and I know that he submitted them along with the awards he submitted on me for the same missions we flew together." Based on Colonel Collins's comments, I queried the Air Force Awards and Decorations Branch in the DCS/Personnel organization and learned that there wasn't a record of any such submissions. Perhaps when they were sent to PACAF Headquarters, the award recommendations were returned to the 8th TFW for corrections after Col. J. J. Burns and Lieutenant Colonel Collins had rotated back to the United States. Administration can be a black hole if not properly supervised by professionals. At this juncture, Brig. Gen. John J. Burns was the deputy director for General Purpose Forces in AF/XOOR at the Pentagon. I never contacted him about the subject.

Back at Manby, Sheila had learned that we could rent a "spinner," a device that extracted most of the water from a wash prior to hanging it out on the line. In addition, she found some kerosene heaters that would drive the overnight chill from the house long before I could get coal burning in the fireplaces located in every room. It wasn't until just prior to leaving Manby that I learned to bank a fire under the ashes so it would last through the night and still be hot enough to start fresh coals burning in the morning.

Easter was then a national British holiday of about ten days, long enough for us to tour northern England and Scotland. We purchased a fourteen-foot-long "caravan" (British for camper) for the trip. To my amazement, it could sleep all five of us and had a small kitchen. It was a good investment. The first stop was the home of Brian Bevan, my classmate at Harvard. Brian was, and still is, an exceptionally gifted individual; outgoing, athletic, and a rugby player. He could play any song you could think of on his guitar and could sing with the best of them. He and his family lived in Cockermouth, in the hilly Lake District of England replete with hills to climb and lush valleys full of colorful flowers during the spring.

From Cockermouth, we visited Glasgow, Loch Ness, Edinburgh, York (a walled city), and what seemed like a hundred castles. All the cities and villages we visited had more charm and history than is possible to even touch on here. It was a treat for children and parents alike. Sheila was taken with the beautiful brass carvings that adorned churches and crypts and, back at Manby, joined a group of ladies who spent their idle time making brass rubbings, some of which still hang in our home in Colorado Springs. We also visited Stonehenge and the impressive stone monoliths that were put in place by prehistoric man for what reasons anthropologists are still searching to discover. Another surprise was that wives and sweethearts were not allowed in the officers' mess except for special occasions—of which there were many. Prior to leaving the United States, we were informed that there would be many "fancy dress balls," and we should come prepared with the proper attire. Always frugal, Sheila went shopping and came home with roughly a dozen formal gowns for the expected occasions. She looked wonderful in all of them, so I forced her to keep about five, even though it emptied the family savings account. For me, the air force formal attire would do. When the first "fancy dress ball" was put on the calendar, we discovered that "fancy dress" translated to costume party, vice formal dress. All wasn't lost though. With a couple of masks, a wand, and tiara, Sheila, with her formal gowns, was transformed into Cinderella, a fairy princess, and so on.

Time passes quickly when you're working hard or having fun! At RAF Manby, it was the latter, and soon it was time for graduation and a follow-on assignment. To my great surprise, my assignment was to the Thirty-Sixth Tactical Fighter Wing at Bitburg AFB as the assistant director of operations (ADO). This was exactly what I had hoped for but had never expected. What a plum assignment! Doubts started creeping into my thoughts regarding what this job entailed. My last operational assignment was as a major, as instructor pilot, and chief of academics at the FWS. This was the pinnacle for a fighter pilot, but it wasn't an operational unit with all the requirements of being ready to deploy and fight on arrival. My American air force classmate, Colonel Bishop, was assigned to stay on at Manby, taking the place of Col. Bob Lines. We were both pleased.

The reporting date at Bitburg Air Base was, of all things, July 4, 1971. We had two weeks to relax and enjoy Europe as we wound our way through the Eiffel Mountains to Bitburg, Germany. We spent time in London and southern England, all very enjoyable, and ended up at the White Cliffs of Dover. There we took a ferry boat across the English Channel to Calais, France. It was dark when we arrived tired and well fed, so we turned in for the night at a caravan camp not far from where the ferry boat docked. As was our practice when traveling with the caravan, I got the children up and dressed and then chased them outside to play while Sheila prepared breakfast. There was not enough room inside the caravan for five people while preparing a meal. When the two oldest returned from playing with children from all over Europe who were also staying at the camp ground, Scott, the second oldest, said, "These kids have funny voices!" It was his first exposure to non-English-speaking people. Sure, England was a foreign country, but they spoke English with a funny accent and some unusual expressions and words. Our oldest, Denise, was crestfallen when asked at Grimbleby School on Tinkle Street in Manby how to end a sentence. She replied proudly, "With a period!" Only to be laughed at by her classmates and told by the teacher that sentences end with a "full stop." To their credit and hard work, they learned to speak reasonable German and Italian and were a great help to their parents when shopping or traveling. Traveling through Europe was fun but challenging. After driving on the left (wrong) side of the road for six months, it was difficult to convert back, especially when making a left turn without some oncoming traffic to block the lanes to the near side. We had purchased a new Audi 100 once it was learned we were going to Germany. It seemed to make good sense to have a car, made in that country, with the steering wheel on the proper side of the car. It was the only new four-door car on the lot painted in an ugly (to my taste) bright orange, but it served us well for fourteen years until son Scott totaled it on a dirt road near Sumter, South Carolina.

293

As we moved from northern France across Belgium and into Germany, our drive through the mainly Old World romantic cities gave us a sense of history that cannot be put to words. Bitburg, Germany, is located in the Eiffel Mountains, not far from where the Battle of the Bulge took place in December 1944. The 36th TFW was responsible for two air bases, Bitburg and Spangdahlem. The headquarters was located at Bitburg, home of the 22nd TFS, the 53rd TFS, and the 525th TFS. The first two squadrons were general-purpose fighter units with a NATO nuclear strike mission, in addition to their air superiority, interdiction, and close air support roles. The 525th Bulldogs had the air defense role for the defense of southern Germany. Spangdahlem Air Base was home to the 23rd TFS and the 39th TEW (Tactical Electronic Warfare). All the fighter squadrons were equipped with F-4D aircraft, and the 39th was equipped with EB-66s.

The 36th TFW was under the command of Brig. Gen. Edwin Robertson II. General Robertson served in the US Army as a private for nine months and then entered West Point in June 1944, graduating in the class of 1947. He had an impeccable combat record while serving in Korea flying F-80s and pulling temporary duty as a forward air controller with the Twenty-Fourth Infantry Division. He was awarded the Silver Star for directing attacks against enemy forces that saved an entire battalion. During the Vietnam Conflict, General Robertson was the deputy commander for operations and then vice commander, 31st TFW, at Tuy Hoa, SVN.

The 36th TFW vice commander was Col. Don Payne. Colonel Payne graduated from West Point with the class of 1950. He flew F-84s during the Korean War and F-4s out of Cam Ranh Bay and serving there as deputy commander for operations of the 12th TFW. The deputy commander for operations (DO) was Col. Mike DeArmond. Mike also graduated from West Point with the class of 1950. He was assigned to the 4th TFW in Korea flying F-86s where he was shot down by a Mig-15 on his forty-seventh mission. He spent seventeen months in a Chinese prisoner-of-war (POW) camp. One of the many ways he was tortured involved being tied to a post overnight in a flooded rice paddy with the water freezing around his feet. I wasn't sure, but Mike's tough exterior and extremely low tolerance for poor performance may have been the result of the treatment he received at the hands of his North Korean and Chinese captors. No doubt about it, the 36th TFW was talent heavy at the top. In addition, Gen. Edwin Robertson held two previous operational commands prior to arriving at the 36th TFW. General Robertson and Colonel DeArmond served together in Vietnam, and the latter was a classmate of

Colonel Payne at West Point. With all that talent at the top, I would have to be on my best game all the time, but what a great team to learn from!

We arrived at Bitburg Air Base on the evening of July 4, signed in, and were put up in a VOQ for the night. The next morning, I reported to General Robertson after which he walked me down the hall to meet Col. "Iron" Mike DeArmond. That is when I leaned that there were already two assistant DOs under Mike, and I was number three. My official title was assistant DO for Spangdahlem AFB. My family and I would live at "Spang," but I would report to work at the DO suite of offices at Bitburg. It was understood that I would prowl the ramp and squadrons at Spang during the early morning and late evening hours prior to coming to work and after my day job at Bitburg. The other two assistant DOs were Col. Jesse Locke and Col. P. C. Davis, both older than me and with a lot more experience. Jesse was a solid citizen and highly respected in the fighter community. P. C. had the reputation of being a raconteur and looked a lot older than his years. He was flying F-104s when I went through the F-86 gunnery training program at Willie. He put on an F-104 demonstration during Gen. Opie Weyland's farewell visit, shortly after the F-86F crashed on takeoff. To be honest, there wasn't much for the third assistant DO to do except take care of all the odd jobs that my betters found onerous.

Shortly after I arrived in Germany, Col. Wilber L. Creech paid a visit to Bitburg to discuss some discrepancies the 36th TFW received during a very recent operational readiness inspection (ORI). Colonel Creech, who at that time was on the brigadier general promotion list, was handpicked by Gen. David C. Jones, commander USAFE, to be the USAFE/DO. With this assignment, Colonel Creech displaced a major general and brigadier, the former USAFE/DO and assistant DO, respectively. There was no question that soon-to-be brigadier general Creech was highly regarded by air force leadership. Little did I know then that he would play a big role in my future. During his visit, I had the opportunity to meet Col. "Bill" Creech and form the opinion that he was all business all the time.

Not too long after my arrival at Bitburg, an RF-4C crashed on takeoff at Zweibrucken Air Base, Germany, located south and west of Bitburg. The Thirty-Sixth Wing was tasked to provide an officer to serve as the Accident Investigation Board (AIB) president. All the colonels pointed to the left, and there I was at the far left. The purpose of an accident investigation is to find the root cause and the chain of events that ultimately made the aircraft unrecoverable and led to the crash. The goal is to find the cause so that any material defects or training shortfalls can be corrected to prevent future accidents. If the root cause was found to be pilot error, then all USAF pilots would be briefed on the error(s) and how to avoid it or them. Finding fault was never an issue, although that factor was always on the mind of pilot and aircrew AIB members, influencing their judgments on what the root cause was.

Having never participated in an aircraft accident investigation in any capacity, I had a lot of regulation reading to do on the way to Zweibrucken Air Base prior to convening the board. Assigned to an AIB are, as a minimum, the following members:

board president, a pilot qualified in the type aircraft involved in the accident

safety officer, a trained flying safety officer, usually the senior FSO from a base in the same command

pilot officer, usually a highly experienced officer in the type aircraft involved in the accident. My preference would be someone from the standardization and evaluation flight

maintenance officer, usually a lieutenant colonel with considerable maintenance experience in the aircraft type involved in the accident

flight surgeon

other specialties, as necessary, to fill the technical expertise required to find and validate the root cause

The mishap at Zweibrucken was about as transparent as an AIB president could hope for. The pilot and WSO of the RF-4C that crashed had both successfully ejected from the stricken aircraft and suffered no injuries as a result of the ejection. Both had different perspectives of the accident from their respective cockpits, but their individual recollection of the events leading up to the mishap fit together well. Essentially, the very short flight went as follows: everything up to shortly after getting airborne was normal. The normal procedure for getting an RF-4 in the air is to pull the control stick full aft and hold it in that position until the nose starts to rise. At that point, the pilot pushes the stick forward to a position that holds the nose at ten degrees above the horizon and then applies trim to hold that nose attitude until climb speed is obtained. When climb speed is achieved, the nose attitude and power are adjusted to hold climb speed until the desired altitude is reached.

On the flight in question, just prior to the pilot moving the stick forward to hold the nose in a ten-degree attitude, the WSO's clipboard flipped off of his left thigh and fell into the open space between the radar control console and the aft stick. At the instant the clipboard lodged there, the pilot started the stick forward, which trapped the clipboard between the bottom of the radar console and a knurled nut on the control stick in the WSO's cockpit. At that point, the pilot did not feel resistance to stick movement; but as the RF-4C rapidly accelerated, the clipboard prevented further forward movement of the stick. As a result, the aircraft started to enter a loop at just a few hundred feet above the ground. Putting both hands on the stick and using all his might, the pilot was unable to move the stick forward because of the government-issued metal clipboard wedged in front of the aft control stick. The WSO did not tell the pilot what had happened but tried to remove the clipboard, to no avail. The pilot ordered ejection, and the aircraft stalled and crashed in an open field just off the end of the runway.

It should be noted that the WSO in question was very athletic and an avid body builder. His torso was thick, as were his thighs. He had a habit of wearing the issue aircrew clipboard on his left thigh, which placed the latching mechanism for the elastic band that went around the thigh against the aluminum panel on the left side of the cockpit. In this position, movement of his left leg could dislodge the latching mechanism and cause the stretched elastic band to flip the aluminum clipboard to the center. On takeoff, the WSO usually placed his legs outward so as not to restrict the pilot's ability to have full left and right movement of the control stick.

This appeared to be an open and shut case! All the board had to do was corroborate or disprove the information provided by the crew members of the ill-fated aircraft, who were both very cooperative. Digging through the wreckage, we found the metal clipboard located between the radar console and the aft cockpit control stick. It was no longer lodged in place because of the crash, but marks on the clipboard, radar console, and control stick confirmed it was in the position described by the WSO when the aircraft impacted the ground. Further, the clipboard was deformed and marred, indicating it had been under some considerable pressure. Witnesses' descriptions of the aircraft's flight path prior to and after the crew ejection supported the pilot's and WSO's testimonies.

What remained was to place an RF-4C on jacks, retract the gear, and power the electrical buses on the aircraft with a ground power cart and the hydraulic systems with a hydraulic mule. In this configuration, we placed the metal clipboard from the crash site in the position given in the WSO's testimony, pushed the front cockpit control stick against the clipboard, and recorded the position of the elevator slab. The experts at McDonald Douglas confirmed that the recorded slab position would result in a partial loop and stall if maintained as the aircraft accelerated.

The cause was replicated and confirmed. Now came the hard part: determining if the mishap could have been prevented. In order to do this, we seated the accident pilot in the cockpit of the jacked and powered aircraft in the manner described above. In the rear, we put, in turn, twenty blindfolded WSO volunteers. The volunteers were told to correct any problems they saw when the blindfold was removed. With a new and undamaged clipboard lodged in place between the radar console and control stick with the pilot pushing on the front control stick with all his might, the volunteer WSO's blindfold was removed. In every instance, the WSO saw the clipboard and, with a jerk, dislodged it in a single try. They also communicated the problem to the pilot. In this experiment, we destroyed twenty brand-new, never-been-used, GI-issue aircrew clipboards.

Just as the AIB was wrapping up their investigation, there was a call from General Robertson's secretary to return to Bitburg for a dinner with General Jones, commander USAFE. The word was that General Jones was making visits to the various wings to meet with all the assigned colonels in a dinner setting. Apparently, he was taking stock of the horses in his stable to determine where, in his view, the strengths and weaknesses lay. It was a nice dinner, and an interesting conversation flowed around the table. I kept my mouth shut and listened intently. After dinner, we all retired to a small more intimate room where coffee and sherry were served. After some more small talk, General Jones turned to me and asked how the accident investigation was coming. Trapped into talking, I went over the details of how the AIB Team verified what the mishap crew told us and the evidence found at the crash site. To help the general understand how it was possible for the clipboard to get trapped between the aft cockpit radar console and the knurled knob on the control stick, I described those particular objects in great detail along with the RF-4D takeoff procedure. He listened quietly and thanked me when I was done. Later, Colonel DeArmond, my boss, came over and said, "Nice job on the accident. Too bad you forgot General Jones flew F-4s for two years when he commanded the 33rd TFW at Eglin AFB, Florida." Hopefully, General Jones didn't mind the refresher course on the RF-4 aft cockpit. All that I knew about the general was that he spent most of his career in SAC, flew bombers, and spent time in maintenance—perhaps he wasn't offended that one of the junior colonels in his command didn't study his resume.

Back at Zweibrucken AFB, the AIB Team met for a full week without coming to a unanimous agreement on the mishap's root cause and chain of events that led to placing the accident aircraft in an unrecoverable position. They did agree that the clipboard strap was poorly designed, which allowed the clipboard to be released and flip into the position that initiated the accident sequence. They agreed that the standard clipboard should be replaced with one that would perform the same functions but be made of a deformable material. But two AIB members, both pilots, would not agree with the finding that the aircraft was unrecoverable because the WSO failed to remove the clipboard and communicate the problem to the pilot, who could have released pressure on the stick momentarily. At the end of a week of fruitless discussion, I told the dissenters to write a minority position and I would submit their position to USAFE as part of the full report. At this point, they backed down and signed the report as written. The mishap report did not tarnish the WSO's career, as he was subsequently selected for pilot training and graduated with flying colors. I believe all involved with this AIB learned a valuable lesson in integrity, which I hope stayed with them through the rest of their lives.

I was eager to get recurrent in the F-4D, but Colonel DeArmond, recognizing that I had not flown the jet for nearly four years, was reluctant to have to worry about another "new guy" flying the aircraft. Besides, staff officers don't have many opportunities to fly and stay proficient. Eventually, he relented, and I got recurrent but not without a stumble along the way. My instructor pilot was Lt. Larry Farrell from the 23rd TFS at Spangdahlem. Their squadron emblem was a hawk, and they were known as the Hawks. Recurrency involves two flights, one during the day and one at night, if all goes well. Both involve aircraft handling, numerous instrument approaches, gunnery range work, and aerial refueling. As luck would have it, the aerial refueling came at night behind a KC-97 Tanker. The KC-97s top speed with a load of JP-4 fuel was just a few knots above the F-4D stall speed, so there was not a lot of room, airspeed wise, to play with. Fortunately, the F-4D has plenty of power to keep the pilot from stalling or breaking off of the refueling boom. All went well, and I was scheduled with Captain Smith of Stand/Eval for the check ride. It was a good flight except for one thing: when asked to perform steep turns, forty-five- and sixty-degree bank turns to the left and right, I decided to show the check pilot how to do them aggressively. Bad idea! The tolerance for steep turns, as I recall, is plus or minus two hundred feet of altitude and plus or minus 10 knots of airspeed. I busted the two-hundred-foot limit and that busted the check ride. Before

Captain Smith could say anything, I said, "This is the first time I every busted any kind of check ride. Why don't I practice those steep turns a couple of more times and then we can also practice anything else that you think I need to improve on?" I said that because I wanted to take the pressure off of the captain and also get in some more practice before the recheck. One more training ride with Lt. Larry Farrell (retired as Lieutenant General Farrell) and a passing recheck, I was cleared to fly the F-4D.

Shortly after recurrency in the F-4D, the 53rd TFS (Bulldogs) at Bitburg was tasked to deploy to Bodo AB, Norway, for three weeks in Operation Barr Frost. Bodo was a Norwegian fighter base about two-thirds up the length of Norway from Oslo. It was late summer, and the weather was forecast to be excellent. As the Fifty-Third was preparing for the deployment, a note came down from Brigadier General Creech, USAFE/DO, requesting a colonel from the Thirty-Sixth Wing to accompany the deployment to ensure that nothing bad happened. The note went on to say that the colonel would only be an observer and that command would remain with the lieutenant colonel squadron commander. Again, all the colonels senior to me pointed to their left, and I was handed the short straw once again. Clearly, three weeks of flying in Norway was something most of them would look forward to. The turnoff for the senior colonels was the observer status coupled with the responsibility to make sure nothing bad happened. Like an oxymoron, those two just don't go together.

The squadron deployment to Bodo was impressive! Sixteen aircraft started, taxied, and took off in flights of four at five-minute intervals. I was flying the element lead in the first flight with the squadron commander leading. It was a gorgeous day all across the mountains, plains, and low lands of Germany and Norway. It was about a two-hour flight of sightseeing and then a landing at Bodo, with the advance team waiting for us in the parking area. Much to my surprise, all aircraft landed code 1, ready to fly the next morning. All that was needed was a post flight inspection and refueling. For those not familiar with the F-4D, sixteen aircraft flying for two hours and landing mission capable is remarkable. We were greeted by the Norwegian wing and base commanders and briefed on local area flying restrictions. These could be summed up with, don't fly into Sweden or north of Sweden into the Soviet Union buffer zone.

The Norwegian air force had developed excellent bombing ranges, and there was plenty of open airspace for mock dogfights over the Norwegian Sea. The town of Bodo was situated on a spit of land projecting into the sea in the region of Nordland, well above the Arctic Circle. The base was just a few miles from town. It took a few hours for everyone to get situated in their quarters for the night, but darkness was not a problem. We were in the land of the midnight sun with about twenty hours of daylight during the late summer. I took advantage of the good light, prowling the flight line looking for potential safety problems and found two. There were probably more, but they just didn't register at the time. The first problem was ramp space! The local fighters were F-5s that didn't take much room, so the ramp was built for them, not big ugly "rhino" F-4s with two powerful J-79 engines. Our squadron crew chiefs had set up perpendicular parking, requiring a hard ninety-degree turn in and a quick, sharp, ninety-degree turnout without much wingtip clearance on one side and sod close at hand on the other. The turnout would also blast the aircraft and personnel next in line. The crew chiefs set it up like the ramp back at Bitburg, where there was plenty of room, but that was not available at Bodo. I convinced the crew chiefs that the aircraft should be angle parked, eliminating all the above problems. All that was required was a little yellow spray paint and some minor aircraft towing, and they were all set for the next morning's flights. The other problem was minor. The trip planners reduced the number of fire extinguishers to reduce airlift requirements. Our host provided enough to meet safety requirements.

An unexpected problem occurred the next morning at breakfast. In the spirit of NATO Nation cooperation, it had been agreed that the American forces would eat all their meals in the Bodo Air Base dining facility. Dinner was great, and both enlisted and officers enjoyed the quality and quantity of the meal. However, breakfast in Norway consisted primarily of a variety of raw fish. This did not go well with the fliers and maintainers. Personally, I didn't like it either. I made a quick call back to General Robertson, explaining the problem and asking if he could arrange for three cooks and a supply of typical American breakfast food to be immediately air-lifted to Bodo. Our host agreed to allow the cooks to prepare breakfast in their dining hall with the proviso that Norwegian military personnel could also choose to eat American breakfast food, and we Americans could also choose to eat theirs. It was a deal, and General Robertson delivered on his promise. Over the remainder of the deployment, I observed a few Norwegian Air Force personnel sampling eggs, bacon, sausage, and the like, but no Americans ate the raw fish.

The next day, the host commander took Lieutenant Colonel Lowery and me on a tour through the town of Bodo. It was picturesque, colorful, and looked like it was new. I commented on how new the town looked, to which our host replied, "It is new! The Germans destroyed the old Bodo, burned it to the ground! What you are seeing is less than twenty years old. Because of the German atrocities against the Norwegian people, no German military units had been allowed in Norway since the war, even though we are now allies under NATO. Our government would fall if they were to allow German military units in country!" It was nearly two decades later that a German military unit was allowed to deploy to Norway, and that unit was a small medical team.

I was not in Norway to fly, but if an opportunity presented itself, I was going to jump on it. Then early one morning, when I arrived at the squadron building to sit in on some of the flight briefings for the morning go, I overheard one young lieutenant say to another, "What time did you get in last night?" The response went something like this: "Man, I didn't leave the disco with Ingrid until they locked the doors and didn't get back to the BOQ until four, and I've got a date with her tonight!"

The first speaker then said, "I didn't hit the sack until two and didn't sleep much after all that Norwegian booze."

It was then that I turned around and said, "You're both grounded for today. I'm taking one of your flights, and I'm sure Lieutenant Colonel Lowery will take the other one! If you want to do any flying while you're here, you'd better follow the regulations, which require no booze within twelve hours of stepping to the jet and an opportunity for eight hours of uninterrupted sleep. Perhaps your commander will conduct some random bed checks to make sure you're fit to fly." The mission that day turned out to be a low level to a gunnery range with all the normal gunnery events on the range. The lieutenants evidently didn't believe I would continue checking on their late-night activities because the same kind of behavior sent three more gunnery sorties my way.

Our hosts took Lieutenant Colonel Lowery and me to Andoya Island, where they had a major air base, munitions storage area, and hardened aircraft shelters. The point of the visit was to show us where US Air Force fighter squadrons could deploy in the event the Soviets made threats against our northern Allies or the neutral Swedes and Finns. The weather was really crappy that day: no flying out of Bodo because of bad weather from there north to the gunnery ranges. Our flight was in a passenger aircraft similar to the Beech King Air, a twin-engine seating about ten passengers. The flight was entirely in the "soup," with our escort assuring us the pilots could fly the route blindfolded. After about an hour, the aircraft banked into a left turn and proceeded west toward the Norwegian Sea. Looking out the right side, I saw a rock formation much like the side of a Fjord. At the same instant, the pilot pulled about a three

G 180-degree turn. A few minutes later, one of the pilots came back and reported, "We turned one Fjord too soon. The winds must be stronger than forecast!" What that told me is they were flying "dead reckoning" or time and distance to their turn point to dive down into a Fjord that lead to Andoya Island. I had close calls before, but usually I was in control; now my fate was in someone else's hands, and it wasn't very comforting. The trip was well worth the time. Andoya would make a great operational base because of its location and the fact that it was well protected by the sheer sea walls. It would be almost impossible to attack it without being detected well in advance.

Three days prior to redeployment back to Bitburg, it occurred to me that a report on my observations and activities as an observer might be expected even though nothing had been tasked. Allegedly, the tasking for an observer had come from General Jones, commander USAFE, or possibly General Creech, the USAFE/DO. However, all my dealings were with a lieutenant colonel on the Seventeenth Air Force Plans Staff, an intermediate headquarters above the fighter wings in West Germany, commanded by Major General Sweat. The lieutenant colonel indicated that this was the first time an observer had been sent with a squadron deployment, but the practice would likely be continued. I came to the conclusion that a report would not hurt anything, and if one was requested, I should do it while everything that transpired was fresh in my mind. Also, if the procedure was going to be continued, my thoughts might prove useful to the next guy and preclude the breakfast problem experienced at Bodo.

The report was pithy because I had to type it myself, as there were no administrative clerks deployed with the squadron, and a longer report meant more mistakes and continuous retyping. Single spaced, it was three pages long, with a couple of maps and several diagrams on aircraft parking and some other issues that had come up. There was also a list of things that would have been helpful to both maintenance crews and fliers if they had been part of the deployment package. Once back at Bitburg, I obtained the Seventeenth Air Force lieutenant colonel's mailing address and sent him the package. He must have forwarded the report to Major General Sweat, who passed it along to Brigadier General Creech at USAFE, as General Creech sent me a short note, thanking me for my observations.

For our return, Lieutenant Colonel Lowery broke the redeployment into two groups because of marginal weather back at Bitburg Air Base and Germany in general. There were few alternate air bases in the event the flights would have to divert, and it was smart not to have too many arriving at nearly the same time. Hence, flights of aircraft were spaced ten minutes apart, and groups of flights were separated by thirty minutes. Air refueling was required to ensure that each aircraft had sufficient fuel remaining to execute an approach upon arrival at Bitburg and then, if necessary, divert to an alternate with twenty minutes of fuel in the tanks. Lieutenant Colonel Lowery let me lead the second group of flights, which was very much appreciated. The weather at Bitburg on arrival was better than forecast, and all deployed aircraft landed safely at Bitburg.

Much had happened while we were away. A new wing, the 52nd TFW was being created at Spangdahlem to incorporate the 23rd TFS and 39th TEW Squadrons. General Robertson, just prior to leaving for a position on the USAFE staff as special assistant and then inspector general, assigned me the job of planning all the necessary actions required to stand up the new wing. This included identifying all the operational staff personnel for manning the director of operations staff at the new wing, as well as the additional personnel needed to fill support positions. Some of these positions were in Personnel, Civil Engineering, Logistics, and Maintenance. These people, I assumed, would come out of the 36th TFW, and the experienced people would have to be shared. I suggested to Colonel DeArmond that I should assume I was going to be part of the DO staff of the new Fifty-Second Wing and, therefore, Colonel Jesse Locke should represent the Thirty-Sixth Wing in splitting out the cadre of people for the new wing. The logic for this was to assure that the Fifty-Second Wing didn't get all the dregs. Following that exercise with Colonel Locke, which we felt protected both wings, I created a program evaluation and review technique chart (PERT) identifying all of the actions that needed to take place prior to planting the 52nd TFW flag at Spangdahlem. I had never seen a real PERT chart, but I read about them in management textbooks and had a pretty good idea of how to develop the chart and identify the critical path. General Robertson gave the draft PERT his OK and told the staff to support it. In a few days, we were putting green sticky dots on actions completed on time, along with yellow and red dots on actions that were behind schedule and way behind schedule, respectively. As time drew near to stand up the new wing, Colonel DeArmond was selected to be the vice commander of the Fifty-Second Wing at Spangdahlem AFB, and Colonel Locke became the vice wing commander at Hahn AFB in Germany. I remained as the DO of the Thirty-Sixth Wing, leapfrogging over Col. P. C. Davis, who also stayed at Bitburg.

Now it was an uphill struggle to learn to be a DO. I'd been given all the odd jobs as the third assistant DO and really didn't get to be an understudy to Colonel DeArmond and learn what the critical aspects of his job were or what the leading indicators for future problems were. I was running hard to catch up. At the other end, General Robertson was pulling even harder to teach me how to think as a large-wing DO. I came to work in the morning at 5:00 a.m., hoping to get caught up on the obligatory reading of messages that came down from USAFE and Seventeenth Air Force, as well as read the things coming up from squadrons that would have to be briefed to the commander. I had to pass General Robertson's office to reach mine. Usually, as soon as I sat down, the direct line from his office would ring with questions something like this: "I stopped by the Victor Alert (VA) and found they were performing an unscheduled change out of one of the VA birds, what's going on?" Victor Alert is where the nuclear weapons—loaded fighters and crews were located, ready to launch into the air at a moment's notice. That notice to go to war would come from a Cemetery Net "red dot" message with the correct codes and authentication. It was obvious the general had good instincts; he knew where to look, when to look, and how to look for problems. As hard as I tried to get ahead of him, to go wherever something was happening and be the one to inform him instead of him telling me, there just weren't enough hours in the day. Moreover, I didn't have his instincts forged in the crucible of experience. It was very humbling.

In mid-November, General Robertson called me in his office and told me I was scheduled for an interview with Lt. Gen. William V. McBride. Here, the middle initial is important because there was a major general William P. McBride, mostly known as Willie P. They were worlds apart in experience and personality. Willie P. advertised himself as the "World's Greatest Fighter Pilot," and in his WW II days, I'm sure he was in the same league as General Myers and General Yeager. He was swashbuckling, loud, and cocky. On the other hand, Gen. William V. McBride had most of his experience in big aircraft and was as quiet as a church mouse. It was often said of him that he had the world's largest receiver and smallest transmitter. He preferred to listen, but when he spoke, it said volumes, and you'd better be listening, so the stories went. My boss at the Fighter Weapons School, Lt. Col. Grady Morris, was a lot like that, so I was used to the technique and on guard.

Arriving early for any appointment was one of my trademarks. It's hard to be too early, but a second late can kill an opportunity. It was about thirty minutes of thinking about why I was there and some possible things that I might say, when at the exact minute of the appointed time, the secretary led me into the general's office and indicated a chair. General

McBride said, "You're being considered for a command. Both Soesterberg and Aviano will be needing new commanders shortly."

Soesterberg was a fighter squadron in Holland, known as the Queen's Own Air Force. Aviano was a wing-sized unit in Northern Italy but did not have its own forces. The aircraft and crews deployed there from other bases to sit Victor Alert and practice their gunnery skills at a gunnery range nearby in Maniago, Italy. This was totally unexpected; I hadn't even learned the DO's job and was now being considered for command. All of a sudden, I felt small and inadequate. A lot of silence passed after General McBride spoke, so I finally said, "I'm honored to be considered, sir!" More silence, pregnant silence, awkward silence. The general wasn't going to say anything. Finally, I couldn't stand it any longer and said something like, "I'm really fortunate to be assigned at Bitburg because the leadership there is rich with command experience. General Robertson has great instincts and seems to intuitively know when, where, and how to find the things that need attention."

More silence! Finally, General McBride thanked me for coming to the headquarters and said, "You *may* hear from us in a couple of months."

Col. Billy Rogers replaced General Robertson as commander 36th TFW. Colonel DeArmond and Colonel Locke were gone. This left P. C. Davis and me to run flying operations as the German winter of darkness, fog and thick cloud formations up to thirty-five thousand feet, was impacting our ability to fly a full schedule of training missions. I quickly learned that any hint of weather above minimums, which varied by pilot experience from one-hundred- to a three-hundred-foot ceiling, would motivate P. C. to release the aircraft to fly. On days like this, I would return to the office from a meeting only to find the windows open and P. C. staring into the murk, trying to make it go away—it was never a good sign. Fortunately, we always managed to get all of our aircraft safely on the ground at one of the four bases in Germany.

On one of these dreary evenings when the ceiling was below minimums and all 36th TFW aircraft were safely on the ground and tucked in, ready for a better day to fly, I received a panicky call from Base Operations. The Base Operations officer conveyed to me that a flight of four Italian Air Force F-104s were inbound and low on fuel; they didn't have enough gas to reach any runways but Spangdahlem or Bitburg. Bitburg had a better instrument approach and slightly better runway lighting, so they chose Bitburg. I drove well over the speed limit to Base Operations, and anticipating a potential crash or aircraft in the barrier, alerted the Fire Department to stand by. We heard but couldn't see the aircraft land. Finally, a call came from the flight leader, requesting a vehicle to lead them to the parking area. The fog was so thick, they could not see the taxiway lights or stripes. The truck was dispatched, and before long, four taxi lights of the aircraft could be seen in trail behind the truck. They shut down in front of Base Operations and asked to be refueled.

The flight leader was a colonel and was the wing operations officer from Ghedi Air Base near Milan, Italy. I told him we had quarters for him and his pilots to spend the night and invited them to join me for dinner at the officers' club. They accepted the dinner invitation but said they wanted to fly on to another base that evening. I was appalled that they wanted to take off again when they couldn't see well enough to even taxi. There was no ceiling; the cloud bases were sitting on the ground. The colonel assured me they were all experienced pilots, and the weather would not be a problem if we would provide them a truck to lead them to the takeoff end of the runway. I tried once more to discourage them by reminding the colonel there was not an open airfield within three hundred miles. He smiled and said that would not be a problem. After dinner and a glass of red wine each, I returned them to their aircraft, and off they went. No crashes were reported in the NATO net over the next several days, so it appeared they got home safely. Flying in those conditions in wartime is understandable; doing it on a cross-country lark is stupid and inexcusable. Moreover, the colonel was setting a very bad example for the junior officers. I doubt very much that Italian Air Force Flying Regulations permitted what they did.

Colonel Rogers called me to his office and informed me that I had been selected to command the Fortieth Tactical Group based near Aviano, Italy. The change of command would be on January 2, 1972, just a few days away. In an instant, I was surprised, shocked, and scared. I had not yet learned to be a good deputy commander for operations and said so to Colonel Rogers. He laughed and said, "Work hard, and you'll learn as you go."

I asked, "Are there one or two things that you can share with me that will give me a head start?"

His reply was nothing that I expected. He said, "Never let a woman in your office alone!"

Incredulously, I asked, "How do you do that?"

His response was very matter of fact: "Arrange your office so your secretary can see you from her desk when you're sitting at your desk, and if that isn't possible, have her come in and read a paper or magazine! Good luck!" As I left, I noted that his desk was visible from his secretary's desk, but all the other furniture were out of view. Colonel Rogers also informed me that I was scheduled to visit USAFE Headquarters at Ramstein,

Germany, to meet with the deputy chiefs of staff (DCSs) and General Jones.

The obligatory visit with the USAFE leadership was informative. I could now put a face and personality with each of the names and understand their priorities. It wasn't surprising that Gen. Bryce Poe, DCS/Logistics, told me that aircraft maintenance was the key to operational success and accident-free flying. Gen. Robert Thompson, DCS/Civil Engineering, assured me that most of the money in a wing's budget was in civil engineering and under control of the base commander. Make sure it is spent for the good of the command and not on "pet projects" that benefit only a few, was his caution. Gen. "Bill" Creech, DCS/Operations, was obviously very busy because he said, "I know you're in a hurry so I'll be brief." He then held up one hand with fingers outstretched and spoke to each finger—making five points:

"Know your job better than anyone else in the business."

"Know the make-or-break activities of your organization and manage those above all others!"

"Go where the action is! Don't let anything important go forward without your personal involvement in the planning and execution!"

"Take care of your people, and they will take care of you!"

"Set high standards for yourself and your organization! If you don't know, no one else will!"

When he finished making those points, he wished me luck and shook my hand. As I passed his secretary's desk on the way out, I grabbed a piece of paper and scribbled down his words of wisdom. Later, I had them typed in large font and placed them under the glass of every desk I ever sat behind from that day forward. It became a daily guide and reminder to get out and about in the enterprise.

The last person I was to meet with was Gen. David C. Jones. He told me that Aviano had been a continuing problem in USAFE and that he expected me to get it on the right track. He noted that his policy was to send "help teams" of experts to visit wings and to provide commanders with their findings so they could fix the problems. He then asked me how I felt about his policy. I said, "I look forward to the teams and their findings. I've always believed that a fresh set of eyes, which know where to look and how to look, see things that are routinely missed. And I would hope that the spacing would be such that I would have enough time to correct deficiencies prior to the arrival of the next team." His brows furrowed on that last comment, but he wished me success and shook my hand.

The last thing I did before the New Year holiday was have a meeting with the 36th TFW Social Actions officer. "Social actions" was a politically correct way of saying "race relations." The latter was a big concern for the military because of unrest that had occurred in large cities back in the United States and the fact that the services had reduced their enlistment entrance requirements to meet recruiting goals at the tail end of the Vietnam War. Potential enlistees were placed in one of five categories, with category 1 indicating a high-school graduate, and category 5 indicating someone that had dropped out of school prior to entering high school and had difficulty reading and writing. As a rule, the air force only accepted category 1 and 2 applicants, but the war had pushed it down to category 4 and a few 5s. Lower-education skills placed people in nontechnical jobs such as supply and mess services. These placements led to perceived discrimination and resentment. General Jones had created a Human Relations course that was mandatory for all military and civil service personnel in USAFE. I had attended the course but wanted more one on one with the chief of Social Actions, who was a black air force captain.

He was a patriotic American, a dedicated air force officer, and wanted to help me understand and be able to deal with the problems of the times, not necessarily for my benefit but for the benefit of the organization and the people assigned to the wing. He pointed out that an outlandish afro was more the result of combing out one's hair and usually didn't require a haircut, just some packing down. He mentioned that pseudofolliculitis was a real medical condition often caused by shaving too close. He suggested that I make sure those afflicted with this condition saw a doctor. He also pointed out that some young blacks, when in civilian clothes and wanting to stir up trouble, would wear a dress hat into the NCO club. Older patrons would take offense to this and order offenders to take their hats off. He had the regulations and book of *Customs and Courtesies* with him to show me that, contrary to popular opinion, it was not against any regulation to wear a hat into a building. Rather, that it was just a custom for men to remove their hats when entering a building. If there was a scuffle, more than likely the older NCO would be in violation of the UCMJ, not the young airman wearing the hat. There was a long list of things he shared with me that were basically common sense. Last, he taught me the "brother" handshake and cautioned that under no circumstances use the word "boy(s)" or "girl(s)" when speaking to a group that contained African Americans. Another phrase not to be used was "you people." Further, he encouraged participation in events that honored the late Dr. Martin Luther King Jr. It was all good advice, and it came in handy at Aviano and future assignments. As we parted, he noted that none of the other colonels that were moving up into command positions had bothered to seek out his advice.

I had planned to relax and think about what I might say at the change of command at Aviano. Tradition suggests the outgoing commander gets to say quite a bit, while the incoming commander says very little—I planned to stick with tradition and say very little, except for something that fit the occasion. However, I didn't get the chance to kick back and cogitate. There was the obligatory New Year's Eve ball, followed by the commander's New Year's Day reception, both in mess dress. When Sheila and I returned from the ball, we found that our daughter had been bitten on the ear by her pet hamster. That night, the hamster died, and the thought of rabies came to mind. We froze the rodent as advised by the flight surgeon. After the commander's reception, I drove to Landstuhl Hospital, Germany, where the rodent's brain would be examined for rabies. The procedure took several hours, and I didn't get back to Bitburg until late, only to learn that the commander Sixteenth Air Force, headquartered near Madrid, Spain, would pick me up at 7:00 a.m. in a T-39 for the flight to Aviano and the change of command. I would have to stay there for at least two months prior to returning to Bitburg to pick up Sheila and the children and drive them to Aviano. The problem was there was no government family housing at Aviano. The chief of civil engineers, responsible for leased housing, strongly recommended we should not live in the house currently occupied by the commander. They felt it was a firetrap, not safe for adults and certainly not safe for small children. I packed two large bags of uniforms and flight gear in preparation for the early morning departure.

Lessons Learned

Promotions and reassignments usually lead to new
and bigger responsibilities. It takes a lot of hard
work to learn the new job quickly enough!

Identify the make-or-break activities of the enterprise
and monitor them on a regular basis.

Conduct a personal assessment of yourself to identify what
you know you don't know about your new position. Be brutally
frank with yourself then work hard to quickly fill the voids!

Seek advice from experts in areas where your
experience and knowledge are lacking!

Stand on principle. Don't ever compromise the truth or your integrity!

When moving to a new organization, immediately assess you subordinates' abilities and mentor as necessary!

Take nothing for granted. Go where the action is and praise or take corrective action immediately!

Royal Air Force College of Air Warfare, January
1971, Lt. Col. Pete Front row, right

Col. Pete showing Norwegian hosts F-4D cockpit

CHAPTER 8

Fortieth Tactical Group, Aviano, Italy

Major General McGough III was a silver haired kindly looking gentleman. From his demeanor, I sensed that this change of command was not something he was looking forward to. General McGough enlisted in the US Navy from 1936 to 1939 when he entered the US Military Academy at West Point in 1939, earning his wings in 1942 while still a cadet. Upon graduation in 1943, he entered the Army Air Corps. He flew P-38s in the European Theater during WW II. He later commanded the 81st TFS at both Clovis, New Mexico, and Hahn Air Base Germany, and the Thirty-Sixth Day Fighter Group at Bitburg Germany. While in Germany, he led the Thirty-Sixth Gunnery Team in several gunnery competitions and also led the first conversion from F-86s to F-100s in USAFE. Later, he commanded the 4510th Combat Crew Training Wing at Luke, then the 355th TFW at George AFB, California, and following that, the 835th Air Division at McConnell AFB, Kansas, in June 1965. After a tour in Vietnam and several positions on the Air Staff in the Pentagon, he assumed command of Sixteenth Air Force at Torrejon Air Base, Spain, just outside of Madrid. Clearly, General McGough had a wealth of experience commanding fighter units at the squadron and wing level and was highly qualified to oversee wing operations from his position as commander 16th AF.

Col. Mort Muma, current Fortieth Tactical Group commander, had been at Aviano less than one year and was being relieved because General Jones had lost confidence in his ability to effectively lead the organization. In fact, he was the fourth commander in a row to be relieved early in their command tours. The thought crossed my mind that if I could last a year, it would set a record for tenure.

The change of command was set to take place about thirty minutes after we landed at Aviano. General McGough spent most of that time talking with Colonel Muma and his wife, saying the kind of things you say to someone working directly for you that has been relieved by your boss. It was a gray overcast day, bitter and cold. Transient alert had parked the general's T-39 not far from the area where the change of command would take place. Several hundred enlisted and officer personnel were lined up by squadron for the ceremony. Hundreds of years of tradition down through the ages dictate that the personnel in the organization should witness the passing of the unit flag from the outgoing to the incoming commander, whether they be knights, earls, barons, kings, czars, or colonels. The man holding the flag was in charge.

It was a short, traditional ceremony. General McGough spoke emphatically about the importance of the Fortieth Tactical Group located in the soft underbelly of Europe, as well as the importance of its wartime mission as a deterrent to adventurism by the Soviet Union. He spoke highly of Colonel Muma and wished him well in his new assignment. He wished the group and me success, and it was over. I walked him to his aircraft and saluted as he departed. He would visit Aviano several times over the next few years, and every visit was a great benefit to me. He was a fine man and highly successful leader whom I greatly admired.

There were a few stout souls who waited on the ramp in the cold damp weather until the general departed, to welcome me to Aviano and to introduce themselves to me. The wife of one of the senior officers politely asked me if my wife wore hats. It seemed like an odd question, but I answered politely and truthfully, "Yes, when it's cold." It wasn't long before the vice commander, Col. Bob Brockman, came over and suggested we retire to the officers' club, where most of the officers were gathering, to welcome and meet their new commander. Cold as it was outside, that seemed like a good idea. We picked up my bags that had been tossed out of the T-39 and put them in the trunk of his staff car. Bob pointed out that the Fortieth Tactical Group was spread out over several miles in eleven different areas, making oversight and security more difficult than for more conventional air base layouts, where all facilities were inside one continuous perimeter fence. In a few days, I discovered the security situation was far worse than it initially sounded.

At the O'club, I met most of the officers in the command and their wives. They all seemed professional and looked fit. I also learned there were three major tenants on the base that we supported. There was a

Military Airlift Command Helicopter Rescue Detachment commanded by a black major, the senior minority officer on the base if you discount Polacks. There were two communications organizations, the Fifteenth Communications Squadron with a highly classified mission commanded by Col. Jim McCall, and the 2487th Communications Group commanded by Lieutenant Colonel Wilson. This unit provided all the long haul communications from Germany down into Italy and on into Greece. I'd been in a tenant organization where the host was not supportive, and I vowed not to let that happen at Aviano on my watch. The only two full colonels in the Fortieth were Colonel Brockman and me. All the rest of the key positions were filled with lieutenant colonels and majors. Perhaps this was a good thing, as they were young, energetic, and eager to learn to excel and move up in rank. At the social, the wife of the deputy commander for maintenance came up and asked when Sheila might be able to join me. I suggested that it could be a few months before quarters were available, but perhaps sooner if we were lucky. Then she asked me if my wife wore gloves. Again, I was puzzled at the question but answered it the same way, "Yes, if it's cold outside." There was one person that gave me a little cause for concern; it was Lt. Col. Higgy Higgenbotham, the deputy commander for operations. Higgy was a former Thunderbird aerial demonstration team pilot, very outgoing, and very sure of himself; this could be good or prove to be a challenge, if not a problem.

My assessment of all the people I met was guarded but positive; after all, my predecessor and the three commanders who preceded him were relieved of command. Was it totally their fault, or was it their failure to forge a team working together for a common purpose, or was it incompetence on the part of one or two individuals? Whatever the cause, I had to work with all the cards I was dealt—there would be no replacements for poor performers. Those that didn't measure up had to be nurtured, trained up to snuff, or moved to positions where their limited talents could be fully utilized.

First things first! The next day, escorted by the deputy commanders, I visited all of their offices and toured the work areas that came under them. That night, I had the dining facility provide me a jug of coffee and one of hot chocolate and loaded them into the trunk of my staff car along with dozens of paper hot cups. With these libations, I toured every place on the base where someone was working (e.g., security police posts, security police desk, command post, and flight line where enlisted personnel were inspecting and repairing aircraft, supply, maintenance control, and the Victor Alert area). My first stop was the security police post at the entrance to the flight line and maintenance areas. There was a young black security policeman on duty, and I used the TV detective Colombo technique on him, asking a lot of questions about him. Where his home was, was he married, what did he do in his spare time, did he have appropriate issue clothing for the cold weather, how often did he get relieved for a break, etc.? After about fifteen minutes of conversation, I could tell he was feeling like a valued person rather just another GI. Then I made a big mistake, saying, "Well, I better go visit some of the other boys on duty." The word "boys" turned him off in an instant, and for the next two years that we served at Aviano together, he never seemed comfortable with me around. I'd been warned about the word but slipped back into an old habit of thinking the word "boys" was a friendly term for the last time.

It soon became apparent that the only people at Aviano that were familiar with the Fortieth's Wartime Mission were the senior officers. Most majors and below were only vaguely aware of what had to be done if a conflict erupted, or during an operational readiness inspection (ORI), which simulated wartime tasking, and could come at any time. I decided it was necessary to brief the entire group on the Fortieth's mission and what each major functional area contributed to a successful ORI outcome. Based on the size of the base theater, it would take five sessions over a period of three days to get all the military personnel into the theater. I would start each session off with a twenty-minute overview, illustrating how the Fortieth and its tenants fit into the overall scheme of USAFE and NATO, the mission statement, and the forces we gained that increase in the Defense Condition (DEFCON). After the overview, the briefings listed below would follow:

- Intelligence briefing, Maj. Wendel Lasher, chief of intelligence
- Operations briefing, Lt. Col. Higgy Higginbotham, deputy commander operations
- Maintenance briefing, Lt. Col. Truman Cobb, deputy commander logistics
- Arrival of forces flow and bed down, Lt. Col. Joe Hillner, base commander
- Wrap-up and response to questions, Col. "Pete" Piotrowski

We did a dry run of all the briefings and improved them on the fly. As expected, it took all morning to complete all the briefings, allowing fifteen minutes for questions at the end. The weakest of the lot was the operations briefing by Higgy. Either he didn't know the mission well enough to brief it or he was a poor briefer. With some coaching and prodding, I expected him to rise to the occasion. It was important that he, above all, look good in front of the Fortieth Group personnel.

All the briefings in the first presentation to a full theater were above average except for Higgy. His briefing was, in a word, terrible! There was no time to train him before the afternoon session, so I would give the operations briefing, vice Higgy. There were only a couple of hours to change a few slides and work the transitions, but with a few notable exceptions, our mission paralleled the 36th TFW, at Bitburg, so most of it was material I was very familiar with.

That afternoon, I filled in for Higgy and got good visual feedback from the audience and from Col. Bob Brockman, the vice. Four more sessions, and we were done. As I visited all the work sites on the base, there were a lot of positive feedback from all ranks, most of them saying they had never been briefed on the mission and how all the various units came together to get the job done and done right. They also said they had never received an intelligence briefing that highlighted just what we were up against and how important it was to deter the start of hostilities by projecting readiness to our adversaries.

I mentioned that the Fortieth Group was spread over several miles of the Italian countryside starting from inside the town of Aviano and propagating southeast along the highway to Pordenone, the province capital. For example,

- town of Aviano, enlisted barracks, gym, and dining hall, west of main road
- town of Aviano, BOQs and VOQs, officers' club and base exchange, east of main road.
- just outside of Aviano, civil engineering compound
- farther outside of Aviano, commissary and storage
- even farther outside of Aviano, fuel storage
- Aviano Air Base, Base Operation, command post, maintenance control, and nuclear alert area, ten miles southeast of Aviano
- across the highway from air base, 40th TAC Group and base headquarters
- farther down and across the highway in an agricultural area, weapons storage area including Nuclear Bombs
- farther southeast, group commander's house
- farther southeast, Defense Property Disposal Office (DPDO)

Each one of the above enclaves was a security nightmare, plus the Italians that lived in the area were predominately Communist sympathizers. As the local mayor characterized them, "They demonstrate at the base fences on Saturday then go to church on Sunday—you don't have to worry about them." Still I worried and spent many late night hours driving around with security police patrols to make sure they understood how important I believed their job was.

It was necessary to visit all of the local dignitaries such as the governor, host Italian base commander, commander of Armored Division next to the air base, mayor, etc., and pay my respects. There was an Italian liaison officer, Marc Bartognia, on the Fortieth staff, that was my interface with all of the dignitaries and local population. As we went around on these visits, I asked Marc who was the most important. His response was "Except for the head of the local chief of Carabinieri, you won't meet them, and they are the priest and the chemist (pharmacist)." He further explained that there was not a medical doctor within miles, so most of the people were treated by the chemist or referred by him to a doctor in Pordenone.

Shortly after I had made the obligatory visits to the local Italian leadership, the command section chief administrator brought a stack of paperwork into my office and said in a tone that spoke volumes, "You need to sign these waivers!" Somewhat puzzled, I asked what they were for. He said, "These waivers authorize the local Italian VIPs to shop in the base exchange, commissary, and class six (liquor) store."

"Is that legal?" I asked.

"No," he said, "and we've been written up for authorizing locals to shop on base in the last two IG inspections." If I was going to expect all the people under me to follow regulations, it was important for me to set the example and tone. The staff judge advocate (top lawyer) was born in the local area, immigrated to the United States prior to WW II as a very young boy, earned his law degree, became a US citizen, and entered the air force as a commissioned officer and lawyer. It made enormous sense for him to be the top lawyer on my staff. I asked him how the waivers came about and what would happen if I didn't renew them. He said it was wrong; the troops knew it was illegal and deeply resented it—every time they found a shelf empty, they blamed it on the Italians. Further, he said, it would cause resentment by the local VIPs, but the Italians also knew what they were doing was illegal and would probably get over it. I asked him to find out what each waiver holder liked to drink and smoke. With that list, I purchased a bottle of whisky and two cartons of cigarettes for each person on the list with my own money. Then I went to visit each one with Marc, the liaison officer, explaining that I could not renew their shopping waiver because it was against US laws and military regulations, but I wanted to bring them a gift expressing my appreciation for their understanding. It wasn't a pleasant experience, and I expected some pushback from the Carabinieri, our Italian military neighbors, and the local Italian host base commander. In this regard, I asked each deputy and staff chief to relay to all of their personnel what I had done and to carefully follow host nation laws when off base. Surprisingly, there wasn't any noticeable reaction.

One night, I received a call that there was an altercation at the NCO club between a senior NCO, the club manager (also an NCO), and a young black airman. I got there as fast as I could and found exactly what I had been warned about: the airman, dressed in civilian garb, had worn a hat into the club and, when told to remove it, refused. On seeing me, the two NCOs said they were going to push for an Article 15 (nonjudicial punishment) for failure to remove the hat and refusal to obey a direct order. Armed with the knowledge given me by the Social Actions officer at Bitburg, I got the NCOs off to the side so as not to embarrass them and pointed out they were confusing a custom with a regulation and that no punishment could be given for violating a custom. I further reminded them that on "western night," all those with western boots and hats wore them into the club and for the entire night—how could this be any different? They didn't like it, but my intervention ended the altercation—or so I thought.

The next day, the Fortieth Group senior enlisted advisor, a chief master sergeant, who was my principal go-between to all the enlisted personnel in the command, brought a dozen or so senior NCOs into my office to discuss the incident at the NCO club the previous evening. Apparently, these NCOs felt that I did not support the NCOs involved in the incident as they would have expected. It didn't take long to understand that the senior enlisted advisor and his entourage expected me to support senior NCOs even if they were in the wrong. I explained to them that I would back all my officers and NCOs when they were on the right side of an issue, but I would not and could not blindly support them when they were wrong. It was also pointed out to them that they appeared to have two standards for hats worn in the NCO club—one for country and western attire and one for fashionable black attire. It was wrong to have a double standard, and it was an even greater wrong to try and enforce a double standard under the guise of nonexistent air force regulations. This was going down hard, and I wasn't getting any support from my senior enlisted advisor. To the contrary, it was apparent he was somewhat of a bigot himself. I didn't expect any help from USAFE personnel, and chief master sergeants have a mafia of their own, but I had to try. Much to my surprise, Higher Headquarters indicated there had been reports from USAFE help teams visiting Aviano that there might be a problem in this area. A new chief master sergeant was soon heading my way, by the name of Pat Patterson. Chief Master Sergeant Patterson really made a difference at Aviano and was an outstanding leader in his own right.

Senator Byrd, West Virginia, brought a small entourage to visit Aviano, ostensibly on a fact-finding trip to learn about our mission and how we fit into NATO. The Fortieth was aptly prepared for these distinguished visitors. A group mission briefing was waiting in the conference along with refreshments and several important stops at base facilities to explain what we did and what our needs were budget wise. I met our visitors at their aircraft and drove them to the group conference room. Just as I started the overview briefing, Senator Byrd asked how long the presentation would take and what time the gift shops in town closed. The response was simple and straightforward: the briefing takes an hour, the tour takes an hour, and Lino's Gift Shop closes in thirty minutes. With that, the senator said he was sorry, but there were some things he wanted to buy, and they were leaving early in the morning for Rome. With that, the group got up and went to the cars we provided and drove to Lino's Gift Shop. After they departed, I raced around to all the facilities where air force personnel were standing by to brief the fact-finders, to let them know the schedule had changed and our guests had departed. I saw Senator Byrd and his entourage off with a salute the next morning and hoped that was the last of the congressional boondoggle the Fortieth would have to contend with. For days after they left, all that the troops talked about was what a waste of taxpayers' money the senator's trip was. Not a good public relations thing for the Congress! It was a lesson for me to make sure that I never created the same impression and caused resentment when I visited a unit. The golf clubs, fishing poles, and shopping lists never came along on an official visit in an air force aircraft or vehicle.

Cardinal Cook, archbishop of New York, also paid Aviano a visit, but the tone and purpose were much different. The cardinal ministered to all Catholics in the military and came for that purpose. Most were surprised that such a small, out-of-the-way unit was on the cardinal's itinerary. All personal, regardless of religious preference, truly enjoyed and appreciated Cardinal Cook's visit.

The base exchange (BX) manager came to my office one day to tell me that five airmen had placed orders for jackets with a patch on the back with the words "Freedom by Any Means Necessary" on a shield of three vertical stripes colored black, red, and green. I was enough of a student of black history to recognize that these colors were taken from the first Black Liberation Movement in America. Moreover, General Jones had banned this patch for wear on air force bases in Europe. I asked the BX manager if he could lose the order or at least delay it for weeks or months. My own personal experience with special orders from the BX was that you usually had to reorder at least once, and the goods took months to arrive. So I wasn't asking for more than routine service. But in this case, the custom jacket order was filled in a couple of weeks, and I was notified when they arrived.

In the meantime, I had conferred with Lt. Col. Tony Farina, the JAG, and asked for legal advice on how to proceed. He advised that to ban the jackets at Aviano was a fool's errand! I asked, "How so?" He explained that with the Fortieth Group barracks located inside Aviano's city limits, all an Airman had to do was put the jacket in a gym bag, walk outside the gate, and put the jacket on. I had no jurisdiction outside the base, and they could wear the jackets there with total disregard for General Jones's ban. Moreover, if an NCO or officer believed an airman was doing wrong by wearing one of these jackets and tried to interfere, he could be arrested by the Italian police for causing a disturbance. To add more weight to his argument against the ban, he pointed out that there were a large number of black dependent teenagers and that I had no authority over dependent teenagers, on or off the base. The only authority I had with regard to dependents was to move them out of base housing if their behavior was prejudicial to law and order. This club was not a factor because there wasn't any base housing at Aviano; all married personnel accompanied by dependents, including myself, lived in Italian houses located off base. Dependents, wives or children, could wear the jackets with impunity. The only other action available to a commander of an installation on foreign soil was to ask our ambassador to declare an individual or family persona non grata and send them back to the United States. Clearly, this was not an issue that rose to the ambassador's level.

I mapped out a course of action. First, I would ask the airmen who now owned the jackets not to wear them for a week while we worked together to prepare the way. Second, I asked them to write a thoughtful letter to the base population explaining why the patch was important to them. Third, I would publish their letter if it was worthy, along with a cover letter from me asking the base population to be understanding; after all, the phrase came directly out of our Declaration of Independence, and we certainly believed in and supported freedom for all people. Fourth, I would call General McBride and explain to him the reason why Aviano deserved special consideration on this issue and how I planned to approach to problem. It was not any easy call, but as noted earlier, General McBride was a good listener. When I finished, he said he would have to discuss this matter with General Jones and then would get back to me. The waiting was worse than the call; changing direction, considering all the factors, was full of big challenges. The callback came late that afternoon. General McBride was succinct, as was his style. He said, "General Jones is willing to let you proceed as you described, but understand that we have already identified your replacement should your plan fail, and we have an aircraft and crew standing by—don't screw it up!" It is always understood that if a commander screws up, whether its aircraft accidents, poor leadership, or whatever, you're toast, so I wasn't taken aback by the warning.

The airman in question, or someone helping them, wrote an articulate letter explaining their feelings and purpose that I would have been proud to have written. I had already composed my letter to put on as an introduction, and both were published in the *Daily Bulletin* for distribution on the following day. The jackets came out of the closet and were worn openly around the base. There was no apparent response in the negative. According to Chief Master Sergeant Pat Patterson, the jackets were worn regularly for about a week or two then disappeared from sight and were never seen again. I suspect that he and some other highly respected senior black NCOs and officers spoke with the airmen after a week passed and suggested they made their point and perhaps it was time to move on. Whatever the reason, the jackets never caused one iota of a problem and passed out of sight quietly! Another bullet dodged!

The 40th TFG was overdue for an operational readiness inspection, so we practiced all of the elements of this demanding test on a regular basis. The mantra I established for the unit was "We do our job to ORI standards every day—we are not just trying to look good—we are training to go to war on a moment's notice!" This concept appeared to be working; every aspect of the mission was getting measurable better. In this regard, I learned that the 36th TFW had failed their ORI before it had hardly started. I seemed that Col. Don Payne, vice commander, took the second shift in the command post when the tasking for a conventional load out of aircraft was sent by the inspector general (IG). Colonel Payne apparently spent too much time studying the tasking for subtle nuances before requesting the munitions, called for in the tasking, be transported from the bomb dump to the flight line. The time lost in getting the munitions to the flight line made it impossible to load 50 percent of the wing aircraft in the twelve-hour time limit. The lesson was not lost on Aviano, and we went over our procedures in considerable depth to ensure there were no inherent delays in our procedures.

The call from the command post came very early in the morning. The call was cryptic: "The ORI Team aircraft is on short final for landing at Aviano!" A recall of key personnel was ordered to ensure we had all the talent necessary to handle the tasking without running critical personnel resources out of crew duty time. For example, aircrews, weapon loading crews, aircraft maintenance personnel, and security police could only be on duty for twelve hours at which time they had to be relieved. Now for certain, if the United States and/or NATO were at war, these limits would be waived if necessary to prosecute the war; however, in being tested under an ORI, these limits were sacrosanct for safety.

I tossed on a flight suit and hurried to the command post to meet the IG who was already there. Brig. Gen. Edwin Robertson was the IG and chose to be present for our readiness test. He was all business and handed me a sheaf of papers setting the stage for the coming readiness test and introduced me to a colonel who would remain in the command post as his representative. He was our go-to guy for clarification of tasking if there was ambiguity. This would prove to be a key point in twenty-four hours.

An ORI at Aviano starts slowly, as our wartime forces come from the 401st TFW based at Torrejon, Spain, and it takes several hours for them to prepare for deployment and then fly to Aviano. While this is taking place, the 40th TFG prepares for their arrival, increases security to DEFCON 4, and moves B-61 nuclear bombs from the storage area on the other side of the highway to the Victor Alert area in preparation of "Mirroring the Victor Alert." If it were a real DEFCON 4, the fighter unit at Aviano would be preparing to fly back to England or Germany to fulfill their wartime tasking, and the aircraft sitting alert with nuclear bombs would be traded out by the aircraft coming from Spain. During an ORI, the forces at Aviano did not redeploy; however, we had to demonstrate that the Victor Alert (VA) could be replaced in twelve hours from the start of the ORI. This was not a strenuous timeline unless the aircraft arriving from Spain arrived broke and required extensive maintenance to return them to combat-ready status. However, moving additional nuclear bombs to the area was a critical step. This required coordination with the Carabinieri (federal police) to close and secure a portion of the only highway to the town of Aviano. Nuclear safety and security was a pass/

fail Item and had to be done with precision and care. Any real-world incident involving a nuclear weapon, termed a "broken arrow," would be briefed all the way up to the United States president. With the B-61 bombs safely transported to the Victor Alert area, we had time to get the group deputy commanders together and do some contingency planning for the next anticipated tasking. One of the considerations is crew rest for the arriving personnel. We learned that the aircrews, load crews, and maintenance personnel had been recalled at 0600 hours, Aviano time. They would turn to pumpkins at 1800 hours and have to go into crew rest. Anticipated arrival time was 1300 hours, giving us five hours to turn four aircraft and mirror the VA. It was accomplished in four hours. Another critical event passed.

If the ORI progressed as anticipated, the next event would be a full conventional load out of the remaining F-4 aircraft. The pass/fail criterion was loading out 50 percent of the aircraft in twelve hours. The only problem we could foresee was bringing in too many munitions load crews to accomplish this tack and then running out of load crew, crew rest, and not being able to accomplish follow-on tasking in time to meet ORI criteria. Load crew work schedules would have to be managed carefully. In this regard, I asked General Robertson's representative in the command post what the 50 percent number was. This may sound silly and trite; after all, 50 percent of twenty-four is twelve, right? Not so in an ORI! The number could be twelve, it could be ten, or it could be eight, depending on how the IG treated the four aircraft in VA loaded with B-61 nuclear bombs. If he only considered the remaining twenty aircraft, the 50 percent number would be ten. If he considered all twenty-four aircraft with no consideration of the VA, the number would be twelve. On the other hand, if he did that and gave credit for the four VA aircraft, the number could be as low as eight. The correct number was important if we were going to carefully manage load crews and pilots to accommodate follow-on tasking. General Robertson's CP representative answered our question in writing. The specific pass/fail number to be loaded in twelve hours was *ten aircraft*.

The conventional tasking order arrived in the dead of night with both Colonel Brockman and me in the CP along with Lieutenant Colonel Baumgartner, chief of maintenance. We pulled the trigger on specific numbers of personnel that could accomplish the tasking, and everyone swung into action. It was like watching a ballet. I left Colonel Brockman in the CP, took a two hour nap, and went to the flight line to watch the load out progress. The bombs and fuzes had been delivered and positioned near the aircraft. Load crews were just arriving, and pilots had already preflighted the aircraft to ensure the ones loaded were ready to fly. For the next several hours, I prowled the flight line checking the Form 781 of loaded aircraft to make sure the entries were correct, the aircraft was in commission, and that the arming wires for the fuzes of loaded bombs were installed correctly and of the proper length. As time passed, it was evident that ten aircraft would be loaded in less than nine hours well under the pass/fail criteria, and all available aircraft would be loaded in under twenty-four hours, the second criteria. Colonel Brockman, Colonel Cobb, Lieutenant Colonel Baumgartner, and I had conferenced several times about the need to call in another load crew to ensure compliance with the tasking but decided it wasn't necessary.

As the twelve-hour time limit ran out with eleven aircraft loaded and the twelfth almost complete, I came across General Robertson also observing the load out. He informed me we had *flunked* the ORI based on the failure to make the load out. I was floored with his announcement and asked how that could be. He said the criteria were twelve aircraft, and we didn't make it! I responded that his representative in the CP gave us the number ten in writing, and we were managing to that number—how could we fail given that information? He curtly replied, "He wasn't authorized to tell you that. You flunked, period!" He then said he could pack up his team or he could stay and continue the ORI as a training exercise; it was my choice. I opted for them to stay and continue so we could benefit from the experience. We passed all the remaining criteria, which included sabotage, runway repair, chemical attack, and a variety of other tests. The complete ORI lasted a week.

When I went home that evening, after about thirty hours of leading the effort along with the leadership team, I found Sheila and the children already asleep. When she woke up, I gave her the news that we had flunked, and it was likely I would be reassigned. Without giving the news much thought, she said, "Don't worry, you're doing a good job—it'll pass."

The ORI outbriefing wasn't very pretty. General Robertson wrote us up for lacking a war-footing attitude and an absence of urgency, plus the failure to meet the load-out criteria. One of the points he made about attitude and war footing was the fact that after their twelve-hour shift ended, some group personnel (mostly security police) played a pickup game of softball back in the cantonment area. Subsequently, as I was driving him to his aircraft, I mentioned that the people playing softball were out of duty time and could not be used in the exercise for another twelve hours, that I thought it was better for them to play ball than go to the club or into town and drink. I also told him I accepted the failure, but the only criterion we didn't pass was the controversial number of aircraft, which were provided to us in writing. To this, he responded, "I could have passed the Fortieth, but I'm convinced you can do much better, and that wouldn't happen if you passed. I'll recommend to General Jones that you get to take the retest in ninety days."

General Robertson suggested that we could move much faster if we considered that the crew duty day for the arriving forces started when they got off of the aircraft at Aviano, vice when they were recalled at Torrejon, Spain. For clarification on his suggestion, I sent a message to USAFE/IG/LG/DO requesting authorization to establish the crew duty start time as the time they landed at Aviano. The response to that request never got out of the USAFE Headquarters; evidently, General Robertson's idea wasn't universally accepted and never was approved.

Over the weekend, I came up with some ideas of how we could do a lot better in terms of time to complete tasking and to show a higher sense of urgency. One of the paperwork issues that caused us problems is that most of the aircraft that deployed to Aviano were F-4Ds, whereas the aircraft that deployed in for the wartime mission and ORIs were F-4Es. The differences between the two were not significant, but by regulation, none of the weapons loaders assigned to Aviano could load conventional or nuclear weapons on F-4Es unless they were certified as trained on the F-4E variant and passed a rigorous standardization and evaluation test. Further, they would have to undergo training every six months to stay current. That was easy to fix; Fortieth load crews were sent to the 401st at Torrejon for training and certification. This provided us two additional F-4E load crews that could be used to mirror the VA and for the conventional load out. Moreover, they would be fresh with twelve hours of crew duty time when the deploying forces arrived because they would be left in crew rest until that time. Further, all of the unaccompanied or single enlisted personnel at Aviano had never experienced an ORI; the one just experienced was their only real exposure to a wartime tempo. Even though they had all trained extensively, the weeklong simulated wartime scenario created a much greater sense of urgency and understanding of what was required. Lieutenant Colonel Cobb also suggested that we use the dead time from ORI team arrival to the arrival of deploying forces to preposition stocks of ground equipment where we knew they would be needed once the munition load outs started. His idea was folded into the plan and paid big dividends.

Prior to the retake, a message from the embassy in Rome stated that the Palestine Liberation Organization (PLO) was planning to break into a nuclear storage area and steal a nuclear weapon, and Aviano was a likely target. This made sense to me, as our nuclear weapons were outside the base in an agricultural field. It was necessary to harden this facility and make sure that if it was breached, no PLO could escape alive, let alone with a nuclear weapon. We had the required number of guards inside and outside the compound, but there was little protection against an armed force. The civil engineers in conjunction with the chief of security police were asked to design, build, and install steel-reinforced concrete fighting and concealment positions that would withstand rocket-propelled grenades and .50-caliber machine gunfire.

Once these fighting positions were installed, I asked the Italian commander of the "Ram" Armored Division that shared the southeast fence line with the airbase if he would agree to respond with two armored personnel carriers to defend the munitions storage area. While this general was not supposed to know there were nuclear bombs in the storage area, the Italian government did, and I was convinced they would have told him. I just told the Italian general I was concerned that terrorists would attempt to embarrass our respective governments by gaining access to the bunkers. What I wanted him to do was move two on-alert M113 tracked vehicles with .50-caliber machine guns to the storage area fence line and train their guns down the fronts of the two rows of bunkers. If anyone inside the storage area moved, they were requested to shoot until our response team could join up with his M113s. When he asked about the safety of our guards, I told him they would be sheltered behind the concrete firing points outside the line of fire. When he agreed to provide the requested support, I provided him, his deputy, and their G-3 a handheld radio and chargers so that they could be reached immediately when needed. The radio turned out to be a real status symbol. I also took them on a tour of the storage area and showed them the concrete firing points where our guards would take a defensive position if the area came under attack. We practiced the response at night on two separate occasions.

Nuclear weapons were most vulnerable when they were transiting from the weapons storage area to the flight line or returning from the flight line to the storage area. The escort force was beefed up, but it was impossible to predict the size of a PLO force; top cover was needed to prevent ambush during the critical transient. For this, I approached the major who commanded the helicopter rescue detachment on base. They worked directly for Search and Rescue Headquarters in the United States, and anything they agreed to would have to fit within their normal training missions and flying hours. After explaining the PLO threat to him, I asked if he would put up a helicopter with a security policeman on board anytime nuclear weapons were being convoyed between the storage area and the flight line. Without hesitation, he agreed, with the proviso that he could not exceed his flying hour authorization but would hold a couple of hours in reserve to the last day of every month. In preparing for the ORI retake, we had two convoys, and the helicopter escort procedure worked extremely well.

Another message from the US embassy in Rome warned that the Italian terrorist organization called the Red Brigades was planning to take as a hostage a senior American military officer in northern Italy. There were only four American senior officers in northern Italy, an army brigadier general at Land South in Vicenza, Italy, about one hundred miles southwest of Aviano, and three colonels at Aviano, Colonel Brockman, Colonel McCall, and me. The message suggested changing routes to work on a daily basis and increasing security. So much for suggestions! There was only one road from the leased house where we lived to the 40th TFG. We could go the wrong way but then had to come back the same way if we were going to work or to visit any of the base facilities. What was of greatest concern to me was Sheila and the children; we lived on the economy several miles from the base. There was no security except for the lock on the door, and it was not possible to have security police guard my house or any other of the family quarters. However, the Italians certainly knew of the threat because the Red Brigades had murdered a number of high-ranking Italian officials, including a chief justice. Shortly after receiving information of the threat, I noticed Carabinieri police cars parked just down the street from the house, as well as Italian soldiers in jeeps not too far away. Still I thought it better if Sheila and the children took some time to visit her parents, but she would have none of it; she wanted the family to be together. I tried to explain that the people I was concerned about were not common criminals, but terrorists that placed no value on human life. She wasn't leaving, and that was the end of the conversation. To my knowledge, none of the other colonels' families left the area either.

Major General McGough decided to test the Fortieth Group prior to the IG's return and set up a squadron deployment from Spain along with a mini evaluation team to grade our performance. General McGough came along to observe and to offer pointers based on his experience. It was a very helpful practice with his team collecting information that would help us to refine our plans and make our readiness for war even better. When it was over, General McGough asked me to join him for lunch at the dining facility for a personal debriefing. Most of it was positive with several suggestions to tighten the control loop. He applauded the security improvements in the munitions storage area and the helicopter coverage of nuclear convoys. As we were finishing, the deployed fighter squadron commander came over with some suggestions. As he went down his list of ideas, I was somewhat negative, noting that we had already tried some of the things he was suggesting, and they didn't work, and not very enthusiastic about the rest. General McGough was silent through these discussions, but when the squadron commander departed, he said, "Pete, that was really stupid on your part! You should have listened to what he had to say and thanked him for his suggestions. All he was trying to do was be helpful! What you've done is convince him that you have a closed mind. That is one person who will never offer you another helpful suggestion!" This wasn't exactly the way I wanted the visit from General McGough to end, but it was a valuable lesson that I took to heart and tried to apply for the rest of my career and postretirement work. At first, I tried to rationalize my negative behavior because my boss was there, but that didn't ring true. It was the first honest realization that I didn't have to think of all the good ideas, just recognize one when I heard it and give credit where credit was due.

The IG team was again about to land at Aviano for the reevaluation. We were so ready this time, the events seemed to be in slow motion. The thought of considering the gaining forces fresh when they arrived had never been approved, but the two resident F-4E qualified load crews really made a difference. Mirroring the VA alert aircraft took less than two hours. Further, the conventional load out was accomplished on all of the remaining aircraft in just over the time limit for half of them. Usually, the conventionally loaded aircraft didn't fly with live ordinance but were downloaded and then reloaded with practice bombs. Once they were reloaded, the force was sent on a low-level route ending at the nearby Maniago Gunnery Range. The pilots had to achieve satisfactory scores to retain their combat-ready status. The next event was usually a nuclear load out simulating that a conventional war between NATO and Warsaw Pact Forces was going in the enemy's favor, and NATO had to resort to nuclear weapons to halt vastly numerically superior Warsaw Pact Forces.

General Robertson had been reassigned, and the new IG was working hard to make sure he didn't leave Aviano looking like a Santa Claus. He was considerate enough to ask when the best time would be to move real nuclear weapons for the force load out. This required twenty more nuclear weapons in addition to the four moved the previous day to mirror the VA. It was mid-September, with daylight and darkness equally split. I suggested anytime around dawn when there was sufficient light and the Italian highway that had to be closed and crossed would have little traffic at that time. The IG input for the nuclear load out came at 4:30 a.m., and that is when the clock started. The nuclear munitions handling personnel and security police escorts were recalled immediately, and the process of loading trailers and forming a convoy of twenty B-61 bombs was started. The helicopter detachment commander was alerted for the airborne escort. The IG was sitting next to me in the command post, monitoring all communications and activities. The last big event of the ORI was set in motion. Word came in that the convoy was formed and moving out of the double fence required in foreign countries for nuclear assets. The helicopter with a senior security policeman (SP) on board was already airborne over the convoy. The SP called with the observation that the field was full of armed men, approximately thirty or more. What now, were we under attack by the PLO? I turned to the IG and asked crisply, "Is this an IG input?"

His immediate response was "*No*, this must be real!"

The reason for my question to the IG was that sometimes, the IG would script an input that cannot be done virtually to add stress and test the unit's response. I was hoping that was the case. The airborne SP had already called the security response force, and the SPs escorting the convoy had ordered it back into the storage area, and the SP commander, monitoring the communications net, requested reinforcements from the Carabinieri. Everything was coming together to combat the threat, when the next call came in from the airborne SP. "The convoy is safe inside of the storage area, and the gates are secured. The armed men in the fields are shooting." The chief of the Carabinieri arrived at the road crossing and informed the SPs there that today was the opening day of the local hunting season for small game. The armed men in the fields were hunters shooting at rabbits and pheasants and, except for a potential stray shot, were not a threat to our convoy. When that word was relayed to the command post, there was a sigh of relief all around, including the IG. After consulting with the chief of the Carabinieri about a safe time for the convoy, he opined that the hunters would abandon the fields about noon for lunch and to celebrate their success and would not likely return for three or four hours. I suggested to the IG that he consider a second input that might coincide with the Carabinieri chief's suggestion. That was easy for him, but my problem was load crew, crew rest. Fortunately, Lieutenant Colonel Cobb was waiting for the convoy to arrive at the flight line and two-man controls to be established at all the aircraft shelters where the aircraft were housed prior to calling for the load crews. The loading time criteria were not that tight, and he didn't want to burn their time prior to absolutely needing them.

The IG cancelled the previous tasking and submitted a new tasking that arrived over the Cemetery Net at 10:00 a.m. All the safeguards were once again put in place, including the airborne helicopter. The helicopter detachment commander and his pilots were certified heroes in my book and were proud of the part they played. The IG was ecstatic over the helicopter idea and promised to write a letter to the military airlift commander, the four-star commander who owned the Search and Rescue Forces, commending them for their spirit of cooperation and support of critical nuclear weapons movements.

Everything from then on went exceptionally well, and Fortieth Tactical Group personnel earned many kudos for exceptional performance during the ORI. Unfortunately, the highest ORI rating that can be earned on a retest is satisfactory. The IG, to his credit, went out of his way to make the point that while the overall performance was outstanding, the highest rating that could be awarded was satisfactory. The ORI debrief took place on Friday morning, enabling me to give Fortieth Group personnel a well-earned three-day weekend. As an afterthought, the Italian liaison officer was asked to research all the local holidays and events that might lend themselves to the use of firearms or demonstrations that, without forewarning, might cause us undue concern.

While the ORI was fresh in my mind, it seemed appropriate to start thinking about an air force compliance inspection. These inspections looked deep into how the unit was run and its careful adherence to regulations and directives, hence the term "compliance." The first place to start is the previous inspection report when the 40th TFG was rated the *worst* in the air force over the previous five years by the air force inspector general—no way to go but up, but not without considerable effort. The vice commander and each deputy commander were assigned a portion of the last inspection report for reviewing corrective actions taken on each write-up. I randomly spot-checked corrective action in all areas covered in the report. One such visit is instructive on why personal follow-up is important. The personnel section had been written up for failure to properly fill out AF Form 123. I found the individual responsible for the personnel actions recorded on the specified form and asked to see the corrective action and some of the forms. His response was positive: "That deficiency is no longer a problem, that form has been rescinded!" After some small talk about how important personnel actions were to each and every air force member and thanking him for his good work, I started to leave when the thought struck me: Did the air force replace Form 123 with another form with a different number? I asked the killer question and got a positive response. When I reviewed a handful of the new forms, I found the same discrepancy on the new form that the IG inspectors found on the old 123 Form. The sergeant and I went through the entire file folder, finding about 40 percent lacking a specific entry. The response to all previous corrective action follow-ups, of which there were several, had always been AF Form 123 has been discontinued; the problem no longer exists. The sergeant and I talked about what could be done to prevent the omission from occurring. It was his idea to use red file folders for those forms that were identified as problem areas. It turned out there were three that fell into that category. He further promised to make a note on the outside of the file folder of what the nature of the problem was. It was a good session, and I believe I was there to help him find ways to eliminate problems, not tell him how to do his job.

Colonel Brockman and I both liked to get out of the office and get our hands dirty, looking for problems to be fixed, and to learn more about what goes on all over the base. We finally came up with a contest of sort, and that was who could find something that existed or was happening on the base that the other didn't know about. In this regard, we both discovered things that were novel or otherwise unknown, but he won the grand prize! In his prowling, Colonel Brockman found a locked portable shed in one of the hardened aircraft shelter loops where our gained squadron aircraft were parked. With no squadron deployed to Aviano at that time, there was no reason for the shed to be locked, and who would have the key? He called the Civil Engineering Squadron and Fire Department because both units are supposed to have master keys or individual keys for all buildings, etc. Neither unit had a key for this facility, so they cut the lock and opened the shed. Inside, we found twenty-four AIM-9 air-to-air missiles. AIM-9s cost more than a million dollars each and are rigidly controlled by serial number. Some unit somewhere in Europe or the United States had deployed to Aviano in the past and left these valuable assets behind. Our theory was the unit bought so many souvenirs of alabaster and "globe bars" that the dedicated airlift for their redeployment couldn't haul out all of their military equipment and personal purchases, so they left the AIM-9s behind. The who was never solved at our level; however, when these assets were turned into the Supply System for reallocation, the serial numbers on each AIM-9 would reveal who was accountable for them.

I thought it so important to be a "walkabout and hands-on commander," that I had standing instructions to my secretary, Mary Ellen Stemper, to order me out of the office every morning at 9:00 a.m., or following the staff meeting, and not let me back in until 5:00 p.m. This meant coming in early and staying late to process all the paperwork that came across the desk, but it was worth it based on all the problems I uncovered from listening to the people doing the work that needed to be done. It was obvious that a better system of getting problems and gripes surfaced was needed. The only complaint input at the time was a formal complaint to Colonel Brockman, which was hardly used. The other option was the hotline, which was transcribed by one of the admin clerks. The problem with the hotline is that the complainant was usually drunk, profane, and not very coherent when calling the hotline. I wanted something better, and the "Commander's Gram" was born to serve this purpose. The Commander's Gram was a single sheet of paper with that title and started out with "Dear Colonel Pete, I want to bring the following to your attention." This was followed by a number of lines, and at the bottom, there was a place to check "Anonymous" and a place to check "I desire a personal response" and a place for the complainant's name. Several locked oak mailboxes with a place to hold these forms were placed in key spots around cantonment and work areas. The only person who could open the Commander's Gram mailboxes was the senior enlisted advisor, Chief Master Sergeant Pat Patterson. The purpose of the boxes was advertised in the *Daily Bulletin* so that military dependents and Italian employees would know what they were for and how to use them. A week went by, and there were no inputs. The thought occurred to me that I needed to "salt" the boxes. So I used my daily walkabout visits to identify things that needed attention and turned them into Commander's Grams and stuffed them into different boxes in the dark of night. One of them was a complaint from a male dormitory that all the tips of the pool sticks had been missing for over two weeks. My first inclination was to send this to the Special Services Office responsible for recreational equipment. The proposed response was an eye-opener that went something like this: "The pool sticks are broken because you broke them. When you stop breaking them, we will start fixing them!" That response was the epiphany that pushed me into writing all the responses myself. Then I sent the response as an action item to the responsible agency. The rule for corrective action was two days maximum. When I wrote the pool cue response, it read like this: "Thank you for bringing the broken pool cues to my attention. When you return to the squadron this evening, you will find that all the old pool cues have been replaced with new ones. The old ones are being repaired. In addition, your first sergeant has a repair kit to replace the tips when they come off. Again, thank you for bringing this matter to my attention!" Signed with my signature.

The responses to anonymous complaints were placed on the bulletin boards all over the base. In time, there were so many that separate bulletin boards were needed to prevent crowding out the purpose of the original bulletin boards. The best ones were published in the weekly base paper. There was always a crowd at the Commander's Gram bulletin board near the base exchange. I think the troops got a kick out of sending anonymous notes to the commander and getting a corrective response. After a while, people started signing their Commander's Grams, requesting a personal response. This was good, but the information wasn't getting out, so we started putting Sergeant Smith and Captain Smith on the Gram and the response so they could be put on the bulletin board.

Oddly enough, I started getting signed Commander's Grams from the Social Actions staff. I processed them just like all the others, but after several came across my desk, I called Captain Scott, the Social Actions chief, and asked him why he didn't just send me official letters like the rest of the staff. His response showed creativity and a lot of humor, "I use the Commander's Gram because you always answer them in two days—an official letter might take two weeks!" I laughed and told him to write letters, otherwise his records could be challenged by the IG, and that I would be more responsive." I used the Commander's Gram rather successfully at every level of command, except as air force vice chief, because I wasn't the boss.

A message from Gen. David Jones, CINCUSAFE, addressed "Personal from General Jones to all commanders," was short and to the point. It read, "The next time I visit your base, I expect you to show me how you do an aircraft records check." Colonels get very few, if any, personal messages from four-star generals, so it really got my attention. Every pilot does a records check every time he/she flies, but it's not as thorough as the one done monthly by the aircraft crew chief to reconcile the Form 781 with all the master records in supply and the engine shop.

I picked up the hotline to Lieutenant Colonel Cobb, and the voice on the other end said, "I got the message and assume you want to do a records check. I'm looking for an aircraft that is due for one, so it's not a wasted effort. I'll call you as soon as the crew chief comes in with the forms."

About an hour later, Colonel Cobb and I walked around with a crew chief as he went to supply to rationalize all of the back-ordered parts for his F-4D. Then to the engine repair shop to make sure that the engine time in the Form 781 for both engines agreed with the master file in the engine shop. After those two stops, I sat down with the crew chief to review every write-up, called "delayed discrepancies," that had not been closed out by a maintenance action to repair or correct the problem. There were pages of delayed discrepancies, none of which prevented the aircraft from flying, but several reduced its ability to perform a vital mission such as air superiority or an air-to-ground attack delivery like "dive toss." A pilot's impression might be that this aircraft can take off and land but not much else. What Truman Cobb and I discovered is that many of the parts ordered to close out a discrepancy had been cancelled by the Air Logistics Repair Center responsible for the part. No reason was given; the order was just cancelled. We made a comprehensive list of all the cancelled orders and sent a message to the depot, requesting action with a courtesy copy to USAFE/LG (Major General Poe). The reason for General Jones's message was starting to sink in; wing commanders needed to get involved to put pressure on the depots; otherwise, all the Form 781s would be full of discrepancies with a part ordered date, where the part had been cancelled without notification. Hence, it would never be reordered. You had to wonder, was this something the depots were doing to look good with regard to back orders?

We also observed that the "buck sergeant" crew chief had to stand around and wait for someone to give him the time of day so he could update the Form 781. I decided we needed a records check desk, where the crew chief would come and call the supply and engine personnel to come to him. After all, the mission was to "fly, fight, and win," and the crew chief with his/her aircraft was the instrument that made it all possible. We also created a records check checklist that was printed in large font to hang above the desk. Last, we agreed that if a Form 781 was dirty and dog-eared, it would be reaccomplished with a new Form 781 holder, dividers, and pages. I spent the rest of the morning working with the crew chief to build a new and neat Form 781 and signed the forms, indicating I had conducted the records check. From then on, I performed a records check once every two weeks just to make sure that the system didn't fall back into its old ways.

A few weeks later, there was a USAFE Wing Commanders' Conference, and I had an opportunity to have dinner with a number of my fellow wing commanders, all more senior and more experienced than I was. During a break in the conversation, I asked if they had conducted an aircraft records check. The answer was uniformly no for a variety of weak reasons. "No, I haven't had the time," "No, I don't know how to do a records check," etc. I knew they were in trouble if General Jones followed up on his promise to observe them do a 781 records check when next he visited their wing. General Jones had served as a maintenance officer in SAC for a couple of years prior to moving to TAC and commander of the 33rd TFW; there was no question in my mind that he had his finger on a problem that he forced me to discover.

While at Ramstein AFB, home of Headquarters USAFE, I happened to be walking down a hall when General Creech came out of his office. He asked me how "Higgy" (deputy commander for operations) was doing. I answered honestly, "I'm glad you asked. Higgy is not carrying his weight and is the weakest deputy on the Group Staff. I'd like to get a replacement for him."

General Creech's response was not what I'd hoped for. He said, "Higgy's just being Higgy, you can carry him."

At this Commanders' Conference, it was noted that a review of all postflight inspections revealed the average number of discrepancies found was twelve. The point was made that if your postflight inspection (PFIs) aren't uncovering this many discrepancies, the crew chiefs are not doing their jobs properly! Armed with this insightful information, I called a meeting of the deputy commander for maintenance, chief of maintenance, and maintenance supervisor to pass on this information and that we needed to tell the crew chiefs that they should be finding, on average, twelve or more discrepancies. Following my comments came a pregnant silence. Finally the maintenance supervisor, a highly regarded chief master sergeant, opined, "Sir, if we tell them to find twelve discrepancies, they'll find twelve or maybe thirteen to make you happy. Most of these will be bogus, like loose rivet or loose screw, fixed on the spot." He went on to say, "What we need to do is send the quality control (QC) team out to redo the PFIs to see if they find discrepancies that were missed by the crew chief. If they do, it will be reported to the crew chief and be a motivator for them to do a more thorough job. We'll keep sending QC to do follow up inspections until we don't find any more missed discrepancies. Then we'll do this periodically so the crew chiefs don't backslide." His suggestion made enormous sense, and I thanked him for having the courage to disagree with my bad idea. Last, I asked to be trained to do a PFI at night just to see how difficult a PFI could be and why crew chiefs were missing discrepancies. It was another eye-opener.

A PFI is the last inspection of the day, unless the aircraft is undergoing maintenance that might require a follow-on inspection. Because the PFI comes after the last flight of the day and normal servicing, it usually takes place during hours of low light and darkness. The tools for a PFI are a two-cell flashlight, rag, and checklist. The rag is important because if some fluid leak indications are found, they are wiped away and rechecked later. This helps determine if it's a real leak or just residual fluid from servicing or previous maintenance. It was dark and drizzling when I found my way to the aircraft to be inspected. Starting at the nose and moving around the aircraft clockwise, the major items that are of concern are fluid leaks, oil, hydraulic fluid, and JP-4—even seeps matter. Also chafing on wire bundles and hydraulic lines in the three-wheel wells are an indication of misalignment, wire bundle clamps installed incorrectly, or being pulled loose by g-forces in flight. Equally important, loose rivets and screws could result in these small items being ingested into the engines, causing significant damage and potential shutdown in flight. It was hard to read the checklist with the flashlight and even harder to detect things of interest. It took nearly two hours, and the crew chief, following after me, found some chafing on wire bundles that I missed. To me, the message was clear: we needed better lighting, even during the day, when looking into the crevices and corners of wheel wells. Lieutenant Colonel Baumgartner advised that the group could purchase mobile electrical power carts, called Lightall, that came equipped with two powerful articulating lights. They also had 110-volt AC outlets that could be used to power handheld lights on extension cords.

The carts weren't heavy and could be easily moved from aircraft to aircraft by hand. Great idea; we ordered enough carts and extension cord lights on one-hundred-foot cords to handle simultaneous PFIs on 25 percent of the normal complement of aircraft plus spares to allow for cart and extension cord repair. The equipment was well received by the crew chiefs, and the number of discrepancies discovered on PFIs increased, probably because crew chiefs could see what they were looking for. Moreover, the time to conduct a PFI dropped by a significant percentage. I did another nighttime PFI using the Lightall power cart and extension light with a 100-watt bulb. As Mark Twain would say, "It was like the difference between lightning and lightning bug."

True to his word, General Jones sent "help teams" to improve the group's compliance and performance. One team stands out in the number that came and went. This was an unusual duo of an air force captain from Social Actions at Headquarters USAFE and a Native American who spent most of entire adult life in prison for a variety of offenses, mostly hard drug possession and distribution related. They would spend a week immersed in the sea of young enlisted personnel and then outbrief me on the problems they had uncovered. Quite frankly, they didn't discover anything that Chief Master Sergeant Pat Patterson hadn't already brought to my attention, but their inputs often caused me to change the urgency or emphasis I placed on resolving problems. I suspected that my predecessor didn't give them the courtesy of listening to and accepting their inputs, and that may have led to his early departure from command.

I learned that there was an unofficial organization on the base called the Black Positive Action Committee, or Black PAC, that met monthly to address issues that warranted their attention. The Black PAC was led by a black staff sergeant and his wife, a schoolteacher in the Department of Defense School System, or DODS. I found out where he worked and made it a point to pay a visit to that area and ask if it were appropriate for me to come to the monthly meetings. He welcomed my presence but noted that it was his meeting and that I shouldn't try to take it over. With that restriction well understood, we shook hands, and I was there in civilian clothes sitting in the back row with Sheila at the next meeting.

There were probably fifty people present, and the attendance was multicultural. People brought up issues, and occasionally, the sergeant, or his wife, would ask if I had any comments on something that was brought up. It was a good forum, and I was pleased that the sergeant and his wife had developed it. On several occasions, I picked up homework for presentation at the next meeting.

Sometimes there were surprises. At one meeting, it was reported that a fight erupted between a black and a white airman at the bowling alley. Blows were struck, and it lasted for several minutes prior to the security police arriving on the scene and breaking it up. The question put to me was, "What are you going to do about it?" I was caught unprepared; there had been no mention in the "blotter" of a fight in the bowling alley, as there should have been if the security police were called. Everything that happens on a military installation appears in the blotter if it, in any way, touches the SP, a phone call reporting a noise, for example. I read the previous day's blotter every morning and was always surprised of how many things went on in a small installation that would otherwise go unnoticed. I honestly explained that I was totally unaware that there had been a fight but would get back to them at the next meeting with what had happened and what action was being contemplated.

With that, the young wife of a white airman sitting in the front row turned to me and said, "You call yourself the commander, and you don't even know what's going on, on your base!"

My response was not very comforting. I said, "I'll try to do better at meeting your expectations!" What struck me hard was the fact that this young woman, probably not even out of her teens and with perhaps a year of association with the air force, had honest expectations that a "commander" knows everything, or at least almost everything, that goes on within the command. It was impossible for me to meet that standard, but I vowed to myself to try harder.

The result of the bowling alley fight investigation revealed that the two airmen involved were buddies, had a couple of drinks, and got into a minor tussle that looked more serious than it was. The security policeman dispatched to the bowling alley knew both men well enough to be called a friend. He got them to stop fighting and shake hands, and they left together. The security policeman was counseled for not entering the fight in the blotter; he was trying to do the fighters a favor. The fighters were counseled by their squadron commander for causing a ruckus. If it happened during an intramural baseball game, it would have been a routine matter resolved by teammates and coaches. The matter was reported back to the Black PAC at the next meeting, and all were satisfied.

At another meeting, the allegation was made that punishment for similar offenses was different along racial lines. The feeling was the black airman received more severe punishment than white airman for the same offense. The offenses referred to were nonjudicial offenses covered by Article 15 of the UCMJ. Punishments for Article 15 offenses are under the discretion of squadron commanders with advice and guidance from the base legal staff. At that time, all bases had an area defense counsel (lawyer) that had an office in a separate building from his fellow lawyers who performed in the prosecutor role. Again, I promised to get the facts and report back to the Black PAC at the next meeting. There weren't many article 15s given over the previous twelve months indicating a good citizenship overall. As I recall, there were about eight Article 15s issued during the previous year, and they were divided equally between racial groups. Because there were fewer black airmen than white airmen, there was an indication of greater resort to punishment if the offender was black, but that was a different issue. There was no dispute that the offenses committed by the eight deserved some action to get the offender's attention. Article 15 action gives a commander wide latitude. He could take a stripe, which was harsh because it could take years to get it back, and a loss of a stripe meant a commensurate loss of pay for that entire period. The commander could also take up to two months' pay, which was also harsh but lasted only a short period of time. The mildest punishment was restriction or extra duty. When the eight Articles 15s were evaluated, it was obvious that black airmen in all cases received lesser punishments. That begged for further investigation. In the final analysis, conversations with squadron commanders revealed that they took family situations into account. A higher percentage of the black airmen were married, some with young children. Commanders took less money from these airmen because they didn't want to cause a hardship that would primarily impact the family. The briefing to the Black PAC meeting brought forth lots of questions but, in the end, put to rest the allegation that blacks at Aviano were being unfairly treated.

At the next Black PAC meeting, there was a very troubling allegation that deeply disturbed me. It was alleged that the area defense counsel lawyer, Capt. Corky Willis, was wearing a Confederate flag on his uniform. "I'll get back to you on this" was the promise made. The next morning, Lt. Col. Tony Farina was explaining to me that Corky was a skydiver and captain of a skydiving team. They called themselves The Rebels and wore a Confederate flag on the sleeve of their flying suits. It seemed Corky also wore his captain's bars on his ball cap. I asked Tony to bring Corky to my office. He was wearing the flying suit adorned with the Confederate flag; evidently, he had been alerted to what transpired the previous evening at the Black PAC. After some discussion, Corky reminded me he was a Native American, full-blooded Cherokee from Georgia, and didn't have a bigoted bone in his body. Nonetheless, I believed he was separating himself from his likely clients and could not fulfill the role as area defense counsel as long as he wore the Confederate flag patch. I explained to Corky that most of his clients, as area defense counsel, were minorities, and there was a widespread perception among that group that he was a racist because of the Confederate flag he wore.

I asked him, for the good of the Aviano community, to remove the Confederate flag from his flight suit. He refused! Then I ordered him to remove it to which he complied, by dramatically tearing it off. Another problem solved, or so I thought.

Two days later, I received an official letter from Capt. Corky Willis requesting a Redress of Grievance on the order I had given him to remove the Confederate flag from his flight suit. Not knowing what a Redress of Grievance entailed, I called for my JAG, Tony Farina. Tony was very uncomfortable explaining to me that a Redress of Grievance would go all the way to the secretary of the air force unless I reversed my position on the order to remove the flag. If I held to my position, it would be necessary for me to write a letter explaining my actions to the commander at Sixteenth Air Force and, from there, to General Jones, commander USAFE, and then on to the secretary of the air force for final adjudication.

I stuck to the principals that I believed in and wrote what I thought was a reasoned and compelling reason for the action I took and direct order given. I don't know what Gen. Sandy Moats, then commander

Sixteenth Air Force, might have said in his cover letter up the chain; however, a month later, I received a terse Letter of Admonishment from General Jones for taking inappropriate action and exercising poor judgment with regard to Capt. Corky Willis. The day I received that letter was not my best day, but General Jones hadn't relieved me yet. There was plenty of work to do and things to make better, so I put the letter behind me and got lost in the job. A couple of months had passed when a call came from the USAFE /JAG. The JAG relayed the information that the secretary of the air force had found in my favor on the Redress of Grievance and reversed General Jones's position. He also informed me that he too believed that Captain Willis had soiled his reputation at Aviano and could better serve the air force at another location in Europe. At first, I was elated with the news then realized that the reversal had not likely pleased my boss, General Jones—you can't win them all!

Some personnel changes occurred that greatly improved the Aviano leadership team. Col. Roy Salem arrived to become the base commander, and Lt. Col. Bill Garner arrived from Bitburg AB, Germany, to take over as the deputy commander for operations. In addition, Major Goggle arrived to take commander of civil engineers, and Maj. Dick Huggins took command of the supply squadron. All of these new arrivals were highly competent in their technical disciplines and demonstrated exceptional leadership qualities. With these additions, the Fortieth was well led as any tactical fighter wing in Europe.

The movie *Shaft* was coming to Aviano, and this was creating a lot of excitement among the young black enlisted community. Richard Rountree played the leading role of a black James Bond—like detective. The base theater was in the cantonment area where all of the enlisted barracks were located. I thought it important that Sheila and I take in the movie to experience the reaction firsthand and perhaps, by our presence, dampen any possible overreaction. We attended both showings; it was a good movie packed with action. For those too young to remember the early seventies, there was no nudity, no profanity, and no gore, although a few "bad guys" died at the hands of Shaft.

Sheila and I left the theater, believing the movie had been an uplifting experience for the base community at large and went home for a night's rest. The phone rang at 2:00 a.m. with the chilly message that a riot was building near the two supply squadron barracks. I donned a flight suit and headed to the cantonment area about ten miles northwest. As I came through the gate, I found security policemen in riot gear and armed with M-16 automatic weapons. I told the chief of security police, who approached me on foot, to get the armed force away from the barracks and out of sight and not to interfere unless they perceived there was going to be loss of life.

When I walked up to the group of perhaps one hundred young blacks gathered outside the barracks, I noticed graffiti spray painted on the barrack's exterior walls. The graffiti spelled out "N#%*^& Go Home, KKK." In an instant, I was surrounded by the troops, all whom I knew and had spoken to a number of times. Each was holding a piece of paper with the same words written on them. I learned that when they returned to the barracks after the movie, they found these slips of paper inside their rooms, evidently slipped under the door. They were hurt more than angry and had armed themselves with baseball bats, pool cues, and similar things handy in the barracks. I asked them to give me a chance to catch and punish the perpetrators for the crime they had committed. I promised to take action immediately and asked for their help. With that, I was offered names of a number of white NCOs whom they considered rednecks. I reminded the airmen that they all had unblemished records, and anything they might do on their own could adversely affect them and would not, in any way, help bring about justice. We talked for at least two hours, and it appeared I was making progress. About this time, one of the usual, very vocal complainers jumped up and entered the barracks, saying he was going to bust some "honky" heads. I followed him in to make sure that no one got hurt but not exactly sure when to act. It was my luck day! The charge of quarters (CQ) was a black sergeant, married with a family, and an outstanding performer on the job. He stopped the angry young black airman, saying, "Give me that bat and get back in your room, nothing is going to happen in my barracks!" That was the end of that threat.

The crowd was dispersing, and with another repeat promise to take immediate action, I departed the scene for my office. I had a big chalkboard in the office to plot future courses of action and then murder-board them in my own mind. This was an excellent tool to take a look at what happened and who might be behind it. I drew some horizontal lines and labeled them White Redneck, Other White, Black NCO, and Usual Black Troublemaker. Then I made three columns and labeled them Highly Likely, Not likely, Not Possible. After some thought, I started checking the squares. What emerged was that a white person of any rank writing the graffiti on the wall, if discovered, would have been immediately accosted—it was too high risk and highly unlikely. All of the minority NCOs that I knew were career military with a strong sense of duty and responsibility. They were hard over against discrimination and bigotry but worked through the system to resolve problems and right wrongs. The only group that, if caught in the act, could get away with it without a severe beating was the young vocal complainers. They could dismiss it as a prank to pull the honky's chain if caught in the act. This logical exercise gave me a pretty good idea of who painted the graffiti on the barracks walls and wrote the notes, but proving it was going to be a problem. It was Saturday and nearing dawn. I decided to recall the entire group by squadron and have every member fingerprinted. I wasn't sure what good it would do, but if one of those slips of paper was undisturbed, or if the paint spray cans at the scene had clean prints, it might be helpful. Most important, it would send a signal to the young men at the barracks that I was doing something.

The next thing that needed to be done was to call General Jones and report what had happened and what I was doing. The command post put me through to General Jones's quarters, and I explained what had transpired, whom I thought was behind it, and what I was doing. When I finished, he said, "It is important to do something! It sounds like you've got your arms around it. Keep working at it. Good luck!"

I showed up at the head of the line at the headquarters squadron and was fingerprinted along with all the rest of the squadron personnel. I had a loud speaker system set up and spoke to all Fortieth Group personnel, explaining what happened and how hurtful it was to a large segment of our population, and asking for everyone's understanding and help in finding the culprits. While we were being fingerprinted, I had the civil engineers repaint the two supply squadron barracks to cover the inflammatory graffiti and eliminate the constant reminder of what happened. Later, I was surprised to learn that three young black airmen, including the one I followed into the barracks that morning, refused to be fingerprinted. That was our first big lead, not that they weren't in the mix of suspects to begin with. I asked Chief Master Sergeant Pat Patterson to solicit their help in solving the crime and if they were willing to bring them to my office so I could hear their views. It was an interesting session; they all had three or four honky NCOs that they opined were the guilty ones.

Time passed slowly, and there was a different mood throughout the base. People were suspicious about who might have done this and not sure where it would lead in terms of community strife, although there were no overt problems. Then the big break came! A black sergeant from the supply squadron, living in the barracks because he chose not to bring his family over to Italy, returned from temporary duty (TDY) at one of our remote sites in Italy. When he entered his room, there was a folded piece of paper just inside the door. He was well aware of the problem once he set foot on the base, and like the good citizen he was, he carried the paper without touching it to the security police. Bingo, we had two sets of fingerprints on the paper. First, the security police and OSI screened all the fingerprints that had been taken the previous Saturday morning—there were no matches. It had to be the three who refused have their fingerprints taken. The OSI chief came to me, suggesting I have another meeting with the three prime suspects to see if they had any more leads and to offer them a cold soda once they arrived. Further, the OSI chief suggested that once they had all taken a drink, my secretary should come in with a message that there was an in-flight emergency and I was needed in the command post. The plan unfolded just like the OSI suggested. Just after the meeting started, Mary Ellen brought me a glass of Coke and offered our guests a glass. They all went for the free soda and took a sip as soon as she passed them on a tray. Moments after she departed with the empty tray, she came bursting back in with the "in-flight emergency" message. Everyone was excused with the promise that we would get back together that afternoon. Eureka, the prints on two matched those on the paper with the inflammatory notation. Two were immediately jailed, and they ratted on the third member whom we also suspected and who was also immediately jailed. In just a few hours, a crowd of black NCOs gathered at the jail; they were angry at being duped by these young men and even angrier at what might have happened if reason hadn't prevailed from the outset.

I called General McBride and passed on the news that the perpetrators had been caught; the evidence was solid—they had confessed and were being held in the base jail. I also noted that there was an outcry against them from the entire Aviano black community, and if it were possible, it would be better for all concerned if they could be held for trial at another base. A few minutes later, I received a callback from General McBride, saying that Brig. Gen. Tom Sadler, commander of the Airlift Wing at Rhine-Main, would be flying down in a C-130 to retrieve the prisoners and take them to Rhine-Main, where they would be held for trial. All three served prison time for their actions and received dishonorable discharges from the air force. General Sadler called me after landing back in Germany and told me, when the three perpetrators were asked why they committed the crime, their response was "Things were getting too good at Aviano, and we had to stir things up so blacks would focus back on discrimination." He also told me that as soon as the three realized they were at Rhine Main AFB, they demanded to see two black airmen that were troublemakers at his base. His suspicion was that there were minority cells throughout Europe that were in constant communication and circulated ideas to create problems. Gen. Tom Sadler became the air forces top cop and retired as a major general in August 1983.

In a few days after the arrests and relocation of the three perpetrators, everything settled back to normal, and the atmosphere was conducive to get in some much-needed flying time. Nighttime was always a good time to fly because of the requirement for night landings, and night weather was even better for filling some of the obligatory currency squares. Ceilings were low in the Poe Valley, but not so low that alternates were required for flight clearance purposes. Having to land at Rimini and Ghedi, Italian Air Bases near Milan and along the mid-Adriatic, would not be a problem and would give me another opportunity to visit Fortieth Group Personnel station there holding custodianship of nuclear weapons committed to NATO for these Italian F-104 units.

Takeoff and climb-out were normal, and getting above the murk under the stars was relaxing after grinding through all the vexing problems on the ground. Once the drop tanks burned out, I flew over to Pisa and asked the controller if traffic would allow me to shoot some ground controlled approaches (GCAs). The ceiling was about three hundred feet, and with a two-hundred-foot minimum, we would break out long enough for a glimpse of the illuminated and famous Tower of Pisa, at that time leaning somewhat precariously. The first four GCAs were perfectly flown, on heading, on glide slope, on speed, and missed approach executed smartly at two hundred feet AGL with the field directly in front of the F-4's pointy radome. The controller was Italian but spoke perfect English with just a twinge of colloquialism. On the fifth and last GCA prior to heading back to Aviano, I was really relaxed and getting a little lazy. No matter, the approaches were flown over the Tyrrhenian Sea, so a few feet low on the glide slope was not critical, just sloppy. As we came down the glide slope, the controller called, "Dropping twenty feet low." Power was added with one click of up trim. A few seconds later, he called, "Forty feet low on glide slope." More power and another up click. I didn't want to make a big correction to get back on the glide slope because big corrections beget more big corrections to go in the other direction, and soon you're chasing your tail. The next radio call was a call to action; the controller said, "You a still forty feet below the glide slope. If you no pull it up, you gonna busta your ass!" With that call, I got the F-4 back on the glide slope, still well above minimums, and completed the GCA. We thanked the controller for the practice and headed for home.

Weather approaches at Aviano were another matter. Getting a little lazy and sloppy here would get you killed in a New York minute. The

Alps rose up very abruptly from the piedmont just behind the base and eight nautical air miles from the runway, which paralleled the Alps. Traffic patterns were always flown to the south of the runway to keep you farther from the mountains, but that meant a turn to the north was required to line up on the final approach. In weather and at night, even in the clear, I always checked the minute hand on the clock at the turn and monitored the needle that pointed to the TACAN on the base. Patterns were flown at 250 knots, or four nautical miles a minute. From the time the turn was started from the downwind leg to the base leg, you had just a little over two minutes before you were into the rocks. My personal limit on the base leg was one minute. If I wasn't started on a turn to final within that time frame, or the needle pointing to the TACAN passed the runway heading, it was a hard turn to the south for a try at another approach. The GCA was very professionally run, and we were safely on the ground with just over two hours of night weather time and five weather approaches—just another good day in the office.

Maj. Gen. Bryce Poe was highly regarded by his peers and staff as a real hands-on expert in logistics and maintenance. Moreover, he liked to visit USAFE Air Bases and see firsthand how well aircraft maintenance was being done.

He flew down to Aviano and asked for a VOQ room and a staff car. When I asked if he would join Sheila and me for dinner at the house or at the O'club, he declined, saying he came to work not to socialize. The next morning, we had breakfast together at the dining facility, and he debriefed me on his findings. Most of what he had to say was positive: checklists and technical data being used properly, etc. Then he told me the horror story that he observed while hiding behind some aerospace ground equipment (AGE). Two airmen were installing wing drop tanks on an F-4D that was scheduled to deploy back to its home station in England. They had one drop tank on the MJ-1 hydraulic lift and were looking for the special grease that was required for lubricating the tank posts prior to snapping them into position under the wing. The lubricant was a silicone gel that would remain fluid and slippery at temperature below minus thirty degrees centigrade, the kind of low temperatures found at forty-five thousand feet in wintertime. When they realized they forget to get the grease from supply prior to coming out to the aircraft, one airman said to the other, "Grease is grease," as he wiped some cup grease off the axle of the fire extinguisher standing near the aircraft. At that moment, Maj. Gen. Bryce Poe jumped from his hiding place with a shout and holler before they could contaminate the drop tank posts.

The cup grease would solidify at the temperatures of high altitude flight, and if a pilot found it necessary to jettison those tanks to save the aircraft, for example, to extend the range to reach a runway when running low on fuel, the tanks would not jettison. Drop tanks are also usually jettisoned in combat as soon as they were empty of gas to lighten the aircraft and improve its performance over enemy territory. I suspect those two airmen will never forget that experience and have told the story of the major general observing them from behind a bunch of AGE well past midnight. It was a good lesson for me, and for years after, I prowled the flight lines under my command. However, I didn't usually do it from a hiding place.

Major General Poe was a highly decorated war hero. After graduating from the Colorado School of Mines at Golden, Colorado, he attended West Point, graduating with the class of 1946. He was assigned to the Eighty-Second Tactical Reconnaissance Squadron in Japan and transferred to Korea when war broke out in 1950. He flew ninety combat missions, including the first jet recce mission. During the Vietnam War, he served as the vice commander of the 460th Tac Recce Wing (TRW) flying 213 combat missions. Prior to assuming duties as USAFE/LG, he commanded the 26th TRW at Ramstein, Germany. Major General Poe received his fourth star a few years after his visit to Aviano and took command of the Air Force Logistic Command, headquartered at Wright-Patterson AFB, Ohio.

One of the many things that promoted unity and togetherness at Aviano was the fact that there were about two thousand American military isolated in the Poe River Valley on a flat agricultural plain about forty-five miles northwest of Venice. As a result, there were a lot of social events sponsored by the officers' wives' club and the NCO wives' club. The frequency was about one of each every two months. Club meals were excellent and low cost. Good bands playing the popular music of the day played at both clubs on Friday and Saturday evenings. Casual social activity was high; most everyone knew everyone else.

Word reached Aviano that the Headquarters Air Force IG and his team had arrived in Europe, headed by Lt. General Lou Wilson, known as "Whip" Wilson. The last time Aviano was inspected by the air force IG compliance team, it failed and was rated the worst unit in the United States Air Force. Clearly, it wouldn't be long before they descended on Aviano with nearly a hundred expert inspectors digging deep into every aspect of our operation. The Aviano mantra was, "We do our job correctly every day so we don't need to do anything differently when inspectors come to visit!" This was known to every man and woman at Aviano, and to the best of my knowledge, they were living by it based on my seven to ten hours of prowling the base every day.

The call from the command post was short: "IG team on short final." I jumped in the staff car and raced to the flight line to greet the IG and his team. The team leader introduced himself and handed me a list of demands, or "needs" to be more politically correct. These involved billeting for about eighty people, office space, large meeting room, and vehicles for the team to get around in. I drove him to a spare office in the cantonment area, while calling motor pool to dispatch a number of cars to the area where they would be working. The colonel thanked me for the hospitality and asked me to pick him up the next day, at 1300 hours, for a windshield tour of the base and all of its remote areas. He also asked that the *Daily Bulletin* for the next four days carry an announcement that the AF/IG would be hearing complaints from 0800 to 1400 hours at a specific location in the cantonment area. According to our IG arrival plan, the command post had already called all of the Fortieth Leadership Team and advised them the IG team had landed.

This was a compliance team; there was no simulated wartime tasking or flying involved like in an ORI, where the commander is essentially the orchestra leader directing most of the activity. In a compliance inspection, the inspectors invade all of the work centers, dig through all the records, and hardly ever say a word until the final outbrief. The wing or group commander is just a bystander and has no role in influencing the outcome at this time. If the groundwork has not been laid with the organization working as a team, doing all the right things over an extended period of time, it is definitely too late to expect a good outcome. All I could do is get out and about and cheer the team on.

The next day, after lunch, I picked up the IG team leader and started driving him all around the many dispersed locations that made up Aviano Air Base. These included two cantonment areas, the warehouse area, the fuel storage area, the motor pool area, the commissary area, the headquarters area, the nuclear and conventional munitions storage area hidden in the cornfield, the flight line, Victor Alert and command post area, and last, the Defense Disposal Property Office. As we were driving along the road paralleling the taxiway to the Victor Alert area, there was a small isolated Quonset hut. He asked what was in the building. I told him it housed the base fire extinguisher repair shop run by a technical sergeant Jones, who did an outstanding job keeping us equipped with over seventy-two ready-to-go fire extinguishers for our gained aircraft. He said, "I'd like to visit the shop," so we stopped and went in. I had visited the shop numerous times and was very confident that the outcome of the visit would be positive. The Quonset hut was not heated, so Technical Sergeant Jones, with material provided by the base civil engineers, had built a small windowed office inside that had an efficient kerosene heater, where he did the paperwork and took his coffee breaks on cold winter days. The ceiling on the office was flat. When we walked in, there was a ladder placed against the office, and the colonel asked, "Why the ladder, what is up there?"

Technical Sergeant Jones replied, "Nothing, sir. I just keep the ladder for repairs." Of all the times I'd been there, I never noticed the ladder nor thought about looking at the top of the office. I started to get a bad feeling. The IG colonel scrambled up the ladder and grabbed some things he could reach and brought them down.

"What is this?" he asked. Then Technical Sergeant Jones started explaining that when Wheelus AFB, near Tripoli, Libya, closed in the late 1960s, all their parts for repairing fire extinguishers were airlifted to Aviano and stored in his shop. With that, we left and finished the tour in time to get the colonel back to their meeting room for their daily wrap-up at 1700 hours. I called Major Huggins, chief of supply, to meet me at the fire extinguisher repair shop ASAP and raced back there. When I arrived, the entire pile of rat-holed fire extinguisher parts were loaded on a flatbed truck, and a big front loader Caterpillar was standing nearby.

"What are you guys planning to do?" I asked.

"Bury this stuff so they'll never find it" was the response.

Before I had time to lose my temper, Major Huggins arrived with the right answer: "Take all these parts over to Supply Warehouse no. 2. I've got guys standing by ready to code them and enter them into the supply system for disposition." I explained to all the helpers who were going to bury the parts that they could all get court-martialed for attempting to destroy government equipment. Moreover, it was wrong headed to think they could pull something like that off, considering the IG team chief, Technical Sergeant Jones, and I were witnesses to the discovery. They all looked down at their shoes sheepishly and agreed it was a dumb idea—they were just trying to protect Technical Sergeant Jones.

I said, "We can all protect him by doing the right thing, so get this load to supply right now," and both Major Huggins and I followed them to make sure there were no parts thrown off along the way.

I remembered back to the only visit Lieutenant General McBride made to Aviano. As we drove by the fire extinguisher repair Quonset hut, he opined, "That looks like trouble sitting out there all alone. You better check it out!" I did visit many times but didn't have his instincts that build with years and years of command experience. The next day, the IG team chief called and asked for another windshield tour. After picking him up, he asked to see the sanitary landfill site and any other dump sites that were used by the 40th TAC Group. Off we went to the landfill and then drove the perimeter fence. I thought he was checking to see if the fence was in good repair. After a couple of hours, he asked where we hid the fire extinguisher parts. I told him we didn't hide them; they were in Supply Warehouse no. 2 being coded and entered into the supply system. My word wasn't good enough; he wanted to see them for himself! When we arrived at the warehouse, there were just a few of the fire extinguisher parts left on the floor; the rest were already entered into the supply computer and stored in the proper bins ready for disposition from USAFE/LG. The supply troops had worked through the night to get it done. He expressed some surprise at what had taken place, so I asked him what he expected would have happened. His response floored me! He said, in most cases, they found unauthorized parts and equipment buried in the base landfill to hide it from the IG. He went on to say that on one SAC base, they found an entire dump truck loaded with unauthorized equipment buried in the base landfill. If he had just asked, we could have saved an entire morning of driving around remote parts of the base.

One of the inspectors was Col. Lou Bush, one of the Fighter Weapons School instructors I served with. In fact, Lou was one of the instructors that gave me the oral test when I was accused of cheating on the first phase test. We taught the same course at the Weapons School, he for the F-100, and I for the F-4. In my book, he was a man of great integrity and a bona fide top gun! One day, during the ongoing inspection, we passed in a hallway, and Lou said, "Pete, I don't know what you're doing, but keep it up." I took that as a signal that the inspection was going OK, but it wasn't over, and I was concerned about how the fire extinguisher parts would be treated.

Lt. Gen. Lou Wilson arrived on Friday, one day before the inspection outbrief; he asked that I take him on a tour of the enlisted barracks. I was comfortable that it would go well, as I had spent a lot of time and invested considerable discretionary dollars in barracks improvements, although they still had a long way to go. As the general walked through the main entrance door, the first sergeant called the building to attention—you could hear everyone snap to—a good sign. While still walking forward, General Wilson gave a loud "at ease" and immediately turned into a dormitory room. In the room, a young black airman was in the process of putting a second leg into a pair of pants. The General shouted, "Don't you come to attention when a senior officer walks into your room?" A pregnant silence followed; the airman had a confused look on his face.

I suggested, "General Wilson, I believe the airman, whom I know to be one of our really good men, is confused by the fact that you gave 'at ease' just as you stepped into his room. I think he was trying to get his pants on to be presentable." General Wilson laughed, and a crisis was avoided. Following that, the first sergeant preceded the general and bellowed "Room Ten-hut" for every room we came to. As far as I could tell, the general was OK with the men and the barracks.

General Jones elected to fly down to Aviano for the IG inspection outbrief on Saturday morning. I met him at the flight line and drove him to a meeting with Lieutenant General Wilson prior to the formal briefing in the base theater. Then I drove both generals to the theater for the briefing. The theater was jam-packed, and troops were standing in the back. The team chief gave the briefing, and I could not have asked for a better outcome than if I had written it myself. It was noted that no one came to lodge a complaint with the IG, and that was a first! There had never been zero complaints in any previous compliance inspection! The 40th TAC Group received an outstanding rating and was rated as the best unit the air force IG had evaluated in the previous five years. It was a proud moment for all the people who had worked so hard to do the right thing every day.

While driving General Jones back to his aircraft, the general turned to me and offered his congratulations, then said, "Pete, your timetable was too slow. You should have been at this point a year ago."

There was a smart-ass inside of me that wanted to say, "General, if you had sent the IG in a year ago, you'd have gotten the same results!" What I did say was "Yes, sir!"

After General Jones and the IG team departed, the Fortieth Group had a picnic and field day so all could share in the glow of the outstanding rating they had earned and richly deserved. The days that followed were full of visits to all the areas, thanking the people for their hard work and encouraging them to keep doing their job the right way and not to slack off just because the IG wouldn't be coming back for at least another three years.

The command post call came very early on a sleepy night. When I answered, the voice said, "We are in receipt of a Blue Dot 21 that needs your attention!" Still half asleep, I rogered the call and assured them I'd stop by in the morning to read the message and stumbled back into bed. My head hadn't hit the pillow when the phone rang again, and the voice said, "Colonel, we are in receipt of a Blue Dot 21 message, repeat, a Blue Dot 21. We need you in the command post immediately!" The cobwebs of sleep were blown away; "Blue Dot" was a real-world message to change DEFCONs and task a wing; something big was happening. I donned a flight suit and sped to the command post in the main operating area.

To step back for a minute, all the exercises and peacetime transmissions had a preamble of "White Dot"; these had to be answered, but they weren't urgent. Blue Dot signified a change of DEFCON and tasking, a Red Dot carried the codes for a nuclear weapon release, and a Black Dot cancelled previous messages and was usually associated with cessation of hostilities. Answering years of White Dot messages and the fog of sleep had caused me to fail to comprehend the significance of the initial call.

It was October 10, 1973. The Arab and Israeli Yom Kippur War was in its fourth day, and the little public English language news piped into Aviano indicated the conflict was not going well, by historical standards, for the Israelis. Evidently, they had underestimated the effectiveness of the mobile SA-6, surface-to-air missile (SAM) systems provided to Egypt by the Soviet Union. The Israeli Air Force was getting low on aircraft due to SAM losses. The Blue Dot 21 message raised the US Forces DEFCON in Europe from 5 to 4 and tasked the Fortieth to deploy four F4Ds to Israeli as soon as possible. Further, these were to be our best aircraft with regard to mission capability and time to mandatory engine change. Deployment instructions would follow shortly. DEFCON 4 meant that the Fortieth should increase its readiness and security without creating any visible indications of doing so. Basically, this latter part of the instruction meant we couldn't do a recall. The deputy commanders were expected to be at work around at 0700 hours, so I didn't bother to call them and ask them to report in early. Then I went down to the Maintenance Control Center, a twenty-four operation, and asked them to pick out the six best aircraft based on the records they had. I was planning to launch six aircraft, two as spares, in the event problems surfaced when they got airborne. When the aircraft were identified to me, I went out and checked the Form 781s in the individual aircraft. They looked good, better than most—the deployed unit that owned these aircraft would not be happy when they found out they were going to lose them. All six were equipped with wing-mounted drop tanks, eliminating the need to load them for the trip across the Mediterranean Sea. Weather would not be a problem, as the entire area from Spain to Turkey was enjoying crisp clear fall weather. I asked the command post to query USAFE/CAT (Contingency Action Team) to find out if an air refueling tanker would be available, as I didn't want the aircraft to enter a combat zone with just the minimum fuel required for landing.

When the deployed aircrews came in for their normal gunnery range missions, they were briefed on the situation. I asked their squadron commander to pick volunteers to form four primary crews and two spares. If possible, I wanted pilots and WSOs with combat experience in Vietnam leading the flight and elements. Last, these selections would be coordinated with the parent wing. Two other flight crews were sent out to preflight and "cock" the six aircraft, so all the fliers had to do was start taxi and take off when it was time to go. Flight planning information was received from USAFE, providing communication frequencies, call signs, tanker rendezvous, and the rendezvous point and time for joining up with Israeli fighter aircraft. These fighters would meet our incoming aircraft about fifty miles out to sea and escort them to the base where they would land and turn over the aircraft. This escort was essential to preclude our arriving aircraft from being mistaken as an enemy force and shot down. The aircrews would return on one of the several USAF cargo aircraft that were delivering needed supplies to the Israeli Air Force and Army. Backward planning provided the required takeoff time. USAFE would provide the final release based on that time. Crews had sufficient time to return to their quarters and pack a bag with toilet articles and clothing that might be needed.

The spare aircraft would fly down range about five hundred miles to the refueling point, take on some fuel along with the primary aircraft, and return to Aviano if there were no aborts for aircraft or refueling problems. This was real, and everyone involved was intensely committed to get it done right and on time. The final release came, and the F-4s departed. About three hours later, the two spares returned. If something had gone wrong, we would have heard about it, but there was no feedback from USAFE.

I was hoping I would never have to review a racial discrimination investigation, but hope wasn't good enough, and one came across my desk that had a bad odor to it. Two Aviano wives applied for a job as test proctor for the college and correspondence courses under the Base Education Office. One applicant was married to a NCO, had thirty hours toward a master's degree, and thirty-three months of teaching experience. She was black. The other applicant was married to an officer. She had eighteen hours toward a master's degree and nineteen months of teaching experience. She was white. The white woman was awarded the job, and the black woman filed a racial discrimination complaint. The Social Actions Office investigated the complaint and elevated it to me because it involved a senior civil servant and PhD. I interviewed the two ladies in question and found both women petite and roughly the same size, attractive, very articulate, and dressed in a professional manner. I also learned that their qualifications were as stated in the Social Actions investigation. Both said they wanted the job because it expanded their experience, paid more than teaching, and required less hours away from home than teaching. The last thing was to interview the gentleman running the Base Education Office that was the subject of the discrimination complaint. He was very professorial, competent, and seemed to fit the job. I asked why he selected Mrs. X over Mrs. Y. for the proctor position. His answer created some doubt in my mind when he said both were equally qualified for the position. I called him on this and asked how he came to the conclusion that thirty hours of master's work was equal to eighteen hours of master's work, and that nearly three years of teaching experience was the same as a year and a half's experience. He opined that those numbers were close enough and that he thought Mrs. X would fit into his staff better. I countered with "How many minorities do you have on your staff?" When he answered none, it was not a surprise. I offered him an easy way out by saying, "If I thought you consciously discriminated against Mrs. Y, I would have to direct the base commander to fire you, but I'll give you the benefit of the doubt. However, I am overturning your decision and directing you to award the position to Mrs. Y."

Those decisions and actions are never easy, but they are always necessary. Two days later, I was the subject of a discrimination complaint by the husband of Mrs. X, for finding against his wife's selection to the proctor's position. This created a sticky situation. The investigator had to be someone outside my command and preferably someone senior to me in rank for his report to be above suspicion. The only one at Aviano that met those selection criteria was Col. Jim McCall, commander of the Fifteenth Communications Squadron, a tenant unit. I asked him if he would conduct the investigation and that I would accept his findings if they were counter to mine. He agreed and redid the entire investigation with the same results.

Water for the Roverado Plain, where most of the base personnel lived, came from deep reservoirs in the Alps that collected snow and runoff from the heavy winter blanket that covered the mountains. The water was safe and was delightful to the palate. The water traveled to Aviano and the surrounding area by aqueducts, some of which were several centuries old but were most adequate—that is, until a major earthquake on the border with Yugoslavia cracked the dam and destroyed parts of the viaduct. With a few shakes of continental plates, the water supply was cut off, and all air force families at Aviano were caught by surprise and left without water. This included all the families because there was no base housing for anyone. Single and unaccompanied enlisted personnel living on base still had water because, in years past, base civil engineers had drilled deep wells that fed the two cantonment areas and the commissary. This included the flight line area, both clubs, the gymnasium, and transient quarters for both officers and enlisted.

Water collection points were set up on base for families to come and get water in five-gallon containers. The base exchange sold these containers at cost. I showed up every evening with four containers along with other husbands and wives to get water for our house. Showers at the gymnasium were reserved for family members. It was a distraction, but everyone was in the same situation—there was no privileged class; we were all in it together. It was at least two months before the dam and aqueduct were repaired and put back in service. While it was a difficult situation, everyone pitched in to help those families with limited transportation, and the community came closer together because of the minor crisis we faced.

General Moats scheduled a Sixteenth Air Force Commanders' Conference at his headquarters at Torrejon AFB, Spain. It would kick off with a dinner and go all through the next day, followed by a social that evening and departures for home bases the next day. The squadron deployed to Aviano at that time was from Bitburg Air Base, Germany, and a major from that unit volunteered to fill the backseat so he could visit with some friends at Torrejon while I was tied up in the Commanders' Conference. He carried an instructor pilot rating and, by regulation, became the pilot in command (PIC) responsible for anything that might happen, such as an in-flight emergency, etc. About forty-five minutes into the flight, I noticed that there was a lot of aileron trim holding up the right wing. This could indicate the right wing was heavier than the left because the right drop tank was not feeding properly or not at all. The major IP thought that would not be a problem and that we would have sufficient fuel to reach Torrejon. Now this wasn't just any F-4D IP; his wife was the daughter of four-star general Jack Catton, commander of the Air Force Military Airlift Command (MAC), headquartered at Scott, AFB, Illinois. I silently questioned his judgment and started to calculate the fuel needed to reach Torrejon Air Base with the minimums required on initial approach; to me, it looked like we would be below the minimum even if the forecast winds were slightly lower than predicted. Plus we were carrying a napalm tank, converted to a baggage pod, on the inboard pylon to accommodate all the baggage needed to dress properly for the social events and conference. While the drag and weight of one napalm tank wasn't much, it made the fuel calculations look a lot better than what we were actually consuming.

It wasn't long before the fuselage tanks started feeding the engines, indicating that all the fuel in the drop tanks and wing tanks was already consumed or wouldn't feed. At this moment, it was clear we were low on fuel and less than halfway to our destination. The major still insisted we could make it, or, if necessary, stop short at Zaragoza Air Base, get the tank fixed, and refuel. I asked him what he would do if I wasn't trying to get to the Commanders' Conference. He replied that he would probably turn around and return to Aviano. With that, I told him, "OK, now that you're still making good sense, you can still be an IP."

Landing with a full drop tank on one wing that didn't feed is not a problem; it just requires some left pressure on the control stick to hold the wing up as the airspeed decreases and the trim becomes less effective. When we taxied into the parking place, it seemed there were a lot of happy faces to greet us—even Lt. Col. Bill Garner, the DO. Upon opening the canopy, we learned that an F-111 with hydraulic failure took the barrier at Torrejon just prior to our scheduled arrival and closed the runway for over an hour. With our fuel state, we would have had to land on the taxiway, a much narrower strip of asphalt with less margin for error when landing with a full drop tank.

It seemed like everything was behind us, ORI, compliance inspection, near riot, and the Fortieth was running smoothly. Every deputy commander was doing an exceptionally fine job. I was spending most of my time looking for things that needed attention or they would turn into problems, or things that, with a little extra effort, could get a lot better. I started digging into compliance inspection reports and ORI reports on other wings in USAFE. Every ORI report had high lights and low lights. If several reports identified that a particular problem was occurring over and over, I went to the deputy commander responsible for that area, and we both went to see if the problem was occurring at Aviano. The IG also highlighted the units that were rated best in USAFE in a particular area. Flying safety might be an example. Whenever I found a "Best in USAFE" rating, I called the wing commander, congratulated him, and then asked if I could come and visit to learn what he was doing. They really couldn't refuse. It only took one day, out and back in an F-4, and I could capture one or more good ideas. Then the responsible deputy commander, section chief, and I would try and make the concept even better and apply it to Aviano. I was like getting free advice and catapulting your organization into the best of the best.

Major General Creech paid us a visit and took dinner with Sheila and me at the officers' club—it was a nice evening, and we hung on every word because he didn't waste any and was always giving sage advice. The following morning, he wanted to visit the Victor Alert area, talk to the aircrews on alert, and then have breakfast with me at the VA dining facility. It was a casual low-key morning, and as we were having breakfast, General Creech asked me if I knew how I was picked for the command job at Aviano. The answer was no; I hadn't a clue and certainly wasn't prepared for the challenge when I arrived on scene. He smiled and asked, "Do you remember the bar frost report you wrote?"

"Yes, but I sent it to Seventeenth Air Force and never expected it amount to anything, why?"

"Well, General Sweat Sent it to me, and after reading it, I sent it to General Jones with a note, saying, 'This kid seems to have his head screwed on right—let's give him a command and put him in the crucible.'"

I thanked him for his confidence, while thinking, *You never know who's watching what you do or reading what you write. Always do your very best in everything you do.*

One of the last big things that happened at the 40th TFG while I was there was a farewell salute to General Goodpasture, SACEUR/ CINCEUR, by Allied Forces South. General Goodpasture was highly regarded in all NATO nations, and Italy was no exception. The salute would culminate with a large force parachuting into the nearby Italian Army Reservation by airborne battalions, brigades, and divisions of several NATO nations, and a battalion of the crack Eighty-Second Airborne Division from Fort Bragg, North Carolina, was representing the United States. The Fortieth didn't have a direct role; however, Aviano Airfield was a recovery and pickup point for the Eighty-Second Battalion, and I wanted to make sure the Fortieth did everything we could do to support them, including medical support from our hospital if necessary. As I wandered around the base, I ran into a short bandy rooster of an army brigadier general by the name of Max Thurman. I saluted respectfully and asked if there was anything I could do for the general. He looked at me with piercing eyes and asked, "Who are you?" When he learned I was the Fortieth commander, he said, "Yes, I have a list of things I need and rattled off five things of which I only remember two: an ambulance with doctor, nurse, and corpsmen, and night lighting at their assembly point on the base. How long will it take you to get these things done?" he asked.

"Two hours, unless you need them quicker!" I responded.

"That will do," he said, and we parted with a salute. The next time I ran into Gen. Max Thurman, he was wearing four stars and serving as the army vice chief of staff, and I was the air force vice chief of staff. We became very good friends and often skied together when he came to vacation at Keystone, Colorado.

Aviano had settled into a smooth routine, and I was logging more flying time, primarily because the leadership team was exceptionally strong and very little bubbled up to me. The 52nd TFW that I, in a small way, participated in creating was deploying the 23rd TFW "Hawks" to Aviano for gunnery training at Maniago Range nearby. I was looking forward to their arrival and hoping to get reacquainted with some of the aircrews that I flew with two years previously. When the aircraft arrived and had gone through their PFIs, as was my habit, I reviewed all the Form 781s to get a feel for the condition and quality of aircraft that were temporarily under my control.

What I found was very disturbing and presented a serious challenge! More than half of the deployed aircraft had a notation in the forms that read as follows: "The autopilot has been disabled and disconnected from the Stability Augmentation System IAW (in accordance with) Fifty-Second Wing Maintenance Directive XXX." This notation was in direct conflict with a USAFE/LG directive promulgated by Maj. Gen. Bryce Poe that stated in part, "The F-4 autopilot must be maintained in serviceable condition and operating properly with the Stability Augmentation System. If this directive is not complied with, the aircraft is grounded." General Poe would not, on his own, promulgate such a prohibition unless it had been coordinated with and approved by General Creech, DCSOPS, chief of safety, and General Jones, commander, USAFE. The wing directive could not trump a USAFE directive, hence nine of the aircraft that arrived that afternoon should not have flown, and I had no choice but to ground them until the autopilots were repaired and working harmoniously with the Stability Augmentation System. I was harking back to my first flight in an F-4 eight years previously at the Fighter Weapons School. The aircraft was dynamically unstable in pitch for some unknown reason. Capt. Lee Kriner, the IP, put the aircraft safely on the ground once the fuel was burned down to where there was only fuel in the forward fuselage tanks, creating a very safe stability margin. The F-4 autopilot, which only provided altitude hold and heading hold, was quite primitive by commercial standards at the time, but it was the first military aircraft that I had ever flown that had an autopilot. No one seemed to really understand the relationship between the F-4 autopilot, Stability Augmentation System, and the flight controls. There had been numerous accidents over the years that implicated the interrelation of these systems and likely led to the USAFE/LG directive. I suspected that the reason for the wing directive was convenience and C rating; shortage of parts may have also pushed them to look for a convenient way out of maintaining the autopilot. On the other hand, no other wings seemed to have the problem based on the sampling that came to Aviano.

I notified the 23rd TFW squadron commander that the number of flights planned for the next morning would have to be curtailed because of mandatory aircraft grounding due to inoperative and disconnected autopilots. He tried to push back but without success. The next call to Gen. Tom Clifford was going to be a little more difficult. General Clifford was a colonel when he assumed command of the 52nd TFW when it was reborn on January 2, 1972, and was promoted to brigadier general in that position—obviously, he was well thought of at USAFE. General Clifford was a tall man with an athletic physique, and polished in his speech and manner. I explained that nine of the deployed aircraft were grounded in accordance with the USAFE maintenance directive that required an operational and integrated autopilot to satisfy mission capable requirements. He pushed back with "That is all covered in the wing directive that explains fully how the autopilot can be properly and safely disconnected."

I pushed back with "A wing directive cannot overturn or trump a command directive. Unless you can provide me a copy of a USAFE waiver for the 52nd TFW, I have no choice but to keep those nine aircraft on the ground until they are repaired."

He said, "Well, I'll just take the monkey off your back and bring them home to Spangdahlem."

"Fine, as soon as you can provide a USAFE release for a one time flight, I'll be happy to turn them loose."

That last comment was a "Checkmate"; the aircraft were on my base and my responsibility until they were fixed or a waiver was granted, otherwise, any mishap occurring from a flight was my responsibility. As a parting comment, I advised General Clifford that I had formed a "Tiger Team" to repair the autopilots in the 23rd TFS aircraft but didn't have enough parts to fix all of them and that anything he could do to provide parts would be appreciated.

The following evening, while catching up on the paperwork at the office, the direct line from the battle cab in the command post rang. It was General Clifford; he had flown down in an F-4 and was requesting that I come to my command post to meet with him. I drove to the command post, thinking this wasn't going to be pretty or easy. General

Clifford had also asked the 23rd TFS squadron commander to join the discussion. I didn't mind the two on one, but it was going to be harder to reason with General Clifford with one of his troops in the room. The general was very cordial and offered me a copy of his wing maintenance directive, authorizing the autopilot disconnects. I read it out of courtesy and then commented, "If General Poe will approve this, we will comply. Do you mind if I get him on the phone?" To my surprise, he agreed! We went command post to command post and asked the USAFE duty officer to connect us with General Poe. General Poe was not on station, so they connected us with his deputy, a crusty colonel who had spent his entire lifetime in aircraft maintenance. He was the gold standard in my book, and I respected him. General Clifford explained his wing directive and asked that the colonel (I regret forgetting his name) to approve implementation of the wing directive. I don't remember the deputy LG's exact words, but it bordered on something like "All Fifty-Second Wing aircraft that are not in compliance with General Poe's directive are grounded wherever they are. Your wing directive has no standing and should be rescinded immediately! Have your LG send me a list of parts you need to fix the autopilots, and I'll see what I can scrape up for you!" I felt sorry for General Clifford, but I couldn't understand why he tried to bluff his way out of a bad situation of his own doing. Moreover, the substance of the call we just had with the USAFE deputy LG would get passed around the headquarters to Generals Poe, Creech, and possibly Jones—not a good thing. In addition, the immediate and precipitous drop in C status for mission aircraft would raise eyebrows all the way up to the air force headquarters and the DOD.

General Clifford returned to his aircraft and flew back to Spangdahlem. I suspected that he was in violation of crew rest and that the aircraft was one that should have been grounded—but it was a transient aircraft and not my responsibility.

It was winter 1974, and I'd been in USAFE three-plus years of a mandatory four-year tour: with the Air War College with the RAF in England, assistant DO for Spangdahlem while living there and working at Bitburg, then DO at Bitburg and moving there, then two years at Aviano as 40th TAC group commander; time had passed quickly. What was on the horizon?

Col. Carl Cathy had a similar job as commander of the air force operation at Zaragoza, Spain. The mission there was primarily gunnery training for the fighter wings in England and Spain, where both the weather and national law limited training opportunities. Spain, with its largely sunny weather and gunnery range complex, was the go-to place for fulfilling mandatory gunnery and flying requirements. The main difference between Aviano and Zaragoza was the Victor Alert and munitions storage at Aviano.

Carl graduated from West Point in the class of 1957 and earned a master's degree in Aeronautical Engineering at MIT, courtesy of the air force, a few years later. With those impeccable credentials, it wasn't surprising that he pinned on Eagles with less than fourteen years' service, what was referred to a "fast burner." When the promotion list for brigadier general came out, Carl would call and complain, "Pete, we didn't make the list, what did we do wrong?"

My response was always "Carl, I'll never get promoted to general, but as for you, you're too young and don't have enough time in service—you just have to get older!" And sure enough, when he had about twenty years' service, he was promoted and eventually retired as a lieutenant general.

Carl also liked to float rumors, fishing for any information about potential moves in USAFE. One day, he opined that I would be moving from Aviano to Torrejon to take command of the 401st TFW. I liked that rumor because the 401st was a great assignment, a full tactical fighter wing located just outside of Madrid, Spain. Moreover, just two years previously, then colonel Creech was sent there to put the place in order, and he did. As a result, it was probably one of the better-run wings in USAFE, even though he had been gone for some time. It was my observation that once an organization got in a rhythm, it kept that rhythm for a few years even if poor leadership stepped in. Command at that level was hard work and required long hours, six or seven days a week, but it was also the most personally rewarding job in the air force because you were working closely with the people who were training to go to war if the call came.

In mid-February 1974, I received TDY orders to Washington DC with reporting to Maj. Gen. Willie Y. Smith, air force director of doctrine at Headquarters USAF. The notification was so close to the reporting date that it didn't appear there was a way for me to get to Washington in time for the scheduled meeting. If I could get to Milan Airport for a direct flight, there was a slim chance I could be in DC in time for the meeting, but the window of opportunity was shrinking. Then I was informed that Maj. Mike Moore, deputy to Lt. Col. Bill Garner, was driving his family to Milan Airport for a flight to the United States. Mike promised that he could get me there on time and came by the house to pick me up in his Ferrari sedan for the trip. Once on the Autostrada to Milan, I got a glimpse of the speedometer and saw the needle at 175 kmh. I asked if the tires were rated to handle that speed. He said,

"Colonel Pete, this is an export model. We're traveling at 175 mph, and the tires are good to 225 mph." With a gulp, I settled back and watched the scenery whiz past. Mike passed a lot of cars as we sped along the Autostrada, but nothing passed us.

The rest of the trip was routine, and in two days, I was standing in front of General Smith's secretary along with five other colonels. On the dot, we were all ushered into the general's office, all in the dark as to why we were there. The general explained that the current chief of staff, General George S. Brown, had decided to establish a group of six colonels to pontificate on the direction the air force should be taking as it moved forward into the future. This concept somewhat followed a group formed prior to World War II called the Air Tactics School at Maxwell Air Force Base, Alabama. He noted that our respective major command commanders had nominated us for this "study group"; in my case, that would be General Jones. He then took us down the corridor to Lt. Gen. "Dutch" Huyser's office, AF/XO. General Huyser spoke with us for a few minutes and then took us to General Brown's office, CSAF.

General Brown was a big man, with broad shoulders and an athletic figure. He seemed very relaxed as he laid out our future. The group would exist for one year, no longer. No one was in charge and had the authority to tell others what to do. Then looking at me, he said, "Pete, as the ranking colonel, I expect you to manage your budget, approve TDY, hire the secretaries, and in general, keep the others out of trouble, but you're not in charge." Then he went on to say that he was hoping we would come up with ideas for his consideration that would improve the air force in a big way, not just on the margin. He was kicking us out of Washington because if it was easy for the staff to get their hands on us, they'd use us to solve the day-to-day problems that were biting us in the butt. He wanted us to have the opportunity to kick back and think about the future. He also said that he didn't care if we didn't produce anything, if we worked as a team or worked as individuals, and if we wrote one paper, many papers, or no papers. Last, he said no matter what happened, we would all be better for the experience. As a final note, he said he wanted us to visit all current air force four-star generals and get their views on where the air force should be going. At the same time, he wanted us to read the two-volume history of the air force, written by air force historian Dr. Futrell, before we put pen to paper.

Gen. Robert E. "Dutch" Huyser escorted us back to his office and made it clear that regardless of what the chief said, he, General Huyser, expected us to produce a number of scholarly papers. Following that short meeting, Gen. Willie Y. Smith escorted us back to his office. There, he made it even clearer that within two weeks of reporting to Maxwell AFB, he expected us to produce a list of topics that we believed were worthy of investigation. Subsequently, he wanted the first draft of a paper within a month after visiting all the air force four-star generals. So much for General Brown's concept of kicking back and pontificating the future of the air force.

With that final guidance, General Smith told us to return to our current duty stations, wait for orders, and start cleaning out our desks and preparing our successors. Upon returning to Aviano, I told Sheila what had happened and that if she had any unfinished shopping she needed to take care of that immediately. She made plans to take the children to her parents' home in Arizona and then, when the school term ended, to their ranch near Coeur d'Alene, Idaho, their retirement home. Col. Bob Brockman had recently rotated to the CONUS, and his replacement was Col. Robert Miller, who seemed like a competent successor, but that wasn't my decision.

The air force gave us about thirty days to think about the next assignment and what it might mean for us before they pulled the trigger and cut the orders for us to relocate to Maxwell AFB, Alabama. Sheila made commercial travel arrangement from New York to Arizona and then on to Idaho. We departed for New York on March 18, 1974.

Lessons Learned

Have a vision for your command or enterprise. Develop a
plan for the vision with milestones along the way. Make
sure that everyone in your command/enterprise knows the
plan and the intermediate goals. Get buy-in and ensure your
subordinates at least two levels down know their goals.

Make sure that everyone in the enterprise knows
its purpose and what is important.

Know the make-or-break activities of your enterprise
and manage those above all others!

Motivate and train your subordinate leadership team!

Set high standards for yourself and your enterprise/organization!

No enterprise of any size or significance can be run from the CEO's office!

All levels of leadership have to get out and about; it is both educational and motivational! Hands-on leadership works!

When a crisis erupts, immediately do something that has the appearance of resolving the issue! This will buy time for you to actually resolve the issue in a less-stressing environment!

There's nothing better than the farmer's footsteps to make the crops grow!

Always remain true to your moral compass!

Col. Pete with Chief of Carbinarri & translator escorts paying
respects to Governor of Pordenone Province, Italy

Col. Pete & Carol Cobb pining eagles on Col. Truman Cobb, 40th LG

40ᵗʰ Tactical Group Leadership Team, Aviano, Italy

Col. Pete & Col. Brockman pinning eagles on Col. Salem, Aviano, Italy

Lt. Gen. Lou Wilson, Air Force IG arrives at
Aviano with team to inspect 40th TG

CHAPTER 9

The Six-Man Group

I arrived at Maxwell AFB in late April after spending a few days with Sheila and the family in Arizona and getting the children in school to finish out the school year and receive credit for their work in Italy and Arizona.

All six of us showed up on nearly the same day and started getting acquainted.

The players were

Col. Stewart Bowen, from Headquarters Air Staff
Col. Robert Kennedy, from Systems Command
Col. William "Moon" Mullins, from Tactical Air Command
Col. John L. Piotrowski, from USAFE
Col. Robert Reed, from Air Defense Command
Col. Leonard Seigert, from Strategic Air Command

The alleged story about the birth of the group was that each of the major command commanders was asked by the chief to nominate their best and brightest colonel. From this list, General Brown would pick six for the Maxwell study effort. It sounded very flattering, but Col. Larry Welch wasn't there, and neither were several very shiny colonels that I had met along the way—so much for the best and brightest? Whatever, we were there, and it was time to go to work.

The first task was to decide who would share offices. I had not previously met any of these officers, except for Moon Mullins, who was aide to Maj. Gen. T. Ross Milton when I stopped by his Thirteenth Air Force headquarters at Clark Air Force Base in the Philippines as I worked my way home from Bien Hoa in April 1963. As a result of this past meeting, Moon elected to work share an office with me. Bob Reed paired up with Bob Kennedy, and Stu Bowen and Len Seigert paired in the middle office.

Administrative details were immediately taken care of regarding office space, office furniture, secretarial staff (selected but not put on the payroll until the immediate travel stopped), and order supplies for our work. Then it was time to start thinking and debating among the six the worth of various topics. This led to installing big whiteboards in each of the three offices for listing topics and murder-boarding them. It became a favorite pastime to gather in one of the offices and discuss potential topics, listing them and their merits on the whiteboard.

The second order of business was to carry out General Brown's direction to read the two-volume set of Dr. Futrell's history of the air force, about one thousand pages total, and to visit all the four-star generals in the air force. The purpose of the latter was to record their concerns going forward ten to twenty years into the future. We checked out three sets of Dr. Futrell's classic work from the Air University Research Center in the main library and started reading. Those books accompanied us on all our trips and sparked considerable discussion on events that shaped the air force. I personally enjoyed the fully recorded Army Air Corps/Air Force history and the evolution of Air Force Doctrine. It was very educational, useful as a touchstone for the work ahead, and filled in many voids and gaps in my professional education.

I worked with the executive officers of all the air force full generals in Europe to see if we could conveniently connect with all of them with one swing through Europe. This would include deputy CINC Europe at Stuttgart, Germany; CINCUSAFE at Ramstein, Germany; senior military representative to NATO in Brussels Belgium; and the SHAPE chief of staff, just outside of Brussels Belgium. Fortunately, we were able to fit all of those visits in eight days and were soon on our way.

To say that we were very privileged to have the opportunity to visit more than a dozen air force four-star generals, nearly all of them leading major air force commands, is a gross understatement. What we heard and learned would fill a book in and of itself. There were at least two threads that ran through all of their comments, and these were taking care of our people and force modernization. When the Vietnam War ended in December 1972, air force personnel numbered 1.2 million strong, and many pilots were transitioned from bombers and transports to fighters to spread the combat burden. This resulted in former Strategic Air Command lieutenant colonels with two or three hundred hours of flying time in F-4s commanding Tactical Air Command Fighter Squadrons full of captains with three thousand hours and two or three combat tours. This imbalance in experience caused dissension because the younger pilots perceived their leaders were not capable of adequately leading them in combat. With regard to modernization, the F-4 was designed by the navy for protecting a carrier battle group from attacks by Soviet Blackjack bombers and issued to the air force by Secretary of Defense Robert McNamara. This third-generation jet fighter proved inadequate in the air superiority role against older Soviet MiG-17s and 21s. On the other hand, the F-4 served us well as a fighter bomber performing interdiction and close air support missions. The air force needed to replace the obsolete F-100s, aging F-105s, and inadequate F-4s with aircraft that could handily achieve air superiority over contested territory and better support ground forces in the close air support mission. A high-low affordable mix of F-15s and F-16s was the goal, but force structure reductions would be necessary to pay for the proposed aircraft buy.

Back at Maxwell, the "Six-Man Group," as we dubbed ourselves, turned to addressing the list of topics requested by Major General Smith. First, we addressed the structure of a study paper. Working as a team, we settled on a format that we believed would serve the chief and provide a solid starting point if the idea presented in the paper was going to be staffed for further consideration and perhaps a follow-on full-blown effort. The format we settled on is outlined below:

> Title: Describing the purpose and scope of the paper
> Executive Concept Description: one paragraph
> Expected Benefit, Initially and Over Time if Implemented: No more than one page
> Rough Order Magnitude of Cost in Dollars and Turbulence: No more than one page
> Detailed Concept Description: No more than five pages
> Recommendation: One pithy paragraph

Next, we started proposing concepts that seemed to distill out of what we had heard to date from senior air force leaders. Every idea that was offered was written on the whiteboard. When the board couldn't hold any more words, we started winnowing the ideas and writing down on paper what remained. After several iterations over three days, we had about thirty survivors of the winnowing process. These were typed out and a copy provided to each member. We would do this again in a few months after more exposure to air force senior leadership and when some of the initial "hot ideas" started to look sophomoric. We sent the proposed study outline and list of topics to Major General Smith to close out that obligation.

The next set of visits were across the United States, including NORAD, Air Defense Command, Strategic Air Command, Military Air Lift Command, Air Force Logistics Command, Air Force Systems Command, and the Tactical Air Command. Again, these visits were most informative, with the senior commanders being very candid about their concerns for the future. General Clay, commander of the Air Defense Command, the US component of NORAD, made a comment that was very insightful when he said, "When I came to work yesterday, I thought about disestablishing ADCOM because it is no longer useful. Today, I came to work convinced that ADCOM must be revitalized and expanded because it is more vital than ever with the Soviet bomber modernization program!" General Clay was also dual hatted as commander of the binational parent command NORAD. Thirteen years later, when I took command of NORAD, I came to understand what he said and why he felt compelled to say it.

The visit to TAC deserves a few words because Gen. Robert Dixon was the only commander that followed up on our visit. General Dixon, known as the "Tidewater Alligator" for his gruff hard-nose demeanor, rolled out the red carpet and spent nearly two days with us. The visit started with a dinner with General Dixon and his general officer staff. The next day was a full nine-hour day of briefings on TAC, covering missions, units, and issues. The briefings were comprehensive and revealing. That evening, there was a social hour mixing with his staff for discussions on the issues. The next morning, General Dixon met with the six of us in his conference room. Colonel Mullins, the most junior of the group, was seated to his immediate left, then by date of rank, three on a side, ending with me on General Dixon's immediate right. General Dixon started the meeting by saying he had spent considerable time educating us on TAC and was giving each of us an opportunity to ask one question of him before departing. I don't remember the questions that the rest of my fellows asked, but I remember mine. I asked the general his thoughts on the adequacy of the munitions contingency stockpile of ninety days for NATO and one hundred eighty days for Korea. His response was direct, profane, and scared the hell out of me! He said, "You self-serving son of a bitch, one more goddamn word out of you, and I'll kill you on the spot!" As I started to respond, he repeated, "One more word and you're dead!" Then he got up and returned to his office through a back door.

We departed through the side door, where I turned and asked my fellows, "What did I do to set him off?"

Their universal answer was "Nothing, you were last. He had that outburst planned all along but had to wait until the end, or none us would have asked a question." You don't easily forget something like that. It never crossed my mind that I would work directly for General Dixon in the not-too-distant future.

Back at Maxwell AFB, we all did a power read of Futrell's air force history and then started to work off of the list we had made and forwarded to General Smith. One day, when I was the only one in our suite of offices, a Major General James V. Hartinger walked in and wanted to speak with the man in charge. I explained that no one was in charge, by direction of the chief, but I was the ranking colonel and would do everything I could do to help. He started out with "Evidently, you don't know who I am, so let me set you straight! I'm the Air University vice commander and commandant of the Air War College. This is my building you're living in, and I would have thought you had the good sense to come by and introduce yourselves!" What could I do but apologize for our oversight and bad manners. In the next minute, I learned that Major General Hartinger was at one time the youngest colonel in the air force, then the youngest brigadier general in the air force, and the best fighter wing commander. Further, he received a Battle Field Promotion in Italy and then attended West Point, where he was an All-American Lacrosse player and enshrined in the Lacrosse Hall of fame. Last, that he would soon wear four stars and become the air force chief of staff. I thought to myself that this man has the biggest ego I've ever come across and would be someone to give a wide berth—if possible.

When the rest of the Six-Man Group returned, I shared my experience with them. None of them knew Major General Hartinger, or of him, so I didn't feel too bad for not recognizing him. Because of General Hartinger's umbrage at our lack of courtesy toward him and the Air University command structure, I made an appointment with Lt. Gen. Felix M. Rogers, Air University commander, and paid my respects.

Lt. Gen. F. Michael Rogers, as he preferred to be known as, was a distinguished hero of WW II. He was commander the 353rd Fighter Squadron equipped with P-51s in the European Theater of Operations and shot down twelve enemy aircraft, becoming a double ace. In 1949, he entered the intelligence field and served as the air attaché at the US embassy in Madrid, Spain, from 1953 to 1957. Subsequently, he served as an intelligence officer in the Air Staff and Joint Chiefs of Staff. He was also assigned to the Office of the Assistant Secretary of Defense with duty at the State Department. Following a number of staff assignments, he was appointed commander of the Air University in November 1973. Subsequently, in August 1975, he was promoted to the rank of general and assigned as commander Air Force Logistics Command, at Wright-Patterson AFB, Ohio. He wore a large handlebar mustache reminiscent of those I saw on British officers while at the Royal College of Air Warfare in England. He was very articulate and spoke with a very subtle British accent. As I left, it occurred to me that General Rogers and General Hartinger were worlds apart in their personalities.

Once the Six-Man Group settled in at Maxwell AFB, the real work started—grinding out papers for General Brown. Bob Reed chose to write on merging the fighter aircraft and radar assigned to ADCOM (the US component of NORAD) into the Tactical Air Command. The payoff for this merger would provide significant savings in personnel at the staff level because there was near total duplication for pilot, weapons controller, and maintenance personnel management, maintenance and logistics staff, maintenance quality control, aircrew standardization and evaluation, flying and ground safety, etc. Moreover, moving aircrews and weapons controllers from ADCOM to TAC would create a larger pool for worldwide assignment and reduce the time that personnel would have to spend overseas. Worldwide assignments would provide personnel a greater mission perspective and provide a larger pool of personnel for remote assignments. Bob Kennedy immersed himself in a program called JTIDS, or Joint Tactical Information Distribution System. JTIDS was still in development, and Bob felt the benefits it promised needed greater analysis and exposure. I don't recall what Stu Bowen, Len Seigert, and Moon Mullins started out to write about, but I chose two topics that I alternated on. When one got stale, or I ran into a cul-de-sac, I would switch to the other. The first concept involved a phenomenon observed at Aviano that suggested behavior of young airmen was adversely affected by seasonal changes. It was something that might go unnoticed by a senior officer serving less than two years in command. I served nearly twenty-nine months at Aviano, and the repeating seasonal behavior patterns appeared obvious to me. The second paper addressed a concept receiving a lot of attention at the time called "Limited Nuclear Exchange or Response." The concept suggested that it was possible, even likely, that the Soviet Union and the United States could move away from their well-established deterrent postures and start lobbing handfuls of nuclear weapons at each other to test their respective resolve. Just looking at population distribution and potential targets in both countries suggested that such a concept greatly favored the Soviet Union because normal wind patterns would result in lower numbers of downwind delayed causalities across sparsely populated Siberia. Nonetheless, the widely acclaimed "strategic thinkers" of the day seemed to believe this was a possibility, if not feasible, phase of the Cold War.

Base housing became available for five of the Six-Man Group; Stu Bowen decided to leave his family in Washington DC because his children were enrolled in elite private schools. Once we had a house to move into, Sheila and the children arrived by train from the farm in Idaho, and we were a family once again.

Just as things were settling into a routine, we received a TWX from General Dixon with the following message: "Personal from General Dixon to the Six-Man Group. I spent two days educating you on the issues facing TAC. I would like you to come back and brief me on what you are doing with regard to the future of the air force. Warm regards, Bob Dixon."

I immediately called a meeting and, after handing each a copy of the message, asked, "Who would like to accompany me on a return visit to TAC to brief General Dixon?" The silence was deafening! Next, each member was polled to make certain their intentions. No one would commit to return to TAC; in fact, they absolutely refused to even consider it. It boggled my mind that five colonels would choose to ignore an invitation—no, more like a command—from a senior four-star general. It seemed like career suicide! As we walked back to our office, Moon must have realized that General Dixon selected him for this assignment. Perhaps more importantly, Moon was likely to be reassigned back to TAC with the opportunity to command a wing. He couldn't afford to ignore the general's invitation to return and brief on what we were doing. In a soft voice, almost like he didn't want to say it, Moon said, "I have to go—I'll go with you." It made me feel a lot better, not having to go back to TAC and face General Dixon alone after the previous encounter, but I wasn't looking forward to it by any means.

General Dixon's invitation was a call for action and attention to detail! First, we strategized about the form, style, and approach to the briefing. Moon's intelligence from his associates in TAC told him that the general despised any form of pleasantry or superficial comments. Accordingly, we agreed to keep our comments restricted to the briefing material. We chose twenty of the projects that were sent to General Brown via Generals Smith and Huyser. The format chosen for white papers was used for the briefing format. The words on each chart were kept to a minimum and one slide was used for each white paper topic. We also agreed that when General Dixon entered his conference room, we would stand at attention until he sat down but would not say a word. When he sat down, I would call for the list of topics and follow that with the first white paper Chart. I would talk to this chart until he stopped asking questions or nodded his head as an indication to move on. I would buzz for the next chart for Moon to talk to it, moving back and forth in a *Huntley-Brinkley* format. Moon and I did a dry run of the briefing at least a dozen times, asking each other questions to force a deeper understanding of the material we would be covering.

We flew up to Langley AFB, Virginia, and had a good night's rest prior to the early morning briefing time. The TAC conference room chart flipper helped us get set up and briefed us on the various means of calling for the next chart. He also warned us that General Dixon would sometimes clandestinely buzz for the next chart just to put the briefer on edge, and if that happened, just switch to the chart that came up because it wouldn't be a mistake on the chart flipper's part. He put out name tags for those who would be attending the briefing. Moon was seated on General Dixon's immediate left, and I on his immediate right—the same seats we were in when I got my butt ripped to shreds just six weeks earlier.

A few minutes before the scheduled time, the flag officers on the TAC Staff started to fill the conference room; the briefing was to be given to a full house. Moon and I exchanged glances, wondering if this was a good or bad thing for us. When General Dixon entered the room, all present came to attention and waited for him to take his chair. Not a word was spoken by anyone. As soon as General Dixon was seated, the introductory and overview chart came up, and I said, "General Dixon, these are the topics that will be covered." I spoke to the next chart, adding a little more detail than was on the chart. He nodded. Up came the following chart, and Moon started to speak. General Dixon cut him short, asking if the format was consistent throughout the briefing.

When the answer was yes, General Dixon said, "I got it!" With every head nod, a new slide came up. When the slide on "Seasonal Impact on Behavior" came up and he saw that two of the bases in the study were TAC bases Seymour-Johnson AFB, North Carolina, and England AFB, Louisiana, he wanted to understand the purpose of the study and why those bases were chosen. He was satisfied that they were chosen because the study was structured around four bases in the north and four in the south to determine if there was a statistical difference between cold and warm climates. With that, the briefing moved to a close, with a chart that solicited comments and questions.

General Dixon told us that our briefing was one of the best he'd ever received and then berated his staff for not using a similar format for briefings they presented to him. He also directed Brig. Gen. Don Payne, DCS/Personnel (the same Payne that was the vice commander at Bitburg when I was the DO), to follow up on the behavior study and keep him informed. I never heard from Brigadier General Payne, although the TAC/DCS/Personnel was sent a copy of the completed study after it was published.

Moon and I were happy to escape from the conference room. I suspect General Dixon rolled right into a staff meeting after we left.

Back at Maxwell AFB, every member of the Six-Man Group was deep into the research and writing mode. I found myself vacillating back and forth between the two primary studies I was working on. When I ran into a wall or got stale on one, I would jump to the other until I had a blazing glimpse of the obvious on the other study and would then shift back. This kept me fresh and really interested in what I was doing. Attending night school for an MBA at Auburn University also helped keep the mind from growing stale, and the statistics course grounded me in what was needed to do the proper analysis for the behavior study.

The Six-Man Group lost its champion in the summer of 1974. Gen. George Brown, who formed the group and gave us direction, was selected by the president to move up to become the chairman of the Joint Chiefs of Staff (CJCS) on July 1, 1974. Gen. David C. Jones, my former boss as CINCUSAFE, was chosen by the secretary of Defense for the vacated position and endorsed by the president to become the new air force chief of staff. In my view, these two great air force leaders were worlds apart in style and vision. I did not think General Jones would continue the group, and if he did, we would be studying the issues he thought needed to be studied. I was pleased to be wrong on both counts.

Time passed quickly, and the holidays were soon on the horizon. This was going to be the first real Christmas for the Piotrowski family in years. In the past, something the air force wanted me to do immediately always got in the way.

The call from General Jones's senior executive came in mid-December. He informed me that General Jones was extending me an invitation to travel with him and a small selected group on a three-week trip through the Pacific starting on January 3, 1975. Was I available? he asked. The only acceptable answer was yes! It wasn't long before I had TDY orders and started planning for the trip. The itinerary started in Washington DC, then Alaska, Japan, Korea, South Vietnam,

Thailand, the Philippines, and finished in Hawaii at Hickam AFB, where General Jones would outbrief Gen. Lou Wilson, commander PACAF, on observations throughout the Pacific. The one thing I hadn't been told was what General Jones had in mind for me to do on the trip. The only thing I was told is to report to Lieutenant General Roberts, DCS/Personnel, at the Pentagon early on the morning of January 3. I arrived at Andrews AFB, Maryland, on January 2nd and rented a car at Base Operations and spent the night in visiting officer's quarters at Bolling AFB, Maryland, wondering what was expected of me.

Early the following morning, I was standing in front of General Roberts's secretary's desk, asking if the general had some guidance for me. In a few minutes, I was reporting to General Roberts. It was then that I learned that the "chief" wanted me to "grade" the performance of wing commanders at all the air force bases and wings we would visit over the next three weeks. His description of my proposed duties set me back on my heels. My immediate response was "Sir, I can't do that!"

General Roberts came back with "You can't or you won't?" I tried to explain that, first, I was unequipped to evaluate wing commanders' performance, never having been on an inspector general team; and, second, even if I had that kind of experience, I didn't believe an accurate assessment could be made in one or two days at an air base by one person. I noted that my only experience of being on the receiving end of inspections is that it took large teams of highly experienced experts over a week to evaluate a wing. The general paused for what seemed like a long time and then asked if I would go on the trip, walk around the bases visited, and if I saw anything worth reporting, prepare a memo for him. I agreed, thinking that it was going to be a three-week boondoggle because I felt that I would not find anything worthy of reporting in the short time that I would have on PACAF Air Force bases, bases and missions that were completely unknown to me. Then General Roberts asked me if I would take several valises of classified documents (the chief's travel-smart books) to the KC-135 aircraft sitting in front of Base Operations at Andrews AFB. General Roberts explained that he was riding on the chief's helicopter to the flight line at Andrews and didn't want to complicate matters by dragging the valises along. I offered to take them immediately but learned that some were still in last-minute updates, and he needed to proofread them prior to giving the valises to me. He noted that departure from Andrews Air Force Base was 1600 hours on the dot.

It was only 0915 hours, and I didn't think there would be a problem for me checking out of the VOQ, turning in the rental car at Base

Operations, and getting myself, my luggage, and the valises to the aircraft in plenty of time. I returned to General Roberts's office at 1100 hours, only to learn that the books were still not ready. At noon, they still weren't ready, and I started to feel a little uncomfortable in the gut. It was after 1300 hours when to valises were turned over to me. It took time to walk to visitors' parking at the Pentagon, which was a long haul from the river entrance. I decided to take Highway 95 South to the Beltway and then the Beltway east across the Woodrow Wilson Memorial Bridge to Maryland and Andrews AFB. It was the least complicated route and only about a ten-minute longer drive than the more direct route that traveled over a lot of surface roads and was not well known to me. All was going well heading east on the Beltway with the WW Bridge only a mile or so ahead when the road turned into a parking lot. These jams normally clear in a few minutes, and it was just after midday, not rush hour. After ten minutes of traffic gridlock, I convinced a couple of drivers to move slightly so I could get to the shoulder and hopefully make it to Highway 1. This goal achieved, I pulled into the first business I came across, a car dealership, and asked to use their phone. When the chief's executive officer came on the line, I explained where I was and that the bridge was expected to be closed for hours because a semitrailer was jackknifed and on its side, closing all lanes. Highway 1 would get me back on the Beltway going west back to the Pentagon, but I needed some directions from him to make all the correct turns once I reached the Pentagon. Then came a deadly silence—maybe he didn't know the route either? The brigadier general came back with "If you don't know the way, my directions won't help you" and hung up.

Back I went, and with the Pentagon on my right and a fork in the road in front, I stopped and got out of the car, flagging down the first police car that came into view. When I explained my predicament and asked for directions, there followed an ominous pause—could it be he didn't know the way either? Finally, he said, "I can't lead you to Andrews, it's against the law. However, I'm going that way myself. Just follow me, and when I give a wave out the window, turn right and you'll see signs to the air base." On we went, and with the signal, I turned right and saw the signs. All the while, I was thinking of plan B: what to do if I didn't get there in time? Take a commercial flight to Anchorage, Alaska, just across the road from Elmendorf AFB. If I didn't catch up with them in Alaska, I would fly commercially to Tokyo, where Yokota AFB, Japan, the second stop on the Itinerary, was located. A mile down the road, there was an accident, and traffic was held up—so close and stuck again! I ran up to the accident scene and explained my problem to the on-scene commander.

Again a helpful police officer said, "Pull off on the shoulder and proceed carefully—but don't cause another accident."

The chief's aircraft came into sight at 1530 hours, and the entrance door was open with a ladder in place. At least I could get rid of the top secret documents, and perhaps buy some uniforms and toilet articles at the first stop, Elmendorf AFB, Arkansas. Then I noticed the suitcases under the aircraft wing—they were mine. When I climbed aboard the aircraft, there was an outburst of applause and laughter. The chief's exec called ahead and alerted Major General Gabriel, DCS/Operations, senior officer on board, that I was stuck in traffic. He had someone pick up my bags and check me out of the VOQ. Now my only problem was the rental car; if I didn't turn it in, the bill when we returned would be roughly $1,500. I didn't think Sheila would believe my story about the traffic jam. Then I learned the chief had been called down to the Sec Def's Office and was running at least an hour late—there was plenty of time to turn in the car and settle down a highly elevated heart rate.

The chief's aircraft was divided into two compartments, with a bedroom in the very back. Up front, there were two adjacent tables, one on each side of the aircraft, with seating for four at each table. Aft of these tables was the galley where food was prepared for the aircrew and passengers. Aft of the galley was another two-table area, and further to the rear, the bedroom. Luggage for all on board was loaded in an unfinished space aft of the bedroom. General Gabriel informed me that General Roberts would be sitting at his table and invited me to sit there also. I suggested that it would be better for me to sit with a couple of brigadier generals and a colonel across the aisle. He directed I sit next to him, and that was the end of that discussion.

It took only a few minutes to get airborne once the chief and Lieutenant General Roberts climbed on board. It should be noted that the chief's KC-135 aircraft was based at Wright-Patterson AFB, Ohio, with its primary mission as a test platform for prototype avionics equipment intended for installation on various types of air force aircraft.

About an hour into the flight, General Roberts was informed by the aircrew that they had discovered an equipment malfunction that was not an emergency but needed to be corrected. The crew planned to stop at a Strategic Air Command (SAC) base for repairs prior to leaving the lower forty-eight states. The most convenient KC-135 base was Wurtsmith AFB, Michigan, located just slightly off of our route of flight. The en route stop was approved, and the wing was notified that a planeload of Pentagon generals were unexpectedly dropping in on them with a broken KC-135 aircraft. I can assure you this is not what a wing commander wishes for! To their credit, maintenance personnel did a great job with no further problems occurring during the following three weeks of travel!

The first planned visit was Elmendorf AFB, home of Alaska NORAD region, Alaskan Air Command, and the Twenty-First Tactical Fighter Wing. There were also two active air defense alert locations at Galena and King Salmon airports located along the western and northwestern reaches of Alaska. In addition, there were several radar sites along the coastline feeding data to a central command and control site. At that time, the 21st TFW was equipped with F-4Es. Elmendorf was also home to a Priority A Storage area (tactical nuclear bombs). The Alaskan Air Command did not, at that juncture, have a nuclear mission. The weapons were stored and maintained at Elmendorf AFB for uploading on F-111 aircraft, based in the lower forty-eight states, en route to targets in the Far East in a crisis.

Without the unplanned stop in Michigan, the team would have arrived at Elmendorf in time for dinner with senior officers from host commands. However, actual landing time was around midnight. Nonetheless, Lt. Gen. James E. Hill, commander Alaskan Air Command, hosted a cocktail party with heavy hors d'oeuvre. Lieutenant General Hill and his senior staff gathered with General Jones and party on one side of the room, while I hooked up with the 21st TFW commander and his staff on the other end of the room. The conversation among the wing leadership soon found its way to the subject of Human Relations Training (HRT), a four-day program mandated by General Jones shortly after he became air force chief of staff. In his previous assignment as CINCUSAFE, General Jones established a similar program throughout air force bases in Europe. I found them quite helpful at Aviano, Italy, in forming a common understanding between whites, blacks, and other minorities on their sensitivity to perceived discrimination. As one black NCO at Aviano told me, "If you're black and not paranoid, you're crazy!" I attended the first class at Aviano and saw a significant difference in the attitude of most participants at the end of the week. As a result, I personally opened all HRT classes at Aviano and sat through the first day to show that the program had my full backing and support.

The 21st TFW colonel in charge of maintenance and logistics (DCM) was very outspoken against HRT, blaming it for robbing him of the personnel needed to properly maintain the Wings F-4s and achieve an acceptable C status rating. I asked the wing commander, vice wing commander, and deputy commander of operations how they felt about the HRT Program. Their response was muffled and generally in support of the DCM. I pointed out that General Jones was only fifty feet away and that I would ask him to come over and explain why such a program was vital to the air force if that would be helpful. When they declined the offer, I pointed out that the program was doomed to failure if they didn't fully support HRT in a very positive way. Without their support, the effort and time spent by their personnel in the HRT Program would be largely wasted.

Following the HRT discussion, I informed the wing commander that I would like to visit the Priority A Storage Area and, following that, visit some security police posts and then visit with some aircraft maintenance personnel working on the flight line. He assigned his vice commander, Col. Ed Tixier, as my escort for the visits to start later that morning.

Colonel Tixier picked me up at 0800 hours. The social didn't break up until 0200 hours due to our very late arrival, so it was a short night. Elmendorf AFB is located next to Anchorage, Alaska, and normally experiences a relatively warm winter because of the Japanese current flowing along Alaska's southern coast. That day was an exception, with the temperature hovering just above zero degrees Fahrenheit with dense fog that limited visibility to about ten feet. The road to the Priority A Area paralleled a fence that I assumed was the base perimeter fence. Peering through the dense fog, I noticed a hole in the fence large enough to drive a pickup truck through. When asked if it was the base perimeter fence, the colonel replied, "No, it is the nuclear weapon storage fence." Two or three hundred feet later, we arrived at the Priority A entry point. A staff sergeant in charge of the on-duty force did an excellent job of checking our credentials and asking Colonel Tixier if he was going to escort me into the area. This was necessary because I wasn't authorized to enter, but the colonel had access indicated on his security badge as well as escort privileges. Once inside the secure facility, I asked the sergeant how long the hole in the fence had been there. He replied, "Almost a month!" I then asked if he had reported the hole to his superiors, to which he responded, "Every day since the snowplow ripped it open!" Then he produced a stack of discrepancy reports (DR) signed by him and the other shift supervisors. Colonel Tixier was speechless when I asked if this problem had surfaced during any of the wing staff meetings over the previous month. "No" was the response. I then asked the sergeant if it was OK for me to submit a DR and sign it. He seemed pleased that I would do so. Then I asked if there were any other problems that we should know about. To this, he responded that locks on the vehicle access gates were broken, and they could not secure the Priority A Area. He added that it was taking several extra security police to provide the required two-man access control at the hole and the broken gates. I filled out and signed another DR.

After leaving the Priority A Storage Area, I asked Col. Ed Tixier to take me to Security Police Operations where I checked the day's blotter. Air Force Security Police keep blotters just like municipal police do. Sure enough, the next to the last entry in the blotter was Colonels Piotrowski and Tixier's visit SP Post no. X, Priority A Area. Then I asked to see the previous three months' blotters. A quick review of these historic documents revealed that none of the appropriate commanders from wing down to squadron level had visited the Priority A Area in the previous three months. Nor had the Alaskan Air Command or wing senior enlisted advisors visited the area. No surprise that things were not getting fixed! The Priority A area was off the beaten path; it was winter, and not many people in leadership roles were venturing out in the cold. Next, I visited some of the security police guarding the flight line and the supply squadron. I didn't find anything to report from those areas except that no one in a position of leadership or responsibility had been visiting those locations either. It was a recipe for low morale and for bad things to happen.

The next stop was Yokota Air Force Base located on the outskirts of Tokyo, Japan. I had visited Tokyo several times when I was stationed at Osaka, Japan, in the 67th TRW—but this was the first time I had set foot on Yokota. The base was home to Fifth Air Force and the senior American military officer in Japan. While Yokota had an operating runway, it did not host an operational mission; in that respect, it was different than most air force bases and should have been a lot easier to manage. We arrived on Sunday. Not much was happening, so I just wandered around the base, visiting places that were open, such as the base exchange, bowling alley, recreation center, dining facility, etc. It was eerie; the base was almost a ghost town, which suggested to me that most of the young airmen were off base, perhaps living off base with a girlfriend.

I had dinner at the dining facility and joined three young airmen who were unlucky enough to have an unoccupied chair at their table. I was in uniform and introduced myself as part of General Jones's visiting team. To my surprise, there were only about a dozen enlisted personnel eating dinner. I asked my usual questions: "How long have you been in the air force?" "How long at Yokota?" "Where are you from?" "What do you do in your off time?" "How is the air force treating you?" etc. Pretty soon, I had them talking but didn't learn anything except they had never spoke with a colonel before. While sitting at the table talking with the airmen, there was a loud pounding on the window nearby.

I ran to the window and found a three-star general (Fifth Air Force commander) shouting, "Where's the door?" I pointed in the direction of the door, and he took off. I went to the door in the chance that he might want to know who the strange colonel was sitting in his dining hall. He was questioning the mess checker (the man responsible for verifying the people who came in were authorized to eat there or collecting the meal fee from people like me). The general's questions were "Where do I park my car?" "How much is the breakfast meal?" "Where is the chow line?" "Where are the trays and silverware?" Then he went off to get the layout of the dining facility in his head. At least he was smart enough to come there that evening to find out what he didn't know because he was hosting a meeting with General Jones and the top enlisted NCOs the following morning. He'd served as Fifth Air Force commander for eighteen months but had never been to the dining facility—not a good sign. I was there the following morning having breakfast with some more enlisted personnel. The dining facility was crowded, so the troops had come back from town.

Following breakfast, arrangements were made to visit all the enlisted dormitories accompanied by each squadron's first sergeant. The dormitories were all in good order and clean. The one anomaly was the variation from squadron to squadron in the pictures displayed in the rooms. One squadron had animal pictures, dogs, cats, wild animals, etc. Another had landscapes. One had nude pinups of which many were gross and distasteful. When asked about the dormitory standards, the first sergeant responded that he didn't know of any. Next question: "How long have you been here, and when is the last time you met with the air base wing commander?"

His response was "Two years, and never met or met with the air base wing commander."

My next call was with the air base wing commander, Col. Robert Reed. After some general conversation, I commented that there seemed to be some confusion among the first sergeants on what the standards were for dormitories, specifically what was suitable for display on the walls. To that, he responded that his standards were published and clear. At this, he took a loose-leaf binder from the shelf behind him and leafed through it until he found an article he published in the base paper under the rubric of "The Commander Speaks." He held it up to me and said, "Here are the dorm standards, clear as can be." I was astonished that he expected first sergeants and the troops to read articles carried in the base paper. I told him that the only two people that I was sure who read the similar articles that I wrote were the editor and my wife; and that if my wife thought it was good, she would send it to her mother. Then I asked him when was the last time he met with the first sergeants. His answer was "Never—I don't consider it necessary to meet with first sergeants." I was beginning to get the picture: he spent all his time in his very nice office that was well appointed and ran the wing by telephone calls and base newspaper articles that no one ever read. We had a long talk about "hands-on walkabout leadership" and that he needed to get out of his office. I also pointed out that his base newspaper articles had no authority and could not be enforced. Further, that any standards should be promulgated in base regulations and that he should sit down with the first sergeants and squadron commanders at least monthly. I encouraged him to communicate down two levels to be sure that his words got to the working level. I also suggested that he pass out information at his weekly staff meeting that was relatively important to get down to the troops—then follow up by asking enlisted personnel if they had heard X. I suggested he would find out which of his subordinate commanders were not getting the word out. When I did this at Aviano, I discovered that security police, supply, and the helicopter squadron always got the word; the rest were rather sporadic, and it was necessary to lean on the commanders of those units.

Security Police Operations was next on my list, and it was no surprise that neither Colonel Reed nor his deputy had visited one of their security police posts within the previous six months.

Yokota Air Force Base, Japan, lacked leadership and involvement at the wing level. NCOs were carrying the leadership load, making decisions as required.

It was time to board and fly to Osan Air Base, Korea. Osan was a diverse and complex base and the closest base to the South Korean capital of Seoul and the demilitarized zone (DMZ), the no man's land dividing North and South Korea. Not surprisingly, Osan AB was home to the Fifty-First Fighter Wing with aircraft on five-minute alert, and the Korean Combined Air Operations Center (KCOAC) with intelligence feeds from multiple intelligence agencies and satellites. It was also home to the largest air force hospital on the Korean peninsula. The Fifty-First Tactical Fighter Wing had a proud heritage in Korea as achieving the highest number of MiG-15 shoot downs during the Korean War. The 4th TFW, located at Kimpo (K-14) across from the 67th TRW that I flew with, was a very close second in MiG shoot downs. I hit all the regular hot spots that quickly revealed spotty or lack of leadership, security police, base supply, dormitories, dining halls, and enlisted clubs. Every location visited indicated the base was being well led and run. Air force personnel in the middle officer and enlisted ranks were positive on the mission and their respective organization.

Next stop, Kunsan Air Base and the Eighth Tactical Fighter Wing located in central west South Korea. The 8th TFW that I flew with testing the Walleye electro-optical glide bomb in Vietnam had been relocated from Ubon, Thailand, to Kunsan AB. The wing commander was Alfred M. Miller Jr., also known as Wolf 13. The Wolf call sign was a tradition started at Ubon AFB during the Vietnam War, with Col. Robin Olds as Wolf 1. Wolf 13 indicated that Colonel Miller was the twelfth wing commander in succession following Col. Robin Olds.

Colonel Miller was a hands-on walkabout leader that did a lot more than just drink coffee in the flying squadrons with his fellow fighter pilots. His footprints could be found all over the base. Unlike a lot of the bases I visited, the security police blotter revealed that he regularly visited security police posts around the base at all hours of the day and night. All wing personnel that I spoke with were very positive about their mission and high on the wing leadership all the way down to their immediate supervisors. Wing statistics in F-4 in-commission rates, flying hours, and other traditional measures indicated the 8th TFW was one of the air force's best by just about any measure. I told Colonel Miller that he was doing a great job and thanked him for the hospitality. He was later promoted to brigadier general and subsequently retired as commander of General Supply Center in Richmond, Virginia, on July 1, 1981.

The next stop was a surprise! While airborne, it was announced that General Jones was taking us to Tan Son Nhut Air Base on the outskirts of Saigon, South Vietnam, and Headquarters Seventh Air Force. The purpose of the visit was to gather data on how well the South Vietnamese government was doing in their fight against the North Vietnamese Army and their surrogates, the Viet Cong. General Jones was no stranger to South Vietnam (SVN) and Tan Son Nhut, as he served there earlier in the Vietnam War as deputy commander for operations and subsequently vice commander Seventh Air Force. General Jones asked me to visit a Vietnamese Air Force Electronics Maintenance Facility and then look into US Air Force personnel morale issues at Tan Son Nhut Air Base.

It was a Saturday and early afternoon. During my two tours in South Vietnam, I learned that the Vietnamese military did not usually work on Saturday and never worked or flew missions during the siesta period from about 1200 to 1500 hours. Therefore, I was surprised to find the maintenance facility full of Vietnamese Air Force (VNAF) personnel, and every maintenance position manned with a junior grade office or senior grade NCO. On the other hand, I didn't see any actual work being accomplished such as taking electronic test equipment readings or removing and replacing parts. When I asked questions of those VNAF personnel that introduced themselves in English, I didn't get answers that made any sense from a maintenance standpoint. It was all a show for General Jones's visit. However, I did learn that VNAF pilots preferred the AT-37, a converted trainer aircraft, over the AC-119 Gunship. The AT-37 was fun to fly but had no range and carried very little ordnance for close air support or interdiction missions. On the other hand, the AC-119 was a workhorse that could be airborne for hours, carried a commensurate amount of firepower, and could deliver that ordnance from above the small arms and light AAA threat. The AC-119 should have been the aircraft of choice for the VNAF, but all they wanted were spare parts for the AT-37. I passed these thoughts to General Jones.

Linking up with Lieutenant General Roberts, we toured some of the USAF enlisted facilities and the tent city that most air force enlisted personnel were housed in. I got a strong whiff of marijuana when we were still one hundred yards from the first row of tents. This was not going to be good. It wasn't long before a puzzled look crossed General Roberts face, and he asked me what the odor was. I told him it was marijuana (MJ) and plenty of it. When we entered the first tent, it was obvious that most of the occupants were stoned on booze, MJ, or both. Lieutenant General Roberts called for security police and ordered the arrest of all the troops in the tent. A second tent followed the first, and I could see people fleeing other tents in droves. Lieutenant General Roberts left for a meeting with local air force commanders and joined General Jones to give him my report prior to his meeting with SVN president Ky. President Ky arrived as we were talking, and General Jones introduced us. I remarked that I knew General/President Ky when he commanded the 1st VNAF Squadron equipped with A-1 aircraft at the other end of Bien Hoa Air Base from the Air Commandos. I also mentioned that Brig. Gen. Gary Willard was a good mutual friend. Capt. Gary Willard was an exchange officer flying combat in A-1s with then Captain Ky. With that, President Ky took, from around his neck, the lavender flying scarf he was wearing and gave it to me, along with a warm handshake. I still have and treasure that memento.

Bangkok, Thailand, was our next stop, where there was no work for me. General Jones planned this stop specifically to visit with Brig. Gen. Harry C. Aderholt, known to all Air Commandos as "Hinny." I worked for then colonel Aderholt when he commanded the First Air Commando Wing, Hurlburt, Florida, succeeding Col. Chester Jack and Col. Ben King. I was the wing weapons officer and tasked by Colonel Aderholt to support Capt. James Ahman in writing and editing a Wing Global Operations Plan for Counterinsurgency Operations. Shortly thereafter, I was reassigned to the Air Force Fighter Weapons School as an F-4C/D instructor pilot.

Currently, Brigadier General Aderholt was assigned as chief of the Military Assistance Group (MAG) Thailand, and the senior air force officer in Thailand. General Jones was interested in getting General Aderholt's views on insurgencies taking place in the region. General Aderholt, on the other hand, was bullish on reestablishing an Air Commando unit with the original charter of 1961, flying A-1, A-10, and C-47 type aircraft and fighting insurgents in Allied countries, as well as training their aircrews. General Aderholt was both very passionate and very persuasive in these discussions.

The team stayed in Thailand to review operations at U-Tapao Air Base in South Central Thailand. U-Tapao was a B-52 Base and home for the B-52s that pounded North Vietnam in the early 1970s that brought the North Vietnamese to their knees and thus to the bargaining table. Equally important, the pounding B-52s gave Hanoi led to bringing our POWs from prison camps in North Vietnam, home. The visit to U-Tapao was brief, so it was necessary to visit the hot spots and try to get a sense of how well the wing leadership was doing. The security police visits didn't raise any alarm bells; however, the next stop at the NCO club did. The club was packed probably because it offered the troops a place to party when the work on the flight line was done. Good booze was very cheap. It was the first club I'd been to, including my tours in Vietnam and at Ubon, Thailand, where there were topless dancers. The reader must understand that the only enlisted personnel on B-52s were the gunners that operated the tail gun stingers remotely. It was primarily an all-officer crew consisting of pilot, copilot, navigator, bombardier, and defensive system operator or electronic warfare officer. Therefore, I suspected that most of the NCOs at the club were largely in the maintenance, munitions, security police, or other support career fields. When the band stopped playing and the showgirls stopped gyrating, the topless women went and sat down at tables, presumably with their boyfriends. The tables seated about six, one nearly naked girl, her boyfriend, and four others leering at the topless go-go dancer. This seemed like a perfect scenario for a lot of fights provoked by comments or touching. I asked the club manager about the provocative situation and if it caused a lot of fights. He said that there were two or three fights a night, but no one got hurt very bad. I suggested that it would be a very good idea for the girls to have robes that they could put on when they went to the tables, or better yet, have a back room where the entertainers could go and relax for fifteen minutes or so when on break instead of sitting with the audience in their skimpy costumes. He looked at me like I was crazy and said this was combat, not Washington DC. Actually, U-Tapao was in a very friendly and peaceful location—this was 1975, and the United States was no longer in combat, except perhaps for some Special Forces in a covert role.

The next stop was at Clark Air Force Base located near Manila in the Philippines. Not far away was Subic Bay, the largest US Naval Base west of Pearl Harbor, Hawaii. Clark AFB was the largest air force installation in the Western Pacific. It was a major logistic transshipment point and also a major repair facility for forward based aircraft. I recall flying B-26 Aircraft from Bien Hoa, South Vietnam, to Clark AFB, Philippines, for major repair work that was beyond the capability of the First Air Commando Detachment in SVN. Clark AFB was large both in area and number of personnel and home of Thirteenth Air Force Headquarters, also known as the "Jungle Air Force," from its operations in World War II throughout the Pacific Region. Subsequently, the US Air Force pulled out of Clark AB at the request of the Philippine government. This request came about the same time that volcanic ash from Mt. Pintubo's volcano on Luzon covered Clark with over two feet of ash, collapsing most buildings and ruining all machinery and vehicles.

I spent most of the day and early evening with security police. They gave me a tour of the base perimeter and showed me the many gates that had been installed by gangs of Philippine thieves that preyed upon the base. It was evident that these gangs found it easier to install a gate in the chain-link fence that replicated, in every way, those built by air force civil engineers. Evidently, it was much easier to drive in, pick up their booty, and drive out than climb over the fence. Moreover, some of their take was very large, like the full-size fire truck that was stolen and found years later in a remote village. The civil engineers kept replacing the locks on these gates with the toughest and best locks available; nonetheless, they were removed and replaced with locks that the thieves had the keys to. The "thieves' gate" that got my attention was the one located about two hundred yards from the edge of the conventional munitions storage area. Conventional munitions are stored in steel-reinforced concrete "igloos" with one opening covered with a very thick steel door. After the concrete has "cured," igloos are covered with an overburden of dirt about four feet thick. Over time, the igloos become overgrown with thick native grasses that camouflage the storage area from the air. However, from the ground, they are very discernible. The Clark AFB munitions storage area held thousands of tons of high-explosive bombs of the WW II and Vietnam era. In the hands of Maoist terrorists in the Southern Philippines, these munitions could be very deadly, raising the question of, why not an internal fence around the storage area?

Later that evening, I cleaned up, put on a suit, and walked over to the NCO club. Perhaps I should have worn a uniform, but if I wanted to learn what was going on, mufti seemed like the right choice. At the NCO club, I ordered tonic water with a twist of lime and leaned back against the bar to observe the activity. All seemed normal, so I asked the civilian-clothed gentleman standing alongside, "Where is all the action?"

His response caught me by surprise: "If you're looking for sex, there will be one hundred prostitutes here in just a few minutes."

I responded, "I'm here TDY for a couple of days, how does that work?"

He said, "See all those chairs along the wall? Buses will drop off the prostitutes from the nearby towns, and they'll sit in those chairs waiting for someone to ask them to dance."

The wait wasn't long before dozens of young women dressed up in formal gowns poured though the NCO club front door and headed for the chairs. They all looked like they were in their late teens or early twenties; on the other hand, Oriental women always looked younger than their age to me. It wasn't long before I noticed one of the women looking at me and beckoning me to come over to her. I did, and she asked, "Would you like to dance?"

"Yes" was the instant response! "You have to buy dance tickets," she responded. At the club cashier's window, I purchased two dollars worth of twenty-five-cent tickets and returned to the young woman. Two dollars was good for two foxtrots, and she collected the tickets. It reminded me of the "dime a dance" clubs that were featured in movies about New York City set in the late 1940s and early 1950s. As I walked her back to her chair, she asked if I would buy her a drink, so we went to a table where a waitress took our drink order. She ordered in her native tongue, and I asked for tonic water. Normally, cocktails were priced somewhere between fifty cents and a dollar in the Far East clubs, but the tab was three dollars. When her tiny glass of amber liquid arrived, I tasted it—not surprisingly, it was sweet tea. Following some small talk, she asked me if I would like to spend the night with her. I said I didn't have a car and was staying on base in the barracks. She said all I had to do was get on the bus with her when it was time to go, and I could stay with her at mama-san's place. That was enough for me; the NCO club was harboring a prostitution ring, selling dance tickets, and gouging the troops for tea. I thanked her for the time, went back to the BOQ, and mapped out the next move.

The following morning, I was back at the NCO club and asked to see the club manager—this time, I was in uniform. The club manager was a crusty chief master sergeant. When I asked about the prostitutes and phony drinks for two dollars, he denied everything. I asked him to show me the members-only bar, which in earlier times had been known as the "stag bar." However, in deference to the increasing number of career women in the air force, both officers and enlisted, the Air Staff in the Pentagon under General Jones had mandated the change to "members-only bar," indicating that guests, including nonmilitary spouses, were not welcome in that sanctuary. In response to my request to see the members-only bar, the club manager said, "We don't have one of those. We only have a stag bar!" Inside the stag bar, I noted the walls were covered with life-size *Playboy* nude centerfold pictures—probably thirty or more in number. I asked the chief where the nude male pictures were. He was taken aback, responding, "What kind of club do you think this is?"

I responded, "If you have life-size nude women for the male NCOs, you should also have life-size nude male pictures for the female NCOs who come in here—otherwise, you're discriminating against the women." That comment didn't set well with him, so I switched the subject to happy hour, asking the club manager when happy hour was held in his club.

His crisp response was "Ten until two."

Somewhat surprised, I asked, "Ten at night until two in the morning?"

"No," he said, "10:00 a.m. until 2:00 p.m. every day!"

"You mean you encourage the NCOs to come in and drink for four hours in the middle of the workday and then go back to their offices, shops, and flight line and supervise the enlisted force—that's crazy, and its wrong. What's more, General Jones, our chief of staff, has mandated that happy hour will only last two hours in any given week and will be accompanied by generous portions of free food to ensure the drinking did not occur on an empty stomach. You are in violation of all of his directives!" With that, I left the club both aggravated and puzzled! How could all of these gross violations of good conduct and order occur right under the noses of a three-star general and his senior enlisted advisor, the wing/base commander and his senior enlisted advisor, and all of other commanders on the largest base in the Far East? The answer had to be that they had forgotten or otherwise ignored that their responsibilities for leadership extended all the way down the chain of command. Further, that the senior enlisted advisors had become part of the problem, instead of being key members of the leadership team. All of these observations were relayed to General Jones and Lieutenant General Roberts.

The trip was all but done. There was a courtesy stop scheduled at Hickam AFB, Hawaii, where General Jones would spend some time outbriefing Gen. Lou Wilson, commander PACAF. This was the same Lou Wilson who inspected Aviano AFB, Italy, when I was the commander and awarded the 40th TAC Group the accolade of "Best Unit in the Air Force." He was promoted to general and assigned as commander PACAF shortly after the Aviano AFB inspection.

About three hours out of Hawaii, General Jones came forward to where I was sitting with Lieutenant General Roberts and Major General Gabriel. He asked General Roberts to prepare a trip report that he could use to outbrief General Wilson and leave behind for General Wilson to use as an action paper. When General Jones left, General Roberts looked across the table at me and said with a wry smile, "Pete, you've only got three hours before we land to get that report written."

I had to believe that General Roberts was not expecting the requirement to prepare a trip report; otherwise, he would have laid on the tasking at the beginning of the trip. I answered with a positive "Yes, sir, I'll get right on it, but I'll need some help. Would you please ask the other general officers for their inputs and place a call for a secretary to be standing by when we land at Hickam?" He took care of those requests, and I started writing up my input base by base according to the itinerary, planning to insert the other generals' inputs as I received them. As it turned out, the remainder of the team, several major and brigadier generals and one colonel, only added a few paragraphs. In the final analysis, General Jones's trip report turned out to be mostly my discoveries and observations.

By the time the plane landed at Hickam, the trip report was finished in handwritten rough draft. At the PACAF Command Section, we learned that General Roberts's call had come too late to keep a secretary on hand but that we were free to use any of the typewriters in the Command Section. I was surprised to learn that the Air Force DCS/Personnel didn't have any more clout than that. I immediately started typing, and General Roberts was proofreading and editing as each page came out of the typewriter. By midnight, we were finished; some pages were totally redone due to extensive editing by General Roberts. Both the general and I were there early the next morning to "hold hands" with the secretary who came in early to put the trip report in its final and correct format for General Jones's signature. While we waited for the trip report to be typed, General Roberts asked me what I would like to do when the one-year tour on the Six-Man Group ended. I said, "Sir, the most rewarding job in the air force is wing commander. I would like very much to have the opportunity to command one of the big fighter wings in the United States, or anywhere else for that matter."

His response was reassuring: "We've got a couple of fighter wings that are coming open, and I will make sure you get one of them."

My work was done! All I had to do was stay out of trouble on the flight from Hickam to Andrews AFB, Maryland. It certainly had been both a unique experience and outstanding education on how things could go wrong on air force installations when the leadership was not "minding the store," to quote an old bromide. Just as we were about to board the chief's aircraft for the last time, Lieutenant General Roberts pulled me aside and informed me that the other colonel on the trip, a career logistics professional, was on the brigadier general promotion list that had just been released for publication. The colonel was a friend and richly deserving of the promotion, and I said so to Lieutenant General Roberts. The general went out of his way to say that I was not eligible for promotion because of my youth and not to be disappointed. In response, I explained that because of my enlisted background and rather pedestrian night school college education, I did not have any expectations of getting promoted and was ecstatic that I had reached the rank of colonel and had the opportunity to command.

A few hours out of Hawaii heading east, General Jones called me back to his compartment and and asked me if I thought the Air Commando Unit of the early 1960s could be reconstituted, primarily in the counterinsurgency role. I replied that anything done once could be redone but that the air force had changed considerably in the intervening fifteen years. Fighter pilots were flying high-performance F-4 aircraft for the large part, the F-15 was moving into the operational force, and a lightweight fighter was on the horizon. This was a far cry from 1961 when pilots were flying a plethora of second-generation jet fighter aircraft and itching for a fight. I noted that most of the aircraft suited for operating in a third-world country were gone. To be suitable for a third-world country, an aircraft had to be inexpensive, easy to fly, in the USAF inventory, and relatively easy for a third-world country to maintain. What was needed was a high-performance but relatively simple T-28 like trainer aircraft with a turbo prop propulsion system. The USAF didn't have such an aircraft, and I wasn't sure that anything like it existed in the free world. Looking back, I regret that I wasn't more positive. Such a force was needed then and is still needed for training and assisting third-world countries like those in South America and Africa that are continuously embroiled in fighting insurgent groups or drug lords. At this writing, the USAF is considering such an aircraft for the COIN Mission. However, the air force budget for FY2013 is in such dire straits that the proposed COIN procurement is unlikely to survive.

About two hours' flight time to the West Coast, a call came to the chief that there was serious trouble at Minot AFB, North Dakota. We learned that a large number of black airmen, mostly security policemen, had locked themselves in the Minot dining hall and were issuing demands. It was noted that they were armed with their M-16s. At that juncture, Gen. Russell E. Dougherty held the reins of Strategic Air Command, one of the finest officers I have ever known. Russ, as his colleagues knew him, was a bomber pilot during WW II and, after the war, was encouraged to go to law school. He practiced military law for a short period and then came back on flying status in SAC. Prior to assuming command of Strategic Air Command, he was the SHAPE (Supreme Headquarters Allied Powers Europe) chief of staff. General Jones called me back to his private section of the plane and told me to "stay loose," as he might want me to visit northern tier bases and find out what the problems were behind the action taken by the black security policemen at Minot AFB.

At Andrews AFB, I gathered my luggage and headed home to Sheila and the family—it had been a long and hectic three weeks. A few days after getting back to the Six-Man Group, a call from Lieutenant General Roberts told me to be at Andrews AFB in two days and link up with Brigadier General Osway. We would be visiting three northern tier air force bases, Grand Forks, Minot, and Ellsworth; the first two located in North Dakota, and the third in South Dakota, near Mount Rushmore.

I arrived at Andrews AFB, Maryland, Base Operations way ahead of time and started looking for General Osway. I walked round and round for what seemed an eternity without locating the general. There was a brigadier general Iosue in Base Operations, but obviously not the man I was to meet. In desperation, I asked General Iosue if he had seen General Osway. To my embarrassment and surprise, his response was "That's me." His name was an Italian spelling that was pronounced "Osway." After a brief introduction, we boarded a T-39 Sabreliner and flew to Grand Forks AFB, North Dakota. My instructions were to find out what is troubling the black community on base in general and, more specifically, black security policemen. With that general guidance and my experience at Aviano AFB, Italy, I decided to look at the BX, commissary, barbershop, and beauty shop to see if the base stocked periodicals and products that I knew were desired by black military personnel and their families. Considering the northern location, these products were not likely to be found in the surrounding civilian communities, which were largely

99.9 percent Caucasian. In the magazine racks, there were current *Jet* and *Ebony* publications. At the card rack, there were birth announcements featuring babies with dark hair and dark faces, and every form of greeting card, including birthdays, anniversaries, and friendship; all had several card choices that would be appealing to minorities. Hair care products in the BX, commissary, and barbershop and beauty shop had items, combs, etc. that appeared to the kind preferred by black Americans. This was a big plus for Grand Forks. Arrangements were made for me to visit security police (SP) guarding B-52s in the afternoon, early evening, and early morning. Temperatures were forecast to drop into the minus thirties that night, but I thought my air force top coat with liner would keep me warm for the brief periods I would be out in the cold. Wrong again!

The shift NCOICs who accompanied me on these rounds were all very professional and knew their men by their first names. I made the decisions of who to talk to and where to go to prevent a canned route with selected personnel. It didn't seem to matter where I directed we go; all the SPs I spoke with were men I would be proud to have in my command. As we neared a SP post, the NCOIC and I would both get out of the truck and advance on the post. In every case, the SP challenged us with the familiar question: "Who goes there?"

The NCOIC would respond with "It is Master Sergeant Jones and Colonel Piotrowski!"

"Advance and be recognized" came the familiar answer. Once recognized, the NCOIC would relieve the SP of his post, taking his weapon and standing guard while the airman and I moved out of hearing for some conversation. The standard *Columbo* technique was employed.

> How long have you been in the air force?
> How long have you been at Grand Forks?
> Where are you from?
> Are you married, do you have any children?
> What do you do in your spare time?
> How do you rate the air force so far?
> Have you been issued warm-enough clothing for days and nights like this?
> How often do you get some relief while on guard duty?
> Is there anything that would make it easier or better for you to do your job?

Usually by the fourth or fifth question, they would warm up to the conversation, and I could get an assessment of how they felt about the wing and the wing leadership. The next morning, I went to the SP Operations Desk and reviewed the previous day's blotter. All the SP posts I had visited had reported the fact that I was there. Then I went back six months, reviewing all the blotters for that period. It was obvious that the wing leadership believed their SPs were an important part of their overall mission because the wing commander, vice commander, base commander, SP group commander, and senior enlisted advisor all regularly visited the SPs on post. They evidently all believed in hands-on walkabout leadership.

With Grand Forks AFB, North Dakota, as a calibration data point, the next stop was Minot, another double wing Strategic Air Command base, home to both an ICBM Minute man Wing and a B-52 Bomber Wing. The only differences: it was colder, forecast to be about forty degrees below zero that night; and it was where the security police had barricaded themselves in the dining hall in a mass protest. I made arrangements to go out on the flight line with a security police shift supervisor at both 10:00 p.m. and 2:00 a.m. to cover both night shifts. While waiting for the evening hours, I visited the base exchange and commissary.

At the base exchange, I could not find any articles that would relate to black airmen and their families stationed at Minot. For example, all the birth announcements and greeting cards of every sort had babies with white faces, and most had blue eyes. The magazine rack was full of fashion, outdoor, body building and weekly news magazines. However, there was no *Jet*, *Ebony*, or other magazines popular with the black community. There were lots of blue jeans and Western hats on display, but none of the broad-brimmed hats typically worn by black males in that time frame. The dress racks displayed no colorful dresses that were popular with black women. The lotions department was void of any hair care products and combs favored by the black community. I asked the base exchange manager why there were no items of any kind in the store that catered to the black community. His response was "I keep ordering them but never receive any shipments." I then asked if he asked for assistance from the exchange headquarters in Texas. His response was "It's not that big of a problem. They can go to town and get anything they want." I didn't consider that a satisfactory response or solution—after all, there was a riot, so to speak, on Minot by black airmen in the security police group.

With some time to spare, I drove to the town of Minot and visited some of the stores—I couldn't find any that displayed products that would be favored by black military personnel stationed at Minot. With nothing for them on base or in town, the only way minority personnel could get things they desired was to have them sent from friends and/or family that lived in major metropolitan areas or in the South.

It was late January 1975, and it gets dark early in the northern latitudes. I dressed warm for the flight line visit, a layer of long waffle underwear, dress blues, and a uniform trench coat. I could have borrowed a parka but wanted to look like an air force colonel, not just another olive drab lump. A technical sergeant picked me up at the BOQ a 10:00 p.m. sharp. There was a moderate wind blowing and pushing the cold through multiple layers of clothing like ice daggers. Without much conversation, the sergeant drove right up to a guard post next to a B-52, rolled down his window, and told the airman with an M-16 rifle over his shoulder, "There's a colonel from the Pentagon that wants to talk to you." He didn't get out of his truck and relieve the airman of his guard duty responsibilities; he just dropped me off and drove a few feet away to sit in his warm truck with the motor running.

I shook the airman's hand and introduced myself. The first thing I noticed was that he was not wearing a parka but rather a fatigue jacket more suited to a mild day in Texas. I asked why he wasn't wearing a parka and learned that his parka was a little soiled and was in the dry cleaners. I walked back to the truck and asked the technical sergeant for his parka and gave it to the airman to wear. After that small gesture of humanity, the airman and I chatted. I learned that not many senior people ever came out on the flight line; I was the first colonel he'd seen in a long time. It didn't take but ten minutes before I was so cold that words were difficult to form. I had to cut the conversation short and get back in the truck and warm up a little prior to the next guard post. I spoke with six security policemen on that shift and went back to the BOQ to warm up and rest up for the next series of flight line visits.

The second round of visits went pretty much the same. No security guard was ever relieved of his post to talk to me, and the security police supervisor sat in his warm vehicle while the guard and I chatted. It wasn't a very large sample size, and it wasn't random because the shift supervisor selected all personnel visited. However, it was evident that all airmen on post that I spoke with were well trained in their career field and believed their job was important. It was also evident that their supervisors up through the air division commander did not make periodic visits to check on the security police. The next morning, I went to the security police group headquarters and asked to see the blotters for the previous night and the previous six months. I found my name listed as visiting all of the posts on the previous two shifts. However, I only found one or two instances where a security police squadron commander, security police group commander, or member of the wing or Air Division staff visited the flight line, and those were in the early fall months, when it was warm.

I could sum the whole situation up as apathy with regard to the security police and apathy with regard to black military personnel and families stationed at Minot. I provided a written report to Brigadier General Iosue on my observations.

Subsequently, we visited Ellsworth AFB, South Dakota. It was a Strategic Command installation with both bomber and ICBM mission responsibilities. During the day, I visited the base exchange, commissary, barbershop, and beauty shop. I found these facilities were well stocked with products favored by the black community. This surprised me following the visits to Minot AFB facilities, where similar products were totally absent. I sought out the BX manager and asked her how she was able to stock minority-related products when other neighboring bases failed. She related that she had similar problems with the normal BX supply chain, so she ordered direct from the product distributors. Since she started going direct to commercial suppliers, her BX was always well stocked with the products favored by minority customers. Problem solved and customers content. Every aspect of Ellsworth AFB that I visited, I found professional, well run, and properly supervised.

General Iosue and I returned to Washington DC via T-39, and I caught a commercial flight back to Montgomery, Alabama, and Maxwell AFB. It wasn't more than a week or so when a call came from General Iosue, directing me to visit Eglin AFB, Florida, to find out what the racial environment was there. And if there were problems, find the root cause or causes.

Fort Walton Beach, Florida, in the early spring sounded a lot better than North Dakota in the dead of winter. I rented a car and drove to the Florida Panhandle and checked myself into the visiting officers' quarters (VOQ). My first stop the next morning was the Eglin AFB Social Actions Office. To my surprise, the office was a flurry of activity with phones ringing off of the hook. When there was a brief lull in the activity, I approached the major who seemed to be in charge and introduced myself, saying I was representing Genera Iosue, AF/DCS/Personnel, with regard to the racial climate at Eglin AFB. He gave me a strange bewildered stare and asked, "How did you get here so soon?" We were definitely having trouble communicating, so I asked him if I could have a cup of coffee while he told me what the frenzy was all about.

The coffee was excellent and hot; the conversation was even hotter. The major told me that the racial climate in Fort Walton Beach and surrounding towns had always been hostile to blacks with regard to housing, services, and social activities. Moreover, that Eglin's senior leadership seemed tepid at best in working at improving the situation with the city mayors and councils. He went on to say that it was almost impossible for black couples to find rentals near Eglin. No matter what rank or financial well-being a black couple enjoyed, there were always disqualifiers that prevented them from finding a decent rental in a respectable neighborhood. They either had to live tens of miles away or in run-down shanties. He went on to say that there had always been hope that things would change for the better without some acting out like there had been at Minot, North Dakota, or Del Rio, Texas, but those hopes had been shattered the previous evening. He then related the incident about the armament center commander, an air force major general, who attended an on-base intramural basketball game between his headquarters squadron and a team from another base unit. His team was not faring all that well in the match-up, and at one point, the general got up and shouted for all to hear, "Get those (N-word) off of my guys!" The Social Actions chief was there and heard it himself. It was a key game, and most base units were represented. The reason for the frenzy in his office was that just about everyone on the base was calling in to report what happened and asking what Social Actions was going to do about it. I asked if he had an appointment to see the general and learned that was an action in progress.

With all that as a backdrop, I asked the major to give me a comprehensive rundown on the issues, where to look, whom to talk to, and what civilian agencies I might want to talk to, such as rental agencies, that were most troublesome. It wasn't long before I had a big list of places to go and people to talk to. I also wanted to head down the road to the Air Commando Wing where I served five years just a decade ago. It would be a useful to compare the military/city relationships at Hurlburt AFB with those at Eglin AFB just twenty or so road miles apart. My discussions with two real estate agencies left me with the impression that the Social Actions major was correct in his assessment of Fort Walton Beach and Shalimar realtors. I posed as a unit commander expecting some transfers in from another base, all married with families, and about half of them black. They said they could probably accommodate the white military families, but there were few rentals for black families.

My trip to Hurlburt AFB revealed that the leadership attitudes were as different as night and day with those I was exposed to at Eglin AFB. The personnel I spoke to were also very upbeat about their assignment and their Special Operations Mission. I went back to the Eglin AFB Social Actions Office only to find that things had worsened with regard to the previous night's shouting of racial slurs by the senior commander at Eglin. There was a request from Social Actions for something of an apology from the center commander, but none was forthcoming. I called Brigadier General Iosue and gave him a thumbnail sketch of the situation. He then connected me with Lieutenant General Roberts, AF/DCS/Personnel. General Roberts asked me if I could see a pathway to some kind of resolution to the situation, both near and long term. I reluctantly told him I didn't see any way to recover from the previous night's racial slurs from the center commander in front of a crowd of two hundred-plus people. That incident was the topic of all conversation across the base, and people were waiting for some kind of resolution that would clear the air and lessen the tension. In my opinion, the center commander had to be replaced, and replaced with someone who would work hard to improve the racial climate on Eglin and with the surrounding communities as well. Further, a joint effort with the Hurlburt wing commander would help because people from the different commands, Air Force Systems Command and Tactical Air Command, shared the same problems. General Roberts pushed back, asking if there wasn't another path that might work without removing the center commander. I replied that I couldn't see a solution because the man had already refused to make an apology for his incendiary remarks, and time was against him—the situation would only get worse. He thanked me for my work, and the phone went dead.

My work at Eglin was complete, so I checked out of the VOQ and pointed the rental car north toward Montgomery, Alabama, and Maxwell AFB. I felt bad because tensions were ramping up, and there was no indication the air force had the stomach to pull the center commander. When I showed up at the Six-Man Group office the next morning, there was a message stating that the center commander was retiring, and a replacement was announced. The air force did what was necessary to alleviate a very bad situation and start down a better road for a very important installation, home to four very important missions—all would have suffered without a dramatic signal and personnel change at the top.

A month or so later, General Roberts asked me to come to Washington to participate in a round table discussion reviewing racial problems at a number of bases and the actions being taken. It proved to be a very useful session, and it was obvious that General Roberts was on top of race relation problems across the air force. A lot had changed in the few months since the incident at Minot AFB, North Dakota. Inspection teams conducting ORIs and compliance inspections were paying more attention to support services like the BX, commissary, and special services, as well as commander/supervisory involvement with the troops. Such things as visits to the flight line and other places where airman were on duty 24/7 with little or no supervision were now on the IG checklist. Gen. Bryce Poe, who taught me that one hour at night on the flight line was the best hour a commander ever spent, would have been proud.

As the meeting was breaking up and I was getting up to depart, Lieutenant General Roberts called out, "Pete, would you like to know what your new assignment is?"

"Yes, sir," I responded, thinking of his promise to give me another job as a wing commander.

The general said, "You're going to Kessler Technical Training Center as the vice center commander!" My spirits sank; being a vice commander at a training base was a real letdown and, in my view, a nothing job with little or no responsibility. I asked across the distance between us if the assignment was negotiable. He said it was and to give him a call. I felt a little better, but not much. My feeling was that this was an indication that Lieutenant General Roberts was trying to tell me that my usefulness to the air force was waning, and I was headed for second-class assignments.

After General Roberts left the room, General Iosue grabbed me by the arm and spun me around, saying, "What the hell is wrong with you—you don't question an assignment made personally by the DCS/Personnel. You better drop any thoughts about calling him for another assignment!" Based on General Iosue's advice, I never made the call; I was reluctantly going back to Keesler AFB, Mississippi.

When I returned to Maxwell AFB, Alabama, I told Sheila the bad news that my standing in the air force was seriously downgraded and that we were being assigned to Keesler AFB as the vice commander to a major general Shotts. Further, that I didn't have much choice because if I declined the assignment, it would result in mandatory retirement in seven days, which would be stupid because we hadn't done any planning for life after the air force. I suggested to Sheila that we take the assignment and plan to retire after serving the obligatory year of service following a PCS (permanent change of station). During that year, I would write a resume; we would make plans about what to do next considering what looked best for us and the children's education. She agreed; we had a transition plan to civilian life, and it only included the air force for another year.

With all the travel and time associated with the trip through the Pacific with General Jones and team, as well as the follow-on Social Actions temporary duty, the plan to earn an MBA at Auburn University fell by the wayside—another fifteen hours of MBA credit in the trash basket.

Based on the anticipation of an early assignment notification, I finished up all my papers associated with the Six-Man Group Charter. The paper on "Seasonal Effect on Human Behavior" was becoming very popular as all the human relations incidents occurred in the months predicted by the analysis embedded in the study—January, April/May, and August. Orders arrived, requiring that I proceed immediately to Keesler to replace the outgoing vice commander who was being reassigned. Apparently, Lieutenant General Shotts did not like being without a sidekick! Sheila and the children would stay behind so they could finish school, while I became a geographical bachelor in Biloxi, Mississippi. While I hated another separation, it could be a good thing. I could learn the job, spend a lot of time roaming the base at all hours, and spend time sitting in classrooms evaluating instruction and course material. I had the feeling that not much had changed at Keesler since I left in January 1955 for K-14 Air Base, Korea—twenty years earlier.

Lessons Learned

Always have the courage to do and stand up for what is right.

After being in a leadership position for a while, a person gets comfortable and stops seeing what is going on throughout the enterprise—get out and about! Getting out and talking to people in their comfort zone can be very revealing.

If an area of the enterprise is ignored, it will generally flounder, so get out and about!

Develop the instincts to discover problems. Know where to look and what to look at.

Commanders and leaders have the responsibility to look after their personnel 24/7, not just on a pleasant summer day when it's convenient!

There are always indicators of problems; find out what they are and monitor them at least weekly or monthly.

Opportunity is more often where you find it,
not where you want it or expect it!

Human nature is fairly constant over time; look at inspection reports
of other organizations with similar missions and personnel makeup.

CHAPTER 10

Keesler Technical Training Center

Orders to report immediately to Keesler AFB, Mississippi, came unexpectedly. Evidently, the previous vice commander, Col. Walter H. Baxter III, was reassigned in March 1975; and Maj. Gen. Bryan M. Shotts, center commander, wanted the position filled as soon as possible. It should be noted that Colonel Baxter III retired in August 1982 in the grade of major general. Colonel Baxter's wife elected to remain in their house at Keesler until their children finished the school year, so Sheila and the family stayed at Maxwell until the vice commander' house was vacated. Sheila and the children were getting tired of double moves and family separations. However, they also needed to finish the school year, so I kissed them all good-bye and drove southwest to Biloxi. We did get together over the Easter weekend and colored Easter eggs, somewhat of a family tradition. We had been married just over thirteen years and moved twelve times. In the nine years prior to marrying Sheila, I had moved twelve times, not counting Korea or Vietnam. While the navy uses the recruiting slogan, "Join the navy and see the world!" the air force certainly was keeping us on the go and covering a lot of geography in the process.

General Shotts (nicknamed "Let's Go Shotts") was a tall lean man with an outgoing nature. He made me feel welcome and encouraged me to offer my opinion on matters that came to the Command Section. The only real job for vice commander was to act as the KTTC inspector general and hear all complaints that came before him. I soon learned that no complaints came to that level. My own experience at Aviano told me that there were always problems. But when they didn't bubble up, it was because people didn't believe anything would be done to resolve their complaint or that there would be retribution against them for raising an issue. Something had to be done to open the pipeline so that military personnel assigned to Keesler had a viable grievance channel! General Shotts would not likely allow me to put out the mailboxes that worked so well at Aviano, so another means had to suffice. Perhaps getting out and about for several hours each day with the persona of Peter Faulk, the Hollywood detective (Columbo) that just kept asking questions, would open people up.

As noted earlier, I had been stationed at Keesler twice previously, in 1952-53 as an enlisted student radar technician, as an aviation cadet in the Electronic Warfare Officer course, and as a second lieutenant from July 1954 to January 1955. With that background, I was quite familiar with the training routine at the various tech schools. The KTTC was involved in three major training areas for both officer and enlisted personnel. These were administration, electronics, and intelligence collection. The base and training routines were very predictable in terms of student loading and the material presented in the classrooms. One could almost look five years ahead and be relatively certain of the tempo and educational content at Keesler. The only thing that would perturb these two elements would be an unexpected war like the Korean War in June 1951 and the Vietnam War, which started for me in the fall of 1961 but came into mainstream American consciousness in 1964. By the summer of 1975, the only thing on the horizon was the low-rate personnel drawdown following the end of the Vietnam War and the inevitable collapse of South Vietnam once the Congress shut off financial support to President Ky.

Without much else to do, I visited all of the various schools and sat through classroom sessions, met with the group commanders of the major school curriculums, and became familiar with their concerns. To my surprise, their greatest concern was the fact that General Jones, CSAF, and Lieutenant General Roberts, DCS/Personnel, had implemented a program to eliminate "dead time" in the training flow. This was for both enlisted and officer personnel going from their initial entrance training, OTS, ROTC, and Air Force Academy for officers and basic training for enlisted personnel until they started their follow-on training. In my experience as an airman, I had ninety days from the time I arrived at Keesler AFB until the actual start of technical training. During these ninety days, I pulled KP and performed other cleaning and maintenance details. As an officer, there was little delay in the flying training program until I arrived at Williams for F-86 Gunnery Training where I had about sixty days of nonproductive time—updating departure and approach manuals at Base Operations.

The reason for their concern over the new policy on dead time was the expected loss of "detail manpower" to cut the grass, paint the buildings, etc.—essentially to do all the things operational personnel did at operational bases. If they expected to be comforted by me in their concern that they might have to do some minimal manual labor—they were sorely mistaken. I reminded them that not only did operational officer and enlisted personnel prepare for combat, undergo ORIs, experience frequent deployments, work long hours and extended weeks, and stand alert 24/7, but they also maintained their facilities and the environment around them. I pointed out that their workweek was a fixed five days, and the workday for instructors was six hours. It was time they got off of their butts and joined the real air force. It was not what they wanted to hear. Eventually, the slack time from arrival at a training base to starting class was reduced to a maximum of three days. This was just about enough time to "sign in" at all the necessary places, get a base decal for a car or motorcycle, fill out the obligatory paperwork that comes with a new duty station, and find out where their classroom was located. In addition, fluff was trimmed out of a number of courses. As a result, the operational utilization of enlisted personnel on their first four-year enlistment was raised from about 75 percent to 85 percent, or a gain of about 146 days on average. This continued to improve over the next two decades.

From my previous assignments at Keesler, I remembered the many stories about airmen being given "knockout drops" at local bars and rolled for their money. Now that I had responsibility for the safety and well-being of all personnel at Keesler, it was imperative that I visit some of the trouble spots. I called the head of the OSI (Office of Special Investigation) and asked if he could give me the names of some of the current problem business establishments so I could get a feel for the off-base difficulties our young recruits might encounter. He said it wasn't safe for me to go alone but that he would accompany me on visits to the worst offenders. His last comment was to dress a little "scruffy." When the knock came and I opened the BOQ door, he took one look and said, "Colonel, not that scruffy!" He was wearing a sport coat with open collar; I had on cut-off jeans and an old shirt used for working around the house. After cleaning up from scruffy, we visited several places and had conversations with "hostesses," who were oversolicitous. I realized that owners had upgraded their venues but not their business model. When we were done, I asked the OSI chief if he could get the word out to the troublesome bars that the Keesler vice commander was very concerned about incidents at their establishments and would be making more undercover visits over time. It is doubtful the visits and warning had any effect, but the incident rate seemed to decline.

One of the good things about the vice commander's job at Keesler was the secretary I inherited. Claire was a middle-age woman, raised in the local area, who was a superb writer. For the first few weeks, she would type out the dictation that I gave her or the letters I had written in long hand. When finished, she would come in and most often say, "You really don't want to send this letter, do you?" When asked why, she would explain very politely why it was a very bad letter and then would offer her version of a proper letter that got the message across. Her letters were so well written and to the point, while being civil, that we immediately adopted a new approach.

I would call her in and hand her some correspondence and say, "Please provide me a response that does the following." In short order, she would provide a perfect reply. Seldom did I ever change a word. Claire taught me how to write properly and civilly, maybe even graciously on occasion.

The weeks passed quickly, and June arrived; it was time to drive to Maxwell AFB, Alabama, and pick up Sheila, our children, and dog, Samantha. Samantha was Denise's pet acquired when I first arrived at Maxwell. Samantha was a Brittany spaniel and would double as my bird dog during hunting season. The trip was short and uneventful. The only problem was there were two houses that we were offered to choose from. One was small but on the Back Bay and next to the commander's house. The other home was being vacated by the regional hospital commander. It was larger but on the other side of the base. Sheila liked the larger house, but when General Shotts opined that it would be nice if I lived next door so we could drive to the office together and discuss important issues in private—that sealed the deal. It proved to be a good choice but not because of the opportunity for issue resolution. In nine months, I don't believe we ever talked business, but rather because we bought a small sailboat, and Denise and Scott learned to sail. Scott also spent a lot of idle time fishing off of the dock catching croakers, a fish that resembled a bluegill. Perhaps the best feature of living on the Back Bay was the shrimp boats laden with fresh-caught shrimp that motored by on their way to seafood processing plants. They would sell us bait shrimp for one dollar per pound. These bait shrimp never saw a hook but tasted mighty good either freshly boiled or in a variety of delicious dishes that Sheila prepared.

General Shotts was born and raised in the Biloxi area and grew up with most of the local business leaders. He was a true Southern gentleman, and it appeared awkward for him to deal with the discrimination issues that found their way to the front office. When I brought them to his attention, he gave me carte blanche to resolve them. This gave me some important work to do. In this regard, I spent a lot of time with the Human Relations (HR) office and was their "come-to guy" when something came up that they couldn't handle at their level. The head of the Human Relations office was a young black captain with a charming wife. He introduced me to the president of the local NAACP chapter, a practicing dentist who had grown up in the area. He was a wise and thoughtful man who proved to be very helpful but always behind the scenes. One situation comes to mind where his advice proved most helpful. A black female nurse brought a complaint to the HR office that she had been discriminated against in one of the most popular local restaurants. It was fine dining establishment called Mary Mahoney's. The complaint was that the nurse was seated when she arrived at Mary Mahoney's but then sat there for over an hour without being offered a menu or waited on while others who were white that arrived after her were waited on by her waiter. After nearly two hours of waiting, she left. She claimed that she was appropriately dressed for the occasion. This was important because in the South during that era, you dressed for dinner. As a historical note, the restaurant was set in a red brick building where slaves were housed prior to being freed after the Civil War. Sheila and I had dined there many times and knew Mary, the owner. I asked the HR director if he would take his wife to the restaurant, at my expense, as a way of testing the environment. We agreed it should be on the same night of the week on which the alleged incident occurred. The report was favorable; the HR director and his wife were, in their view, treated no differently than any other of the clientele and had a very enjoyable evening. We thought that perhaps a single black woman might fare differently than a couple, so we found a young black woman that agreed to be a test case, again at my expense. The results were the same! The young woman experienced a very enjoyable evening with excellent service. The results were puzzling, so I spoke directly with the nurse who filed the complaint. She was convincing in her account of the alleged discrimination and was also an attractive young lady. Next, I called the president of the local NAACP chapter. He assured me that Mary Mahoney did not discriminate, was a personal friend of his, and that he and his wife had dined at her establishment many times without any hint of discrimination. He opined that the nurse's experience was likely the result of one waiter who knew it was against Mary's policies but saw an opportunity to vent his personal bigoted beliefs on the nurse.

He suggested that I tell the story to Mary and give her the opportunity to straighten out any discriminating members of her staff. Armed with the time and date of the alleged discrimination, I spoke with Mary. To her credit, Mary invited the lieutenant to dine at the restaurant as her guest. Case closed, and hurt feelings wiped away.

Students attending classes at Kessler tech schools were different in 1975 than they were in 1953. They were more mischievous and with somewhat less respect for authority. At about 0200 hours one morning, I received a call that there was a bomb threat against one of the female student dorms, and the building was being evacuated. Bingo, the thought immediately came to mind that some young male student in a nearby dorm thought it would be a great thing to get all the female students out on the grass in their "baby doll" pajamas, or perhaps less. I raced over to the dorm area, but it was too late. There were about three hundred scantily clothed young women shivering in the early morning air and about twice the number of young men from nearby dorms mingling with the women. I called for more security police (SPs) to help round up the women and get them back in their dormitory. The fire chief reported that they found no bombs in the building. I'm not sure that we got all the women back in the dorm, but I was absolutely certain that there would be another bomb threat the next evening.

I gathered all the firemen and SPs around me and told them I wanted a detail of SPs and fireman positioned, but hidden, near the dorms about midnight because there were going to be more bomb threats. Next, I told them that the women would be kept in the dorm with the firemen and SPs knocking on doors for suspicious items and only physically checking the common areas. Also they had to have female SPs to check the lavatory and shower areas. If there were no female SPs, then I would provide a detail of female NCOs they could brief on the appropriate clearing procedures.

The following two nights, there were bomb threats called in against the same female dorm. As briefed, the women were kept in their rooms. Not surprisingly, all the nearby men's dorms emptied out at the time the "bomb" was supposed to go off. No bombs were found. I half expected a fourth attempt, and we were prepared for it, but it didn't happen. These were simple problems compared to ORIs and night in-the-weather aerial refueling an F-4D from a KC-97.

General Shotts was TDY when the SP Operations Desk called at midnight to inform me that there was a man on one of the base water towers, armed with a rifle, and shooting into the base housing area. I donned a flight suit and headed for the water tower. When I arrived, a SP hidden in a group of trees briefed me over the base mobile radio system that the man appeared to be a drunk civilian who came over a nearby perimeter fence and climbed the ladder to the catwalk around the water tank. They reported that the man had fired several shots into the ground and did not appear to want to damage anything but rather to goad the SPs into shooting him, Suicide by police! Good thing the air force had mature, well-trained, and disciplined SPs, or this guy would have been dead because at least three SPs had him in their gun sights. I was also hidden in the trees but, after a few minutes, decided to move into the open and try reasoning with the man. A real challenge because he was apparently very drunk.

Once in the open and bathed in the red glow coming from the light on top of the water tank, I introduced myself as Pete and asked if there was anything I could do for him. He replied, "I was in the Sea Breeze Bar with my girl when she up and left with another guy. Can you find her for me?" I told him we would try and pretended to speak into the handheld radio ("brick"). The SPs said they were in touch with the Biloxi Police and would have them check out the Sea Breeze Bar. Meanwhile, I was having a conversation with our "tower guy," trying to coax him down ostensibly so he could help us try and find his girl. After a few minutes, he asked, "Who the hell are you?"

I said, "I'm Pete, remember!"

He replied, "I know you're Pete, but who the hell are you?"

I figured this was no time to be cute, so I said, "I'm Colonel Pete, the Keesler vice commander, and I can help you locate your girlfriend if you'll come down the ladder!"

To that, he said, "I hate colonels!" A shot rang out, and a bullet hit about fifty feet from where I was standing.

I said, "No need to shoot. We're friends, and I can help you!" Another shot, only this time, the impact was a little closer. "Well, if that's the way you feel, I'll leave," and I walked back into the shadows and crouched behind the staff car.

With that, the SP NCO that had been hidden and had briefed me on the situation when I arrived on scene walked into the red glow and said, "I'm glad you got rid of that son of a bitch. He's a real pain in the ass." In ten minutes, the NCO talked the guy off of the water tower and to the fence where he helped him crawl back over and into the arms of the waiting Biloxi Police. The SP NCO was awarded a Commendation Medal for his cool headedness and quick thinking. He's one of the very few people that called me a SOB and pain in the ass to my face, and I thought it was cleaver and appropriate; moreover, he was decorated for it.

Earlier, I mentioned that Colonel Rogers, 36th TFW commander, warned me to never let a woman in my office unless my secretary could see me or have her come into the office. Good advice, and I was about to find out why! Claire buzzed on the intercom that there was a woman who wanted to see me about her husband. "OK, send her in" was the response. In came a rather attractive woman dressed only in a bikini, followed closely by Claire, holding a newspaper. Claire sat down, pretending to read the paper but was really interested in the proceedings. The woman asserted that her husband, now stationed in Europe, wasn't answering her calls or letters and wanted me to get him on the phone for her. I patiently explained that I wasn't her husband's commander, but even if I was, I had no authority in domestic matters unless they lived in base quarters. It got nasty, and I got the feeling she was going to take off some of her rather skimpy clothing and then accuse me of molesting her. I asked Claire if she would escort the woman out and buzzed the executive officer for assistance. Fortunately, she went loudly but without assistance. Thank you, Colonel Rogers, for your good advice!

Sheila served as an advisor to the Keesler Officers' Wives' Club (OWC), and she sometimes told me about issues brought up by the membership that provided some insight on officer morale in general. One such story, however, had some serious overtones. Sheila said the OWC tabled a vote on a membership application because she asked them to allow me to comment on the issue at hand. A male spouse of a female officer applied for OWC membership. The OWC president and board, after a brief discussion, mostly centered on the title "Officers' Wives' Club" decided to vote down the application. I asked Sheila if I could speak to the OWC Board, as the issue was much larger than they thought. I pointed out to Sheila that federal law prohibited discrimination based on race, ethnicity, religion, gender, and age. And while the OWC was not a federal organization, it did meet at the officers' club located on a US government installation, therefore denying membership could lead to the OWC being forced to meet off base if the applicant decided to push the issue. I also pointed out it could get messy and embarrassing for the OWC. I discussed the issue with General Shotts, and he OK'd my meeting with the OWC Board and outlining the issues to them.

Sheila arranged the meeting with the OWC president and board, and I explained the alternatives. Allow the male spouse to join, and there were no issues. Deny the male spouse membership, and nothing might come of it. On the other hand, the applicant may file suit on the basis of Title IV of the 1964 Civil Rights Act. If the later happened, the OWC would be forced to hold their meetings and functions off base at a commercial establishment. Then too, if there was adverse publicity surrounding their discrimination, it might be hard to find a commercial enterprise that would host their activities. After I departed the meeting, the OWC voted to accept the male spouse's application for membership, and over time, they were glad they did for a whole host of reasons. For example, the male member did all the high wire and ladder work necessary to appropriately decorate the officers' club for the various balls and functions the OWC sponsored. He presented demonstrations on self-defense, how to perform simple maintenance on cars when husbands were on temporary duty away from Keesler, and other related subjects. He turned out to be their go-to guy for a lot of things husbands failed to tell them.

It was announced that General Shotts was selected for promotion to lieutenant general and assigned to command Fifteenth Air Force, Strategic Air Command at March Air Force Base. He needed to be replaced, and a change of command was scheduled for August 1, 1975. The incoming commander and his wife arrived a day early to participate in a Gulf Coast—wide reception for the incoming commander. General Jones CSAF was there for the reception and to officiate at the change of command the following day. Normally, the next level commander conducts a change of command. For Keesler Technical Training Center, this would be Lt. Gen. George McKee, commander, Air Training Command located at Randolph AFB, Texas, near San Antonio. On the other hand, General Jones may have had a close relationship with General Shotts from their days in SAC and wanted to officiate.

Two things stood out about the new commander and his wife. First, the incoming commander was very hard of hearing and, in a social setting, often didn't know he was being addressed, which made him appear very aloof and distant. His wife experienced a near-death episode as the result of an allergy to animal dandruff. As a precaution, she spent her first night at Keesler in a base hospital suite because no one in the Housing Office could guarantee that pets had not been in the distinguished visitor quarters, and no one wanted to take a risk that could threaten her life. Plans were being made to completely renovate the commander's quarters. Something must have happened at the evening reception that caused the air force to revise its plans. The following day, I offered to assist the incoming commander in any way he might find useful in the transition. His response was a terse, "That won't be necessary."

That afternoon, there was a receiving line with General Jones, General Shotts, and the incoming commander. All the guests went through the line. Subsequently, it was announced that there was a change in plans: the major general designated for command of Keesler was sorely needed elsewhere, and Maj. Gen. Skip Scott and his wife Sally were inbound for the change of command and would arrive in two hours. When Skip and Sally arrived, there was a change of command between Generals Shotts and Scott and a second receiving line. It was a strange experience with a great outcome. General Scott was a superb hands-on commander.

General Scott's version of the events described above is repeated below to complete the story. On the morning of the change of command at Keesler (three-hour time difference), Skip and Sally were driving from McClellan AFB, California, where he was stationed, to the Bay area to attend a change of command of a friend and colleague. They were stopped by a California State Highway patrolman and told to return immediately to McClellan AFB where a plane would be waiting for them. At McClellan, Skip was informed that he had been selected to command the Keesler Technical Training Center and that a T-39 aircraft was standing by to fly him there as soon as he and his wife had packed appropriate clothing. When they deplaned at Keesler, they were immediately escorted to the officers' club for the reception and change of command.

General Scott was a pleasure to work for, and I learned a great deal about leadership and courage from him. One event stands out in my mind: There was a formal dining out scheduled in honor of all the technical schools under the center. It was an annual affair. At the head table were seated the commander, vice commander, mayor of Biloxi, and two other local dignitaries, and all of our wives. Extending out perpendicular from the head table were long tables, one for each of the technical disciplines taught at Keesler. Next to the head table were seated the school group commanders and a distinguished guest from the community, such as the Chamber of Commerce president, bank presidents, etc. Staff and instructors from the respective school filled the remainder of each long table. It was a formal yet congenial evening, and it appeared that most military members and guests had a good time. For some, it was the first time they had an opportunity to hear General Scott talk about the "state of Keesler" and the way ahead.

As we were leaving the officers' club, the wife of the Chamber president caught up with General Scott and Sally, who were just ahead of me. I heard her complaining loudly that she had been seated next to a black officer and his wife, stating she would never set foot on Keesler again unless she could be assured she would never be embarrassed like that in the future. General Scott turned to her and in a calm but stern voice said, "I will solve your problem. You will never again be invited to or welcome on Keesler Air Force Base. We do not condone or tolerate racism!" Then he turned on his heel and left the officers' club. Problem solved, and I'm sure the word got out to the community at large. Further, I don't ever recall seeing the Biloxi Chamber president on the base for the remainder of my assignment there.

On September 1, 1975, General Roberts received his fourth star and took the helm of the Air Training Command (ATC) at Randolph AFB, Texas. His promotion to full general broke the long-standing tradition that a three-star general would command ATC. He was now General Scott's boss and the man who sent me to Keesler. Commanders routinely visit the bases under their command; as a result, I got to see and speak with General Roberts occasionally. He was always friendly and brought up many of the things we did together while I was on the Six-Man Group, such as the trip across the Pacific with General Jones. It was easy to like General Roberts because of his personality and ever-present good humor. It was easy to respect him because he was one of the top fighter pilots in the 1950s and had the trophies to prove it. Still I regarded him as the man who indicated it was time for me to retire, and the date when I could put in my papers was only nine months out.

General Scott was somewhat of a do-it-yourself kind of guy, as was I. One Saturday, I saw him working on the family car and walked over to see if I could help. I had a wide range of tools plus timing light, a cylinder pressure gauge, and a unique clear glass body spark plug that allowed you to see the flame color in the cylinder when the engine was running. It was designed for tuning a carburetor and worked like a miracle. The general had a large battery powered radio next to his car and was listening to the Air Force Academy vs. Notre Dame Football game. The general's oldest son graduated from West Point Military Academy, and he had two sons attending the Air Force Academy, both on the football team. The general also graduated from West Point and was a running back for the Black Knights on the Hudson. The Air Force was winning, and the score at halftime was 31-10, in favor of the Air Force. It appeared to be a sure thing the Falcons would win with that kind of lead and momentum. At the start of the second half, Notre Dame put in their freshman quarterback, an unknown by the name of Joe Montana. If you're not familiar with that name, you know and care nothing about football. The final score was 34-31, with Notre Dame defeating the Falcons. The general's car was repaired, but there was no fix for his disappointment on the game's outcome.

Lieutenant General Hartinger, now commander Ninth Air Force, was coming to visit the Air Borne Command Control and

Communication (ABCCC) C-130 Squadron based at Keesler. I was selected to pick him up at Gulfport, a small town located about fifteen miles to the west. Gen. Jim Hartinger was his usual self, quite loquacious about the things he was doing at Ninth Air Force located at Shaw AFB, and that he planned to bring Col. Bob Reed (Six-Man Group) in to command the 354th Tactical Fighter Wing (TFW) at Myrtle Beach Air Force Base, Georgia. One thing he said struck me as somewhat backward looking for him and meant as advice for me: "When you're number two, you don't say much, do you?" His comment somewhat explained how he could be so outgoing and vocal in his own right and be absolutely silent unless asked to comment in the presence of Lt. Gen. Felix M. Rogers, Air University commander when Jim Hartinger was his vice. I think he intended the remark as friendly advice or perhaps a warning to a colonel as the vice commander under a major general. It only took a little self-reflection to realize that I had been a little pushy with my opinions, and it would be wise to back off. There were some personality dynamics at work as well. General Shotts had been in command for two or three years before I came on board. He was very comfortable in his position and with the local community. As a result, he had given me free rein in a number of areas. On the other hand, General Scott was just taking control and needed to be convinced that I was a team player and not a loose cannon with a personal agenda.

There were storms on the horizon—real storms called hurricanes that visited the Gulf of Mexico every summer and fall from June to November. We had lived at Fort Walton Beach in the Florida Panhandle for five years and never had been threatened by a hurricane; hence, Sheila was unfamiliar with the potential fury of these storms and the devastation the accompanying storm surge can have on buildings in low-lying areas near beaches. In this regard, the highest point on KAFB was only twelve feet above sea level. There was a Defense Meteorological Satellite Program (DMSP) downlink van at Keesler, so I visited the site and got the latest fix on the hurricane meandering around out in the gulf. According to the satellite picture, the path the hurricane was on looked like it was heading directly for Biloxi. The Hurricane Hunter C-130 Squadron was also based at Keesler, and their "over the eye" collections provided the same indication. The storm did not have the really low pressures of a "killer" storm, but it was packing a wallop. General Scott was at San Antonio for a conference, so it was my responsibility to prepare the base and make sure all the students and permanent party personnel were safe. We put all the students in windowless concrete block buildings that served as their schoolhouses for the night or until the storm passed and the base was out of danger. The local sheriff and the mayor of Biloxi ordered evacuation of all personnel living in low-lying areas, which included the base, Biloxi, and nearly the entire county. After putting plywood over the windows in our base house, I helped Sheila load the car for evacuation, recommending she go as far as Jackson, Mississippi, and spend the night in a motel there.

Then I went to the office and made sure that all but essential personnel were directed to go home to protect their property and care for their families. Security police made sure that all on-base personnel were in shelters or had evacuated and then took up strategic positions for what might come. My office became my command center as I tracked the storm from the base weather station and local TV. It was about 1800 hours when it became apparent that the storm was tracking more to the east than directly at Biloxi. The counterclockwise rotation of a hurricane puts the brunt of the storm surge and the highest winds on the east or northeast side of the storm, so it appeared Biloxi and Keesler would not get the full force of the storm, but Mobile, Alabama, and Pensacola, Florida, would be pounded. Shortly after that news, Sheila called from our house, saying that she had been on the road for several hours but had not made any northerly progress because the road was jammed with evacuees. Because she was only a few miles out of town, she decided it was safer to ride out the storm with me instead of in the car stuck in traffic. By the time she drove from the house to the headquarters building, the winds were blowing 50 mph, and the rain coming down in sheets. The winds may have gone up as high as 60 mph as the storm passed over Mobile, Alabama. Keesler came through largely unscathed, and life, for the most part, returned to normal the next day.

As mentioned in the earlier write-up on Keesler, enlisted students marched to and from school. The classroom hours were 0600 to 1200 hours, 1200 to 1800 hours, and, if necessary to meet operational unit needs, from 1800 to 2400 hours. The formations of students starting class at 1200 hours and those returning from class at 1200 hours were timed so the incoming class passed in review just a few minutes before the outgoing class. This allowed the general, vice commander, or a group commander to take the pass in review and see all of the students or at least two-thirds of the student on a daily basis. On occasion, when the general was tied up, I had the opportunity to take his place on the reviewing stand and return the salute of the enlisted person acting as the formation commander. I had been one of the troops in at least 150 formations when I was an electronic and radar technician student. I always considered it an honor to take the review when the general was away or tied up. Basic training, where enlisted personnel are trained to march, among other things, was cut from twelve weeks to nine weeks, and finally to six weeks to increase the time enlisted personnel spent being productive in operation units. As a result, in my opinion, they didn't march nearly as well as we did twenty years earlier. I could be biased in this assessment.

The assignment at Keesler provided for a lot of good family time even though the house was so small that my predecessor had converted the two-car garage into a family room. The converted garage and kitchen is where we spent most of our time. We enjoyed the main gulf beach and our private beach on the Back Bay, sailing on the Back Bay and getting to spend every night and weekend at home. The local cuisine was also excellent. Denise had many friends from the neighborhood and school, and Scott was thick with Buddy Martin, the son of Colonel Martin, who lived next door. I think Buddy was the living proof that most American boys wanted to live the life of Huckleberry Finn. Buddy was an adventurer and managed to include our Scott in most of his nefarious schemes. This included building a raft of driftwood and other wooden scraps and attempting to cross the Back Bay a distance of more than a half mile. Fortunately, the raft came apart before they went fifty feet from shore, and Buddy's mother heard their screams that broke out as soon as they became immersed in the cold water.

Shortly after the Christmas holidays, General Roberts called to tell me that I was on the brigadier general promotion list and offered his congratulations. As I would learn later, the commander of a major command like SAC, TAC or ATC submits to the chief a list of colonels in his/her command that they strongly believe should be promoted. General Roberts must have put my name on that list; otherwise, I would not have been promoted below the zone to BG the first time eligible. I also later learned that the BG promotion board chaired by a four-star general and made up of major generals, while aware of these names, are not obligated to promote anyone on these four-star lists but rather promote based on the merit reflected in the individual officer's records. Evidently, the work on the Air Staff, at Bitburg, and Aviano was well documented in performance reports. The call and the promotion were highly unexpected; nevertheless, I wasn't so giddy or in disbelief that I didn't remember to thank General Roberts for his confidence and support.

When I told Sheila the "good" news, it didn't seem that she was nearly as excited as expected. Clearly, she played a large part in my success as a wonderful and gracious hostess to many official gatherings and of course doing the lion's share of raising our three children. She carried an enormous additional burden with our youngest being severely handicapped. Perhaps she was looking forward to my retirement and living a more normal life—something like we were enjoying at Keesler with reasonable workdays and most weekends free. Regardless, I knew she would always be there to support me. She was a remarkable and wonderful wife and still is to this day.

Weeks passed while I wondered what future assignment was in store for me as a newly promoted brigadier general. I was hoping for the job of division commander at one of the two-wing Tactical Air Command Bases. Luke Air Force Base near Phoenix, Arizona, was one of them. This would be perfect for Sheila, as her parents and brother would only fifty miles away in Mesa, Arizona, a few miles east of Phoenix—close enough to visit on weekends or holidays but far enough away that it wouldn't be a distraction. However, the odds were that a staff job in the Pentagon or at one of the Air Force major commands like TAC or USAFE, or a Joint Headquarters was in the wind.

The next call from General Roberts was to inform me that my next job was to be the initial "squadron commander" of the Airborne Warning and Control Wing (AWAC) equipped with E-3A aircraft. I was stunned—squadron commander? I thought I had passed that level years ago; besides, I was a fighter pilot, not a tanker or airlift pilot, and the E-3A was built around the Boeing 707-320 commercial airliner, one of the largest long-range aircraft until the B-747 entered service. I halfheartedly thanked General Roberts for the "good news" and turned to ponder this disheartening and unexpected turn. Further, I would be working directly for General Dixon, and my two brief encounters with him ended on sour or false notes. After a few minutes of remorse, I returned General Roberts's call and thanked him profusely for this "wonderful and challenging" assignment and promised to not let him down. I told him that I was somewhat taken aback because I was expecting some stuffy staff position.

Claire's buzzing on the intercom broke into my thoughts, telling me General Dixon was on the line. Normally, this meant that the general's secretary was on the phone, waiting for the lower-ranking person to pick up before the senior officer picked up on his or her end. I picked up the handset and said, "Pete here."

The voice on the other end bellowed, "This is Bob Dixon, I know who you are. I placed the call!"

My response was timid: "Yes, sir!"

General Dixon then said, "I'm calling to welcome you to TAC and AWACS. Do you know why I hired you?"

My response was "No, sir, I don't have the faintest idea."

General Dixon said, "Neither do I!" and he hung up. General Dixon was in rare form and certainly let me know that he was the boss and would be looking over my shoulder. It was going to be an interesting assignment.

Shortly after the phone call with General Dixon, orders came, and we were on the road again. Housing was not yet available at Tinker, AFB, Oklahoma, so Sheila and the children spent time with her family in Mesa, Arizona, while I drove northeast to Oklahoma City and Tinker AFB, where an initial cadre of Airborne Warning and Control (AWAC) personnel was forming.

Lessons Learned

Vice commanders or the number-two person in any endeavor don't say much! Rather they are like a duck on water in a windstorm, clam to the observer, but paddling like hell to keep their boss well informed on all issues!

Find out what your boss is uncomfortable with, or out of touch with, and cover those areas like a blanket!

Have the courage to do what is right

Stamp out discrimination whenever and wherever it appears in your enterprise!

Always, always go where the action is!

Always thoroughly investigate reports of discrimination, and document the results.

Walkabout and hands-on leadership always builds morale and carries the day!

When the situation permits, make sure the time you spend with your family is quality time!

Maj. Gen. Skip Scott pinning the Legion of
Merit & MSM medals on Col. Pete

Col. Pete eating in the Mess Hall with enlisted personnel

Maj. Gen. Skip Scott & Sheila pinning faux stars on Col. Pete after his selection for promotion to Brig. Gen.

CHAPTER 11

AWACS and the E-3A

Tinker AFB, Oklahoma, just outside Midwest City was like no other base I'd ever been stationed at. It was a large sprawling complex dedicated to logistic support of a number of air force operational aircraft, aircraft jet engines, and a plethora of supporting components. One of the aircraft supported was the KC-135, an airframe similar to the Boeing 707-320B the E-3A was built around. Tinker AFB, also known as the Oklahoma City Air Material Area (OCAMA), also performed depot level repair on the TF-33 engine that powered the E-3A, four on each aircraft. In keeping with this mission, OCAMA was led by Maj. Gen. Carl G. Schneider and his deputy, Brig. Gen. Leighton R. Palmerton. OCAMA along with four other depots were directly subordinate to the Air Force Logistics Command located at Wright-Patterson AFB, near Dayton, Ohio. Brigadier General Leighton Palmerton and I were on the same promotion list, so he was in his first general officer assignment, just as I was. A mixed military and civilian staff of colonels and senior executive service civilians supported the generals. The workforce consisted of more than twenty thousand civilian craftsmen and supply experts who did the repair and made sure the repaired parts were catalogued and warehoused or shipped immediately to units in need of the parts. Major overhauls were also performed at the depot. It was amazing to see KC-135 and B-52 aircraft torn down to their skeletons to check for corrosion and cracked structural members. The E-3A was the first active duty operational unit located at Tinker. This, in my view, would likely require some changes to the day-to-day operations and attitudes of a longtime depot operation. An

F-105 Air Force Reserve Unit was located on the far side of the base. This unit was under Twelfth Air Force and TAC and the commander, Brig. Gen. Roger P. Scheer, was someone I could relate to. In a few years, he would be promoted to major general and assigned as commander of all air force reserve forces from November 1986 through October 1990.

Air force personnel were already populating the 552nd AWAC Wing with key personnel, and several were on hand to greet me when I reported in. Some of them that I recall forty-four years later are

Col. Dave Underwood, 552nd provisional commander;
Col. Don Sperry, designated as the 552nd vice wing commander;
Col. Jerry Mack, designated as the 552nd director of operations;
Col. Pat Hays, designated as the 552nd director of logistics;
Lt. Col. John R. Farrington, a.k.a. "Jack," designated commander of the 552nd Flying Training Squadron;
Lt. Col. "Mack" McGlaughlin, designated director of resources; and
Lt. Col. Wally Brug, designated commander of the 963rd AWAC Squadron.

There was also a host of senior noncommissioned officers in maintenance, flight engineers, and radar surveillance technicians, many of whom were on the E-3A test team at Boeing. The latter meant they were highly experienced on the Boeing 707-320B and all the exotic systems that made it an E-3A. Even though there were dozens of them, they were a very small cadre compared to the thousands of newcomers that would soon populate the 552nd Wing.

Shortly after my arrival, it became apparent that Col. Don Sperry, a very bright and talented individual, was initially slated to be the wing commander, and I was a last-minute revision to the original plan. If this was true, perhaps it was because I had demonstrated the skills and instincts to be a successful wing commander, and also had a strong radar and avionics background both helpful to build an AWACS wing from the ground up and bring it to operational status. No matter how or why I was given the job, it was my responsibility, and there was no time to waste in getting started and setting goals.

Neither the Systems Command developing the E-3A nor the Tactical Air Command who would operate it at home and abroad in peace and in war had developed a Program Evaluation Review Technique, or "PERT" Plan, for the fielding the system. There were no metrics or planning tools for measuring how well the wing was progressing toward its scheduled initial operational capability (IOC) that was to occur shortly after the third E-3A was delivered to the wing. There will be more discussion about IOC demonstration and achievement later.

It was obvious that a PERT plan was needed, and there was no one in the initial cadre that had the grasp of the enterprise or the ability to draft such a plan. I would have to do it—and the sooner, the better. Housing was not yet available at Tinker for the family, so Sheila elected to take our children to visit her parents in Idaho rather than struggle with temporary quarters and two moves. Without the family, I had plenty of time to lay out a PERT based on planned E-3A deliveries. Clearly, the number of operational E-3As on the ramp dictated the number of flight crews and mission crews, the number of trained and certified maintenance personnel, the number of trained software personnel, the tempo of training, and the support equipment and facilities. While it was easy to fall into the trap that the number of aircraft was the sole driver, we learned quickly that the support equipment, known as Aerospace Ground Equipment, or "AGE," in that era was also a significant driver of aircraft in-commission rates. The AGE that supported the E-3A was new, different, complex, and often cranky.

Memorial Day weekend was the ideal time to work on the PERT. I ordered a two-hundred-foot roll of four-foot-wide graph paper and some drafting tools and templates for creating the 552nd/E-3A PERT covering the period from June 1, 1976, until May 31, 1978. This would encompass the arrival of the third E-3A and IOC in the spring of 1978, a period of 730 days. With each one-inch square of the graph paper representing one calendar day, the PERT chart would be sixty-one feet long and occupy two walls of the wing conference room. There were four subcritical paths laid out on the graph paper. There was a subcritical path for flight crew training, one for mission crew training, one for maintenance personnel training, and one for E-3A Software System buildup and their personnel training. Personnel arrival and specific equipment delivery were covered in their respective paths. The critical path for the wing was developed as a result of the four subcritical paths. Circles indicated routine events and accomplishments, whereas critical events were denoted by triangles. Colored dots were used to indicate success or failure. If an event was achieved on time, a green dot was located next to the circle or triangle. If the day passed without achieving the event but there was a work-around path, a yellow dot was located next to the event circle or triangle. If there were no work-arounds, a red dot would be placed on the chart. Finally, when the event or activity was finally completed, a green dot would be used to *partially* cover the yellow or red dot with the appropriate date. This method of color-coding success and/or failure gave the viewer an immediate picture of where problems were building and where the path ahead appeared less risky.

By the end of the Memorial three-day weekend, I had filled in most of the known scheduled events and laid out a skeleton PERT for all four subcritical paths based on the simple logic of how long it took to train and certify a flight crew, mission crew, and maintenance personnel. On the following workdays, each of the deputy commanders responsible for operations, maintenance, and software validated or corrected my initial drafting. The deputy commander for resources filled in all the expected completion dates for facilities, and the personnel officer provided the expected schedule for the arrival of officers and enlisted personnel.

When the PERT was completed, it was hung in the conference room where all wing staff meetings were held. A red vertical rod, indicating the current calendar date, moved on a track above the PERT chart. During staff meetings the appropriate staff member briefed the status of items to be achieved on the date, and colored dots were affixed to the chart based on the status. Red and yellow dots were briefed weekly thereafter until the event or activity turned green. The homemade PERT turned out to be an effective and useful management tool, as well as an efficient way to brief distinguished visitors on the wing's progress to IOC.

Most of the newly assigned 552nd Wing personnel were transfers from the two EC-121 "Warning Star" organizations, the 551st and 552nd AEW&C Wings; AEW&C stands for Airborne Early Warning and Control. Many had been flying barrier patrols over the Atlantic and Pacific Oceans for years in those four-engine Constellation aircraft. Many had also flown in Project "College Eye" during the later years of the Vietnam War. The aircraft and crews were based in Korat RTAFB, Thailand; however, their missions were flown over the South China Sea approximately twenty-five nautical miles east of Haiphong, NVN. The aircrews and mission crews loved the venerable old EC-121, were dedicated to the mission, and were looking forward to a roomier modern aircraft with a significantly upgraded radar, communications, and computer suite. They didn't require any motivation. All I had to do was provide resources and a little guidance and then get out of their way. They were wonderful to work with and were key to our collective success. General Dixon visited the wing four times while I was in command. Two were perfunctory and therefore easy; the other two, much more challenging. The first visit coincided with the formal activation of the 552nd Wing on July 1, 1976, which fortuitously coincided with my promotion to brigadier general, both with refreshments and short speeches. General Dixon presided over both events and was charming, instead of his usual probing self. With Sheila and the children staying with her parents in Idaho, she missed the pinning and playing the traditional role of a military wife in pinning rank on one shoulder, with the officiating officer pinning the other. Mrs. Carl Schneider, wife of the Oklahoma City Air Material Area (OCAMA) commander, a charming lady, filled in for Sheila.

General Dixon seemed impressed with the PERT chart and asked questions about the critical path. He was particularly interested in the work-arounds associated with the yellow dots and the current status of the fixes proposed to turn the red dots to green or yellow. After some detailed discussion about the PERT chart and the 552nd Wing buildup, General Dixon looked at me and said, "I'm thinking of a seven-letter word starting with S—what is it?" I put my hands behind my back and started thinking of words that started with S. "Safety" came immediately to mind, but that was only six letters. "Screw up" was seven letters, but it was two words. General Dixon's aide was sitting behind him and was mouthing a word, but I couldn't lip-read it.

I finally said, "General Dixon, I give up. I can't think of a relevant seven-letter word starting with S."

He responded with "'Sponsor'—what is your sponsorship program for incoming personnel?" With that mystery behind us, I called for backup chart two hundred, and up came the sponsorship briefing. About twenty-five charts into that briefing, General Dixon said, "That's enough, take me to my aircraft!" I took him to his aircraft and rendered honors as he taxied away from the ramp. His parting words were "So far so good. Don't screw it up!"

General Dixon was a certified American hero, a man to be admired and feared. After earning a degree in Literature at Dartmouth College in June 1941, he couldn't wait for America to get into the war raging in Europe, so he went to Canada and enlisted in the Royal Canadian Air Force (RCAF). There he earned his pilot wings in November 1942 and then went on to the RCAF Astro Navigation School and was awarded navigator wings. Upon completion of flying training, he was transferred to Scotland, where he checked out in the Spitfire. As soon as he was current in the Spitfire, Pilot Officer Robert Dixon was assigned to the 541st Royal Air Force (RAF) Reconnaissance Squadron. In 1943, after the United States entered WW II, he was transferred to the Army Air Forces, Seventh Photographic Group, Eighth Air Force. In 1944, Major Dixon assumed command of the Fourteenth Photographic Reconnaissance Squadron assigned Mark XI Spitfires, P-38s, and

P-51s. His unit flew recce missions all the way to Berlin in support of operations in Europe. He was shot down on his sixty-fifth mission while flying a recce mission of the Merseburg, Germany, oil refineries. He was captured and interned as a POW until freed by Allied forces in May 1945. Perhaps his intolerance of mediocre performance came from his internment as a POW.

The next nine months were full of challenges and frustrations. Much of the AGE support equipment was new to the air force and designed just for the E-3A. It was complicated and hard to maintain. We calculated that about 50 percent more was needed than programmed. Moreover, at least one of each peculiar item was required to support a deployment of one or two E-3As. Lead times for these items was way into the future, so we had to do a better job of maintaining them. The three items that come to mind are:

> the glycol cooling unit that was required to cool the E-3A radar when maintenance procedures required the radar to be running on the ground,

> a much more powerful electrical ground power unit to power up all aircraft systems on the ground, and

> a ground air conditioner to cool the electronics when troubleshooting systems

The wing was equipped with two unique simulators, one for training the flight crews and the other for training the mission crews. The flight simulator was state of the art for the mid-1970s. The cockpit had six degrees freedom of motion and a terrain model board for takeoff and landing and other traffic pattern work. It also incorporated an air-refueling module that was very realistic. With these two simulators and mission software created by the in-house software team, ground training proceeded at a pace in keeping with our projected needs.

The strongest and most capable leader in the wing was Col. Jerry Mack, Wing DO, who, in an earlier assignment with EC-121s (the first 552nd Wing) while supporting combat operations in Vietnam, conceived and wrote the draft Operational Requirements Document (ORD) for the E-3A. He was assigned to the Air Defense Command (ADC) to continue refining the ORD and maintain support for the E-3A in ADC. However, an air force reorganization would shortly transfer ADC radar and interceptor responsibilities from ADC to TAC, resulting in the

E-3A acquisition and mission also transferring to TAC. Colonel Mack also spent two or more years on the E-3A test team at the Boeing facility near Seattle, Washington, and was qualified as an E-3A instructor pilot and E-3A mission commander. He played a key role in building the wing and a significant player in the ultimate success of the E-3A and the 552nd Wing.

Under Colonel Mack, there were two other officers that were instrumental in getting the wing going in the right direction and ultimately off the ground and operational. These were Lt. Col. Jack Farrington, commander of the AWACS Training Squadron, and Lt. Col. Wally Brug, commander of the first operational E-3A Squadron, the 963rd. Colonel Farrington was tireless in his efforts to keep all the training programs on a pace that would have trained crews ready to fly when the first E-3A arrived. He also demonstrated excellent judgment of talent and character when picking the instructor cadre and forming the standardization and evaluation team. On the other hand, the task of forming and leading the first E-3A Squadron was a daunting task. I worked closely with Jerry Mack and Wally Brug in formulating the crew composition, crew substitution rules, and how the squadron was organized. The two choices for the latter were organized around the functional activities of the crew force or around the mission. I felt strongly about the latter. It took a lot of time, energy, and logic to forge a mission orientation—but I was convinced it was right and the only way to ensure mission success.

A functional arrangement would have resulted in each discipline being headed by a wing chief of the function (e.g., chief pilot, chief navigator, chief flight engineer). A chief mission commander, a chief senior director, a chief weapons controller, a chief radar technician, and three other chiefs of technical career fields would represent the mission crew. These functional chiefs would write the Officer Efficiency Reports and Airman Proficiency Reports, respectively, and be responsible for each respective career field development. In the functional arrangement, there would be no one officer or NCO on any given crew with clout over the members of the crew. Crew discipline and poor performance in flight would be subject to the review and opinion of the functional chief on the ground-—not exactly a good way to go to war or an approach that General LeMay would approve of.

In a mission orientation model, the aircraft commander would write the OERs of the flight crew and would have an input on the mission crew commander's OER. The mission crew commander would write the OERs and APRs of all other twelve personnel on the mission crew. The squadron commander would write mission crew commander's OERs. Flight crews would be formed crews with only one position substitution on any given flight. Mission crews would also be formed crews with only two position substitutions allowed on any given flight. Teamwork is critical to mission success in both the cockpit and in the back end. Teamwork is the result of practice and working together as a team. Weaknesses of team members are recognized and compensated by others on the team and then trained out. Teamwork at the level required in combat and during an aircraft emergency is not possible with the sandlot mentality of a "pickup" team. The enlisted crew force did not accept the crew concept when it was put forth, nor ever, for that matter. They saw this as an encroachment on their opportunity to have many personnel under their supervision and therefore a better chance for promotion. It took weeks of meetings with senior and chief master sergeants, lots of one-on-one discussion, and finally a declaration that the subject was closed and the mission concept would stand. This was accompanied with the adoption of a chief over each career field with responsibilities for keeping the career field informed of technical modifications to their equipment, mission crew procedural changes, Weighted Airman Promotion System (WAPS) testing, and career field progression. The latter was intended primarily for lower-grade airmen new to the career field.

In the late fall of 1976, an incident in the Headquarters Squadron collocated with the Command Section remains indelible in my mind's eye. The wing was scheduled to receive a congressional delegation to review progress toward operational status. During the night, a snowstorm passed through the area and deposited nearly a foot of snow on the streets and sidewalks that led to the 552nd Headquarters Building. As I was going over the presentation for our visitors, loud voices erupted just outside the door to my office. The wing senior enlisted advisor (chief master sergeant) and headquarters first sergeant (M.Sgt. Paul Boyden) were standing nose to nose, somewhat upset with each other. Nearby, a tall slender black airman second class (two stripes) orderly room clerk was standing at attention. I learned that the chief had ordered the airman to shovel the snow. The airman had reported for duty in his class A uniform as appropriate to support the scheduled DV visit. The airman responded positively to the order to shovel the walk but requested permission to return to his barracks and change into fatigues and boots for the detail. The chief took this as a rejection of his order and threatened the airman with an Article 15. At this point, the first sergeant came to the defense of the airman. That's when I appeared on the scene. The visit was still a couple of hours in the future, and the airman's request to change uniforms seemed reasonable. With that, I got the chief aside and told him to back off, and everything worked out fine with the walks being cleaned prior to the DV's arrival. Subsequently, I learned that the senior enlisted advisor started working behind my back, telling the wing NCOs that they could not count on my backing. To a degree, he was correct; I would not back any NCO that was giving bad or unlawful direction to his personnel. When I learned from several chief master sergeants that the senior enlisted advisor was working against me, vice keeping me abreast of problems associated with our enlisted force and helping to build moral, I had to replace him.

The incident related above was long forgotten, and many years had passed when I received a call from the same young airman, now a *chief master sergeant*, thanking me for interceding on his behalf and saving his career in the air force. Looking back over the years, we had a nice chat on the turning points in our respective careers.

Part of wing manning included the assignment of Capt. Terry McKenzie as my executive officer. Terry was a master weapons controller, so he knew the business of AWACS and was previously assigned at TAC Headquarters as an E-3A project officer under the deputy director of operations for support systems, headed by Brig. Gen. Robert Russ. Terry was a workaholic, and I appreciated his energy and work ethic. He came to work early and stayed late. On the other hand, there was just a slight chance that TAC assigned him as my exec to keep tabs on me, as I had come from outside the Tactical Air Command. Terry did a fantastic job, and his experience as a weapons controller was very helpful as I worked through a minefield of training and personnel issues. He served me faithfully then subsequently commanded a Tactical Radar Unit under Ninth Air Force when I was the commander, and was my executive officer at NORAD and USSPACECOM in the late 1980s.

Things were not busy enough building the wing and planning for the future, so on September 11, 1976, the air force realigned the Seventh Airborne Command and Control Squadron, based at Keesler AFB, Mississippi, under the 552nd AWAC Wing. The missions were somewhat related, but the difficulty of getting from Tinker to Keesler made the span of control difficult. The unit was known as the "ABCCC," standing for "Airborne Command, Control, and Communications," and was led by Col. Hugh Cox, a strong and charismatic leader. It only took one visit that included a training flight on ABCCC to convince me that Colonel Cox needed top cover and occasional guidance, but not close supervision. All of his aircrews and controllers were highly experienced and flying one of the safest aircraft in the air force inventory in a relatively benign environment. Essentially, the ABCCC was an extension of the Tactical Air Control System, except without radar to track the aircraft under their control. Control was accomplished by radio calls and position reports. The ABCCC was radio rich and could converse with forward air controllers assigned to army units engaged with the enemy and air force fighter flights that could provide close air support to ground forces in need of fire support outside the range of corps or division artillery. For its time, it was a very effective link between air force fighter forces and soldiers and marines on the ground engaged with the enemy and in immediate need of fire support.

A landmark test highlighting what AWACS could do against a determined and dense threat supported by standoff jammers to clutter the AWACS Planar Array Radar plus "Red" aircraft equipped with pylon-mounted pod jammers was conducted on November 10, 1976. The 552nd mission commanders, senior directors, weapons controllers, and surveillance technicians participated in the test. However, the wing had not yet received its first operational aircraft; therefore, the two E-3As participating in the test were test aircraft from the Boeing Development Test and Evaluation (DT&E) test force.

Two guide words characterized the tactical test during both the planning and execution phase. These were realism and safety! Safety was paramount due to the density of the threat in a compressed airspace and a vital consideration in planning the test. In addition, because of its scope and complexity, TAC test "fail-safe" procedures were required. For example, if there was a complete communications failure between ground-based command elements or AWACS, established fail safe procedures would immediately have stopped the air battle and facilitated the safe, orderly movement of aircraft to predetermined altitudes and locations, and then sequenced them to their recovery bases.

A Red Force consisting of three hundred aircraft attacked the E-3A defended airspace in three consecutive, time-compressed waves to overwhelm the AWACS radar and weapons controllers. The ability to evaluate E-3A radar performance in a dense clutter environment of chaff and jamming was made possible by Red Force standoff and carry along jammers and chaff dispensers. The ECM force consisted of B-52s, EB-57s, and Navy EA-6Bs. Both the B-52s and EB-57s also dropped chaff to screen the attacking force.

The Test Concept called for a much smaller Blue Force of 133 interceptors, approaching one-third of the Red Force. In addition to fighter aircraft, the Red Force was supported by an RC-135 Signals

Intelligence collection platform and the ECM aircraft listed above. All Blue Force interceptors were under control of the mission commander aboard AWACS. There were two E-3As in the test, a primary and a backup. Both AWACS would be radiating and monitoring the battle space. The primary E-3A mission commander would control the defensive battle, pitting the vastly outnumbered Blue Force against the invading Red Force.

Col. Jerry Mack was the mission commander on the primary AWACS, which was operational for the duration of the test. Brig. Gen. "Pete" Piotrowski was mission commander on the backup aircraft, monitoring the air battle but was never required to take over control of the defensive air battle. All together 413 of 443 scheduled sorties were flown in support of the test. Approximately 97 percent of Red Force aircraft were successfully intercepted by the Blue Force under AWACS control. A few of the Red Force aircraft survived because Blue Force aircraft were out of range or otherwise engaged in completing intercepts. None of the Red Force attackers, with the mission of finding and destroying the E-3As, were able to find either the primary or backup E-3A.

Gen. Robert, J. Dixon called the test "a magnificent professional performance by all participants." A short TAC test results briefing prepared for General Dixon was subsequently briefed to the House Armed Services Committee and all fourteen participating NATO countries.

I was on my way to Europe to brief the TAC test to the NATO AWACS Committee representing primarily England and West Germany to provide information that would "hopefully" lead to a decision to purchase the E-3A for NATO. The British were pushing for the E-3A, but they were firm that if a decision to purchase NATO E-3A was not reached by the end of 1977, they would withdraw from the NATO AWACS program and build a competing concept known as Nimrod. Representatives from Germany were dragging their feet on a decision and asking for more information as a delaying tactic.

While waiting for military air transportation in Washington DC, I was called by the executive office from AF/PR (Programs) and directed to provide the briefing to the Air Staff Board comprised of major generals on the Air Staff. The briefing was well received, but there were questions on exactly how effective the E-3A was and why weren't all the attacking aircraft engaged. They wanted their questions answered, and following that, the major general heading AF/PRP wanted me to brief the House Armed Services Committee early the next morning. Maj. Gen. Jasper Welch, head of Air Force Studies and Analysis (AF/

SA), offered to have his analysis team evaluate the test data and develop an acceptable metric. I stayed with Maj. Gen. Jasper Welch and his analytical team, thinking I could help. Just short of midnight, one of the analysts produced a bar chart showing five-minute increments of the entire air battle. One bar in each five-minute increment represented the number of Red aircraft that could have been engaged considering time and distance. The adjacent bar indicated the number of Red aircraft that were engaged in that five-minute period. The chart showed that, on average, 97 percent of the aircraft that could have been engaged were engaged. Essentially, the 3 percent that was missed could be attributed to the tempo of the battle and the fact that there were only nine consoles available in the initial E-3A design.

Traditionally, three consoles were occupied with surveillance technicians that detected aircraft radar tracks, "hooked" them with a "track ball" action, and identified them as friendly, unknown, or hostile. Once this action was taken, the computer would display the track's ID number, velocity vector, and their altitude. Weapons controllers seated at three consoles would take action to put friendly fighters on hostile tracks to engage them and, on unknown tracks, to identify their type and nationality. The seventh console would be used by an ECM officer/ weapons controller to mitigate any clutter, natural or hostile, that was interfering with the E-3A radar. The eighth console supported the work of the senior director who distributed the engagement workload among the weapons controllers. The ninth console was a floater and could be occupied by the mission commander in a benign environment, or perhaps an additional surveillance technician in a dense air traffic environment, or an additional weapons controller in a dense high-tempo air battle. During the tactical test, Col. Jerry Mack and I stayed on our feet so we could observe all of the consoles and understand the complexity and phase of the battle. The vacant chair was filled with either a surveillance technician or weapons controller at the direction of the senior director. Subsequently, modifications to the E-3A would add three more consoles, bringing the number to twelve, and later three additional consoles, bringing the total to fifteen. These later upgrades would have enabled a near-perfect score for AWACS in the tactical test.

Early the next morning, I called General Dixon to inform him that the general running AF/PRP and chairing the Air Staff Board had directed Major General Welch to develop charts that would more fully and technically explain the TAC test. General Dixon was planning to brief all of his four-star colleagues at the next corona (meeting of all air force four-star generals) on the TAC test, and I wanted him to know about the new charts prepared by Air Force Studies and Analysis. Well, General Dixon never passed up an opportunity to chew me up and down, like only the tidewater alligator could, for not driving down from Washington after midnight to get his approval on the two new briefing slides. He opined that there was plenty of time to drive from the Pentagon to Langley AFB, Virginia, and back to brief the Congress.

I briefed the AWACS Tactical Test results to the House Armed Service Committee using the two bar charts showing exactly what could have been accomplished based on aircraft positions and what actually was accomplished by the weapons controllers and their supporting fighter aircraft. Ninety-seven percent of perfect was deemed a pretty good performance. While there were skeptics, the large majority opined that the rigorous test demonstrated the merits of the E-3A and validated the air force program to procure thirty-four E-3As at a cost of $150 million each—the most expensive aircraft in the air force inventory at that juncture.

The following day, I was on the way to Europe to brief the NATO AWACS Committee on the tactical test results. Again, the briefing was well received, and the British representatives moved to take a decision to purchase the E-3A. However, the German representatives urged caution and wanted more data on the production aircraft performance once they were operational. Again, the RAF stated their position to drop out of the NATO AWACS Program and develop Nimrod if a decision on the E-3A was not firm by the year's end. This all came to a head in a subsequent meeting described later in this chapter.

Gen. David C. Jones, air force chief of staff, was a big proponent of AWACS, perhaps because he flew on the prototype when it deployed to Europe for in situ testing in the early 1970s while he was CINCUSAFE. Without his support, the program would likely have died. Originally approved as an air defense requirement, the E-3A was shifted to the Tactical Air Command because support for air defense of the United States was on the decline, and ADCOM was scheduled for closure. TAC had other signal requirements, like the F-15, to replace aging F-4s and become the air dominance fighter for the next four decades. If not for General Jones's support, the E-3A may never have gone into production.

One of General Jones's visionary ideas was called "Big Picture." Big Picture involved converting the E-3A display to a television signal that could be easily transported from an AWACS on orbit along the East German border to the National Military Command Center (NMCC) in the Pentagon and/or the Emergency Situation Room under the White House. The concept was predicated on the idea that any attack by a near peer nation would be initiated by a massive air attack with land forces close behind. Thus, with the E-3A radar picking up the leading wave of attacking aircraft and the live video transmitted in near real time to the NMCC and White House Situation Room, the president and secretary of defense could see the opening air attack and not have to rely only on verbal reports. In addition, General Jones envisioned equipping forward air controller jeeps (now Humvees) with Identification Friend or Foe (IFF) beacons. These beacons are coded with four octal numbers that are interrogated and read out by ground or airborne radar, like the E-3A. The code dialed into the IFF could indicate ground unit identification and status. If the first three digits were used to denote companies, they would accommodate 512 units, or the equivalent of fifty-six brigades. Status examples given in the last digit could pass eight messages. Examples might be, "in contact with the enemy," "need resupply," "need fire support," "need medical evacuation," etc. The beacon location on the E-3A display would reveal the unit's location.

To test his thesis, General Jones had Boeing fabricate an arm that would mount on an E-3A console and hold a television camera the proper distance from the display to produce a full-screen picture. Video stream was transmitted to a receiver within line of sight and then retransmitted via satellite to command centers. Once the concept was proven in flight, General Jones took advantage of a visit by his German Air Force counterpart to demonstrate it.

An E-3A training mission was scheduled in the tidewater area south of Washington DC, and the appropriate communications and video displays were set up in the Andrews AFB officers' club. Linkup was accomplished, and the air picture, along with intercept training for the onboard weapons controllers, was easily discernible on the large television screen. The demonstration was going as planned until the DVs arrived; at that moment, the display was lost.

General Jones took the apparent disaster in stride as I spoke with the crew and learned that the display the camera was mounted on had crashed. However, they were working on moving the camera from the starboard console in the front row to the adjacent console. The move would take about five minutes. Time passed slowly as General Jones was describing the concept to his guests when the screen video came up as promised. I hand-signaled General Jones that we were operational, and he brought the DVs over to the TV display. I explained the symbology and asked the senior director aboard the AWACS to go to full range and hook some of the tracks approaching New York from the east. The DVs were clearly impressed with the Big Picture concept. General Jones then pointed out some of the vehicle-borne IFF beacons that were "squawking" a variety of codes, simulating a unit's designation and status. It was an impressive demonstration, and the impact of the Big Picture concept was not lost on the GAF Chief.

After the demonstration, I followed up on the fault that shut the video down for several minutes. It was a known computer software problem that was being corrected, but the fix had not yet been deployed to the field. Some of the messages that flowed through the computer from the radar had an extra bit. These extra bits were stripped off into a buffer at the first console that received the message stream. That console was the starboard console on the first row. When the buffer filled up, that condition shut down the console. If the mission ran long enough, the second console in the serial distribution would shut down as well, and so on. Fortunately, the Boeing technician responsible for the TV modification carried an Allen wrench on board the aircraft—just in case.

On the other hand, taking tools on board an AWACS scheduled for a mission was strictly forbidden by wing regulations. This was necessary to preclude tools from being lost on the aircraft and getting into the electrical cabinets or control linkages and causing serious damage to electrical components. In this instance, the transgression was forgiven.

With that Big Picture success behind him, General Jones aimed higher. He had Lt. Gen. Bill Creech, assistant chief of staff, plan a demonstration in the NMCC for the president, cabinet members, secretary and deputy secretary of defense, senior members of OSD, chairman JCS and senior staff, service chiefs, and senior service staff. Again, I was designated as the briefer.

Lieutenant General Creech invited me to come to his Pentagon Office on Monday prior to the Saturday briefing for a dry run. I was there early and ran the briefing by General Creech. It was a briefing that had been given in different forms all over the world, and I wasn't expecting many changes. Wrong again! Anything going to President Carter and his cabinet had to be ratcheted up in quality a notch or two.

General Creech had a unique way of making notes. Each note was written on a full sheet of paper, even if it only had two or three words on it. This worked great at staff meetings, as each sheet could be a taken individually to its rightful recipient or staff agency. As I recall, there was a sheet of yellow legal paper being ripped off for just about every other slide. Fortunately, these were not slide changes, just phrase and sentence changes to the briefing. It's important to note that I didn't read briefings; I spoke to the charts, and the script was largely memorized. When the briefing was finished, General Creech "suggested" that I come back Tuesday morning to run the "new" briefing by him. Tuesday was a lot like Monday, only there were fewer changes and yellow sheets. Wednesday's dry run was almost an "attaboy," and Thursday's only brought forth about a dozen changes. It should be noted that the briefing consisted of about 250 slides with dual presentation for about 125 dual slide changes. The E-3A was going to be live over the Nellis Ranges with a small short scenario coming at the end of the briefing. To stay in the allocated airspace, the E-3A had to make a 180-degree turn. It had to be a hard turn, which caused the screen display in the E-3A to freeze during the turn, as the planar array antenna could not compensate for the steep bank angle. General Creech did not like the picture freezing and didn't want the cadence of the Big Picture briefing to be interrupted with a technical explanation on why the display froze. He recommended that I give a short tutorial on the E-3A electronic countermeasures (ECM) resistance during the time the picture was frozen so the audience wouldn't see it.

There was a final dry run on Friday with only about a half-dozen changes. They were really minor changes, so I asked General Creech if he would wave these, as I had the briefing down pat and the real presentation was the following morning. General Creech gave me one of the pained looks he was famous for and said, "Pete, if you can't hack it, it'll be good enough without the changes." The gauntlet was thrown down—the choice was mine. I practiced the briefing with the changes about twenty times between then and going to bed Friday night; I was as ready as I could be.

Saturday morning, General Creech and I met in the National Military Command Center (NMCC) Presentation Center to check the visuals on the big screens. I normally like to use a pointer in my right hand because I'm right-handed. That was OK until I crossed in front of the screen to get to the lectern and the microphone, where I would communicate to the E-3A as "Bronco Control" during the live demonstration. General Creech didn't like the loss of time nor crossing in front of the screen, so I had to immediately adapt to using a pointer with the left hand.

The NMCC Presentation Center started filling up, and it was near show time. General Jones, air force chief of staff, was sponsoring the briefing, so I took the cue to start from him. President Carter had cancelled, but his cabinet, the senior DOD staff, all the JCS flag officers, and the service chiefs accompanied by all their service staff, three stars, were there. The briefing went exceptionally well, except for one-millisecond hesitation when I was describing an E-3A screen picture taken over Central Europe and the Mediterranean. I used to describe the entire body of water being displayed as the Adriatic, Mediterranean, and Tyrrhenian Sea and paused ever so slightly as I was digging in the gray matter for "Tyrrhenian."

At the end of the presentation with the live E-3A picture as a backdrop, I asked for questions. This was the "big picture": to inform the assembled national and military leaders that they could see a conflict, air, land, and sea, starting halfway around the world—with the picture coming to them with the speed of light. As I was answering questions, the secretary of state interrupted, asking what that slow moving object could be crossing the border from Mexico into Southern California. I glanced at the screen and saw that an E-3A surveillance technician had hooked a track, highlighting it on the screen with a velocity vector, airspeed, and altitude. Checking the time, I noted that it was 9:30 a.m. in DC and 6:30 in California, just short of daylight for the time of year. My response was "Sir, I can't tell you what that aircraft is or is doing. However, based on the flight path and time of day, I suspect it is a plane full of drugs being smuggled from Mexico into the United States with the plane landing at an abandoned desert strip at dawn." The secretary of state's astute observation coupled with my response brought the briefing home and made the "big picture" point far better than the briefing.

As the distinguished guests were leaving, General Creech came forward to the podium and said, "Good briefing, except for your short brain hiccup in the middle."

Back at Tinker and working the day-to-day issues of running a wing, the call came to return to Washington DC to brief President Carter on Saturday at the Emergency Situation Room (ESR) in the White House. On Thursday, I had permission to scope out the ESR—projectors, etc.—and determine when I had to arrive at the gate to arrive at the ESR at least one hour before the presentation. Secret Service personnel accompanied me to the ESR and covered every move I made. I asked where the president sat. The response was "Why do you want to know?"

"So I can position myself to be looking at the president and at the screen."

"OK. He sits in the chair on the side nearest the screen." I pulled the chair back from the table to make it easier for President Carter to sit down, only to discover it had a very dark stain on the gold upholstery. Then I asked where others sat. "Why?"

"So I can change this chair with someone else's chair—this one has a bad stain on the seat."

"Don't worry about that. The president spilled his coffee on the chair. He doesn't care." Well, I cared and exchanged the chair with the one where the chairman JCS usually sat. There were two doors to the ESR, so I asked which door the president used to enter the room. "Why do you want to know?"

"So I can be facing the door and be ready to start when the president comes into the room. Where does the other door go?"

"You don't need to know." Next, I moved the president's chair away from the table so it would be easy for the president to sit down without delay. "Why are you doing that?"

"I only have thirty minutes with the president, and I don't want to lose any of it while he moves his chair around." Next, I checked out the slide trays, found out where they kept the spare bulbs, checked to make sure the access doors to the bulbs were functional, and adjusted the picture on the screen for size and clarity. When I was satisfied with my preparations, I left.

Saturday morning, I was in the ESR with about an hour to spare— checked everything out and stood by to demonstrate the Big Picture concept to President Carter. Essentially, the Soviets could not mass an air attack two hundred miles behind the East German eastern border without an AWACS on orbit in West Germany detecting the pending attack and transmitting the live video to the Pentagon's NMCC and the White House ESR. The live video could also convey the status of US naval and ground forces with IFF codes displayed on the live video. Decisions could be made on real-time visual evidence.

It wasn't long before the secretary of defense, chairman JCS, and air force chief of staff arrived, followed by the director of the National Security Council. A few minutes later, the president walked through the door and took his seat. The briefing started without hesitation, highlighting the Big Picture concept. Soon, the president was asking questions, but not the kind I had anticipated. He was asking for technical details and the frequencies of the E-3A radar, how many transmitters (klystrons), was there frequency diversity to counter narrow band jamming, could the radar operate during aerial refueling, etc. It seemed that President Carter failed to see the strategic importance of the Big Picture in his crisis decision-making role, but rather that his nuclear engineering background drove him into the arcane details of how the E-3A worked. Fortunately, as the wing commander, I was well into E-3A technical details, and as an E-3A simulator pilot and part-time surveillance technician, I knew how the system worked. When the briefing and questions abated, President Carter noted that he was hosting Chancellor Helmut Schmidt of Germany the following week prior to a G-7 meeting at Williamsburg, Virginia, and asked chairman JCS, Gen. George Brown, if I could be available to brief the chancellor. The chairman responded in the affirmative.

The following Saturday, I was at the ready in the White House ESR waiting for the president and chancellor to walk into the ESR for the Big Picture briefing. My gut feeling was that the chancellor would want to spend his private time with President Carter discussing our dire economic situation and the US "stagflation" economy, with the country dropping into recession with interest rates at nearly 20 percent. Truth is, I don't know what happened, but they didn't come to the ESR. Evidently, things other than AWACS were on the chancellor's agenda, and I was able to return to Tinker and building up the 552nd to achieve its IOC.

The first E-3A, tail number 75-0557, was scheduled to arrive at Tinker AFB on March 23, 1977. The ceremony was scheduled for the following day to accommodate any potential slips in E-3A arrival time. The arrival ceremony was scheduled for midmorning on the twenty-fourth. Aircraft 75-0557 arrived on time and was placed in a distant hangar to keep it out of sight. The plan was to have the full wing assembled in our hangar with the DVs on an elevated podium where they would overlook the wing personnel and out onto the ramp. They would be able to see the aircraft taxi from its hide and stick its nose into the hangar two minutes after the DVs were seated.

As a long-time fighter pilot, I must confess that the E-3A is an impressive-looking aircraft from any angle! When it turned the corner and started to push its nose into the hangar, there was a hush and then a cheer from the assembled masses—their real journey into history was about to start. There were a number of distinguished speakers, Gen. Robert Dixon for TAC, Gen. Bill Evans from Air Force Systems Command, Maj. Gen. Larry Skantz, E-3A program manager from Electronic System Command, and Maj. Gen. Carl Schneider, our host and commander OCAMA. As host for the event, it was my responsibility to start the ceremony and introduce the guest speakers. General Dixon chose to speak last and after a few biblical quotes, one of which was from the prophet Isaiah: "'And the Lord asked who shall I send, who will go for us?' And Isaiah said, 'Here I am Lord send me!'" He ended with the words spoken harshly through clenched teeth, "I wish you hard work!" My first thought was what a downer to end the arrival ceremony on, but in an instant, I realized he had said exactly the right thing—only hard work and lots of it would enable the wing to succeed. It was my job to make sure all the wing personnel understood the true meaning of his words. There were cake and refreshments for all personnel to partake of as I drove the DVs to their waiting aircraft. General Dixon's parting words to me were "Don't screw it up."

Now that the 552nd had ownership of an E-3A, it was time to start testing our tornado evacuation plan. Oklahoma City was in the center lane of Tornado Alley, as the swath of land from Dallas, Texas, to Kansas City, Kansas, was referred to by locals. Tornado season lasted approximately sixty days from mid-April to mid-June, but those powerful twisters could arrive earlier or much later, depending on cold front movement and moisture coming northwest from warm gulf waters.

That evening at standup, I learned that our first E-3A arrived without any major discrepancies. I was eager to fly a training sortie or two the following day. To my surprise, Col. Pat Hayes wanted to keep the aircraft on the ground for two days to let his maintenance team closely examine it, fix all the discrepancies they had parts for, and in general, make sure the aircraft was ready for flight. As much as I wanted to get the bird in the air and log some training sorties, it seemed like the prudent approach. Further, I didn't want to push back on my senior staff at that juncture without a very good reason for doing so.

While maintenance went over the aircraft, Colonel Mack and I went over the procedures that I mandated for monitoring the aircraft when it was in the traffic pattern. My flying background was all single-engine or two-engine fighter aircraft, essentially small nimble aircraft with one pilot. The exception was the B-26 and C-131, which had two R-2800 engines. The B-26 was crewed with one pilot; the C-131, a pilot and copilot. Generally speaking, fighter wings always had an instructor pilot in a small air-conditioned glasshouse referred to as "Mobile Control" because it could be towed to any of the available runways and was always located just off the runway at the desired touchdown point. It was the Mobile instructor pilot's responsibility to ensure that aircraft in the traffic pattern were properly configured with regard to their gear and flaps, to order pilots to "go around" if an approach looked unsafe, and to render assistance to pilots with in-flight emergencies. In addition to Mobile Control, fighter wings always had an officer assigned as the Supervisor of Flying, or SOF, who had access to a vehicle with radios that could tune in ground control and tower frequencies, as well as always receiving on "Guard Channel." The SOF was the ultimate authority, unless the commander or deputy commander for operations were present, when it came to in-flight emergencies, recalling aircraft to land immediately because of deteriorating weather, or diverting aircraft to alternate airfields if the runways were closed because of an accident or weather.

On the other hand, large aircraft organizations believed that the pilot and copilot, plus perhaps a flight engineer, and navigator in the cockpit provided sufficient eyes and ears to preclude stupid mistakes, such as landing with the gear up. There were enough people in large aircraft cockpits to read emergency checklist while the pilot maintained control of the aircraft or to read detailed technical data to the pilot in an emergency. My key staff on the flying side thought I was going way overboard with the Mobile and SOF concepts. To their dismay, I mandated that a SOF be identified for every day we flew. Further, that a SOF truck be equipped with every radio that might be needed and that the SOF be positioned adjacent to the landing point of the runway whenever an E-3A or KC-135 front-end trainer were in the traffic pattern.

The morning E-3A 0557 was to fly its first training flight under my command, I was in the SOF vehicle along with Col. Jerry Mack and the real SOF. We observed the aircraft configuration as it took the runway, and everything looked normal. We heard Tinker Tower clear 0557 for takeoff and saw the engines power up. As the aircraft started to move, we all observed liquid streaming from a panel low and just aft of the cockpit. Colonel Mack shouted, "Abort, abort—engine shutdown, engine shutdown. Evacuate, evacuate!" With great relief, we saw the aircraft stop, the engines cut off, and the entrance door open.

After the fire trucks washed away the spilled JP-4 jet fuel and cleared the scene, maintenance personnel opened the panel to the lower bay of the aircraft. They discovered a Marman clamp connecting two four-inch diameter fuel lines had come loose, allowing tens of gallons of JP-4 to be pumped into the lower bay and then out on the ramp. The clamp had obviously been loose for some time with just enough pressure to hold the connecting fuel lines together. It could have come apart while the aircraft was en route to Tinker or when the aircraft taxied to the hangar for the arrival ceremony. We were indeed fortunate that there were three sets of eyes in the SOF truck as 0557 started its takeoff roll. A disaster of epic proportions had been avoided. After that incident, everyone supported the SOF concept, and there were other events where the SOF saved the day. After the Marman clamp was refitted and tightened and all other Marman clamps inspected and torqued, the first E-3A training flight took place on March 31, a week after the arrival ceremony.

Running an operational wing was a 24/7 job and always full of surprises! Building an operational wing with a very complex and sophisticated aircraft that was new to the air force inventory, and with newly assigned personnel arriving every day with no tangible relevant experience to the mission or aircraft compounded a commander's job factorially. A few examples will help illustrate these assertions.

Col. Jerry Mack and his chief of standardization and evaluation informed me that our best pilot and first instructor pilot (IP) in the E-3A would be Maj. Jim Sterk. Upon reviewing his records, I realized that Major Sterk had flown only the B-52 after graduation from pilot training. I suggest to Colonel Mack that our first IP should be one with thousands of hours in the KC-135, a predecessor to the Boeing 707 with many of the design features and flight characteristics of the E-3A. For example, the B-52 had eight turbojet engines, levitated on takeoff, and accommodated crosswinds by aligning the landing gear with the runway while the aircraft crabbed into the wind so that the flight path was down the runway. The E-3A had four turbofan engines, took off and landed like a normal aircraft, and in a crosswind, aligned the fuselage with the runway and killed the crosswind drift with a wing low slip. Besides, I opined the optics were all wrong. If one of our pilots upgrading to the E-3A had a tire blow on landing because the tire was defective and the E-3A sustained some damage, critics will fault us for using a B-52 experienced pilot, vice a KC-135 experienced pilot. Colonel Mack was questioned about the second-best pilot and where he fit in the list of most qualified candidates to be instructor pilots. His immediate response was Maj. Morry Hardy, a high-time KC-135 pilot who was only a scintilla behind Major Sterk. I decreed that Major Hardy would be designated the first IP, and Major Sterk could be the second IP to start training our initial cadre of pilots, but not the first. Feelings were hurt, but in a few weeks, all was forgotten, and there was plenty of flying for all E-3A instructor pilots. As a note, Col. Jim Sterk later became the 552nd wing commander.

One of the senior officers at Tinker AFB, fundamentally responsible for the 552nd AWAC Wing's success as well as the overall program in general, was not a member of the wing, but part of the logistics team in the Oklahoma City Air Material Area (OCAMA). This was Col. John Bradshaw. Colonel Bradshaw came over to my office and made me an offer I couldn't refuse. He offered to pay for and build a Joint Logistic Center (JLC) in the 552nd Wing complex. Colonel Bradshaw had done all the planning and design of the JLC, which would include positions for 552nd supply personnel, Boeing representatives, and logistics personnel from OCAMA. He already had a signed commitment from Boeing Company for twenty-four-hour manning, six days a week. His office would provide OCAMA logistics reps 24/7 as long as the wing would do likewise. It was a win-win proposition. All I had to do was provide a suitable location in the wing maintenance complex, and Colonel Bradshaw would do the rest. The JLC was a state-of-the-art facility, with Colonel

Bradshaw providing all of the computers and large-screen displays showing the current status on all part requisitions, part's locations, and estimated time of part delivery from any source. It was a model for all future aircraft acquisitions.

Colonel Bradshaw did more than conceive and build the JLC; he improvised several unique programs that helped keep the E-3As flying locally and all over the globe. Some of his brainstorms are listed below:

ELOPE (E3A Layaway of Peculiar Equipment): OCAMA at Tinker AFB repaired the TF-33 jet engines that powered the E-3A. They also repaired all the associated TF-33 sub-system (e.g.; fuel pumps, fuel controls, etc.) Most of the remaining E-3A systems were supported by other logistic centers. For example, the planar array radar and klystrons were repaired and warehoused at Warner Robbins Air Material Area (WRAMA) near Atlanta, Georgia. If a radar part was needed to repair an E-3A at Tinker, it would take about a week after the part was requisitioned before it would arrive at the 552nd Maintenance Complex. Colonel Bradshaw recommended that all parts unique to the E-3A, regardless of where they were repaired, should be warehoused at Tinker AFB. Control and movement of these parts would be held at their primary repair facility. With Tactical Air Command support, ELOPE was approved by Air Force Logistics Command and implemented immediately. This program alone increased the E-3A mission capable rate by ten percentage points because there was no shipping delay when a part was needed.

SAVE (Save E-3A Valuable Equipment): A number of expensive parts were coded as nonrepairable, which meant that when removed from the aircraft because they were malfunctioning, they were simply thrown in the trash and a factory replacement requested. Colonel Bradshaw suggested that all of the failed nonrepairable coded items be saved and placed in an empty warehouse at Tinker. After six months of collecting these items, Colonel Bradshaw and I would determine if there was good reason to generate a repair contract for selected high failure rate items. We discovered that some of the expensive items coded nonrepairable by Boeing were indeed repairable. One example that I recall was a machined aluminum tube in the radar cooling system. Glycol cooling liquid flowed through the tube, while an electronic sensor attached to a flat base on the tube with four screws and safety wire measured the pressure providing feedback to the pump. The machined tube cost $1,500 and was relatively indestructible. The sensor cost $75 and was the part that failed. Colonel Bradshaw funded a local contractor to replace the sensors for a very small percentage of the total assembly cost. There were many other examples that saved taxpayer dollars.

REMOVE (Rapid Evacuation and Movement of Valuable Equipment): A study conducted by Colonel Bradshaw highlighted that it often took days for a broken part to move from the 552nd Maintenance Area into the repair cycle. He established a broken part pickup cycle that ensured failed parts were in the repair cycle within four hours. This increased the availability of parts significantly.

Chicago Connection: Colonel Bradshaw's fertile mind led him to study commercial air traffic movements. His study determined that if an E-3A part was needed anywhere in the world, it would get there in less than twenty-four hours if it was at O'Hare International Airport, Chicago, Illinois, by 2:00 p.m. any day of the week. He contracted with a package expediter at O'Hare to personally transfer parts from an incoming commercial aircraft from Oklahoma City, Oklahoma, to the specified outbound aircraft. This prevented a potential abort for a fire warning system failure during the Bundestag E-3A demo, and countless times on deployments to Europe, Iceland, the Pacific, and the Middle East.

Colonel Bradshaw is one of my heroes and became a close personal friend. Regrettably, his parent command, Air Force Logistics Command (AFLC), apparently didn't fully value his creativity and innate ability to get the right things done quickly. He retired as a colonel and has a family farm in Kansas and home in Colorado Springs, Colorado.

New E-3As were arriving at the rate of about four a year, and by the end of 1977, there were three or four E-3As on the ramp at Tinker. Flight crew training was progressing very well, as the incoming pilots were highly experienced in large multi-engine aircraft. Trouble is that flight crew training competed with mission crew training, and the two were not compatible. For example, flight crews required lots of landings and instrument approaches of all types, ground-controlled approach (GCA), instrument landing system approaches (ILS), audio direction finding (ADF), and some other ancient stuff found in third-world countries. Flight crews were also required to practice a heavy dose of in-flight emergencies. None of this training was compatible with eight hours of orbiting at thirty-five thousand feet and conducting intercepts for surveillance technician and weapons controller training. Getting the scheduling priorities right to generate formed combat-ready crews was of first-order importance.

One of the buildings constructed for the 552nd was an academic facility for all classroom training for aircrews, mission crews, and maintenance personnel. It was state of the art with various projection capability and lots of whiteboards for diagramming and presenting material to the students. I wanted to sit in on some classes and get a feel for the quality of instruction and the student learning level. What I saw appalled me, not the instructors or their presentations, but the way the classroom appearance had deteriorated. Walls brand new a year ago were rubbed by chairs, smudged in all manner of ways with backs of chairs, soles of boots, etc. I asked the chief instructor to call a meeting for me at the close of the academic day so I could speak with the instructors. At the appointed time and in a casual setting, I praised them for the quality of the education and the progress the wing was making in just about every facet of the buildup to initial operational capability and operational status. Then I expressed my disappointment in the state of the facility that was just a year old—the room we were in was a good example of the smudges, smears, and deterioration of the facility. I noted that the attitude of the students was largely set by their first impression—and that right now, it was a bad one. I noted that it was Friday, and this evening, the civil engineers are going to drop off paint, brushes, rollers, drop cloths, masking tape, and everything needed to paint the classrooms back to like new. I suggested that anyone who wanted to join me in the effort, to meet me at the building at 7:00 a.m. on Saturday. I would bring a case of cold beer that we could share when the painting was finished. I was hoping that maybe half the instructors would join me.

The next morning, I arrived a few minutes early dressed in blue jeans and an old faded shirt to find the entire instructor cadre there. I said, "Good morning, all. I'll take the next room down the hall, the one I'd been in the day before that was in such pitiful shape." When I opened the door and turned on the lights, I was greeted with a freshly painted room. I don't know when the NCOs started painting, but the entire facility was done—every room had been freshly painted before I arrived. I had difficulty finding the words to thank them for their effort and broke out the chips, pretzels, and beer. It seemed a little early for cold beer, so I asked the NCO club to provide an urn of coffee and doughnuts. There were about as many instructors as there was bottles of beer, so no one was going to get anywhere near the driving limit.

In the flying game, bad things happen unexpectedly from all directions. Early one morning, the command post informed me that one of our airborne E-3As had experienced a complete hydraulic failure. Flight controls were manual, so aircraft handling wasn't a problem. The E-3A was built around the Boeing 707-320B airframe, which had a manual emergency gear lowering system, backed up another system using stored compressed air, so lowering and locking the gear in place should not be a problem. Stored compressed air was also used for emergency braking, but emergency braking was touchy, and that sensitivity could cause blown tires and result in an aircraft swerving violently, causing damage to the landing gear itself. Tinker did not have long runways, and the winds were such that the shortest runway was in use. The crew did an excellent job of landing and stopping the aircraft after burning down the fuel to lower the weight, lessening the landing airspeed and also the potential for fire.

I was waiting at the ramp to congratulate the crew for their handling of the airborne emergency and to learn what maintenance had to say about the hydraulic failure. While talking to the flight crew, a technical sergeant emerged from under the main gear wheel well with a micrometer and announced with authority that the failure was the result of "ovality"! My response was "What is ovality?" Immediately, I was informed that "ovality" is the term used when hydraulic lines are bent, resulting in a major axis that is 5 percent greater than the minor axis. This errant bending causes stress in the tubing, which results in premature failure in the major axis of the bend. I asked the sergeant to check several other bends in the hydraulic tubing. The result of his inspection was "ovality" in every bend—the problem was systemic. Immediately, all other aircraft were checked, and all hydraulic line bends that could be easily accessed were out of limits in ovality. I grounded all the aircraft. Stupidly, I grounded all the E-3As without first consulting with the TAC/DO or General Dixon. On the other hand, safety of flight rests on the shoulders of the wing commander. I knew many wing commanders who were fired for loss of aircraft and deaths of pilots and crew members. I never heard of one being fired for acting prudently in the face of adversity. General Dixon never said a word to me about the E-3A grounding and backed me to the hilt on the issue. After he retired and was no longer a tidewater terror, I wish I had asked him why he let me off the hook on this issue while constantly threatening to kill me on several other trivial matters.

That evening, I received a call from the Boeing Aircraft Company's CEO. The gentleman told me that my grounding of E-3As at Tinker was giving the Boeing 707-320B a bad reputation and causing concern throughout the commercial aviation community. He followed up with a request for me to return the E-3As to flight status. I told him I would not start flying the E-3As until I was convinced they were fixed. He then asked me what it would take to change my mind. I responded that I had just told him that the hydraulic problem must be fixed before any E-3As under my command would fly again. I reminded him the E-3A hydraulic system was vastly different than those on commercial airlines and that his airline customers did not have a problem. He hung up. Following that conversation, I wondered if the test aircraft at the Boeing plant near Seattle, Washington, had experienced hydraulic line failures from ovality. They had put far more hours on their test E-3A than the 552nd AWAC wing had on any of our line aircraft—had they covered up the problem?

Technically, the problem was significant because there were many places in the aircraft that could not be reached without taking off the exterior skin. Fortunately, some very bright engineers and scientists at Boeing developed a method of cutting and then shrink welding the new tubing in place that would withstand the five thousand pounds per square inch (PSI) pressure that ran through the lines. The ovality problem originated when Boeing engineers changed the 707-320B hydraulic pressure from 3,500 PSI to 5,000 PSI to drive the thirty-foot diameter-rotating antenna on the E-3A. This change in pressure mandated that the tubing be changed from one-half-inch internal diameter (ID) aluminum to one-half-inch ID stainless steel. Stainless steel is much stronger than aluminum; hence, even though the pressure was greater, the wall thickness of stainless steel tubing was thinner, resulting in a smaller outside diameter. It was the smaller outside diameter of the stainless steel tubing along with the fact that the Boeing engineers did not foresee the need to change a bushing in the tube bending machine that caused the ovality problem in every bend made in the stainless steel tubing. With hundreds of bends in the E-3As hydraulic lines, it only took a few hours of flight time before one would fail. The recovery was painful, but the wing never experienced another hydraulic failure after the repairs were made.

With the hydraulic problem fresh in our minds, another E-3A safety issue arose. While taxing to the runway and completing preflight checks, one of the instructor pilots reported that he could not move the aileron control (yoke) from the right aileron up to the down position. He radioed that with both the pilot and instructor pilot using all their arm strength, they could not move the yoke from the position it was in. The aircraft was taxied back to the ramp to awaiting maintenance personnel. It was suspected that foreign objects left in the wing control cable chase had jammed the cables. The first step was to remove all the panels from the cable chase and inspect the channel. Much to our surprise, the cable channel was full of odd tools, rivets, and other debris. No one could point to any of the junk in the cable chase as causing the controls to lock up, but we were all sure that this was the problem.

I called the senior Boeing representative at Tinker and asked him to come out to the aircraft. He seemed shocked to see all the junk left in the aircraft and called Boeing to report the incident. Shortly, Boeing's chief test pilot called me to tell me that we didn't have a flight control problem. He related that the Boeing 707-320B was made with larger ailerons than the KC-135 Air Force pilots were familiar with to provide increased roll rate authority for the newer and larger aircraft. He went on to say that with more than a 10-knot wind from behind the aircraft, and the ailerons rolled full over in either direction, the wind against them would prevent even the strongest pilot and copilot from rolling the ailerons back to neutral or to the opposite extreme. Assuming the aircraft was taking off into the wind as they normally were, neutralizing the ailerons was never a problem. He went on to say that even taking off with a 10-knot tailwind (unusual but could be necessary), the ailerons could be neutralized as soon as the aircraft accelerated enough to get air flowing across the wings from the front. His pointing out this little known fact about the E-3A eliminated our concern about locked flight controls and highlighted that there was a lot we still had to learn about the aircraft. On the other hand, his words did not relieve my concern about the danger of foreign object or trash in the cable trace, causing the controls to jam. At that time, we had three aircraft on the ramp and had thoroughly inspected all three aircraft's cable traces. All were full of manufacturing tools and trash. I took pictures and sent them to the CEO of Boeing Commercial Aircraft. I'm sure he wasn't amused and didn't send a thank-you for returning his tools and parts.

In addition to maintenance and manufacturing issues, the 552nd was a tenant at Tinker, and the host was not meeting my standards for taking care of our personnel. Three examples are given to illustrate the issues we faced.

Barracks inspection is an important command function for both squadron and wing commanders. I went through the barracks monthly with the first sergeant when the troops were at work. On one such inspection, I noticed that more than half of the barrack latrine sinks were missing the rubber sink stoppers that were usually hooked to a chain tethered on the faucet. I also noticed a sign posted at the end of a row of sinks encouraging water conservation. I envisioned the troops shaving with the hot water running full blast because they couldn't collect hot water in the sink. Fixing the problem appeared simple: all the civil engineer had to do was order a couple of dozen rubber sink stoppers, give them to the first sergeant, and the problem was closed. I asked the first sergeant to make it happen and moved on to more important things. A few days later, the first sergeant brought me a letter from the base commander stating that they were going to replace all the barracks sinks the following year, so there was no need to spend money on rubber sink stoppers. What stupidity, they were running hundreds of gallons of hot water down the drain and would continue to do so for at least another year. It was also my experience that things like sink replacements get moved into the future when higher priorities arise. Stupid and fiscally irresponsible! I asked the first sergeant to bring me a sample of the sink stopper and a count of how many we needed. With the sample and number of stoppers needed in hand, I drove into Midwest City to a hardware store and purchased what we needed plus 20 percent. The bill was under ten dollars.

Back in the office, I penned a note to the base commander, stating that I shouldn't have to do his job and requested he reimburse me for the amount of the enclosed receipt. He must have been really offended because he went crying to the ALC vice commander, Brig. Gen. Leighton Palmerton, who stormed into my office, demanding to know why I sent such an offensive note to the base commander. After a short acrimonious discussion without Leighton recognizing the need to keep the dormitories in good shape, I pulled a picture out of my desk drawer and showed it to him. It was an eight-inch-by-ten-inch black-and-white picture of General Dixon when he was a major general serving as the Seventh Air Force director of operations in Vietnam. He had just returned from a RF-4C Reconnaissance Mission over North Vietnam and was walking with his arm around the shoulders of the RF-4C crew chief. The caption was "We are a Team." My comment was "This is how my boss feels about our enlisted personnel—would you like me to elevate this issue to my four-star boss and your four-star boss?" General Palmerton spun around and left the office. Somehow, my instincts told me that picture would come in handy someday. On the other hand, I never did get my six dollars and change back for the purchase of the sink stoppers.

I personally briefed all the newly arriving personnel assigned to the 552nd Wing. They were divided into three groups: airman up to the rank of sergeant, noncommissioned officers (NCOs), and officers. It seemed important for the commander to be the first one (or almost first one) to brief them on the E-3A mission and to inculcate them with how important the E-3A was in both tactical and strategic operations, and exactly where we were in building the wing to its full operational capability. They also needed to know that if they encountered problems in doing their jobs correctly and professionally how to resolve those issues. They also needed to be informed on the problems the wing was struggling with in reaching initial operational capability and how those problems were being dealt with. The obvious point that they were the ones that were at the heart of the mission was heavily emphasized—and that it was my responsibility to make sure they had the proper tools, accurate and up-to-date technical data, sound training, and the guidance to ensure the mission was successfully accomplished. I also introduced them to the Commander's Gram Program and assured them if they sent me a CG, they would get a personal response mailed to them or posted on the bulletin board if it was anonymous. These briefings took place weekly at the beginning and biweekly as the number of new arrivals tapered off. Last, I asked them if they had encountered any problems or if there were any issues that they wanted to bring to my attention. Generally, there were no issues raised; but one day, a technical sergeant said that he had a hard time finding the places on base that he needed to go to for in-processing. He said there were no signs leading from the main gate to finance, personnel, security, and the hospital. As you can imagine, if you didn't turn in your financial records, you wouldn't get paid, nor could you file the forms necessary to be reimbursed for moving from the previous assignment to Tinker. Personnel records had to be turned in to ensure the Air Force Personnel System knew where you were. Security registered your car and provided base decals for automobiles. Security was also where you applied for your security badge providing access to the flight line and hangars. Hospital records were hand-carried to the new base hospital to ensure base medical personnel would have access to you and your families medical history to ensure proper treatment if someone was injured or became ill.

As soon as the words were out of his mouth, I winced recalling the difficulty I had in locating the same facilities. I had to repeatedly ask for directions sometimes two or three times because the activities weren't well marked, and it was possible to drive right by them without seeing the facility. I asked the technical sergeant to hang around for a few minutes while I called for a base photographer. We all got into my staff car, and we drove out and back through the main gate and to all the possible intersections where there should have been signs with arrows providing direction to the important facilities for new arrivals. There were none, and the Tinker base map that was mailed to every new assignee at their previous assignment was of little help. The map highlighted the industrial and contracting facilities that were important to the OCAMA civilian workforce and job applicants, but of little interest or importance to 552nd personnel.

When the pictures were printed, I hand-carried them to General Palmerton, explaining that just a few signs at strategic road crossings plus a visible sign near the curb at each important location would make it a lot easier for personnel arriving for the 552nd. I emphasized that we needed these people on the job not driving around the base looking for the security or finance offices. I even offered to pay for the signs. Leighton was polite and said he would ask their senior enlisted advisor to look into the problem. Two days later, I received a note from General Palmerton, stating that the OCAMA senior enlisted advisor advised him there wasn't a problem because everyone knew where these facilities were located. How obtuse and uncaring can base leadership be? True people that had worked at OCAMA for several years knew where these facilities were. My concern was for the military personnel assigned to the 552nd driving through the main gate for the first time. Out came the picture of General Dixon and crew chief that I carried to Leighton's office and made him the same offer: put some signs out so my people can navigate the base, or I'll raise the problem to General Dixon. I knew General Dixon would love ripping into someone over the signs. In two weeks, the signs were in place.

There were a number of female airmen living in Tinker enlisted dormitories, mostly two to a room. Rooms were about fifteen feet by fifteen feet—not very large for two people by current standards. These rooms were furnished with two single beds, two dressers, two upholstered chairs, and a desk and chair. The beds took up considerable floor space, and there wasn't much room left for anything else. Several enlisted women got together and wrote me a Commander's Gram requesting their dorm be furnished with double stack beds like they had in basic training. Instead of writing a response, I arranged a meeting with them because I wanted to make sure they knew what they were asking for and would not have buyer's regret. They assured me they would not backpedal and that more floor space in their barracks rooms was the most important thing to them. The request was turned over to the 552nd senior enlisted advisor to make it happen. A few weeks later, he informed me that there were no standard air force beds or bed adapters available to stack the beds. The bed adapter is a steel pipe about 1.5 inches in diameter that attached to the top of one bed and the bottom another, allowing the beds to be safely and sturdily stacked.

The next step was to have a meeting with the female airmen, the 552nd Wing senior enlisted advisor, and his counterpart at OCAMA. At the meeting, I was told that there were beds available but that there were no bad adapters to be found anywhere in the air force. Hence, the "girls" would have to be satisfied with their current beds. When the chief master sergeant uttered "girls," you could sense the tension from the female airmen. I tried to be light when I said, "Chief, there are women, or females, in the air force, but there are no 'girls'—please refer to the women properly."

Then I took on the bed adapter issue. I noted that the Oklahoma City Air Material Area could construct a B-52 from raw metal with all the skilled personnel, machines, and technology at its disposal. Clearly, they could make a few bed adapters in their extensive sheet metal shops! I would not take no for an answer. What I wanted from them was a certain date when the bed adapters would be available. In just two weeks, the bed adapters had been fabricated, and the female airmen had the floor space in their dorm rooms they desired. I had always believed in the saying, "Don't ever pass up an opportunity to make something easy happen."

The initial manning and training issues were being overcome, and the wing was making good progress until we hit a roadblock in Mission Crew Initial and Continuation Training. Mission commanders, senior directors, weapons controllers, and surveillance technicians, all central and critical to mission accomplishment, needed live intercepts. They needed to detect, decide, act, and engage unknown or hostile aircraft. The Air Defense Command had twenty-six fighter squadrons, Tactical Air Command with twenty-five fighter wings with roughly 1,875 fighter aircraft, so it would seem there were plenty of interceptors and targets for the mission crews to work with. Not quite so, all these pilots had mission requirements of their own, and it took a lot of imaginative scheduling to accomplish all of their mandatory requirements every six months to include all their weapons qualifications, night refueling, etc. We would park an AWACS near one of the heavily used gunnery ranges and catch the flights as they came off of their last gunnery event. If the AWACS mission crew was good, they could split a four-aircraft flight into singles and get four valid intercepts executed in less than ten minutes and before the flight ran into minimum fuel. At some point, it would be necessary to waive or reduce "live" continuation training interceptor requirements based on proven performance and work in the simulator. At this juncture, both the flight and mission simulators were operating twenty-four hours a day and six days a week.

One evening, working late at the office on Friday, I came across a message (they were called TWXs in those days) from the vice chief of staff, Gen. William V. McBride, to General Dixon, commander TAC, with the 552nd/CC as an info copy.

The message was very short and said, as I recall, "The Japanese Self-Defense Force is interested in AWACS and is sending twenty-two JSDF Service members to fly on an AWACS Mission. Please accommodate but do not compromise flight and mission crew training.

Warm regards, Bill." My first impression was the request was in direct conflict with itself. There were no empty seats on E-3A training sorties—and we were behind schedule in turning out mission-ready crews. There were thirteen extra seats in the rear of the aircraft, but these were always filled with students and instructors who would rotate into console seats as soon as a student achieved the desired level of proficiency expected for that mission. Clearly, we would lose twenty-two training days for every sortie the JSDF personnel flew on. I wondered how General Dixon would react and didn't have to wait long to find out.

It was Saturday morning after a late night prowling the flight line. I was still in bed and half asleep when the phone beside the bed rang. It was General Dixon on the line, not his secretary or the command post. I picked up the phone and said, "General Pete here."

His curt response was "Dixon here, can you do it?" I quickly assumed that he was referring to the vice chief's message that said fly the JSDF without any cost to training.

My response was short: "No, sir!" The phone went dead. General Dixon got his answer and hung up. My next thought was, *This is not going to be pretty.*

I went to the office and called in my exec, Capt. Terry McKenzie; the DO, Col. Jerry Mack; and Lt. Col. Jack Farrington, commander of the Training Squadron. I didn't know what was going to happen next, but when it did, I needed quick and accurate answers. An hour hadn't past since Dixon's curt phone call when Captain McKenzie brought in a TWX from General Dixon to General McBride. It said, "Reference your message, either rescind or recant! Warm regards, Bob." That was all it said. I was wondering who drafted the original message about the JSDF because that action officer was in real hot water by now. The phone rang; it was Maj. Gen. Jim McInerney, a friend and a certified hero during the Vietnam War, flying Wild Weasel SA-2 suppression missions in the F-105 and later as squadron commander of the F-4G Weasel Squadron. He was awarded the Air Force Cross for his heroism and probably deserved the Medal of Honor. Maj. Gen. Jim McInerney, currently the chief of Air Forces Foreign Military Sales in the Pentagon, had written the message for General McBride to send to General Dixon. He wanted to know what he could do to put the fire out and calm down General Dixon. I explained that it wasn't that we couldn't fly the Japanese, but we couldn't do it without a significant loss in training. Moreover, that the 552nd Wing was behind schedule in reaching IOC due to things like the hydraulic system ovality problem. It was pointed out that the qualifying phrase "at no loss in training" is what set General Dixon off—it was a contradictory request, and it offended him. I suggested that he prepare a nice message recognizing that the 552nd would lose some training opportunities, but that it was important to get the JSDF on board with the E-3A. A message of that sort was sent to General Dixon; the waters calmed, and the Japanese flew a number of sorties, putting the training schedule in a much deeper hole than expected.

There were four new buildings associated with the bed-down of the E-3A at Tinker AFB. One of those three was for the flight simulator with several degrees of motion and a large terrain model. The second was for the mission simulator that replicated the back end of AWACS. There was also a building dedicated to lead in training with a number of classrooms. The fourth new facility was squadron building that provided rooms for the squadron commander and his/her personnel, mission briefing rooms, and other miscellaneous rooms for the Training Squadron, and the 963rd, 964th, 965th Operational Squadrons. The latter, when fully populated, would have roughly 680 officers and enlisted assigned.

One pet peeve of mine was bulletin boards that were mandatory in a squadron area. They were usually ugly with papers haphazardly stapled on the board. I wanted something better, something uniform, and something that was a source of pride rather than embarrassment. To stimulate good ideas, I obtained supplies from the civil engineers and constructed a sample bulletin board. It had a thin plywood backing overlaid with three-eighths inch corkboard and covered with maroon fabric. Maroon was the scarf color and tail flash of the 965th Squadron. This was all set in a frame. It was sized to hold two rows of eight-and-a-half-inch-by-eleven-inch papers with four in each row. At that time, the air force had six mandatory things that had to be displayed on a squadron bulletin board. I can't remember all of them, but there had to be the Detail Roster, Ground Safety Bulletin, Flight Safety Bulletin, etc. This left two spaces for anything the squadron commander wanted to post. To ensure that there was uniformity, there were prongs that would fit holes from a two-hole punch (those were popular in those days) for each of the eight pages to be displayed. In addition, there were one-fourth-inch clear plastic covers that were drilled to fit the prongs that laid over the pieces of paper. Each of the six mandatory topics had labels above them. I took this masterpiece down to the squadron building and told the commanders that the board I made was just a sample of what would be acceptable to me. But what I really wanted to do was sponsor a contest among the squadrons to see who could come up with the best "BB" prototype. The commanders would choose the winner, and I would pay to have four professionally made—one for each squadron. This exercise fell into the category of setting high standards for your organization.

There was considerable creative work improving on the sample I made. They chose the one they collectively liked best, and the Commander's Bishop's Fund bought them. When they were delivered, the squadron commanders, first sergeants, and I assembled on the bottom floor at a doorway into a squadron area and selected the best spot for the BB. The two civil engineers assisting us mounted it to the wall, and it looked very professional. With that, I said, "Measure the distance from the corner of the outside wall and from the floor and install the rest just like this one." To understand what happened, next the reader needs to picture that this is a very large two-story building with two squadrons on the first floor, one on each side, and two on the second floor. I went upstairs to see how the second floor installation was coming. The two civil engineers didn't see me in the background as they prepared to install the BB.

After making the obligatory measurements, one said to the other, "If we do what the general said, the BB will stick into the doorway twelve inches."

The other said, "I don't care. The general said forty inches from the exterior wall, and that's what we're going to do!" Hearing that, I ran forward and stopped the installation before they could put a hole in the wall. The problem was that the stairwell between the first and second floors changed the end wall and doorway relationship on the second floor. I ran around to the other second floor squadron and stopped them from a county option on their exterior wall. The two upstairs squadron commanders and I picked a suitable location for the BB, and they were then professionally and permanently installed.

I can still replay that moment in my mind, when the technical sergeant civil engineer said, "I don't care. The general said forty inches, and that's what we're going to do!"

I was much more careful when I gave directions after that and usually added, if that doesn't look right, get back with me! And I can still recall being told countless times as a junior officer and action officer in the Pentagon, "Well, that's what the general said," meaning one of my superiors.

Things were going reasonably well with lots of progress in both flight crew and mission crew training. It seemed like a good time for me to check out in the E-3A and earn the respect of the fliers in the 552nd. General Dixon scheduled a commander's call at Langley AFB, and that afforded me an opportunity to inform the general, in person, that I was going to start my checkout in the E-3A. As soon as I got the words out of my mouth as part of some one-on-one polite conversation, he grabbed me by the collar and pulled me closer as he said, "Damn it,

Pete, if I wanted a pilot, I'd have picked a captain for your job. I want you to manage the wing!"

I blurted out a "Yes, sir!" but went ahead with the checkout anyway. Actually, I was flying a lot as it was, only all my time up to the pilot checkout had been learning the mission equipment and working with the mission crews.

Progress was being made toward the criteria previously identified for IOC. As we started examining the criteria, we realized that the people that wrote it didn't understand much about the E-3A. As I recall, the criteria was very specific and required the wing to maintain a twenty-four orbit one thousand nautical miles from Tinker AFB when there were five aircraft assigned. It sounded reasonable on the face of it. However, it was a stretch to believe the wing could maintain a mission capable rate of 60 percent, or three aircraft out of five, with the limited spare parts available and the steep learning curve for our maintenance team at that juncture. Also, it would take approximately three hours for an aircraft to arrive on station, and with a maximum of twelve hours endurance, on-station time would be limited to six hours. Three aircraft could provide a total of eighteen hours of continuous radar coverage on orbit. The first aircraft would have to recover and take off again in less than six hours. Considering the postflight, preflight, and refueling times and any repair time, it seemed to be an impossible tasking. I briefed the TAC Staff on my assessment of the IOC requirement and recommended that TAC just declare us having achieved IOC when the following conditions were met: five aircraft assigned, seven flight and mission crews certified mission ready, a sufficient number of trained maintenance personnel, and a war readiness spares kit (WRSK) filled to an 80 percent level. The TAC Staff adopted the recommendation, and IOC was declared when the aforementioned criteria were achieved. Filling the WRSK to 80 percent took longer than the other criteria, and IOC was declared on April 16, 1978, just a little over one year from the first flight at Tinker.

On Saturday, May 29, 1978, General Dixon relinquished command of the Tactical Air Command to General Jones and subsequently was retired by General Jones. There wasn't a change of command, as apparently, General Dixon did not like General Creech and would not allow him to participate. At General Dixon's retirement reception, there were posters that declared his concept for leadership was to keep the staff in chaos, giving more than one deputy chief of staff (DCS) or director the same tasking pitting one against the other. That strategy certainly worked to achieve his goal of creating chaos.

On Monday, May 1, 1978, General Creech drove from the Pentagon down to Langley AFB and assumed command of the Tactical Air Command (TAC). Subordinate TAC commanders were notified by the TAC command post that General Creech had assumed command and was in his office at TAC Headquarters. There was a new and demanding sheriff in town!

Shortly after taking command of TAC, General Creech scheduled a Commanders' Conference at Langley AFB for all wing and center commanders. The message announcing the conference stipulated the dress for the conference would be flight suits for all meetings and business suit for the evening socials. In addition, commanders would travel to the conference in their wing aircraft. This would be his first opportunity to articulate his policies and tell us what he believed was important for his subordinate commanders to focus on. This was going to be interesting and informative.

> Several important issues were brought up at the conference. Four are listed below:
>
> Commanders should fly often to ensure they were highly proficient and had a good grasp of their flying operations.
>
> Every wing with the same type aircraft would be required to fly the same number of hours per aircraft assigned per year. The number of sorties to be flown by each type aircraft was taken from an analysis of all TAC wings.
>
> Every squadron achieving the monthly quota of the annual flying-hour goal would earn a three-day weekend at the end of the month.
>
> Every squadron failing to achieve the monthly quota will fly the last weekend of the month.

For example, the RF-4 Wing at Shaw AFB, South Carolina, was flying a higher sortie rate than the RF-4 Wing at Bergstrom AFB, Texas, even though Texas offered better flying weather. Among those wings flying the same type aircraft, the one with the highest average sortie rate was identified as the TAC Standard. Standards were achieved and raised every year for the next three or four years.

Commanders had the discretion to schedule more hours/flights during seasonal periods of good weather than in the months of bad weather.

- The wing and squadron monthly hour goals would be posted on a signboard at entrances to the base. These signs would reflect the cumulative monthly achievement with plus and minus signs and numbers to denote if the squadrons were ahead or behind schedule.
- When monthly flying hour goals were met, the wing commander could give squadrons a three-day weekend at the end of the month. If flying hour goals were not met, the last weekend was a work and flying weekend.
- Self-help projects to improve base facilities were encouraged and expected.
- A TAC-wide paint scheme, primarily earth tones, was introduced with the objective of getting all wing buildings and signs painted within the next two years.

At the end of the first day, we all loaded into buses to drive by the aircraft flown into Langley AFB by each wing commander. General Creech graded their appearance as we drove by. Aircraft appearance ranged from outstanding to abysmal. General Creech made the point that all of TAC's aircraft should mimic the best-looking aircraft seen on the ramp, that commanders needed to instill pride in their crew chiefs and maintenance personnel, and that no one could take pride in a trashy-looking plane. The E-3As were in such demand for training and operational sorties that I didn't have one to fly to Langley for the conference and escaped the grading. The E-3A was a handsome and majestic airplane but just couldn't compete in a "beauty contest" with the latest of sleek fighters.

As a result of the direction provided by General Creech at this Commanders' Conference, aircraft flew more sorties, there were three-day weekends when the sortie rate was achieved by a squadron prior to the end of the month, and wing commanders spent more time flying than sitting behind their desks. Morale was on the rise, and the combat capability of the command grew exponentially.

At subsequent Commanders' Conferences, General Creech introduced new concepts such as the Combat-Oriented Maintenance Organization (COMO) and Combat-Oriented Supply Organization (COSO). Under COMO, General Creech directed that one-third of the line maintenance organization be assigned to each of the three squadrons in a wing. These maintainers would wear the patch and scarf of the squadron they were assigned to and would work out of a flight line building next to the Squadron Operations building. They would only work on their squadron's aircraft, and the crew chief's and assistant crew chief's names would be painted on the aircraft behind or below the pilot's name. Crew chiefs and their assistants would be cross-trained to perform a number of tasks that were previously "unionized" so that only specialists could do the work—removing panels was one such task. Removing a panel was a simple task only requiring a Phillips head screwdriver. Prior to cross training, panel removal could only be accomplished by an airman with a "sheet metal" specialty code, often significantly delaying the start of maintenance actions until a "specialist" arrived at an aircraft, requiring panel removal to get to a black box. In each line maintenance facility, there would be a sortie board displaying how the squadron planned to achieve its monthly sortie goals. Also displayed would be the actual sorties flown. Thus, every maintainer was constantly aware of whether his/her squadron was ahead or behind schedule and whether it was likely they would earn a three-day weekend or work the last weekend of the month playing catch-up. It was a great motivational tool, and sortie generation increased without an increase in manning or parts. COMO also provided a good bond between the pilots and maintainers and as such when a squadron deployed its own maintainers went with their aircraft. Under COMO, the wing chief of maintenance was still responsible for quality control inspections and training.

COSO was similar to COMO. Supply personnel were assigned to work out of a squadron maintenance facility and also wore the squadron patch and scarf. High-use parts were stored in this flight line facility so when they were needed, the parts were immediately available—no longer were parts delivered from a distant warehouse with about the same delivery priority as a shovel or lightbulb for the civil engineers. If a part located in the warehouse was needed, one of the squadron supply personnel would go get it. They were motivated to get the aircraft back flying because their three-day weekend depended on it.

Once standards for flying were established and working, General Creech turned to standardizing other things that varied considerably from base to base that should have been in the same ballpark but weren't. One glaring example was payment of per diem to an individual following a temporary duty assignment (TDY). Officers and airmen were required to pay all expenses out of their own pockets (except for airline, bus, and train tickets) and then be reimbursed when they returned from travel.

This required a visit to the Finance Office on base and completion in quadruplicate of a form that was submitted for payment. The time one had to wait for payment varied from thirty minutes to thirty days across TAC bases. General Creech decreed that if one base could reimburse per diem expenses in thirty minutes, the rest of the bases could do likewise. The TAC standard was established as thirty minutes. Immediately, a great hue and cry came up from the bases that required weeks to reimburse service members. "How can we ever get payment down to thirty minutes when we have weeks of forms to process?" shouted the multitude.

"Work overtime until you catch up. Every base has the same number and skill level of finance personnel. There is no reason to be behind" was the response from General Creech. In a month or so, all TAC bases were reimbursing personnel for TDY expenses while they waited a few minutes for the paperwork to be processed and approved. Every activity was examined, and standards were applied where applicable—it worked, and all TAC personnel and their dependents benefited.

Returning to aircraft sortie rates and COMO, General Creech gave the 552nd a reprieve from COMO because of the low number of E-3A assigned when the program was established. He gave me the authority to establish COMO when I felt the time was right. I believed that at least a total of eight E-3As, four per squadron, were required for COMO to ensure some flexibility for major maintenance and still meet a typical squadron flying schedule.

When the eighth E-3A arrived on the ramp from Boeing, I advised operations and maintenance staffs that flight line maintenance personnel would be divided into two squadrons to match the 963rd and 964th Operational Squadrons. It was explained that these squadron maintenance personnel would only work on their squadron aircraft, would deploy with the squadrons, and would wear the squadron patches and scarves. Operations liked it; maintenance didn't! But that was typical of their different mind-sets, and while I tried mightily to convince maintenance that ops were not their enemy, it was a very hard sell with Colonel Hayes and his staff unhappy with the COMO concept.

A week went by, and it was immediately apparent that the 963rd Squadron flew a very high percentage of scheduled sorties, while the 964th was having trouble getting aircraft off the ground. I mentioned this observation to Colonel Hays, the LG. He thought it was just a "getting started" issue. After the second week of similar performance by the two squadrons, I suggested there was a systemic problem in the 964th maintenance. Colonel Hays opined that 964th Squadron was assigned all the older aircraft, and the 963rd got all the newer ones. In response,

I pointed out that the oldest aircraft was only two years out of the factory and virtually brand new and low in flying hours. However, if he was convinced this was the problem, I directed him to transfer the two newest aircraft to the 964th and the two oldest aircraft to the 963rd. With some grumbling, he made the swap. At standup (when we finalized the next day's flying schedule based on the current day's results) that evening, I noticed that our hangar queen (an aircraft that seldom flew) that transferred to the 963rd was scheduled to fly the next morning. Later that night, I went out on the flight line to chat with the maintenance crews and get a sense of morale and attitudes. There was the hangar queen with several maintenance personnel from the 963rd readying her for the morning flight, her first flight in three weeks. I asked the crew chief, whose name was freshly painted on the aircraft, if he thought his plane would make the mission. He was enthusiastic and positive when he said, "She's ready, and she'll fly in the morning!" True to his word, the plane flew and completed the scheduled AWACS mission.

That visit with the hangar queen crew chief on the flight line gave me a clue that it was leadership, not maintenance skills or aircraft age, that made the difference between the two maintenance squadrons. I asked my new senior enlisted advisor, Chief Master Sergeant Jones, formally from the maintenance career field, to spend some time on the flight line and find out why one squadron was performing so well and the other seemed clueless. The chief was back the next morning with his report. It was almost laughable that he was able to come up with the answer so quickly. What he learned was, when the two line maintenance squadrons were formed from the previous single entity, people were selected from the pool by their new commanders. A major with extensive experience in the repair shops that supported the line was picked to be the new 964th Squadron maintenance officer/squadron commander. Personnel were chosen for each squadron like how pickup ball teams were formed when I was a kid: a coin was tossed to see who got the first pick, and they rotated back and forth for each succeeding choice. The original flight line maintenance officer/squadron commander knew all the superstars and picked them for their talent and leadership skills. The newly appointed 964th maintenance officer/squadron commander did not know any of the people or their performance and must have made his choices based on height and looks. Moreover, the new maintenance officer had never worked the flight line—he lacked the instincts and was poorly supported by his senior NCOs. The senior enlisted advisor's report sounded very plausible, so I asked for his recommended course of action. His response surprised me because it was so simple: "Return the major to the repair shops and replace him with the senior maintenance officer from the other line squadron—he has the maintenance savvy and the leadership skills to succeed. Also take the 964th maintenance NCOIC off the line and replace him with the next ranking NCO." As I suspected all along, it was a leadership issue; replace two people at the top was all that the senior enlisted advisor recommended to solve the problem. I directed those actions be taken and waited for some tangible results. In less than one week, both squadrons were very competitive in making the schedule. And both squadrons started earning three-day weekends at the end of the month. Transitioning to COMO proved once again that strong motivational leadership is central to the success of any enterprise.

NATO was considering a purchase of E-3A aircraft, and I was selected to brief each NATO nation's leadership on E-3A demonstrated performance, such as the TAC test, aircraft availability and reliability, based on nearly two years' performance. Maj. Gen. John Pustay had been leading the NATO Policy and sales effort and achieved a lot of traction with the Europeans. However, now that the E-3A was flying and there was solid evidence of its "big picture" and "deep look" capability, it was deemed appropriate by General Jones to put an operator in the mix.

The first visit to Brussels to sit in with the NATO nation's representatives was a lot like watching grass grow—nothing happened that was apparent to me. Essentially, the British representative stated that a decision to purchase E-3As for NATO had to be made by November, or England would go it alone with the development of their Nimrod concept. The German representative said they couldn't be rushed and needed more time and information. An important fact of the agreements to date was that the NATO E-3A along with the NATO crews would be based in England, at Waddington Royal Air Station. Hence, the British stood to gain financially with infrastructure funds and the money the international pool of maintenance personnel and operational crews would spend in the local area.

The Nimrod was a solid state design with solid state phased array radar in a bulbous nose and another in a similar feature aft of the horizontal stabilizer. In theory, it was better than the E-3A because there were no aircraft features to blank the radar. However, it would be more difficult to develop the software necessary to correlate tracks, as they passed from one radar field of regard to the other.

A second meeting produced similar discussions from the British and German representatives, even though I was providing hundreds of pages of information on E-3A system performance, system reliability, and system availability. At the third meeting, there was no agreement on the part of the Germans, so the British, true to their word, pulled out and accelerated their work on the Nimrod. Shortly after the British pulled out, it appeared that the German Defense Ministry had all the information they needed and agreed with the remaining NATO nations to go forward with the purchase of E-3As for NATO. As a direct result of finessing the Brits, the main operating base went to Geilenkirchen in the northwestern part of West Germany near the Belgium border. Score one big political and financial victory for the Germans. On the other hand, while the British developed and tested the Nimrod, they never put it in production, primarily because of the cost.

The German Defense Ministry's decision to go forward with AWACS led to the Bundestag's request to fly a number of ministers aboard the E-3A to observe firsthand what AWACS could do in improving the air defense of West Germany. Accordingly, the wing was directed to deploy a single E-3A to Ramstein AB, Germany, to support the request. All the missions would be flown out of the then West German capital, Cologne Bonn's commercial airport, for convenience of the ministers. Three sorties were planned, one each day, to accommodate the number of ministers who requested to fly in the E-3A on an operational mission. The risk of getting all three sorties off in succession was more than moderate, especially when you factored in that one flight out of Cologne Bonn was actually three sorties per day: a flight to Cologne Bonn to pick up the ministers, the demonstration flight out of Cologne Bonn, and then returning there to disembark the passengers and conduct a wrap-up briefing and answer questions, followed by a short flight to Ramstein AFB to prepare the aircraft for the next day's mission. It would have been desirable to operate out of Cologne Bonn airport; however, they did not have the support equipment required for the E-3A—ramp space and security was also a problem. The time of year was late November, early December, and so low ceilings, poor visibility, and cold weather were also a consideration.

The deployment to Ramstein was uneventful, as were the preparations for the next day's flights. Prior to the deployment, a briefing was prepared to inform the Bundestag Parliamentarians about the E-3A and the mission between the period after takeoff and arrival on orbit over West Germany. The briefing was in 35 mm format and projected on a screen pulled down from the aircraft ceiling in the aft section of the E-3A. Also in the aft of the aircraft were three rather tall communications cabinets and thirteen seats for additional crew members on extended sorties or student crew members on training missions. The slide projector was attached to the top of one of the communication cabinets and projected over the heads of the seated Parliamentarians. In addition, each day, several strudels were ordered from a local German bakery for our guests, along with several carafes of coffee in addition to the normal fare for the crew. If they didn't enjoy the flight, perhaps they would remember the hospitality. The first mission went flawlessly; the Soviets even put up a Mig-25 flying at Mach 3 parallel to the long leg of the orbit along the East German Border.

After landing at Cologne Bonn airport, the Parliamentarians and I went to a DV lounge in the terminal where I answered questions about the mission. They were most curious about the paucity of air traffic over East Germany and Poland compared to that in the West and wondered if the Soviets had invented a means of jamming or spoofing the E-3A radar. It was noted that there was hardly any commercial air traffic in the east and no private aircraft compared to the west. It was also noted that this lack of commercial and general aviation traffic made it very easy for the surveillance technicians to detect a change in the traffic that might indicate an attack was in progress. In addition, IFF beacons on army jeeps were used to signal reports of "enemy" action observed by ground forces. I also pointed out that the minimum velocity detected by the E-3A ground-looking radar was roughly 80 mph. Our experience showed that this would detect most of the high-speed vehicles on the German autobahns so that minimum was raised to over 120 mph for the demonstration so the road traffic would not detract from the demo.

The second flight was not so benign. During the flight briefing at Ramstein, Major Sterk announced that the wet runway and light winds would not allow the pilots to safely abort takeoff if an engine were lost on the takeoff roll just prior to liftoff. I asked the major how bad the situation was. His response was "We need two hundred feet more runway." Now anyone who has calculated the go/no go distance for takeoff knows that two hundred feet on one of those graphs is about the width of a pencil line—but that was the major's calculation. A hush came over the room—the crew was wondering if I would waive the two hundred feet; losing an engine on takeoff was not a common occurrence, and this was a presidential level demonstration. I had worked tirelessly to instill a strong sense of safety into the crew force and was not going to destroy all that hard work by violating my own rules. My response to the major was "We will just have to wait until the conditions improve." I then asked how much fudge we had in the planned takeoff time.

"Thirty minutes" was the answer! As I got up to check the winds and RCR (runway condition reading) myself, Major Sterk burst into the briefing room with "The winds have shifted to directly down the runway.

We now have two hundred feet to spare—it's a go!" With that, we all raced to the E-3A to get airborne prior to an unfavorable shift in the surface wind.

All went well until we got on orbit. As I was instructing one of our guests on the display symbology and showing him how to "hook" a track of interest, there was a loud boom just outside the starboard wall of the fuselage. The Parliamentarian looked at me for an answer; I told him that we were near thunderstorms and that a lightning bolt must have passed close to the aircraft—nothing to worry about. However, I knew it was an engine stall on the inboard starboard engine, which was very uncommon. I excused myself and went to the cockpit, where I discovered that the pilots had climbed to forty thousand feet to avoid turbulence, thus the combination of altitude and rain were starving the engines for oxygen. On my direction, the pilots requested a lower altitude, and the engine stalls subsided.

On returning to Ramstein, I learned that an additional Parliamentarian wanted to fly, but we had no more seats—I said no to the request. Next, I was informed that the engine fire warning light would not illuminate when the test light switch was placed in the on position—that was an abort item. I went to the aircraft to talk to the technician working the problem. He opined that it would be the wiring harness that was defective, probably from chafing due to vibration in the number four engine nacelle or the connection at the light itself. He was presently checking the harness. I asked if we had the parts in stock and if he had the time between now and the morning preflight to complete the troubleshooting and fix the problem once discovered. He said the parts were not in stock, but he had the time if he had the parts. Our wing logistician had worked out a means of getting parts to Europe by buying a seat on a direct flight from Chicago to Frankfurt, Germany. We could make the last transatlantic flight if we had the courier and part on a flight out of Oklahoma City by 2:00 p.m., CT. At that moment, we had about two hours to spare. I directed the technician to immediately order the parts that could possibly be needed. He refused, citing AFM 67-1 and stating it was against regulations to order a part until it had been determined the part was needed, and he didn't know what was needed. I explained to him the importance of the mission, that our wing was the only user of E-3A parts in the world! Again, he declined, saying it was wrong to violate the regulation. It was probably the second or third time in my career that I gave a direct order, this time to order the parts immediately, and followed him to the phone to ensure he did so. As it turned out, the problem was in the light socket, which was repaired in just a few minutes after discovery. The part arrived in time and was flown back to Tinker on the E-3A and returned to supply channels when we redeployed.

Next came a phone call from General Creech, asking me why I declined to take the additional Parliamentarian on the next day's flight. The answer was "There are no more seats available—all are being occupied by aircrew or Parliamentarians!"

"Where do you sit on takeoff?" he asked.

"I sit in the jump seat."

"Put someone else in the jump seat and strap yourself to one of those big communications cabinets in the rear—they're designed to take a crash landing." I spent a lot of time the next morning explaining to the crew that the sale of AWACS to NATO might hinge on one Parliamentarian's vote, so I was going to strap myself to a communications cabinet for takeoff and landing. It was not something I wanted the 966th Training Squadron to emulate, just to get a few more students airborne for training missions.

The last demo flight came off without a hitch—the deployment was a resounding success. We met all our objectives plus one. After completing the debriefing session with our Parliamentarian guests, I climbed aboard the E-3A and asked the senior director, Maj. Jimmy White, for a piece of strudel, saying in part, "I ordered the strudel, I paid for the strudel, and I want to eat a piece of the strudel!"

Major White looked at me from over his crumb covered mustache and said, "General, two out of three ain't bad." The crew had eaten all the remaining strudel while I was debriefing the Parliamentarians. "Two out of three ain't bad" became somewhat of a prized saying in the wing. However, to keep the record straight, when the aircraft got to altitude on the return flight to Tinker AFB, Major White trotted out five big trays of fresh strudel of different flavors. We were all stuffed with strudel by the time the flight was halfway home.

The E-3A was a proven system, and every Unified commander wanted *some* in his theater—permanently. Problem was that not enough aircraft had been delivered on the thirty-four aircraft buy to satisfy these requests, nor had enough crews been trained to combat-ready status to fully man the aircraft if we had them. As a result, there were many deployments to Okinawa, Korea, Alaska, and the North African littoral.

CINCLANT/SACLANT had a unique problem and somewhat personal problem—Admiral Kidd could not and would not tolerate Soviet bear bombers or recce aircraft flying over his carrier battle groups in the Atlantic at low altitude. He wanted E-3As on alert at Langley AFB, Virginia, not too far from his headquarters at Norfolk, Virginia—and got them. He also wanted E-3As on alert in Iceland, augmenting the three ground radar there and covering the Greenland, Iceland, United Kingdom gap—also known as the GIUK gap. The wing was directed to open up a detachment at Keflavik Airfield, the international airport for the capital of Reykjavik. I selected Lt. Col. Ed Zampa to command that detachment. It was a good choice, as he did an excellent job building morale in a difficult environment and making sure that all flights were professionally planned, briefed, and executed.

The winter weather at Keflavik Air Base is bad enough to frighten even the oldest and boldest of fliers. The southwestern part of Iceland is not very cold, just snows most of the time that coats the runway with packed snow or ice. The result is very slick runways and poor stopping conditions. Over the years, Icelanders in that area developed a very unique method of improving runway conditions. They cook sand in huge oven hoppers and spread it on the runway while it is hot. The sand melts down into the ice and snow, forming a very gritty surface, enabling commercial aircraft, the E-3A, and 57th Fighter Squadron aircraft to land almost normally. When the conditions were determined unsafe, E-3As and fighters diverted to bases in Scotland, principally Lossiemouth Royal Air Force Station just below the fifty-eighth parallel.

The 552nd received just a couple of days' notice that we were hosting the NATO nations' military representatives to that august international body. They were to arrive at 0900 hours, receive the wing briefing, tour an aircraft, both simulators, the software development facility, the academic training facility, and maintenance shops, then have lunch and return to their aircraft at 1300 hours. The weather forecast for that morning was snow, and lots of it. By late afternoon of the day, prior to their arrival, it started to snow, and a walking tour of three groups of five was out of the question. I needed six staff cars to drive our guests from point to point. The Air Logistics Center, our host, was asked for support. They said they couldn't support the request and suggested rental cars. That would put a huge dent in the wing budget. Reluctantly, I asked wing officers, starting with the colonels and squadron commanders, if they had a late-model four-door sedan that they would be willing to drive our guests around the flight line to the O'club for lunch and return to their DV aircraft at Base Operations. I would drive my staff car to escort the US military rep and the senior mil rep heading up the group. That left twelve members requiring four cars. By morning, I had a fleet of four-door Cadillacs parked outside wing headquarters. I went over the tour routes for each of the cars and drivers. All the officers proffering their cars were flight or mission crew members and could answer just about every question that our visitors might ask. The drivers were invited to sit in on the wing briefing so that we would all be telling the same story to our guests. Crisis averted.

The 963rd Squadron was deployed to Okinawa as part of a major PACOM exercise. I went along to fly top cover for Lieutenant Colonel Brug and observe the operation. I wasn't the least bit concerned about Wally's ability to lead his squadron effectively and safely, just an opportunity for me to fly and learn more about mission systems operation. It was something of an ORI, and the squadron was taking hits for OPSEC (Operational Security). The IG had tapped our phone lines, and E-3A crew members were saying too much about the flight schedule when talking on the phone. Lieutenant Colonel Brug called a squadron meeting and gave everyone a warning about OPSEC and said he would pull out all the phones if there was one more violation. There was, and that was the end of all the unsecured phones; he pulled out every one right out of the wall. My kind of guy! On the other hand, it appeared that no matter what was done to mask E-3A operational schedules, the IG could pinpoint takeoff times almost to the minute. Missions were over twelve hours with refueling. A full crew of seventeen, plus a straphanger or two like me, required thirty-four to forty in-flight meals. Flight lunches were picked up one hour and thirty minutes prior to takeoff. The IG simply staked out the flight kitchen and watched for the crew van to pick up a large number of prepared meals. I told the IG I wasn't going to allow the crews to eat stale food just mask takeoff times. He backed off of the silly stuff.

Everything was going fine in Okinawa when real-world tasking was received to redeploy the 963rd detachment to Riyadh, Saudi Arabia. Apparently, a flare-up between South Yemen and Oman caused concern in our key Arab ally in the Middle East. There were a number of women in the detachment as well as one or two personnel of the Jewish faith. I called Headquarters Air Force to ask if they wanted me to send those people back to Tinker and send people from Tinker directly to Riyadh. The answer was no; the Air Force was going to push the Saudi military to allow USAF women to drive and not be required to wear burkas when in town. The redeployment went without a hitch. All squadron personnel were put up in first-class hotels. One of the squadron's intelligence officers, an attractive young female lieutenant, was an Olympic class diver and went to the hotel pool clad only in her bikini. I'm told that the next day, there was a new Saudi law prohibiting women from swimming in hotel/motel pools. Dictatorships can craft and pass new laws rather quickly, even overnight, in proven fact.

Once NATO nations learned that German ministers received flights on an E-3A to seal their support, most of twelve remaining nations wanted an E-3A deployment to their country, or perhaps a briefing to their Parliament. Norway wanted to test AWACS ECM resistance and received support from the US government to do just that. They also wanted a briefing to the Norwegian Parliament to explain how the E-3A radar achieved its jam resistance. I was given the responsibility for the briefing and invited to be a guest at the US ambassador's residence on the outskirts of Oslo. The residence was very imposing, sitting high on a hill overlooking several acres of manicured grounds. In the entrance hall, there was a life-size stuffed horse and Andy Warhol's signature painting of a Heinz Tomato Soup can. The first evening, there was an informal dinner for members of the Norwegian government, which gave me an opportunity to talk about the AWACS in a casual setting and answer questions.

The flight test took place the following day. The E-3A was to fly a surveillance orbit over some mountainous terrain with the mission of detecting any aircraft approaching the AWACS. There were a couple of Norwegian Air Force officers on board the AWACS to observe the test and ensure there were no dirty tricks—just a really good radar with excellent side-lobe suppression and a very narrow main beam. The Norwegian Air Force flew a number of aircraft equipped with electronic jammers to screen the fighters approaching the E-3A at very low altitudes in the mountain valleys. They may have also deployed some ground jammers to the area, but I'm not certain of that. Regardless, the E-3A planar array radar picked up the fighters at maximum range for their altitude and tracked them all the way to the E-3A. The Norwegian government was very pleased with AWACS performance and supported the NATO procurement. There may have been some questions about the effectiveness of their own ECM equipment.

Months later, two E-3As were deployed to Okinawa to participate a major annual South Korea exercise. One of the goals for AWACS was to establish data links with the US Army's missile minder for patriot surface-to-air engagement systems and with the US Navy Aegis cruisers and destroyers. The data link was known as Link 11 and was used to control engagements with the F-106 in the CONUS and exchange friendly, unknown, and hostile tracks with compatible systems. For example, the US Navy's E-2 radar surveillance aircraft and the US Army missile minder that fed tracks into their surface-to-air (SAM) air defense systems. On the first day of the Joint/Coalition Exercise, the E-3A communication technicians failed to link up with any of the compatible army and navy systems. On the second exercise day, the E-3A was loaded with our most experienced communications technicians; but again, they failed to link up with any other Link 11 system. Our best communication technicians were sure they were doing everything correctly but, out of desperation, asked the navy to loan us one of their Link 11 experts to fly on AWACS for the third day. As the story was relayed to me, when the air force techs broke out the crypto codes prior to arriving on orbit, the navy chief assisting them said, "You have the codes for the wrong Zulu day and time!" In this context, "Zulu" stands for the day and time at the zero meridian, which runs through Greenwich, England. Greenwich Mean Time is the standard used throughout US military services worldwide for operations to ensure all activities are time synched. After some discussion, the navy chief convinced the E-3A crew that in the Pacific Command (PACOM), Zulu Time was based on Honolulu, Hawaii time. With the crypto codes for Honolulu, Hawaii, set in Link 11, all the systems linked up, and it worked every time after that revelation. I guess worldwide did not include the Pacific region.

When that Joint/Coalition Exercise was finished, we were tasked to brief President Park about E-3A capabilities on the E-3A using the same slideshow setup used for the German Bundestag. After the E-3A landed at Osan Air Base near Soul, about fifteen South Korean Secret Service personnel descended on the aircraft to ensure it was safe for their president. They went through the aircraft very, very thoroughly and announced it was safe for President Park. I didn't have the heart to show them the doors that led to the front and rear lower lobes that housed most of the esoteric AWACS gear, such as the six klystrons that generated the RF signals radiated from the planar array antenna—one for each unique frequency. On the other hand, I knew there were no threats to President Park lurking in those lower bays.

At the appointed time, a caravan of six long black limousines drove onto the flight line and made a beeline for the stairs leading to the E-3A rear entrance door. When they were about forty feet from the foot of the stairs, they started a left-hand circle at speed that was just short of squealing the tires. After about three circles, the caravan stopped with a limo adjacent to the E-3A stairs. A man got out of the front and stood by the rear limo door. Nothing happened, the man reentered the limo, and the high-speed circle began anew. After three false starts, the caravan stopped; President Park exited the rear door and sauntered to the bottom of the stairs, where I was waiting along with two of his bodyguards. After President Park was comfortably seated and served coffee, the briefing began. Following the AWACS briefing, he was given a tour of the aircraft, exiting the front door where the limos were waiting.

When the Joint/Coalition United Nations Korean exercise was over, an E-3A landed at Clark AFB, Philippines, to provide a similar AWACS briefing and aircraft tour to President Marcos. The visit by President Marcos went without the fanfare and dramatics experienced in Korea and was well received with lots of questions.

Upon returning to Tinker AFB, Oklahoma, I decided to take on a challenge that had been put on the back burner while working NATO AWACS issues. This challenge was maintaining the unique Aerospace Ground Equipment (AGE) that supported the E-3A. The in-commission rate for unique AGE hovered just above 50 percent, and the individual pieces of equipment had the appearance of something in a salvage yard. I moved the AGE NCOIC to another supervisory job and put in a highly regarded senior master sergeant with the charge to bring AGE up to the level of other aspects of maintenance. This would require an in-commission rate of 75 percent, and a not-mission-capable maintenance (NMCM) of less than 20 percent. It must have been a bigger challenge than I expected because the senior master sergeant put in his retirement papers after being in the job for only six months.

What that meant is I had to find a top-notch NCO with a reputation for making good things happen with less than nineteen years service so he or she couldn't retire if the going was too tough. I found the man and promised I would work with him to bring AGE up to par with the rest of maintenance. The master sergeant and I called a meeting of all the AGE maintenance personnel and informed them of the following:

> The base civil engineers would paint the outside of their building to match the rest of 552nd facilities.

> All of us, me included, would paint the inside of the building white to provide better illumination in their work areas.

> The AGE workforce would be divided into three groups to match the existing flying squadrons. The AGE associated with each squadron would have a circle on each side that matched the flying squadron colors of blue, maroon, and yellow.

> AGE maintenance personnel would receive new toolboxes and new snap-on tools as necessary to help them to improve their efficiency.

All of the AGE groups achieving an average monthly in-commission rate of 75 percent would enjoy a three-day weekend.

I would visit the AGE shop on a random basis and rate the appearance of their AGE equipment. The group with the best-looking AGE would get a bonus prize day off monthly.

It took a couple of months of walkabout visits to the AGE shop and discussing with the maintainers about what needed to be done to help them achieve their goals. After about three months, two of the groups earned a three-day weekend, and one of those two earned the bonus prize additional day off.

An assistant deputy undersecretary of defense called to inform me that I had been selected to command and build the NATO AWACS Wing at Geilenkirchen, Germany. I thanked him for the advance alerting, saying I was ready for any assignment the air force and DOD wanted me to have. However, I was thinking that I had already done three years of building the 552nd to operational status and a couple of real-world deployments. A four-year tour in NATO building a second AWACS Wing would brand me as an expert "one trick pony," with little value to the air force for a follow-on assignment. Dutifully, I called General Creech to pass on the information given me by the assistant deputy undersecretary, asking when I might expect orders. He said, "You've already been with AWACS too long, and I have more important things for you to do in TAC. How does commanding a numbered air force sound to you?"

"Sounds great, sir. I'm ready, and right now, the 552nd is in great shape, with no major issues."

A month later, I received a call from Lieutenant General Gabriel, commander of USAF Forces Korea and deputy commander United Nations Forces Korea. He was about to lose his air force director of operations, a two-star position, and was alerting me that he would be calling General Lew Allen, air force chief of staff, to have me reassigned to Korea as his director of operations. I really liked General Gabriel; he was very affable and always pleasant to work for. He was my direct report when General Dixon brought me into TAC to command and build the 552nd AWAC Wing. I remember well when I previewed the TAC Test briefing to General Dixon; he really raked me over the coals for about an hour. When the briefing was over and General Dixon had left the room, I went over to then major general Gabriel and apologized for the lousy presentation. He smiled and said, "Pete, that was a B+. You can't get any better than that in this conference room!" I told General Gabriel it would be great to work for him again and thanked him for his confidence in me. It would be a great assignment and an opportunity to get back into flying late-model fighter aircraft.

After hanging up, I called General Creech and relayed the gist of the conversation with Lieutenant General Gabriel. General Creech said in part, "It would be a great job, but I've got a command for you and need your talents in TAC."

Just when I thought I was finished globe-trotting to market AWACS, I was tapped by the Air Staff to go to Iran and help the Shah's Air Staff complete their bed-down planning for the E-3A purchases that Congress was considering. It was the fall of 1978. Col. Don Kutyna, from the E-3A System program officer at the Electronic Systems Command (ESD), was selected to accompany me. He was the E-3A R&D expert, and I was the operator. The flight to Tehran, capital of Iran, was uneventful. We were met by American embassy staff and taken to the Ministry of Defense, where we met a major general who headed the Iranian Royal Air Force (IRAF) Planning Staff. The following morning, Colonel Kutyna and I were flown to a number of Iranian Air Force bases where we met the commanders and toured the facilities and met some of the IRAF officers and enlisted workforce. Three of the bases visited were Bandar Abbas, Khatami at Esfahan, and Shiraz. From our perspective, Shiraz was the odds on favorite for bedding down the E-3A. The local area had a high tech industrial base, and Shiraz Air Base was receiving United States Navy F-14s with significant high-tech support from US industry.

When the tour was finished, it was Thursday, with the Holy weekend starting that evening. For whatever reason, a military attaché in the US embassy asked me if I wanted to do some hunting over the next two days. It seemed the nearby Alborz Mountains were overrun with very large and nasty wild boar. Because pork was forbidden to touch, these huge pigs were rooting up the local farmers' crops, and the unarmed farmers were unable to do anything about the wild boar, let alone touch them. I said I would be happy to scour the mountains for wild boar and, armed with a 12-gauge pump shotgun, went hunting. An embassy staff member picked me up in the morning, dropped me off in the mountains at a rendezvous site, and picked me up at the same location in the evening. This went for both Holy days, and I had a great time hiking through the western coastal mountains—but to no avail. Not one wild boar did I see, but I did find lots of places where they had torn up the local crops. When I later commanded CENTAF, the experience paid big dividends in developing our supporting plan for CENTCOM's 2004 War Plan.

On Sunday, Col. Don Kutyna and I were back at work in the Iranian Royal Air Force Headquarters working with their chief of plans. We explained that from our perspective, Shiraz was the best choice for an E-3A bed-down location based on all the important support factors. Two of these were: a large pool of highly skilled personnel to draw from, and a large thriving city to support a significant increase in operational and maintenance personnel; moreover, Shiraz AB was an excellent airfield with a long load-bearing runway.

The Iranian major general heading up the planning function listened patiently and then went over to a large map of Iran hung floor to ceiling on a wall and pointed to a vast desert area at least a hundred miles southwest of Tehran. While pointing, he said, "The Shah en Shah (King of Kings) wants to put it here—why, can't he do that?"

I said, "There is nothing there, no roads, no city, and no electrical power generation to support a large industrial complex like an E-3A Wing."

The general countered with "The Shah en Shah is well aware of those limitations. That is exactly why he wants to put the E-3A unit there. We will have to dig wells for water, build roads for access to the site, and put in electrical power generation to support the airfield and the city that will eventually support it. This will take a couple of years, but the E-3As will not be produced and delivered for at least three years—so the airbase and the city will be ready before the airplanes arrive!"

"Why are you doing this when you don't have to?" I asked.

The general responded that there are many Bedouin tribes in that region. "They have no way to get supplies or take their trinkets to market for sale. They have no reliable source of water and no electricity to improve their lives. Putting the E-3A unit there will solve all those problems and put the E-3A out of range of Saddam Hussein's Scud missiles. Iraq is our mortal enemy, and we need the AWACS and the F-4s and F-14s we are buying from the United States to keep the Iraqi Air Force in check!" He went on to say, "You and Colonel Kutyna have to convince your air force and the US government that everything would be in place prior to arrival of the first E-3A and that the airbase would be far better than anything we had seen on our tour of existing Iranian air bases." We carried that message back to Washington DC, and Congress with USAF support approved the sale of E-3As to Iran.

General Rabbi, chief of the Iranian Royal Air Force, his wife, and two generals from his staff paid a visit to Tinker AFB, Oklahoma, to fly aboard AWACS and tour all of the support facilities. He wanted to get a firsthand view of what it took to support a large number of E-3As. General Rabbi, trained in the flight simulator and his staff, received a back-end orientation in the mission simulator. General

Rabbi demonstrated he was a good pilot and subsequently experienced no difficulty in flying the E-3A. I went along on his E-3A flight to ensure that he didn't pressure the instructor pilots to do anything out of the ordinary. Sheila, my wife, entertained Mrs. Rabbi by taking her shopping in one of the newest malls in Oklahoma City. Sheila related that Mrs. Rabbi almost fainted when she realized that she left a leather bag she was carrying at one of the stores. Fortunately, it was still there when they returned—that's when she confided to Sheila that she was carrying nearly $400,000 worth of gold bars in that bag. That would equate to about twenty-five pounds of gold. On his departure, General Rabbi gave me a gift of a case of premium caviar (seventy-two cans) and a case of vodka. The value of these gifts far exceeded the sixty-five-dollar gift value limit allowed. I called the US government gift repository for instructions on where to send the caviar and vodka. I was told to get two witnesses and donate the gift to the officers' club to sell over the bar and for appetizers. I believe the O'club made higher profits for the following two months.

Regrettably, President Carter convinced the Shah en Shah to abdicate and sent Gen. Dutch Huyser, USAF, to Iran to convince the service chiefs to allow the ayatollah to return to Iran. They did and were summarily executed within two weeks of the ayatollah's return. Mrs. Rabbi escaped and found her way to the United States, where she established a residence on the West Coast. The United States has had nothing but problems with Iran ever since.

General Creech called to inform me that there was a slight change in his reassignment plans for me due to fiscal constraints and the political environment. Air Defense Command was going to be disestablished on October 1, 1979, and their air defense aircraft and ground radar would be transferred to the Tactical Air Command under First Air Force to take advantage of economies of scale. Those concepts sounded a lot like Col. Robert Reed's Six-Man Group paper becoming reality. Unfortunately, he went on to say, "The mood in Washington is against creating a new headquarters to replace an old one (First Air Force in lieu of Air Defense Command). Therefore, the new entity would be called Air Defense TAC (ADTAC), and the commander would be dual hatted as the deputy commander of TAC for Air Defense and Commander ADTAC." What games politicians play! Further, he noted there was no money in the budget for this to happen until October 1, 1979; however, there was money in the budget for Brig. Gen. Neil Eddins, my replacement to arrive at Tinker in late May 1979 as my special assistant. General Creech opined that we could get along during the overlap and that I could mentor General Eddins during this period, so there would be no momentum lost during the change in commanders.

Colonel Eddins had a storied career as an air force fighter pilot. He was assigned to the Air Force Fighter Weapons School in the late 1950s as a test pilot flying the F-100 Saber. While there, he was selected for the air force Thunderbird demonstration team flying in the slot position from 1959 to 1961. In 1966, he was a flight commander in the 388th TFW flying F-105s out of Korat Royal Thai Air Force Base (RTAFB), Thailand. In January 1967, he was reassigned to Nellis AFB, Nevada, and became commander of the Thunderbirds until February 1969. Following operational assignments in the European Theater, he returned to Thailand as the vice wing commander of the 432nd TFW at Udorn RTAFB in March 1975. Shortly thereafter, he was reassigned to the 388th TFW at Korat RTAFB as the wing commander. The 388th rotated back to Hill AFB, Utah, in December 1975, with Colonel Eddins retaining command of the wing. In May 1977, he moved to TAC Headquarters as the assistant deputy chief of staff for logistics. Subsequently, he took command of the 1st TFW at Langley AFB, Virginia, equipped with F-15s.

After commanding two fighter wings and a deep immersion in logistics, he was well equipped to take the 552nd helm. I don't remember a change of command where Neil and I exchanged the wing flag. He just took over and of course was well known to all wing personnel after serving as my "special assistant" for nearly four long months. Brigadier General Eddins must have done a good job in leading the wing forward, as they continued to excel in every challenge handed to them. General Eddins was rewarded with a promotion to major general with an assignment as the US Military Training Mission commander in Riyadh, Saudi Arabia. He is retired and living in Henderson, Nevada.

In late September, Sheila, my wife, and I bid farewell to the hundreds of people in the 552nd AWAC Wing that made it all happen and headed our cars northwest to Peterson AFB, Colorado, on the outskirts of Colorado Springs. I wasn't expecting an overwarm welcome, as my job was to take over command of their air divisions, sage centers, Fighter Interceptor Squadrons, and ground-based radar; and transfer these assets to the Tactical Air Command. Essentially, ADTAC would become the US Force provider to NORAD along with the Alaska NORAD region and Canadian NORAD region.

Lessons Learned

Set high standards for yourself and your
organization—it becomes contagious!

Never violate Higher Headquarters regulations or
your own rules without first taking responsibility and
accountability because you are setting the example.

Determine the right course for your enterprise
and have the courage to execute!

Do not blindly stand behind senior subordinate
leaders when they are wrong!

If you need to violate an established rule to accomplish
the mission, document the event/activity and tell
your superiors—don't ever try to hide it.

Always reward creativity and speedy execution of difficult tasks!

Seek the counsel of subordinates who've demonstrated the rare trait of
telling you the truth as they perceive it, even though it may be painful!

Leaders do not have to be the originators of all good ideas. They
just have to recognize and seize upon them when they hear one!

Reward and applaud good ideas whenever and wherever you find them.

You'll never know what is happening at the lower levels of your
enterprise unless you go there unannounced and without an entourage!

There is nothing so rewarding as creating a team
effort in pursuing a worthy goal!

Never pass up an opportunity to fix something that is easy!

Gen. Dixon & Sheila pinning stars on Brig. Gen. Pete
with Scott & Denise observing. Tinker AFB, OK

Col. Jerry Mack hosts Dining Out. Brig. Gen. Pete & Sheila to his
right. Col. Mack was the heart & soul of AWACS, Tinker AFB, OK

E-3A AWACS & crew. Five flight crew on left, thirteen
mission crew on right. Tinker AFB, OK

Maj. Gen. Pete showing NATO officers how to
operate surveillance console. Tinker AFB, OK

Gen. Creech, Commander TAC, pins stars on
Maj. Gen. Pete. Langley AFB, VA

Secretary of the Air Force, Hans Mark awards Maj.
Gen. Pete the Zukert Management Award. Former Air
Force Secretary Zukert on right. Pentagon, VA

Brig. Gen Pete checks out in the F-15, Luke AFB, AZ

CHAPTER 12

Air Defense TAC (ADTAC)

The older children, Denise and Scott, were not enthusiastic about leaving Midwest City and moving to Colorado Springs, Colorado. We had been in Oklahoma for over three years, and they had formed strong bonds with their schoolmates and neighborhood friends. Denise made arrangements with the family of a close friend to live with them until graduation from high school with her longtime classmates. Scott didn't go to such drastic lengths to stay in Oklahoma. Sheila and I finally overcame their resistance without resorting to force, and off we went.

The North American Aerospace Defense Command (NORAD) was and still is a binational command manned by both Canadian and American forces and personnel. The command was established on May 12, 1958, at Ent AFB in Colorado Springs, Colorado. It was widely known for its hardened and deeply buried survivable command center in Cheyenne Mountain located along the Front Range just south of the city. Gen. James E. Hill was the NORAD commander at the time of my arrival. General Hill was a highly decorated WW II fighter pilot in P-47s, with five kills, making him an ace. Later, he saw combat in Korea flying F-80s, where he shot down a MiG-15, giving him a total of six aerial kills. He flew 127 combat missions over Europe and 128 in Korea, for a total of 255 combat missions. His combat decorations include the Silver Star, Distinguished Flying Cross with three Oak Leaf Clusters, and Air Medal with forty Oak Leaf Clusters. He was promoted to the grade of general on December 21, 1977, when he took command of NORAD and ADCOM. At that juncture, Lt. Gen. Kenneth Lewis,

RCAF, was the deputy commander of NORAD, and Maj. Gen. Warren Moore was the deputy commander of ADCOM. I'm reasonably sure that General Hill did not support the air force's decision to transfer his NORAD regions, Interceptor Squadrons, and AC&W radar sites to ADTAC. Nonetheless, he was very gracious and welcomed me aboard when I reported to him and informed him that I was ready to assume the role of his component commander on October 1, 1979.

In 1979, NORAD consisted of the headquarters located in a large windowless building on Bijou Street, a few blocks northeast of downtown Colorado Springs. It was comprised of the USAF Air Defense Command (ADCOM) and the Canadian Air Command located near Winnipeg, Manitoba. Operational forces consisted of the Alaskan NORAD Region at Elmendorf AFB, Alaska, the eastern and western Canadian regions, and six US NORAD regions and several subordinate air divisions in the continental US (CONUS). In the CONUS, there were twenty-three Air Defense Fighter Interceptor Squadrons with forty-six alert locations, where two fighter aircraft, flight crews, and crew chiefs stood alert 24/7/365. Any unknown aircraft penetrating the North American air defense identification zone (ADIZ) without a flight plan or not arriving within five minutes of the forecast time at the ADIZ would theoretically result in scrambling a pair of these fighters to intercept and identify the unknown aircraft. Alert pilots were eager to fly, so there was no hesitation to "scramble" them to intercept an unknown.

These Fighter Interceptor Squadrons were spread over the periphery of the lower forty-eight states as tenants on SAC, TAC, or MAC bases. Air defense squadrons were normally commanded by a lieutenant colonel, with a major as the operations officer and second in the chain of command. For example, the following Fighter Interceptor Squadrons were located at the bases indicated:

Squadron	Aircraft	Location
2nd TFITS	F-106	Tyndall AFB, FL
5th FIS	F-106	Minot AFB, ND
48th FIS	F-106	Langley AFB, VA
49th FIS	F-106	Griffiss AFB, NY
57th FIS	F-4E	Keflavik AB, Iceland
83rd FIS	F-106	Castle AFB, CA
87th FIS	F-106	Duluth IAP, MN, then relocated

87th FIS	F-106	K. I. Sawyer AFB, MI
95th FIS	F-106	Tyndall AFB, FL
318th FIS	F-106	McChord AFB, WA

Air Defense Fighter Interceptor Squadrons in the CONUS were under the command and control of a NORAD region commanded by an air force brigadier general. Every CONUS NORAD region was collocated with a semiautomated ground environment (SAGE) center. Each SAGE center was built around a vacuum tube era computer that processed tracks of aircraft in the region. The SAGE computer also enabled surveillance technicians and weapons controllers in the SAGE center to identify "unknown" aircraft (referred to as bogeys) in the region's airspace and conduct intercepts to visually identify them with fighter interceptor aircraft sitting five-minute alert. The alert area was usually located adjacent to the end of a primary runway on the airfield. The alert area contained hangars for two alert aircraft. Above the aircraft were sleeping quarters for the pilots/aircrews, a dining facility, and a recreation area. The recreation area usually contained a television, small library, and an exercise area. When a pilot or flight crew were "scrambled or flushed," they slide down a brass fireman's pole into the aircraft hangar bay. Normally, pilots/aircrews and crew chief were on alert in the alert facility for forty-eight hours. There was also a command and control individual in the alert area to verify the scramble-or-flush order. When aircrews arrived at the facility for alert duty, they preflighted and "cocked" their aircraft for immediate engine start and taxi. Once they entered the cockpit on a scramble or flush, all they had to do was start the engine and signal the crew chief to pull the chocks. It was expected that the aircraft would be airborne within five minutes from the time the Klaxon horn sounded. This five-minute time to get airborne was routinely met. If the alert crew had not been scrambled to identify an unknown during their forty-eight hours on alert, they would normally be scrambled at the end of their alert cycle to fly a training mission. While the alert force was airborne and available to conduct an intercept if required, replacement crews and aircraft were placed on alert and cocked.

CONUS NORAD regions and SAGE centers were located as follows:

Region Designation	**Region Location**
20th NORAD region	Fort Lee, VA
21st NORAD region	Hancock Field, NY

23nd NORAD region	Duluth, MN
24th NORAD region	Malmstrom AFB, MT
25th NORAD region	McChord AFB, WA
26th NORAD region	Luke AFB, AZ

In addition, ADTAC was responsible for the surveillance radar in Iceland as well as those along the distant early warning line across the Arctic Circle in Greenland, Canada, and Alaska. There were still a number of aircraft control and warning radar sites operated by ADTAC, where there was insufficient FAA radar coverage over the ocean approaches to the United States and across the ADIZ. There was also a Nike SAM air defense site on Key West, Florida, to defend the southern approaches to Florida from low-flying Cuban aircraft. NORAD was both a binational and Joint Command. The binational nature of NORAD was represented by the two Canadian NORAD regions and about 170 Canadian officers and enlisted on the NORAD staff and in the Cheyenne Mountain command center. Maj. Gen. William Cooper, USA, represented multiservice jointness as the NORAD chief of staff. When the Nike site on Key West was closed in 1980, Major General Cooper, an air defender, was transferred to Germany as the commander 32nd RADCOM.

Clearly, ADTAC was a widely dispersed geographic command. The span of control was also very large, with six brigadier generals directly reporting to me. Running ADTAC was a big step up from commanding the 552nd Wing. On the other hand, everything had been in place and up and running for some time. There was no start from a clean sheet of paper, as had been the case at Tinker. All I had to do was to quickly find the weak areas and bring them up to standards that I felt comfortable with, and blend ADTAC into TAC. The really big challenge was transforming the air defense culture, which was highly decentralized and autonomous, down to the Fighter Interceptor Squadrons and radar sites. The "culture" of any organization is usually the hardest place to influence change. Further, there is no document or charter that defines an organization's culture. It just is what it is and difficult to describe or get your arms around.

Col. Ralph "Sox" Bowersox was assigned to ADTAC as vice commander, a direct lift from the former ADCOM/DO. "Sox" was a highly experienced and well-respected member of the air defense community. The rest of the staff were also direct transfers from the ADCOM organization. Most were highly competent in their field and had spent their entire career in the air defense world. Up to this point in time, air defense interceptors were solely all-weather interceptors and not found in the tactical commands, such as US Air Forces in Europe (USAFE), Pacific Air Forces (PACAF), and Tactical Air Command (TAC). Jet interceptors started with the F-86D, F-89, F-94, F-101, F-102, and F-106—none of these aircraft were flown in the Tactical Fighter Commands with the exception of the F-101 which had a nuclear strike missions in Europe.

Advanced pilot training for interceptor pilots emphasized instrument flying and ground-controlled intercepts by weapons controllers in SAGE sites. Interceptors were vectored to the target aircraft and directed by weapons controllers when to fire their rockets or guided missiles. They had no training in dog fighting or air-to-ground weapons delivery. With regard to the air-to-air mission, ADTAC fighters were expected to encounter Soviet bombers and reconnaissance aircraft, not fighters. As to the air-to-ground mission, air defense interceptors were not equipped to carry and release air-to-ground munitions. Accordingly, air defense fighter pilots rarely transferred out of the Air Defense Command prior to 1966 because they were not trained in the requisite skills required in the tactical forces. This changed in the 1966 time frame during the fighter buildup in South Vietnam to carry the fight into North Vietnam. Col. "Sox" Bowersox was one of these wartime converts to tactical fighters and flew a one-year tour in F-105 "Thuds" with all missions flown over North Vietnam. Sox would have excelled in the tactical forces; however, with over twenty years' experience in air defense, he was reassigned to ADCOM after his tour in Vietnam and subsequently to ADTAC. Colonel Bowersox, as my vice commander, was very helpful in balancing my lack of experience in air defense. He knew all of the pilots in ADTAC by their first names, had flown often with all of the squadrons, and was well respected by all the generals running the air divisions/regions. He also knew the Interceptor Squadron commanders and which ones needed constant oversight.

General Creech dropped into Peterson AFB, Colorado, one evening with very little advance warning on a swing through TAC's western bases in Twelfth Air Force. He arrived two days after our household goods arrived and still in boxes in all the rooms except the kitchen. In the short time we had after notification and prior to General Creech's arrival, Sheila ran out and bought some groceries for dinner, including a shank of prime rib. I met General Creech at his aircraft, a T-39 Sabreliner, and drove him to the Antlers Hotel, where he had reservations. On the way, I offered him our dinner menu and said I could pick him up from the

Antlers and bring him back to the base after he had a chance to freshen up. He very graciously declined, saying that he wanted to have a quiet night and get to bed early.

When I returned home, I told Sheila we were off the hook for dinner and could get started with the unpleasant chore of unpacking for our fifteenth move. Just as we started opening boxes, General Creech called with the news that the Antlers's kitchen was closed for renovation, and he would like to take us up on our dinner offer. It was about an hour round trip to downtown Colorado Springs and back, which gave Sheila sometime to prepare the meal. I opened some red wine and cleaned up the kitchen before leaving. After dinner and brandy, General Creech said he'd like to see the house. It wasn't much—two stories, small in size, and every room full of unpacked boxes. General Creech didn't say a word as we led him through the quarters. I didn't think our assigned house on Selfridge Avenue was even suitable for colonel's quarters, but it was on Peterson AFB general's row and where we would spend the next eighteen months. It was a good thing we could live on base, as I spent the greater part of that time TDY. Our next-door neighbors were Maj. Gen. Bruce Brown and his wife, Claudine—wonderful people, and we're still the best of friends. Bruce was erudite and a deep thinker; Claudine, very charming and gracious. Gen. Bruce Brown was also the source of several four-star butt chewing from General Hartinger. That vignette will come later and in sequence.

On October 1, I showed up at the office set aside for the ADTAC commander at the Chidlaw Building and introduced myself to my secretary and senior enlisted advisor. My secretary turned out to be an air force technical sergeant and one of the best I was ever privileged to work with. My opinion of her professional skills was reinforced by her eventual promotion to chief master sergeant. The executive officer was Maj. Terry McKenzie, who volunteered to move from Tinker AFB to Colorado Springs to help get the command staff quickly transitioned to my work and leadership style. Colonel Bowersox then took me around to all the other rooms in the Chidlaw Building, where the ADTAC Staff were now hard at work, translating all the former NORAD regulations into TAC and ADTAC regulations and field instructions. The talent that I inherited from ADCOM was impressive. On the other hand, I reminded myself that the transformation of culture had to start immediately and asked the exec to set a date for the first Commander's Call so I could address everyone in a more formal manner, set the tone, and establish goals. One of those goals would be to move ADTAC from the Chidlaw Building in Colorado Springs to Langley AFB, Virginia. Moving

ADTAC to Langley would enable achievement of all the manpower savings envisioned in the transition from ADCOM to TAC.

It turned out to be a fast immersion into Air Defense Interceptor Operations. On October 2nd, Maj. Gen. Bruce Brown invited me to attend an Accident Board Investigation Report on an in-flight mishap involving the 5th FIS based at Minot AFB, North Dakota. The board president, a colonel, briefed all the events leading up to the mishap and the board's findings. It was a classic failure of leadership! Very briefly, the 5th FIS was tasked to deploy six F-106s. Such deployments were then referred to as "Six Packs"—I didn't even like the sound of that term associated with aircraft deployments. The squadron commander, a lieutenant colonel, turned over the planning for the deployment to a captain in the squadron. The captain's plan was simple to brief but difficult to execute. The deployment was to be accompanied by a KC-135 tanker also based at Minot AFB. The KC-135 would refuel the fighters when they reached predetermined levels of fuel. The plan called for all six fighters to line up in flights of twos behind the tanker when it took the runway. When the tanker and "chicks" were cleared for takeoff, the flights of two would take normal element spacing, roughly eight seconds, and join on the tanker's right wing in echelon formation. When all aircraft had joined, there would be six F-106s in wingtip formation with the lead F-106 flying wingtip formation on the tanker. For the nonfliers, "in echelon" means that when lead turns away, all wingman fly level, looking at the underside of lead, unless "show formation" is briefed, then they fly in the same plane as the lead (KC-135) aircraft's wing. When a lead aircraft turns away or toward the flight, all wingmen stay in the plan of lead's wing. In normal formation, a turn into the wingmen is always flown the same as show formation (i.e., in the same plane). The length of a KC-135 wing and six F-106s creates considerable vertical movement for the number six aircraft when the KC-135 makes a thirty-degree bank. There was no backup deployment plan for bad weather.

On the day of the deployment, the ceiling was about two hundred feet and the visibility low. Minot was just above minimums. At the F-106 flight briefing, with the KC-135 tanker crew in attendance, the captain asked the KC-135 aircraft commander if he would hold the KC-135 below the clouds until all six of the F-106s were on his wing and then start a climb into the weather. The aircraft commander replied that the Strategic Air Command (SAC) had only one climb profile for a KC-135 and that he was obligated to follow that profile, which was a continuous climb, as soon as the aircraft reached climb airspeed. The captain then briefed that all three elements of F-106s would use minimum spacing for starting their takeoff roles. This was an attempt to ensure that all three elements would get on the KC-135 wing prior to the tanker entering the clouds. Everything was now in place for the accident to occur. When the gaggle of aircraft taxied onto the runway, the tower called, asking if they wanted to amend the planned departure, as the weather was deteriorating. The squadron commander, flying the lead F-106, replied no. This was his last opportunity to change the plan and call for a standard radar trail departure until all aircraft were above the clouds. Once VFR on top with the tanker on radar, they could join up.

The KC-135 rolled and started his standard climb profile. The lead F-106 element joined shortly before the KC-135 entered the clouds. The second pair of F-106s was just about joined up when the tanker entered the weather, but managed to achieve a "hairy" join up. The third pair of F-106s was closing too fast when the first five aircraft went out of sight. Element lead declared "lost wingman," which dictates a prescribed angle of bank turn-away from the flight for a predetermined number of degrees. For example, if number 2 is joining on lead and loses sight, the pilot declares "lost wingman" and turns at a fifteen-degree bank for a fifteen-degree heading change. If number 3 as an element lead with number 4 on his wing declares "lost wingman," he turns with a fifteen-degree bank for fifteen degrees, but number 4 banks thirty degrees and turns to achieve a thirty-degree heading change. This has been the standard for decades to ensure that aircraft in weather do not run into each other. Once a lost wingman procedure has been declared and executed, each pilot calls the controlling agency and requests assistance for rejoin or continuing the mission as single aircraft.

The pilot of the number 5 aircraft (element lead) and the pilot of the number 6 aircraft (wingman) had not briefed the number of degrees they would turn if "lost wingman" was declared. The element lead turned hard right; his wingman was not as aggressive, and number 5 cut the radome off number 6, his wingman. All this happened in the weather at low altitude. Both pilots were able to maintain control of their aircraft and get to visual conditions above the clouds, where they could check the airworthiness of their aircraft. Both aircraft recovered safely. However, the cost of repairing them was well over $1 million; hence, it was a class A mishap. The Accident Board president said that the board found the accident was caused by a failure of leadership.

Leadership failure: The commander approved an operational plan that did not have a backup provision for use in the event of inclement weather.

Leadership failure: The commander allowed a highly flawed plan to be briefed when the weather was known to be at minimums and forecast to remain that way for several hours after takeoff.

Leadership failure: The commander did not revise the plan during the actual flight briefing or at the end of the runway prior to takeoff. A radar trail departure is a standard procedure and could have been a legitimate audible to the pilots from the commander in the briefing room or on the runway prior to departure.

Last leadership failure: The commander did not assign a more experienced pilot such as operations officer or a flight commander as part of the mission planning team.

Maj. Gen. Warren Moore, vice commander ADCOM; Maj. Gen. Bruce Brown, NORAD/DO, and Brig. Gen. William Lindeman were in attendance and started conferring about the board president's findings. A major concern was that the squadron commander was handpicked by General Hill and was one of his favorite field grade officers. All of a sudden, General Moore said, "Wait, this isn't our problem—this is Pete's problem. He assumed command of ADTAC yesterday, and he now owns the 5th FIS."

My response was "Well, gentlemen, this all happened months ago on your watch, but I'll take the action needed because it's my squadron going forward!" Then I told the board president I concurred with his findings and asked, "What is the flight status of the squadron commander?"

"Still flying," I was informed.

General Moore turned to me and asked, "What action do you plan to take?"

I responded, "Warren, I can't have a squadron commander who can't exercise discipline and leadership with regard to our mission. I will relieve him immediately and ground him at the same time to ensure he doesn't get in another aircraft and do something else dangerous or stupid. The operations officer will be the acting commander until Colonel Bowersox and I can find a suitable replacement." That is when the board president chimed in and informed me the squadron commander himself caused a midair collision when he turned the wrong way into his wingman when leading a two-ship formation in a pitchout for landing at Peterson AFB. I believe both aircraft were lost, but the pilots ejected safely. Such a mistake was beyond comprehension!

The fact that the squadron's disastrous plan was allowed to proceed without anyone from the air division collocated with the squadron intervening was also cause for alarm. Clearly, over the years, air defense squadrons had become little autonomous operations with little or no oversight. Colonel Bowersox and I would change that with lots of visits to fly with the squadrons and visits to the parent air divisions.

General Moore offered to tell General Hill about the actions that I was planning to take so he wouldn't find out from the grapevine. I offered to carry my own mail, but he held firm, saying I didn't need to beard the lion on the second day of my new command. Sadly, he didn't tell General Hill, and the general came across the former squadron commander in the halls of the Chidlaw Building about a month later and learned that he had been relieved of his command and assigned to ADTAC headquarters.

NORAD Headquarters and the Chidlaw Building were somewhat of an unusual arrangement. The building was named after Gen. Benjamin Chidlaw, USAF (ret.). The general graduated from the US Military Academy in 1922 and entered the Army Air Service. He received his wings in January 1924 and was assigned to Clark Field, Philippines, in the Third Pursuit Squadron. He flew the Air Mail in 1934 and was later assigned to the Second Bomb Group at Langley Field, Virginia. At Langley, he entered the logistics field and became involved in jet engine development in 1939. As tensions began to rise prior to WW II, he was promoted to major in March 1940, lieutenant colonel in September 1941, colonel in March 1942, and brigadier general in November 1942. He saw action in the Mediterranean Theater as deputy commander Twelfth Air Force and later commander of the Twenty-Second Tactical Air Command in Southern Europe. After the war, he was promoted to general on July 29, 1951, and assigned as commander of the Air Defense Command at Ent Air Force Base in Colorado Springs, Colorado. General Chidlaw also became commander of the Joint Service Continental Air Defense Command on September 1, 1954. Evidently, this is where US Army AAA and SAMs were folded into ADCOM and later NORAD. He retired from that command on May 31, 1955. Subsequently, Ent AFB became the support base for ADCOM and NORAD, and the headquarters of NORAD and ADCOM moved into the Chidlaw Building, named after the general. The arrangement was rather unique in the military—that is, to have a major war-fighting headquarters in a commercial building located within a short distance from two military installations, Peterson AFB and Ent AFB.

The Chidlaw Building was a complete headquarters complex. It had three floors, with one located underground; it had no windows except on the entrance doors to a vestibule that led to a secure entrance; and it contained the following support facilities:

NORAD Command Section
ADTAC Command Section (formerly ADCOM)
Headquarters Command Sections for NORAD and ADTAC
sufficient office space for all staff personnel
conference rooms
secure briefing facilities
secure communications complex with links to Cheyenne
    Mountain Complex
printing plant
civilian guard facility and recreation area
small base exchange and food store
executive dining facility
cafeteria
exercise room
commercial bank
Ent credit union

In summary, the Chidlaw Building replicated everything that was available at Peterson and Ent Air Force Bases for approximately $1 million in annual lease fees plus the cost of the Civilian Guard Force. It was expensive to operate in the center of Colorado Springs, Colorado. There may have been some attraction for the Chidlaw location by the NORAD commander. The "movers and shakers" of Colorado Springs provided a house and estate to the commander of ADCOM and NORAD when these commands were first formed for the price of the then "housing allowance." I've never seen the house but have been told on reliable authority that the house was in the Broadmoor five-star hotel area and consisted of a few acres of grounds to include a swimming pool and tennis court. This house was considerably closer to the Cheyenne Mountain Complex and to the Chidlaw Building than Peterson AFB. However, when Gen. David C. Jones became chief of staff of the air force, he determined that it was unethical for the commander NORAD/ADCOM to receive such a large financial gift from the community. I believe, at that time, it was permissible to accept a gift of $65 from a US citizen if it could not be politely refused, or a gift of $165 from a foreign official if it could not be politely refused. Gifts valued over $65 or $165, respectively, that could not be refused without offending the giver were turned over to the US government. Clearly, the property that was made available to commander in chief (CINC) NORAD exceeded by several hundred dollars the gift limit on a monthly basis. As a result, General Jones requested that the then

CINCNORAD, Gen. Daniel "Chappy" James, move into quarters at Peterson AFB, Colorado. This was really a downsizing, as there were no suitable general officer quarters at Peterson AFB until recent construction in 2010.

With the Minot F-106 mishap corrective actions behind me, I became recurrent in the T-33 and started flying with an ADTAC T-33 Squadron located at Peterson AFB. The mission of the squadron was to provide a credible jamming threat to ADTAC AC&W radar sites and to support the periodic performance calibration of the same radar. There were roughly a dozen T-33s in the squadron, and they were not heavily tasked; as a result, they provided excellent transportation for me to get around the country to visit Fighter Interceptor Squadrons, radar sites, air divisions, and SAGE centers. I needed to put the calipers on the commanders at every level and work the transformation and culture change issues. It was a treat to be back in the T-33, an honest aircraft without all sorts of computer assist in flight controls and stability augmentation. One aircraft, one engine, and one pilot had a nice ring to it.

Two of my favorite questions when talking to commanders at all levels were "Who are your two strongest officers and NCOs?" and "Who do you worry about when you're relaxing at home?"

The answers that caused me to probe much deeper were "All of my officers and NCOs are outstanding!" and "I don't have anyone in this squadron that I worry about!" The law of averages suggests there is a bell-shaped distribution of personnel in all units unless we're talking about the Thunderbirds or the Six-Man Group, and there was even someone in the Six-Man Group that I worried about on a continuous basis.

One of my many squadron visits took me to McChord AFB, home of the Twenty-Fifth Air Division and the 318th Fighter Squadron. Checkout in the F-106 was still on the near horizon, so I couldn't fly with the squadron; on the other hand, that afforded me more time to spend in maintenance shops, on the flight line, and talking with the pilots. The Twenty-Fifth Air Division commander hosted a cocktail social that evening so I could get to meet more of his personnel as well as spend more time with the squadron pilots and their families. The squadron commander appeared to be a solid guy and one who would not let the junior pilots run the operation into a ditch. However, the squadron operations officer, a major, proved himself a maverick of the first order. He had a little too much to drink and decided to take me on, in front of his subordinates, on the issue of low-level flying. His hypothesis was that the squadron pilots should be allowed to fly low levels down to fifty feet above the terrain. I pointed out that their mission was to intercept unknown aircraft penetrating the ADIZ under GCI Control and, if those aircraft were determined to be hostile, to engage them under CGI Control; further, if DEFCON One was declared, to engage (at that time) Soviet Bear-H bombers under GCI Control. I also pointed out that there was no indication that Soviet bomber pilots were training to fly low-level penetration routes. That being the case, I could not find any reason to fly below 1,500 feet above the terrain, which was the altitude for a visual landing pattern in the F-106. On the other hand, if all the air division commanders could justify low-level training flights at no loss of intercept training, I might consider low-level route flying at five hundred feet. Unfortunately, with most of the squadron pilots looking on, the operations officer continued to try and justify low-level flying at fifty feet AGL—anything else was un-American, or cowardly, and a lot of other comments that are unfit to print. I chose to disengage because the major had lost control of himself, and that was obvious to all. So I just walked over to and started a conversation with members of the air division. Squadron pilots took the major in tow and, I suppose, home. What I just experienced, laid on top of the recent aircraft mishap, was very unsettling. It seemed that bad judgment was running amuck in the Fighter Interceptor Squadrons. It all reinforced my belief that the culture had to change immediately before there were more serious consequences.

I asked Colonel Bowersox to visit the 318th Squadron and put the calipers on the squadron commander, operations officer, and flight commanders. Following his visit, his advice was to remove and replace the squadron operations officer because he was providing negative leadership. He felt that all the flight commanders were fine and would provide better direction with the operations officer gone. With Sox's reinforcement of my understanding of the situation, I called the air division commander and directed that he remove and replace the operations officer. When I later learned that he picked a just promoted major to move into the operations officer's job, I had serious reservations. The young major had very little experience as a flight commander and, in my opinion, would have difficulty in exercising leadership over his former fellow flight commanders. Normally, it is not a good idea to move someone up above his peers in the same organization but rather move the person into a new organization where they would not have to rise above all the former close friendships or rivalries.

One of my goals was to transition the Fighter Interceptor Squadrons (FIS) from their traditional orange flight suit to the olive-green version worn by USAF Fighter Units around the globe. Perhaps this might, in some small way, move the air defense culture just a scintilla to the right. Only two classes of aircrew wore orange flight suits: test pilots, and test aircrews at Edwards Air Force Base, California, and other locations, and FIS pilots. The theory was that the international bright orange would make it easier to locate a pilot or aircrew that had ejected from a disabled aircraft. Since all test flight work and close to 100 percent of FIS flying was done in North America and predominately in the lower forty-eight states, there was no concern for hiding from the enemy. However, all ejection seats were now equipped with emergency beacon locators that are automatically initiated when ejection from an aircraft occurs. Further, most, if not all, aircrews are provided personal beacon locators that report a downed aircrew's location covertly through satellites. There is no reason for FIS pilots to wear orange flight suits, and we wanted to get them to look like all other fighter pilots, except perhaps for the swagger. The requirement to transition to the olive drab flight suit was promulgated with the proviso that FIS pilots could wear their current issue of orange flight suits until they were no longer serviceable or presentable. End of subject, or so I thought.

It was time to check out in the F-106. I'd never flown an interceptor or air defense fighter, only tactical fighters, although the F-4 came close. Further, I'd never flown a delta wing aircraft, so there was much to learn about the aircraft. Tyndall AFB, Florida, was the training base, and the Second Fighter Interceptor Training Squadron (2 FITS), the schoolhouse. In addition, I would have the opportunity to spend a little time getting to know Maj. Gen. William "Earl" Brown, the commander at Tyndall. Earl was well known throughout the air force, especially to that small group of heroes who were sent to fight the air war in Korea. The two most famous fighter wings in South Korea were the 4th TFW based at Kimpo AB and the 51st TFW at Suwon AB, both not far from the capitol, Seoul, Korea. Earl was a solid citizen with a distinguished flying career from the early days of aerial combat in Korea followed by a number of tough assignments. It seemed that everyone knew Earl. If his name was mentioned in casual conversation, three of four people would say, "I flew with Earl in (fill in the blank). He's really a great guy!" He was reassigned as commander of Seventeenth Air Force at Sembach in Germany and later promoted to lieutenant general. Earl flew 125 combat missions in the F-86, mostly flying wingman for three of the Korean war's most highly decorated aces, Maj. Gen. Boots Blesse, Col. Jim Jabara, and Maj. Manuel "Pete" Fernandez.

Earl once described what it was like to be a wingman in combat to these great aces: "It's like driving down the Beltway around Washington

DC in rush-hour traffic, all the time looking backward while hanging on to your leader's wing." I would agree that is an apt description. In fluid four formation, proven effective in the Korean War, a wingman's role was to keep looking behind the formation to ensure it wasn't coming under attack.

Later, Earl flew the F-4 in combat over North Vietnam. He was shot down on March 30, 1970, and rescued. While waiting for the choppers to pick them up, it is reported that his backseater (GIB) turned to Earl and said, "Earl, we're getting too old for this crap!" (or words to that effect). Earl would have been approaching forty on that occasion. Earl was also a world-class Alpine skier and, while stationed in Germany as a lieutenant general, won the European command— sponsored ski competition in the giant slalom event. As an aside, I had the pleasure of knowing all three of those great aces.

The F-106 was about the thirtieth aircraft that I checked out in. An air force pilot cannot expect that level and variety of experience today. Perhaps he/she will have the opportunity to fly five or six different aircraft, and two or three of those will be trainers. In the early fifties, when I started flying, aircraft became obsolete in three or four years after going into production. A good example was the F-86, famous for a favorable 14 to 1 kill ratio against the MiG-15. Two years after the Korean War ended, they were obsolete and were being flown to Davis Monthan AFB, Arizona, in the mid- to late 1950s, to be mothballed in the "boneyard." The only F-86s flying at that time were used to train foreign pilots at Luke AFB, Arizona. The F-100 came next, also manufactured by North America, and became operational in the late 1950s. It saw combat in South Vietnam in the midseventies, although obsolete as a frontline fighter at that time. On the other hand, F-15s and F-16s introduced into the air force inventory in the late 1970s and early 1980s are still our frontline fighters though their basic designs are thirty to forty years old. At this writing, a pilot stays in one or two operational aircraft most of his/her flying career.

The F-106 was truly a pilot's dream to fly—solid aerodynamics, superb and powerful J-75 engine, excellent range and endurance, and flew like a real airplane. It was easy to land and very stable at all speeds. The only thing I didn't like about the aircraft was the metal bow that went longitudinally across the top of the canopy with a longitudinal centerline brace that went from the bow to the fuselage forward of the windscreen. It seemed to be a big hindrance to a pilot's vision; however, if intercepts are conducted with the aid of both ground and internal radar, the pilot is always looking in the cockpit at the instruments and radar display. The F-106 also was also equipped with an infrared search and track (IRST) system, which was used to aid the onboard radar in tracking low-flying aircraft by their IR signature. On the other hand, if AWACS controllers were controlling an F-106, they could track both the F-106 and its target at low altitude out to 225-plus miles. The F-106 landed like most other aircraft, unlike crashing the F-4, so getting rated in the "Delta Dart" was easy and enjoyable. I could now go fly with all the squadrons in ADTAC. Tyndall still had operational F-101s for test purposes and offered me a chance to fly it—unfortunately, the opportunity never materialized because of other pressing business. For aviators, the F-101 held the time to climb record for many years. On the other hand, its high horizontal stabilizer and elevator could be blanked out by the wing at high angles of attack and cause the aircraft to pitch up violently, often causing a loss of control.

As snow started to fall and the mountains to the west of Colorado Springs turned white, Sheila asked Claudine Brown what people in Colorado did in the winter. Claudine's answer was "Most of us ski." With that, Sheila went down to the Broadmoor Hotel, which, at that time, operated two ski lifts and offered skiing on three slopes, two of them being reasonably challenging—at least for beginners. She purchased five days of group lessons for herself, daughter Denise, and me at the Broadmoor.

When she told me we were all taking ski lessons, the response was predictable: "I'll break a leg, get grounded, and lose my job as commander ADTAC."

To which she countered, "At your age (forty-five), the air force doesn't need you flying fighters—it's a young man's game. They wouldn't miss you in the cockpit one bit." I didn't argue that point but noted that I was just getting ADTAC up and running; it took long hours, and I didn't have the time. That is when I learned the lessons didn't start until 8:00 p.m. and that she would bring a change of clothes to the office on her way to the Broadmoor—pretty much "checkmated."

My last-ditch stand was "Return the tickets and get a refund!" They weren't refundable! My Alpine skiing career started the following Monday, and we became a skiing family. We even brought her brother Hal and his family into the ski fanatics circle. I'm the only one still skiing at this writing in 2011. I started Club Racing with the Peterson AFB Ski Team and then the Air Force Academy Recreational Ski Team for several years. Currently, I just run the Giant Slalom National Standard Race (NASTAR) Courses at Breckenridge, Keystone, and Vail Resorts. Essentially, you race against a pacesetter who receives a racing handicap by racing against one of the US Ski Team GS racers at the beginning of the ski season. All NASTAR pacesetters across the United States receive a handicap from the same US Ski Team racer, thus the standard. For the last twenty years, I've been in the top three, Gold Medal Division in my age group, at one of the above-mentioned ski resorts or the state of Colorado. Alpine skiing is the closest I've come to the exhilaration found in flying an F-86F or F-16A.

Integrating Air Defense Forces into TAC, both operationally and culturally, was hard work, and progress was slow but measurable. On the other hand, the Air Control and Warning Radar Squadrons were much easier to integrate. The surveillance and tracking radar sites were located along the northern border with Canada, along the Atlantic and Pacific Coasts, as well as some along the border with Mexico. There was also a balloon borne radar (known as Fat Albert) based at Cudjoe Key in the Florida Keys. This aerostat lifted a modified F-16 radar to an altitude of twelve thousand feet above sea level to detect low-flying aircraft out to a distance of 165 nautical miles from its moored location. It covered most of the air approaches from Cuba to Florida with sufficient warning to get an interceptor airborne from Homestead AFB, Florida, in time to close with incoming aircraft prior to them reaching the landmass of Florida. The aerostat not only lifted the radar but also carried a gasoline-powered generator and data transmitter to send the radar detections and system telemetry to a ground receiver at the site. There were limitations to the system. The aerostat only carried enough fuel for twelve hours of operation; there were wind speed limitations that required the aerostat to be lowered and secured, and there was a problem associated with salt from the gulf waters collecting on the tether cable and causing lightning strikes on the cable. If lightning hit the tether, it would likely cause it to fail and release Fat Albert into the atmosphere, causing a hazard to aircraft in flight. A free-floating aerostat could also be an embarrassment to the United States should it land in Mexico or another foreign country in Central or South America.

Fat Albert came loose from a lightning strike during my time as commander, and it became somewhat of a comic embarrassment. The tether was struck by lightning during an evening storm, and the aerostat was blown out to sea. As it got colder, the pressure inside the aerostat was reduced, and Fat Albert flew just a few hundred feet above the gulf over some of the prime commercial fishing areas. In the early morning hours, a commercial fishing boat spotted the aerostat and tied onto the cable for salvage rights and hopefully a big check from the air force. As the sun heated up the balloon, it started to rise and pulled up on the boat. With a little more solar heating, the balloon started lifting the stern of the boat out of the water, eventually breaking free and causing major damage to the boat. During this ordeal, the boat's captain radioed his prize catch and position to shore, and ADTAC was alerted that Fat Albert was drifting at altitude toward Mexico. Fighters were scrambled to shoot down the balloon, but the 20 mm projectiles only put small holes in the balloon and failed to cause it to deflate and fall into the Gulf of Mexico. Another element of fighters was scrambled with AIM-9 missiles aboard. The AIM-9 was equipped with an infrared (heat-seeking) sensor, a proximity fuze, and an explosive fragmenting warhead. The AIM-9s ripped the aerostat apart, and the remains sank into the gulf far short of Mexico.

Currently, there are upgraded versions of Fat Albert on the Florida Keys and in southern Texas along the border with Mexico.

There was an event in Cheyenne Mountain on November 9, 1979, that eclipsed any concern that NORAD and ADCOM personnel may have had about the formation of ADTAC and the transfer of air defense air divisions, Fighter Squadrons, and AC&W radar units to the Tactical Air Command. This event was the false missile warning that caused Strategic Air Command crews on alert to start B-52 engines and taxi those aircraft loaded with nuclear bombs to the end of the runway and stand by for orders to launch. The false missile attack warning also caused the command director in the Cheyenne Mountain Command Center (CMCC) to "flush" the air defense fighters on alert around the United States for survival. Fortunately, the defense duty officer (DDO) in the Pentagon NMCC asked enough questions to cause the command director in the CMCC to realize the data they were seeing on their displays was false.

This false missile attack warning was caused by a civilian contract worker testing a module of software designed to cause missile-warning software to dump exercise or training inputs when a real-world missile track message was fed into the system. Obviously, this module was critical to ensure that a crew training or exercise event did not mask a real threat. Exercise and test track messages ended with "tags" that identified them as synthetic tracks. Real-world missile event messages from satellites and radar were generated without tags and were instantly recognized by NORAD computers as real. When real-world event messages entered the NORAD computer, a module of code in the computer immediately dumped all synthetic inputs from the system and forced the real data to the command center displays in NORAD, Strategic Air Command (SAC), and the National Military Command Center (NMCC).

The midnight shift in CMCC was drawing to a close. The crew was running through a standard exercise when the contractor entered the NORAD 407L computer cage and loaded a "Russian strategic launch scenario" message set absent any "tags" to indicate it was synthetic. The fail over module worked as designed—all exercise data was dumped into the bit bucket, and the displays started showing hundreds of strategic missiles coming toward the United States from Soviet land-based missile fields and submarines in the Atlantic and Pacific Oceans. The command director and crew started running their checklist. The defense duty officer (DDO) in the Pentagon alerted to the "strategic attack" on North America by the display in the NMCC called on the red phone to establish a Missile Event Conference. After several minutes of tension and high drama, it was determined the missile attack warning was false—but it never should have happened!

Some of the reasons "the false missile event" never should have happened are listed below:

Any test on the 407L software and performance should have been scheduled.

The CMCC command director and crew should have been informed of the test when they came on duty.

The CMCC command director should have been asked for permission to start the test prior to insert the tape.

The 407L computer cage should have been locked, and only the command director should have been able to provide access.

Data streams from satellite downlink sites and missile-tracking radar sites arrive at the CMCC in two formats. High-speed data go to the 407L computer. Low-speed data go to a teletype located on the counter just behind the command director's position in the CMCC. No data coming in on the teletype is an indication of a failure in the system and that further analysis is required.

Missile Warning Center personnel in the CMCC should have called all three of the satellite downlink sites to ascertain if one or more of sites were forwarding real-world missile launch messages to the CMCC. There is a downlink site in the United States, Pacific Region, and Europe. All three are on direct line ringdown phones. This is now a standard procedure for all detected missile launches anywhere in the world.

The gravity and potential consequences of the false missile event were not covered up or allowed to pass without serious and thorough review. A very high-level review team descended on NORAD and the CMCC. Many procedures were changed and safeguards established. The command director position was elevated from a colonel to a brigadier general. It takes five crews to provide 24/7/365 coverage; accordingly, the services were required to come up with an army brigadier general, a rear admiral (lower half), two air force brigadier generals, and a Canadian brigadier general. This structure continued until after the Berlin Wall came down, heralding the Soviet Union's demise, and then reverted back to colonels as command directors.

Some of the changes brought about were more window dressing to imply improvement but didn't make much sense. For example, some of the responsibilities of NORAD were given to other commands, disrupting unity of command and making it more difficult for commander NORAD to ensure proper support for the mission.

Gen. James E. Hill retired on December 31, with thirty-eight years of honorable service in a change of command with Lt. Gen. James V. Hartinger (pronounced "Hart-in-grrrrrr"). The position of CINCNORAD had been downgraded to three stars because the Congress took some four-star positions away from the army and the air force. The air force chose to downgrade NORAD and the Air Training Command. The Pacific Air Force (PACAF) also lost a star for a while, as the air force favored some of the other major commands. As mentioned in chapter 8, I came to know General Hartinger while assigned to the Six-Man Group at Maxwell AFB, Alabama, where the general was vice commander of the Air University and commandant of the Air War College. As a result of our previous association, it was easy for me to adjust to his style of leadership. After the Air War College, General Hartinger was promoted to the rank of lieutenant general and assigned commander of Ninth Air Force at Shaw AFB, South Carolina. His wife died unexpectedly in their quarters on Christmas Eve night while on that assignment. He was subsequently reassigned to command Twelfth Air Force at Bergstrom AFB, Texas, near Austin, Texas, prior to assuming command of NORAD. It was at Bergstrom where he met and married his second wife, Mickey. Mickey survived Jim and still lives in Colorado Springs, Colorado. She attends the yearly NDIA Ball, which honors General Hartinger's memory and service to the nation with an annual award. General Hill and his wife retired in Colorado Springs with a vision of an increasingly greater role of satellites and space systems in the defense of the United States and in commercial roles around the globe. At that time, the United States and the Soviet Union dominated space with their military systems. In addition, there were a few commercial satellite communication systems. General Hill founded the US Space Foundation with the help of his former executive officer, Col. Dick McCloud (a former Air Commando) and senior enlisted advisor, Chief Master Sergeant Chuck Zimkas. The Space Foundation has grown considerably and annually hosts a Space Symposium attended by thousands from around the globe. Over time, it has morphed into an internationally renowned organization and renamed simply "Space Foundation."

Air National Guard Air Defense Squadrons were starting to transition from the F-106 into the F-4. The F-4 offered twin-engine reliability, a better, more powerful radar, and the capability to carry four AIM-7 long-range radar guided missiles and four AIM-9 infrared (IR) guided missiles. Both of these missiles had more powerful warheads than the AIM-4 missiles carried internally by the F-106. The F-4 also consisted of a two-man crew with the weapon system operator in the rear cockpit operating the radar, relieving the pilot of that burden. Last, the F-4 fleet was very large and offered better logistics support than was available for the F-106. The only disadvantage of switching to the F-4 was a loss of a little range and endurance, but that was a minor consideration.

With the transition of Air Defense Squadrons to the F-4, a multirole fighter, there was talk of adding a tactical "designated operational capability" (DOC) to Air Defense Squadrons and giving them a deployment responsibility for overseas contingencies. This did not happen in the near term, but was on the horizon. I had an occasion to discuss the use of dual DOC air defense fighters with the then air force chief of staff, Gen. Lew Allen. I suggested that perhaps it would be advisable to identify the minimum force of air defense units required to protect vital, if not critical, assets such as the nation's capital, New York City, and Los Angeles. The chief responded that all dual-capable air defense units would be deployed to support an overseas contingency if required. That, to me, was the handwriting on the wall. When the World Trade Towers and the Pentagon were attacked on September 11, 2001, there were only six dedicated Air Defense Squadrons with plans to drop to only four.

One event that I inherited from ADCOM was the William Tell Air Defense Gunnery Meet held annually at Tyndall AFB, Florida. Air Defense Squadrons were selected to compete based on their overall performance. Roughly seven squadrons competed, one from each air division, plus an F-4 Squadron from the Tactical Air Command had been invited to the competition for the past few years. The F-4 enabled TAC to enter the competition because it had both the onboard radar and air intercept missiles (AIMs) to perform the air defense mission. As commander of the 552nd, I attended a William Tell Competition when an E-3A was providing airborne control of intercept missions. My impression was that William Tell was more of an excuse to have a party and was run more like a rodeo than a serious professional military-sponsored competition. I intended to change that. Instead of a somewhat undignified outdoor award ceremony where local onlookers and animals were allowed to wander through the venue, it would be a formal indoor ceremony with senior distinguished visitors handing out the awards. Individuals and team members would receive little statuettes (somewhat patterned after Oscar) of a fighter pilot in a flight suit.

I quickly learned that William Tell cost money—not a lot, but even $5,000 was a lot more than I had discretionary authority over. I asked TAC for a contribution, and grudgingly they offered $1,500. I put the arm on Maj. Gen. Bruce Brown to see if NORAD could match that $1,500. He agreed to ask General Hartinger for $1,500. The remainder of the money came from ADTAC; it appeared the event was fully funded.

On November 4, 1979, three thousand or more Iranian students (?) invaded the US embassy in Tehran, Iran, and took sixty-six Americans hostage and held them in captivity. While in captivity, these Americans were repeatedly threatened to be tried and imprisoned or executed for their alleged crimes as spies. These were dark days for America but did not appear to impact my command. Subsequently, on April 25, 1980, President Jimmy Carter announced that a covert rescue attempt to free these hostages had been aborted at a remote desert location in southern Iran. Further, that several USAF aircrew aboard a C-130 aircraft had been killed when a navy CH-53 helicopter crashed onto their C-130 after completing a refueling prior to evacuating. All other Americans and aircraft involved in the rescue attempt were safely flown out of Iran without discovery. It was a dark day for America and especially the hostages being held in Iran.

In early May 1980, I was notified by General Creech that I had been chosen by the then chairman of the Joint Chiefs of Staff (JCS), Gen. David C. Jones, to be a member of the Desert One Rescue Review Team. General Creech opined that I had been chosen because of my extensive prior experience in Special Operations. I was to report immediately to Admiral (retired) Holloway at the Pentagon. I called Colonel Bowersox and told him he was the acting commander and that I would be in touch from the Pentagon.

At the Pentagon, the following Monday, I found Admiral Holloway in a suite of offices located within the JCS area. There I met the Colonel Executive Officer assigned to support Admiral Holloway and his Desert One review team members as follows:

> Admiral Holloway, USN, retired 1978 as chief of naval operations. Expertise: Admiral Holloway served in the WW II in the Pacific as a destroyer gunnery officer and flew combat in Korea and Vietnam as a fighter pilot.

> Lt. Gen. Sam V. Wilson, USA, retired 1977. Expertise: Intelligence General Wilson was military attaché to Russia and director DIA.

> Lt. Gen. Leroy J. Manor, USAF, retired 1978. Expertise: Special Operations. General Manor planned and directed the rescue raid on Son Tay, NVN.

> Maj. Gen. James C. Smith, USA. Expertise: land military operations. Gen. Smith was the most highly decorated army general on active duty.

> Maj. Gen. Alfred M. Gray, USMC. Expertise: marine operations. General Gray and I would later serve together on the JCS.

> Maj. Gen. John L. Piotrowski, USAF. Expertise: SOF and fighter operations.

As listed above, the Desert One Rescue Evaluation Team consisted of one active duty and one retired member from each service.

The following day, General Jones met with the Desert One Review Team and told us that he wanted the team to report the unvarnished truth on why the rescue attempt ended in failure; no stone should be left unturned to get to the facts, the causes, and the truth.

There is one fundamental and overarching consideration in planning and conducting a hostage rescue. The fact that there is going to be a rescue must not leak or it will likely lead to an ambush and massacre of the rescue force. It could also lead to the killing of all the hostages. Secrecy is always paramount in planning and executing a rescue operation!

The Desert One Review Team, under Admiral Holloway's leadership, was immediately immersed in briefings on how the rescue plan evolved, to include force selection, training, logistics, preparation, intelligence, Desert One location selection, and execution. We learned that the DOD responded immediately to the hostage taking on November 4, 1979. Within a day or so, a planning cell in the Pentagon deduced that any rescue attempt would have to come covertly from the sea. Immediately after their finding, a squadron of eight CH-53 mine-sweeping helicopters was moved from Little Creek Navy Base, Virginia, under an appropriate cover story, to a clandestine desert training location in the western United States. It should be noted that navy CH-53 helicopters were selected over air force CH-53 helicopters because the navy version had folding rotor blades so they could easily fit in the elevator that transported aircraft from the hangar deck to the flight deck of an aircraft carrier. As the rescue plan started to take shape, navy helicopter pilots used to flying at five hundred feet above the wave tops towing a "mine-detecting/defeating sled" in VFR weather were learning to fly nap-of-the-earth on the darkest of nights. They were also learning to fly nap-of-the-earth with the rather crude night vision goggles available at that time. Not all navy pilots made the transition in the time available, so Marine Corps and air force helicopter pilots already trained in low-altitude night flying took their place.

In the sixteen months between the hostage taking and execution of the rescue attempt, there were many starts and stops and alterations in the planning and training for the eventual rescue. The starts and stops were the result of the mercurial nature of Ayatollah Khomeini and his puppet government. One week, they were going to try and execute the hostages; the next, they appeared to be seriously considering the release of all hostages on some Muslim religious holiday. Every time it appeared the hostages might be released, the training slacked off or stopped, and rescue plans were revised based on the latest intelligence collected.

There was a significant lack of specificity on where the hostages were being held, how many Revolutionary guards were guarding them, and the condition of their captivity. For example, were they chained, handcuffed, or free to move about in their cells? Out of this darkness came the light when the Republican guards released a pregnant woman; later they released an African American naval officer. There may have been one other hostage set free, but I only recall the above two releases. As a result of these captive releases, the rescue team learned that the hostages were being held in two locations, vice one. This required a significant beef up in the rescue force. They also learned that the Guard Force was more robust than anticipated, and the facilities the hostages were being held in would be harder to penetrate. The beefing up of the rescue force would play a major role in the eventual Desert One abort.

The rescue plan that was implemented and executed was a drama of six individual acts. The review team was briefed in detail on all six acts, but we were only asked to report on the cause of failure of the first act, which aborted at Desert One. I am sworn to secrecy on what would have transpired in the subsequent five acts if the abort had not occurred.

Col. Charles Beckwith, commander of the fledgling Delta Force, was appointed commander of the rescue team and planned accordingly based on the intelligence available to him. Initially, the rescue force that would free the hostages in Tehran could be moved forward from the refueling and trans loading point at Desert One with four CH-53s.

Accordingly, eight CH-53 helicopters were flown onto a carrier in the Arabian Sea; a 100 percent overage based on the passenger loading of Delta Force and released hostages to compensate for maintenance difficulties. This would prove to be correct for helicopter aborts; however, as Colonel Beckwith gained knowledge from the released hostages on the true nature of hostage captivity, he increased the rescue team to the point that it took six helicopters to move them forward from Desert One. There was a failure to increase the number of CH-53s aboard the carrier to twelve to retain the 100 percent overage for maintenance failures. This oversight proved to be a critical mistake.

To ensure that actual flight training for the rescue attempt did not create the leak that all the planners and rescuers were working so hard to avoid, the actual number of CH-53s and MC-130 required for the mission were never used in a nighttime practice scenario. Only half of the actual aircraft in the rescue attempt ever practiced a nighttime landing, refueling, and passenger cross-loading with night vision goggles in the US western desert. These were four CH-53s and four MC-130s. In talking to some of the rescue aircrews over the years, some insist that a full complement of aircraft rehearsal was accomplished, but the official briefing from the planners said this did not happen. It is also likely, based on comments from the actual aircrews, that the sand at Desert One was not near as compact as existed in the locations where they trained. Accordingly, there was considerably more sand blown into the air from prop and rotor wash at Desert One than aircrews experienced in training—not only because the sand was more easily blown into the air but also because there were twice as many props and rotors lifting the sand. Hence, in the actual rescue attempt, aircrews had to deal with far less visibility during ground operations at Desert One than they had experienced in training.

The number of personnel that were involved in the planning, preparation, and execution of the rescue attempt outside of the actual team was very limited and also highly compartmented. This was driven home to the review team when we called on Admiral Hayward, vice CNO, to get his views on the operation and his professional opinion on what might have led to the failure. Admiral Holloway's exec scheduled the appointment and provided Admiral Hayward's staff the purpose of our visit. When we were ushered into his office, Admiral Hayward said to us, "I don't know why you're here."

To which Admiral Holloway responded, "I told your staff that we wanted to get your views on the Desert One failure!"

Admiral Hayward then said, "I know that, but I still don't understand why you came to see me—I wasn't allowed to know about Operation Eagle Claw!" I don't know about the rest of the team, but it shocked me to learn that the vice CNO wasn't read in on what was largely a naval operation for the first two acts of the rescue attempt. His comment best captured how few people were read in on the operation and how compartmented the planning was.

The review team was privileged to visit Delta Force and observe some of their training operations and entry procedures. The entire team was seated in their "shooting house" in a living room setting along with some manikins. Some of the manikins were holding babies and groceries, while others held guns and knives. The door was closed, and the lights went out—it was darker than the inside of a whale's belly. A few minutes later, with the muffled sound of an explosion, the door blew off followed by fifty or more muzzle flashes penetrating the darkness. The lights came on to reveal that all the manikins with weapons were full of holes in the chest and head. Our rescuers had on night vision goggles and smoking guns in hand. It was an impressive demonstration.

We also went to Hurlburt AFB, Florida, to visit with the First Special Operation Wing and fly in both their MC-130 and HH-53 on nap-of-the-earth penetration missions over the Eglin AFB, Florida, Range Complex. I also took the opportunity to also fly on an AC-130 Gunship as a 105 mm Howitzer loader and observe the first round accuracy of that big gun. The target was a truck, and from ten thousand feet, the first round was a direct hit. The fire control technology was vintage 1970s—I'm sure it's significantly better today—and the air force has improved the AC-130's overall firepower with more powerful automatic weapons like the 30 mm Gatling gun with flatter trajectories and significantly increased lethality.

Lt. Gen. Sam Wilson was also doing a lot of data collection from the various intelligence agencies. He was investigating Soviet collection means and what capabilities they had to detect rescue force training and what they might have been able to deduce from it.

After the CH-53s were flown aboard the carrier, they were always below deck when eyeballs or sensors could have detected them on deck. They only flew at night, and only flew low level over the water. The carrier also moved closer to and further away from the Iranian coastline several times to ensure that no alarm bells would go off when they moved closer to execute Operation Eagle Claw.

In the spring of 1980, Ayatollah Khomeini was again threatening to try and execute the hostages only with more fervor than before. Pres. Jimmy Carter was briefed repeatedly on the progress in planning and training for the rescue attempt. In early April, he was informed that in two weeks, the window for executing Operation Eagle Claw would close until September. This was because there would not be enough hours of darkness during the summer months for the CH-53s to approach the Iranian coastline in darkness, refuel at Desert One, and proceed forward to their "hide" all under the cover of darkness. Based on this knowledge and the strident tone in Tehran about executing the hostages, President Carter gave the go-ahead. The reader needs to know this to understand the extremely difficult conditions President Carter faced when he took this decision. He had to give the go-ahead immediately or wait rather helplessly for the next six months.

With the data collection drawing to a close and the analysis under way, the team turned hard to the work of writing the report and vetting the conclusions. It was fourteen-hour days, seven-day weeks to get the job done, so I could return to my family and command. Besides, when you're TDY and the job to be done is measured in progress not just days on the calendar, the motivation is to get it done and move on! However, I did get permission to leave one late Friday night and return Sunday night to spend some time with Sheila, our seven-year-old daughter, and four-year-old son.

Anyone who has had experience with reviewing aircraft accidents knows that the investigator starts looking for the root cause of the mishap. The root cause is the first event in a chain of events that makes the accident unavoidable. The same logic was applicable to our investigation. To go forward from Desert One required six mission-capable helicopters on the ground refueled and able to go on to complete the next act in the drama. Only five mission-capable CH-53s arrived at Desert One, so the senior Eagle Claw commander, an air force lieutenant general at Masirah Island, Oman, called a mission abort with the approval of President Carter. The abort was called prior to a refueled CH-53 landing on top of an MC-130, setting the cargo aircraft on fire and killing all but one of the crew members in the MC-130. The reason for the refueling was to enable all the flyable helicopters to reach the carrier. The MC-130s carrying Delta Force had sufficient fuel remaining to reach their base as planned. Starting from the five, vice six, flyable helicopters at Desert One and working backward in the planning and training process is instructive in the investigative process.

It appeared the highly compartmented planning and adherence to a very strict need-to-know policy, which excluded senior naval flight officers like Admiral Hayward, limited the review process that might have uncovered the potential for CH-53 mechanical failure during the flight from the carrier to Desert One. As a maintenance officer and pilot for most of my career, studying maintenance data and failure trends was second nature. A review of CH-53 "meantime between critical failures" revealed statistically that about 60 percent of the helicopters taking off from the carrier would arrive at Desert One in mission-capable condition. Five out of eight was predictable. It was also likely that there would be more failures during the flight to the hide site.

The failures that occurred in flight were "blade indication malfunction" (BIM). That crew landed their helicopter immediately according to their flight manual emergency procedures. Fortunately for them, another CH-53 had them in sight with their night vision goggles, landed, and picked them up. A second CH-53 suffered some instrumentation failure that required the pilot to fly nap-of-the-earth solely with the aid of night vision goggles. After several hours of this, the pilot felt he was so fatigued, he could no longer proceed to Desert One without crashing the helicopter and killing the crew. He climbed to altitude and flew back to the carrier—arriving very low on fuel. The third CH-53 lost one of their hydraulic systems in flight. I was told on very good authority that a CH-53 could fly safely with one of its two hydraulic systems operational, but could not take off in this condition. Hence, the original calculation of eight helicopters was correct based on the earlier composition of the Delta Force Hostage Rescue Team requiring four in-commission CH-53s at Desert One. However, this requirement was not recalculated when the rescue force grew in number, requiring six helicopters at Desert One and therefore roughly a dozen helicopters on the carrier. A check of the space available on the carrier hangar deck revealed that it could have held twelve helicopters, and the navy had far more than twelve CH-53s in its inventory.

About the time that I arrived at this conclusion and submitted my findings to Admiral Holloway in draft form, I received a late-night phone call in my quarters from an air force four-star general. The general, in very plain language, told me it was common knowledge among senior officers that I was trying to pin the blame on someone and to back off or my air force career was over. That came as quite a shock, as our working papers were not circulated outside the review team office, and I was not trying to blame anyone. I was just evaluating the planning process and looking for a root cause and the truth, as requested by General Jones, chairman JCS.

I didn't sleep a wink that night, mulling over my analyses and wondering if I had completely lost my objectivity, being overcome with zeal without realizing it. I wanted to finish the job I was assigned and provide some insight to others who might be tasked to plan and execute highly sensitive covert missions in the future. Further, I wanted to do what the chairman asked us to do—to shed light on the facts of why the rescue mission failed! By morning, a plan had come together. I went to Admiral Holloway's office and asked his exec if I could speak with the admiral. In a matter of seconds, I was standing before the admiral and said, "Admiral Holloway, I've been working long hours, seven days a week, trying to find a root cause from all the data we've collected. You've seen most of my work, so you've got some idea of the validity of it and the support for it. What I would like to ask of you is that you put my work under the microscope! If you find that I've lost my way or my objectivity, please let me know and give me some guidance!"

Admiral Holloway's response went something like this: "Pete, you've produced far more credible work than anyone else. Right now, the report is resting largely on your mechanical failure analysis! I'll give your papers an extra scrubbing. In the meantime, keep up the great work you're doing!"

The weight on my shoulders was lifted, and I proceeded to continue with a full court press effort. I had a strong suspicion of how word got to the senior air force leadership to tell me to back off. It had to start with one of the other team members going up their chain. I believe Major General Gray was sensitive about a marine helicopter pilot crashing his refueled CH-53 on the MC-130 that provided the refueling, and killing several air force SOF aircrew members. We had spoken about this event, and I pointed out to General Gray that the mission abort occurred when only five mission-capable helicopters arrived at Desert One. The unfortunate accident occurred later and wasn't a subject for our report. I also made the point that the CH-53 mishap investigation would most likely be conducted by the Marine Corps because the pilot was a marine. As an aside, the marine pilot had a stellar career and retired as a general officer. Enough said.

The review team finished its work and stood by as Admiral Holloway and others reviewed the draft report of the Desert One failure. Except for polishing and improving readability, the report stood as written. I never heard from that senior air force general again on the subject of the Desert One Failure Report. An unclassified copy of the report is available on the Internet and can be found by googling "The Hostage Rescue Mission Report, Admiral Holloway."

Back home, Sheila and Denise were doing well, with good neighbors like Bruce and Claudine Brown looking after them. Thanks to Colonel Bowersox, ADTAC was also doing well. General Creech said it was time to start planning to move ADTAC to Langley AFB, Virginia, where additional manpower savings could be achieved by merging our respective support staff. As it turned out, there were a lot of people on the ADTAC Staff that had repeatedly extended their assignments at ADCOM because they liked the quality of life in Colorado Springs and Colorado in general. The state offered unlimited scenic hiking trails, mountains, streams full of trout, and thirteen destination ski resorts. It was anticipated that a number of the senior officers and NCOs with over twenty years of service would retire rather than leave Colorado Springs and their homes of many years. Planning for the move was given to Maj. Terry McKenzie, who really excelled at working out all the details on challenging problems.

The call from Colonel Bowersox was unexpected. When I picked up the phone, Sox said, "Boss, I just crashed a T-33 on landing and broke both the wings." I asked if he was in the hospital, only to happily find that he and the other pilot, one of our standardization and evaluation pilots—the best of the best—were without injury. Sox went on to tell me that while flying at altitude, they lost the ability to control the elevator with the stick. However, they found that they could control aircraft pitch attitude with the elevator trim. Elevator control in ancient aircraft like the T-33 was purely mechanical by a metal cable that ran from the bottom of the control stick to the tail section linkage on the elevator. On the other hand, the trim tab on the elevator was controlled electrically by a motor actuated by the trim knob on top of the control stick. Sox and his copilot decided to try and land the aircraft in an attempt to save it, vice flying to a desolate area and bailing out at a safe altitude and recommended airspeed. Their plan was working just fine until they were rounding out just prior to touchdown and ran out of trim and could not keep the nose up. The aircraft hit hard and broke the wings. The accident investigation team discovered that the locking mechanism to prevent the elevator linkage from coming uncoupled had been removed. It was suspected that a maintenance person had purposely tried to cause the accident. Aircraft maintenance records identified the person who had performed work in that area. He confessed, was court-martialed, and convicted of his crime. The cost of replacing the wings on the decades old T-33 was less than $100,000, so the mishap was not characterized as a major accident.

Bills for the William Tell gunnery meet were coming in and needed to be paid. I went to Major General Brown for the $1,500 he promised to obtain from General Hartinger. When I asked for the money, he gave me the Polish salute with an "oh shucks," or something like that, followed by "I forgot to ask the grrrr!" Later that evening, while still in the office, I received a call from General Hartinger. He was upset that I had asked Major General Brown to intercede for me and gave me the longest and harshest butt chewing I had received in my twenty-eight-year career. He was speaking so loudly, I could lay the phone down on the desk and still hear him very clearly. When the general finished venting his anger on me, he hung up. That culminated a long day, so I went home. There I received another call from General Hartinger; he had thought of a few more unpleasant things to say!

The next morning, shortly after arriving at the office, the phone rang, and it was General Hartinger asking me to come to his office. The in-person butt chewing was much louder and of higher quality than those over the phone. That butt chewing from General Hartinger was definitely a record. In total time, it lasted over an hour and stretched over two days—could it be a service or world record? When I mentioned the three verbal abuses to General Brown later that day, he opined that I got off easy compared to his experience on the same issue. The $1,500 was forthcoming, and all the bills did get paid.

Aerial gunnery meets are always high risk both in the air and on the ground. The teams want to win and may take risks that they would not consider in day-to-day flying operations. It was important to take a look at how things were coming together and the attitude of the host commander. Maj. Gen. Chuck Horner had recently assumed command at Tyndall AFB, Florida, taking over from Maj. Gen. William "Earl" Brown.

Maj. Gen. Chuck Horner and I were neighbors at Williams AFB, Arizona, when we were both going through F-86F Gunnery School. He was a make-it-happen kind of guy, and I just wanted to make sure he was making the right things happen. I came away with the feeling that Chuck was on top of everything and knew where and how to look for trouble if it was bubbling up anywhere. We also went over the award ceremony, and both were convinced that all the loose ends had been run to ground. I planned to return to Tyndall AFB, Florida, and William Tell three days prior to the end of competition and participate in the awards ceremony.

Sheila and I were just sitting down for dinner when the phone rang about 5:00 p.m. on Friday evening, October 3, 1970. The voice on the other end identified itself as belonging to some colonel in the JCS. The voice then said, "Pack your bags for a warm climate and report to the Pentagon, room 2Axxx, in the morning at 8:00 a.m." I responded by saying that my bags were packed for a warm climate because I was heading for Tyndall AFB, Florida, to host the William Tell awards ceremony, and the JCS would just have to do without me. The voice snapped back with "Lieutenant General Gorman, director JCS, is ordering you to be in the Pentagon tomorrow morning, and you better be there!"

I responded, "OK, I'll be there, but I need you to arrange military airlift because I don't think I can get there commercially because of the late notification."

The voice said, "That's your problem—be here!" There was a redeye flight through Denver arriving in Washington about 6:00 a.m. I was on it with a few more changes of clothes stuffed in the travel bags. Sheila feared I was headed for another trip into the unknown. She was right!

Upon arriving at the designated room in the JCS area the next morning, I found a large room full of about three hundred people. All the services were represented in the room, including several brigadier and major generals. I noted that Major General Lawrence, USA, was there. He was often referred to as "Lawrence of Arabia" because he served as the commander of US Military Training Mission to Saudi Arabia for a few years. It was alleged that he was highly regarded by Prince Sultan, Saudi Minister of defense, and considered an expert on the Arabian Peninsula. It was noteworthy that Iran had attacked Iraq on October 1 over a border disagreement involving the Shatt el-Arab waterway three days prior to this gathering, and the buzz was that this meeting had to do with that conflict. With General Lawrence in the mix, I wasn't concerned that I would be called on to do anything; he was the expert, and I'd never been to the Middle East. Wrong!

After about an hour of just hanging around the edge of the crowd and listening to the talk, Lieutenant General Gorman entered the room, and all became quite. The general asked, "Is Gen. Pete Piotrowski here?"

I raised my hand from the back of the room and said in a loud voice, "Here, sir!"

General Gorman responded with "Pete, you stay. Everyone else can leave!" There was a definite unease coming over me at this point.

When everyone else had cleared out of the room, I approached General Gorman and shook his hand. He said, "Pete, the chairman (Gen. David C. Jones) was in Saudi Arabia when Iran attacked Iraq. The king called for General Jones and asked for help in protecting his kingdom. We assembled this group to be ready to respond. I just got off the phone with the chairman, and his direction is to send you with a team of five to the kingdom to provide that assistance. He mentioned that the king was told you are the world's expert in air defense. Pick your team, and we'll cut the orders and get you on your way."

I responded to this tall order with "General Gorman, I don't know any of these people or their credentials. If you would please ask your personnel expert to pick the five best people of this bunch that are suited to the tasks that lie ahead of us, I will be pleased to lead that team!"

The General said, "That's a deal, I'll get back with you shortly!"

After lunch at the Pentagon cafeteria, I returned to the meeting room to find three colonels, one lieutenant commander, and one major waiting for me. Two of the colonels were from the air force, the other from the army. The lieutenant commander was obviously navy, and the major from the army. Their experience and skills were the following:

> Col. Walter C. Hersman, USAF, fighter pilot, combat tour in Vietnam, attaché to Jordan and fluent in Arabic, retired as a brigadier general
>
> Col. [name forgotten], USAF, communications expert
>
> Col. Joseph House, USA, Air Defense, Hawk expert, combat tour in Vietnam
>
> Lt. Cdr. Joseph C. Strasser, USN, Aegis commander, combat tour in Vietnam, retired as a rear admiral
>
> Maj. [name forgotten], USA, Hawk expert, combat tour in Vietnam

With a little pep talk from me on the importance of our mission, we were on our way. In the process of getting visas, talking papers, and the like, I learned that the current USMTM commander was Maj. Gen.

Charles "Chuck" Donnelly Jr. I knew Chuck well enough to know that he would not be pleased to host a team that was essentially there to do his job as the US military advisor to the king and prince sultan, minister of defense. It was going to be a tough sell, but I thought Chuck would understand and we could work as a team. Wrong again!

When the team landed at Riyadh, Saudi Arabia, courtesy of a C-5, we processed through Customs and were then met by a representative of USMTM. The rest of the team was taken to their lodging, while I met with Maj. Gen. Chuck Donnelly. His first comment was "Welcome to Riyadh. What the hell are you doing here?" I explained that the king had asked General Jones for help in preventing an air attack from Iran on Saudi Arabia's very vulnerable Ghawar oil production and storage facilities near Abqaiq and Ras Tanura, respectively. Accordingly, General Jones felt obliged to send some additional personnel specifically to do that job. I suggested that my team would work closely with USMTM, that we would share all our ideas with him and his key staff, and that all of our message traffic would be provided to him for review prior to transmission. There would be no secrets between us. However, it was made clear that while he could review our message traffic, he could not edit it or refuse transmission. That review part seemed to calm him down but didn't make him happy.

I learned that a high percentage of USMTM personnel were stationed in Dhahran on the east coast; only General Donnelly and his key staff were housed in Riyadh, the capital and location of the Saudi Ministry of Defense. The US ambassador and his staff lived in Jeddah on the Red Sea coast along with all other ambassadorial teams. It was obvious that the king didn't want a large foreign presence in his capital city. Nonetheless, our team would be based at Riyadh in a compound provided for General Donnelly and the USMTM staff in the capital region.

The next morning, General Donnelly introduced our team to Lieutenant Colonel Fahad, director of operations of the Royal Saudi Air Force (RSAF). Normally, a two- or three-star general would hold position; however, Lieutenant Colonel Fahad was a prince of high standing, and that is all that mattered. Our visit fell during the period of Ramadan. This made it a little more difficult for the team to schedule visits to meet with senior Saudi military officials because they were fasting and a little out of sorts during the day. Lieutenant Colonel Fahad stated the king and defense minister, Prince Sultan bin Saud, were concerned that the Iranian Revolutionary government would use the Iran/Iraq war as an excuse to attack the enormous wealth-producing crude oil storage facilities on the small island of Ras Tanura in the Persian Gulf. Our mission was to offer ways to improve the defenses of these facilities. He added that he would personally make sure that the places we needed to visit in carrying out our mission were open to us.

Based on Lieutenant Colonel Fahad's remarks, we laid out our visit plans. Colonel House and the major would visit the eastern Hawk air defense missile site installations and also speak with the contractor providing maintenance and logistic support. Our naval team member would visit with the RSNF and determine its capabilities for radar surveillance and air defense. Colonel Hersman and his colleague would scope out the command and control relationships between the services for air defense and also look at their fighter basing to see if it was appropriate for the threat. As a team, we agreed to meet every evening at six o'clock at the USMTM HQ to go over our data, lay out future visits, and assess if we had sufficient information for a report. My first task was to hitch a ride on the forward-deployed AWACS and find out what the day-to-day air traffic over Iraq, the Persian Gulf, and Iran looked like. It would be a ten- to twelve-hour flight and would give me plenty of time to pick the brains of the E-3A mission crew who had been conducting surveillance missions over the area for several days.

The AWACS flight was very useful, as it set the baseline for friendly aircraft in the area and the means for identifying potentially hostile air traffic in Iraq and Iran. The E-3A surveillance radar also provided an extended picture of general air traffic over the Persian Gulf and Saudi Arabia. Two days later, I visited the RSAF Air Control and Warning (AC&W) radar site on a hilltop northwest of Al Jubail. When I arrived at the radar site, an Englishman said he provided contractor support for the radar and he would escort me to the site commander's office. When we entered the commander's office, I was introduced to a young RSAF major. We drank Chi and spoke briefly about the purpose of the visit when the major said, "Mr. Dickerson will take you to the tactical room and introduce you to the controllers on duty."

As we walked down a dark hallway (radar and AC&W sites are always dark), I asked, "Mr. Dickerson, what exactly do you do at the site?"

He replied, "Everything. I train the operators and the maintainers, do the maintenance, and when they don't want to work—run the radar and track the aircraft. I'm taking you down to the tactical center because the major doesn't know the way. He's never been there—in fact, he's never gone beyond his office." His comments did not bode well for operational readiness and ability to engage incoming hostile aircraft. As we got closer to the tactical center, he advised me, "Don't ask the so-called operators any technical questions. They don't know anything about the system. In fact, some of the officers you will see don't even work here. They have been ordered to sit at the consoles to make it look operationally capable." We entered the room, and he made introductions to about eight officers sitting in front of radar screens and staring at the three tracks crawling across the displays. They didn't "hook" any of the tracks or touch any switches. I asked one of the so-called operators if the air traffic I was seeing was typical for this time of day. He said yes. This confirmed what the Brit told me, as when airborne in the E-3A on the previous day, I saw about ten times the traffic in the same area. As we departed the tactical center, I told my escort I'd like to pay my respects to the commander prior to leaving. He commented that wouldn't be possible because he left for the day as soon as we departed his office earlier that morning—that he normally wasn't at the site past 10:00 a.m., and it was almost noon. I asked how old the radar was and about its capability. He opined that the design was about twenty years old and that it didn't have much electronic countermeasures (ECM) capability, but that it was still a good AC&W radar manufactured by Marconi.

The next day, I was back to Al Jubail with our team's command, control, and communications expert, exploring the area for a higher vantage point for a radar looking out to sea. We found a hill that was perhaps one hundred feet higher than where the current radar was sited. That difference doesn't sound like much of an advantage, but getting above the salt layer over the Persian Gulf provides a significant improvement in detection of low-flying aircraft. Also the radar equation shows that an increase of one hundred feet increases the detection range of an aircraft at wave tops by fourteen nautical miles. The site also provided much better coverage of the approaches to Ras Tanura and the crude oil storage facilities located on the island. There were no docking facilities for oil tankers there. Instead, there were large pipelines going out to buoys moored in the Persian Gulf. A tanker would simply pull up alongside one of these buoys, connect to the hose, and have their tanks filled with crude in very short order. There was no messing around with taking on pilots, using tugs, and mooring the tanker—it was efficient and fast to fill up at Ras Tanura.

The team studied the disposition of RSAF fighters, and to us, it looked unbalanced when compared to the perceived threat. Their newest and most capable fighter, the F-15, was based in the Central Highlands, whereas the threat was in the east, closest to their wealth-producing oil facilities. I visited the chief of the RSAF, a major general, and discussed the possibility of relocating an F-15 Squadron to the modern and sprawling Dhahran Air Base. The air chief explained to me that my suggestion was not doable. The F-15s were in the highlands to protect the summer palaces of Saudi Royalty located in the cooler higher altitudes from attack. When asked what the threat was, he replied, "Israel!" He also noted that the Saudi government paid Pakistan to deploy a division of Pakistani soldiers in the northwest to counter a ground attack from Israel. When I suggested both of his scenarios were highly unlikely, especially in the light of the close relations between the United States and the kingdom, he didn't give my comment much credibility. When I asked if it were possible to deploy a squadron of F-15s to Dhahran should intelligence sources indicate an attack on Ras Tanura or the oil fields at Abqaiq was likely, the air chief then explained that Saudi Arabia was made up of six military districts, each commanded by an army major general. All the forces in a military district belonged to that commander. If a tank, plane, or soldier from one district moved or deployed into another military district, it would immediately be transferred to the gaining commander. Hence, no military district commander would allow any of his forces to move to another military district because he would lose them permanently. He went on to explain that this was to prevent the massing of forces that could result in a coup on the monarchy. Therefore, it was not possible to move any forces like an F-15 Squadron to the east even for a few days. Once those F-15s landed at Dhahran, they could never go back to where they came from. That put an end to any further meaningful discussion. The only aircraft available to defend Ras Tanura and Abqaiq were the F-5Es based at Dhahran. For armament, they carried two 20 mm M-39 cannons internally with a reduced ammunition load, and two AIM-9 missiles externally. The F-5E armament was considerably lighter than the F-15, which also had an internal 20 mm Gatling gun and carried four AIM-7 radar missiles submerged in the fuselage and four AIM-9 IR missiles on wing pylons. More importantly, the F-15 had a long-range look-down, shoot-down radar for detecting and engaging low-flying aircraft.

With this in mind, I visited the F-5 Squadron and met with the major general military district commander whose headquarters was also at Dhahran. While in conversation with the district commander, a young Saudi major wearing a flight suit walked into the office. Immediately, the district commander got up from behind his desk and stood against the wall, while the major sat in his place. It was immediately apparent that this was no ordinary major. I introduced myself and learned that he was Maj. Bandar Sultan, son of the defense minister, Prince Sultan bin al Saud. The major was the F-5E Squadron commander, a very high-ranking prince and, in a few years, would become ambassador to the United States for over two decades (1983-2005). He became the ambassador at age forty-four. Major Bandar generously invited me to fly with his squadron to assess their combat capability.

Not being current in the F-5, I arranged to fly an air defense training mission in the backseat with our USAF F-5E liaison officer. It was a productive and demanding mission with regard to air defense. I was pleased that they used an airborne E-3A to set up and control the engagements up until the "merge." This was beneficial to both the E-3A mission crew, the F-5E pilots, and to the air defense of the region as long as E-3As were deployed to Saudi Arabia. While on the flight line at Dhahran, I met some of the Northrop contractors who were maintaining the F-5s and learned that Col. Truman Cobb, USAF (ret.), the deputy commander for maintenance at Aviano AB, Italy, headed up the maintenance activity for Northrop at Dhahran. From his team on the flight line, I learned that money was not an issue for the Saudis, and their F-5Es were always fully mission capable, and there never was a parts shortage.

The army team members had been thoroughly going over the local Hawk capability and deployment. Their assessment was binary! The Hawk battery was in excellent condition; all the technical order (TO) modifications and updates were accomplished immediately upon receipt, and the battery was combat-ready. On the downside, the battery was located west of Dhahran. The city high-rise buildings blocked radar coverage over the Persian Gulf from the unit's organic radar. Accordingly, the Hawk battery was totally ineffective in engaging aircraft approaching from the east, from Iran. Another limitation was that the battery was only manned for an eight-hour period during the day.

This important finding resulted in a visit with the chief of the army staff, a major general and head of the Royal Saudi Land Forces (RSLF). The army chief was much more outgoing than other high-ranking Saudi officers I had met, and we had some far-ranging discussions on defense of the kingdom. The first order of business was the team's recommendation to move the Hawk battery to the east side of Dhahran so the radar could detect, track, and engage incoming hostile aircraft over the Persian Gulf. To this, the General said, "Such a move was impossible." The reason was that soldiers had to be home in time to take their wives shopping; otherwise, the family would starve. Women were not allowed to drive, not allowed to have access to bank accounts, nor should they be seen out in the souks without being accompanied by an adult male member of the family. If the Hawk battery were moved seaward of Dhahran, the soldiers would not be home in time to take care of their family responsibilities. Moving the families was out of the question as well.

Checkmated by tradition! I asked the army chief whom he thought would win the Iraq/Iran War. He didn't hesitate to say, "The Persians will win because Arabs do not have the stomach for a long drawn out war." He went on to say, "Arabs favored the lightning strikes of their historical mode of warfare and would soon grow weary of a long war, hence the Persians would eventually win." He didn't envision how the Scud missiles with poison gas warheads would devastate and decimate Tehran. Nor did the United States! The slaughter of Revolutionary guards as they attempted to invade across the southern marshes near Basra also exacted a heavy toll on Iran's army.

It was essential to pay a call on the US ambassador, his deputy chief of mission, and the military attaches, who would be expected to have some opinions on how to ramp up the Saudi defense posture looking east. General Donnelly provided one of his in-country C-12 aircraft (King Air) to take me to Jeddah where all embassies were located. While I was in Jeddah, the US ambassador invited me to a social function attended by a large number of western European attachés. During a conversation with the British air attaché, he asked, "Don't you blokes care about the shipload of Chinese CSS-2 missiles that arrived here a few weeks ago and transshipped overland to the south?"

"What CSS-2 missiles?" I asked. He then told me that a ship loaded with CSS-2 missiles arrived in the dead of night and that the missiles were off-loaded before dawn and moved southeast over land. Somehow, our intelligence community missed all that. After I reported this to the US chief of mission, the missiles were located in the "Empty Quarter" (Rub' al Khali) a few weeks later. When discovered by US Intelligence sources, they were already operational. It was reported that the Saudis only received conventional warheads for their CSS-2. However, the missile is capable of being loaded with either high explosive or nuclear warheads.

Our navy team member was hot on the trail of improving shipborne air defense in the Saudi Navy Forces (RSNF). While we were in country, the RSNF received their first PCG-1 Corvette from the United States. As I recall, it was docked at the navy base at Al Jubail, not far from the radar site visited shortly after our arrival in country. The ship was equipped with an air search radar and some close-in air defense capability. The air search radar gave it a "picket ship" detection and track capability if it patrolled in the Persian Gulf fifty miles or more east of Ras Tanura. Aircraft approaching the Ras Tanura oil storage area from the east could be detected about 120 miles from the island and possibly engaged by aircraft on Combat Air Patrol (CAP). We learned that the ship was going on patrol in a few days, so we went to Al Jubail to watch the activity. From our observation point, we saw the sailors going aboard ship about 8:30 a.m. The PCG-1 moved away from the pier at 10:30 a.m. and seemed to maneuver on the horizon twenty or so miles out to sea. To our surprise, it returned to the pier at 2:00 p.m. Shortly thereafter, the sailors came ashore and left the area. The next day, we learned that the ship was not intended to stay at sea because the sailors had to be home in the evening to take care of their families or they would starve. At best, we could expect the PCG-1 to be away from the pier for about four hours during midday, five days a week, at the most.

I went shopping in the local souk one evening with one of the USMTM officers who knew the local customs and would keep me out of trouble. There I intended to purchase something made out of gold for Sheila and perhaps a watch for myself. The gold souk was without a shopkeeper when we entered. There were perhaps six other people waiting with thousands of dollars in gold jewelry sitting on the counters and hanging in display on the walls. No one touched anything! To steal was to lose a hand on "Chop-Chop Friday." In the watch souk, I picked out a watch and was haggling over the price with the owner. We were about five dollars apart when the evening call to prayer sounded. We were still bargaining when a religious policeman took his baton and ran it around the open door frame. The owner threw the watch at me and took the twenty-dollar bill from my hand. I won the deal but only because he didn't want to get beaten by the religious police. When we walked out the souk, the curbsides were full of women in black burkas waiting outside the local mosque for their husbands to return. Evidently, only men are allowed in the mosques. While shopping, women wearing a burka would put their hands between the burka veil and their face, pushing the veil outward so they could look down to see merchandise they were interested in.

On a second trip to the souks, I purchased some frankincense and myrrh. I had learned that these hardened modules of tree sap were highly valued in biblical times because they were used to fumigate garments and make them smell fragrant. With the shortage of water in desert areas, the Bedouins could obviously not wash their clothes as we do today. They made small tripods of sticks over which they draped their garments. Under these garments, they ignited frankincense or myrrh, which gave off a sweet-smelling smoke. We had a washing machine and dryer at home, so I bought these two items that allegedly two of the three wise men gave to the Christ Child to give as Christmas presents to family and friends. I've often wondered if it was sold in the souks for tourists or it was still used for original purpose by Bedouins of the desert.

In one of my several conversations with RSAF Lieutenant Colonel Fahad, I learned a little known fact that Saudi men were, by their laws, allowed to have four wives and that divorce was a mere formality should a man want to rid himself of a wife. The only requirement was for the husband to provide for his former wife in the manner to which she had become accustomed. That was probably easy for former husbands to accomplish because women had so little legal standing, I suspect, they wouldn't complain. In addition, I learned that most Saudi men only had three wives at any given time. With only three wives instead of four, they could date because they were "single" in the sense they had an opening. Hence, Saudi men with three wives dated other women until they found one they liked better than one of the three current wives. Then they would divorce one and marry the new love while retaining their "bachelor" status.

An army colonel and significant prince commanded the Royal Saudi Army Air Defense Artillery Forces. He was out of country when the Iran/Iraq war started but came home shortly thereafter. The team made several attempts to arrange for air tracks from the RSAF radar at Al Jubail to be forwarded to the Hawk battery west of Dhahran. The colonel rebuffed every attempt to exercise appropriate passage of radar tracks from the RSAF radar to the RSLF Hawk battery, saying that the RSLF did not take orders from the air force. Working through the Dhahran district commander, we arranged for an exercise to demonstrate the combat readiness of Saudi Forces. In this readiness test, the F-5Es would play both aggressor and defender. Two elements would go out over the Persian Gulf and return at ten thousand feet above sea level heading toward Dhahran. The tracks on these aircraft would be used to divert F-5s from CAP to engage them. At the same time, these radar tracks would be sent to the Hawk battery for them to simulate engagement. The exercise was to start at 0001 hours on a Monday. At 2359 hours, the prior night, the air defense commander reported all his forces down for extensive maintenance—thus avoiding the readiness test. Subsequently, the colonel/prince convinced his father, defense minister Prince Sultan, to declare the Saudi Air Defense Artillery forces a separate branch of service equivalent to the RSLF (army), RSNF (navy), and the RSAF (air force), thus avoiding any further harassment from our team or USMTM personnel. He had a stellar career. Eleven years later, he was the commander of Royal Saudi Land Forces during Desert Storm.

In addition to our work with the Saudi Forces, the team sent daily messages to the chairman JCS (CJCS) about our activities and suggestions for air defense upgrades that required US approval and material support. In total, I suspect we sent over sixty suggestions on ways to robust the air defense capability of Saudi Arabia from Iranian air attack. One of the suggestions that I recall was to install US Air Force and/or US Navy radar warning and homing receivers (RHAW) on the tops of tall buildings and towers near Dhahran and Al Jubail RSNF Navy Base. The concept was that Iranian F-14s and F-4s that would likely be employed to attack Saudi oil facilities would have their airborne radar on to detect and shoot down any aircraft coming up to intercept them. The RWAH gear would pick up their radar transmissions providing direction to the aircraft or flight of aircraft. These signals could be sent to a central location where the time angle information could be used to pinpoint the attacking aircraft locations. Relatively cheap and simple to do! The response from the JCS staff was "It won't work if the Iranians don't turn on their radar." Their response was factually correct, but most likely tactically wrong, and our suggestion was a step in the right direction. The role of Higher Headquarters is to support people in the field, not fight against them.

Somewhere along the way, I was contacted by a Saudi army general in charge of their helicopter program. Evidently, he had the authority to choose what helicopters to buy and how many of them to purchase. I don't recall his name, but he was a high-level prince, as only a Prince could have so much authority. He invited me to have lunch with him at the Riyadh officers' club. I met him there at the appointed time, and he led me to a table where we would dine and then to the buffet table. The buffet contained enormous amounts of just about anything one could think of. The spread was huge and extravagant! He explained that he traveled frequently to the United States to go to helicopter demonstrations, to visit Saudi helicopter pilots in training, and for other various related reasons. I also learned that he purchased a replica of the *Gone with the Wind*'s Tara, home of Scarlet, where his wife lived, as she refused to live in Saudi Arabia. He wanted to know if there was anything he could do for me and our team that would provide him additional reasons to travel to the United States. I explained that our team had no authority to offer advice on procurements—that was the USMTM mission, and he should contact General Donnelly in this regard.

I noticed that there were only two other people at the Saudi O'club for lunch. I asked, "What time was it customary for Saudi officers to come to the club for lunch?"

His response was unexpected: "We never come here!"

To which I asked, "Why is that?" I should have known the answer.

He said, "We don't dance, we don't drink, and our wives cannot be seen in public by men who are not close relatives—why would we come to this club?"

To that I asked, "Why do you have this opulent club and such an expansive buffet if you never use it?"

His response again floored me: "Because you have them!" I never heard from him again. After about three months of looking for solutions to robust the Saudi Air Defenses, whether these solutions were easy, difficult, hard, or impossible (cultural), we had offered many solutions, but all were turned down as impossible. At this juncture, Lieutenant Colonel Fahad informed me that the chief of the Saudi Defense Staff would like a briefing on the team's assessment and suggestions for improving their air defense posture.

After several brainstorming sessions, the team settled on a "stoplight" chart with the various Saudi military capabilities, including Command and Control, down the ordinate and the words "Location, Training, Manning, Maintenance, Effectiveness, Overall" across the abscissa. The chart was ugly, mostly red and yellow except for maintenance, which was provided by United States and other national company teams such as McDonnell Douglas for the F-15s, Raytheon for the Hawks, Northrop for the F-5s, etc. For example, the Hawk, F-5s, and F-15s were rated as follows:

Item	Location	Training	Manning	Maint'	Effective	Overall
HAWK	Red	Green	Green	Green	Red	Red
F-5	Green	Green	Green	Green	Yellow	Yellow
F-15	Red	Yellow	Green	Green	Red	Red

On the right, there was a slide that came up that explained all the reasons for the color coding of each system. The F-15 was the best and most flexible system for defending the Kingdom's vast oil facilities in the east from air attack. However it was coded red because of mal positioning and because all F-15 ammunition and missiles were under lock and key, and only the district commander could approve opening the ammunition bunkers. The F-15 was also yellow because without access to ammunition and missiles, pilots could not train adequately. It took at least two days for a decision to open the munitions storage bunkers to be made and implemented. Another anticoup procedure!

When the briefing was finished, the chief of the defense staff asked in a pained voice, "What can I do to fix these problems?"

My answer was "Absent changing the culture and implementing our recommendations, there is little you can do except hire mercenaries to provide for the air defense of your East Coast and oil facilities." I also pointed out that the oil-producing and storage facilities were also vulnerable to naval bombardment as well.

The team kept hard at reviewing Saudi Air Defense capabilities and sending messages to the JCS. However, I believed that our days in Saudi were drawing to a close, and we would be going back to the Pentagon shortly for an outbrief with Lieutenant General Gorman. During this period, I was invited to attend a social and dinner by Truman Cobb, my former maintenance officer. They lived in a Northrop Compound with perhaps as many as six hundred people living in apartments within the compound. None of the wives could drive cars because of Saudi law prohibiting women from driving, so every American wife had a chauffeur to take her wherever she wanted to go. The chauffeur was provided as part of their husband's employment agreement. Contracts were for four or five years, and the workers were handsomely paid. They could save about $500,000 in four years if they didn't blow it all on vacations just to get away from the desert when they could. I learned that all of the couples that had a drinker in the family also operated an alcohol-making still. It was against Saudi law, but everyone turned a blind eye as to what went on in the compounds. The still operators specialized, producing only one type of liquor. For example, there were gin, vodka, bourbon, scotch, etc. producers. To be polite to the hosts, I let every one of the proffered blends touch my lips but didn't drink any even though I was told repeatedly that it had been three years since anyone went blind from the homemade hooch! I also learned some trade secrets; all the stills produced the same "white lightning" product. This basic alcohol was modified by putting "oak chips" in a sealed jar to make bourbon, or filtering it through a charcoal mixture several times to replicate the taste of scotch. They were very creative and proud of their alcohol beverage selection.

Off to Oman

I was right about leaving Saudi Arabia soon but wrong about the going-home part. The team received orders from the chairman JCS to relocate to Oman, where we were tasked to forge a memorandum of agreement with the Oman government for US Forces to make port calls and to exercise with the military forces of Oman. That seemed like "mission impossible" for a team comprised of air defense and command and control subject matter experts. It appeared to me that developing a government-to-government memorandum of agreement was what US ambassadors and the state department did to earn their pay. Nonetheless, military officers do what they're told, and off we went on another great adventure. The US embassy in Jeddah assisted us with visas and getting reservations for us in a British-run hotel in the ancient capital of Muscat. The only thing I knew about Oman prior to going there was that the legendary Sinbad the Sailor was from Oman and sailed a dhow to China.

The team arrived in Muscat and took a cab to the hotel where we had reservations made by the US embassy in Jeddah, Saudi Arabia. We were pleasantly surprised to find the hotel was owned and run by a British hotel chain. The rooms were nice and in a Western motif. Typically British, it had a pub that catered to Westerners (Muslims don't drink), was open to women, and half the waitresses and bartenders were women—quite a change from the Kingdom of Saudi Arabia. We quickly learned that Oman was led by Sultan Qaboos bin Said al Said. We also learned that Sultan Qaboos had been educated in England and, shortly after returning to Oman, was imprisoned by his father for wanting to modernize the country. With the aid of the British who were seconded to Oman, Qaboos escaped and overthrew his father to become the sultan. He was a little more gracious to his father, the former Sultan, banishing him to exile in England. In gratitude for the help he received from the British, Qaboos turned over the defense of Oman to British flag officers who were seconded to him from the British Defense Ministry. I believe seconded officers were paid by the British and also by the sultan—not a bad deal. As a result of this arrangement, the Oman Air Force was led by RAF Air Vice Marshal Eric Bennett (equivalent to a USAF major general), the Oman Army by an RA Maj. Gen. Ken Perkins, and the Oman Navy by an RN commodore. Most of the air force leadership and pilots were British and flying Jaguars made in England—a good but somewhat dated fighter. They also had trainers and some utility aircraft.

The next morning, we found our way to the American embassy located in a rather run-down two-story building in the old part of town. I suspect the building was several hundred years old. It housed both the embassy and quarters for the ambassador and his wife. It didn't take but a few seconds to learn that Ambassador Marshall W. Wiley did not like the US military; in fact, it was more correct to say that he hated the US military. He soundly blamed US Armed Forces for destroying Vietnam and told us, in no uncertain terms, he would not allow us to destroy *his* country! I immediately suspected our team was tasked to work the agreement with Oman because the ambassador refused to move in that direction. He served a tour in the US Navy in the 1940s and became a career diplomat in 1958, serving in Yemen, Lebanon, Jordan, Egypt, Iraq, and Saudi Arabia prior to assuming the ambassadorship in Oman. He was certainly an expert on the Middle East and spoke Arabic like it was his first language.

When Ambassador Wiley stopped his tirade against the military to catch his breath, I took the opportunity to assure him that we would seek his guidance every step of the way and no correspondence would leave Oman without his review and approval. It seemed like the right thing to say, but I believed, if necessary, I might have to retract the approval authority. When he assimilated what I said, his personality flipped, and he became cordial, shaking our hands and welcoming us to Oman. More importantly, he assured me he would arrange for me to meet with Air Vice Marshal Eric Bennett, RAF, who, in his opinion, was the mover and shaker of the British flag officers seconded to Oman.

In two days, I was meeting with Air Vice Marshal Eric Bennett, while the rest of the team met with his staff. AVM Bennett was quite a surprise, less than five feet tall and in all respects very tiny. After some light conversation about my exchange duty with the RAF at their Air War College, he pointed out the Air College commandant, Commodore Saunders, was a close friend. After coffee, we turned to business. Eric's primary concern was that the US ulterior motive was to break the British lock on foreign military sales to Oman. I did my best to assure him that we had no such intentions and regarded the relationship between the sultan and the British military as unassailable. On the other hand, the location of Oman on the Arabian Sea made it an ideal port of call for US fleets in that area and also provided an excellent opportunity to build on our relationship with very fundamental maneuvers and exercises that would greatly benefit Oman's military forces. I also pointed out that a closer relationship with the United States military might cause South Yemen to rethink its repeated encroachments in the Dhofar region in western Oman. The latter struck a responsive chord—but it was just the beginning of weeks of wrangling. I don't know why it took so long—maybe diplomacy has to marinate for a month regardless of how beneficial an arrangement between two countries might be.

Back at the hotel, the team held its regular daily recap meeting. After dinner at the pub, I was doing some reading and mapping out a long-range approach for negotiations with AVM Bennett when the phone rang. A voice at the other end identified that I was speaking with the Oman minister of the interior and that he and the minister of defense wanted to meet with me in the Palm Grove across the street from the hotel in thirty minutes—under the two tallest palms. I agreed and immediately called Colonel Hersman and told him about the meeting. I said I wasn't sure what this was all about but that I would call him when I returned to the hotel and that if I wasn't back by morning, to inform the ambassador. With that, I headed out to find the two tallest palm trees and the two Omani ministers under them.

Muscat is at fifteen degrees north latitude. It was late December and quite dark at 8:30 p.m. I spotted what might be the tallest trees and headed for them. It was pitch black under the trees, and I couldn't see much but heard "psst, psst" and turned toward the sound. Before me, there were two men in formal Omani robes with khanjar daggers tucked into the sash that circled their waists. These khanjars were decorated with jewels, and the sheath looked to be silver. Their robes contained a lot of gold thread, so I assumed they were whom they purported to be. In hushed voices, they introduced themselves and told me they knew why the team was in country and believed a memorandum of agreement with the United States on closer military-to-military relations would be good for Oman and would give their traditional enemies pause. However, they were concerned that AVM Bennett would not negotiate in good faith and in the best interest of Oman. They wanted to know what transpired at the meeting that morning. I gave them a thumbnail sketch of what transpired and assured them I appreciated their support for our mutual goal. They requested that I meet them at the same location at 8:30 p.m. after every meeting with AVM Bennett. After the meeting with the two senior ministers, I felt that there might be a reasonable opportunity to achieve our objective. Back at the hotel, I called Walter and gathered the rest of our team to brief them on the meeting. We agreed that it was in our best interest to not share information about the meeting with the Omani ministers with the ambassador at this juncture.

Progress was slow because AVM Bennett was procrastinating and also taking flights to visit other Arab and African nations where the British had sway with local military leaders. Perhaps he was looking for consensus or just gathering information on their experience with US relationships. Regardless, after several visits with AVM Bennett, he signaled that he might support a memorandum of agreement for joint exercises and exchange visits with US military forces. The number of meetings with ministers under the tallest palm trees equaled the meetings with AVM Bennett. With a glimmer of hope that an agreement might be achievable, our team set to writing a draft memorandum, with everyone participating.

The basic guidance to the team was to keep it short and simple. After a few days, we had something I was willing to take to Ambassador Wiley. I fully expected immediate rejection and a lecture on why he wasn't going to let the US military ruin "his country" and prepared some counterpoints.

When Ambassador Wiley was handed the draft memorandum, he read it over twice and said in a cordial manner, "I can approve this if you agree to two changes."

"What are the changes?" I asked, thinking he had found a way to gut the paper and kill it with kindness.

To my great surprise, he said, "We should change it to a memorandum of understanding because it will be easier to get it approved by the sultan's cabinet, and there is a redundant sentence in the third paragraph that adds nothing and should be removed." Agreement was immediate, and he had it retyped on embassy stationery for his signature and gave me a copy. Mission accomplished. He also approved a cable back to Lieutenant General Gorman, reporting that Ambassador Marshall W. Wiley had agreed to carry our "jointly written" memorandum of understanding to the Oman government for approval. The team hung around until the first round of reviews had been approved and then left for home with a good feeling of having accomplished something important. Little did we know at the time that our memorandum of understanding would play a critical role in support of Desert Shield and Desert Storm and that I would make several more visits to Oman in another capacity.

With regard to Saudi Arabia, I believe we convinced the chief of the defense staff that, absent a change in culture, there was little likelihood that malpositioned Saudi Military Forces could defend the kingdom fighting only between the daylight hours of eight to five.

On the way back to Colorado Springs, Colorado, I stopped by the Pentagon and back-briefed Lieutenant General Gorman on any issues that he might have had about the team's activities in Saudi Arabia and Oman. He was curious as to how the chief of the defense staff reacted to the outbriefing with the stoplight charts that were mostly red in the Effectiveness and Overall capabilities. I reported that the Saudi general kept asking me how to fix the various problems, and when I gave him the correct answers, his comments were always "That will not work here!"

On returning to ADTAC in the winter of 1981, Colonel Bowersox grabbed me and said, "We've got to have a conversation!" I was prepared for bad news but not for what he had to say. But first some background on the Strategic Air Commands (SAC) Bombing and Navigation Competition called Proud Shield and Giant Voice and perhaps other names since it originated in the late 1940s. The competition's goal was to motivate SAC aircrews to improve their combat skills and then recognize and reward the best of the best. To the competitors and the rest of the air force, the competition was simple known as the Sac Bomb Comp. This competition was held every year since its inception, except for 1972 and 1973, when it was cancelled because of the war in Vietnam. It was the continuous armada of B-52 over North Vietnam that brought the war to a halt and the start of meaningful peace talks in Paris.

In 1980, when low-altitude ingress by B-52s and FB-111s was the approved penetration strategy, SAC invited air defense fighters to participate by attempting to intercept bombers en route to their targets. Air defense fighters from all regions participated, and the squadron with the highest number of validated intercepts was invited to the Bomb Comp Award Ceremony held at Barksdale AFB, Louisiana, home of SAC's Eighth Air Force. The SAC competition was global, and British Vulcans, Australia's F-111s, and USAFE F-111s were invited to participate. In SAC, preliminary competition started in early fall, and I was able to fly as a nonparticipating wingman to an F-106 from the Eighty-Third Fighter Interceptor Squadron from Castle AFB, California. Our two-ship hovered over the desert route that B-52 and FB-111 crews would travel to their target. It wasn't too difficult to spot them in the clear desert air even with their camouflage paint schemes. However, seeing them wasn't good enough! They had to be spotted early enough to drop in behind them and achieve a successful simulated missile engagement. To catch a B-52 in an F-106 was relatively easy, but the FB-111 was a much tougher adversary flying at just under Mach 1. My element leader was only able to get in missile range on about half of the F-111s he spotted. I was just along to observe so was not permitted to call out adversaries that I saw. It was excellent training for the F-106 pilots, and General Ellis, commander SAC, is to be congratulated for inviting ADTAC to participate.

The SAC Bomb Comp Awards Banquet was normally held in November, and all SAC aircrews in the finals were invited to attend, as was the 318th FIS from McChord AFB, Washington. The 318th was the winner of the Intercept Competition by a wide margin. Col. Ralph Bowersox attended on my behalf as commander ADTAC. There were numerous awards for bombing, navigation, refueling, and important aspects of the mission, such as closest to the scheduled time-of-bomb on target, etc. At the Bomb Comp Award Ceremony, there were two new trophies to be awarded, the General Curtis E. LeMay trophy for the best combined score in high- and low-level bombardment and the trophy for the best air defense squadron. General LeMay would be present to award the trophy named in his honor.

Colonel Bowersox told me there had been a problem at the officers' club the evening prior to the Bomb Comp Award Ceremony. The General LeMay trophy on display in the O'club was stolen! He said that as soon as he learned of the theft, he immediately thought the 318th was involved. He didn't think that any of the SAC attendees would dare play such a prank—the punishment would be swift and harsh. Colonel Bowersox said that he immediately went to the squadron commander's room at the motel where the 318th pilots were staying. He noted that it took some time to get off of Barksdale AFB, as the base was locked down, and all departing cars were being thoroughly searched. When the door to the squadron commander's room was opened, he found the LeMay trophy sitting on a table with the squadron commander and pilots seated around it. After a few questions, he learned that the squadron commander had taken the trophy from the O'club hidden under his flight jacket and out the gate to the motel. This was not difficult because it had not yet been reported stolen when the car with the commander and trophy departed though the guarded gate.

Colonel Bowersox then ordered the squadron commander to return the trophy to the officers' club immediately, which he did. Again, this was not difficult, as the security force was only searching outbound traffic. He later learned that they placed the trophy in a women's restroom commode stall. Fortunately, it was discovered by a cleaning woman the next morning and heavily guarded until it was finally presented to the winning SAC aircrew that evening. I asked Colonel Bowersox if he had reported the incident to General Creech or anyone else in TAC. He said no and opined that no one outside the squadron knew of the culpability of the squadron commander in the trophy theft. I asked if the squadron commander had been relieved and replaced by the air division commander, also resident at McChord AFB, Washington. Again, he replied in the negative.

My next move was to call the major general, Twenty-Fifth Air Division commander. When he came on the phone, I asked if he was aware of the incident; he replied in the affirmative. I then asked why he hadn't relieved squadron commander of command for this bizarre and foolish behavior in front of his squadron pilots, for exercising extremely bad judgment that could have resulted in a shocking embarrassment to TAC and General Creech, and for grand theft. His response was a tepid "It would have ruined his career." I reminded him that I had cautioned him not to place the major in command of the squadron because he was too young and immature, that the major had proved me right, and I wanted him removed immediately, the very next instant! He started defending the major, saying that removal from command would ruin the major's career! I reminded him that the major damaged his ability to command, and there had to be some consequence for his actions; otherwise, the major's actions would prove a terrible example of leadership and judgment on the air division commander's part and for all the squadron pilots and likely all the NCOs and airmen.

When he started to continue support for the major, I cut him short and said, "Listen very carefully! My next call is to General Creech because he deserves to know what happened, and I want him to hear about the incident from me, not from some other source. This will come out because someone will talk, and it will spread. When I speak with him, I can say one of two things! The first thing I might say is that you refused to relieve the major, so I relieved you and the major for exercising such terrible judgment. The other option is that you relieved the major of his command and that I strongly supported your decision! Which of these comments do you prefer I say to General Creech? You have ten seconds to answer!"

His response was "Tell him that I relieved the major."

My response was "Relieve him of command and move him to your staff in the next ten minutes!"

With that settled, I hung up and called General Creech. To say the least, General Creech was not pleased with what had happened and instantly asked why he was hearing about it so long after the incident. I replied that Colonel Bowersox said that he didn't feel that he had the authority to put the air division commander on the carpet and told me about the incident the instant I walked in the office after returning from the Middle East. Further, that the air division commander was waiting for me to return before taking action but had a close eye on the squadron and squadron commander. I reminded General Creech that he issued me this general after I fired his predecessor and that I knew he held the replacement in high regard. End of story!

The word came down from TAC that there was a schism at the Fighter Weapons School, and it was finding its way into a rewrite of the Tactics Manual. What I heard were phrases like "If you're the wingman and believe that you have better situational awareness than your leader, assume the lead and strike out on your own. You don't have to make a radio call; the rest of the flight should follow your lead." This was not only bad guidance; it was deadly and likely to result in the loss of the entire flight! It was easy to recall the days when I was a wingman and sometimes thought I could be a better leader than the one I was assigned to fly wing on. However, most of my leaders were veterans of WW II and Korea and had been tested in the crucible of combat. They were savvy, and I was eager but very green. ADTAC had its own Weapons School for Air Defense Tactics that pertained to the F-106 in the Active Force and Air National Guard and F-4 in the Air National Guard. The thought occurred to me that the same wrongheaded thinking might be creeping into the Air Defense Tactics Manual. I called Maj. Gen. Earl Brown and asked him to set up a meeting with the Air Defense Weapons School instructors that afternoon, as I was heading for a jet and would be there in about five hours.

When General Brown met me on the Tyndall flight line, I got to the point quickly and asked for a draft of the Tactics Manual rewrite. Sure enough, the same thinking was incorporated into the Air Defense Tactics Manual. In addition, there were phrases to indicate that any wingman could assume flight lead anytime the former thought that they had better situational awareness. But no one could explain to me how a wingman could "assume" he was better informed. There was also some verbiage that stated flight leaders couldn't be trusted, and wingman should strike out on their own whenever they felt compelled. The conference room at Tyndall's Fighter Weapons School was filled with senior captains, majors, and lieutenant colonels, all highly experienced and skilled in their profession as fighter pilots. The best of every unit are selected to attend the Fighter Weapons School, and only the best of the graduates are invited back to become instructors. I asked them one by one if they understood that they were telling the lieutenants in the operational squadrons that they themselves, the writers of the revised manual, could not be trusted and that only the inexperienced were capable of properly executing the mission. Each one in turn spent a lot of time studying their shoelaces searching for an answer—but none came. I suggested they do some soul-searching about their role as flight leaders and if they really thought it a good idea for their wingman to depart at will in combat without so much as a "you're on your own lead" radio call. I told General Brown that I would personally review the draft manual word by word prior to publication and suggested he do the same prior to sending it to me. The late afternoon and night session we had at Tyndall AFB must have been worthwhile, as the draft Air Defense Tactics Manual I received for review was in good order. All the new think free will garbage had been expunged.

In late May 1981, General Creech called, saying he wanted me to take Maj. Gen. Larry Welch's place as the TAC deputy commander for operations, as Larry was moving to a new position.

My replacement at ADTAC was Maj. John L. Pickitt, a fine officer whom I held in the highest regard. The move of ADTAC to Langley AFB, Virginia, was already planned, funded, and ready to get started when General Pickitt came on board. He executed the move flawlessly. Subsequently, General Pickitt was promoted to lieutenant general and became the director of the Defense Nuclear Agency (DNA). The DNA was later renamed as the Threat Reduction Agency. General Pickitt retired from that position a few years later and resides in South Carolina.

Lesson Learned

Courage is the most important characteristic of leadership because all others depend on it. Not the courage to take the machine gun or charge the hill, but the courage to do what is right!
—Gen. George C. Marshall

Courage is rightly esteemed the first of human qualities . . . because it is the quality that guarantees all others.
—Winston Churchill

When your gut tells you that something is not right, follow your gut feeling, it is right 98 percent of the time!
—Gen. Wilbur L. Creech

I should have listened to my gut and not allowed the air division commander to persuade me into letting that young major take command of the 318th FIS.

Always be true to your moral compass.

Every commander has the responsibility to ensure that the guidance promulgated to subordinates in his/her command adheres to principals proven in the crucible of war.

No one is entitled to continue in a position of responsibility if they fail to exercise sound judgment and act responsibly.

Be agile and be prepared to successfully tackle any assignment you're given.

Leadership of any enterprise should be entrusted to
someone with a mature understanding of the responsibilities
as well as the leadership skills to succeed!

Maj. Gen. Pete checks out in the F-106. Tyndall AFB, FL

E-3A & 57th FIS F-4s, Keflavik, Iceland patrol
the Greenland, Iceland UK Gap.

CHAPTER 13

TAC, Deputy Commander for Operations

Sheila could not travel with me to Langley AFB, Virginia, because the end of the school year was just a few weeks away and to move our school-age children at that time could have been prejudicial to their grades and learning. Even more important, our oldest, Denise, was graduating from high school and was accepted to the Air Force Academy. Sheila definitely wanted her to have the honor of walking across the stage to receive her diploma and honors. Sheila also wanted to be there to turn her over to the academy, as a parent should. In addition, her parents were driving up from Phoenix to attend their granddaughter's graduation and spend time with Sheila and the kids. At the other end, I would be moving into Maj. Gen. Larry Welch's quarters. General Creech had started renovating the quarters at Langley, and the gap after Larry departed and our delayed family move would give the contractor time to complete the renovation before Sheila and the two remaining children arrived. Another separation was not good, but there were some advantages to mitigate being apart.

I knew three things about Maj. Gen. Larry Welch: he was brilliant, very effective, and a workaholic—a nice combination that would put a lot of pressure on me to measure up to the bar he set. On arrival, I learned that Larry was going to Shaw AFB, South Carolina, to take command of Ninth Air Force, one of the premier numbered air forces with twelve wings under its command. He would also be getting his third star with the assumption of command.

We had a few days of overlap where he briefed me on all the issues that were in work and clued me in on some of General Creech's hot buttons and a typical week's schedule. Larry also showed me detailed plans for the SCIF (Sensitive Compartmented Intelligence Facility) that was being built in the TAC Headquarters building. Larry warned me that this was a very important project for our boss and to be sure to visit the construction site at least once a week to check on progress and ensure fidelity with the blueprints! He also pointed out that General Creech had personally initialed each page of the blueprints to signify he had approved them. He noted that Lt. Gen. Thomas H. McMullen, the vice commander, should be my best friend and the go-to guy when I needed advice. General McMullen was also a workaholic. I don't think I ever got to my office before he was in the building, and generally left work prior to him, even though it might be 9:00 or 10:00 p.m.

I was convinced the DO was a very busy person because I had two civil service secretaries and two majors as staff to support me in handling the work that passed through the office. There was also a brigadier general as the assistant deputy commander for operations (ADO). I can't remember the man's name, but he generally handled the command and control issues and backed me up on the flying issues, and vice versa. Tactical Air Command (TAC for short) was a very large and complex organization. It consisted of three numbered air forces, three centers, twenty-five fighter wings, six regional air defense regions, dozens of Air Defense Fighter Squadrons, and all the air defense radar from the Arctic to Key West, Florida. It was also the lead command for developing requirements for new aircraft and weapons associated with those aircraft. In addition, TAC was the air component of three Unified Commands (i.e., Atlantic Command (LANTCOM), Southern Command (SOUTHCOM), and US Readiness Command (REDCOM)). In 1979, CINCREDCOM was tasked by the National Command Authority (NCA) to form the Rapid Deployment Joint Task Force (RDJTF) as a separate subordinate command. Ninth Air Force became the air component of the RDJTF with forces assigned drawn from Ninth Air Force, SAC, and MAC. Ninth Air Force was then and still is the air component of CENTCOM. The TAC/DO and his/her staff are at the heart of supporting all these air component responsibilities.

Shortly after arriving at Langley, I was briefed in on the F-117 Stealth Fighter Program. It was deep black at the time—meaning, it was very closely held and only people with an absolute need to know were briefed on the program. The TAC/DO was the echelon of command above the F-117 Wing that was forming out at a classified location in the western Nevada desert. A "test" squadron equipped with A-7 aircraft with the mission of evaluating avionics had been formed under the command of Colonel Sheppard, a fighter pilot and former Thunderbird team member. The A-7 Squadron was a cover for the activity that was taking place at the covert airfield in a remote desert location under the control of the Department of Energy (DOE) Nevada test site. The Nevada test site was where nuclear warheads were detonated underground for stockpile stewardship. New designs were also tested there to measure the yield and other critical design factors.

New hangars to house the F-117s were under construction at the same time that F-117s were coming off the Lockheed Skunk Works production line and shipped to another desert location where the wings were reattached and all systems checked out. For years, the F-117s would only fly once in the daytime from that classified location for an airworthiness and functional check. After landing, the test pilot write-ups would be corrected, and then the F-117 would be flown to the covert location under cover of darkness where hangars were being built to house and hide them from overhead surveillance. From then on, for years, they would only be flown at night and never out of their hangars from before first light until after dark. The F-117 fuselage was faceted and covered with radar absorbing material. As a result, its radar signature was miniscule, and the F-117 was only detectable by ground and airborne radar from very, very close range.

The A-7 had been chosen for the cover story because stealth fighter test pilots believed A-7 flight characteristics and computer-driven weapons release systems were very similar to the F-117. Moreover, squadron pilots had to have something to fly on a regular basis when they were not flying stealth fighters at their secret desert location. Pilots and maintenance personnel along with essential Lockheed technicians and engineers would fly from the Las Vegas, Nevada's McCarran airport early Monday morning and return Friday evening and Saturday morning, depending on simulator and flying schedules. Undercover FBI and Air Force Office of Special Investigation (OSI) personnel prowled the bars, casinos, and bistros of Las Vegas to determine if anyone was talking about the project. These reports were available to me, the local wing commander, and others responsible for the program. Nothing of significance was reported for the years that I was responsible for the program.

My biggest concern was the wing commander. I really can't put my observations into an apt description; the best I can say is that his behavior was a departure from the norm. I wasn't looking forward to sharing my observations and opinions on Colonel Sheppard with General Creech. As I learned at Aviano, the bond between Thunderbird pilots across the years was very strong—my concern was that General Creech would not agree with my recommendation to relieve Colonel Sheppard. Further, I did not know what General Welch may have reported based on visits he may have made to the fledgling F-117 unit. To my surprise, General Creech listened quietly to my report and then said, somewhat sadly, "He has to go! I'll find the right man to replace him." The follow-on F-117 Wing commander was solid, strong, and an effective leader.

After settling down into the humdrum routine of a staff officer, an internal problem hit my desk. The two major aides asked for some private time, so we had a meeting. They were concerned that fraud was being committed by the two civilian secretaries supporting the TAC/DO's office and that I was an unwitting party to the crime. They pointed out that both secretaries came to work at seven, worked until six, and ate a brown bag lunch at their desks, charging eleven hours of work each weekday and five hours on alternate Saturdays, or about sixty hours a week. "How long as this been going on?" I asked.

"Ever since the mid-1960s, when one of your predecessors hired them and tolerated their work habits, or for about sixteen years" was their response. The majors presented their view that one secretary should come in at 7:00 a.m. and work until 4:00 p.m. with a one-hour lunch period. The second would come in at 10:00 a.m. and work until 7:00 p.m. with an hour for lunch. They opined that there wasn't sufficient work in the office for four people, so they suggested one of the two majors should come in at 6:00 a.m. to open the safes and get the paperwork organized for me. The second would come in at 11:00 a.m. and work until I left and then close the office. Both would work a minimum of nine hours per day, plus whatever was needed on weekends. Their pitch made a lot of sense to me, so I screwed up my courage and scheduled a meeting with the civilian secretaries for the first thing the next morning. The majors also pointed out that one of the secretaries kept a small TV under her desk and watched soaps all day. They argued that it was unprofessional and a big distraction to those who waited in the outer office for an appointment with me. The TV was so well hidden that I hadn't noticed it, and the sound didn't come into my office because the door was always closed for privacy and security of classified documents. Another reason I might not have heard the TV was my hearing was degraded because of too many hours on the flight line and around aircraft with their engines running.

I explained to the two civilian secretaries that I had been keeping track of the hours being worked and decided that I was demanding too much of them and that my recent assessment of the workload indicated their long hours were not necessary. The tall one complained that she needed the overtime to pay her daughter's college tuition, and the other complained that she just needed the money. I applauded their work ethic but offered that I could not be a party to using taxpayers' dollars to pay wages that were not justified. There was a lot of hand wringing, but I held firm, and the new hours started the following day. I held the tall lady back when that part of the discussion ended and told her to remove the TV from under her desk. I wasn't sure whether either one of the secretaries would show up for work the next morning—but they did. More importantly, they didn't file any civil service actions against me. A side benefit was that there wasn't much small talk after the schedule change, and the majors thought I was a certified hero for having the courage to do the right thing.

The occasional F-16A (single-seat) aircraft ran into the ground on a low-level mission without the pilot attempting to eject. It wasn't epidemic, but any loss of life is taken very seriously. There weren't any clues as to why, and never any witnesses, as low-level training missions were largely solo events over uninhabited areas. The leadership at the wing level and at TAC headquarters suspected pilot inattention or carelessness was the cause. Then we got lucky! An Air National Guard pilot flying out of Buckley Field, Colorado (now Buckley AFB), located just east of Denver, Colorado, was flying at thirty-five thousand feet when he found himself recovering consciousness with the aircraft stalled, heading straight down like a lawn dart. He looked around the cockpit, checked all the red warning lights, and realized that all four computers that ran the flight controls on this electric/fly by wire jet had failed. Then he ejected. He survived to tell the accident board what he observed prior to ejection. Equally important, the medical examination after he was picked up indicated that he had experienced a high number of negative Gs that likely caused him to black out. The evidence for this diagnosis was the burst blood vessels in his eyes. In addition to the flight computer failures, the pilot also noticed that the aircraft had experienced multiple electrical generator failures.

A call to the F-16 Program Office at Wright-Patterson AFB, Ohio, and to General Dynamics (GD), who designed and produced F-16s at their factory in Fort Worth, Texas, brought a team of F-16 experts to Langley AFB, Virginia, for an accident postmortem. What we heard bordered on criminal negligence, if not gross incompetence!

The GD engineers were asked to describe how the electrical power generation system in the F-16 worked, how the flight control computers were powered, and what happened to aircraft flight controls when the flight control computers lost generator voltage in flight.

TAC leadership learned that electrical power for the F-16 was generated by the primary generator that ran off of a power take-off (PTO) shaft driven by gears connected to the F-16's F-100 jet engine. If the primary generator failed or electrical power from that generator became unusable due to large voltage or frequency excursions, electrical power automatically shifted to the backup generator. The backup generator was on the same PTO shaft as the primary generator, so if the PTO was causing a problem, the same problem was also resident in the backup generator's electrical power. Not a good design for dependable redundancy. Should the backup generator fail, a hydrazine generator took over and provided electrical power for about fifteen minutes. However, it was likely that electricity from the hydrazine-driven generator would not meet the voltage and frequency specifications of the flight control computers. I asked if the flight control computers were connected to the aircraft batteries should the generators fail. The response was "No, because it was possible that the aircraft battery voltage could be lower than specified and damage the computers." I noted that this bordered on the height of insanity because if the flight control computers (FCCs) shut down, the aircraft crashed, essentially turning the FCCs into dust. The engineer came back with "The batteries will only power the FCCs for about twenty minutes, and we didn't consider that sufficient." I retorted that there was hardly a point in the entire United States that a pilot couldn't reach a suitable runway in fifteen minutes if F-16 electrical generators failed. After some discussion, it was agreed that the first and immediate step was to connect the FCCs to the F-16 battery and to add a preflight step for the crew chief to check the F-16 battery voltage prior to flight and make an entry in the Form 781. It was also agreed that GD had to expedite development and production of a better electrical generating system with greater reliable and graceful degradation.

The next topic was, what happens when the FCCs fail or are deprived of electrical power? The GD engineers first told us what every F-16 pilot learns in ground school—that there are four identical FCCs in the F-16, and there must be three operational for the F-16 to fly. The reason for this is that at least two of the four computers must agree with the response to every input from the pilot or sensors. If one fails, it is highly likely that two of the three remaining will agree, and the F-16 will fly properly. However, if one of the four computers failed, a red light in the cockpit would illuminate! The pilots' handbook (Dash-1) advises that if one of the four redundant flight computers fails, the pilot should land the aircraft as soon as possible (ASAP)! In over six hundred F-16A/B flying hours, I've only seen that red light come on twice, so it is not a very common occurrence.

The GD engineers then told us that if the electrical generators failed, as they did in the Buckley Air National Guard incident, the elevator would revert to its null position, and at normal cruise speed, this would result in a nine negative G pitch over! After a noticeable outburst from the senior officers present in the room, General Creech asked, "Why did you do that, and why not a 1.5 G pitch-up so the pilot could eject instead of becoming a smoking hole in the ground?"

There was no immediate answer, but when a response was offered, it was something like "It was a convenient thing to do in the design process." The conclusion to this discussion was direction to GD to reprogram the software so that the null position of the elevator when the FCCs failed would cause the F-16 to pitch up mildly at normal cruise airspeeds. This would be an urgent engineering change to the entire F-16 fleet. Immediately, word was sent to all F-16 Wings about the mishap findings as well as the immediate and longer-term fixes to the F-16 fleet in TAC, PACAF, and USAFE. The next step was to visit the F-16 Wings in TAC and fly with one or two of the squadrons, primarily to demonstrate that the generals at the TAC Headquarters believed the aircraft were safe to fly. Connecting the FCCs to the aircraft battery was a relatively easy flight line fix, and it didn't take long before the entire fleet was modified. I don't recall another "lawn dart" incident once this modification was initiated. There was still some unease in the wings and squadrons, and it was important to keep them current and fully informed about the upgrades in progress. As General Creech would occasionally remind me, "The only reason TAC Headquarters exists is to support the wings and squadrons, not the other way around." I took the liberty to underline his advice because it applies to every enterprise anywhere! For example, most, if not all, revenue generated by any business is achieved in the field, not at the headquarters with corner offices, executive suites, and big conference rooms.

There was an Air Defense Squadron, the 48th FIS, equipped with F-106s located on the far side of Langley AFB. The Forty-Eighth also had an evaluation flight of T-33s for calibrating East Coast radar sites.

I was still current in both the F-106 and the T-33, so I could fly either aircraft for official travel or currency purposes. The T-33 was the better choice, as it was far cheaper to maintain and cost less per hour to fly. Moreover, the F-106s had an important strategic defense role in the Capitol region just north of Langley. Therefore, I made arrangements to fly with the T-33 flight for most of my official business travel to Tactical Air Command bases. I was assigned one pilot to fly with, a first lieutenant, Randy Galloway, who had spent a tour as an Air Training Command instructor pilot and was in a lead-in assignment to fighter aircraft. Randy was a top-notch pilot and demanded the best of me—no slack for seniority from him! I liked that because he was bringing me back up to my former top gun skills. He was also a skilled waterfowl hunter, and we spent a few hours in duck blinds together harvesting geese, black ducks, and wood ducks. We still are good friends and hunt together annually.

The tasking came midafternoon from Commander Readiness Command, Gen. Don Starry, USA, to plan a contingency operation to completely destroy the Cuban Air Force! This plan was in support of another operation that was being considered for Central and South America. The latter operation would entail large numbers of support aircraft flying between the western tip of Cuba and the most eastern part of Mexico. It was envisioned that the Cuban Air Force had to be neutralized to prevent them from interdicting the flow of support aircraft to and from their objective. The tasking said that General Starry, CINCRED, would visit TAC at 0900 hours the following morning to review our plan. General Creech gave me the tasking and directed he be briefed on the plan at 0700 hours in his conference room.

In my view, the tasking consisted of three related parts. The most important part was the plan itself; second, a war room, where we could show visitors from Higher Headquarters the enemy order of battle and the weight of force we were putting against each element, as well as the expected battle damage; the third part, a detailed briefing of the plan was paramount. The planned operation to destroy the Cuban Air Force had to be explained in a cogent and compelling manner.

The planning went to the current operations staff supported by TAC's intelligence staff. Building a war room in the TAC Command Section space went to TAC civil engineers and TAC/Intel. I provided some general guidance, such as first attack would commence at one hour prior to nautical dawn preceded five minutes earlier with electronic countermeasures (ECM) aircraft that could blind or degrade Cuban Air Defense surface-to-air missiles (SAMs). The first attack would be followed by F-16s attacking each target with general-purpose bombs to ensure that nothing remained operational to include runways, fuel storage farms, and maintenance facilities. The TAC civil engineers were tasked to turn a ten-by-fifteen-foot storage room into a war room with cork walls, floor to ceiling. Next, intel was tasked to provide photographs of all Cuban operational airfields and air defense sites. Each airfield and air defense site order of battle would be identified with a line connecting the description to the site's location on a map of Cuba. This would be placed on one side of the room. On the other side of the room would be the friendly forces wall depicting the bases, type aircraft, and weapons loads. In addition, there would be a flow chart showing the aircraft routes and flow over the targets. Last, the TAC briefing team, resident on the DO staff, was tasked to work with the mission planners and capture the execution in a briefing format. Then I went home, picked up a shaving kit, a fresh uniform, and some snacks, and returned to the office—it was going to be a long night.

I could not have been more pleased; the civil engineers turned that storage area into a room that any chief executive would be proud of. But that should not have been a surprise because General Creech had been bringing the command up by its bootstraps with self-help, and the CE shop had been at the forefront—they knew and lived TAC standard.

When the war room construction was complete, the intel shop began bringing in a wall-to-wall map of Cuba, photos, and order of battle data—things were starting to take shape. I started to have some confidence that we would pull this off in time for General Starry's visit at 0900 hours. I toured the war room and provided some last-minute guidance along with a bushel of kudos. Next was a review of the briefing with some last-minute revisions. Then we rehearsed and rehearsed it in front of the DO planners and intel folks who collaborated in developing the war plan.

At 0700 hours, the office direct line lit up, and General Creech said he was ready to take the briefing. It flowed well, and in my view, the story was compelling and crisp, and detailed how the mission would unfold if executed, with an expected results wrap-up. When the briefing was done, General Creech leaned back and paused for a few seconds. Then came the questions: "Why so few sorties? Did we run out of aircraft? Did we run out of ramp space for additional aircraft? Did we run out of bombs?"

The answer to all his questions was "No, sir, but our calculations showed that both the first attack and the follow-on attack each achieved a 90 percent probability of destroying every target. I double-checked them myself and believed we would more than accomplish the mission with the forces and weapons load specified in the plan."

General Creech responded in a fatherly tone with, "Pete, no plan ever survived first contact with the enemy! Double everything for insurance." And that we did prior to General Starry's arrival.

Following the briefing, I took General Creech to the just-completed war room. He was ecstatic with the quality and completeness of the room and the elegant and complete order of battle work done by his intel staff. It was obvious that he was pleased with the effort when he said, "We'll bring General Starry here first so he can get a complete grasp of the situation prior to the briefing." When CINCRED arrived, he spent nearly an hour in the war room, asking detailed questions about the Cuban readiness state of their air defenses and fighter aircraft.

Subsequently, he applauded the briefing and gave General Creech a "well done." As I recall, at the end of the briefing, General Creech opined that we could probably accomplish the mission with a lower force level, but he wanted to make sure that nothing could shoot or fly following the last wave of attacks. As an aside, General Starry was a large man but lean. He rose through the ranks in the Armor Branch and was wearing a tanker uniform with a red bandana hanging from a rear pocket in true tanker fashion. He was revered in the army and passed away in 2011.

The mission was never executed! However, planning it provided us a template of what could be done in little more than half a day. The only thing that wasn't done was cut the tasking order (fragmentary order) stipulating time over target, refueling orbits, frequencies, safe passage corridors, rescue cap, etc. Once General Creech and General Starry approved the plan, a warning order would have led to the development of a fully executable plan.

Tactical Fighter Gunnery Competition was suspended, as the Vietnam Conflict demanded more and more fighter resources and replacement aircrews. The demands of a gunnery competition seemed out of place and counterproductive, and Gen. Walter C. Sweeney Jr. suspended the competition. During the last competition in 1962, an F-104 won most events and overall honors. It should be noted that the F-104 was the least capable aircraft model in the TAC stable to win a comprehensive gunnery meet. It was the superb flying by the pilot of the F-104 that carried the day.

General Creech was always looking for ways to increase competition because he firmly believed that competition made us better wherever it existed. And he had plenty of evidence to support his conviction. Examples were the flying hours program, competition between squadrons in every wing, COMO, COSO, base appearance, aircraft appearance, and all the support activities where he established standards and goals for just about every aspect of a TAC wing/base activities. He called me up to his office and asked, "What do you think about resurrecting the Global USAF Tactical Fighter Gunnery Competition?"

My answer was "Sir, that would be fantastic!"

He came back with "I'm glad you like the idea because it's your job to make it happen—get cracking! We'll call the competition Gun Smoke 81."

It wasn't just my job to make Gun Smoke 81 come off as the air force's premier flying competition. Maj. Gen. Jack Gregory, commander of the Fighter Weapons Center, the host commander at Nellis AFB, Nevada, where Gun Smoke 81 would be held, also had a lion's share of the action in readying facilities and gunnery ranges. Nellis consisted of a plethora of ground and air gunnery ranges that stretched from Las Vegas into the Navy China Lake, California, Range Complex and Edwards AFB, California, covering thousands of square miles. General Gregory was a good friend and one of the finest tactical commanders in the air force. It would be a pleasure to work with him on developing the road map and milestones along the way to execution. The road map detailed all the events and timeline as well as rehearsals along the way to the opening ceremony and eventually the awards ceremony. It included all the minute details to ensure everything was just right to support the units that would deploy to Nellis, vie for the trophies, and be in the winners' circle.

I had considered myself an expert planer who accounted for all possible contingencies. However, after working with Major General Gregory on Gunsmoke 81, it was obvious that he was the master of details and work-arounds for the unexpected.

The awards ceremony would be the "icing on the cake," with several air force senior generals taking part, led by Gen. Lew Allen, CSAF. Gen. John Roberts, one of my former bosses and commander of the Air Force Training Command, a legendary fighter pilot and top gun of one of the earlier gunnery competitions, would be in attendance and a presenter. Maj. Gen. Fredrick "Boots" Blesse, USAF (ret.), another legend in his own time, would also be in attendance. Boots wrote the booklet *No Guts, No Glory*, a primer for fighter pilots on how to achieve victory in aerial combat. I have a shop worn copy in my library; it was well read by fighter pilots of the Korean and Vietnam Wars because it was the only authoritative document on the subject. Moreover, the author was a double ace, with ten confirmed air-to-air kills. Boots also was a competitor in one of the first Global Gunnery Competitions and *won every event* and was truly the top gun.

Gen. Jack Gregory and I met several times at Nellis AFB to go over all the details, starting with the arrival briefings, range briefings, event briefings, squadron facilities, ramp rules, departure and arrival rules, and rules about the rules. We set up the awards ceremony, checked the DV seating on the stage, and made sure there was plenty of room between the two DV rows of chairs so that it would be easy for senior officers to walk between the rows with people in the chairs. The public address system was thoroughly checked with a hot backup. We had a plan for just about every possible contingency. That is about the time General Creech informed me that I was the master of ceremonies for the awards ceremony. We checked the newly purchased trophies for each event and the overall winner. The trophies would either be locked up or, if on display, guarded by two security policemen. I didn't want to relive the stolen trophy incident that occurred at the SAC Bomb Comp two years prior. One of the biggest problems was trying to provide rules and guidance for the pilots and events that would lead to a fair competition. For example, the A-10 could not compete in the air-to-air "dart" engagement for the lack of a lead computing gun sight by design. The A-10 was strictly a close air support aircraft and a tank destroyer, and excelled in both of those roles.

By all accounts, Gun Smoke 81 was a resounding success! The pilots loved it, and the gunnery scores showed that the best of the best qualified for the competition, and that they were experts at their trade. There were no mishaps or disqualifications for pushing the envelope, and no fights at the O'club bar. Most importantly, Gen. Lew Allen, CSAF, and General Creech were pleased with the spirited competition and the results—Gun Smoke would be a biannual gunnery competition going forward until world events would necessitate a suspension.

Being a staff officer in a major headquarters is always full of surprises. Most of the correspondence addressed to General Creech came to me for advance reading and research, if needed, to ensure the commander had complete information when he read the correspondence. Sometimes it required preparation of a draft response as a courtesy, although General Creech usually personally wrote all letters he signed. One morning, a letter in the stack gave me a sever jolt in the pit of my stomach. It was a glowing report of Maj. Hal Hornburg's F-15 demonstration at Chanute AFB, Illinois, signed by Maj. Gen. Norma Brown, center commander. It was so glowing that it was inflammatory and detailed how Major Hornburg violated just about every rule spelled out for demonstration pilots. These demonstrations were one of General Creech's ideas for showing the prowess of TAC fighters and pilots in support of countless requests for aerobatic demonstrations by the Thunderbirds, which could not possibly be met due to their packed schedules. Each demonstration pilot was certified by General Creech, me, or both of us, availability permitting. The certification was done in situ alongside the runway at show center. Minimum altitude was five hundred feet AGL. This was a hard floor, and any dip below that was resulted in immediate disqualification. I had a stake in the game because I certified Major Hornburg, whose full-time job was chief of standardization and evaluation of the First Tactical Fighter Wing at Langley AFB, Virginia.

I called Hal and told him to drop everything and come to my office immediately. When he arrived, I gave him Gen. Norma Brown's letter to read. He quickly turned red and said, "This is a bunch of lies—not one bit is true." I told him I believed him, but the letter had to go to General Creech, so I was going to call Gen. Norma Brown to get her side of the story, and I wanted him to stay put in case I needed him. When I got Norma on the phone, I thanked her for the letter and asked if she could confirm the details in the letter about the pilot's performance. Her response was disgusting but saved the day: "I wasn't at the open house and didn't write the letter. My chief of staff did." She put him on the phone so he could vouch for the contents. His response was similar: he didn't go to the show either, just made up some stuff that he thought would please General Creech. Neither the general nor her chief of staff was a flier. Thus, knowledge of flight discipline requirements was not one of their strong suits. There was one phrase in the letter that convinced me that it was a complete pack of lies. In part, the letter said that when Major Hornburg departed Chanute to return to Langley, he did a roll on takeoff and buzzed the crowd at treetop height. In fact, the runway at Chanute AFB would not support F-15s, and the demonstration was flown from another location. As a word of caution, I suggested to General Brown that she not sign letters when she had no knowledge of the content. Next, I hand-carried the letter to General Creech and gave him the facts. He just shook his head in disgust. Major Hornburg went on to an illustrious career. He was promoted to the rank of general on November 14, 2001, when he assumed command of the Air Combat Command. After Desert Storm, all bomber and tanker aircraft in the USAF were transferred to TAC, and that command, no longer predominately a fighter force, was renamed by Gen. Tony McPeak, CSAF, as Air Combat Command (ACC).

Aircraft mishaps are always tragic. A valuable combat asset may be damaged or lost. Public and/or government property may be extensively damaged. And of course, the most precious asset, the lives of pilots, crew members, rescue personnel, and bystanders may be terribly altered or lost. Accident boards are formed to determine the train of events that led to the mishap with focus on the key event that made the mishap inevitable. The board's business is serious with the ultimate goal of preventing or reducing future aircraft accidents from the same cause. Some accidents are the result of flawed engineering design, like the F-16 accident described previously. Others are the result of aircraft designs accepted by the air force that have aerodynamic quirks like adverse yaw! Adverse yaw can cause an aircraft to depart normal flight if the pilot is the least bit inattentive during a critical phase of flight. The F-100 and F-4 fighters fell into this category. On the other hand, F-15 and F-16 aircraft are so aerodynamically stable that you have to work hard to cause them to depart normal flight. For example, the F-15 has a pair of handles on the canopy bow—called chicken handles; if the pilot has somehow caused an F-15 to depart from controlled flight, all he/she has to do is let go of the control stick, and the F-15 will return to normal flight. This assumes there is enough altitude for recovery. A computer to which the pilot makes inputs flies the F-16. Prior to flight, the pilot is supposed to tell the computer the configuration of the aircraft. Things like external fuel tanks, ordnance, etc. are entered into a computer display. The computer then limits the number of Gs that can be applied by the pilot. There have been instances where the pilot purposely did not enter external fuel tanks in the aircraft computer's data base to get a G advantage in air-to-air combat tactics training. When this happens, there is a much higher probability the aircraft will depart from controlled flight. Then there are accidents that are the result of bad judgment on the part of pilots. Bad judgment is the hardest cause to correct. One thing learned in reviewing accidents is that wing commanders are universally loyal and supportive of pilots under their command—as they should be, unless circumstances strongly dictate otherwise. The following incident is a case in point.

On a reasonably good weather day at Hill AFB, Utah, an F-16 failed to stop normally and engaged the far end "barrier" (about a 1.5-inch braided steel cable) stretched across the runway about one thousand feet from the end. The barrier is intended to stop aircraft before they go beyond the end of the runway, and it did just that. Hill AFB, Utah, is at an altitude of 4,473 feet above sea level. At this altitude, the air is considerably less dense than at sea level. All aircraft fly on density altitude. Hence, when the airspeed indicator monitored by the pilot is showing 140 knots on final approach, the aircraft is actually going about 165 knots per hour. This is the actual velocity the tires and brakes must dissipate in order to stop an aircraft on the runway. Recommended pilot technique for stopping an F-16 on landing is to employ aerodynamic braking by holding the nose high until the elevator can no longer hold the nose up, and then apply normal braking to stop the aircraft. Apparently, the combination of airspeed on final approach, point of touchdown, and pilot technique after landing did not stop the F-16 in time to prevent it from taking the barrier.

Maintenance personnel were in the process of extracting the unharmed aircraft from the barrier when a second F-16 flown by a student with IP in the rear cockpit entered the landing pattern. Normally, in this situation, the IP would tell the student to make a low approach and go around. This would be the prudent course of action because if the second aircraft also had a stopping problem, it would most probably crash into the aircraft already in the barrier. The likely outcome of this would be two aircraft totally destroyed and three pilots killed. Unfortunately, the IP allowed the approach and landing to continue. During the landing and rollout of the second F-16, there was confusion as to which pilot (the IP or student) was in control, and the second F-16 departed the runway into the grass medium, broke the nose gear, and caused over a million dollars in damage. Some might say that was a good outcome because it didn't run into the F-16 in the barrier. The accident board, after completing their investigation, found that the IP was at fault for not taking control of the aircraft and/or not telling the student to go around because of the other F-16 in the barrier at the end of the runway. It must be understood that air force regulations state that if there is an instructor pilot in the aircraft, that instructor pilot is the pilot in command and is responsible for the safe operation of the aircraft. In the instance where there are two instructor pilots flying in a two cockpit F-16B, one will be designated as the pilot in command, to sign the flight plan and be responsible for the safe operation of the aircraft.

General Creech's policy was for the TAC/DO to receive the accident investigation briefing in the morning and offer advice if warranted. General Creech would then take the briefing in the afternoon. After the briefing, it was customary for General Creech to invite the wing commander into his office to offer advice on what corrective action, if any, the commander might take and to encourage him to continue aggressive combat training, and not revert to conservative measures as a result of the mishap.

I took the briefing and found the accident board did a very creditable job in analyzing the mishap and determining the cause that ultimately led to the accident. Basically, they determined that the IP of the second F-16 that ran off of the runway failed to exercise sound judgment by allowing his student to attempt a landing with an aircraft in the barrier. Further, the IP failed to take control of the aircraft when the student was unable to maintain control of F-16 on the runway after landing. The wing commander then had the opportunity to concur or offer his own assessment of the mishap. The wing commander elected to disagree with the board's findings and argued that the F-16 ran off the runway because of severe wind gusts that occurred at the time of landing. I asked the wing commander if the tower had recorded the wind gusts on their instruments, if any personnel on the flight line were injured, if any flight line equipment had been overturned or damaged, etc. Last, if he had found any witnesses that could validate his claim of sever wind gusts. The answer to all these questions was negative. I then asked the board president if he investigated the possibility of a microburst of wind that could have caused the mishap. He responded that they ran this possibility to ground and could not uncover even a scintilla of evidence to support the wing commander's claim.

I invited the wing commander to my office for lunch and encouraged him to agree with the board's findings absent any witnesses or meteorological recordings to support his claim of severe wind gusts as the cause. He held firm to his position! I then asked, "What is the status of the IP involved in the mishap? Has he been subject to a requalification check ride? Has he been decertified as an IP?"

The wing commander said he saw no reason for any of these actions—"He is a good IP!" he said. I pointed out that he was responsible for the aircraft as an instructor pilot and failed to maintain control of the student or the aircraft. Therefore, his judgment and skill as an IP was in question. I suggested he might want to seriously consider some of the actions I recommended prior to the board president's briefing to General Creech. To this, the Wing Commander gave no response. I saw big trouble ahead for him and encouraged him to reevaluate his position. As an aside, my job was not to save wing commanders from their own stupidity or folly, but rather to ensure the board president and his team had conducted a thorough investigation and identified the chain of events, including the cause, that ultimately led to the mishap. In addition, I believed that it was my responsibility to be perhaps the first dispassionate adult to tell a wing commander his thinking was seriously flawed.

When General Creech took the briefing that afternoon, nothing changed. The wing commander took the opportunity to disagree with the findings and presented his version of the severe wind burst as the true cause of the mishap. General Creech asked about the status of the

IP and then approved the board president's report and thanked him for the effort. He then asked me to accompany him to his office. He asked, "How did the wing commander travel to Langley?"

"He flew to Langley in one of his wings, F-16s" was my response.

Then General Creech said, "Find him and tell him he's fired and to travel back to Hill AFB, Utah, commercially—I don't want him flying another TAC aircraft! Call the 388th vice commander and tell him he's in charge until a replacement arrives. Also tell him to ground the F-16 IP involved in the mishap and have him recertified as a line pilot!" After locating the former 388th Wing commander and telling him he was to fly home commercially, I made sure he didn't have access to the F-16 aircraft he flew to Langley. Then I called the 388th Wing vice commander and passed on General Creech's guidance. In addition, I suggested that he send an F-16B with two pilots to Langley so that the second pilot could bring their F-16 sitting on our ramp home to Hill AFB. This was an extreme case of a wing commander overreaching to find a reason to justify exceedingly bad judgment on the part of a pilot in his command. Col. Pete Kempf, commander of the 4th TFW at Seymour Johnson AFB, North Carolina, was reassigned to the 388th TFW at Hill to fill the void. Pete was a strong no-nonsense leader and held a number of key leadership positions including commander of Twelfth Air Force prior to his retirement. Pete was also a Bootstrap classmate of mine at the University of Nebraska at Omaha in 1964.

A troubling letter arrived on General Creech's desk. It started out with the salutation "Dear Boss, I quit," and went on to explain why—it was written by Capt. Ron Keys stationed at Luke AFB, Arizona. The letter piqued General Creech's interest, so he invited the captain to TAC Headquarters to explain why he felt compelled to leave the air force. Essentially, what Captain Keys told General Creech is that the senior officers in his squadron were unfit to lead. I believe one of the captain's comments was "Our squadron commander is incapable of leading a four-ship flight, but if he could, he couldn't find the range complex or hit a target." Unfortunately, we found Captain Keys's story to be true and replicated in many fighter squadrons throughout TAC. In a way, the Vietnam War caused this situation—the unintended consequences of personnel actions. After many or most of all TAC fighter pilots completed their second or third combat tours in Vietnam, the air force started rotating bomber and tanker pilots into F-4 Replacement Training Units (RTUs). Most of the SAC pilots sent to F-4 RTUs were majors, some were even lieutenant colonels. When they finished the RTU course with less than one hundred hours of F-4 flying time, they were sent to

Vietnam. Because these RTU graduates were low in fighter experience, they served a year as wingman. Upon returning from Vietnam, many were retained in TAC and assigned to F-4 Fighter Wings. Their rank resulted in assignments as squadron commanders or squadron operations officers—second in command of a squadron. Most, if not all, were incapable of improving the skill sets of their subordinates and often set negative examples because of their lack of experience. Most captains that started in the fighter track after commissioning were far more experienced and more capable than the officers placed over them.

As a result of Captain Keys's letter and the investigation that followed, General Creech initiated the Fighter Pilot Shortfall study that resulted in a comprehensive briefing of the same name. What the study revealed set off alarm bells throughout tactical air forces worldwide. Essentially, we learned that there was a great demand for fighter pilots in TAC, PACAF, USAFE, AAC Headquarters, the Pentagon, and Unified Commands (now called Combatant Commands). Examples of the latter are CENTCOM, EUCOM, NORTHCOM, PACOM, and SOCOM. I'm reminded that the AF/XOXFMC Plans Branch that I served in as a major and lieutenant colonel was populated with fighter pilots, but our work was largely related to nonflying activities, such as the Bare Base Program and Conventional Munitions Stockpiles. In fact, the study showed that more fighter pilots were leaving their flying assignments and going to headquarters assignments than there were fighter pilots coming into the wings from Combat Crew Training Squadrons. If this trend were allowed to continue, there would be a significant downgrade in combat capability in the USAF worldwide fighter force.

A very comprehensive and compelling briefing was developed on the Fighter Pilot Shortfall, and General Creech gave it to everyone that came to visit TAC. The word was getting out, but nothing was being done to correct the situation, thus the problem continued to grow.

About this time, General Creech informed me that Lt. Gen. Tom McMullen had been selected to command the Aeronautical Systems Division of the Air Force Systems Command and that the chief had approved my promotion to lieutenant general to serve as TAC's vice commander. That was so unexpected that I was speechless. At the same time, he told me that I would have to continue living in the DO's quarters, as he had scheduled the house designated for the vice commander for upgrade. No problem; Sheila would prefer to bypass another move and some more broken china.

A few days later, General Creech woke up with a severe muscle strain in his back. Apparently, he slept with a window open, and a cold breeze caused a major back muscle to lock up. He couldn't come to work, and the doctors heavily medicated him in attempting to loosen the muscle. He was down for about a week. It was late summer and very nice outside in the tidewater area, so we met every day at 9:00 a.m. at the patio table behind his quarters facing the James River. At these meetings, he would give me his instructions for the key issues TAC was addressing. On what turned out to be the last of those meetings, General Creech informed me that the pinning ceremony for my third star would take place the following morning. Following the pinning, I would fly to the Pentagon and give the Fighter Pilot Shortfall briefing to the air force chief and the air council (all the three-star generals on the air force headquarters staff).

Things didn't quite work out as planned. I reported up for work at the DO's office about 0600 hours as a major general only to be informed that the pinning ceremony was cancelled. Further, I was to go back to my quarters, put the third star on my uniform, and get ready for the trip to the Pentagon. General Creech was much better and would present the Fighter Pilot briefing to the Air Staff—but he wanted me along just in case he had a relapse. I went back to quarters and laid my uniform blouse on the bed, and Sheila set up our camera on a tripod so we could take a picture of her and me pinning the third star on the epaulets. Things don't always go as planned!

Uncharacteristically, General Creech sat in the back of the T-39 Sabreliner and offered me the opportunity to fly the jet to Andrews AFB, Maryland. The weather was poor with rain and low clouds, so it required a GCA to about a two-hundred-foot ceiling. I was along as a backup for the briefing just in case the muscle spasms returned due to the cold and damp weather. As we were walking down a Pentagon corridor to the chief's office, General Creech said, "Pete, you're out of uniform!"

With a quick check, I asked, "How so?"

His response was "You forgot to take off your name tag!"

To which I stupidly replied, "Sir, the name tag is optional for three-star generals. No one is going to know me, so I thought I'd wear it when away from TAC."

"Take it off!" was the curt response. Nonetheless, I always wore the name tag when travelling away from TAC. Wearing the name on the uniform saved a lot of embarrassment on the part of junior officers and airmen whom I came in contact with; officers and airmen who didn't have any idea of who I was without it.

General Creech was probably the best briefer ever in conveying an important message, and he was no less with the chief and the air council on the Fighter Pilot Shortfall. Immediate steps were taken by the personnel staff in the Pentagon and at the air force personnel center at Randolph AFB, Texas, to ensure that there was the requisite experience in fighter squadrons all over the air force to provide leadership in aerial combat to "Fly, Fight, and Win." As a footnote, about twenty-five years later, Capt. Ron Keys was promoted to the rank of general and given the privilege of commanding Air Combat Command.

While I was promoted and officially the vice commander of TAC, General Creech requested I continue to wear both hats, the vice and the DO, because he had not yet selected a replacement for the DO position. He asked me to continue working out of the DO office because the workload was heavier there, and the assistant DO needed to have immediate access to me along with the directors of the DO staff. Staying in the DO office would also reduce the traffic through the command suite.

The call came unexpectedly. General Creech asked how progress was coming on the Classified Planning Room (CPR) or SCIF. "It's on schedule. The framing of rooms is nearly completed, and drywalling is in progress" was the reply. He invited me up to his office to accompany him on an in-progress inspection. I grabbed up the drawings along with a tape measure and raced up the stairs to the command suite. General Creech was waiting and asked me to take him to the CPR. I immediately took this as a test to see if I knew where it was without hesitation or missteps along the way.

When we arrived at the CPR, his first comment was "This is all wrong! These rooms are a lot smaller than I wanted them to be! Someone has made changes behind my back!" I realized what was happening—it happens to anyone who has designed a building with rooms and saw it when the foundation was laid and then again when the rooms were roughed in. The facility always looks bigger before the walls go up. I pulled out the tape measure and suggested we measure each room wall to wall and check them against the drawings. I held on to the tag end of the tape while General Creech took the readings. Every dimension was within one fourth of an inch (plus or minus) of the specified dimension on the initialed drawings. General Creech wasn't happy, but he agreed that the rooms were the correct size and that progress was on schedule. I uttered a silent thanks to Larry Welch for his foresight and the warning he gave me on the CPR. The CPR was shortly put to good use during the Grenada invasion and rescue operation.

The First Air Commando Wing was executing a nationally directed covert mission—it was really deep black. I called Brig. Gen. Hugh Cox,

1st SOF Wing commander, on a secure line to find out how the mission was progressing. He informed me that the mission had been completed, and the aircraft, an MC-130, was departing the area. I was relieved that all had gone well until he added that the crew had elected to stay airborne for another two hours to set a world record for C-130 endurance. At that, I noted that the mission was so black, they could never talk about it, and the endurance record would never see the light of day, or be recognized. I opined that the crew had to be fatigued by the mission and being airborne for about twenty-four hours and to call them on a secure radio and tell them to land ASAP. After a few minutes, Hugh called me back and said he was unable to contact the crew but would keep trying. Brig. Gen. Hugh Cox worked for me when he commanded the C-130 ABCCC Squadron at Keesler AFB, Mississippi. His unit was a direct report to the 552nd AWACS. Hugh was an exceptionally gifted officer and an outstanding leader. I was confident that he tried repeatedly to make contact. Somewhere there are retired and aging MC-130 crew members that set an endurance record but cannot tell anyone where, when, why, or how it happened.

During my tenure as TAC/DO, the First Special Operations Wing was assigned to TAC as it had been since its inception as Jungle Jim in the spring of 1961 when I reported to the unit as a captain with six months in grade. The air force inspector general, Lt. Gen. Howard Leaf, had recently conducted a compliance inspection of the Air Commando Wing and, while finding them "satisfactory," found their morale low. The IG attributed this to the fact Air Commandos were assigned to TAC, a predominately fighter command, whereas the First Wing was equipped with C-130s and helicopters. As a result of this finding, the IG suggested the morale would be improved if the 1st SOW were assigned to the Military Airlift Command (MAC), a command equipped largely with cargo aircraft and a few helicopters. General Creech and I, in our own council, came to a different conclusion—that Air Commandos and TAC were kindred souls because our mission was to fight wars and, in the process, destroy the enemy and his forces. On the other hand, MAC was in the business of hauling cargo and personnel to where it and they were needed. Their mission involved avoiding the enemy, if at all possible, as they had no means of defending themselves or successfully engaging the enemy. Nonetheless, the Air Staff established a forum whereby Maj. Gen. Duane Cassidy, MAC/DO, and I, representing TAC, would debate the issue of "should 1st ACW be transferred from TAC to MAC to improve their morale?" The mediator of this/these debates was Maj. Gen. Perry M. Smith, deputy director of plans on the Air Staff. Major General Smith had been the vice commander and then commander of the Thirty-Sixth Tactical Fighter Wing at Bitburg, Germany. Prior to that, he had several assignments as a line fighter pilot including a tour at Ubon AB, Thailand, flying F-4Ds over North Vietnam in 1968.

During our discussions on the future of the 1st SOW, Major General Smith seemed heavily biased toward the air force IG recommendations that the wing be transferred to MAC. Perhaps it was because both the AF/IG and General Smith served on the Air Staff, and he felt compelled to support the Air Staff's position. I argued that Gen. Curtis LeMay correctly assigned the Air Commando Wing under TAC because it was a combat unit with the purpose of seeking out the enemy and destroying them wherever they could be found. Further, that Air Commandos had thrived under TAC over the twenty-one years since their 1961 baptism in the crucible of combat in Vietnam. I further pointed out that the fundamental principal for organizational structure was the strategic purpose or mission of an organization. In this regard, the 1st SOW was correctly aligned under the Tactical Air Command, a war-fighting organization, vice an airlift organization—even though the airframes were highly modified C-130s and CH-53 helicopters. Last, I opined that Headquarters TAC and Ninth Air Force would do a better job of working the morale issue by flying with the various squadrons—and that I was committed to begin flying with my old unit, the 1st SOW, immediately.

No agreement was reached at the meeting with the understanding a follow-on discussion would be scheduled in the near future. I back-briefed General Creech on my impression that Major General Smith appeared biased toward implementing the air force/IG recommendation. We then set upon planning our strategy for the proposed follow-on meeting with the Air Staff. As we were about to wrap up, General Creech said, "Instead of expending a lot of time and effort on this issue, let's find out what General Gabriel's position is on this." He immediately placed a call to the chief's office and spoke with General Gabriel. I heard one side of the conversation that ended with "Well, Chief, if that's what you want, we will make it happen as smoothly and transparently as possible!" Then he turned to me and directed that I call Brig. Gen. Hugh Cox and tell him that his wing, the 1st SOW, would be transferred to MAC as recommended by the air force/IG. The transfer process would start as soon as congressional delegations were notified and the programmers could affect the change—that TAC would do everything to make the transition go smoothly! I knew that General Creech did not agree with the move; I also understood that TAC had a lot on their plate, and the fight with the Air Staff was a big distraction and could lead to problems on other issues down the road. As an Air Commando "plank holder," with five years as a snake eater and member of the Air Commando Hall of Fame, I strongly believed the move might immediately provide a small boost in morale but would be short in duration. While the aircraft were more alike, the missions were vastly different, like the "difference between lightning and lightning bug," to quote Mark Twain. I was convinced it is the mission, not the vehicle, that bonds.

Less than ten years later, the Joint Special Operations Command (SOCOM) was formed to incorporate Air Force Air Commandos, Navy Seal Teams, and Army Special Forces under a single war-fighting command for exercising and execution worldwide. MAC retained the service Title 10 responsibility to "organize, train, and equip." However, when SOCOM received acquisition budget authority, some of the low-cost "equip" responsibility was shared with SOCOM.

Maj. Gen. Jack Gregory, commander of the Fighter Weapons Center, called and informed me of the unthinkable. It was midmorning on January 18, 1982. Four Thunderbird aircraft had crashed while practicing a "line-abreast loop" at their practice site near Indian Springs Air Base, Nevada, northwest of Las Vegas. Thunderbird leader and all three wingmen that made up their signature diamond formation were all killed in the crash. The pilots and their positions were lead, Major Norm Lowery; Captains Willie Mays and Pete Peterson, who were flying left and right wing, respectively; and slot pilot, Capt. Mark Melancon. They were flying T-38s at the time of the crash. General Creech had already received a call from Jack and was aware of what had happened—he was devastated over the loss of lives. It was standard procedure for all practice maneuvers to be videotaped and voice recorded from the ground so that the leader and pilots could review the film later, much like professional and college football coaches review practice and game films to discover mistakes and take corrective action. On the day of the crash, video recordings were made including the crash—however, the voice recorder wasn't working, so the calls from leader to wingmen and between solo pilots were not available. During the various maneuvers, T-Bird leader is continuously making calls to his wingman. Having a recording of those calls for the accident investigation would have been extremely valuable in isolating the cause of the mishap. General Creech obtained copies of the tapes of the successful line-abreast loops and of the one resulting in the crash. He studied these for hours and, by overlapping good loops over bad, was able to deduce that the mishap loop was more oval than the successful loops. This observation gave rise to the premise that a foreign object was dislodged in flight and somehow fell into and jammed the elevator flight controls of the lead aircraft. The accident film also revealed that the pilots of aircraft on the wing evidently saw the ground coming into their peripheral as they approached the bottom of the loop and started to pull up, but it was too late.

The nation was in the first years of President Reagan's administration and still suffering from the economic downturn of President Carter's "stagflation." General Creech was concerned about the future of the Thunderbird Aerobatic Team and the possibility that few in the DOD would have the courage to fund rebuilding the team. On the other hand, the F-16 was operational and perfectly suited as a platform for an aerial demonstration team. The F-16 was powerful, nimble, and larger than the T-38, so it was easier for the spectators to visually acquire, and it could pull over nine Gs!

General Creech wanted to discuss potential selections for the accident board president. He was looking for a general officer with fighter experience and maturity that could lead (vice follow) the board members. He also wanted to find someone who was not currently assigned in the Tactical Air Command so there would be no question of the board president's independence. Said another way, there shouldn't be any suspicion of command influence. I suggested he consider Brig. Gen. Jerry Larson. Jerry was a former Thunderbird, so he would be an expert on the various maneuvers flown by the team, including the line-abreast loop, which they were flying when the mishap occurred. Jerry was also a graduate of the Air Force Test Pilot School and spent a tour at the Fighter Weapons School on the weapons test side. I had flown with him as a data recorder in the backseat on several test missions and had enormous respect for him. General Creech considered my suggestion along with several other potential candidates and eventually selected Brig. Gen. Jerry Larson for the unpleasant task of identifying the series of events that ultimately led to the crash. Regrettably, it was a bad choice. Ultimately, Maj. Gen. Tom Swalm, a former Thunderbird leader, found the root cause of the mishap in his capacity as president of the collateral board. The collateral board follows the accident board and is formed to determine if there is fault should there be any litigation against the air force.

While the accident board was at work, General Creech assigned me the job of rewriting the Thunderbird playbook. It was the authoritative manual that described, in exquisite detail, how each maneuver was to be performed. I suggested that it might be better if a former Thunderbird pilot was called in for the job. Wrong! General Creech said, "I want you to do it because you've never been a Thunderbird and are not emotionally attached to any of their maneuvers! You'll take out all the garbage and make the show much safer." Then he gave me some advice he received from Group Captain Douglas Bader, RAF, after a solo show he, Captain Creech, flew in Europe as leader of the Skyblazers.

Group Captain Bader advised, "Select maneuvers that will thrill the spectators, and fly them so well, you will please your fellow aviators! Not the other way around!" What the group captain meant was, don't pick maneuvers that are on the ragged edge because the average spectator will never know the difficulty you've surmounted—only the professionals will know! You'll have put yourself at great risk but will have added no value to the demonstration. Group Captain Bader knew what he was talking about! In practicing for the Hendon Air Show on December 14, 1931, then pilot officer Bader crashed while attempting a "dairy turn" and lost both his legs. This was the same maneuver he watched Captain Creech perform solo in an F-100C under a very low overcast. Bader, through sheer willpower, returned to flight on artificial legs eight years after his mishap. During WW II, he was credited with twenty-one aerial victories over German fighters, mostly ME-109s, plus several probable aerial kills that could not be confirmed. Following successful engagements with two ME-109s on August 9, 1941, his Spitfire went down over France, and he was interned as a POW. During the bailout, one of his prosthetic legs was trapped in the aircraft. Out of respect for Bader, the Germans allowed a British transport to airdrop a replacement for the prosthetic leg lost in the downed aircraft over the POW camp.

Rewriting the T-Bird playbook was tedious work—it was more than one hundred pages thick detailing dozens of air show maneuvers. I expunged several routines that did not meet the Bader Test, upped the minimum altitude on most maneuvers that survived, and rewrote several to reduce unnecessary risk while retaining the spectator pleasing factor. General Creech was the arbiter of all changes and approved 99 percent of all the revisions and removals. Once the word got out that I was ravaging the T-Bird playbook, I received calls from just about every former living T-Bird leader and wingman. It seems like they correctly heard that I was eliminating or revising their signature maneuvers, one they created to add to Thunderbird lore—it was their legacy. I had the best top cover one could have in the air force, so it was easy to be understanding but absolutely unrelenting.

General Creech was successful in getting support for rebuilding the Thunderbirds in the F-16, a perfect platform for aerial demonstrations. The new challenge was developing an appropriate paint scheme. Traditionally, Thunderbird aircraft were painted with a silhouette of this legendary Native American bird on the underside of the aircraft and a field of stars on the vertical stabilizer. This was something only General Creech could do and he did, but he liked to bring me along as an apprentice. We spent hours checking the stars on the tail to ensure they were randomly placed. Random was defined as no three stars in a straight line. I recall that it took three paint overs to get the random factor correct. The silhouette of the Thunderbird on the bottom of the fuselage was a similar matter. General Creech and I would lay on the concrete under the aircraft for an hour while he sketched modifications to the outline. We'd be back the following day to study the new paint scheme. Many things had changed in the paint scheme since the original Thunderbirds were formed under the leadership of Maj. Dick Catledge at Luke AFB, Arizona, in May 1953. One of those changes was the location of the number that designated the position that a given plane flew. For the previous couple of decades, the number was quite large and centered on the vertical stabilizer (fin) of the aircraft. General Creech wanted to return to the roots of the Thunderbirds with the "Native American Thunderbird" on the vertical fin and the position number on the F-16 air intake below the leading edge of the wing. Lead always flew the number 1 aircraft no matter what aircraft it actually was. Thus, if the number 1 aircraft was down for maintenance, a crew chief would paint the number 1 on one of the spare aircraft prior to the show. It made it a lot easier to repaint the number when it was reachable from the ground and did not require a hydraulic lift or maintenance stand to reach the center of the fin twenty feet above the ramp. On the other hand, I received a large number of phone calls from former Thunderbird pilots complaining about the relocation of the number. Why it was important to them, I'll never know or understand. However, the caller was easily deflated when I told them the T-Bird paint scheme was being ably handled by General Creech, and they would have to call him about the issue. To my knowledge, General Creech never received any calls on the number location; they knew better.

General Larson and his supporting staff on the accident board had completed their work and came to TAC Headquarters to brief their findings. They found pilot error as the primary cause. Most of us who had reviewed the materials available to us disagreed with the findings. One of the biggest pieces of evidence that convinced us the accident board was wrong was the pathological evidence that proved the leader, Major Lowry, had both hands on the control stick when his plane hit the ground. This indicated that at some point in the loop approaching the 270-degree point from the start, he was compelled to put more effort into getting the required g-force to complete the loop. However, the video showed no evidence of induced increases in g-forces all the way to impact. The fact that both hands were on the control stick prevented Major Lowry from calling the flight and telling them to pull up. The radio button is on the throttle where the pilot's left hand rests from the start of taxiing to the runway until engine shutdown after the flight. These points were brought up several times; however, the accident board was firm in their findings. Many accidents are the result of pilot or aircrew error; this was not one of them!

The reason for an accident board rests in the need to find the cause so that corrective action can be taken. The accident board findings are not releasable to the public. Following an accident board, a collateral board is formed to find if there is "fault" for litigation purposes. Collateral board findings are releasable to the public. As mentioned earlier, General Creech appointed Maj. Gen. Tom Swalm president of the collateral board. Tom was and still is a good friend and colleague, and led the Thunderbirds from May 1973 until January 1976. During this period, he flew 290 shows and countless practice sessions. His current job was commander of the Tactical Air Warfare Center at Eglin AFB, Florida.

The accident scene was relatively undisturbed except for the removal of the pilot's remains. It was available for General Swalm to examine every inch of the ground for clues that would support the eventual findings of his board. Notwithstanding the findings of the accident board, there was still lingering suspicion that the mishap was caused by a foreign object lodging in the elevator control mechanism somewhere between the cockpit and the elevator itself. Here is a simple description of the how a pilot's inputs to the control stick are transmitted to the elevator. When a pilot moves the control stick forward or aft to cause the T-38 to descend or climb, a ridged linkage from below the pivot point on the stick travels rearward through the fuselage to a spring that connects to the elevator. The spring is quite strong but provides enough flexibility to dampen, as well as isolate, turbulence effects on the elevator from being induced on the control stick. This spring from all the mishap aircraft except #68-8156 (lead's aircraft) had been found and were judged to be normal. After several days of searching, General Swalm found the spring from the leader's aircraft—it was abnormally stretched and elongated. The spring was examined by engineers and determined that it had been stretched by Major Lowry as he tried mightily, with both hands, to move the elevator up, thus causing the nose to climb and avoid hitting the ground. The elevator had to be jammed by an unknown foreign object lodging in the linkage aft of the spring as the aircraft floated over the top of the loop at less than one G for the elongation to occur. This elongated spring from the elevator linkage provided conclusive evidence as to the cause of the crash.

With both the accident and collateral boards completed, it was time to get to the business of resurrecting the Thunderbird Team. With the loss of the leader and wingman of the signature "diamond" and introduction of a new aircraft, it was necessary to start from the beginning. As commander of the Tactical Air Warfare Center, I believe General Swalm was current in the F-16 and, as a former Thunderbird leader, was the logical choice to rebuild the team. He spent weeks converting the new and approved playbook maneuvers to F-16 airspeeds and altitudes. For example, every air show maneuver has an entry airspeed and altitude above the ground that must be met to ensure safe completion at five hundred feet above show center. There is also a fudge factor for altitude and temperature. For example, a loop conducted at Houston, Texas, (sea level) with a temperature of eighty degrees Fahrenheit would require less airspeed/ altitude at entry and over the top than the same maneuver in Colorado Springs, Colorado, at 6,400-foot elevation and ninety degrees Fahrenheit. These all had to be worked out prior to training the individual team pilots, and that took several additional months.

The first F-16 painted in Thunderbird marking and colors arrived at Nellis AFB, Nevada, on June 22, 1982. Starting in August 1982, Maj. Jim Latham was leading a two-ship team through all the maneuvers and building from there. When the Thunderbirds opened their 2003 (fiftieth anniversary) season, their first public show was the 1,339th flown in the F-16, still a highly capable frontline combat aircraft.

My secretary walked in and announced that the flight suit manager from some air logistics center was on the phone and needed to speak with me. The conversation was informative and short. The flight suit manager was calling to get funding to pay for and ship the last remaining five thousand international orange flight suits to one of our ADTAC Fighter Interceptor Squadrons. The bill for the flight suits was approximately $1.7 million, and he was sure the squadron didn't have that kind of money in their supply account and wanted to know if TAC would pay the bill. My response was "No! Please don't honor any requests for orange flight suits from TAC units! Thanks very much for the call!" While I was initially angry, it soon brought a smile to my face. The FIS units were planning to get their hands on about one hundred years' worth of international orange flight suits to forestall ever having to switch to the olive drab flight garb under the guidance of "wear what you have until no longer serviceable or presentable." I gave Maj. Gen. John Pickitt a heads-up on the clever but failed-end run his troops tried to execute.

The TAC/DO position had not yet been filled because General Creech was having difficulty finding someone that could meet his expectations. Uncharacteristically, he asked for my opinion on my replacement. The answer was easy—Maj. Gen. Robert Reed! Then Colonel Reed had been one of the Six-Man Group at Maxwell AFB and, in my view, the best of the bunch. Since then, he successfully commanded the 354th Wing at Myrtle Beach, South Carolina, and was currently the Air Defense Fighter Weapons Center commander at Tyndall AFB, Florida. While at the Six-Man Group, Bob and I had several discussions on how big a role motivational leadership played in being a successful wing commander. He believed management was key, and motivational leadership played little if any role. I tried to convince Colonel Reed otherwise throughout the year we served together but failed. His first command at Myrtle Beach AFB, South Carolina, caused him to see the light that it was leadership, not management, that girded the loins and spirits of warriors! From that point forward, he established an enviable record as commander and leader.

General Creech accepted my recommendation, interviewed Bob Reed, and hired him on the spot. After that, whenever we were together, General Creech would tell me that of all the things I did for him and TAC, recommending Bob Reed for the DO job was the most important. Shortly after Bob Reed was on board at TAC, General Creech called me into his office and said, "Pete, you're a great staff officer, but you're the best field commander in the air force, so I'm letting you go to command Ninth Air Force." Then he went on to say, "Don't move into the new vice's quarters—you'll be moving down to Shaw AFB, South Carolina, as soon as Lt. Gen. Larry Welch's new assignment can be announced."

Lessons Learned

The primary role of Higher Headquarters is to support
the forces in the field, not the other way around!

Listen to what people in the geographically separated
units are saying! They are where the action is.

Whether engaging the enemy or generating profits, always organize
around the strategic purpose/mission of an organization!

It is leadership, not management, that wins the day and battles!

People are led, and things are managed in any successful enterprise.

"Morale is to things as three is to one!"—Napoleon. Personally, I believe it is at least ten to one.

Have the courage to do what is right!

Maj. Gen. Pete escorts Vice President Bush to see the Stealth Fighter at a Top Secret Location

CHAPTER 14

Ninth Air Force

The change of command took place in October 1982 at Shaw AFB, South Carolina, with General Creech officiating. When it was over, General Creech and General Welch left Shaw AFB in separate aircraft. General Creech flew back to Langley AFB, Virginia, and General Welch to Washington, where he would receive his fourth star and assume the job of vice chief of staff under General Gabriel. The 363rd TFW was the host organization at Shaw AFB commanded by Col. Dick Carr.

In October 1982, Ninth Air Force was also the air component of the Rapid Deployment Joint Task Force (RDJTF) under the command of Gen. P. X. Kelly, USMC, but change was in the wind. On January 1, 1983, the JCS stood up Central Command (CENTCOM), a Unified Command that assumed all the responsibilities of the RDJTF. At that juncture, CENTCOM's Area of Responsibility would encompass the Middle East Arabic and Islamic states from Libya to Pakistan, including, among others

Libya	Sudan	Egypt
North Yemen	South Yemen	Saudi Arabia
Oman	Bahrain	Jordan
Iraq	Iran	Syria
Qatar	Kuwait	UAE

CENTCOM, commanded by Gen. Bob Kingston, USA, was comprised of four service components: army, navy, air force, and Marine Corps. The army component was the Eighteenth Airborne Corps commanded by Lt. Gen. Jack V. Mackmull, a bull of a man. He also possessed a very astute understanding of air power and its application. Jack was the ultimate army pilot inducted into the Army Aviation Hall of Fame for his legendary contributions to army aviation. He had three combat tours in Vietnam as an aviator. Lieutenant General Mackmull passed away on April 3, 2011. I don't recall the navy component commander's name, but it really doesn't matter; the rear admiral was on the staff in PACAF and didn't have any forces. Evidently, some would be assigned when needed. Lt. Gen. Ernest (Ernie) C. Cheatham Jr. commanded the marine component. To say that Ernie was a giant of a man was an understatement in every sense. During a break in his military service in 1954, he played defensive tackle in the National Football League for both the Pittsburgh Steelers and the Baltimore Colts. After returning to active duty, he was awarded the Navy Cross for heroism as commander of Second Battalion Fifth Marines during the 1968 Tet Offensive in Vietnam. The air force component was commanded by yours truly with forces assigned from Ninth Air Force, Air National Guard units, MAC Airlift, and SAC Bombers, with liaison officers from the latter two commands. CENTCOM's air component was called Central Air Forces, or CENTAF. The acronym was specifically designed so as to not confuse people with the NATO Command AFCENT and was plural to indicate the control of more than one air force, as was the case in Desert Storm.

Brig. Gen. Charlie Bishop was the 9th AF vice commander. Traditionally, a numbered air force vice commander provided oversight on the assigned Air National Guard (ANG) units. Ninth Air Force was assigned all the ANG Squadrons east of the Mississippi, and that kept Charlie pretty busy and on the road most of the time. I was pleased to find that TAC ANG Squadrons were far more disciplined than those in the Air Defense Command and subsequently ADTAC.

Col. Jack Van Loan was the Ninth Air Force director of operations. Jack was a longtime fighter pilot shot down flying F-4s over North Vietnam and held as a POW for several years. Like many of the POWs that I worked with after they were repatriated, Jack had little tolerance for those who were not totally committed to the mission. Jack was also always in pursuit of perfection. The only thing I had to do was pull on the reins lightly once in a while when Jack was too hard on his staff or the TAC wings assigned to Ninth Air Force. Jack also spent a lot of time on the road flying with the various wings and bringing back issues for us to work on their behalf.

The command section was actually smaller in manpower than the deputy command of TAC for operations (DO) at Langley AFB, Virginia. I don't believe the workload was less but was delighted with the quality of the people supporting me. Col. Chuck Peters was the chief of staff and a tough, demanding taskmaster. From time to time, I could hear him chastising someone who had turned in a shoddy piece of staff work for my review. One of those sessions from Colonel Peters was all it took to motivate one to raise the quality of their work. There were two secretaries in the command section, Jean Cook and Midge Hickman. Both were pleasant, efficient, and a joy to work with. On the other hand, Jean presented a slight problem. Her chair was modified with yellow "egg carton" foam tied to the back with orange bailing twine—not exactly your best first impression for visitors to the command section. I asked Col. Chuck Peters to help me understand the problem. Chuck told me that Jean suffered from severe back problems, and the arrangement she had on her chair was the only way she could tolerate sitting for any period of time. Thinking I might convince her to try some orthopedic chairs made especially for people with back problems, I approached her on the issue. What I received in return for my good intentions was a look of determination and fury that spoke volumes about "don't you dare touch my chair"—checkmated by a young lady turned lioness that weighed no more than one hundred pounds.

That night, I measured the back of the chair and asked Sheila if she would *please* make a slipover cover that would hide the foam and bailing twine on Jean's office chair, but to make it of light material so as to not change the medicinal quality of the foam and to match the office decor. Angel that she was and still is, Sheila came to the office and took some photos of the office that weekend when everyone was gone, picked up some sample material and brought it to the office the following weekend, found a good match, and made the slipcover. The following weekend, we went back to the office with the finished slipcover. I trimmed the ragged foam to match the curvature of the chair back, and on went the cover. It looked great, but would Jean accept it?

The following Monday, I was in early, along with Colonel Peters; he gave the modification a thumbs-up, and we waited. An hour or so later, I heard voices outside the door. Shortly thereafter, Jean came in with my morning cup of coffee. All she said was "It looks nice and feels good!" The first battle was won, and I had a friend for life. I reflected for a moment on what Gen. Larry Welch might have thought about Jean's chair and immediately realized that with his intense focus on work, he probably never even saw it.

The only other person that hung out in the Ninth Air Force command section was Maj. B. J. Hall, formerly General Welch's officer aide. He had only been brought on board a few months prior to my arrival, and after a brief interview, we (B. J. and I) agreed that he would continue on as my aide. He was an F-16 instructor pilot (IP) and would be able to fly with me on the many business related trips I would be taking throughout Ninth Air Force, TAC, and the army units that 9th AF supported. One very nice thing about taking trips with an IP is that you never stop learning about how to exploit the weapons systems as well as sharpening your pilot skills. But there is another important benefit. When my day started at 0600 hours, the IP can start his/her duty day at noon; therefore, the IP duty day doesn't run out until midnight, and you can fly back to Shaw AFB, South Carolina, when the work is done without violating crew rest requirements. Of course, part of that time, you're a passenger in the backseat—that's the only downside.

The first JCS tasking given to CENTCOM was to plan for the defense of Iran against a Soviet invasion. More specifically, the tasking called for a plan to delay a Soviet army group advancing toward the Strait of Hormuz—it did not call for the defeat of a Soviet force invading Iran. A Soviet army group could consist of eight to twelve divisions. The purpose of this hypothetical Soviet invasion would be to reach and take control of the Strait of Hormuz and close the Persian Gulf to oil tankers—thus putting an oil stranglehold on the Western World, especially the United States, which was increasingly more dependent on Saudi Arabian oil. Forces assigned for this plan were as follows:

> the US Army Eighteenth Airborne Corps commanded by Lt.
> Gen. Jack V. Mackmull, comprised of
>> Twenty-Fourth Infantry Division (heavy)
>> Eighty-Second Airborne Division
>> 101st Air Assault Division.
> the II Marine Expeditionary Force commanded by Lt. Gen.
> Ernie Cheatham Jr. comprised of
>> Second Marine Division
>> Second Marine Aircraft Wing
>> Second Marine Logistics Group
>> 22nd MEU
>> 24th MEU
>> 26th MEU
>> supporting units

CENTAF, comprised of MAC, SAC, and TAC units and CENTAF Headquarters forward

Planning began immediately upon receipt of the tasking, starting with the intelligence staff looking for potential interdiction choke points from the Soviet western border with Iran to the Strait of Hormuz. I immediately fell back on my own experience in Iran when my host dropped me off in the Alborz/Zagros Mountains for a wild boar hunt. I spent two days wandering around in the hills looking for pigs. What I remembered most was the torturous winding roads hanging on the edges of the mountains, especially on the outside curves. I suggested to the intel team working on targeting for the plan that they look at potential lines of communications (LOCs) that the Soviets could use from the border between Azerbaijan and Iran to Bushehr where the coastal mountains gave way to the Southern Plains. They came back with hundreds of pictures of road segments that could be easily interdicted with one-thousand or two-thousand pound general purpose bombs dropped from F-16s with their precision bombing system. With the F-16, you could put a bomb through the roof of a pickup truck. Surely you could hit the road the truck was on. Not only could we stop Soviet armored divisions every few miles of their journey, but we could also destroy their vehicles as they jammed up along the road. On the other hand, CENTAF forces had to deploy and be ready to interdict immediately on arrival. If the deployment order wasn't executed immediately on detection of a Soviet invasion, we would be giving up interdiction opportunities to a Soviet force that would be speeding south and setting up air defense SAMs and AAA along the route. It was also envisioned that we could do "quick turns" at Iranian airbases at Shiraz and Bushehr to increase the number of sorties daily by eliminating the time lost flying back to Saudi Arabian bases. I visited the air bases at Shiraz and Bushehr during the time spent in Iran on their AWACS bed down and found they were very capable of supporting third and fourth-generation fighter aircraft.

CENTAF's annex in support of CENTCOM's 2004 Plan had to provide for the bed down of forces, tactical airlift, in-flight refueling orbits, air superiority combat air patrols (CAPs), close air support (CAS), AWACS orbits, and B-52 bombing sorties. In addition, there were safe passage routes to and from the target areas, weapon loads for every sortie, communication frequencies, and a plethora of arcane details to execute the plan. Medical evacuation of wounded personnel was also a very high priority in the planning process. As it is often said, the devil is in the details. Because of my concern for delays in the execution decision at the highest levels, I directed that the staff actually print out the fragmentary (frag) orders for all the interdiction and CAP sorties for the first seven days following arrival. Also aircraft like the F-15 and F-16 capable of engaging opposition aircraft would deploy from the United States with a full load of air-to-air missiles and 20 mm ammunition. It was essential to plan for the worst-case scenario. In this regard, it was foremost in our minds that the Eighty-Second Division and the 101st Division were lightly armed and would be depending on the air force to provide immediate CAS and make up for their shortfall in long-range artillery support. Most importantly, I felt it extremely important that we tracked our C-130 airlift capability to evacuate Eighteenth Corps ground forces from Iran with their equipment and in a rapidly deteriorating situation, without their equipment. To meet this requirement, our ops team had to coordinate very closely with the 18th TOC to stay on top of the situation as well as monitor the availability of tactical airlift.

The Marine Expeditionary Force was planned to go ashore at Chabahar along the Iranian southern coast. It was unlikely that their landing would be opposed, as Chabahar was a considerable distance from the Strait of Hormuz as well as the most probable route a Soviet incursion would take.

With Op Plan 2004 planning in progress, it was time to check out in the aircraft flown throughout Ninth Air Force. These were the F-15, F-16, F-4 and RF-4, A-10, 0-2, and 0V-10. There were no two-seat aircraft in the A-10 inventory, so I wrote that aircraft off as one to fly because it didn't make sense for me to devote the amount of time required to get prepared to fly the A-10. In addition, a blown tire on landing would bring the naysayers in the media down on all general officer commanders flying with their operational units. I was already current in the F-15 from ADTAC. The F-16 was first on the list, followed by the F-4/RF-4, the 0V-10, and the 0-2.

The F-16 checkout took place at MacDill AFB, Florida, just outside Tampa, Florida. MacDill had the reputation of being a well-run wing with an excellent training record. The F-16 Ground School was very professional, and the simulator was a modern computer-driven marvel compared to the F-4 simulator, which was a little better than a Link trainer of WW II vintage, except for challenging F-4 pilots with compounding emergencies to cope with. The side stick controller that replaced the traditional control stick between the pilot's legs was somewhat awkward at first. This little device, no more than four inches high, moved only about one-tenth of an inch front to back or side to side. It worked on pressure, not movement, and translated the pilot's commands through transducers to the F-16 flight control computers. Side stick control movement was hardly perceptible to the pilot, if at all, but it took about fifteen pounds of pressure in any direction to achieve full flight performance allowed by the flight control computer.

The F-16, like the F-15, was powered by an F100 engine made by Pratt & Whitney, and subsequently, as a result of the Fighter Engine Competition by General Electric's F101 engine. The F-100 was a modular engine with four major sections: compressor, combustion chamber, turbine, and afterburner. The turbofan design with afterburner was a tremendous breakthrough in jet engine design, providing exceptional takeoff thrust in full afterburner, yet also providing excellent range with the 0.36 to 1 bypass ratio. On the other hand, the modular design and short turbine blade life put a heavy workload on F-15 and F-16 Wing engine repair shops. Essentially, the F100 engine produced temperatures in the combustion chamber that caused the tips of the turbine blades to melt, shortening their useful life. Temperatures in the J79 engine installed in the F-4 should not exceed 680 degrees. Temperatures in the F100 engine, at max power, were approximately 1,100 degrees, which resulted in significantly more thrust as well as increased stress on their turbine blades.

Students transitioning into the F-16 from fighter lead in training in the F-5 and more experienced pilots, like me, with a few hundred hours in the F-15, were treated alike on their first F-16 sorties. We were not allowed to use the afterburner; the aircraft would accelerate so quickly in afterburner that the gear door speed would be exceeded before the student pilot could place the gear handle in the up position to raise the gear. As a result, the gear doors would be ripped off due to the excessive air pressure on them. Even without using the afterburner, many an instructor pilot had to abruptly raise the F-16 nose and point the aircraft at a steep climb angle to slow it until the gear came up. A couple of flights without afterburner allowed the student to quicken his/her reflexes and get the gear up before disaster struck. The F-16A/B had super quick acceleration—now that is a nice problem to have.

After a couple of aircraft handling flights accomplishing stall series and the like, it was time for a trip to the gunnery range. As of that time, I had approximately twenty-three years flying fighter aircraft from the F-86 to the F-4 with manual depressible gun sights. Hitting the target in those aircraft was all about pilot skill and their ability to instinctively compensate for wind drift, dive angle error and airspeed error. Most, if not all of the time, the pipper (gun-sight aim point) was nowhere near the target at weapon release due to compensation for the aforementioned errors. The A-7 was the only previous aircraft where the pilot could place the pipper on the desired target at weapons release. I had flown the A-7with the Taco ANG Squadron at Tucson, Arizona, but did not have the pleasure of flying it on a gunnery mission.

The F-16 was, in a word, fantastic as a gunnery platform! As we rolled in on the bombing target, the IP said, "Drag the 'death dot' to the target (a pickup truck) and hit the pickle button when it's on or as close as it's going to get to the target."

I pulled up with 4 Gs at bomb release, and the range officer said, "Bull's-eye!" Looking back over my left shoulder, I could see white smoke from the spotting charge at the base of the truck.

"Not bad," the IP said. "Now try holding the death dot on the driver's door of the truck momentarily prior to bomb release."

I did, and the range officer said, "Bull's-eye!"

The IP said, "Now put the death dot on the window of the driver's door." Another bull's-eye, with smoke from the spotting charge coming out of the truck cab. This was incredible! True, my decades of experience helped me get the death dot on the target, but it was the computer aided by the radar range and range rate input that did all the calculations so that the bomb hit wherever the death dot was. Students upgrading in the F-16 were combat-ready after a few sorties. Strafing was a little more challenging because of the much higher speeds and rudder sensitivity. However, after two strafe passes, I was tearing up the target. If I went into combat again, I wanted it to be in an F-16!

After visiting all the wings and spending a couple of days with each one, I came to the conclusion that I had nine strong wing commanders, one acceptable wing commander, and two that I had to mentor. If mentoring didn't work, then I had to move them on to something they were capable of doing well. In this regard, Lt. Gen. Jack Gregory, now commander of Twelfth Air Force at Bergstrom AFB, Texas, and I spent a lot of time talking about our needs for strong colonels with a proven track record to put into tough, demanding command positions. There just weren't enough of them to fill all the critical jobs. It was then that I learned that when generals talk to other generals, the conversation is mostly about people because we were always looking for the next person to put into a tough, demanding job.

Sheila, my wife of twenty-one years, and I had made fourteen military moves and lived on base, in government housing, for seven of those assignments. With the exception of Langley AFB, Virginia, all the houses were very inadequate. For example, as vice commander at

Keesler, the house was so small, we carpeted the garage and used it for a family room. At Peterson AFB, as commander ADTAC, I sealed off the dining room with drywall to make a bedroom for our youngest child. The 9th AF commander's house was another disaster; it had a generous allotment of room for entertaining but very little for the occupants. For example, the master bedroom was so small that there was barely room for our queen-size bed, a dresser, and one chest. The bed had to be pushed against the wall to make space for the rest of the furniture plus some walk-around room for Sheila. She needed to be able to get up at night for our handicapped son, so I slept against the wall. To get up without disturbing Sheila, I had to scoot down the bed and off the end. The master bathroom was so small that the sink counter rested on the bathtub, making it almost impossible to pull a shower curtain around it to keep water off the floor when showering. Also, in order to enter the bathroom and close the door from the inside, it required walking around the door and snuggling up against the tub. You wouldn't stay two nights in a motel like that—we were there for three years! However, I had the house upgraded for my successor and good friend Gen. Bill Kirk.

There is an unwritten rule for general officers and their wives, and that is, never improve your quarters, or you will be investigated till long after your retirement. On the other hand, you can identify the problem, come up with a logical solution, and have the fix implemented after you have departed so you are not the beneficiary. In this regard, I invited the TAC civil engineer to visit Shaw and look at a number of potential construction projects to improve support for the mission and quality of life for the base population. One of these was the 9th AF commander's house master bedroom and bathroom. A plan to move a section of the wall out three feet solved both the bedroom and bathroom space problem. Funding was approved for some future date after I departed. Once orders were approved for my next assignment, construction started. Bill and his wife were inconvenienced for a few weeks, but when the work was done, they enjoyed an adequate bedroom—a place where we spend somewhere between one-fourth to one-third of our lives.

The commander's house had a two-car carport with no place to store lawn and gardening tools and other stuff required to maintain the outside appearance of a house, which every military housing occupant is required to do. I drew up a set of plans to turn the carport into a garage under General Creech's self-help program. If the plans were approved by the base civil engineers, they would supply the materials, and it was up to me to provide the labor—the most expensive part of any project. The plans were approved with two additions—to meet Fire Protection code, the interior, walls, and ceiling had to be drywalled with five-eighth-inch material, and fluorescent lights had to replace the old inadequate Edison bulbs. I scheduled the project for the Christmas/New Year's week and took leave. All future Ninth Air Force commanders enjoyed the "Pete Piotrowski Memorial Garage."

A pilot and aircraft were lost at Myrtle Beach AFB, South Carolina, on a gunnery range mission. The aircraft crashed during the recovery from a dive bomb event. There were no radio calls, and no one on the ground or in the flight was looking at the mishap aircraft during its last few seconds of flight. The accident board found the cause as pilot error, as there was no evidence of aircraft, airframe, or engine malfunction. A visit to the 354th TFW was in order to put the leadership under the microscope. After twenty-four hours on base and discussions with the commander, vice commander, and director of operations, I was convinced the aforementioned mishap was caused by a laissez-faire attitude on the part of wing leadership, as well as lax discipline. I gave General Creech a thumbnail sketch of my findings and told him the wing was on my radarscope. Not too long after that, the 354th lost an A-10 flying a low-level mission. Again, nothing was found wrong with the airframe or engine, and no one saw the aircraft during the last few minutes of flight. Another accident board found the cause to be pilot error. Another call to General Creech, only this time I suggested that the wing commander be relieved and replaced by a stronger individual. He cautioned me that firing a wing commander immediately after an aircraft accident would send a chill throughout TAC, putting all the wing commanders into a defensive crouch, and would have an adverse impact on realistic training for combat. The 354th commander kept his job, at least temporarily. Just a few months later, the 354th was invited to deploy a squadron to Nellis AFB for Red Flag. For those who don't know, Red Flag is a simulated war held periodically at Nellis AFB, Nevada. It is as close as one can come to actual combat with the exception of not being shot at with real bullets. Each day, Blue Force strike packages are "fragged" against targets in red territory on the Nellis Range Complex. These Blue Force aircraft have to penetrate a Soviet Integrated Air Defense System (IADS), evade and/or negate aggressor force aircraft, dodge smoky SAMs, and destroy the targets on the range. While deployed to Nellis AFB, Nevada, for Red Flag, the 354th almost burned up one of their aircraft on the ramp undergoing routine maintenance. The aircraft was loaded with infrared flares that are ejected to defeat a simulated incoming air or ground launched missile. The 354th technician sent to disarm the flare system was unqualified (not trained or certified) to do the job and inadvertently jettisoned all the flares loaded in the aircraft's dispenser on the ground under the aircraft. The main tires caught on fire, and without quick thinking and action by others, the aircraft would have been engulfed in flames and would have endangered all the other aircraft on the ramp. When I was sure I had the correct story, I called General Creech ASAP, relayed the incident, and said, "Sir, we can't afford this guy any longer—he has got to go!"

His response was, "Fire him this minute—put the vice in charge until we can find the right guy to take over."

It wasn't until the next Red Flag that I received another trouble call from Maj. Gen. Jack Gregory, who, at that juncture, was still the Fighter Weapons Center commander. Jack called to inform me he was ordering the Louisiana ANG A-10 Squadron off Nellis AFB because their "tail flash" was stirring up a racial storm, and they would not remove it. The offending tail flash was "Coon Ass," and black airmen from Nellis units and visiting squadrons were deeply offended. I learned at Aviano that perception is reality and concurred with Jack's action and urged him to get the LA ANG gone ASAP.

The following day, I called the Louisiana Air adjutant general to discuss the issue. When I suggested that the words "Coon Ass" be removed from their A-10 tails because it was very offensive to black airmen and to me as well. He pushed back hard, saying that "Coon Ass" was a Cajun expression, referring to Cajuns, not blacks, and was a state motto. In response, I inquired if he had "Coon Ass" painted on the doors of his staff car and if the governor had the words "Coon Ass" painted on his state-funded limousine. Then I reminded him that all the Louisiana license plates that I had ever seen carried the motto "Sportsman's Paradise," not Coon Ass. The conversation digressed to the point where the AG said he would not direct the words be removed from the A-10 tails. Whereas, I told him that Louisiana Air National Guard aircraft with those words on the tail would not be welcome, nor would they be serviced at any Ninth Air Force Base, nor would they be invited back to Red Flag. I added that I was also certain that they would not be welcome west of the Mississippi at Twelfth Air Force Bases and wished him a good day. What surprised me is that it took him nearly a week to call back and say the words were being painted over and asked if the restrictions could be lifted. I thanked him for taking the appropriate action and told him his aircraft were back in good standing. I passed the word to Jack Gregory and thanked him for his immediate and tough stand.

Col. Peter Kemp was the wing commander at Seymour Johnson AFB, North Carolina, a classmate of mine going through Bootstrap to earn our bachelor's degrees. He had a keen mind and was a no-nonsense kind of guy. Some even felt he was too tough. I felt very comfortable with him in charge of the Fourth Wing. Then out of the blue, General Creech called and said Pete was being transferred to Hill AFB, Utah, to take command of the 388th Wing there. As mentioned earlier, serious leadership and discipline problems surfaced in that wing, and they needed a proven leader to go in and clean up the mess and put the wing back on the right course. Col. Larry Huggins moved in to take over the Fourth Wing.

Rumor had it that Gen. John W. Vessey, USA, chairman of the Joint Chiefs of Staff, had asked each of the CINCs to brief their primary war plan at a recent CINCs' conference and was disappointed with their performance. This would have been in 1983, when combatant or Unified/Specified commanders under the Unified Command Plan were given the title of commander in chief, or CINC for short. Examples would be CINCCENT, CINCEUR, CINCPAC, CINCSAC, etc. Secretary Donald Rumsfeld changed all those titles to combatant or regional and functional commanders. Not too long after the story about the CINC's poor performances on briefing their war plans made the rounds, Lt. Gen. Jack Mackmull called and invited me to support him at a conference Gen. Shy Meyer, army chief of staff, was holding at Fort Leavenworth, Kansas. Seems that General Meyer was tasking his principal corps commanders to brief how they would employ their forces in an opposed river crossing. Participating were the I Corps commander from Korea, the V Corps from Germany, and the Eighteenth Airborne Corps from Fort Bragg, North Carolina. As General Mackmull explained to me, he didn't have the artillery support or tanks that the heavy armored corps had to execute the assigned mission. His plan was to tell the army chief that the Eighteenth Corps and Ninth Air Force were an air/land battle team. As such, that I would first brief how Ninth Air Force/CENTAF would provide air superiority over the river crossing, isolate enemy forces held in reserve, and soften/destroy the opposing forces before he executed the river crossing. In addition, that prior to D-day and H hour, we had agreed on the apportionment of fighters to close air support and interdiction. With that introduction, I briefed the air portion of our air/land battle scenario, and then Jack briefed General Meyer on the actual river crossing—then together, we took questions from the chief. Jack won a big "attaboy" from Gen. Shy Meyer, CSA, as the only corps commander that had sense enough to understand we were a joint team and should fight as such. It was an eye-opening experience and helped me considerably as CENTAF worked to fully develop an air supporting plan for Ops Plan 2004.

Visiting CENTCOM's area of responsibility (AOR) was necessary and expected. My first visit was to Egypt and Pakistan. Egypt was important because Pres. Hosni Mubarak was friendly to the United States and had signed a peace treaty with Israel a few years earlier at Camp David during President Carter's administration. It was also strategically important because it provided the USAF with a covert bomb storage area filled with weapons that could be loaded on B-52s as well as tactical fighters. In addition, Egypt provided a covert air base down in a deserted area of the country for E-3A Operations known to airmen as the Black Hole. Maj. Gen. Stanton (Stan) Musser was the chief of the Office of Military Cooperation in Egypt and the senior military advisor to the US ambassador. Stan was a good friend, and an F-4 pilot with extensive combat experience in Vietnam. He also flew with the Thunderbirds in the F-4. The Egyptian Air Force was converting to F-4s, and Stan was the best-possible choice to assist and lead them through the conversion. He was a great motivator and an inspirational role model.

It was a very informative trip and left me with confidence that Egypt would be a strong supporter of CENTCOM and CENTAF if the need arose. Before I left Egypt, I spent an evening watching the light show at the foot of the Great Pyramids and Sphinx. It provided a brief but compelling history of one of the great civilizations of all time. With a few hours to spare prior to departing for Pakistan, General Musser arranged for me to visit the National Museum of Egypt. Surprisingly, there were few exhibits available for public display because the facility was so small. However, I was treated to a warehouse tour where untold treasures of that ancient civilization lay in boxes or crates, waiting to take their turn to be put on display in the limited space available. It is a tragic shame that so much history of the ancient world could not be made available for public viewing. It is now 2011, and former president Hosni Mubarak is in the final days of trial for crimes against humanity. Elections are scheduled for November 2011, with the Egyptian military a temporary and transitional authority. Our toehold on the western edge of the Middle East is in serious jeopardy.

Arrival in Pakistan was considerably different than being met by an old friend in Egypt. The Air Force T-39 that brought Maj. B. J. Hall and me to Islamabad International Airport unloaded us and our baggage on the tarmac, and then departed. We waited for about thirty minutes for someone to pick us up, but no one came. There wasn't much activity at the airport, and nothing looked like a terminal, just some scruffy-looking characters riding around the ramp on a variety of typical airport support vehicles. They spoke no English or wouldn't admit to it, and I spoke only a few Arabic phrases learned in Saudi Arabia and Oman a few years earlier. Major Hall set out on foot to find someone who spoke English, and I sat atop our luggage heap on the ramp. After what seemed to be a very long time with the sun long past below the horizon, Major Hall returned with an air force officer who was waiting for us at a VIP lounge somewhere else on the airport. He took us to a hotel in Rawalpindi, the major city outside of Islamabad. It is important to note that Islamabad was a new city still under construction. It resembled the Washington DC Mall in that all the buildings were of white marble and all were government buildings. There were no shops, hotels, or other commercial enterprises. The support structure for Islamabad was in Rawalpindi, about twenty miles distant.

Later that evening, the Pakistani Air Force (PAF) chief of staff hosted a reception for us so that we could meet and get to know a number of his staff. The PAF chief was a very gracious man educated in England and spoke the English language fluently. We spent considerable time together discussing their purchase of F-16s and the pending conversion to that weapon system. He gave me a tour of a couple of their air bases and showed me their current fighter, the MiG-19, an aging and limited weapons system. The MiG-19 was a twin-engine fighter with the engines stacked vertically in the fuselage, very similar to the British Lightning. The PAF chief said the MiG-19 was a maintenance nightmare. An engine had to be removed after fifty hours of flight time, unless sooner because of failure, and the removal and replacement took three days. A typical flying program would require both engines to be removed every two months.

I was allowed to visit a number of PAF air bases to develop an understanding of their air discipline and technical capability. In a word, it was a lot like visiting an RAF base, as most of their training and traditions were vested in what the Pakistanis learned and inherited from the British while under their rule. I was convinced that they could easily transition to the F-16 and would find it a much easier aircraft to fly, fight with, and maintain. A trip to the famed Khyber Pass between Pakistan and Afghanistan, the fabled invasion route between east and west, was scheduled but never realized. The PAF chief said there was heavy fighting in the area, and it wasn't safe. As a last resort, I was flown by helicopter to within viewing distance of the Khyber Pass as it sloped up from Pakistan to Afghanistan. After seeing the pass, it was abundantly evident why invaders chose that route. On both the north and south edges of the Khyber Pass, impenetrable mountain ranges rose that stretched for hundreds of miles. This was my only visit to Pakistan; there were too many other places to visit in the region that were key to CENTCOM responsibilities.

Back at Shaw, there were problems. A visit to the 33rd TFW at Eglin AFB revealed a severe weakness at the top. The Thirty-Third was a choice assignment because of its location on the Gulf of Mexico with virtually unlimited air space over the Gulf for air-to-air training. Also the Thirty-Third was a tenant with everything provided by the host, except aircraft maintenance, so all the commander and his staff had to focus on was flying, maintaining the jets, and keeping the aerospace ground equipment that supported F-15 maintenance activities in good working order. During my short visit, I requested to spend time in the engine shop and on the flight line. It was planned to be a short visit: an afternoon and evening with the troops, dinner with the wing commander, and leave the next morning.

Upon arrival, we were to visit the engine shop. That was my primary focus because of problems associated with the PW F100 engine turbine blades. The wing commander picked me up at the T-39, and off we went to the engine shop. But there was a problem: the wing commander couldn't find the entrance to the facility. I saw some people in the distance looking around the corner of a building, so I suggested we go there. Sure enough, it was the chief of maintenance and the engine shop chief waiting for us to drive up. I was relieved to find that the shop chief was on top of the F100 engine problems. To my surprise and delight, they had spare engines on hand and no holes in the aircraft on the flight line that needed to be filled with engines. The turbine blades were getting better; hence, the F100 engine problem was slowly but steadily improving.

It was now about 5:00 p.m., and flying was largely over for the day; it was a good time to visit the flight line, talk to some F-15 crew chiefs, and check aircraft 781 Forms. These forms can be very revealing on how well an aircraft is being maintained. For example, a cross-check between delayed maintenance waiting for parts and the supply status of parts will reveal how good the coordination is between maintenance and supply activities. Also a plethora of delayed discrepancies may not ground the aircraft but will limit the training that can be accomplished on any given flight and reveal a cavalier attitude on aircraft maintenance. What happened next was a shocker. I pointed out an F-15 with a crew chief doing a postflight inspection and suggested we stop there. I introduced myself to the crew chief and shook his hand, telling him how much I appreciated his service and his work and asked if I could do a Form 781 check. As an aside, there is a requirement for a maintenance supervisor to review every possessed aircraft 781 forms monthly. If this crew chief's forms were in good shape, he'd have my signature in the 781 for bragging rights. His response was most informative! He said, "I know who you are, General, but who is the colonel with you?" He was talking about his wing commander who should have spent about 20 percent of his time flying with the squadrons, 40 percent on the flight line, and the other 40 percent in the maintenance shops. He should have also been presiding over the obligatory monthly commander's calls where the troops would get to know him and his policies. I had a big problem with this wing commander! Sheila and I had dinner with the wing commander and his wife that evening, and while I hate to admit it, his wife was far better equipped to lead the wing than her husband.

Shortly after returning to Ninth Air Force, I sent staff pilots down to the Thirty-Third to fly with the squadrons and to give me a feel for the wing commander's visibility in the organization. In addition, I looked in depth at all the data coming out of the wing that shed light on their maintenance activities and flying performance, and how well they were meeting their flying hour goals. All the feedback and data mining substantiated my initial assessment. I needed to replace the wing commander, not because he was taking the wing in the wrong direction but rather because he was providing no direction at all and was not visible to anyone but his secretary, as he spent most of his time in his well-appointed office. I called General Creech and informed him of my assessment and need to replace the current commander. He agreed with my finding and explained that selecting a wing commander was a two-step process. I had the privilege of selecting wing commander replacements, but he had the first right of refusal, which meant he could decline my recommendation.

That seemed fair, so a call was placed to TAC Personnel for a list of highly regarded colonels who had the experience and potential to successfully command a tactical fighter wing. I scrubbed their records, conducted several interviews, called the current commanders of the top-three contenders for their endorsement, and made a selection. One of my interview questions was "What is the most difficult thing you've had to do in your air force career?" I passed my selection to General Creech and stood ready to set the assignment process in motion, only to be notified that my selection was declined. Well, I thought, let's make this easier by selecting someone from the TAC/DO staff who had worked for me and that I knew General Creech was high on. This individual later wore four stars, commanded a Specified Command, and then became the air force chief of staff. Again General Creech did not approve of my selection. The pressure was starting to mount! After two more refusals, I called my predecessor, Gen. Larry Welch, now vice chief of staff, USAF, for a gut check.

He just laughed when he heard the names of the people whom General Creech rejected and opined. "They are all outstanding officers and good choices to command a wing. General Creech is just sending you a message, and that is, 'If you spend 95 percent of your time selecting your subordinates, you will have enough spare time to address all the problems that result from those selections.' It reminded me that General Creech had said the thing when I took over ADTAC. General Creech rejected a total of eight nominations for commander of the 33rd TFW. The ninth that he approved was Col. George Forester, 363rd TFW/DO at Shaw AFB. George did a stellar job leading the Thirty-Third Wing to win several notable awards—for example, winning the William Tell Air Defense Gunnery Meet twice.

A couple of visits to the 4th TFW at Seymour Johnson AF, North Carolina, left me with mixed emotions. The wing was converting from F-4Ds to F-4Es, a significant upgrade in combat capability as well as a major change in handling performance and systems. The squadron commander leading the conversion struck me as well suited for the challenge and doing an exceptional job of orchestrating the transition. He had rock-solid answers to all the questions I put to him as he toured me around his operation. His name was Lt. Col. Richard B. Myers, who later became the fifteenth chairman of the Joint Chiefs of Staff. On the other hand, the wing commander, Col. Larry Huggins, seemed to be over his head. When asked, "Who is your weakest squadron commander?"

The response was "They are all great. I don't have any weak subordinate commanders!"

When asked, "What do you worry about before you fall asleep at night?"

The response was something like "That there will be an increase in rainy days this summer, and we'll have a difficult time meeting our sortie goals." Summer rain is not something commanders worry about as a general rule. This guy was either clueless or not willing to give honest answers. I put the Fourth Wing on my list of places to visit often; the commander needed mentoring. My second visit left me more perplexed. Colonel Huggins took me to several maintenance facilities as requested. He characterized all of them as the best in TAC. I knew that wasn't true; several were barely average. One 4th TFW maintenance facility visit I remember vividly because it was so bizarre. It was to the pylon and bomb rack repair shop located on the far side of their runway and some distance from the main maintenance area. When we walked through the entrance door, I gave everyone "at ease," introduced myself to the shop chief, and shook his hand. Then I turned to the nearest airman, a three-striper, shook his hand, and asked him a series of questions:

> How long have you been in the air force?
> How long have you been stationed at Seymour Johnson?
> Are you married?
> Is your wife happy with your quarters?
> What do you and your family do for recreation?

All the questions were designed to establish a report and demonstrate that I cared about the individual, which I did. Then we talked about the workload: did the wing lose any sorties for lack of the equipment they repaired, was the backlog of things to repair high, were they working overtime? When I finished talking with him, I looked for someone else to talk with. The shop was deserted; about fifteen airmen escaped? This was highly unusual! Airmen and sergeants generally seek the opportunity to talk to their wing commander and high-ranking officers for bragging rights back at the barracks or at the NCO club. I asked the NCOIC of the pylon and release shop where all his personnel had gone. His weak response was "I guess they all went to the chow hall." That didn't make any sense, as it was only 1030 hours. Lunch wasn't for at least another hour. As we drove away, I asked Colonel Huggins if anything at the shop struck him as unusual. His response was "No, they're the best in TAC."

Every week, the latest incident report (IR) from the Air Force Safety Center at Norton AFB was dropped into my "in basket." The incident report was important reading for commanders at all levels, as it covered accidents, foreign object damage (FOD) to jet engines, and other incidents on every flying unit in the air force. I looked for trends; it didn't matter to me where they happened. It was reasonable to assume that every flying wing had the same level of manning (approximately 90 percent) and drew from the same pool of personnel, so skill and experience levels were about the same at every wing. The only exception to this generalization might be the Thunderbirds maintenance team. Therefore, if a unit somewhere in the air force was having problems, it was just as likely to happen in one of your units sooner rather than later, unless it was a leadership problem.

The current incident report had me scratching my head and reaching for the phone but I decided not to be knee jerk. I would wait to see if the adverse numbers at the Fourth Wing repeated the following week. The IR listed more foreign object damage (FOD) and afterburner (AB) blowouts on takeoff for the 4th TFW than all other air force wings combined equipped with F-4s during the previous week. That was highly unusual and signaled something radically wrong. I knew from eighteen years of flying and maintaining F-4s that FOD was caused by sloppy maintenance discipline, but I had little experience with AB blowouts, which were very uncommon. The next week's IR revealed that nothing had changed; the Fourth Wing led the entire air force in FOD and AB blowouts. Not exactly confident that Colonel Huggins, his vice, and his LG were viewing the situation the same as me, I once again checked my urge to call the Fourth Wing and decided to wait another week. The third IR in a row showed no change to the problems at the Fourth Wing, so I called Colonel Huggins and asked him what he was doing to correct his FOD and AB blowout problems. I was stunned when he responded with "What problem?" I referred him to the past three incident reports, which he evidently didn't read or, worse, didn't comprehend the situation.

"Get back with me tomorrow morning with your corrective action" was my crisp response.

The previous 4th TFW commander was Col. Pete Kempf a bright, no-nonsense guy that I first met when he was a first lieutenant in two of my classes at the University of Nebraska while earning our Bootstrap degrees. He was in the Military Airlift Command (MAC) at the time flying C-141s. Subsequently, he called me at Hurlburt AFB when he was TDY there. I took him up for a weekend flight in an AT-28 chasing down Special Forces undergoing jungle training in the swamps on Eglin AFB ranges. The experience convinced him he wanted to be a fighter pilot and, with MAC's consent, was able to make the transition. Colonel Kemp had been "short notice" transferred to take over the 388th TFW at Hill AFB, Utah, where there were serious problems attributed to the previous wing commander. Under Pete Kempf, the 4th TFW was at the top of its game; under Colonel Larry Huggins, I was quickly coming to the conclusion it was running on momentum and lacked strong leadership.

The following morning, Colonel Huggins informed me that he had appointed a major from one of the flying squadrons to conduct an investigation and at the same time had told his deputy for maintenance and chief of maintenance to take corrective action. A week later, he called and informed me the investigation was complete and asked if I wanted to take the briefing at Shaw AFB or Seymour Johnson. I said I would fly in early the next morning, take the briefing, and spend some time with his maintenance team. At 0900 hours, the following day, the investigating officer was going through a stack of charts depicting the airflow through the PW J-79 engines mounted side by side in the F-4 fuselage. To my absolute amazement, the major was saying that the airflow across the left and right side of the F-4 nose to just aft of the front cockpit where the engine intakes extended out from the fuselage was such that foreign objects could not be carried into the engines by airflow. He was implying it was an act of God! I stopped the briefer and asked Colonel Huggins if he had received and approved the findings being briefed to me. He nodded yes. I asked the maintenance colonels, lieutenant colonels, and chief master sergeants if they concurred with the findings. They all nodded yes. I suppose they would agree, as they didn't want to accept or admit it was their fault. With that, I told the assembled group that I started flying the F-4 shortly after it entered the air force inventory in 1964, and FOD was essentially the result of undisciplined maintenance, and if they could not or did not understand, that I would prove it to them. Further, I pointed out that the AB blowout problem was unrelated to the FOD issue, and they hadn't even addressed that. I turned to Colonel Huggins and told him the problem was leadership, not God, but if it turned out that God didn't like him, then he would have to go because I couldn't afford to continue offending God.

I cut the visit short and, on arriving back at Shaw, went directly to the 363rd TFW engine shop and spoke with the chief master sergeant who ran it. I had been to this engine shop many times to confer with the shop chief and his technicians whenever there was a problem identified with the PW F100 or J79 engine, or errant engine maintenance practices. I went to the shop to get a hands-on education on each problem and the corrective action required. Then as I visited other wings in the command, I could go out on the flight line or in the engine repair shops and see if engine maintenance and repair was being done correctly.

I asked the engine shop chief if he had time to go to Seymour Johnson AFB in the next day or two to see if he could find the problem that was leading to the astronomically high FOD and AB blowout events there. We agreed that FOD was likely caused by undisciplined airframe maintenance, whereas the AB blowouts had to be the result of faulty engine maintenance—two distinctly different areas to investigate. He said he was available to go but needed Colonel Carr's OK. I called Colonel Carr from the shop and received his OK for his 363rd Wing's engine shop chief to be gone for a couple of days.

It was about noon the following day that the chief called and said he had located the cause of both problems, and if they weren't fixed immediately, there would be more serious problems in the near future. He had only been at Seymour Johnson about two hours! I asked what he had discovered. It was like the old bromide "It's as plain as the nose on your face!"

What the Chief said was "There are no experienced personnel on the flight line! All the 'stripes' have migrated into the air-conditioned back shops. The only personnel working on the flight line are 3 levels right out of tech training school. Many have not even been certified to accomplish the tasks they are being directed to do. The engine people sent out on the line are not qualified to adjust the afterburner linkages! That is why there are so many AB blowouts. The sheet metal and other technicians are not familiar with the requirement for all screws and rivets forward of the intakes to be absolutely tight and inspected after every maintenance procedure in that area." It was that easy for an experienced supervisor to find the cause of all the problems. The real question was, why didn't the tens of highly experienced maintenance supervisors at the Fourth Wing find the problem? In my view, it was poor and absent leadership at the top. I called Colonel Huggins immediately, informed him of the cause of the current engine problems the wing was having, and told him he was damn lucky that he didn't lose an aircraft because it was going to snowball over time. I directed that he spend at least two hours every day on the flight line at random hours to ensure that the staff, tech, and master sergeants forced back on the flight line were performing or supervising the work there. I also directed him to write down the names of young airmen doing various tasks and then to check their training records to make sure they were trained and certified to do the work. A serious incident, perhaps the loss of life and an aircraft, had been averted! I was very unhappy with myself for waiting three weeks to jump on the problem that was evident in the weekly incident reports.

For those not familiar with air force technical training lexicon and skill levels, a short tutorial is in order. Airmen graduate from formal technical training with a 3 level Air Force Specialty Code (AFSC). The navy and the army use different acronyms. For example, the army uses MOS (Military Operational Specialty). When an airman arrives at an operational assignment, he or she is trained on specific tasks associated with a weapons system, the F-4E at the 4th TFW, for example. Once the trainer is satisfied that a 3 level airman is proficient on a given task and can accomplish it without supervision, he/she is certified on the task. Once certified, they can be sent to do the job by themselves. For a given AFSC, Avionics, for example, there may be fifty tasks someone with that AFSC working on F-4Es can be certified on. The dispatcher must ensure that only people certified to do specific troubleshooting and repair are sent to do it. As airmen gain experience and rank, they can achieve a 5 level, generally associated with sergeants and staff sergeants; a 7 level, associated with technical and master sergeants; and a 9 level, associated with senior and chief master sergeants. Seven and nine levels are usually the result of years of experience and advanced schooling. Generally speaking, it would take at least a 5 level to task train and certify a 3 level on a task. Proficiency is continuously verified with quality control (QC) inspections performed by "experts" after a task has been completed and signed off in the Form 781.

The air force had three primary fighter commands: TAC in the CONUS, USAFE, in Europe, and PACAF in the Pacific; and CENTAF was emerging as a fourth under CENTCOM. In addition, there was the Alaskan Air Command that was tied to NORAD. General Creech, as commander TAC, had the responsibility for working with Air Force Systems Command in the development of new weapons systems or the modification of operational systems. It was his responsibility to ensure priorities for development and modifications were harmonized among the fighter commands. Each year, tactical force commanders would convene at TAC Headquarters to argue for new development starts and establish priorities. Most of them wanted the same things but not necessarily in the same priority. For example, USAFE might have as their highest priority a laser-guided Maverick antitank weapon to defeat Russian tanks in a NATO/Warsaw Pact conflict; whereas, PACAF might argue that the highest priority be given to the advanced medium-range air-to-air missile (AMRAAM) so they could defeat Soviet interceptors at extended ranges while penetrating to assigned targets on the Kola Peninsula. I was invited to attend one of these meetings because CENTAF was taking on a much larger role as the air component of CENTCOM and would be the only air component in combat over the next two decades.

The meeting was a gathering of Eagles for two days: General Creech was the host, Gen. Larry Welch represented the Air Staff, Gen. Jerry O'Malley came from PACAF, Gen. Chuck Donnelly from USAFE, Lt. Gen. Lynwood Clark from AAC, and me, from CENTAF. It was fascinating to watch the "big dogs" debate the various programs and lobby for their program of choice. There were two dominant players in the room: General Creech and General Welch, and then a significant gap to the next level. Rumors throughout the air force over the past ten years had General O'Malley as the odds on favorite to become the air force chief in his time. On the other hand, it was clear to me, after seeing these senior officers working the priority issues, that it would likely be

Gen. Larry Welch who would be selected by the SECDEF when the time came for Gen. Charlie Gabriel to retire. To be fair, I knew General Welch and what he was capable of; this was my first exposure to General O'Malley.

The air force gave 9th AF/CENTAF the responsibility for managing all forward propositioning of resources in the CENTCOM area. There were seven cargo ships loaded with conventional weapons anchored off the island of Diego Garcia in the Indian Ocean. Thousands of trucks, other vehicles, maps, bare base shelters, and a field hospital were stored in warehouses in Sudan and Oman. In Sudan, the warehouses were leased and behind security fences. In Oman, the warehouses were located on Omani air force bases and afforded protection by Omani security forces. At each location, there was a handful of air force sergeants maintaining these resources valued in the billions of dollars. It was my responsibility to ensure they were properly taken care of and ready to go to war, and the AF personnel were safe and properly supported. On my first trip to Sudan, it was immediately obvious that the sergeants at Port Sudan on the Red Sea were at great risk. There was no communications, no phone lines, not any means of communicating back to the embassy in Khartoum. If they got hurt, sick, or there was an attack against them or the warehouses, there was no way to call for help or evacuation. That needed to be fixed immediately! I had studied a stand-alone system for long haul communications called Meteor Burst. Essentially, it consisted to two briefcase-size packages with a transmitter, receiver, and typewriter in each segment. It would only handle a message of about 140 characters, but that was sufficient to call for help, a doctor, or evacuation. I also thought that a twenty-foot boat with a large-enough outboard motor and auxiliary fuel tanks would allow them to escape to the beach and onto Saudi Arabia. They could also use the boat for fishing and other recreation. Arrangements were made to get the Meteor Burst system purchased and delivered immediately, one briefcase segment to the US embassy in Khartoum and the other to the troops at Port Sudan. It could also be used to order needed parts and keep both ends proficient in using it. How Meteor Burst worked is interesting. The operator types a message and hits the transmit button. Short bursts of "hello" with an address are repeatedly sent into space to reflect off of the ionized tail of small meteors coursing through the ionosphere. When the angle is right, the "hello" is received at the intended receiver at the other end, which then transmits back, "I received your hello—send the message!" The originating segment then automatically sends the short message. Evidently, both the hello and actual message reflect off of the same meteor tail, which may last for several seconds. Amazing, but it works and will cover distances up to 1,500 miles. The airmen's living conditions in Port Sudan were marginal as well. The large house accommodated the five men reasonably well, and they had a maid for cleaning and a cook to prepare their food. On the other hand, the water was unfit to drink and had to be filtered through a rare earth complex filter to extract all the junk that was in the water. They took me up to the rooftop to show me the gunk that was being trapped by the filter. After the filtering process, the water was boiled prior to cooking or drinking. All vegetables and fruits had to be soaked in a bleach solution for thirty minutes and then thoroughly rinsed in the filtered/boiled water prior to eating. If it wasn't the end of the world, you could see it from there in Port Sudan.

Quality of life throughout Oman was much better, rivaling Western civilization, largely because of British influence over several decades. It made me proud to realize it was the memorandum of understanding forged by our team in 1980 that led to CENTAF's ability to preposition goods in Oman. There was a new ambassador in Muscat who was much friendlier to US military personnel looking after the propositioned stock. Most of the military goods propositioned in Oman were vehicles. Engines needed to be run every so often and fuel tanks kept at five gallons so they could be driven on and off airlift aircraft without exceeding the fuel allowed. Vehicles had to be driven short distances to ensure the tires didn't take a set, and repairs had to be made to keep them operational. The maintainers, all sergeants lived in hotels nearby, had rental vehicles to drive to and from work and had access to excellent global communications. There was also an air force major in Oman that had some responsibility for all AF personnel in country. Visiting Oman was important for morale and to ensure the work was being done and done right, but not nearly as important as Port Sudan, where personnel were at risk, and the political situation was also very volatile!

Back in the United States, it was time to participate in a CENTCOM exercise called Roving Sands held in the western desert area. CENTAF was the largest player because it was easy to move aircraft from air bases in the east to others in the western United States. The MEF also participated in large numbers as well as the lightly armored units of the Eighteenth Airborne Corps. On the other hand, it was expensive to move much of the 24th ID, although the headquarters always played as did their Tactical Operations Centers (TOCs). The navy didn't play at all except for the admiral and a small headquarters staff.

These CENTCOM Roving Sands set in the desert were really good for the air force elements because it brought in SAC bombers and MAC airlifters that we normally didn't get to work with on a regular basis. It also gave the CENTAF staff and me an opportunity to spend some time with the SAC and MAC liaison flag officers. They would become a full-time part of the staff when we deployed to the Middle East. As I mentioned earlier, the MEF would be largely unopposed for their amphibious landing at Chabahar. Hence, the Marine Air Wing operating out of an existing airfield about twenty miles north of the beach would not be gainfully employed. On the other hand, the light forces of the Eighteenth Corps, supported by CENTAF, would be trying to hold back several Soviet armies. In this regard, I would send a message to CINCCENT, General Kingston, requesting that the Marine Air Wing be "chopped" to CENTAF for tasking to support the engaged land forces. CINCCENT would always accept my recommendation and direct Lieutenant General Cheatham to accept CENTAF tasking for his air wing. General Cheatham would always refuse to accept the tasking and inform the commandant of the Marine Corps on his refusal message.

General Kingston's staff and senior commanders always met about 2100 hours every day during Roving Sands to hear General Kingston's assessment of the day's operations and set the stage for the following day's planning session. The CINC always asked for comments, so I asked General Cheatham why he refused to accept tasking from CENTAF when his Marine Air Wing was doing flyovers for the unopposed marine battalions doing close order drill. On this particular occasion, General Cheatham asked the CINC to clear the room except for the flag officers. When everyone had left, General Cheatham checked all the doors and the presentation room to ensure no one was listening. Then he said, "If I allow the Marine Air Wing to be tasked by CENTAF, you will have another marine general to take my place in the morning!" That was a shocker, and no one said a word. Then Ernie went on to say that if CENTCOM deployed into combat, he recognized that two separate tasking of air assets didn't make sense and would at best create confusion, and that he would accept CENTAF tasking! General Kingston, General Cheatham, and I shook hands on that commitment. For the remaining Roving Sands exercise, I continued to ask for tasking authority; General Kingston continued to support it, and General Cheatham continued to refuse with copy to the commandant, Gen. P. X. Kelley. In theory and in the pretend world, the marine air/ground team was inseparable.

Every morning of these joint exercises, the CENTCOM leadership team met together to be briefed on the current situation and receive the CINC's guidance on going forward to include the weight of effort for the land battle. Each component commander would then interpret his guidance and provide him feedback on how they would support it. For example, I might respond

> Fifty percent of the F-15 sorties would be on airborne caps with the remainder on ground alert.

> Fifty percent of F-16 sorties would interdict and isolate LOCs and the enemy forces in reserve.

> Thirty percent of F-16 sorties would be on five-minute ground alert for close air support missions.

> Twenty percent of F-16 sorties would be held in CAS reserve or flown as interdiction sorties as the land battle dictated.

> Fifty percent of the A-10 sorties would be on airborne alert for immediate requests.

> Fifty percent of A-10 sorties would be on five-minute ground alert.

> If General Kingston or his land component commander, Lieutenant General Mackmull, wanted to modify the air apportionment, it would be discussed at that time.

Following this meeting, CENTAF planners would prepare a draft frag order to support the CINC's guidance. Within two hours, General Kingston would tour the CENTAF war room, evaluate our response to his air/land battle plan, and tweak it as necessary. The frag would then be published, and the sorties would flow as directed. There was never any question in my mind or any of the staff that it was a joint effort and that every day and every contingency was flown and fought jointly. It was a constant irritant to me to hear the Beltway Bandits and armchair strategists, especially those who never heard the sound of gunfire, opine that the services weren't joint enough. Perhaps in other Unified Commands, there was a scintilla of truth in what they railed about—but not CENTCOM! Title 10 Code requires that the services organize, train, and equip. But when their forces come together under a "combatant commander," they plan and fight as a joint team!

CENTCOM exercises were a huge benefit to CENTAF forces, especially the ones that were external to Ninth Air Force. Most units enjoyed the opportunity to deploy to unfamiliar air bases, maintain their aircraft from, and test the validity of their war readiness spares kits (WRSK), live in tent cities, plan and operate from a frag order, and harmonize a strike package consisting of several units via telephone. Strike package commanders also practiced rendezvousing fifty or more aircraft in the strike package on air refueling orbits and forming them up into a comprehensive lethal force inbound to a highly defended target complex. The flying portion of these exercises lasted from seven to ten days, and lots of valuable lessons were learned and corrective action taken prior to the next one. It was these exercises and the fundamental 2004 Plan that became the foundation of Desert Shield and Desert Storm. However, the enemy forces, target sets, and geography of Desert Storm were vastly different, and the approach taken by Lt. Gen. Chuck Horner, commander, CENTAF, was unique, innovative, and highly effective.

Lt. Gen. Jack Mackmull stormed into my makeshift command section, demanding to know why the air force wouldn't evacuate his troops from a mock battle situation along the exercise FEBA (Forward Edge of the Battle Area). I'd received a heads-up earlier from the MAC liaison that they had denied a request for airlift because the crosswinds at the forward landing strip were significantly above the C-130s prescribed safe limits. I told Jack that if we were in real combat and his forces were being overrun, we would attempt to evacuate the ground forces. On the other hand, it was an exercise, and none of his troops were in danger. If I ordered aircraft to land at that airstrip, we could have people killed in the process of attempting to land or, worse, loaded with soldiers trying to take off. What I could do in the spirit of the exercise is provide a maximum effort of close air support to defeat the hypothetical enemy trying to overrun his battalion. Jack didn't like my response and was pushing hard for air evacuation. So I asked him how often he ordered his Eighty-Second Airborne Division to conduct practice parachute jumps when the winds were *well above* safe limits. That ended the conversation. Roving Sands exercises were conducted annually, and that was about the extent of our large-scale realistic joint training. In 2011, CENTCOM conducted and their deployed forces participated in over twenty Joint/Coalition Exercises annually.

General Creech called to inform me that a new infrared technology was being tested on an F-16 at Edwards AFB, California. Edwards was the Air Force Flight Test Center where all new aircraft modifications were tested for flight and operational suitability. General Creech must have known that I was getting a lot of flying time in the F-16, both on the gunnery range and on cross-countries, and was quite proficient in the aircraft. The upshot of all this was that General Creech had made arrangements for me to participate in one of the Low-Altitude Navigation and Targeting Infrared Night (LANTIRN) system. He wanted the opinion of someone with a lot of combat experience and one who had pioneered high-performance aircraft night attack and close support operations at the Fighter Weapons School. This sounded like a good opportunity to fly the F-16 with a new and revolutionary capability!

Major Hall coordinated with the Edwards Flight Test Center project officer for available dates of scheduled testing. There was a convenient window of opportunity, and we jumped on it. Major Hall also obtained coordinates of the route I would fly with the LANTIRN pod so we could fly it during the daylight prior to landing at Edwards. The test route was through the mountains north of Edwards AFB and into the adjoining ranges of Navy China Lake. The route was just short of an hour long and required doing several tactical ridge crossings where the pilot rolls the aircraft inverted just prior to reaching the ridgetop and pulls down like a Split S maneuver prior to rolling back upright, flying down the back side of the ridge. I was attempting to fly at two hundred feet above the ground level (AGL) but was unable to maintain that altitude even with pulling 6 Gs as we bottomed out in the narrow valleys between the ridges. My impression of the route we flew is that it was going to be a real challenge on a video screen at midnight.

Because I was long past meeting crew rest requirements and we were trying not to lose too many days on the trip, I would fly in the rear seat of an F-16B with a LANTIRN IP in the front seat. It was a really dark night with about a five-thousand-foot overcast and light rain dotting the canopy when we took off. The IP demonstrated the LANTIRN system at five hundred feet AGL, then two hundred feet AGL, then one hundred feet AGL, and then he gave me control of the aircraft. After about one minute at two hundred feet AGL, I was comfortable with the system and flew the aircraft for the remainder of the route. It was an amazing system, revolutionary for its time, but very primitive compared to the capability now fielded in 2012. The IR display showed terrain feature for about one mile in front and to the side of the aircraft up to about sixty degrees on either side. A terrain following radar displayed a horizon bar representing the altitude selected—in my case, two hundred feet AGL. As the radar detected a rise or descent in the terrain, a separate bar that looked like a little aircraft floated above or below the two-hundred-foot horizon bar. All I had to do was keep the two bars superimposed by flying the aircraft up or down as indicated by moving the aircraft image on the screen. LANTIRN allowed the pilot to select the maximum number of Gs that would be experienced to maintain the horizon bar and aircraft image on the screen superimposed. Ours was set at 4 Gs, which was a fairly soft ride. The radar not only looked down but also looked forward. As I rolled inverted to crest a ridgetop and then back to level flight at two hundred feet AGL following the terrain down the back side of mountain, the radar would range the distance to the valley floor and determine when I needed to start the 4 G pull to avoid crashing in the bottom. Nice! And it was a lot smoother ride than my visual flight in the sunshine along the same route earlier that day.

The IP also let me do some pull-up/dive bomb attacks using the inertial navigation system for a queue to pull up to eight thousand feet AGL, roll inverted, and acquire the target on the LANTIRN screen. The death dot worked the same on LANTIRN as it did on the basic gunnery system. The targets were small isolated buildings in the desert and at road junctions. The LANTIRN system was like magic, and the transition only took about one minute to get adjusted to the mechanism. Another nice feature was that if you wanted to initiate a turn, you could queue the LANTIRN pod to look forty-five degrees in the direction of the turn. If there was high terrain that exceeded the G setting for the flight, an alert would appear on the screen.

It was hard to get to sleep that night, thinking about the revolutionary LANTIRN system. The air force would own the night—nothing or no one could hide. Camouflage wouldn't hide or mask objects like tanks, aircraft, or even troops because the IR detectors in LANTIRN pod would see the temperature difference between the background and military personnel and equipment.

Major Hall, a highly qualified F-16 pilot, and I talked at great length about the LANTIRN pod and my flight the previous night. He confided in me that he had great reservations about the technology being ready for the average squadron pilot. However, after hearing how easy it was for me to adapt to LANTIRN in a few minutes with my modest proficiency in the F-16, he was sold on the concept!

When we returned to Ninth Air Force the next day, I called General Creech and relayed my experience with LANTIRN. Essentially, I said that if a fifty-year-old pilot required only one minute to transition into the LANTIRN nighttime role, a twenty-some-year-old that was flying the line regularly and played computer games would find it second nature. I recommended he favorably consider giving LANTIRN his highest priority for introduction into the F-16 fleet.

During one of the many late-night phone calls with Lt. Gen. Jack Gregory, each of us looking for colonels who displayed exceptional qualities to put in tough demanding jobs, Jack mentioned that he had his butt chewed by General Creech. He went on to say that General Creech had visited Nellis AFB and discovered the stag bar at the O'club featured topless dancers on Friday nights. Any form of nudity was a no-no in TAC, and General Creech blamed Jack for letting it escape his detection. I suspect General Creech was really angry at himself because the weapons center was a direct reporting unit to TAC Headquarters that just happened to be in Jack's backyard. As I expressed my sympathies for the injustice, Jack interrupted and said, "Pete, I'm just calling to tell you that you've got a problem at Langley!" I hung up and immediately called Col. Butch Viccellio, 1st TFW commander at Langley and host to TAC Headquarters. I directed Butch to go immediately to the NCO club and personally confront the club manager about topless dancers or whatever! Then take appropriate action and call me back. A few minutes later, I received his callback, saying the club manager assured him they didn't have topless dancers and there wasn't any problem. I smelled a rat but didn't have time to trap it, as General Creech called to tell me about his undercover investigation.

It seems that General Creech called the NCO club and asked, "Where's the action?"

The response was "Depends on your pleasure. We have topless mud wrestlers for the guys on Friday nights and topless male strippers for the ladies on Saturday nights!"

Then he went on to say, "Pete, you better clean this mess up right now!"

I called Colonel Viccellio back and informed him that he had been lied to by his NCO club manager in response to a direct question. Further, I directed him to have a very serious and pointed talk with his senior enlisted advisor who had to have known about the topless mud wrestlers and the topless male go-go dancers and did not share that information with his commander. My suggestion was that he relieve these two disloyal NCOs from their current positions and also issue to them a letter of reprimand for the various offenses they committed.

I then employed General Creech's ruse to call all Ninth Air Force Officer and NCO clubs to find out "where the action was" for a TDY guy. I learned that the MacDill AFB officers' club had topless Jell-O wrestlers on Friday nights. I immediately called the wing commander to put an immediate stop to that activity.

Two flights of F-15s from the First Wing at Langley AFB, Virginia, were deploying to Jordan to conduct some training operations with the Jordanian air force. King Hussein of Jordan was a pilot, flew his own royal jet, and had flown extensively with the Jordanian air force. It provided an excellent opportunity for me to arrange a trip to coincide with the First Wing deployment. The king was just wrapping up a visit with the First Wing pilots and on the way to his aircraft when I arrived by T-39. After taking off, the king (in the left seat) executed a low flyby down the runway at about ten feet above the ground. He was low enough and close enough that we could see him waving through the pilot's side window. All the Jordanian fighter pilots were ecstatic with the show.

The Crown prince, King Hussein's younger brother, educated in England, invited me to a traditional Bedouin lunch to celebrate the successful completion of the joint exercises. Prior to lunch, he expressed the need for Jordan and the United States to become closer allies and suggested exchanges like the one just completed were excellent ways to get to know each other and encouraged more of the same. The Crown prince gave me a history of the Hashemite Kingdom, and I presented him with a book of Fredrick Remington's sketches and paintings; after which he led me into a large room where fighter pilots of both countries were waiting. He stopped on one side of a small table about thirty inches across and gestured for me to the opposite side. The table was about waist high and covered completely with a large mound of rice topped with a leg of lamb. We waited as attendants came and poured hot goat's milk over the lamb and rice. Then he said, "Bon appétit," and grabbed the lamb with his right hand and ripped off a piece of flesh. As I continued to observe my host, he squeezed a handful of rice into a small log and downed that. The left hand is considered unclean by Muslims, so I grabbed the back of my flight suit with the left hand and concentrated on keeping it there while attempting to rip some lamb meat off of the carcass with the right—no success there. I tried squeezing rice into a roll and eating that, slightly more successful, so I stuck with the rice. When it was time to leave the table, the carpet around my feet was about an inch deep in rice, and I was still hungry. I would have given anything for one whack at the lamb with a sharp knife; it looked delicious, but I'll never know.

Back at the deployed F-15 Squadron's operations building, I was told that a message had been received directing a flight of four F-15s to fly into Mogadishu, Somalia, with me along at the request of the US ambassador to Somalia. The remainder of the F-15s would fly to Aviano, where we would all rendezvous in a couple of days. I was privileged to fly lead and took the flight to Mogadishu International Airport. The name was a joke. At that juncture, the airport consisted of a runway, taxiway, a couple of small buildings, and a control tower. Upon arrival, the control tower, in good English, cleared us to land. We pitched out and took spacing, with me leading the four-ship. As I descended to about one hundred feet on short final, I saw twenty or more animals getting up from the runway and walking over to the edges. I told the flight there were animals on the runway and to execute a missed approach while I contacted the tower. The tower operator said it was normal for wild dogs to sleep on the black asphalt runway because it was warm, but they would get out of the way as the aircraft were landing and not to be concerned. Well, I was concerned an animal the size of a small dog hitting the nose gear at 120 knots could render it inoperable. The same-size animal hitting the main gear could sever the brake hydraulic lines and force the use of emergency brakes. The F-15 would stop all right, but getting the parts and mechanics to repair the hydraulic lines would take weeks. On the second approach, I slowed the F-15 to the minimum safe speed and looked for animals. As the tower operator advised us, the dogs started getting up a few hundred yards in front of the F-15 and trotting to the edge of the asphalt. As the last F-15 landed, they started returning to their favorite spots and lying down. As we taxied in, it was apparent that appearances were not important in Mogadishu; the sides of the taxiway were littered with crashed aircraft, some of which I recognized as Soviet MiG-21 fuselage skeletons. As I recall, there were enough marine guards at the embassy to provide a twenty-four hour-guard for our four F-15 aircraft.

The following afternoon, the ambassador had a lawn party at his official residence and invited his counterparts from other embassies as well as some high-level Somalis. It was a warm sunny day on a sloping manicured lawn sloping down to the beach about a quarter mile away. A perfect day for swimming, and the sandy beach was covered with people, but no one was in the water even though the Indian Ocean was calm as far as one could see. I asked the ambassador if the Somalis didn't care for swimming or the ocean. "To the contrary," he replied, "there would be hundreds in the water if some idiot hadn't built a cattle meat processing plant just two miles up from the beach that attracted hundreds of Madagascar sharks to the area. The sharks attacked a number of the locals before the government put the water off limits."

Downtown Mogadishu was about four city blocks east to west and north to south. At least that is how much of the four streets, laid out like a tic-tac-toe puzzle, were paved. The natives were small in stature, and their features were very fine, very Anglo-Saxon, vice African. I seemed to recall that the fabled Queen of Sheba allegedly came from Somalia. All the natives were very pleasant and eager to show off the goods they had for sale. It was a pleasant experience. It is almost impossible to believe their society could go downhill so fast in less than a decade.

The F-15 flight to Aviano Air Base, Italy, was uneventful. The F-15 is a great aircraft as a combat weapons system, and a pleasure to fly! I don't recall how I hitchhiked home from Aviano on air force military airlift, but back at Shaw, things were far from normal. The idea of having component commanders brief their major war plan was catching on. General Gabriel, CSAF, tasked all air force component commanders of Unified Commands, like CENTAF, to brief their war plans in support of their Unified commanders at the next scheduled Corona Conference. A Corona Conference was a gathering of the chief and all four-star air force generals. Three Coronas were usually scheduled every year—one in the summer at Homestead Air Force Base located south of Miami, Florida; one in the fall that coincided with the Service Academies' Football Game at the Air Force Academy north of Colorado Springs, Colorado; and one in the Pentagon in February. The latter is the only one the vice chief was able to attend—someone had to run the air force while everyone else was away.

Normally, three-star generals are not invited to Corona Conferences unless they are a deputy chief of staff (DCS) presenting a policy paper for discussion and decision by the air force leadership. However, the fall Corona in 1984 was an exception because General Gabriel wanted all the air force components of Unified Commands to brief their supporting plan to their CINC's major war plan. Accordingly, Lt. Gen. Bruce Brown, commander Alaskan Air Command, and I, representing CENTAF, were invited along with the four-star commanders from PACAF and USAFE to brief our war plans. For some obscure reason, Lt. Gen. Jack Chain, DCSOPS on the Air Staff, called for all the briefers, or briefing preparers, to bring their briefings or outlines thereof to the Pentagon so he could vet them. I thought this was ludicrous because I didn't work for Jack and wasn't going to change a thing in the 2004 Air Campaign Plan that had been approved by my Unified boss, Gen. Bob Kingston, CINCCENT. Evidently, other air force component commanders felt the same way as they sent representatives with outlines to the Pentagon. It was a waste of everyone's time and travel money.

However, when General Creech said he would like to review the 2004 Air Campaign Plan, that was a different matter. General Creech was my air force boss, didn't want to be embarrassed by a sophomoric presentation, and, I suspect, wanted me to do well in front of my betters. Each briefer had a total of thirty minutes behind the lectern. Taking time off for getting on and off the stage and answering questions from the four-stars left no more than twenty minutes for the actual presentation. My briefing was dual-screen presentation with eighty charts on each side. That gave me fifteen seconds per pair of slides. It could be done! The prebrief to General Creech was on Saturday at 1000 hours. B. J. and I flew up in an F-16 early that morning and were at the ready when General Creech entered his conference room and sat down. B. J. was in the projection room taking notes. The actual presentation to General Creech took several hours because he drilled down deep into just about every chart and offered many suggestions. However, he only changed about twenty charts. Mostly, he improved graphic charts by making the data easier to digest. For example, he recommended changing bar charts that depicted the buildup of fighter aircraft in theater to an integral line graph. He also simplified some of the more wordy charts, making it easier for the audience to quickly grasp the information. When it was over, he gave the presentation an A+.

Major Hall was crestfallen, saying we'd never get the changes done in time. He was concerned that General Creech, who would be in the Corona audience when the briefing was presented, would be very unhappy if his recommend changes were not incorporated into the final briefing. It was late Saturday afternoon; we had planned to fly back to Shaw that night and then on to Colorado Springs on Wednesday to be ready for the scheduled presentation on Thursday morning. If slide changes were to be made, our original plan had to be altered to accommodate the graphics shop personnel that would be making changes. To help the reader understand Major Hall's concern, there were no PowerPoint Rangers in the 1980s—we were using viewgraphs that had to be created by hand on paper and then sent to a photo lab and turned into plastic opaque viewgraphs. Each viewgraph than had to be put on a light table and all the "light holes" covered with an opaque substance to prevent the light from shining through. Some viewgraphs had as many as four reveals, a big multiplier. Not to worry, I said. We won't waste time flying back to Shaw tonight. Get Colonel Peters on the phone along with the graphic support team, and we'll go over every chart that has to be changed, line by line and word by word. They can make the changes on Sunday, and we can proof them after we fly back to Shaw. That gives them Monday and Tuesday to complete the production work. We can proof the new viewgraphs as each one is completed and be ready to fly out Wednesday afternoon. When the work was done that evening, we ordered in pizza and shared a bottle of wine, knowing that Colonel Peters would take care of everything on his end.

On Wednesday, the F-16 flight from Shaw to Peterson AFB with a stop at Tinker AFB, Oklahoma, went as planned, and we landed with an in-commission aircraft for the return flight. The 2004 War Plan briefing schedule revealed that I was the first briefer. Good, I would set the tone of the day rather than be a victim of it. If I'm allowed an immodest moment; the briefing went flawlessly! And when the briefing was finished, I laid six inches of preplanned fragmentary order (frag) on the conference table in front of the podium and said, "This is the preplanned frag for the first week of combat. We will not have time to start from scratch in theater! However, if our masters in Washington are slow to take the decision to deploy us, then our preplanned third day of interdiction may wind up being what we actually do on day one. It all depends on how far the Soviets have advanced. Our preplanning is flexible!" There were no questions.

General Gabriel stood up, followed by all the four-stars, and applauded! It was a good moment, and I saw a smile on General Creech's face; the latter was the best tribute of all. Lt. Gen. Bruce Brown was next, followed by Gen. Billy Minter, commander USAFE. General Minter did not brief his USAFE War Plan but rather the Noncombatant Evacuation Plan, or NEO. The NEO describes how American dependents would be rapidly moved from forward bases in Germany back to the United States so they would not become Soviet prisoners. One component commander was so off of the mark that General Gabriel stopped him shortly into his briefing and suggested that he sit down. After the war plan briefings were completed, Lieutenant General Brown and I were excused—the remainder of the Corona was off limits for us.

Jean Cook put the call through to my office; it was from a civil service worker at Shaw AFB. He asked if I would be a guest speaker at the Rafting Creek Baptist Church located just outside the city limits of Sumter, South Carolina. The subject would be fellowship. He assured me that a number of Shaw AFB civilian workforce attended the church. His request seemed reasonable and provided an opportunity to meet members of the local community and some of the civilian workers at Shaw AFB. I accepted. After jotting down some notes on fellowship and leadership, I walked out of the office to tell Jean to put the event on my calendar and to be sure and remind me of the commitment. She turned a little pale and then informed me that the Rafting Creek Baptist was an all-black congregation that conducted full submersion baptism in the creek as part of their services—maybe I should reconsider. I told her that wasn't an option! I couldn't back out of my promise, once committed, short of a war in the Middle East.

The appointed Sunday arrived. I dressed in my best class A uniform and drove myself to the church early to spend some time with the minister and to scope out the facility. The minister was a huge man, about six feet six with a generous girth. He had been a minister at a large church in Chicago, Illinois, where he preached for several years, then moved to South Carolina to get his own parish. He talked me through the proceedings, indicating I would speak right after the baptisms. As it turned out, it was very cold that morning, and baptisms would take place in a large concrete well behind the pulpit.

When the service started, I was seated next to the minister. It was standing room only. I never did learn if that was typical or if more people showed up to see and hear the "general." Everything moved along smoothly. When it was time for the baptism, the support staff removed some flooring from behind the pulpit to reveal a large concrete pit with stairs at one end leading down to the base of the water-filled pit. The minister descended into the pit until he was waist deep in water. About half-dozen male and female children were called up and fully submerged in the pit. The soaking-wet minister introduced me and left to change into dry robes.

The general rule used by the air force for public speaking was that fifteen minutes was about right, twenty minutes was too long, and that anything longer was arrogant and narcissistic. My gut feel was that for this occasion, sermon and all, twenty minutes was acceptable. At the end of twenty minutes, the congregation seemed to just be getting warmed up, and I was getting some verbal feedback from the audience. I rolled on providing examples of fellowship in the military, both in peace and war, and was close to forty-five minutes when the minister returned in dry garb. I concluded and gladly yielded the pulpit to him. He preached for another thirty minutes and ended the service.

As he walked me to the rear door of the empty church, I asked for some feedback. He looked down on me and said, "Well, brother, you left them rather poorly!" That didn't sound very good, so I asked for an explanation. The minister let out a sigh and said, "A sermon in a black Baptist church usually lasts for about four hours. I don't know what the parishioners will do for the rest of the day." I was a little crushed but hoped the parishioners would relax and do something they enjoyed.

Sometime later, I was invited to speak to an Episcopalian congregation. When I arrived at the church, I proudly told the minister I was prepared to speak for as long as he wanted—four hours, if desired. He smiled and said, "Son, in this church, no souls are saved after five minutes, and you start losing converts after ten—keep it short and punchy!" I spoke for exactly seven minutes and opened it up for questions. Some left and some stayed to ask questions—perhaps just to be polite. Congregations were good forums, but you had to know the boundaries for each religious denomination.

I had a number of superstars as wing commanders in Ninth Air Force. One was Col. Bob Baxter, commander of the 31st TTW at Homestead. I first met Bob on the Pacific Trip with Gen. David C. Jones in January 1975. Then lieutenant colonel Baxter was General Jones's aide-de-camp. We were the two most junior officers on the trip and found common cause in our lowly status. I was pleased to find that he commanded the 31st TTW when I took over 9th AF. Bob was really special and the ultimate achiever. He was first in his Air Force Academy class, earned an advanced degree at Oxford, England, as a Rhodes Scholar, first in his pilot training class, and first in his F-15 Combat Crew Training class. Not surprisingly, he rose through the ranks with below-the-zone promotions to every rank above first lieutenant, which is automatic at eighteen months. I didn't have anything to do with his assignment to the 31st TTW, but I suspect he was sent there because Homestead AFB, Florida, home the Air Force Conference Center, was the showcase of TAC and the air force! The Air Staff, TAC, and all Air Force Commands held conferences there. If things didn't go right, the chief, General Creech, and I would hear all about it! It was a pleasure to visit Homestead, because no matter where I looked for trouble, all I found was good order and discipline. I learned a lot from Bob and transplanted it to other wings. Never as, "Colonel Baxter is doing this or I want you to do this," but rather, "I've seen this idea work in other places. Give it some serious consideration. I suspect it will make your life a lot easier."

With this as background, I was surprised when I exercised my "right of refusal" on one of Colonel Baxter's squadron commander selections. When I interviewed his nominee, I found him to be a solid journeyman fighter pilot—I would go to war as his wingman. However, he lacked the fire, vision, and energy that I believed was necessary to effectively lead a fighter squadron and make it better. I called Colonel Baxter and expressed my concern on his nominee and suggested, if that was the best man his wing had to offer, then we needed to tap TAC-wide resources for a better candidate. His response was shocking: "Well, General Pete, it's his turn." Then followed my lecture that assumption of command and promotions is not about turns—it's about giving the best people you have the opportunity to succeed or fail at the next level. I went on to point out that if the air force worked on a system of "it's your turn," he, Colonel

Baxter, would still be looking forward to his promotion to major. He pleaded his case badly but passionately.

In the end, I said, "Bob, you can give him the squadron, but mark my word, you will soon have the unpleasant task of removing and replacing this officer!" Three months later, Colonel Baxter called with another nominee for the same squadron; it didn't take him long to recognize his mistake.

Given Colonel Baxter's past track record, I wasn't surprised when he was selected for promotion to brigadier general and reassigned to the TAC Staff as assistant deputy commander for operations. TAC was a place where General Creech and other senior officers could mentor him and move him to a big challenging job when it became available. Before he could make the move to TAC, his orders were changed to the Pentagon as the deputy for plans, also a great job with a lot of exposure to senior officers who had never heard of Col. Bob Baxter. To everyone's surprise, he elected to retire in lieu of the assignment. Once a general officer or selectee elects to retire, it's virtually impossible to reverse the action set in motion. I called Bob in an attempt to convince him to pull his papers. He said he'd been offered a six-figure job on Wall Street and was not about to pass it up. Serving one's country and fighting her wars when necessary is not about money; it's a noble calling and a sacred commitment to freedom and personal sacrifice! I hung up, both sad and glad that he was leaving. Because Bob didn't serve in the grade of general for two years; he retired as a colonel.

On August 24, 1992, the aircraft and personnel assigned to the 31st TFW at Homestead AFB, Florida, were evacuated in the face of Hurricane Andrew. Andrew destroyed the base and nearby town of the same name. The base was never rebuilt.

Back to the Middle East with a MAC flight to Rhein-Main AB, Germany, and a T-39 Sabreliner to Port Sudan, Sudan. The troops were in good spirits and took me through all the warehouses, showing me how well they maintained all the equipment under their control and shared with me their problems with parts shortages. Apparently, their biggest problem was with vehicle batteries and tires that degraded quickly from the oppressive heat and humidity—something to find solutions for and stay on top of when I returned to the States! The NCOs and I were back out on the desert, discussing issues away from the warehouse, when a Sudanese major general was driven up to our location by his aide-de-camp. We exchanged salutes, even though I was out of uniform, wearing khaki shorts, desert boots, and a short-sleeve civilian shirt. The general informed me that I had an appointment with the Sudanese first vice president, Mr. Tyebe, in two hours and that I should return to my aircraft and fly to Khartoum immediately or I would be late for the meeting. The general spoke very good English, but try as I might to explain that American generals do not meet with heads of state without direction from our president or secretary of state, and I had not been given such permission or direction, he wasn't backing down. The Sudanese general seemed to be getting a little irritated at my reluctance to depart when one of the NCOs came running up with a Meteor Burst transmission from the US embassy in Khartoum, saying I had an urgent meeting in two hours with the Sudanese 1st VP. Off we raced to the T-39 and got airborne without clearance because there were no communication links to anywhere from Port Sudan.

Once airborne, I dug out my travel bag and found a dark suit, white shirt, and tie, changing as fast as I could to become somewhat presentable when the plane landed. As the T-39 taxied in front of the terminal building, I spied a caravan of Mercedes limos lined up just outside the fence separating the aircraft ramp from the access road. When I exited the T-39, a door of one of the limos opened, indicating, I thought, to get into that car. Once inside, the man seated next to me introduced himself as the chief of mission, explaining that an Ethiopian army force had invaded southern Sudan and was moving unchecked into the interior. Knowing that I was in Port Sudan, they came up with the idea that a televised newscast about the US Air Force general responsible for the defense of Sudan was here to determine what actions should be taken to counter the invasion. To give credibility to the news story, I was to meet the first vice president Mr. Tyebe. We would exchange salutes, shake hands, and then go into the presidential palace. After about thirty minutes of small talk and refreshments, we would emerge exchange salutes and hug each other. The greeting and departure would be televised.

When this charade was finished, the chief of mission drove me to a hotel where Major Hall had secured a room for $300. Our per diem was about seventy-five dollars a day, so saving Sudan was going to put a big dent in my budget. B. J. certainly could not afford a $300 room, so he slept on folded-up blankets on the floor of my room.

There was only one TV channel, and sure enough, on the evening news, there was a few seconds of the 1st VP and me exchanging salutes and a hug. The English subtitle said, "American general here to look over the Ethiopian situation!" The next morning, we learned from the TV that the invading force had withdrawn. My face ended the war in just one day. How's that for efficiency? When Major Hall left the room to check with the T-39 flight crew about our departure arrangements, he found two packages outside the door. Both were tied with ribbons, representing the colors on the Sudanese flag, and both had business cards from the 1st VP tucked under the ribbons. I suggested that we leave them wrapped so Sheila could have the pleasure of opening them on my return—whatever they might be. The hotel we stayed in was located at the juncture of the Blue Nile on the east and the White Nile from the west. The Blue Nile was loaded with large nasty crocodiles; the White Nile had none. However, the Nile River formed from the two at that juncture and flowed north to the Mediterranean Sea, had crocodiles that were a constant threat to people and their livestock along the way.

We flew back to Rhein-Main AB, boarded a C-141 to Dover AFB, Delaware, and then another T-39 to Shaw. At Dover, we declared our purchases with US Customs, listing the two packages as gifts of unknown value from the 1st VP of Sudan. The Customs agent squeezed them and shook them then asked if I had any idea of what was in them. I suggested that the large soft one might be a tribal robe, and the smaller one some trinket associated with the robe, saying that I was keeping them as they were presented so my wife could have the pleasure of opening them. He let them go through as is without duty. Sheila was delighted to have the opportunity to open these treasures—that is, until she opened them. The large package contained a leopard skin rug with red glass eyes and broken teeth. Whoever prepared the hide used the actual skull, and the teeth were real—not fake plastic. I suspect the rug had been on the palace floor for over a hundred years. The palace staff were probably glad to have a reason to get rid of it. The smaller package contained a pair of crocodile shoes (high heels) and a matching purse. How they did it, I'll never know, but the shoes fit, and Sheila wore them. If the packages had been opened, they would have never been allowed in the United States, as both animal species were on the embargoed list at the time. We still have the leopard rug, and it has been to show-and-tell several times with our grandchildren.

I went down to MacDill AFB to visit with Col. Ron Fogleman, the recently assigned wing commander. I had some concerns that Ron was flying with F-16 students as their instructor pilot and perhaps wasn't as qualified as the traditional line IP who flew with students several times a week. After reviewing Colonel Fogleman's IP check ride and standardization/evaluation write-ups, it was clear that he was an exceptional pilot and well qualified to be an F-16 instructor pilot for the incoming students from pilot training. Moreover, flying the line with students on a frequent basis provided him good insight on the training squadrons and also the quality of maintenance. In the afternoon, the colonel and I went to the F100 engine shop, always a place with a heavy workload. The atmosphere was a cause for concern. F100 maintenance personnel had been working twelve hours a day, seven days a week for an extended period, and appeared to beat down by the workload. Their morale was in the toilet. I'd learned from Col. Bob Baxter that forming engine repair teams and giving every team a monthly quota with extended days off as a reward when they met the quota prior to month's end worked miracles for him. The F100 was modular compared to the unitary J79 Colonel Baxter had in his F-4 aircraft, but the concept should work with either engine. The shop chief was brought into the discussion but proved very negative about the team/quota concept. One of his concerns was the modular makeup of the engine. The F100 engine modules varied in failure rate and also in time to repair. His point was they didn't repair engines, but rather modules of engines. Then they assembled the good modules with a repaired module and checked its performance on the test stand. I suggested that they give maintenance personnel points for each module repaired, with the more difficult modules earning higher points. I opined they would not get the module points correctly assigned initially, but could adjust as they learned the difficulty relationships. Under the proposed repair concept, a module team would get time off when they achieved the required number of points. Pushback on my team concept was coming from all directions: the deputy commander for maintenance, chief of maintenance, engine shop chief, and the wing commander.

I backed off and was driven by Colonel Fogleman to his office, which was near the flight line and my T-39 poised for the flight back to Shaw. It was Friday evening and time for a decision. Rarely did I give direct orders, but there was proof at Homestead AFB, Florida, that the team concept for engine repair worked, and worked well. I gave the following direction to Colonel Fogleman:

> Go back to the engine repair shop after I leave and give everyone the weekend off! The troops were really dragging and needed a rest.

> Tell the shop chief and his bosses that you will meet with them Monday morning to develop a "point system" for engine modules and start the team concept. Modify the points as necessary as the concept evolves.

> Reduce the workday to ten hours, then nine, then eight. The teams will work as long as necessary on their own to get the points they need for extended time off.

Do not tell them this is my idea, but rather your own idea after you had time to reflect on the discussion we had in the shop.

Don't worry about the loss of a weekend of work. The engine shop technicians are so tired, they wouldn't accomplish much anyway. Moreover, their families or girlfriends will be happy to have them around.

I called Colonel Fogleman in a couple of weeks to see how the idea was working. He reported that they had made minor adjustments to the points, and it was likely that two of the five teams would get from three to five days off at the end of the month. It was a resounding success—thanks to Colonel Baxter's pioneering the team concept. We transplanted the idea to all 9th AF wings, and I shared what we were doing with Lieutenant General Gregory at 12th AF. Jet engines were no longer the primary item for aircraft being grounded.

We also talked about the fact that the MacDill AFB officers' club had been losing money for the last several months. The demographics at MacDill suggested it should be beating all the other 9th AF officers' clubs in making a profit. First, MacDill was host to a large Unified Command, CENTCOM, that entertained hordes of TDY visitors, most of whom frequented the club for their meals. The air force mission at MacDill was Combat Crew Training in the F-16. There were hundreds of TDY students living in bachelor officer quarters and eating at the O'club and partying there at Friday night happy hours. In addition, MacDill was a magnet for cross-country flights to log flying time. With all of the above factors bringing in business, how could the O'club lose money unless their business plan was terribly flawed? I told Ron I'd send the resident auditors from Shaw down to take a look at the O'club books at no cost to him. This was based on my own experience with the O'club at Aviano AB, Italy. Two days after the auditors arrived at MacDill, the club manager, a chief master sergeant, committed suicide. A year previously, he had set himself up as both the ordering authority and the receiving authority for food and other supplies. This is an absolute no-no in any business, but he got away with it for a while! He made deals with suppliers so he could order high, get short deliveries, and split the difference with the suppliers. It didn't take him long to embezzle $400,000 from the club. I regret that he took his life, vice a year or two in prison at Fort Leavenworth's Federal Penitentiary, but that was his choice.

The CENTAF Air Campaign Plan that I briefed at the Corona somehow received a lot of publicity. As a result, requests came from all the service war colleges for me to brief their student bodies. While the briefing was given at Corona in twenty minutes, it took over two hours in an academic setting. The Air Campaign Plan turned out to be very instructive for students in the grade of lieutenant colonel and colonel. It was 1985, thirteen years after the Vietnam War ended; most of the students hadn't served in Vietnam, and certainly none who flew combat missions there had any idea of how a campaign plan came together and how a frag order was generated. At the Industrial War College, there came a question from an army colonel that was new and unexpected. It was "Why didn't you formulate a plan to defeat the Soviets in Iran?"

I told him there were two reasons why the plan didn't envision winning even though that was a distinct possibility if the interdiction phase was as effective as expected. Those two reasons were "First, our masters in Washington tasked us to formulate a plan to delay the Soviet Force in their thrust to reach the Strait of Hormuz for as long as possible. Second, the forces provided for the ground campaign were largely airborne and air assault forces plus the 24th ID and Marine MEF with some armor. By and large, the American forces were greatly overmatched in numbers and armored vehicles by the expected Soviet Army Group!" To say the least, the student body wasn't happy with the answer! On the other hand, I applauded their desire to defeat the postulated Soviet forces. Their feelings echoed mine.

The CENTCOM Army Units CENTAF supported were great places for me to visit, although their commanders were treated far better at Shaw AFB than I was on visits to the field. Their commanders were hosted at the officers' club along with the key 9th AF staff to a six-course meal centered on steak or prime rib. When I visited Eighteenth Airborne Corps at Fort Bragg, or one of their subordinate divisions, we dined on Meals, Ready-to-Eat (MREs) in a tent, and I didn't get to choose the entrée. There was one exception, and that was lunch with Major General and Mrs. Schwarzkopf at their quarters. I met some outstanding army generals in these exchanges: Maj. Gen. Jack Galvin and Maj. Gen. Norm Schwarzkopf, 24th ID; Maj. Gen. Jim Lindsey, Eighty-Second Airborne Division; Lt. Gen. Bill Livsey, Third Army commander; and Maj. Gen. Jim Thompson, 101st Airborne Division.

My favorite army unit to visit was the 24th ID at Fort Stewart, Georgia. They always had something for me to do that helped me better understand what soldering was about. On one visit, Maj. Gen. Jack Galvin drove me out in a driving rain to an M-60 tank on maneuvers. My job was to become a member of the tank crew and fire some projectiles at a tank silhouette two miles down range and barely visible in the distance. The task was fairly simple: position a set of crosshairs on the silhouette, press a button that laser-ranged the distance to the target, alert the crew, and fire the round. The report came back that the sabot round hit the target. Next, we fired an inert high-explosive round that apparently also hit the target. It was pretty close quarters in that tank, and the loader had to squeeze into a small space on the left side so the recoiling gun wouldn't smash him. I jumped out and asked General Galvin if I could fire another round. His face said he wished he could say yes as he told me I'd already fired more rounds than a combat-ready crew was allocated for a year. Sad, but that is all the readiness training the army could afford. Fortunately, the air force had inexpensive practice bombs that simulated a real bomb's ballistics, and aircraft ammunition was much cheaper. On the other hand, a fighter pilot was indeed fortunate if he got to fire an air-to-air guided missile short of real combat.

My next conversation with General Galvin was considerably different. The first call came from the 354th wing commander at Myrtle Beach AFB, South Carolina, to inform me that one of their A-10 pilots had erroneously fired the aircraft's 30 mm cannon on a 24th ID M-60 tank, knocking the turret off of its bearings, disabling the tank. Fortunately, no one was hurt. The circumstances were unusual at best. The Twenty-Fourth was on maneuvers against a hypothetical enemy and called for close air support against some old derelict tanks on a tactical range. The 354th responded with a pair of A-10s who reported to a forward air controller (FAC) for an update on the tactical situation and for marking the target. As this was taking place, a real 24th ID tank crew heard the A-10s overhead and moved to the edge of the clearing holding the derelict tank targets to watch the show. They were standing behind their tank when the airborne FAC marked the derelict tank with a 2.75-inch rocket tipped with a white smoke warhead. The smoke mark was good, but the wind drifted it toward the real M-60 tank with the crew standing behind it. When the first A-10 rolled in to fire its 30 mm Gatling gun, the tank crew realized they were the target and ducked behind their tank for protection. Enough of the depleted uranium rounds hit the M-60 tank's turret to knock it off its bearings. I immediately called General Galvin to report the incident and apologize for the mistake. Imagine my surprise when the general expressed his congratulations to the wing for their marksmanship and his appreciation for what an A-10 could do to support his soldiers in combat. I kept trying to express my apologies, but he kept brushing them aside with praise for the A-10, saying it was the tanker's fault for entering the tactical range and that the tank was easily repaired. Gen. Jack Galvin went on to earn his fourth star as commander SOUTHCOM and then as SACEUR in NATO.

The 347th TFW equipped with F-4s at Moody AFB, Georgia, was a good unit. They were accident-free for a number of years, and maintenance statistics were solid; but in my view, there was something lacking. They just didn't seem to be improving and keeping pace with other 9th AF wings. It was time for the wing commander to move on, and I was very fortunate to break Col. Harold "Hal" Hermes free to take the reins. Unfortunately, the timing was bad, and the TAC/IG showed up about a month after the change of command for an operational readiness inspection (ORI). The wing's performance was not pretty, and they failed the ORI. Senior commanders usually attend ORI outbriefs by the IG for one of two reasons: to congratulate the wing commander for a job well done, or to pick up the pieces and provide help where necessary. I was there for the latter. After the inspector general finished briefing the results of the wing's unsatisfactory performance, Colonel Hermes responded with brevity, saying all the right things. Most importantly, that the IG's report would be his blueprint for getting the wing back on the right track and that they looked forward to the IG's return for the opportunity to prove they could perform their mission in an outstanding manner. Hal was soft spoken and low key, but it was clear to all in the base theater that he was dead serious!

Some will understand that failing an ORI does not enhance the resume of any of the wing's leadership team, whether it is operations, maintenance, or base support. A wing has approximately ninety days to prepare for a retake of the ORI. That three-month period is jam packed with long hours and hard work as the subordinate units that received unsatisfactory or marginal ratings practice to correct their deficiencies. Others that were satisfactory strive for outstanding ratings to prove their professional competence. Every weekend would be full of work, and nights would be used to practice loading out a large percentage of the 347th Wing's seventy-two F-4s with conventional and nuclear weapons. The role of Ninth Air Force was to provide helpers to improve checklists and perform the role of surrogate inspectors when the 347th Wing was ready for a preliminary evaluation.

When the IG ORI team returned, the wing's overall performance was outstanding, even though the best rating that can be awarded on a retake is satisfactory. However, the IG made it clear that the 347th TFW performance was the best they had seen in years and congratulated wing personnel for setting the example for others. Col. Hal Hermes made the difference; there were no other personnel changes in the wing. Hal went on to make the 347th TFW even better over the remainder of his first year in command and was rewarded with a richly deserved promotion to brigadier general for his work at Moody AFB and on previous assignments.

A wide net was cast to find a replacement for Brigadier General Hermes. I talked to senior commanders throughout TAC and reviewed at least a hundred personnel folders of highly recommended colonels. One name kept coming forward—that of Col. Buster C. Glosson, currently in the Fighter Weapons Wing at Nellis AFB, Nevada. His wing commander spoke very highly of him and recommended him for command. I hired him to lead the 347th TFW and officiated at the change of command between him and Brig. Gen. Hal Hermes.

A few weeks later, I was back at Moody to put the calipers on Colonel Glosson and get a feel for how he was doing. At that juncture, the 347th was one of the four premier wings in Ninth Air Force—it was important to keep it running smoothly and at its best. Colonel Glosson assembled his key staff in the wing's conference room and provided me a briefing of how he was going to make the 347th even better. The briefing was full of "I" and "me," as in "I'm doing this," etc. There were no "we," "us," or "our" in an hour-long rundown on the wing. After that, I had some time with Buster as we drove around the base in his staff car. I cautioned him about not giving his staff any credit for anything that was being done in the wing and suggested he be more inclusive with his staff. I also pointed out that the 347th TFW was one of the top performing wings in TAC and that searching out weaker points and making them stronger was a good thing, but that a wholesale makeover of the wing in his image was likely to be a failure. I also pointed out that his predecessor was somewhat of a hero in 347th's history, and he should be careful to credit Hal for the wing's success while striving to make things better where appropriate. I used General Creech as an example, noting that while Generals Creech and Dixon had their differences, General Creech always praised General Dixon, saying words to the effect, "We are fortunate that General Dixon brought us this far. It's up to us to take it to the next level!" I also pointed out that General Creech always used the words "we" and "us." not "I" and "me." There was one thing for certain: Colonel Glosson had energy and ambition; hopefully and with proper mentoring, those traits would benefit the 347th TFW.

I made several more visits to the 347th TFW but never had the opportunity to spend much time on the flight line talking to crew chiefs and maintenance specialists or in the engine shop or other back shops.

It seemed that the chamber of commerce always wanted to host me at some special event or ask me to speak on the future of Moody AFB, Georgia. Several years later, a member of the Valdosta, Georgia, Chamber of Commerce paid me an office call while visiting Colorado Springs. I was the commander NORAD and USSPACECOM at the time. It was good to see Parker Laite, who was always supportive of the 347th TFW, military personnel, and their families. During our conversation, he brought up Buster Glosson and asked if I enjoyed all those social functions they sponsored on the occasion of my visits to Moody AFB. I said, "I had to be honest, and while I certainly enjoyed their hospitality, I would rather have been prowling around the wing and talking with airmen." What he said next set me back a lot. Parker told me that Buster Glosson insisted that the chamber have a function for me on every visit to Moody AFB to get me off the base and out of his hair for as long as they could. Enough said!

It was a sad day, but it was inevitable—Gen. Wilbur L. Creech was retiring, but his legacy of continuous improvements in both combat capability and quality of life would live on. It is almost an understatement to report that his six years as commander were the golden years of the Tactical Air Command. Every measure of the command had improved:

> more flying hours per aircraft and pilot
> higher aircraft in-commission rates, with no increase in spare parts
> more realistic training, more and bigger Red Flag exercises
> reintroduction of worldwide gunnery competition
> high standards for all air base functions
> significantly improved air base appearance
> higher esprit, improved readiness, and much more

It was September 1984 when all the commanders of Tactical Air Command units across the United States gathered at Langley AFB, Virginia, to bid him farewell and welcome in his successor, Gen. Jerome F. O'Malley. As mentioned earlier, Gen. "Jerry" O'Malley was the PACAF commander, and most of us viewed his posting to TAC as a way to better prepare him to move up to replace General Gabriel as the air force chief of staff in a couple of years. At the change of command, General Creech spoke eloquently and graciously about the improvements we had together worked so hard to bring about and cautioned us to keep making the air force and TAC better in combat and on the home front. General O'Malley was gracious and appropriately short in accepting the mantle of leadership for TAC.

Following the obligatory social function, General O'Malley assembled all the numbered air force, direct reporting centers, and wing commanders to start us off in a *new* direction! He went so far as to suggest he was going to bring in some real tactical experts, like Maj. Gen. Fred Haeffner and Brig. Gen. Tom McInerney. The former major general "Fat Freddie," as he was known to his friends, led a storied career that was always on the brink of disaster—like the time he advocated to General Dixon that all F-15s be manufactured with a rear seat facing backward to detect enemy aircraft closing in at six o'clock. Fat Freddie called it the "Janus" concept. Major General Haeffner was credited with downing a MiG-17, plus an assist on another and two more probables during the Vietnam War. He had credibility in the fighter world, but not necessarily as a leader. In that short meeting, I learned that one should never speak poorly of your predecessor's work because it makes you look much, much smaller.

Lt. Gen. Jack Gregory, commander 12th AF, and I just continued on course, knowing that it would all sort out shortly, and it did. At the following TAC Commanders' Conference, TAC received the Air Force Flying Safety Award for the best flying safety record in the air force, and Ninth Air Force for the best record in TAC. Not too shabby for needing new direction.

General Kingston held a Commanders' Conference for his component commanders in the early winter of 1985, where he laid out in some detail the direction for CENTCOM and its components. It was a comprehensive road map and something we could all jointly contribute to. That evening, he served dinner in his quarters followed by further discussions. His aide called me aside and said that I had a phone call that I could take in the kitchen. The caller was Col. Ralph "Ed" Eberhart, General Gabriel's executive officer. Ed wanted to know if I was in position to take a call from the chief. I explained to Ed that there was no privacy at the CINC's quarters, and it would be better if I could call General Gabriel in a couple of hours when I returned to the BOQ. He insisted that the chief wanted to call me and would call the BOQ room at 2300 hours on the dot!

I was puzzled! It was highly unusual for the chief to call someone working for another four-star general; it was usually your boss that called to chew you out for some transgression, and I couldn't think of anything I might have done that would rise to General Gabriel's level. I wasn't looking forward to the call. I left General Kingston's quarters early, poured myself a glass of wine, and waited for the phone to ring! I had been a three-star for almost four years, and there didn't appear to be any other assignments that seemed appropriate for someone with my background. I suspected that General Gabriel was calling to thank me for my service and ask me to retire because the air force had someone else in mind to lead Ninth Air Force. Well, it had been a challenging and fun ride for a guy who, early on, was hoping to reach the rank of major prior to retirement. The phone rang, and I picked up the receiver with "Pete Piotrowski here, sir!"

The voice on the other end said, "Pete, will you accept a fourth star and be the vice chief?"

I was dumbfounded; the only response I could come up with was "General Gabriel, this is Pete Piotrowski—is that whom you wanted to call?"

The response was confirming: "Yes, Pete, will you be my vice chief?"

"Yes, sir, I'll do my best!" Then he covered some of the administrative details about sending my nomination to the White House before it could be announced and that General Welch's reassignment as commander SAC had to be approved prior to the announcement of my moving up. He said I could tell Sheila, if she could keep a secret. Wow, that was a turn of events I could never have imagined.

It was April 20, and I had just finished participating as the guest speaker at the NATO E-3A base in Geilenkirchen, Germany. I left for the BOQ early to get a good night's sleep prior to moving onward to Saudi Arabia and Oman when the call came. It was the Air Force Command Center in the Pentagon calling to inform me that General O'Malley and his wife were killed in a T-39 crash at a small airstrip in Pennsylvania. It appeared the brakes had failed and the T-39 ran off the end of the runway into a canyon—there were no survivors. I asked if the chief had requested my return or was it OK for me to finish my preplanned series of visits with high-ranking government officials in Saudi Arabia and Oman. The duty officer said it was my decision; there was no requirement for me to return. With a heavy heart for the O'Malley family and the air force, I continued my trip.

In Saudi Arabia, I met with Prince Turki bin Faisal Al Saud, one of the most powerful young princes and subsequently the head of the Saudi Intelligence apparatus. Prince Turki gave me a tour of Dhahran Air Base on the east coast of the Arabian Peninsula, and we discussed the deployment of CENTAF fighters to Dhahran in the event of a threat to peace in the region. He was very much in agreement of the concept and promised full support. Promises are always easy to make but sometimes never kept. When Iraq invaded Kuwait in August 1990, Prince Turki and the Saudi government honored their commitments. From Saudi Arabia, I went south across the Rub' al Khali, "Empty Quarter," to Muscat, Oman, where I visited all the propositioned stock locations and maintenance personnel, and met with Air Vice Marshall Bennett prior to departing for Germany and on to Shaw AFB.

On the long flight home, there was ample time to ponder the various permutations that could result from General O'Malley's tragic and untimely death. The senior officers most qualified to take his place were Gen. Larry Welch, Lt. Gen. Jack Gregory, and me. I put myself as most qualified, having served as commander ADTAC, TAC/DO, TAC vice commander, and 9th AF commander in sequence over the past six years. In addition, currency in all TAC fighter aircraft, except for the A-10, was a big plus. I was curious to find out what decisions had been made in my absence. Back at Shaw, I learned that Gen. Robert Russ had been nominated for his fourth star and selected to replace Gen. Jerry O'Malley as commander TAC. Both General Welch and I would continue to SAC and the Air Staff, respectively.

Colonel Fogleman received a richly deserved promotion to brigadier general and was reassigned. His replacement was Col. Jimmy Cash. Shortly after the change of command, there was a tragic accident on a training mission in which the F-16 student pilot was killed when his aircraft plunged into the Gulf of Mexico. I appointed a rated colonel from the 9th AF Logistics Staff to head the accident board and determine the cause of the mishap. While the board was proceeding with their investigation, General Russ called to share with me that he had received phone calls from pilots at MacDill AFB, suggesting that the accident board appeared to be covering up the true cause of the accident. There is always bar talk about an accident until the results are in, vetted by intermediate commanders and their staff, and finally briefed to and approved by the major command commander, in this case, General Russ. If there was something amiss, I had to get to the bottom of it and salvage the accident board's work. Colonel Cash, the wing commander, offered his opinion that the accident was caused by pilot error on the student's part. The mishap occurred on the second engagement in a one-versus-one air-to-air training engagement. There are several "knock it off" (KIO) points in every engagement to reduce the possibility of a mishap. For example, the instructor pilot is supposed to call out over the radio, "Knock it off," when the objective of the lesson has been learned or if it can't be learned because of circumstances. In addition, there is a KIO if either of the aircraft reaches an altitude of ten thousand feet above the gulf. There is also a KIO call if the airspeed of one of the aircraft goes below 200 knots indicated airspeed (IAS).

I asked if I could review the IP's heads-up display (HUD) recording. Colonel Cash called for it, and we both watched it in his office. The HUD tape would show what was happening from the instructor's aircraft perspective and what the instructor pilot was seeing. What the HUD video revealed was very instructive. The first engagement, which started from a neutral position as each aircraft passed abeam each other, was won in short order by the student pilot. His tactics and aircraft control against a much more experienced pilot were excellent. The second engagement also started from an abeam neutral position, but this time, the instructor gained an early advantage and pressed the attack. Clearly, the object of the lesson had been learned, but the IP failed to call KIO and continued to press the attack. In a few more seconds, the HUD display indicated the IP had passed through the ten-thousand-foot floor and still didn't call KIO. The HUD also showed that the IP aircraft was below the KIO IAS and closing on the student, indicating the student's aircraft was well below the KIO IAS—still no KIO. As the IP continued to press the attack, we observed the student's F-16 depart from controlled flight. The student didn't eject when his aircraft departed from controlled flight. Evidently, he was trying to recover the aircraft.

I asked Colonel Cash if he had previously reviewed the HUD tape, and he acknowledged he had. I was tempted to relieve him on the spot for dereliction of duty. Next, I met with the board president, whom I had appointed, and through a series of questions, learned that he had a conflict of interest that he previously failed to disclose. It turned out that the instructor pilot who caused the mishap and student pilot's death was in fact a student of the board president when the latter was an IP at a pilot training wing. They had become friends, and that friendship destroyed the accident board president's objectivity, so I relieved him on the spot and replaced him with another officer to lead the mishap investigation. General Russ was back-briefed on the findings and actions taken.

General Russ was a longtime TAC pilot and wing commander, and served on the TAC Staff as the Assistant DO. But most recently, he served on the Air Staff in the DCS/Requirements and was extremely well respected on Capitol Hill, where he spent a lot of time keeping senators and representatives current on fighter acquisition programs. He was also an avid golfer and found that a convenient way to spend time with important members of Congress on weekends.

On one of his many swings through TAC bases, he spent some time at England AFB, Louisiana, home of the 23rd TFW Flying Tigers, proud holders of the Flying Tiger volunteer heritage. The original Flying Tigers flew obsolete P-40 aircraft under the leadership of Gen. Claire Lee

Chennault against the Japanese invading China during WW II. The P-40 was substantially inferior to the Japanese Zero; however, through superior tactics devised by General Chennault, the Flying Tigers outfought the Zeros by a significant margin. At the time of General Russ's visit, the Twenty-Third Wing was equipped with A-10 Thunderbolt II aircraft. When word from the command post indicated General Russ was back at Langley, I called to ask if he had discovered any problems at England AFB that required my attention. He said there were a few and reeled them off as follows:

> mildew in the shingles on the roof of the golf clubhouse
> tee box markers needed replacement
> golf carts needed to be upgraded with Plexiglas windshields
> most golf carts needed some repair

I was delighted that there wasn't any mission or aircraft maintenance problems that needed attention. I called Col. Peter Foley, 23rd TFW commander, and gave him the report received from General Russ. He heard the problems firsthand and was already taking corrective action. Pete was a solid wing commander; I didn't have any concerns about him and of his ability to lead the 23rd TFW. When I finished talking with Pete, I called the rest of the wing commanders with golf courses on their bases and told them that the appearance of the clubhouse, tee box markers, golf carts, and golf course appearance in general were high on General Russ's list of interest items.

In May 1985, General Gabriel's exec, Col. Ed Eberhart, called to inform that the chief was inviting my wife and me to accompany General and Mrs. Gabriel and others on a swing through Europe. The trip would include stops in Scotland, England, Paris (to attend the Air Chiefs' Conference being held there during the Paris Air Show), Germany, and Turkey. It would be an opportunity for us to get better acquainted with the General and Mrs. Gabriel as well as other senior members of the Air Staff. All we had to do is show up at the hangar where the Speckled Trout, the chief's C-135 aircraft, was kept. The KC-135 was primarily used as a test aircraft for advanced communications equipment that would eventually be installed in Air Force One and SAC's operational aircraft. The unusual name came from the secretary of the KC-135 project office who, I'm told, had an abundantly freckled face.

The trip started exactly on time, with everyone on board anticipating a very informative trip. It was Sheila's and my first opportunity to meet Mrs.

Gabriel, who was a very charming lady with a strong Southern heritage. Our first stop was an RAF Base in northern Scotland. From there, we drove to Saint Andrews, where General Gabriel had a business golf outing with his British counterpart, the chief of the Royal Air Force. Sheila and I shopped the local area for souvenirs. We especially enjoyed the charm and history of the Old Course clubhouse. Watching the British Open Golf Tournament over the years since then has brought back fond memories of the visit and the stay in a quaint hotel on the Old Course that existed years prior to the Revolutionary War.

The next stop was London, where General Gabriel and I continued discussions with the RAF leadership. As our host would say, "It was all good stuff!" From there, Speckled Trout flew the entourage to Paris, where we all checked into a low-end hotel only to find the room rates upward of $300 per day, more than double what was advertised when the reservations were booked. In response to query, we were told that the rates were elevated because the French Tennis Open and Paris Air Show were running concurrently. Everything was more than double the usual fare, even at the McDonald's on the Champs-Elysees just down from the Arc de Triomphe. It was going to be a budget-breaking three days but worth every penny.

The Paris Air Show was very educational! There were a number of pavilions rented by international aircraft and avionics manufactures showing off their newest products. Most were from the United States; the second largest representation was from the Soviet Union flying their latest-model fighter and transport aircraft, including the world's largest, the AN-124. In addition, a number of NATO nations' aerobatics teams flew daily. General Gabriel spent most of his time meeting with air chiefs from around the world. The Paris and British Air Shows continually prove to be a useful conference for cementing relationships, scheduling exchange visits and exercises with friends and allies, and generating interest in foreign military sales of US aerospace products. If memory serves me correctly, General Gabriel hosted a Global Air Chiefs' Conference in Las Vegas and Nellis Air Force Base, Nevada, a couple of years later.

Mrs. Gabriel gave Sheila a course in international antique buying—and to show off her newly acquired skills. Sheila purchased a few items that still grace our home. The Gabriels also arranged for most of the official party to enjoy an evening at one of Paris's finest underground (in the basement) restaurants—it was delightful, even though we didn't have the foggiest idea what we were eating! Due to the strain on the travel budget, most of the staff, along with Sheila and me, were eating at McDonald's the last evening in Paris. We justified it as an evening stroll to the Arc de Triomphe and down the Champs-Elysees! Sheila and I were almost run over by the six lanes of never-ending traffic circling around the arc. Once safely across, a Parisian local showed us the stairs that led to the underground crossing. It was much less stressful getting back to the hotel. Next on the Itinerary was a day-long visit to Ramstein Air Base, Germany, home to USAFE and Fourth Allied Tactical Air Forces. From there, we flew to Ankara, Turkey, where General Gabriel and I met with the leadership of the Turkish air force. When the visit ended, Colonel Eberhart pulled me aside and said that Sheila and I had passed the test and that orders to Washington would follow shortly.

Lessons Learned

If you spend 95 percent of your time wisely selecting your subordinates, the 5 percent remaining is all you will need to run the enterprise!

The success of any large enterprise depends largely on the performance of subordinate units! Therefore, you are always training and mentoring your subordinate leaders!

Leading a large geographically dispersed enterprise requires attention to leading indicators and the knowledge of what the trends indicate. It also requires personal visits to low-performing organizations and a keen understanding of where to look and what to look for!

The ultimate responsibility of the commander is the preparation of subordinate units to prevail in combat. If a subordinate commander is inept, he/she must be replaced for the good and success of the unit in combat.

Three primary ingredients for the success of any enterprise are strong involved leadership at all levels, hard work, and a strong commitment to succeed!

All organizations thrive on strong visionary and involved leadership! Conversely, organizations with weak or uninvolved leadership struggle and usually decline.

Never speak poorly of your predecessor; it only makes you look poorly.

These rules apply equally well to the competitive world of business.

Lt. Gen. Pete checks out in the F-16, MacDill AFB, FL

Central Command (CENTCOM), Gen. Robert Kingston,
CINC with Lt. Gens. Jack MacMull, Ernie Cheatham, and Pete
as Service Component Commanders. MacDill AFB, FL

Lt. Gen. Pete's last flight in the F-16. Shaw AFB, SC

Gen. Pete receives Order of the Sword from CMSgt
Ken Meeks, 9th AF. Shaw AFB, SC

CHAPTER 15

Air Force Vice Chief

On August 1, 1985, there was a quiet pinning ceremony in General Gabriel's office to assume the rank of general and become the air force's vice chief of staff. Theoretically, the position made me the second ranking general in the air force; however, I always paid due respect to those who were promoted ahead of me. The Air Force Civilian Leadership was as good as it can get. Secretary of the air force, Vern Orr, was a good outside man and kept the political wolves at bay as a friend of President Reagan and Secretary of Defense Casper Weinberger. Air Force undersecretary, Edward C. "Pete" Aldridge, had two full-time jobs; the second was as the director, NRO, with an annual budget of over $10 billion. The most important thing for me was to understand how the Air Staff functioned and to meet all the deputy chiefs of staff, or DCSs, most of them I knew from previous assignments, but some I didn't. The first stop was to the DCS/Personnel, Lt. Gen. Duane Cassidy. I knew Duane from our debates on where to assign Air Force Special Operations Forces. He was a hard charger and highly respected with service in both the Strategic Air Command and Military Air Transport Service. Duane explained air force personnel policies, my role in general officer assignments, and the key issues of the day. The session lasted about four hours, and when it was over, I asked Duane if he had ever considered me for the TAC commander's job after General O'Malley's tragic accident. His response was immediate and passionate: "I ran down to the chief's office and said you were the perfect choice to replace General O'Malley—you already commanded half of TAC and had been the TAC vice commander previously and were a disciple of General Creech. General Gabriel's response was 'I want Pete as my vice chief!' and that ended the conversation."

General Gabriel had assembled a great team to support him in running the air force, and it was my pleasure to work with them in helping our chief be a good steward of the air force. In actuality, the chief worked outside the air force on a daily basis with Secretary of Defense Casper Weinberger, Deputy Secretary William H. Taft, and the various DOD assistant secretaries, the JCS, and the Congress. The vice chief generally was looking inside the air force, providing guidance to the Air Staff and the operational commands. The biggest part of the job was getting direction from the chief on the various issues and providing feedback on how things were progressing. The deputy chiefs of staff at the time were

> Lt. Gen. Harley Hughes, DCS/Plans and Operations; background: fighters and bombers. Harley was also the operations deputy for JCS matters—a very important role.

> Lt. Gen. Merrill "Tony" McPeak, DCS/Programs and Resources; background: fighters

> Lt. Gen. Leo Marquez, DCS/Logistics; background: air defense fighters and maintenance/logistics

> Lt. Gen. Bernard P. Randolph, DCS/Research and Development; background: airlift and space systems development

> Lt. Gen. Duane Cassidy, DCS/Personnel; background: airlift

> Lt. Gen. Michael A. Nelson, inspector general; background: tactical fighters

I enjoyed working with all of them; they were a good team of highly experienced professional and very helpful to me!

One of the vice chief's many jobs was to sit on the Joint Requirements Oversight Council, or JROC, to review all Category 1 and 1A acquisition programs. At that time, the JROC consisted of only the service vice chiefs with the JROC chairman's position rotating among the service vice chiefs every six months. Today, with a JCS vice chairman mandated by the Goldwater/Nichols Bill, the JROC is chaired by the JCS vice chairman and the deputy sec def.

At the time, I joined the JROC in the summer of 1985. Gen. Maxwell "Max" Thurman was the army's vice chief, Adm. Ron Hays was the navy's vice chief and JROC chairman, and Gen. John K. Davis was the Marine Corps vice commandant. The JROC was an important body in the acquisition process. Their job was to ensure every individual service requirement was considered by all services as a potential joint requirement. It was tougher than turning lead into gold, as each service didn't want to complicate its acquisition process with joint requirements that would add to the cost and stretch the time to fielding of the system by having to include sister service requirements in the design. However, there were some successes, most of which were in electronics and communications systems. The JROC met as often as required so as not to unduly extend the acquisition process with bureaucratic foot dragging.

Admiral Hays, a highly decorated fighter pilot, was nominated to take the reins of the Pacific Command (PACOM) and moved to his headquarters at Camp Smith, Hawaii. Gen. Max Thurman was next in line to assume the JROC chair for six months. The golden age of the JROC by my recollection was when Gen. Max Thurman served as the chairman. We were friends from 1974 when I met him at Aviano. Always a no-nonsense, make-it-happen kind of leader, things moved smartly and effectively under his leadership. A service chief had to have very strong and cogent reasons to reject a service acquisition from becoming a joint acquisition under his watchful eye. Admiral Hays was succeeded by Adm. Huntington "Hunt" Hardisty as the navy vice and joined the JROC. Subsequently, it was the air force's turn, and I moved into the JROC chair. Every major service acquisition program manager (PM) had to come before the JROC to describe the end product and explain why it was or was not suited to be joined by one or more other services. Whether or not the PM believed there was benefit for his program or for another service to be joined with the program, it was the business of the JROC to probe the issue of jointness to determine if there was merit. It was our collective goal to do what was right in this regard, but at the same time to keep our deliberations and the demands on the PMs minimal to avoid delaying a program with bureaucratic meddling. In hindsight, I believe we were faithful to those principals. Admiral Hardisty was only in the Pentagon long enough to become a good friend, and he was reassigned as commander in chief PACOM to replace Admiral Hays. His replacement was Adm. James "Jim" Busey, another outstanding individual and fighter pilot.

As the vice chief, it was necessary to become space savvy because the air force was the DOD's lead agency for satellites and space launch. Hence, I was immersed in several days of training behind the "green door" leading to 4C1000 where all the USAF and National Reconnaissance Office (NRO) programs were contrived and controlled. At that time, the NRO was a highly classified organization, hidden inside the air force but still an independent organization. Its very existence was classified, and the acronym "NRO" could only be used inside a Sensitive Compartmented Intelligence Facility, or SCIF. The NRO was officially declassified on September 18, 1992, by the deputy secretary of defense, as recommended by the director of central intelligence (DCI). The upside was the air force played a big role in space, both in the "white" open world and the "black" highly classified realm. The downside was that when the services were issued a 10 percent across-the-board budget cut, the air force top line would drop from $100 billion to $90 billion, but we couldn't deficit the hidden intelligence/black space portion. As a result, air force acquisition and day-to-day operations suffered 10 percent more than the other services.

Space system capabilities opened a whole new world of exotic and expensive satellites capable of doing unimaginable things from the far reaches of space. In the mid-1980s, there was a Unified Space Command, Air Force Space Command, Navy Space Command, and a small but extremely well-led Army Space Command. All were bit players compared to the NRO that built and operated most of the nation's intelligence, reconnaissance, and surveillance space systems. Not a lot more can be said here because most of what was highly classified then, still is.

One of the things that I took away from my immersion in space is how the Air Force Space Command (AFSPACECOM) in Colorado Springs, Colorado, was subordinated to the Unified Space Command, or USSPACECOM, a Joint Command under the Unified Command Plan (UCP). Air Force Gen. Robert Herres, who was also commander NORAD and Air Force Space Command, commanded USSPACECOM. I was troubled by the incestuous relationship of General Herres being dual hatted as the commander USSPACECOM and commander of Air Force Space Command, one of his three service components. There were three reasons for this. First, a Unified commander should be seen as evenhanded when dealing with his/her components. That is a hard image to create when you command both the parent and subordinate unit. Second, a Unified commander needs unbridled and honest advice from his service components. The emperor needs to be told he has no cloths. That kind of advice is hard to get when you're talking to yourself or, no better, when the future of vice commander, Maj. Gen. Maurice "Tim" Padden, day-to-day leader of Air Force Space Command, is controlled by General Herres instead of the service chief of staff. Third, there is not enough time in the day, month, or year for one person to effectively lead three diverse commands. At best, at least two will suffer from serious neglect and lack of hands-on knowledge by the commander. Last, and I fully admit, it was a parochial service position. There was no path to grow a replacement for General Herres. Commander USSPACECOM was a nominative position—that is, all three services were entitled and encouraged to nominate a candidate to replace General Herres when it was time for him to move on or retire. Thus, absent a viable air force candidate for USSPACECOM, the job would likely go to the navy, the service with the second-largest space presence, and a vice admiral sitting as General Herres's deputy.

After a few days of convincing myself these thoughts were valid, I presented them to General Gabriel; he agreed and asked me to take the issue to General Herres. Much to my surprise, General Bob Herres quickly agreed and said he would take the reorganization issue to Gen. John W. Vessey, chairman, JCS. This was necessary because General Herres was foremost a Unified commander under the UCP, and any changes to his command responsibilities were the purview of the JCS. The chairman and the service chiefs agreed to the recommendation, and Maj. Gen. Tim Padden assumed command of Air Force Space Command, and General Herres had more time to attend to NORAD and USSPACECOM—a win-win situation. The next step in providing a viable air force candidate for US Space Command was to promote Maj. Gen. Tim Padden to a three-star lieutenant general so he would be eligible to move up, or replace him with an air force three-star.

Service vice chiefs also had the responsibility to substitute for their service chiefs in the "tank." The tank is an arcane term from WW II that then described the room the service chiefs (chief of the army and chief of naval operations along with Lt. Gen. Hap Arnold, army air service chief) met in. Evidently, the entrance was something like getting into an army tank, so the room was dubbed the "tank," and the name survived all changes to the venue. The 1980's version of the tank on the Pentagon's second floor was more like a small boardroom. The rectangular conference table was large enough to seat the five principals, chairman and four service chiefs. Seating was by service rank, with the chairman sitting closest to the presentation screen to his left. Rotating clockwise, the army chief, Gen. John Wickham, sat opposite the chairman. The chief of naval operations, Admiral Watkins, sat next to General Wickham's left. At the far end of the table sat the Marine Corps commandant, Gen. P. X. Kelley. Continuing around the table, the air force chief, Gen. Charles Gabriel, sat on the chairman's right. See diagram. There were additional chairs around the room's perimeter for the JCS-J3 and J5 as well as the service operations deputies (J-3s) or others that may have been invited by the chairman.

Army Chief   Navy CNO

Projection   Marine Corps Cmdt

Screen

Chairmen JCS   Air Force Chief

When the JCS met in the tank, the chairman would first introduce the subject under discussion, provide some background, and then ask for comments. Comments from the "chiefs," or their representatives, always started with the United States Army chief and rotated clockwise as indicated in the diagram above. The air force, as the junior service, was always last to speak. Any rebuttals or additional comments required the chairman's approval.

General Vessey was an extraordinary person. He served in WW II, the Korean War, and Vietnam War. He held every enlisted and commissioned rank in the USA, from private to four-star general. While serving as first sergeant at the battle of Anzio, Italy, he received a battlefield commission and rose to the highest military rank and also the highest military position. When he retired in 1985, at the age of sixty-three, he was the longest-serving active-duty member of the United States Army. Other members in order of precedence were Gen. John A. Wickham Jr., USA; Adm. James D. Watkins, USN; Gen. Paul X. Kelley, USMC; and Gen. Charles A. Gabriel, USAF.

The first time I was in the tank for General Gabriel, it was on the issue of the Strategic Nuclear Retaliatory Force composition. As many readers will remember, the TRIAD stood for the three legs of our strategic nuclear deterrent force. There were B-52 bombers on alert at Strategic Air Command bases; Minuteman ICBMs in Montana, Wyoming, and the Dakotas; and Navy ballistic missile submarines on patrol in the Atlantic and Pacific Oceans. The concept of a TRIAD was to ensure that there could be no systemic defect that would take down more than one leg of this three-legged stool. Whenever there were reductions in the total number of nuclear weapons or advances in their capabilities, the issue of how many of each should be retained on active status was studied, and the overall ratio was a highly debated subject for a number of reasons.

The long-standing air force position was

> Land-based missiles are prompt and will get to their Soviet targets first, and they are immutable.

> Bombers on alert will launch ahead of incoming Soviet ICBMs and SLBMs, destroy residual targets in the Warsaw Pact, and carry the preponderance of megatonage.

> Further, bombers that survive can be reloaded and conduct follow-on attacks.

The navy's position on their "boomer" boats was

> Our submarines on patrol are the most survivable nuclear deterrent.

> It should be noted that nuclear submarine patrol areas was one of our nation's closely guarded secrets, and one patrol area covers tens of thousands of square miles in the broad ocean areas. The submarine went to sea with sealed orders to be opened by the captain when they were safely out to sea. Only the captain and the navigator knew where they were going and where in that vast ocean area they would hide. On the downside, the earlier SLBMs, like Polaris and Poseidon, were short-range SLBMs, requiring the subs to sortie from their hides to their launch areas. Also communications with submerged submarines on patrol was not instantaneous and sometimes tenuous.

Warning of a Soviet ICBM/SLBM launch was a critical piece of ensuring ICBMs were not destroyed sitting in their silos or alert bombers destroyed in their alert areas waiting for an order to launch. In the 1985 time frame, the United States had Defense Support Program (DSP) missile warning satellites in orbit that covered the globe from our eastern shores eastward around the globe to our western coastline, and from about sixty-five degrees south latitude to sixty-five degrees north latitude; therefore, there was only a sliver of the Arctic that offered open water for Soviet SLBM launches that was not covered by the DSP Constellation.

However, powerful radars located at Thule, Greenland; Clear Alaska; Fylingdales, UK, and Concrete, North Dakota, covered the far northern latitudes. These radars, along with others looking outward from the east and west coasts, provided a second phenomenology to confirm what the Infrared DSP satellites were reporting. Satellites provided approximately thirty minutes warning of missile launches in the Soviet Union and twenty minutes warning of SLBM launches from the broad ocean areas. Complementary land-based radars provided about twenty minutes of warning to the president and other senior decision makers. Information from DSP satellites and missile warning radar arrived with the speed of light into NORAD's Cheyenne Mountain Command Center near Colorado Springs, Colorado; CINCSAC's Command Center at Offutt AFB, Nebraska, and the National Military Command Center (NMCC) at the Pentagon. Within three minutes of a missile launch that had the "potential" of reaching the United States or Canada, the NMCC defense duty officer would convene a missile warning conference. CINCSAC held the authority to launch the alert bomber and in-flight refueling force to their precautionary orbits for survival awaiting a presidential order. Thus, there was always sufficient time to survive the alert bomber force in the event of missile attack. The future of the TRIAD was on the Joint Chiefs' docket, and General Gabriel was unavailable to attend. His absence required me to represent the air force in the tank on this contentious issue. I wished the chief, with all his experience on this critical issue, would be there to carry the banner. In addition, Gen. John Wickham, CSA, was his West Point classmate and might be an ally, in that the army did not have a strategic nuclear retaliatory capability.

Lt. Gen. Harley Hughes briefed me on all the main and peripheral issues that could arise in the tank and wished me luck when it was necessary to represent General Gabriel at JCS tank sessions. As mentioned earlier, the air force sat next to the chairman and spoke last; at least that would give me an opportunity to listen to all the discussions and frame my own remarks. When General Vessey came into the room, all rose in respect. He shook my hand warmly and welcomed me to the JCS. He turned to me and said, "Pete, it's OK to tell jokes in the tank, but you cannot tell an ethnic joke, as that would be highly inappropriate! Let me give you an example of what is acceptable. You can tell jokes about the Hittites, as their civilization died out thousands of years ago and there are no living Hittites to be offended. Now there were these two Hittites, Sven and Ollie . . . !" We all laughed, and I knew I'd been had. General Vessey was 100 percent Norwegian from a small community in northern Minnesota. My wife is second-generation Norwegian, and I learned from her father that Norwegians love to tell jokes about Swedes, whom they believe are inferior. Sven and Ollie were always the characters in the jokes my father-in-law told.

The chairman invited the JCS briefer to present the issues that revolved around reducing the number of nuclear warheads on alert as part of the Strategic Arms Reduction Talks (START) that had been introduced by Pres. Ronald Reagan at Geneva, Switzerland, on June 29, 1982. Talks were in progress, but agreements would not be reached into well into the future and signed on July 31, 1991. Our meeting was to lay a foundation of understanding for going forward that would be the basis of future discussions in the tank and eventually the DOD input to START negotiations. After some comments by the chairman, he asked for comments. General Wickham argued for caution; Admiral Watkins spoke for some time about the survivability of nuclear-powered submarines on patrol and the wisdom of cutting less survivable systems if the need arose. General Kelley deferred, saying that the Marine Corps had no nuclear weapons. It was my turn, and I used the opportunity to extol the wisdom of the TRIAD, three distinctly different basing modes, three entirely different delivery systems, and individually designed and tested warheads providing a hedge against systemic failure of a single system that could negate our strategic nuclear retaliatory capability. I noted the warning systems would give decision makers time to execute the bombers and silo-based missiles, ensuring their survivability under attack, adding it would give a potential attacker reason to be cautious. I also noted that traitors had divulged our most closely guarded secrets in the past, but it was unlikely that any one person would have access to all the legs of the TRIAD. Last, I noted that communications with submarines on patrol was not instantaneous, and that when ordered to execute the Single Integrated Operations Plan (SIOP), some, if not most, ballistic missile submarines had to sortie to get within range of their assigned targets. Therefore, a balance should be maintained in the TRIAD going forward.

When I finished speaking, General Vessey turned to me and said in a stern voice, "General, the submarines will be where I tell them to be!" And on that note, the tank session ended. My arguments must have had some validity, as the TRIAD still exists to this day.

Shortly thereafter, General Vessey retired, and Adm. William J. Crowe was confirmed as the 11th JCS chairman under President Reagan on October 1, 1985. Admiral Crowe had a master's and doctorate in Politics from Princeton University and was very savvy in the ways of

Washington, starting from his early days as the assistant military aide to President Eisenhower. He was a pleasure to work for as a member of the JCS. I had a special advantage over the others in the tank sitting on his right and being the last to speak. But more than that, Admiral Crowe was a chocolate eater in a big way. Accordingly, each participating member of a JCS tank session had a bowl of Hershey Kisses wrapped in silver foil in front of them. It didn't take long for Admiral Crowe to devour his allocation with a few dozen silver ball wrappers surrounding his position. Shortly after he finished his, I would push my bowl over toward him. Soon it was gone as well, but I believe that small favor gave me a little edge in debate.

The Supreme Allied Commander Europe (SACEUR) and commander EUCOM was one person, Gen. Bernard W. Rogers at that juncture. General Rogers graduated from West Point in June 1943 as the First Captain of Cadets and a Rhodes Scholar. In 1947, he attended Oxford University in England, graduating with a bachelor of arts in Philosophy, Politics, and Economics in 1950. He later received master's degrees in those disciplines. General Rogers was looking for a replacement for his retiring chief of staff, a nominative position that had traditionally been filled by an air force general. Filling a nominative position meant the service filling the position would temporarily gain an additional four-star billet. As such, there was considerable competition for filling nominative positions. General Gabriel called me into his office and advised me that he was going to nominate me for the position of SHAPE chief of staff and that General Rogers had taken a liking to me during one of the tank sessions we both had participated in. With a resounding "Yes, sir," I left the chief's office, trying to think of a better candidate to serve General Rogers. Being number two was not a desirable position; being chief of staff of a political organization was even lower on the totem pole. Then I recalled Lt. Gen. Thomas Richards had served as Gen. Douglas McArthur's personal bodyguard at his headquarters in Japan. Moreover, he was sent to South Korea in June 1951 to join the Twenty-Fifth Division in countering the North Korean Invasion, and was awarded a Silver Star for gallantry and two battle stars on his Combat Infantry Badge. With General Richard's record in hand, I went back to General Gabriel's office and suggested that Lieutenant General Richards would be a slam dunk to be selected for the SHAPE chief of staff position. He agreed, and General Rogers was delighted to have a soldier hero turned air force general as his chief of staff. This was not a one-time thing; General Gabriel called me in on more than one occasion with the news that some command was in trouble and he was going to send me there to get it back on the right track. All these assignments would have been great opportunities, but there was always someone I knew that was better prepared and also richly deserved promotion. I would discuss these ideas with General Cassidy, DCS/Personnel, and with his support, carry them back to General Gabriel.

It was September 1985, the last month in the fiscal year, usually a very busy time for the air force comptroller and program managers, making sure they would spend all the money appropriated and allocated by Congress by the end of the month. For others, it was time to ensure there was enough money to fly the aircraft through the end of the month to maintain aircrew proficiency. This year, there was a unique problem, and that was to test the Vought ASM-135 Antisatellite Weapon (ASAT) before a congressional prohibition against testing ASATs kicked in on October 1, 1985. The Soviets had a very robust launch capability and a co-orbital ASAT that they tested on a regular basis against their own aging satellites or a unique test satellite target. They would launch their ASAT in the same plane as the intended target satellite and catch up with the victim in two or three orbits. The Soviet ASAT would then close on the victim, orient its "onboard shotgun," and fire a barrage of large pellets at the satellite.

The United States did not have an operational ASAT and depended on long-lasting and high-quality satellites, vice a very robust launch capability. If a conflict erupted with the Soviet Union, the United States could be at a serious disadvantage with regard to intelligence collections from space assets. The ASM-135 ASAT was intended both as a deterrent and an operational capability should it be necessary to degrade Soviet space capabilities. It was important to test it to ensure that it would work and to demonstrate its capability to the Soviets. The ASM-135 did not have a first stage and was designed to be launched from an F-15 that would act as the first stage and also launch the ASAT to arrive at a point in space where it could maneuver to be precisely in the path of its victim. Undersecretary Pete Aldridge, along with the DOD Space Community, had identified an aging satellite that had long exceeded its useful life as the target. The only logical intercept window fell on *Friday,* September *13,* 1985. Friday the thirteenth seemed a little foreboding, but it was the only opportunity before the congressional prohibition kicked in at the beginning of the new fiscal year. Secretary Aldridge gave the go-ahead for the test, and preparations were set in motion. The seeker had to be cooled down with nitrogen up to just prior to being uploaded on the F-15, and the F-15 takeoff was precisely timed to the target satellite's orbit. Once airborne, the F-15 pilot was guided by information displayed on the HUD (heads-up display). Release of the ASM-135 occurred at approximately 1.5 Mach at nearly fifty thousand feet altitude. The test was successful with the ASM-135 sensor package positioning itself directly in the path of the orbiting victim. Approximately six thousand pieces of debris were created in a torus that dissipated over a couple of weeks. No resident space objects were affected by the injection of this new space debris.

It was October 7, 1985, early morning, when the chairman's exec called, requesting that the chief or I report to the chairman's conference room immediately. The chief was out visiting units in the field, so I ran down to the second floor, wondering what crisis had been dropped on the chairman's desk. The room was almost full, and other service chiefs were sitting in the front row, so I joined them. The chairman, who at the time had only been in that position one week, told us that an Italian cruise ship in the Mediterranean had been seized by Palestinian terrorists. The White House wanted it disabled so it could not reach a port friendly to the terrorists and to give the United States time to come up with a rescue plan. The chairman directed his first question to Admiral Watkins, CNO: "Jim, can you disable the ship?"

The response was unexpected. Admiral Watkins said, "We could use a destroyer or cruiser in the Med to take out the rudder with five-inch gunfire."

The chairman didn't seem to care for that approach, so I offered, "Admiral Watkins, don't you have submarines with precision sonar that could take out the rudder or screw by bumping up against it at night?"

Admiral Watkins didn't appreciate my offering naval advice, responding with "Pete, if we did that, the terrorists would probably shoot all the hostages!"

My response was "Well, the Med is full of debris and other junk. I don't believe it unusual for a ship to bump into something, and it's a lot less obvious than a five-inch broadside engagement."

About that time, a navy commander in the back of the room offered the comment, "Admiral, we have a sub in the Med with a hardened sail. We can disable the ship submerged at night." That seemed to satisfy the chairman's need, and he left for the White House to meet with the National Security team. Marine Lieutenant Colonel Oliver, USMC, was at the NSC and recommended that a Joint Special Operations Command (JSOC) team, under the command of Gen. Carl Stiner, attempt to seize the ship if the crisis could not be resolved peacefully. I believe the JSOC could have done the job, but they were never given the chance, and the *Achille Lauro* sailed into an Egyptian port without intervention after executing a disabled Jewish American tourist, Leon Klinghoffer, and throwing his body and wheelchair overboard.

A few days later, the chairman's exec again summoned me to the Admiral Crowe's conference room; again, it was early morning. The chiefs were arriving as I entered the room and took my place in the front row. The chairman said intelligence sources indicting the terrorists who had hijacked the *Achille Lauro* and given asylum in Egypt were planning to fly from Cairo to Tunis on a B727 Egyptian chartered aircraft departing about 9:00 p.m., Washington time. The NSC wanted the US Navy's Sixth Fleet in the Mediterranean, under the command of Adm. Frank Kelso, to intercept the B727 with two sections (flight of four) of F-14s from a carrier and force it down on Sigonella AB, in Sicily. President Reagan approved the plan, and orders were sent to Admiral Kelso to execute the operation with approval for the pilots to fire their 20 mm cannons across the nose of the B727, if necessary, to gain compliance. A carrier-based E-2C radar surveillance plane would support the F-14s by attempting to detect and track the chartered 727.

Admiral Crowe asked Admiral Watkins what he thought the probability would be of intercepting the 727 carrying the terrorists. The CNO replied that the chance of intercepting the right aircraft would be very low, no better than 5 percent. My belief was considerably different than the CNO's, so I gave my opinion even though I wasn't asked. "Admiral Crowe, the takeoff time for the B727 Charter flight is 2:00 a.m., Cairo time—nine local here. There will be no other aircraft taking off at that time flying the Med to Tunis. I've flown the Med many nights while stationed at Aviano, and I can assure there are few, if any, commercial aircraft flying at that time of night. The B727 carrying the terrorists will be the only aircraft in the sky. The E-2C is equipped with a great search and track radar; however, the radar is limited to 250 nautical miles range by design. The air force can provide an E-3A as backup to the E-2C. It has greater endurance and a powerful radar that can pick up a B727 at five hundred-plus miles. All three aircraft, E-3A, E-2C, and F-14, have Tadil A (Tactical Data Link) and can pass tracks without radio communications. The F-14 has a very capable intercept radar and will most likely pick up the B-727 at ranges greater than fifty miles. I believe the probability of intercept is greater than 95 percent." I added that, "The E-3A could stand off from Cairo about three hundred miles and pick up the 727 Charter on takeoff and pass the track to the E-2C. The E-2C could then focus its attention on the synthetic track until its integral radar picked up the skin track for control of the intercept." The CNO said the navy didn't need the E-3A and declined the offer. I fully expected the chairman to recommend the E-3A backup, but he was mute on the idea.

As most readers will remember, the intercept of the B727 was successful, and the F-14s did have to fire warning shots while flying alongside the 727 Charter to convince the pilots to land at Sigonella AB. When US forces arrived at the aircraft, Italian military forces and police had already surrounded it, preventing US personnel access to the terrorists. The Italian government allowed the notorious terrorist Abu Abbas to escape to Yugoslavia, a tragic mistake for justice.

The exchanges with Admiral Watkins left me a bit uncomfortable, to say the least, so I sought advice from my navy counterpart, Adm. Jim Busey, vice CNO. Jim confided in me that Admiral Watkins was difficult to get along with and not very operationally oriented. He shared with me that secretary of the navy, John Lehman, and Admiral Watkins did not speak to each other. Their primary means of communication with each other was by passing notes back and forth. Their other means of communication was to call Admiral Busey and ask him to be the go-between messenger. This seemed to be a very awkward and difficult way to run the navy. On the other hand, Admiral Busey was a superstar and a pleasure to work with.

Changes were on the horizon for the air force. Secretary Orr, a President Reagan appointee, decided to retire and return to California. Secretary Weinberger nominated, and the President approved the appointment of Russell A. Rourke, then serving as OSD's legislative liaison to Congress, to become the next secretary of the air force. With years of experience in OSD and on the "Hill," it was believed that Secretary Rourke would slide right into the new job with no noticeable transitional issues. I could not have been more wrong!

It took a few weeks to realize that Secretary Rourke had developed some work habits that were somewhat foreign to those of us in uniform. A paper was due to Deputy Secretary Taft by close of business on Friday. The chief was on travel, and it was protocol to coordinate any Title 10 (Organize, Train, and Equip) Issues with the secretary of the air force or undersecretary of the air force prior to taking a position paper to OSD. It was midafternoon on Friday, and the Air Staff had fully coordinated on what I believed to be a sound position on the issue at hand. I took the paper to the Secretary Rourke's office for coordination and approval only to be told by his executive staff that Secretary Rourke did not work on Fridays. That was a stunner, and Undersecretary Aldridge was in Houston, Texas, undergoing astronaut training to be the payload specialist on a supersecret NRO payload scheduled for launch on the space shuttle about a year in the future. Not wanting to bypass the new air force secretary, I got agreement from Secretary Taft's military assistant (an air force brigadier) that it would be OK to get the paper on Taft's desk at 0800 hours, Monday morning. I felt pretty good about avoiding an embarrassing situation, but underestimated Secretary Rourke's work routine. A few minutes prior to 0745 on Monday morning, I was standing in front of Secretary Rourke's personal secretary, asking her if the secretary was in. She advised me that her boss usually came in around 1000 hours on Mondays, but it could be as late as noon. Enough of that, I took the issue paper to Secretary Taft's office with the understanding that there was a new sheriff in town, but only occasionally.

Secretary Rourke strived to maintain his relationships on the Hill, built up over the years as Secretary Weinberger's legislative liaison. That seemed like a good idea that could, on occasion, benefit the air force during budget hearings. On the other hand, the long luncheons on Capitol Hill took precious time away from important work in the Pentagon. The B1 bomber was proving to be an exceptional aircraft in everything but engines and defensive avionics. The engine problems were being corrected, but defensive avionics were in big, big trouble. The Air Force Systems Command (AFSC) had made the decision to take Defensive Avionics integration away from the prime contractor and accomplish that job within the air force. Unfortunately, the procurement and integration of the Defensive Avionics Suite was years behind schedule with no definable resolution in sight. Accordingly, the B-1 was under the sec def's Acquisition Review Process, which required a quarterly review in front of Secretary Weinberger and his acquisition experts. Such a review was scheduled in a few days, and it was essential that Secretary Rourke be thoroughly prepared for the tough grilling he would get on the B-1 program by Weinberger and his staff.

Secretary Rourke's prebrief on B-1 issues was set for 1100 hours, but he changed it to 1000 hours. I thought that was a good sign in that he wanted more time so he would be better prepared. When we gathered in the secretary's briefing room, he indicated that he had an important luncheon on the Hill, and we would have to keep it short. After about two charts, Secretary Rourke asked the program manager to jump to the last chart because he didn't want to be late for his appointment. I cautioned the secretary, suggesting that the environment at Secretary Weinberger's briefing would be hostile and that he had better have a firm grasp on all the actions that were being taken to correct B-1 problems. He would not be detoured and left for the Hill with at best a casual understanding of B-1 problems and corrective action being taken by the air force.

At 1355, I accompanied Secretary Rourke to Secretary Weinberger's conference room. All the principals were there, including Dr. David Chu and the chief OSD weapons system operational tester. It was not going to be a friendly session for our secretary, although a few months earlier, all present were his close associates. After the OSD Staff beat up on SECAF for over an hour, Secretary Weinberger ended the session with an admonishment to get the B-1 fixed. When we were out the door and a few feet down the corridor, Secretary Rourke turned to me and said sternly, "Why didn't you warn me?"

I responded with "Mr. Secretary, we tried, but you wouldn't take the time to listen!" I think it was beginning to dawn on him that being secretary of the air force was more than a ceremonial position with close-in parking and a key to the executive elevator.

Lt. Gen. Bernard (Randy) Randolph, DCS/RD, came bursting into my office midmorning of January 28, 1986, asking, "Have you heard the news?"

"What news, what's happened?" was the response. He flipped on the TV hidden in the wall in time to catch a rerun of the space shuttle blowing apart just seventy-three seconds after liftoff at 1138 hours that morning. The nation, led by President Reagan, was immediately in mourning for the seven brave souls aboard shuttle flight STS-51-L.

Randy quickly informed me that Congress had recently directed that all large space payloads be launched from the space shuttle bay and accordingly had cancelled production of the Heavy Lift Titan 4 space launch vehicles. He noted that the United States National Space Programs would be severely impacted for the next year or more. This meant only the highest priority satellites with National Security missions could be launched on the few remaining boosters until the cause of the Challenger tragedy was uncovered, fixed, and the shuttle returned to flight. Undersecretary Aldridge, in his role as director NRO in coordination with the Central Intelligence Agency (CIA), National Security Agency (NSA), and the National Security Council (NSC), would be assessing the space situation and making recommendations to the president. As it turned out, Randy was overoptimistic; the space shuttle was grounded for two and a half years before returning to flight in the summer of 1988. As I recall, the air force, as executive agent for space, launched only four or five heavy payloads in all of 1986. There were about the same number of DOD space launches in 1987. On the other hand, the Soviets conducted approximately ninety space launches, including missile tests, annually during the same period.

On February 3, 1986, President Reagan announced that former secretary of state William P. Rogers would chair a thirteen-person panel to investigate the Challenger accident. President Reagan asked the Roger's Commission to "review the circumstances surrounding the accident, determine the probable cause or causes, recommend corrective action, and report back to me in 120 days." Maj. Gen. Donald Kutyna from the Air Force Space and Missile Center in Los Angeles, California, was one of the Roger's Commission members and a key player in identifying the root cause of the mishap.

One of the perks of being a member of the JCS was going to the White House along with the chairman and the other service chiefs when General Gabriel was visiting Air Force Field Commands. Prior to passage of the Goldwater-Nichols Bill, the chairman was the principal military advisor to the president; however, the service chiefs supported him in that role, offering supporting comments or occasionally dissenting if they felt strongly to the contrary on a given issue. In a sense, this was a good check and balance, because if one Service held a strong dissenting view, the remainder had to be very firm in their views prior to standing before the president. Both presidents I served under, Ronald Reagan and George H. W. Bush listened carefully and asked thoughtful probing questions on the military advice presented to them. It was an honor to be part of that team!

On April 5, 1986, another tragedy struck! This time, it was the explosion of a bomb planted in the La Belle discotheque in West Berlin, Germany. US military personnel stationed in West Berlin regularly frequented the La Belle. Two American servicemen were killed, and seventy-nine more were injured. One Turkish woman was killed, and another 159 people were injured. Several terrorist groups were suspected of the atrocity, until a telex message from Tripoli, Libya, to the Libyan East Berlin embassy was intercepted, congratulating them on a job well done. Immediately, planning was initiated for a punishing retaliatory strike against Libya.

The planning for a retaliatory strike was very close hold. Guidance from President Reagan was that only military targets would be struck with emphasis on those that were directly related to terrorism. The intelligence community prepared a list of targets that satisfied the president's direction. These were vetted by the JCS and then taken to the president by the chairman with representatives of the intelligence community and the National Security Council. Admiral Crowe informed the chiefs (General Gabriel was traveling in Europe at the time) that the president personally selected the targets to be struck. Admiral Crowe also pointed out that he was going to ask General Rogers, SACEUR/CINCEUR, to personally pick up the target list and time over target (TOT), and hand-carry them back to EUCOM. Admiral Crowe also forbade any electronic communications about the attack and gave General Rogers instructions to have the information hand-carried to each operational unit involved in the mission.

Admiral Crowe explained his reasoning for the extra precautions taken to pass the targets and mission specifics to EUCOM. He noted that even the most highly classified data with a header saying "Personal from Chairman JCS to SACEUR/CINCEUR, eyes only" will have to be typed and then taken to the Communications Center, where two or three people will see the message. Then on the other end, at least three people will see the message before it is handed to General Rogers. After the meeting, I called all air force field commanders and told them we were implementing a new procedure for passing very sensitive information. First, they would have to install a fax machine capable of handling top secret (TS) information in their respective command centers. Second, when sensitive information was to be passed from the Pentagon, I would call them from the air force command center, requesting they go to their command center and call me when they were at their TS fax machine, then I would send the fax. The reverse procedure would be used when they wanted to send highly sensitive information to Headquarters Air Force. We used that procedure several times while I was in the Pentagon and later when I was back in the field.

The TOT was 0200 hours on the morning of Wednesday, April 15, 1986, or 2100 hours, Tuesday, April 14, Washington DC time. The JCS met just about every day from the La Belle bombing to the day of the attack to monitor the situation. One day, I suggested to Admiral Crowe that the attack be slipped to 0200 hours on Saturday because that was a Muslim Holy Day, and it was less likely that their air defenses would be fully manned. The Chairman said that was a good idea, but Washington couldn't keep a secret that long, and he was concerned that even waiting until Tuesday was a stretch! Actually, he wanted the strike to occur earlier, but the Sixth Fleet Carriers were in port and had to get to sea, shake a Soviet "tattletale," and practice flight operations for at least one day prior to going into combat. Those were the reasons for Tuesday rather than earlier. Some European governments were notified of the pending attack: England because two air force F-111 Wings that would be participating in the attack were based there, and France because overflight of the F-111s was requested to significantly reduce the round-trip time from takeoff to landing

At one of the JCS meetings, the CNO came into the room with the admonition that the United States would be committing an act of war against the Soviet Union. Perhaps something had leaked, or it was just bad timing, but a Soviet warship with connections to a Soviet Maritime Intelligence Center had just anchored in the Tripoli Harbor. Part of the mission planning called for Navy EA-6B electronic jammers to jam Libyan air defense systems and their command and control links a few seconds prior to our attack aircraft breaking the radar horizon. Admiral Watkins asserted that the jammers would interfere with Soviet ship transmissions. I tried to assure the CNO that only the Libyan radio receivers would be affected, not the transmitters aboard ship. He wasn't having any of that, but the chairman quieted him down.

The day of the attack, DC time, Admiral Crowe called me and asked if I would visit Sen. Barry Goldwater, a former air force fighter pilot, and brief him on the mission against Libya. It was a normal courtesy to brief the chairman of the Senate Armed Services Committee and the chairman of the House Armed Services Committee on any military activities that would put servicemen in extreme danger. Senator Goldwater at that time was hospitalized, recovering from hip surgery. I waited until late in the afternoon when I was informed he would be awake and alert. I took a list of the targets, the units and aircraft participating in the punitive attack, and a map. The senator was very gracious and asked lots of questions about the defenses and the probability of success. He was very positive about the attack, in response to the disco bombing, being the right thing to do. "We can't let these attacks go unanswered!" were the senator's parting words.

Just prior to joining Secretary Weinberger, Admiral Crowe, and other members of the JCS to monitor El Dorado Canyon as the mission progressed, I called Secretary Aldridge and suggested he might want to watch the evening news. As some readers may know, service secretaries are responsible for organization, training, and equipping their service personnel. All operational matters are the purview of the Office of the Secretary of Defense (OSD), the JCS, and combatant/regional commanders. Accordingly, Secretary Aldridge had no knowledge of El Dorado Canyon planning or execution. Nonetheless, I didn't want him to come to work on Wednesday and be the only one in the Pentagon that didn't know his air force went to war the previous evening.

Secretary Weinberger had a small conference room that he used as a command center. He invited the chairman and the chiefs to join him in his command center at 2000 hours, DC time, to listen in on the attack in progress. General Gabriel was in England at one of the F-111 bases, participating in the premission briefing and cheering the aircrews on as they taxied out to takeoff. Lt. Gen. Dick Burpee, an old friend, was the

JCS J-3 sitting between the sec def and chairman; Gen. John Wickham, Adm. James Watkins, Gen. P. X. Kelley, and I were all in the room. We could hear the discussions between Lieutenant General Burpee and Rear Admiral Dave Frost, EUCOM J-3, on the other end of the line as the last hour of the mission unfolded. Admiral Frost was also connected to the Sixth Fleet Command ship in the Mediterranean, which was in turn connected to the Aegis Cruiser acting as the "delousing" ship for the returning aircraft. The "delousing" ship is necessary to ensure that only friendly aircraft are allowed to pass over and return to the carriers, USS *Saratoga*, USS *America*, and USS *Coral Sea* on station in the Gulf of Sidra. E-2s, A-6s, and EA-6s were airborne, and A-7 as well as F/A-18 strike packages were forming up.

Except for the voices at the head of the table, it was quiet in the room; American sailors and airmen were about to go into combat in a surprise attack against Colonel Kaddafi's terrorist infrastructure—nearly a hundred lives were at risk. Twenty-four F-111s had taken off from the 48th TFW at RAF Lakenheath supported by at least four EF-111s, jammers from the 20th TFW at RAF Upper Heyford. Twenty-four laser bomb—equipped F-111s would rendezvous with tankers over the Atlantic, and eighteen mission-capable aircraft would depart the tankers for their targets in Libya; six spares would return immediately to their base in the UK. The French government refused the US request for overflight, so the F-111s from England flew out to sea over international waters west of France, Spain, and Portugal, entering the Mediterranean Sea through the narrows of the Strait of Gibraltar then onto their target in Libya. This added 1,300 miles additional distance to their targets and again on the return.

As the time over target (0200 hours in Tripoli, 2100 hours in DC) approached, the room became very hushed, with everyone concentrating on the mission progress being relayed by Lieutenant General Burpee. A wall-mounted TV tuned to CNN was just off my right shoulder when the reporter announced at 2055 hours, "Now turning to our reporter in Tripoli." That really got our attention! Someone in the room turned up the volume as the screen changed to a picture of the Libyan capital along with a picture of the on-scene reporter.

The voice said, "I'm reporting from the rooftop of my hotel. Tripoli is in a festive mood. There are a lot of people walking and driving through the downtown area. Wait, I hear aircraft, there are bombs dropping on Tripoli Airport! Libya is under attack!"

It was obvious to everyone in the room that the date and time of the attack had leaked, or else someone at CNN had mystic powers. Why would the producer of CNN nightly news switch to Tripoli exactly five minutes prior to the TOT, and why else would the reporter be on the rooftop of a major hotel with a panoramic view of the entire city and surroundings if they didn't know the time and the targets?

It was less than thirty minutes from the CNN announcement when the delousing ship reported that the last mission aircraft had reported in and passed over the ship en route to the carrier. Shortly after that, Lieutenant General Burpee relayed that all navy aircraft had recovered aboard their respective carriers. The next event of the evening was the TV broadcast of President Reagan announcing that US Forces conducted a punitive attack against Libya for their bombing of the West Berlin discotheque that killed three and injured 229 innocent people.

Of the eighteen F-111s that departed south from the tanker, nine were to strike Colonel Gaddafi's military headquarters (Bab al-Azizia), a multistory L-shaped building. Six were targeted against an airfield south of Tripoli used for airlifting military personnel and cargo, and three were going against a "frogman" training facility on the coast. F-111 aircrews were given strict orders to abort their mission if specific mission essential equipment failed en route. The aircraft terrain following radar, podded laser guidance system, and radar homing and warning system were three of those items. Accordingly, only three—111s bombed the Bab al Azizia headquarters/barracks; one missed, four aborted, and one was shot down over the Gulf of Sidra. Two F-111s hit the swimmer facility, and one hit a Naval Academy dining facility, a few miles short of the intended target. Three F-111s bombed the airfield, one bombed a warehouse, believing it was a hangar, and another aborted. Two air force officers were lost in the attack, Capt. Fernando L. Ribas-Dominicci and Capt. Paul F. Lorence.

General Gabriel called about 4:00 a.m., eastern time, to let me know that twenty-three aircraft had landed safely at their bases in England, and one aircraft was presumed lost in the raid. He also reported that the F-111 PAVE TAC pod video cameras had recorded some excellent footage of the damage to the swimmer facility and destruction of aircraft on the ramp at Tripoli Airfield. I thanked him for the on-scene report, got dressed, and headed for the Pentagon. I stopped by Admiral Crowe's office, expecting that he might be in, anticipating meetings at the NSC or with the president. When I walked in the office, he appeared to be in a foul mood as he tossed some photographs across his desk at me. Most of the photographs showed only clouds, but there were a couple that depicted a number of bomb craters near the L-shaped Bab al-Azizia barracks and a large white collapsed tent near the craters. There was also a photo of the swimmer facility, but the view was from the east, and the attack was from the west; hence, no damage showed. As I looked at the pictures, Admiral Crowe growled, "That's from the overhead. That's all we've got to show for last night's effort." I mentioned General Gabriel's report from RAF Lakenheath in the UK and the fact that the F-111s had video film of their attacks. The chairman's mood brightened slightly as he said, "Call your chief and tell him to get his butt back here as fast as the plane will fly. We need those pictures back here for a 2:00 p.m. meeting with the president!" They must have pushed the Mach limit on Speckled Trout because the chief got back in time with the videos we all saw on TV showing the Snake Eye bombs detonating among the Soviet transports parked on the ramp at Tripoli Airport.

Within a few days after the attacks on Libya, a call from Lt. Gen. Brent Scowcroft, USAF (ret.) got my attention. The call was brief; Brent said that a number of influential acquaintances were questioning the courage of the F-111 aircrews involved in Operation El Dorado Canyon, suggesting that there was no justification for so many aborts in a modern twin-engine aircraft—only ten of eighteen aircraft bombed their targets. Brent asked if I could provide him with information that would correct a growing perception among Washington's elite that air force aircrew courage went AWOL when called on to fight. I told General Scowcroft that information on aircraft malfunctions were still coming in from the field, that I would get back with him in a couple of days, and that we could meet in my office to discuss the details.

Lieutenant General Scowcroft was no ordinary retired officer. I had met him and held him in the highest regard, but he was on another level. He graduated from West Point in 1947 and accepted a commission in the USAF, completed pilot training in 1948 followed by operational assignments. Along the way, he earned an MA in 1953 and PhD in International Relations in 1967 from Columbia University, and served as the air attaché in the American embassy in Belgrade, Yugoslavia. He was appointed military assistant to President Ford in February 1972, and in August 1973, he was reassigned as deputy assistant to the president for National Security Affairs under Henry Kissinger.

The F-111 Wings participating in El Dorado Canyon were under Third Air Force in the United Kingdom and USAFE, commanded by Gen. Chuck Donnelly. A call to General Donnelly revealed that Gen. Richard L. Lawson, deputy commander EUCOM under General Rogers, was tightly holding all the information on the mission. However, General Lawson was the de facto commander EUCOM for day-to-day operations. General Lawson was reluctant to release any data but relented when told it was for Lieutenant General Scowcroft. There was a tight connection between the two as General Lawson succeeded General Scowcroft as the military assistant to President Ford when the latter moved to the National Security Council. He appreciated the fact that Brent was trying to help some of the elite in Washington understand why an F-111 flying nearly four thousand nautical miles en route to their targets, with the last two hundred or so miles skimming the waves to avoid radar detection, might experience some critical mission equipment failures. General Lawson provided me the information needed. The time from takeoff to target was roughly eleven hours. On the other hand, mean time between failure (MTBF) for some of F-111 mission critical systems like the terrain following system, and the PAVE TAC pod were in the order of six hours. In lay terms, this means that half of these systems would have failed en route based on averages. In retrospect, F-111 mission critical systems performed better than average for those eighteen aircraft that departed the tanker with all systems go. If France had authorized overflight for these eighteen aircraft, their time to target would have been reduced by more than half, and nearly all F-111s would have been able to complete their missions, and crews would have been far less fatigued. Brent Scowcroft came to the Pentagon, and we met for over an hour, going over the data and mission profile in detail. His pilot background helped a great deal in assimilating the data and understanding that the electronics of that era were still a work in progress. He gained the information needed to help educate his associates. Essentially, it was a lot like the Desert One rescue attempt. Eighteen F-111s was probably the right number if France had granted overflight! However, when they didn't, the extra 1,300 nautical miles flown over international water to their targets exceeded mean time between critical mission failures, causing aborts.

One of the onerous details in the Washington DC was military representation at many of the government-sponsored cocktail party mixers. There was at least one a week, and in the "busy season" two or three. All the sponsors of these social events wanted a four-star flag officer from each service in attendance. The gilded invitations were impossible to refuse; a uniformed four-star from each service had to show up and work the room, making small talk. Most, if not all, of the foreign delegations sent representatives to these functions, and one had to be careful not to say anything that would be considered sensitive. The chiefs I served under, General Gabriel and General Welch, had the first right of refusal, and they took advantage of that prerogative. As a result, Sheila and I spent many of our evenings on the cocktail circuit making small talk and wishing we were elsewhere. It was commonly referred to as "potted palm" duty because that's what we felt like—potted palms as decorations at some of those august venues. We often ran into Lt. Gen. John Pickitt and his wife, Mary, good friends from our days in the Tactical Air Command. At that time, General Pickitt was the director, Defense Nuclear Agency (now euphemistically called the Threat Reduction Agency). On one such occasion when we found ourselves talking with the Picketts, Mary Pickett opined, "Being superficial is so hard!" I found that a very apt description of "potted palm" duty.

Air/land battle was a concept that had been germinating since General DePuy, USA, took command of TRADOC in 1973. Based on lessons drawn from the 1973 Arab-Israeli War came the sharply revised Field Manual 100-5, Operations, dated July 1976. Gen. Don Starry succeeded General DePuy and carried the concept even further. He realized that firepower focused on the forward edge of the battle area (FEBA) overlooked the enemy's second echelon forces sitting in reserve. He refocused the initial effort codified in FM 100-5 and renamed it air/land battle, giving the air force responsibility for close air support and interdiction of an adversary's second echelon forces. TAC worked with TRADOC on the air/land battle concept, and I was the TAC lead in 1981 and 1982, as it was coming to fruition.

In a historical sense, the Air Corps discovered the air/land battle concept following the defeat of American and Allied North African forces in WW II at the first battle at Kasserine Pass in the Tunisia Campaign. Field Marshal Rommel soundly defeated US forces with a feigned retreat and entrapment. US Army airpower in Africa was modest at the time, but to make matters worse, units were assigned to army divisions, and division commanders had absolute control over their Air Corps units. Divisions not in combat held their aircraft back. Following the first battle of Kasserine Pass, Gen. Dwight D. Eisenhower began restructuring the Allied Command. Gen. George S. Patton took command of II Corps, and all air support aircraft were placed under Air Vice Marshal Arthur Conningham. Air Corps units would now be centrally controlled and available to support the Allied commanders' battle plans. Lt. Col. Spike Momyer was there and learned the lessons of Kasserine Pass firsthand. He commanded TAC from 1966 to 1973 and supported the air/land battle concept.

Air/land battle was sent to Unified/Combatant Commands in the mid-1980s. EUCOM, under General Lawson and in concert with Gen. Bob Reed, chief of staff SACEUR, asked the JCS to consider the adoption of a Joint Force Air Component commander as the tasking authority of all combat air forces under a Unified/Combatant commander. Their request was on the JCS calendar when Lt. Gen. Harley Hughes came to brief me on the subject because General Gabriel was on travel. It would be a very rancorous and divisive session, as the Marine Corps was hard over on retaining control over marine air as I had learned as the air force component of CENTCOM. I commented to Harley that I wished General Gabriel would be there because the tank session was going to be very contentious. I was surprised when he said, "Haven't you figured it out yet? General Gabriel doesn't like conflict in the tank and avoids it at all cost! He'll never be there when there is going to be a service fight! Get used to it!" I realized that Harley was right; General Gabriel was on travel during all the divisive sessions while I was the vice chief.

All the principals were in the tank except General Gabriel, and Marine Commandant P. X. Kelley looked to be in a combative mood. The Marine Air-Ground Team was sacred to the corps! Chairman Crowe introduced the subject under review as "Should there be a single tasking authority for air power in a regional or combatant command?" He also noted that EUCOM had raised and supported the position that there should be a single tasking authority for air power. Without further ado or tipping his inclination on the issue, the chairman asked for comments. At this point, I pushed my bowl of Hershey Kisses over to the chairman, knowing I wouldn't have time to eat any of them and needed all the support from the chairman I could get.

> Gen. John Wickham Jr., USA, said he had no position on the issue. However, he believed that organic helicopters used for transportation should not be subject to "centralized" tasking.

> Adm. James Watkins, USN, said he did not have an opinion and was agnostic on the issue. I believe he took this position, believing that Gen. P. X. Kelley, USMC, would defeat the proposal.

> Gen. Paul X. Kelley, USMC, literally rose to the occasion and made his remarks while standing. He argued persuasively that the marine air/ground team was inseparable. They trained together as they would fight together, and that no other external air support would be effective in providing air support to marine infantry. He spoke passionately on the issue for about fifteen minutes.

I was next! I turned to the chairman and highlighted the air force position:

> The air force believed that a single air tasking authority was absolutely essential for a regional combatant command or

task force to deconflict ingress and egress routes into enemy territory and to deconflict close air support tasking at the FEBA. Further, a single air tasking authority was essential for providing deconflicted frequencies and aircraft call signs, electronic countermeasures support, air refueling tankers and air refueling orbits, centralized rescue operations, as well as ground and airborne radar control. In addition, a single air tasking authority was required to publish a comprehensive and deconflicted air tasking order (ATO) that would cover a twenty-four-hour period specifically supporting the combatant commander's intent and follow that with continuous twenty-four-hour ATOs.

Further that, the air force believed and supported the concept that any service, depending on the circumstances, could fill the role of the single air tasking authority (SATA). The decision as to which service would be given SATA would be up to the combatant commander or CINC (in those days).

Then I gave examples of when other services should/would be designated as the SATA.

During naval support of a marine amphibious operation, SATA would be held by the navy for tasking of both naval and marine air sorties coming off of carriers. Once the marines were ashore and had taken control of an airfield or airfields, SATA could transfer the Marine Corps or remain with the navy at the combatant commander's discretion.

Subsequently, as additional forces arrived in theater, and if the air force provided the preponderance of air power in support of the JTF commander or regional combatant commander, the CINC could transfer SATA to the air force.

The decision as to which service would function as the SATA should always rest with the combatant commander. However, this means that each service must develop the capability to perform all of the complex planning functions and publish the ATO.

Then I turned to the chairman and said, "The air force will always support the combatant commander's direction, providing preplanned or on-call air power where he directs. The marine concept holds the marine air/ground team as inseparable. Therefore, marines will always get their own air support, plus whatever the CINC directs. Soldiers will only get air force support. If you believe marines' lives are more important than soldiers' lives, you will support the Marine Corps position. If, on the other hand, you believe marines and soldiers are equally important, you will support the EUCOM and air force position." Before the Chairman could speak, Admiral Watkins opined that if the navy could also function as the SATA, the navy would support the air force and EUCOM position. I responded that which service performed the SATA function would be the combatant commander's decision and could change from one scenario to another, depending on whether the friendly forces were dominantly land or sea based and which service provided the preponderance of air power.

After allowing for further discussion, the chairman called for a vote. It was three to one; with the chairman supporting the majority, it was four to one. I represented the air force in the JCS tank when a lot of important decisions were taken, but this was clearly the most important with regard to the nation's ability to win conventional wars! It also played a big part in the role the air force played in Desert Shield and Desert Storm. Desert Storm was the first real war where a Joint Forces Air Component commander (JFACC) functioned in that role and performed all of the functions enumerated above and more. It was clearly a landmark decision not on the same level as establishing the air force as a separate service, but one that enabled the air force to achieve much of its promise in combat.

To his great credit, General Kelley put out a message "to all marines" the next day, informing the corps of the decision taken and directing that all Marine Corps units at every level support it. I quietly called my counterparts in the services and suggested that if they wanted to fill the SATA role at a combatant commander's direction, they should start building that capability as soon as practicable. The navy was first to mirror the air force's capability in the SATA role from a sea-based platform.

A European travel itinerary arrived on my desk from Air Force Secretary Russell A. Rourke. One of the vice chief's responsibilities was to approve all Secretarial Staff, Air Staff, and Field Commander's travels overseas. It was normally a very routine chore; however, once in a while there was a need to politely suggest a change in the travel plans to ensure the air force didn't wind up in the news in an unflattering way. Such was the case with a trip through the Far East by a senior air force officer. The itinerary included a two-day stop in Hong Kong. To my knowledge, at that time, we did not have any bases or forces in Hong Kong, nor were we planning to sell them any F-16s or other military hardware. It took some persuading to convince the general that an aircraft with air force markings on the tarmac of the Hong Kong International Airport would not garner anything but bad publicity for the air force. The itinerary was appropriately revised to bypass Hong Kong. Secretary Rourke's travel plan was another challenge, and he was my immediate civilian boss.

The secretary's plan called for a weeklong visit to London, a week's visit in Paris, and a third week in Cologne Bonn, at that time the West German capital. In addition, the passenger list included his wife and two adult children that would be home from college and free to travel with their parents. The proposed itinerary presented four major problems! First, overseas trips had to include visits to military installations, not just capital cities. Second, the French kicked all US forces out of France in the 1960s; there was no job-related reason to visit Paris or France for that matter. Third, there were no air force bases near Cologne Bonn, so that was a bad call. Last, children or relatives of generals or service secretaries were not allowed to travel on military aircraft unless there was a special exemption and the sponsor was willing to pay for their proportional cost of the trip. For example, in Secretary Rourke's case, there were two principals and two guests; accordingly, the secretary would have to pay 50 percent of the cost of the trip for his children to ride on the aircraft. The cost to the secretary for his two children to travel to and through Europe would run over $100,000, including half the per diem of the aircrew. I walked down the hall not looking forward to the encounter. The problems with the itinerary were explained in detail to the secretary, suggesting that four to five days in England, one at each of the US bases there, plus an afternoon and evening in London with travel to and from London by car from the closest air base in the UK, in addition, a few hours in Paris for a visit with his counterpart, if an invitation could be arranged, would be appropriate on his way to Germany. Six to seven days in Germany would be appropriate if one day were spent at each of the US base complexes in that country, starting with USAFE Headquarters at Ramstein AB.

The secretary was resolute in his determination to travel on his planned itinerary and to take his children along on the trip. I didn't want to take the problem to General Gabriel, knowing that he wouldn't appreciate having my problem dropped in his lap, so I went to see Deputy Secretary of Defense Taft on the issue. I explained the optic issues with Secretary Rourke's desired itinerary and the fact that the law required that he pay for half the cost of the trip if his two children went along. Secretary

Taft said that he would take care of the problem, and he did. The trip never happened, and Secretary Rourke submitted his resignation about a month later.

Air Force Undersecretary Edward C. (Pete) Aldridge moved up to replace Secretary Rourke and took the responsibilities of director NRO along with him. James F. McGovern was appointed as undersecretary of the air force. It was an easy transition all around.

T-39 Sabreliners used for executive travel in the United States and abroad were getting old and increasingly more expensive to maintain. Replacing the T-39s was a pressing need, but it had to be a really good bargain, or the Congress would never appropriate the dollars for a replacement. Serendipitously, Lear Jet was having financial problems about that time. Dr. Tom Cooper was the assistant secretary of the air force for R&D and an occasional golfing buddy. As far as I could tell, he was as solid as they come and worked hard at getting the best product at the lowest price for the air force. We talked a lot about air force acquisition issues, and I was convinced he was right most, if not all, of the time. Secretary Cooper took it as a personal challenge getting a Lear Jet (C-21) at the very best price for the air force. There was no comparable alternative aircraft in production at the time. Lear offered us a very good price for a large number of aircraft, but Secretary Cooper convinced me not to accept their offer but rather to hold out for a better one. There was considerable pressure to accept Lear's offer, but I held out based on my belief in Tom's assessment of Lear's financial situation and his judgment. He was right, and the air force was able to replace all the T-39s with brand-new C-21 Lear Jets at a little over one million dollars per copy. I'm not a gambler—learned that lesson in a tent on a rainy day in Korea as a second lieutenant when a month's pay was lost in a few hours of gambling with fellow RB-26 crew members. However, I'm sure Dr. Cooper was a fantastic poker player based on the way he handled and bluffed his way through the C-21 acquisition.

Dr. Cooper and I worked a number of acquisition issues together. One that comes to mind is the JSTARS Program. It was a really big-ticket item, comparable to the E-3A AWACS if not both more expensive and complex. Determining who submits the "best value" proposal on such a complex weapon system is a daunting undertaking involving hundreds of engineers with acquisition experience. The Request for Proposal (RFP) published by the Air Force Electronics System Division (ESD) was hundreds of pages long and very specific on the weight given to specific criteria in the RFP. For example, "past performance" on relevant contracts by each contractor could be given a weighting of thirty percent. Dr. Cooper suggested that I invite the commander of ESD at Hanscom AFB, Massachusetts, to come to the Pentagon and brief us on the JSTARS Source Selection Board process, to include how the SSB rated the contractor proposals and whom he selected as the winner based on the ratings given the competing contractors on source selection criteria published in the RFP.

ESD was then commanded by a lieutenant general who brought the briefing to my office. The various criteria are color coded, blue, green, yellow, and red; with blue indicating an area was rated "exceeds criteria," green "meets criteria," yellow "below criteria," and red "unacceptable." Once these ratings are assigned to various RFP criteria on the proposals submitted by each contractor, the Source Selection Board can ask each contractor questions that, when answered, could raise or lower the evaluation score and color coding. Thus, the final briefing would show each major evaluation criteria color coding with some areas having an up or down arrow, indicating that the responses from the contractors changed some of the initial scores and ratings. In this process, the Source Selection Board knows who the contractors are, but the Source Selection Authority (ESD commander) would not. Each contractor's color-coding is in a column headed by a letter of the alphabet. For JSTARS, there were five columns headed by the letters *A* through *E*. On the left ordinate were all the various criteria. At the bottom of each column was the cost of the respective proposal. After the lieutenant general gave us the briefing, we noted that contractor D had more areas colored green and blue and was lowest in cost. In our minds, contractor D was the winner, based on the air force source selection process. When we asked whom the General was going to award the contract to, Dr. Cooper and I were informed it was contractor B! When asked how that could be possible given the costs submitted and the ratings awarded, we were told that the ESD commander and Source Selection Authority (our lieutenant general briefer) didn't think contractor D was the best choice. That was quite a shock, given the source selection process was very rigorous and designed to take opinion and/or prejudice out of the selection process. After a short sidebar with Dr. Cooper, I advised the commander ESD that if contractor D was not awarded the contract, then he better form a completely new Source Selection Board and redo the whole process. If the latter was the course he chose, I would elevate the Source Selection Authority to the Air Force Systems Command commander, with Dr. Cooper participating. Contractor D was awarded the contract, and JSTARS, even as a developmental aircraft, played a significant role in Desert Storm.

I don't know if it was the magnitude of the undertaking and the dollar value of the contract that caused Dr. Cooper to want the source selection reviewed at our level. Was it a poker player's gut instinct? Or did he receive a tip that caused him concern? I never asked, but I held him in even higher esteem after that.

It was June 1986, and the clock had run out on Gen. Charles Gabriel's air force career—it was his time to retire on July 1, 1986, thirty-six years after graduating from the Military Academy at West Point. I was privileged to host his retirement party with all of the air force leadership participating. It was obvious that General Gabriel was one of the best liked and most effective air force chiefs of the post-Vietnam era. The Air Staff worked hard to achieve his goals because they admired him and wanted him to be successful. Gen. Larry Welch was chosen by Secretary Weinberger to replace him, and there was no question in my mind that he was the right man and best equipped to take the job. Moreover, General Welch's tour as a lieutenant colonel with Air Force Studies and Analysis under Lt. Gen. Glenn Kent equipped him with the training and experience to quickly and accurately assess the value of every air force program.

Shortly after General Welch took the reins, a young female air force officer stationed at a northern European NATO base filed a sexual harassment complaint against an air force brigadier general. Resolving the issue quickly and correctly was paramount because the accused was on the promotion list for his second star. The complaint had to be resolved prior to Secretary Aldridge signing the promotion list and making it official. If the list was signed, the brigadier general alleged to have sexually harassed one of his subordinates could possibly retire at the higher grade, and a deserving brigadier general would have to wait another year to be considered for promotion.

I asked the air force inspector general, Lt. Gen. Michael Nelson, to personally conduct the investigation! "Get it right and get it done quickly" was my charge to General Nelson, as the promotions of deserving generals on the same promotion list would be held up until the allegations could be confirmed or dismissed. The brigadier general had worked for me when he was a colonel. His performance was above average, but I didn't recommend him for promotion—evidently, two separate promotion boards felt otherwise for reasons unknown to me and selected him to the grade of brigadier general three years ago and recently to major general.

Lieutenant General Nelson was back in a week with the facts. According to the female accuser, the general, as stipulated in her sexual harassment complaint, had been asking her out repeatedly, but she had always declined for two reasons. One, he was twenty years senior, and, two, married. She had kept a diary that included all of his overtures and also confided in her female roommate about her concerns for the general's advances. What precipitated the sexual harassment complaint was the latest incident where he asked her to meet him for a drink after hours, and when she declined, he grabbed her and kissed her even though she was trying to fight him off. The incident occurred in a hallway during lunch hour and was witnessed by several military and civilian staff personnel passing by in the hallway. Her diary of advances, her roommate's confirmation of events, and the witnesses of the kiss all pointed to a long duration of sexual harassment. As a result of Lieutenant General Nelson's findings and written report, Air Force Secretary Aldridge used his authority to remove the offender's name from the promotion list, and the offender resigned in lieu of legal proceedings. The two-star promotion list, absent his name, was published, and deserving officers were promoted with little delay.

In late August 1976, an onerous issue came across my desk. A number of pilots filed inspector general (IG) complaints when they were refused statements of nonavailability of government quarters when denied billeting at an air force base. In this instance, several instructor pilots and their students, on official cross-country flights as part of their training syllabus, were denied on-base quarters but refused "nonavailability" documentation. The end result was they had to pay for motel rooms out of their pockets for performing an air force training mission. The complaint was not resolved at the command level, so it came to Headquarters Air Force for adjudication. It was time to put Lt. Gen. Mike Nelson, AF/IG, on the road again. Mike was back at the Pentagon within a few days, and the report wasn't pretty. A senior air force general was retiring and had put his relatives up in on-base quarters, which is legal if done properly. However, on-base quarters were filled, so nonavailability documentation should have been issued to the TDY pilots and students, but wasn't! Wrong! In addition, Mike uncovered the fact that the senior officer retiring further abused his authority by using air force personnel and vehicles to take family members on tours in a nearby city. Wrong again!

The total bill for the cost to reimburse the officers forced to stay in motels and the cost of government vehicles, personnel, etc. came to just over $4,500. I called the responsible officer and directed that he send me a check made out to the US Treasury for the full amount. I knew the officer well and was fully aware that he served our nation long and honorably both in peace and war. Unfortunately, in the heady and emotional days of retirement, he lost sight of the fact that no one, regardless of rank or position, is above regulations and the law. As noted above, the check was made out to the US Treasury, not to the air force. Federal law requires that when the services sell equipment or services, the money cannot go to the service but rather to the US Treasury. This is to ensure that the services do not sell government aircraft, munitions, or vehicles to raise money to buy things they might prefer. So in this instance, the air force lost $4,500, but the taxpayers did not.

One day, while representing General Welch in the tank for "information only" briefings on a variety of issues under consideration by the Joint Staff, an air force lieutenant colonel gave a horrible briefing. After the session, I told Lieutenant General Hughes, AF/XO (now AF A-3), to provide the briefer some training and coaching to improve his presentation skills before scheduling him to give another briefing. In response, General Hughes told me the officer in question was assigned to the Joint Staff and that he had no control over the situation. He added, the quality of the briefing was typical of the Joint Staff. This is no longer the case as the Goldwater-Nichols Bill ensures that the services send highly qualified officers to the JCS and other designated Joint positions.

President Reagan signed the Goldwater-Nichols Department of Defense Reorganization Act into law on October 1, 1986. There was considerable debate among the service chiefs about the impacts of the bill on service personnel. Gen. P. X. Kelley, USMC, was strongly opposed to the bill, but it was never clear to me why. The chiefs and vice chiefs hosted a breakfast for Senator Goldwater and Congressman Nichols to provide an opportunity for dialog and to understand why they thought the legislation was necessary. As I recall, General Kelley said something critical of the bill, offending Congressman Nichols, which brought our discussions to an abrupt end.

My own personal opinion was that establishing the position of vice chairman was a good move, providing a full-time backup to the chairman with someone who was imbedded in the Joint Staff. The vice chairman would be a senior four-star flag officer who was fully conversant with the chairman's positions and what was going on in the Joint Staff—thus, eliminating the "Mickey Mouse" acting chairman charade. On the other hand, I was concerned that provisions in the bill that stipulated when officers in the grades of major and lieutenant colonel would attend a service or Joint Staff College and subsequently war colleges would place severe impacts on our top officer's opportunity for battalion, ship, and squadron command. It would also impact their opportunity for operations officer and executive officer in combat-related billets. Evidently, my concerns were groundless, as I haven't heard any complaints in that regard. Another concern was that the chairman would now be the sole provider of military advice to the president. Previously, the chairman and the service chiefs would go to the White House when the president requested military advice. The chairman would provide the president with the majority view of the JCS, and if appropriate, a dissenting service chief would provide his minority opinion. On the two occasions when I was representing the air force at one of these visits to the White House, President Reagan would ask the service chiefs for additional information about their service's ability to perform a specific mission. I believe this amplification was useful to the president in taking a decision but, by law, is no longer required.

Once the Goldwater-Nichols Bill was signed into law, it was incumbent on the chairman, with the consent of the secretary of defense, to select a vice chairman to fill the new but vacant position. One of the stipulations in the bill was that the chairman and vice chairman must be from different services. In this regard, I believe they considered the navy and Marine Corps to be "sea services" and the army and the air force to be "land services." I suspect this provision was to preclude a single service from having three votes on an issue raised in the tank. For example, if the chairman, vice chairman, and service chief were in agreement, there would be three votes to two. This stipulation was honored for the first three vice chairman appointees but fell by the wayside after that.

Admiral Crowe was obligated to pick a senior army or air force officer to fill the vice chairman position. He chose Air Force Gen. Robert T. Herres, commander NORAD and US Space Command. General Herres graduated from the Naval Academy and was an underclassman of Admiral Crowe and well known to the admiral. Thus, General Herres was a logical and comfortable choice.

General Welch called me into his office and said that the position of commander NORAD and US Space Command being vacated by General Herres was a nominative position, one that any service could fill. Further, that he wanted to keep those commands under air force leadership and thus was going to nominate me to the Secretary Weinberger for the position. He went on to say,

> "The current vice commander of US Space Command is the highly respected vice admiral William E. Ramsey, with both a fighter pilot and space background. With Admiral Crowe in

the approval chain, it was going to take a strong candidate from the air Force," and that would be me!

It was an unexpected opportunity to move to another field command position. All the big Tactical Fighter Command leadership positions were filled with people that were not expected to retire in the near future. General Herres had a mandatory retirement date about the same time as mine (thirty-five years as a commissioned officer at that time). It was not envisioned that the NORAD/USSPACECOM position would open up. There really wasn't any command assignment expected to open up until Admiral Crowe chose General Herres to fill the newly created vice chairman's position. I now had a more favorable view of the Goldwater-Nichols Bill. I knew that Sheila enjoyed our earlier brief tour of duty in Colorado Springs and would be pleased to return there for a few years. That was a big plus with twenty-eight military moves behind us.

The vetting of four-star officers to new positions was far less rigorous then than it is now with the requirement for Senate confirmation. An interview with Secretary Weinberger was scheduled. When I arrived and was ushered into his office, the secretary, whom I knew quite well by now, got up from behind his desk and extended his hand, saying, "I'm so glad you've accepted this new position!" That was the extent of the interview; the rest of the time was spent talking about how the vice chairman's position would affect JCS deliberations.

Lessons Learned

Never lose sight that the mission of Higher Headquarters is to support the troops in the field.

Joint Commands, rigorous and realistic Joint Training, and well-led Joint Operations are central to victory in combat.

No matter how many promotion boards (or comparable civilian promotions processes) vet a person in the review and promotion process, failures of character do occur.

If your position is logical and unassailable, you will carry the day. This applies to business enterprises as well.

Classified/sensitive information will leak if allowed to marinate, and to a greater degree, in the political arena.

Mean time between failures (MTBF) is the enemy of extended missions. Planners ignore it at their peril.

No one in a position of high authority is above the law.

No decision at the top should be taken lightly; study the issues, weigh the options, and have the courage to do what is right.

To General John Piotrowski
With best wishes,

Ronald Reagan

Gen. Pete & Secretary of Defense Weinberger
with President Reagan. White House

Gen. Pete & Lt. Gen. Abramson, Dir. SDIO at Secretary
Weinberger's retirement. Pentagon, VA

CHAPTER 16

CINC NORAD and USSPACECOM

Admiral Crowe wanted General Herres in Washington as soon as possible to fill the recently established vice chairman's position and have a full-time backup for his demanding job. Therefore, the change of command for General Herres and me was set for early February 1987. The date for these high-level ceremonies is always dependent on availability of the key principals. In our situation, these were Admiral Crowe, CJCS, and Gen. Paul Manson, chief of the Canadian Defense Staff.

Sheila and I would fly out for the change of command then fly back to Washington so she could take care of all the moving details, tidy up loose ends, and prepare to return to Colorado Springs in a motorcade of two vehicles. I would fly the T-39 back with her to pick up a lot of uniforms and business suits that I would need for a variety of military and social occasions, and then return immediately to take up the reins of NORAD and US Space Command.

NORAD is a binational command with Canada formed for the common air defense of both nations in 1958. NORAD took on new importance during the Cold War with the Soviet Union when the latter developed nuclear and thermonuclear bombs, intercontinental bombers, intercontinental ballistic missiles, and spacecraft. The commander and vice commander NORAD were directly responsible to the US president and Canadian prime minister for air defense of the homelands and assured warning of missile attack. Assured warning was the bedrock of deterrence. Further, NORAD used the distant early warning (DEW) line of radar along the northern reaches of Canada and Alaska for detection of approaching Soviet bombers. It also provided for the mid-Canada line of radar to detect and track unknown aircraft in Canadian air space so they could be intercepted and identified or, when appropriate, engaged and destroyed. NORAD was an important military bond between our two countries with roughly half the personnel in NORAD being Canadian. Less known was the fact that most of the generals/flag officers filling key NORAD billets were Canadian officers.

NORAD Staff:

> Vice commander: Lt. Gen. Don McNaughton, CF
>
> Plans: Brig. Gen. Bruce Burgess, CF, and Brig. Gen. Jack Partington, CF
>
> Operations: Maj. Gen. Lional Burgouis, CF, and Maj. Gen. Ian Patrick, CF
>
> Command director: Brig. Gen. Dave O'Blenis, CF. Dave later came back as a lieutenant general and served as the vice commander NORAD
>
> Brig. Gen. Jerry Putman, USA, command director
>
> Rear Adm. Riley Mixon, USN
>
> Brig. Gen. James Ulm, USAF, command director
>
> Brig. Gen. Jimmy Cash, USAF command director

USSPACECOM, on the other hand, was a relative newcomer established in 1985 and still struggling to establish its niche as a Unified Combatant Command. USSPACECOM was comprised of three subordinate service commands: Army Space Command, commanded by Col. Ronan Ellis, and located in a commercial facility in Colorado Springs; Navy Space Command, commanded by Rear Adm. David Frost, located at Dhalgren Naval Station, Virginia; and Air Force Space Command, commanded by Maj. Gen. Maurice (Tim) Padden, located at Peterson AFB, Colorado. USSPACECOM was collocated with NORAD in a leased commercial facility (Chidlaw Building), northeast of downtown Colorado Springs, Colorado. It was a couple of city blocks from what was once Ent AFB, the support base for NORAD. My former command, Air Defense TAC (ADTAC), was previously located in the Chidlaw Building as a service component of NORAD (1979-1981). Most of the senior officers assigned to NORAD and USSPACECOM were billeted on base at Peterson. The rare exception was vice commander NORAD, Lt. Gen. Don McNaughton, CF, who lived in a leased house in the upscale Broadmoor area.

In my view, there was a significant annual expense to work out of the Chidlaw Building at roughly $1 million rent per year, plus the cost of lots of amenities that would be improved, at no expense, if the headquarters was moved to Peterson AFB. In addition, travel for all the officers and enlisted personnel living on base would be reduced to near zero with little or no impact for personnel living off base. I asked Col. Terry McKenzie to get estimates for the cost of moving and to look for potential space on base that could accommodate both NORAD and USSPACECOM staffs in the same building. Last, I called General Larry Welch, CSAF and informed him that if a move were feasible, there would be significant savings in the first year. He approved the concept if no unforeseen problems arose as the planning went forward. The move, if feasible, was set for midsummer when the current Chidlaw lease expired.

For the reader's edification, the Chidlaw Building, in addition to office space, housed the following activities:

> conference rooms
> theater for large meetings and showing educational films
> small base exchange
> convenience food and sundry store
> printing plant to print and publish NORAD/USSPACECOM
>   directives
> large secure communications facility
> gymnasium
> commercial bank
> credit union
> rest area for nonmission contract employees
> civilian guard force, 24/7/365
> guard force lounge

All of the above and more were available at Peterson AFB at zero cost!

The NORAD mission was well established, and there were many professional Canadian and USAF Air Defenders on the staff and in the field. The Canadian Air Command headed by a lieutenant general was a solid organization and well led. Based on my earlier experience as commander ADTAC, my concerns were with the leadership in the air divisions and the isolated Fighter Interceptor Squadrons. Since ADTAC was formed and moved to Langley AFB, Virginia, in 1981, it had morphed into First Air Force and was currently commanded by Maj. Gen. Buford Derald Lary. Derald, as he was known, spent most of his time in the recce world flying RF-4Cs in the 16th TRS out of Tan Son Nhut Air Base in Vietnam and later in England and Germany with the 10th TRW at Alconbury AB, United Kingdom, and the 26th TRW, respectively. He also commanded the 48th TFW at Lakenheath. He was new to the air defense mission when he took command of First Air Force in December 1985. He inherited the big job of streamlining and reducing the number of air divisions based on increased computational power that was commercially available.

The space mission was new, and there was a paucity of "operational" space expertise in USSPACECOM. Essentially, operation space experience resided in the subordinate Army, Navy, and Air Force Space Commands.

I returned to Colorado Springs on a Friday in late February and, after checking into the VOQ, went directly to Cheyenne Mountain, where I had 24/7 easy access to all of NORAD's and USSPACECOM's command and operational plans. To lead these commands, I had to know, in exquisite detail, all the classified operational plans that were in force day-to-day, as well as those that would be implemented in a crisis. I also needed to fully understand the CINC's responsibilities with regard to missile warning and the protocols for advising the president on Soviet test missile launches, which occurred on a regular basis, almost daily!

When I identified myself to the officer in charge of the security vault and asked for all of the NORAD and USSPACECOM plans, he replied, "Sir, we've got lots of NORAD plans, but there are no USSPACECOM plans here." I was puzzled by the fact that there were no SPACECOM plans in the vault and took all the NORAD plans, a wagon full, back to the Cheyenne Mountain Command Center (CMCC), where I could lay everything out and study without being disturbed. When I got tired of studying, I could walk down into the actual command center and get a tutorial on all of the displays and monitor routine exercises with the DOD Command Center in the Pentagon. It was going to be a long blurry-eyed weekend! It was obvious that NORAD was up to date on their war plans and exercised them twice a year in weeklong exercises that included both air defense activity and redeployment of forces in CONUS, Alaska, and Canada. NORAD's biggest role in air defense at that juncture was the declaration of "unknown" aircraft as "hostile" and as a resource provider. These extended command post exercises culminated with the detection of a Soviet ICBM spasm and providing warning to the National Command Authorities in Washington DC. At that time, a Soviet ICBM spasm was referred to as a Russian Integrated Strategic Operations Plan, or RISOP.

After a couple of NORAD Staff meetings, looking at what happened yesterday, I realized my predecessor only looked at point data. Historical data and trends were ignored. I didn't know whether to be happy or sad about what happened the day prior. On the other hand, historical data displayed in graphs revealed if important aspects of the NORAD and SPACECOM missions were improving or deteriorating. Based on historical data, one could deduce standards and goals for every relevant mission area. I told the senior staff that I wanted to look at historical data in graphic form on a monthly basis with the previous days data compared to the previous year's graph. Back at my office, I started to lay out the kind of charts I wanted to be looking at, when Admiral Ramsey came in with a stack of viewgraphs about eighteen inches tall. "Take a look at these," he said. In response, I started thumbing through them and realized the admiral and I were kindred spirits! The charts he gave me were exactly what I wanted, absent the goals and standards, which needed some historical data to establish.

"Why aren't we using these charts? They are exactly what I'm looking for" was my response.

"Your predecessor found them too busy," said Admiral Ramsey.

"Give them to the staff and tell them to start using them next Monday after filling in all the historical data!" was my guidance.

One of the immediate things we learned was that the time to calculate the ephemeris (earth trace) of a new foreign satellite launch varied wildly over time, from hours to days to weeks in some cases. Based on the historical data, the standard was established as eighteen hours with a goal of ten hours. It was important to know the orbital data on new Soviet reconnaissance satellites quickly so that we could warn all US military commanders when their operations were vulnerable to Soviet overhead collection. It was believed that most Soviet low earth orbiting (LEO) satellites were operational and collecting data within a few hours after injection into orbit. There were a lot of US activities that were important to cover up when in the field of regard of a Soviet satellite. In all, there were dozens of operational space activities that were given standards and goals to measure their performance against.

It was equally obvious that USSPACECOM was way behind the power curve in addressing their Unified Command Plan (UCP) responsibilities in countering and negating the Soviet Space Order of Battle. This would be necessary in the event of a conventional confrontation that might escalate into nuclear exchanges to ensure the US Intelligence and warning satellites would survive, and the Soviets would be degraded. The first order of business for me was to get the staff moving in this direction.

Most of the US Space Order of Battle was in the black world with knowledge of the systems held very closely by the National

Reconnaissance Office (NRO). In fact, the very existence of the NRO was in the "black," and their name and acronym were classified. There were more satellites in the black world than in the acknowledged domain, and it was hard to gain an understanding of what the United States actually had in space and what our true capabilities were. There was a clear need for a "red" and "blue" war room where Soviet and US space capabilities could be displayed. In this regard, it was also important to display both space assets and supporting ground assets to gain an understanding of overall vulnerabilities. Nothing like this existed in USSPACECOM at the time of my arrival on the scene.

Two rooms were identified and turned into classified rooms (SCIFs). Once the rooms were certified for top secret material, the J-2 started populating them with Soviet satellite pictures, specifications, and detailed information about their orbital mechanics, capabilities, and supporting ground stations. Once the red war room became populated with operational data, it became obvious that the Soviet Union had a very robust and geographically distributed ground support capability. I asked the staff if these ground support facilities were included in the US Strategic Integrated Operations Plan (SIOP). No one knew the answer, so a query was sent to the Joint Strategic Target Planning Staff (JSTPS) embedded in the Strategic Air Command (SAC) at Offutt AFB, Nebraska. The mission of the JSTPS was to conduct the intricate and detailed planning for targeting Soviet military capabilities and then produce a detailed SIOP that provided minute-by-minute nuclear weapon impacts on military targets in the Soviet Union and Warsaw Pact nations. The SIOP was reviewed and updated every year based on revisions in Soviet and Warsaw Pact Order of Battle and presented to the president for approval. Word came back that Soviet Space supporting ground sites, launch sites, and booster/satellite storage sites were not in the SIOP. We were giving the Soviets a free ride in space—this had to change immediately. All Soviet Space supporting sites were immediately catalogued and given bombing encyclopedia (BE) numbers. The space-related BE numbers were forwarded to the SAC commander/director JSTPS, Gen. Jack Chain, with a request for immediate inclusion in the SIOP under revision.

The next step was to develop a Space Campaign Plan to be executed by Space Command in the event of crisis or hostilities. The purpose of the Space Campaign Plan would be to execute any or all available options to deny, degrade, and/or destroy the Soviet Space Order of Battle when directed by National Command Authority. I gave the job of developing the Space Campaign Plan to Rear Adm. Jerry Beast, J-3, with support from the J-5 Maj. Gen. Wayne Knudsen, USA. It was an urgent requirement.

It was March 1987, and the Congress was in full budget mode. That involved a parade of senior combatant commanders and service chiefs testifying in front of the very powerful Appropriation and Authorization Committees in both the House and Senate. The process bordered on the ridiculous. It was a five-year defense plan cycle. The current year was funded; the following year, where real money was on the line, was always very tight, if not constrained; but by some magic, the following year was generously programmed, and the out-years programmed funding rose by as much as 20 to 30 percent. The president always provided a fiscally constrained budget for the year under consideration by Congress. OSD would try to accommodate the president's fiscally constrained budget with a percentage cut across the board, or by applying their wisdom in adjusting programs within the services and across the services or some combination of the above. Nonetheless, the current year was always very tight, budgetwise, and the future always looked rosy.

What amused me most about testifying before congressional committees is that the first question was always "Do you support the president's budget?" The obligatory answer was "Yes, I support the president's budget!" Once that initial exchange was over, the person testifying was free to express his or her opinion on any item contained in the budget. Because I was so new in USSPACECOM and NORAD during my first cycle of congressional testimony, General Herres, now vice chairman, was invited to sit with me during my testimonies before these august congressional forums to make sure nothing was overlooked or forgotten by this new guy, or something like that. It was somewhat of a stark contrast between us because I was a warrior asking for systems that would degrade or destroy Soviet space capabilities, whereas General Herres was more inclined to prefer ways to deter. A good example was our testimony before the House Armed Services Committee. Congressman John Spratt, SC, asked if I supported procurement of the antisatellite capability demonstrated on September 13, 1986. I responded in the negative, saying that while the demonstration was successful in destroying a satellite, the concept was poorly weaponized and was not a useful combat capability. I went on to explain that LTV's ASAT required a two-day or longer call-up and needed a lengthy cryogenic cooldown of its seeker prior to loading it on a modified F-15 aircraft. Further, it had very little lateral reach, and thus, the prototype ASAT was neither prompt when needed and could be avoided by the Soviets. Moreover, the buy was for nine ASAT payloads, and that was considerably less than needed to degrade Soviet space capabilities. General Herres, on the other hand, supported the procurement because he believed it would deter the Soviets from attacking US space systems with its operational co-orbital ASAT or its high-power laser system located at Sary Shagan. After the session was adjourned, Congressman John Spratt, SC, came up to me and said, "Good job, we don't fund any conventional systems for deterrence!"

Back in Colorado Springs, I was learning firsthand how our very robust missile warning capability worked and how capable the Soviets were in launching satellites and testing their operational and new ICBMs and SLBMs. The Iran/Iraq War was still ongoing, with the Iraqis launching one or more short-range Scud missiles into the Iranian capital of Tehran daily. These launches provided excellent training for NORAD's Missile Warning Center and for the new CINC. While the Defense Support Program (DSP) satellites were designed with Soviet longer-range ICBMs and SLBMs in mind, the infrared focal planes in these satellites were capable of picking up the dimmer signature of Scud missiles. Hence, each of the five missile warning crews was experiencing four to five Scud, satellite, and test missile launches per week. Their individual and crew skills were well honed, which was exceptionally good for our ability to do the real job of missile warning of an attack on North America.

The Unified Command Plan spelled out the responsibilities of the various combatant commands and delineated the boundaries of geographical commands. The UCP also gave USSPACECOM the responsibility of "preparing to deploy Ballistic Missile Defenses!" To me, this appeared to be the most important responsibility that would fail if it didn't get my full endorsement and attention. I formed a BMD Deployment Task Force under the very capable and energetic brigadier general Donald Lionette, USA. Further, I directed that all correspondence internal to USSPACECOM and also leaving the headquarters be written on a single sheet of paper, with coordination blocks for all the staff agencies. In addition, remembering those days in the Pentagon, as an action officer and vice chief, that the red-bordered JCS papers got everyone's attention as important. So I directed that USSPACECOM's BMD papers be purple bordered because they needed to get attention. Last, every paper had a sequential number, so everyone would know if they missed getting one of the papers. It seemed to work, and I occasionally received calls from other commands and the Strategic Defense Initiative Office (SDIO) that they received paper no. 12 but didn't have no. 11, and would we please retransmit no. 11. The task force briefed me monthly on progress toward deployment and all the outstanding issues. General Lionette, if you never met him, is about six feet three and weighed about 230 pounds, all muscle with a loud commanding voice. He got things done and done right! The right man for the job!

The next big event was moving both NORAD and USSPACECOM headquarters to Peterson AFB. The move was accomplished over a weekend, with everyone on the two staff (including me) pitching in to move all of our office stuff from the Chidlaw Building to Building 470 at Peterson AFB. On Sunday evening, all headquarters' office furniture, safes, equipment, and documents were completely removed from the leased building in Colorado Springs; and on Monday morning, we opened for business in Building 470. The Air Force Space Command, as host for both NORAD and USSPACECOM, saved in excess of $1 million annually going forward indefinitely, not counting cost of the civilian guard force and communications equipment. At this writing (2012), it has been twenty-five years. I had stipulated that the CINC's office had to be in the middle of the building with NORAD on one side and USSPACECOM on the other. Next to my office on one side was the office of deputy CINCNORAD and on the other, the office of the deputy CINCSPACE. No staff officer from either NORAD or US Space Command had to cross "command lines" to get to my office.

Mr. Derek Vander Schaff, DOD deputy inspector general, accompanied by a small team, paid a visit to NORAD and USSPACECOM. His mission was to downsize the number of personnel within the two commands by merging some of the functions or perhaps just cutting authorizations. It was made clear to Mr. Vander Schaff that both NORAD and USSPACECOM were significantly smaller than any of the other Unified or Specified Commands by at least 30 percent, and that NORAD was a binational command with the headquarters manned roughly 50 percent by Canadian officers and enlisted personnel. The thought of merging command functions such as plans, operations, and intelligence would be impractical because of the special clearances required for access to information about our satellites. At that time, all space and satellite information was on a very limited billet allocation. It was extremely difficult to obtain billets for US Service personnel with top secret clearances, and virtually impossible for Canadians. Moreover, Canada opposed Ballistic Missile Defense (BMD).and prohibited the use of Canadian forces personnel in any capacity that involved BMD. This also made it difficult to merge operational and planning functions at that juncture. Nonetheless, Mr. Vander Schaff's team rooted around for about two weeks and published a report suggesting that significant personnel savings were possible and offered his recommendations. We had the opportunity to comment on his findings and refuted all of them. As I recall, no personnel authorizations were lost. However to be fair, as NORAD downsized to six alert sites just prior to the September 11, 2001 attacks, there had been some merging of functions between NORAD and USSPACECOM.

The mixed and frequent launch rate of shorter-range missiles exposed a weakness in our ability to perform both the North American Missile Warning mission and the Theater Warning mission simultaneously. The Canadians flag officers in NORAD insisted that warning of missile attack on North America was paramount and should take precedence. Clearly, from a political and homeland defense perspective, they were right! On the other hand, the shorter-range missiles inbound to NATO nations and our European-based forces would reach their targets in about one-fourth the time of an ICBM launched from the Soviet Union to North America. Hence, warning on shorter range and shorter time of flight missiles could not wait their turn in the telephone queue. The J-3s of both NORAD and USSPACECOM were pounding on the table wanting to be first on the "red phone."

The solution to this conundrum was relatively simple but cost a few dollars. I established a Space Operations Center (SPOC) in the Headquarters Building on Peterson AFB. It provided all of the information displayed in the Cheyenne Mountain Complex (CMCC) with a much smaller staff. It had direct lines to the NMCC in the Pentagon and all Theater Command Centers. It was available 24/7/365, with the manpower taken out of hide. It was a vital addition and gave the USSPACE Staff access to combat operations. It also made it a lot easier for me to make the CINC assessment on missile launches worldwide. It worked like this. In the event of near simultaneous ICBM and IRBM launches, the command duty officer in Cheyenne Mountain would be on the red phone with the defense duty officer (DDO) in the NMCC. Simultaneously, the SPOC duty officer would be on the red phone with the command duty officer (CDO) in CENTCOM, EUCOM, or PACOM. Further, if a Soviet ICBM launch into their test impact area on the Kamchatka Peninsula had a potential for impacting in Alaska or on the West Coast, I could run to the SPOC in two minutes and see the data. The same applied to the shorter-range launches that had the potential for impacting in Europe or the Far East. I could also monitor US Navy SLBM launches from their Atlantic test range to ensure the missiles didn't go awry and threaten land areas in South America or

Africa. Much later, the SPOC would play a much bigger role for my successor, Gen. Don Kutyna, providing him the necessary displays and data to provide missile warnings to CENTCOM Headquarters forward in Riyadh, Saudi Arabia, during Desert Storm.

Lt. Gen. James Abrahamson was appointed the first director of the Strategic Defense Initiative Office (SDIO) and charged with the responsibility of developing the technologies to field a Ballistic Missile Defense (BMD) capability to match President Reagan's vision to protect the nation. I had known General Abrahamson since we were colonels and had worked with him as the director SDIO when I was the vice chief. He had great vision and was a superb innovator and motivator of his team. General Abrahamson called and said that he was going to build a BMD Simulation Center and had identified two potential locations. One was at Hanscom Field, Massachusetts, home of the Electronic Systems Division (ESD) of the air force. The other possibility was at Falcon Air Base about ten miles east of Colorado Springs, Colorado (now Schriever AFB), where Air Force Space Command was commanding and controlling all of our military space assets. I told Jim that if he located his BMD simulation facility at Falcon AB (where there was plenty of high-security real estate), I would use it for training and certifying all of my BMD crews. In addition, I would use it as a temporary command and control facility when a BMD operational capability emerged prior to construction of an operational BMD command and control facility in Cheyenne Mountain. I further suggested that I would add an additional Cheyenne Mountain crew so that each shift would have a full day of training on the Falcon BMD simulator at the end of a three-day shift in Cheyenne Mountain. He said he'd get back to me when he evaluated all the factors weighing on his decision. Construction of the Joint National Integration Center (JNIC) started at Falcon AB in the late 1980s and has been expanding ever since. It has undergone many name changes and is now the Missile Defense Integration and Operations Center (MDIOC).

Lt. Gen. Don McNaughton set the bar high by becoming qualified as a command director in the CMCC. He usually pulled a shift every other Friday evening from 1600 hours until the shift ended at midnight. It was a superb way to demonstrate that the work of the command director and supporting warning centers were central to our ability to do our job. Moreover, it gave him the opportunity to get to know and calibrate all the key personnel in our warning centers. I followed his lead and became qualified as a command director, learning all the various mission responsibilities and running the dozens of checklists. Equally important, the "Swing Shift," as it was called, was subjected to several

Higher Headquarters Command Post exercises. The premier of all these simulation was and still is the "night blue" exercise, which simulates the launch of a Soviet RISOP. The exercise stimulated all of the displays in the CMCC with all events displayed in a real-time domain. In other words, from launches at Soviet missile fields to impacts on Washington DC and critical strategic assets, the elapsed time was roughly thirty minutes. There were key players on the Missile Event Conference and subsequent Missile Threat Conference from DOD, CIA, NSA, state department, and other nuclear CINCs. Night blue exercises were very realistic and excellent training for the combatant commander responsible for advising the president on the nature and magnitude of an attack—should one ever materialize.

Not surprisingly, CINCNORAD's assessment on a missile attack was scripted and conveyed supposedly well-known and clearly understood meanings to those on the other end of the red phone. For example, there were three possible assessment responses:

> No! The activity being reported by space- and land-based sensors does not indicate that this is a state-sponsored attack.

> Concern! The missile events being reported, coupled with other activity (bombers), are not sufficient yet to indicate a state-sponsored attack. Stand by!

> Yes! Space- and land-based sensors are reporting launches from multiple Soviet ICBM fields as well as SLBM launches from both the Atlantic and Pacific Oceans. We have verified that our sensor sites are producing these tracks and believe they are real. This is clearly a state-sponsored attack!

The responses to the president are very coarse "yes" and "no" and are readily and immediately understood without any ambiguity. "Concern" signals that something is happening that is not immediately clear. For example, although highly unlikely, suppose a single Soviet submarine in the Pacific salvos a full load of SLBMs and they are headed toward North America. CINCNORAD would likely assess that the Soviet Union would not risk their survival with just a dozen or so SLBMs. Could this be the "mad submarine captain" acting alone? It is believed that Soviet submarines went to sea with the captain holding sealed launch codes. Or is it possible the Soviets would purposely launch SLBMs at critical Command and Control Nodes, believing that the United States would not launch its SIOP in response to a small number of incoming missiles—thinking it might be an accident or rogue commander acting without authority. The scenario outlined would likely lead to a "concern" assessment. In about nine minutes after the submarine SLBM launch, missile defense radars would acquire and track the incoming warheads and accurately predict their impact points. Knowing the impact points would reveal likely intention of the salvo with sufficient time remaining to execute the US SIOP.

It is noteworthy to point out that in the mid to late 1970s, some strategic pundits suggested that the Soviet Union and the United States might possibly fall into a limited nuclear exchange to demonstrate resolve to launch a full spasm if circumstances continued to deteriorate/escalate. The theory went something like this. The Soviets launch two ICBMs into national parks to demonstrate resolve. Perhaps these national parks were the Wyoming Grasslands and Big Bend, Texas. One would think that would be very obvious. Unfortunately, the computers at NORAD, at that juncture, would associate those "predicted impacts" with the nearest critical military installation. The Wyoming Grasslands might be tagged as Ellsworth AFB, South Dakota, a major Strategic Air Command (SAC) bomber and ICBM base. The Big Bend, Texas, could be tagged as a strike against Dyess AFB, another SAC bomber base. The logic that was programmed into the NORAD computer preceded thoughts of limited attacks and made eminent sense when those programs were written.

The limited exchange theory never found favor with me because so much of the unpopulated land in the United States is upwind of highly populated areas with significant manufacturing capability and defense-related facilities. The Sand Hills of Nebraska are upwind of Offutt AFB, SAC Headquarters, and Omaha, Nebraska. The Rocky Mountains and National Forests are upwind of Cheyenne Mountain, Peterson AFB, Fort Carson, and Colorado Springs, Colorado. On the other hand, a similar situation does not exist in the Soviet Union. Limited nuclear exchanges with the Soviet Union could lead to hundreds of thousands of delayed casualties in the United States but very little of the same in the Soviet Union. I saw it as a very bad concept except for eggheads who were bored with chess or needed a reason to sell another book.

It must have been the summer of 1989 when the JASONs came to visit and review USSPACECOM's planning for Ballistic Missile Defense. The JASONs consist of about thirty PhDs and scientists who, under the aegis of the Institute for Defense Analysis (IDA), take on OSD's most vexing and perplexing problems. Gen. William Y. Smith,

USAF (ret.) was then the IDA director and escort for the visit. In 1974, Maj. Gen. Willy Y. Smith was the "den mother" for the Six-Man Group of which I was a member. I gave them the briefing on missile warning, including the histogram of how long it took to determine, with certainty, that one or more ballistic missiles had been launched against the United States. Included was the time to third-stage burnout of an SS-18 Soviet ICBM and the projected outcome of a Brilliant Pebbles (BP) defense against the first spasm of a Soviet RISOP. For the reader, BPs were the brainchild of eminent scientists, Drs. Teller and Lowell Wood of Lawrence Livermore National Laboratory. BPs were envisioned to be small semiautonomous space-based interceptors capable of engaging Soviet ICBMs. When the briefing was finished, a JASON said, "I can defeat your strategic defense concept!" He went on to say that all the Soviets would have to do to defeat the Brilliant Pebbles is launch about one hundred fake and unarmed ICBMs at the United States. The JASON said, "You would mistake this as a real attack and engage them with your Brilliant Pebbles (BP). After your Brilliant Pebbles were expended, creating a hole in the BP constellation, the Soviets would time their real ICBM launch to fly through that hole and destroy the United States!"

My response was measured! "Yes, you are undoubtedly correct that I could likely be tricked into engaging those fake ICBMs. However, at the same time, I would be advising the president that the Soviets had launched a preemptive attack against the United States and that those warheads would be arriving in about twenty-five minutes. The president would most likely release the SIOP against the Soviet Union and all of its strategic military forces. As you well know, it would take about ninety minutes for the hole in the BP constellation to return to where the Soviets could take advantage of it. Hence, our missiles would impact about an hour before that void was in place." Then I added, "This is not like playing Cowboys and Indians. There are real consequences to causing your adversary into thinking that you have just launched a strategic missile attack. If you are successful in creating that false impression, you may just get a full-fledged strategic retaliatory response." There was no further discussion. I often wondered if that scientist is still a JASON.

General Herres called and informed me that USSPACECOM was on the list of places the chief of the Chinese Space Force wanted to visit and provided me the dates. I guess that was a good thing; improved relationship with the Chinese Communists, or more specifically the Chinese military leadership, could help reduce tensions between our two countries. I started making a list of places that I might take him to visit, the Global Positioning Satellite Constellation control facility at Falcon Air Force Station (now Schriever AFB) was my first choice. General Hartinger had broken ground at this relatively new air force facility about twelve miles east of Colorado Springs in 1981, and it was taking on increased importance in the military space world every day. That and a visit to CMCC Missile Warning Center and Command Post would be more than he would likely expect to see. When the general arrived courtesy of an air force executive jet, I took him to his quarters and made arrangements to pick him up the next morning for breakfast at the Peterson AFB officers' club. While at breakfast, he asked, to my surprise, where I lived through his interpreter. "On base not far from here," I responded. As soon as that information was conveyed to him, he asked if he could see my quarters after we finished breakfast. Yes seemed like the right answer, so I called Sheila, who was an early riser, and told her I was bringing the chief of the Chinese Air Force over to see our house in about thirty minutes. I can imagine the flurry of activity that took place when I hung up on the command post radio phone (we didn't have cell phones yet). When I took my Chinese guest to the house, he bowed to my wife and then clasped his hands behind his back and walked through every room, including the laundry room and the garage as if he was Inspector Clouseau of movie fame. When he finished the tour, he said, "Ding hao," which is Mandarin for "number one." He was obviously being polite because it certainly wasn't a number-one house. In fact, it was a converted BOQ built about four years earlier under General Hartinger's direction. Initially, it was intended to house VIP visitors and had four modest bedrooms opening onto a hall that led to a small social room and a small do-it-yourself kitchen. Prior to General Herres's arrival as CINC Space, the VOQ entertainment space and kitchen were enlarged and a two-car garage added. It was totally inadequate for living and entertaining—as were all the houses Sheila and I lived in as a colonel and flag officer, except for the leased house in Aviano, Italy. Since I retired, new quarters for the commanders of Air Force Space Command and Northern Command have been built, once in the late 1990s and again in 2011. The 2011 edition of quarters are much nicer but just barely adequate.

The Space Campaign Plan was not getting any traction, so I took it back from the J-3 and sketched out what I thought it should be, based on my newfound knowledge of Soviet space capabilities and the campaign plan done at Ninth Air Force. It had to deal with a protracted conventional war such as NATO versus the Warsaw Pact or options that might be useful to show resolve without crossing the nuclear threshold. I handed it to the

"Mission Impossible Team" inherited from General Herres. The MI Team was a group of six field grade officers led by Air Force Col. Dick Stafranski with representative from all the services. They were exceptionally skilled in conceptualizing ways of converting ideas to powerful and descriptive graphics. This was prior to PowerPoint, so everything they developed for briefings had to be converted to viewgraphs in the base photo lab. This created a time lag of about three days verses the current technology of about four hours for a fifty-slide presentation. Once we had the campaign plan in briefing format, it was much easier to both upgrade the conceptual framework and convert the concept to a real plan.

The campaign plan briefing became a best seller even though it was classified top secret because of the adversary capabilities contained within. It was briefed to members of both the House and Senate that held top secret clearances in closed sessions. Once the Congress clearly understood the asymmetries between the United States and the Soviet Union, it was much easier to get funding for critical space projects. Air Force secretary and director NRO, Pete Aldridge, and I viewed Soviet Space prowess through different prisms. Secretary Aldridge rightfully believed our technology was far better than the Soviets and that our satellites lived a longer useful life in space, which was demonstrably true. The downside was that our capability to relaunch after a failure on the launch pad or in orbit was measured in months or, in some cases, well over a year. On the other hand, the Soviets had a very robust launch capability, lots of satellites in the barn waiting to be launched, and the ability to launch satellites in rapid succession.

In one conversation with Secretary Aldridge, I commented that our overhead showed that the Soviets, in preparation for an on-orbit replacement launch, mated satellites with two separate boosters, erected both on separate launch pads, and after what appeared to be a launch readiness check, successfully launched one of the two. The secretary saw this as a weakness, suggesting the Soviets didn't have the confidence to stack, mate, and check out just one satellite for launch. On the other hand, as an operator, I saw this as a great robustness and the ability to launch many satellites in a short period of time. To give the reader some appreciation for the logistics of launch in the late 1980s time frame: It took the combination of Space Industry and the Military Space Launch community several months to prepare and check out a "booster stack," which usually consisted of three booster stages and a couple of strap on solid rockets. This was all done vertically. After the booster stacking was completed, mating of the satellite and attaching the nose cone added another two or three months to the process. Once the satellite was launched and successfully injected into orbit, there was a nonoperational period while the materials the satellite was made of were allowed to "out-gas" so no optical mirrors or sensors would be contaminated. Then there was a lengthy period of on-orbit checkout. All in all, it was a very time consuming and careful process. On the other hand, the Soviet stacked their booster and mated satellites on a horizontal cradle. This allowed for stacking and mating to be accomplished in warehouse-like structures instead of towers hundreds of feet tall. As Mark Twain would say, "It was like the difference between lightning and lightning bug." The Soviets also appeared to bypass a lengthy on-orbit checkout and went operational by the third or fourth orbit.

One Soviet system the US Space Community kept on a close watch was their co-orbital Antisatellite (ASAT) Weapon. They conducted quite a few tests of this weapon against their own target satellites. They would launch the ASAT against a satellite in low earth orbit (LEO), but it would take three or more orbits before their ASAT could catch the victim satellite and cripple it with something like a barrage of shotgun pellets. It was easy for our space and missile track optical sensors and radar to observe the "chase" and the results. By our count, the co-orbital ASAT was only about 30 percent effective, still a very big threat considering our glacially slow replacement process. After the Soviet Empire collapsed and I had retired, OSD sponsored a visit to Russia headed by Dr. Van Cleave and a number of recently retired generals and admirals in February 1992. On that visit, I had the opportunity to meet with several active-duty Russian generals and admirals, including the head of their Space Forces. I told the general in charge of Soviet Space Forces that I had studied their co-orbital ASAT and noted that it was only about 30 percent effective. He responded that they purposely only shot down a third of their intended victims. The rest of the tests were close flybys to test the system without intending to actually shoot the victim satellite because they didn't want to create more "space debris." He said the actual success rate was 96 percent. The United States does a lot of Ballistic Missile Defense System testing with offsets so that we can determine success or failure without actually hitting the target. I suspect the Russian general was telling the truth. This is one example of how "good technical intelligence" can be way off of the mark.

NORAD took on greater responsibilities when Pres. George H. W. Bush appointed former secretary of education William John Bennett as the director of the Office of National Drug Control Policy, or "Drug Czar." Director "Bill" Bennett was able to get President Bush to enlist the DOD into supporting the "War on Drugs." Nothing official came from OSD with regard to what Unified commanders with counter-drug smuggling assets were to do in this regard. In my view, the smuggling of addictive drugs into the United States was a heinous crime that was inflicting great pain on our society, as well as sucking money out of the economy and enriching international criminals. I wasn't inclined to wait for instructions but rather to take action that would lead to interdicting drugs flowing into the United States by air. The E-3A track of a low slow aircraft flying from Mexico's Baja California into the United States just prior to dawn, called out by one of President Carter's cabinet members during the Pentagon AWACS Briefing, was still vivid in my mind.

First, we stood up a NORAD Drug Interdiction Center (NORDIC) in NORAD Headquarters. One of our best intelligence analysts was put in charge of taking all the available data on drug infiltration air routes and displaying it on a large map of the border areas of Mexico and the Gulf of Mexico. Contact was made with all the national agencies doing drug interdiction: Coast Guard, Customs, Border Patrol, and the Drug Enforcement Agency (DEA). The DEA assigned an agent to NORAD Headquarters with a lot of experience in the field; he had excellent contacts with agents still in the field and was totally committed to the mission. When asked how long he had been a federal agent, he showed me his silver badge with a big number 3 on it. He said, "I'm agent number three, Elliot Ness of Al Capone fame was agent number one." That revelation convinced me NORAD had the right DEA agent to assist us in the war on drugs.

As we built up the NORDIC, one of the analysts came up with what I thought was a dynamite idea. She was a former army major in the intelligence field working at the operational level. Her idea was to drive the length of the land border with Mexico, including the Rio Grande River, stopping along the way to talk to ranchers, farmers, and other residents living along the border. She was certain that they knew firsthand what time of day and where light aircraft were crossing the border and the direction they were going. Once she collected this data, we could plot it on our map and then schedule AWACS to conduct surveillance in these areas while doing intercept training. All I needed to do was approve a thirty-day TDY, rental car, and advance her $2,000 for expenses. It made sense to me, so off she went. When she returned, it took almost three full days for the debriefing. It was a treasure trove of regular aircraft sightings mostly just before dawn or at dusk flying low into the United States. She was able to identify a lot of aircraft types, including an ancient C-47. Most of the sightings corresponded with abandoned airfields or desert areas that could easily be used for landing and takeoff, and most were only a mile of two from paved roads with easy access. In addition, she was also able to collect considerable information on overland and river crossing routes that we could share with FORCECOM.

Working with US Customs and the Coast Guard, it was clear that once an E-3A had a track of a potential smuggler, the AWACS mission commander could scramble an F-16 to follow the intruding aircraft; however, it was imperative that we get a civil agency with arrest authority involved. This meant getting a US Customs aircraft modified with an F-16 search and track radar to relieve the F-16. Customs agents could also work with local authorities, County sheriffs and state police, to intercept the intruders once they landed. It was important to the civil authorities that we worked covertly with them to keep the military role in drug interdiction out of the media. The NORAD and TAC's First Air Force budgets were significantly larger than the combined sum of all the civil agencies we worked with. These agencies were concerned that their budgets might be cut if it was known they were getting help from the military. To my knowledge, none of NORAD's and First Air Force support was ever reported in the media. On the other hand, the NORDIC was making a difference in the war on drugs, and we were regularly sharing data with FORCECOM, PACOM, LANTCOM, and SOUTHCOM.

I was invited to the Executive Mansion, next to the White House, to brief on preparations to deploy Ballistic Missile Defenses. It turned out to be a ruse to get me there, so one of the then prominent administration advisors could brief me on a "concept" to place Brilliant Pebbles (BPs) on MX Peacekeeper Missiles. The proposed concept went something like this. Twenty Peacekeepers would have their reentry vehicles replaced with fifty BPs for a total of one thousand BPs that could be placed in orbit. Then if US/Soviet Relations deteriorated and the intelligence community believed we were on the brink of war, the president could order the launch of the MXs loaded with BPs and deter the Soviets from attacking. I pushed back, saying, "If we're on the brink of war, the last thing you want to do is launch MX ICBMs that could be viewed as a 'preemptive' attack!"

The advisor's response was "The Soviets will know that these twenty MXs only carry BPs, and they will know exactly where they are located, so there will be no mistake about what we are doing."

I pushed back again, saying, "Have you ever heard of the fog of war? Do you think that on the brink of war, and with the known limitations of their missile warning systems, that they will remain calm?"

His response was "Yes, they will know that these MXs only carry BPs."

Third pushback! "If your intelligence inputs are correct and the US is on the brink of war with the Soviets, they will know that it takes about ninety minutes for our BPs to reach orbit, to disperse, and to become active. Hence, the Soviets will know that they have about seventy minutes to attack us before the BPs are in position to defend the United States. You may have just pushed them into attacking."

His response was "General, you just don't understand!" To the contrary, what I did understand is that it was a really idiotic concept dreamed up by someone who had never heard the sound of gunfire looking for someone in uniform to buy in.

Every combatant commander has the right and authority to assess the performance of assigned forces under his control. NORAD had been doing this for decades by conducting unannounced visits to air defense alert sites where two interceptors were armed and "cocked" ready to scramble. And two combat-ready interceptor pilots or aircrews sat alert, ready to respond to a scramble when the klaxon sounded in their alert area. The "alert" standard was to be airborne in five minutes or less from the instant the klaxon rang. CINCNORAD or deputy CINCNORAD personally approved these no-notice inspections to ensure they would not impact any known or anticipated activities. Normally, they were scheduled to occur at about 0500 hours to preclude interrupting normal sleep patterns of aircrews pulling alert duty. The fitness of the aircraft to perform alert duty was also evaluated. There was a period of time when aircraft unfit to fly were put on alert because "after all, no one expected the Russians to attack, so why waste a flyable aircraft on alert?" On one such inspection to an Air Defense Interceptor Base in the northeast, TAC personnel barred NORAD inspectors from entering the alert site even though they presented a letter signed by CINCNORAD authorizing the inspection. It is important to note that only the TAC personnel and aircraft inside the wire at the alert site could be subject to this inspection as they were "chopped to NORAD control." TAC was the parent command of US-based Air Defense Alert Forces since ADTAC (now First Air Force) was activated on October 1, 1979. Not only was it disappointing that the planned inspection didn't take place, but it was also a significant waste of taxpayer dollars for cost of commercial air transportation, rental cars, and motels for five NORAD personnel conducting the inspection. I called Gen. Robert Russ, commander TAC, and asked for an explanation. His response was terse: "I have the Title 10 responsibilities for training, organizing, and equipping, therefore, there is no need for your inspections! NORAD Personnel will no longer be allowed to inspect TAC Air Defense Alert Sites!" It was some kind of silly power play, so I didn't waste any time in trying to reason with General Russ. However, I did send a message to Admiral Crowe, chairman JCS, asking if combatant commanders had the authority to evaluate the readiness and capabilities of forces assigned to them and under their tasking authority. A courtesy copy of the message was sent to General Welch, CSAF, and commander TAC, General Russ. The response from chairman JCS came back in very short order for a busy man. It was also terse: "A combatant commander has full authority to evaluate the personnel and equipment assigned and under his tasking authority. This authority cannot be abridged." I sent a team back to that same northeast airbase a few days later.

NORAD funded a software development effort at Tyndall AFB, Florida, also the home of First Air Force, and one of their bases. Twice a year, NORAD hosted a Software Configuration Conference to vet all of the proposed software improvement efforts for the Cheyenne Mountain Missile Warning and Air Defense Software as well as the Canadian East and West Command Centers. First Air Force was one of the attendees, and I chaired the conference. At the end of the conference, all the proposed software revisions and additions were prioritized and man-hours available assigned to the various projects. The Software Configuration Management Plan was signed out by CINCNORAD. The Canadian defense minister assigned personnel and dollars to both US and Canadian software projects, as did the DOD.

A few months following the most recent Software Configuration Control Conference, General McNaughton brought a Canadian officer assigned to software development at Tyndall AFB to report on how our activities were progressing. The Canadian major reported that NORAD projects had been set aside in favor of First Air Force needs by Major General Lary. Essentially, NORAD personal and dollars were not being used to work on NORAD's highest software priorities. After a few minutes of conversation with the major, I was convinced that NORAD's effort and funds had been hijacked. I placed a call to General Lary with the intention of getting our software problems back on track, if in fact our money and manpower were misplaced according to decisions taken by the Software Configuration Control Board. I asked Major General Lary if the reports I was receiving that NORAD's software priorities had been sidetracked to put more effort on correcting First Air Force Regional Center problems were accurate. His response was "Yes, that was correct." He had diverted the man-hours and dollars to resolve his problems. I immediately pointed out to him that his problems were Tactical Air Command problems and that he did not ask my permission to divert my resources to fix his problems! Further, that I would not tolerate the diversion of Canadian forces personnel and funds to solve a US Air Force/ Tactical Air Command problem. Then I advised him to immediately stop what he was doing and revert the effort to support the findings and recommendations of the Software Configuration Control Board (SCCB), and to remember that the software facility was not under his command. To my great surprise, he said he couldn't change course and that his work was more important. Then I asked Major General to look at his left shoulder and tell me how many stars he could see. After a defining pause, he responded two. I then told him I counted four on my shoulder. Now that I had his attention, I ordered him to faithfully follow the SCCB directive or I would take the following actions:

> Inform General Russ that he, Major General Lary, had committed fraud in the use of Canadian funds and personnel.

> Call the General Officer Section of Air Staff Personnel and report his transgressions.

> Write a letter detailing his dereliction of duty, fraud, waste, and abuse in a letter of admonishment for insertion in his personnel folder and promotion file.

> Discuss the matter with Gen. Larry Welch, CSAF.

Those comments seemed to sober him up, and he said, "Yes, sir" in a muted voice. I further advised him that I would be tracking the software revision progress very closely and to not try to pull anything over on me. This usurpation of authority by a flag officer really got my dander up! General Lary retired in August 1989.

Many of air force and USSPACECOM surveillance assets were located outside the United States. It was essential to visit these far-flung assets to understand how everything worked and was lashed together through communication links, meet the people, and thank them for their good work. On one such visit to Europe, a critical operational problem was discovered. Missile Warning Satellites (DSPs) downlinked their data to three locations on planet Earth, the DSP covering the Soviet Union land-based ICBMs and Atlantic-based SLBMs reported to a receiver site in Europe. All the electronics for the DSP receiver and communication links were housed in mobile trailers. While visiting the site, I wanted to check the communications with NORAD's command director in Cheyenne Mountain. I picked up the red ringdown phone and heard only static when the other end picked up. I hung up the phone after a couple of shouts that got no response. The site commander shouted into the communications van about patching in another line. I picked up the red phone again. This time, it was obvious another human was at the other end but was unintelligible. The third try was successful, and while not clear, everything said was understandable on both ends. The NORAD communications officer (J-6), Maj. Gen. Jim Cassity, was travelling with us and arranged for a briefing on the communications problems I experienced and how to fix them the following day. That troubled direct phone line is the same one used every time there is a missile or space launch reported to Cheyenne Mountain's Missile Warning Center by the command duty officer to validate that the launch is real and the DSP is working properly. It is central to eliminating false warnings like the one on November 9, 1979, which put the United States on the edge of going to war.

The next day, a young air force first lieutenant briefed us that the problem I experienced was not uncommon and was the result of high moisture content in the soil in that area. Part of the link traveled across the host country's commercial telephone system, and the responsible host nation agency was not very responsive to the "trouble" complaints submitted by the unit. I asked the lieutenant if he was married and lived on the economy. "Yes" was the answer to both questions. I then asked if they had a telephone in their home. The answer was also affirmative. Then I asked how far they lived from the site we were at and if their phone worked every time they placed a call. Again, the responses were "Not far from the site" and "yes." Then I pointed out that the soil was the same damp soil, the host telephone system was the same for both, and therefore something must be failing within the trailers or in the connection with the host nation's telecom system. My instructions were to first replace the telephone instruments; if that doesn't work, replace all the connections; if that doesn't fix the problem, replace all the wiring. It was pointed out to the lieutenant that if he and his wife received the same bad service from the host nation's telephone system, they wouldn't pay the bill until they received acceptable service. We should also refuse to pay our bill until we were certain that a good signal was successfully passing through the host's system. I strongly suggested they get with the host provider as soon as possible and work toward a solution to the red line telephone communications problem. Clearly, I was getting less and less tolerant of Act of God causes to problems encountered.

On the KC-135 flight back to Colorado Springs, Major General Cassity was instructed to conduct a full month of test calls to every satellite and radar reporting element in the Missile Warning Network.

During the first month, at least one thousand phone calls would be evenly distributed among the sites. Each call would be rated on clarity and the number of attempts to achieve operational clarity. For example, operational clarity was a one, acceptable was a two, and garbled was a three. Operational clarity on the first ringdown was a one, operational clarity on the second attempt was a two, and so on. The objective was an average of 1.1 in both categories. In hindsight, the criteria should have been 1.0 in both categories.

Following the first month of one thousand calls to the critical sensor reporting sites, I met with Major General Cassity and his senior staff for a report on the project. The numbers were dismal. It took, on the average, 2.3 calls to achieve an operationally acceptable connection. The average clarity on the first call to a site was approximately 2.5. Our communications with critical sensor and space downlink reporting sites was abysmal. My suspicion was that it got this way over time and military personal accepted it as "business as usual" for military systems. It would be impossible for this to happen in our personal lives—for example, with our cars, with our domestic water supply, with electrical power from the grid, with our commercial telephone service, etc. Can you imagine the outcry against AT&T if you had to dial three times to get a connection, to the local power company if electricity to your home was only available two days a week, or to the car dealership if your car wouldn't start two days out of three?

My guidance was to change out telephone interments, do continuity checks on all the internal lines, and send "cure notices" to all the commercial service providers. After three months of repeating the "one thousand" calls to critical operational sites worldwide, the report showed we were making progress. The averages for both number of attempts and clarity were hovering right at 1.2 just above the 1.1 goal. I congratulated them for the progress we were making and told the General Cassity and the J-6 Staff to keep working on the problem and making the one thousand monthly calls. As I was getting up to leave, General Cassity mentioned that the averages would be better if it wasn't for one problem line. I asked what line that was and was just about floored with the response. It was our most critical link with a not-too-distant DSP satellite-reporting site. In response, I directed General Cassity to remove the STU-3 encryption phone from his office and personally drive to that site and install it on a commercial line. I would take the STU-3 from my office and deliver it to the Cheyenne Mountain Command Center (CMCC). Thus, we would have a top secret commercial link between these two sites. If the red phone didn't work, they could use the

STU-3s with just a few seconds lost in reporting time caused by having to dial a number. DSP satellites, on the average, would provide all the necessary information on a missile launch in seventy seconds. This included launch location, type of missile, direction of flight, and a large projected impact area. The command duty officer in the CMCC had just under three minutes to get all available information from the sensor reporting site for the Missile Event Conference with the National Military Command Center (NMCC) in the Pentagon and the National Command Authority. Hence, a few seconds of delay on the telephone connection was insignificant compared to the need for an intelligible connection. It took nearly six months to get immediate clarity on all the key voice communications links. We also implemented immediate trouble reports on all communication link incidents.

The South Korean air force chief sent an invitation, asking me to speak at their Air Force Academy. Because of our close defense and military ties with South Korea, I accepted the invitation. This also provided an opportunity to visit an optical space track site located on a mountaintop in South Korea. I also took the opportunity to take along a major from Army Space Command who was an expert with GPS Sluggers, the ground receiver purchased by Col. Ronan Ellis for use by army forces. As mentioned earlier, a Slugger was small enough to fit in the large leg pocket on an army or Marine Corps fatigue uniform. A refueling stop in Hawaii would provide the opportunity to visit Adm. Hunt Hardisty, CINCPAC, and show him and his J-3 what the revolutionary GPS Slugger could do for Pacific Land Forces. I also planned to visit Gen. Wally Nutting, commander United Nations Forces Korea (CINCUNK), and demonstrate the Slugger. The speech at the South Korean Air Force Academy simply opened the door for all these important activities along the way.

At Camp Smith, Hawaii, the army major demonstrated both the precision and the operational value of the GPS Slugger. The flag officers assembled by Admiral Hardisty to take part in the demonstration were to a man unimpressed. The army general said soldiers use maps and are proficient in land navigation—they didn't need GPS satellites, or Sluggers—just something else to weigh a soldier down. The admiral from CINCPACFLEET said that all navy ships were equipped with two Inertial Navigation Systems (INS), and these provided very precise navigation for their ships. In addition, all ship's navigators were very proficient in celestial navigation. The Pacific Navy didn't need Sluggers either.

In Korea, the major and I took the Slugger to General Nutting's headquarters, where the major put on a good show. Prior to leaving on the trip, he looked up several potential key military targets in North Korea and put their coordinates in the Slugger. While standing outside of CINCUNK's headquarters, he pulled up the bearing and precise distance to each North Korean target in the database. General Nutting was unimpressed, asserting that soldiers were very proficient in land navigation with maps. However, he asked if the Eighth Army (his US Command) could borrow twenty Sluggers during the next Ulchi-Focus Lens exercise just to try them out. Ulchi Focus Lens is a large-scale South Korean and United States annual exercise.

General Kim, chief of the ROKAF, hosted a dinner in our honor at a swank Seoul hotel. Sheila and I stayed at the hotel that night, so it would be convenient to meet up with General Kim and his wife early the following morning for about a one-hour helicopter flight to the ROK Air Force Academy. The ROK Academy was nestled in a mountainous rural setting much like our own US Air Force Academy north of Colorado Springs, Colorado. While I was speaking to the Korean cadets, Mrs. Kim took Sheila to visit a nearby village.

Speaking through a translator is always difficult for me because the translation pause always puts me off the rhythm that I'm used to for any given briefing. All the stops and restarts make it rather jerky. Moreover, it takes about twice the usual amount of time. As I recall, following the briefing, there were some really thoughtful questions on the capability of satellites to support war fighting in real time.

When there were no more questions from the academy cadets, General Kim and I rejoined our wives for the helicopter ride back to Seoul. Unfortunately, low clouds had moved in, making it difficult for the pilots to find a clear visual path through the mountainous terrain. After about twenty minutes of nail biting flying under the clouds through narrow canyons, General Kim directed that they land at a nearby airfield where we could climb aboard a ROKAF C-130 and fly in the weather (IFR) to Seoul. The helicopter parked a short walk to the waiting C-130, and we were soon airborne again, flying in the clouds at about twenty thousand feet. The C-130 was configured for troop transport; hence, we were sitting in red canvas sling seats along the length of the fuselage facing each other. There were about twelve passengers total in the aircraft.

Without warning, there was a blinding flash and what sounded like a large explosion in the cargo bay aft of the flight deck. When my eyes recovered, I could see a large black pockmark in the cargo bay floor just aft of the bulkhead separating us from the flight deck. Above that black scar, there was a half-dozen cargo tie-down chains dangling from a horizontal bar. The plane had been struck by lightning, and the path through the aircraft chosen by the electrical charge went from the dangling chains to the metal floor of the cargo bay. The explosion and flash was the result of that lightning strike jumping a six-inch air gap. Some of the passengers were on the floor, praying; Sheila was shouting at me, "Are we OK? Are we going to crash?"

Wanting to say something simple to reassure her, I said very calmly, "All four engines are still running, and we're still in level flight—everything will be just fine." Sitting across from me, General Kim was on a headset with boom mike talking to the flight crew, so I concluded that everything was OK in the cockpit. We landed at Seoul with everyone visibly relieved that we were safely on the ground. General Kim started to apologize for the lightning strike, but I cut him short, saying that I was extremely proud of the ROKAF flight crew professionalism that we had the privilege of flying with. He reacted to my words like a heavy burden was lifted from his shoulders. Later that evening, Sheila said she was happy that we would be flying the rest of the trip in our KC-135, above the clouds instead of in them.

The following night, I visited an optical tracking site on a mountaintop in South Korea known as GEODSS. Optical space tracking telescopes can only track satellites late at night under a clear dark sky, so I arrived at 2000 hours and stayed until 0200 hours. The visit was very instructive with the crew teaching me how to generate a satellite track with an optical telescope. Separating out the stars from satellites was easy because all the stars appear to move opposite the earth's rotation, whereas satellites travel in different paths relative to the stars. I was pleased to find the site workforce very professional and dedicated to the important task of developing accurate ephemeris data on satellites operated by potentially hostile states. Their professional approach and work ethic is not necessarily found in teams that work late at night with minimal or no supervision.

Before we left Korea, General Nutting, CINCUNK, made arrangements for the general officers traveling with me and Sheila to visit the demilitarized zone (DMZ) between North and South Korea. It was several hundred yards across at the point we were standing looking across a vast open space into North Korea, looking at North Korean Soldiers who were studying us through their field glasses. Sheila, always one for detail, noted that some of the North Korean soldiers appeared to be loading their rifles. As a second lieutenant, I had seen the DMZ many times from the vantage point of an RB-26 flying just along the edge of the DMZ locating and fingerprinting their air defense radar systems positioned just north of the demarcation line. It looked a lot less foreboding from the ground.

There was a program called TENCAP, which stood for Tactical Exploitation of National Capabilities. The idea was to take data from highly classified national satellites and provide a capability to forces in the field or at sea that was very useful as long as the users could not deduce the source, thus protecting the deep black source. It was the spring of 1989, and a dozen or so space and satellite savvy soldiers, sailors, and airman were briefing me on potential TENCAP Projects. From this list, we would select up to three that USSPACECOM could showcase when it was our turn to put on TENCAP demonstrations to other Unified and Specified (U & S) Commands in 1992. These demonstrations were called "Power Hunter." Sponsorship for these TENCAP demonstrations rotated among the U & S Commands. On the list were the usual good ideas that would make war fighting a little less opaque for the warfighter—something all senior military commanders try to achieve! My ultimate goal, in this regard, was to enable the war fighter to task satellites directly and then have the data collected sent to a terminal in their geographical area immediately available to the combatant commander and his/her forces.

One project on the list of topics to be presented and pruned down to three was "DSP Theater Missile Tracks Direct to PAC II Batteries," which seemed out of place. So I asked, "Why would we want to send missile tracks to patriot batteries?"

The answer was "Sir, the army has modified the PAC II with a ballistic missile shoot-down capability. Getting an early queue with DSP generated tracks would greatly extend the engagement range of the PAC II against Scud missiles. This would enable the crew to narrow their search volume and acquire the incoming missile at longer ranges."

I apologized for my ignorance on the PAC II and asked, "If that is the case, why should we wait until 1992 to make this happen, and where is the PAC II Battery you want to ship DSP data to?" The reply suggested a recently deployed PAC II to West Germany should be the recipient based on the Warsaw Pact's arsenal of Scud missiles. After some discussion, we selected topics for USSPACECOM's future Power Hunter Demonstration, but also made the DSP to PAC II an immediate high-priority requirement.

DSP satellite data processed at ground stations could usually produce a threat missile track fifteen seconds after missile motor burnout, and our goal was to get the data to the PAC II 150 seconds after a missile track was produced. The enhanced Scud had a time of flight from launch to impact of about seven minutes. Thus, receiving a DSP track would give PAC II operators about a two-or three-minute advantage over their organic search radar. In our test of this concept, threat tracks were stripped off at a DSP ground processing site, reformatted, and shipped over a Navy Intelligence Communications link that had global reach. In July 1989, the project was confirmed as an operational success. The time achieved was slightly shorter than the established goal. I was very pleased that the operators and staff had been able to pull this all together and create a real operational advantage for Army Air and Missile Defenders in the EUCOM AOR. Now we needed to make this an operational reality on a global scale.

I called Lieutenant General Kutyna, commander Air Force Space Command, and directed that he take the demo capability and make it a real, reliable, 24/7/365 operational capability. He pushed back, saying that the air force was concerned that the "tap" on the DSP ground processing site might contaminate the data and impact our strategic missile warning capability. Further, they didn't like the idea of DSP data going to the field without being vetted through the Missile Warning Center in the CMCC. I countered his arguments, saying this was theater data; the PAC II could not engage a threat missile until it's organic radar had the Scud threat missile in track, which was a second phenomenology validating the track. I also pointed out that "diodes" had, for decades, proved that they limit electron flow to one direction. He could put one or more diodes in series to ensure there would not be a reverse flow of electrons corrupting DSP data.

General Kutyna wasn't budging and had the weight of the air force and NRO behind him, so I chose an alternate approach. I sent letters to the commanders of Army and Navy Space Commands, the other service components of USSPACECOM, and offered them the opportunity to operationalize shipping DSP Track Data to PAC II and any other service missile engagement capability. Both Army and Navy Space Commands came back with a positive "We want to do this" response. I sent their responses over the AFSPACECOM, asking which service he preferred to work with. As suspected, Air Force Space Command saw the light and requested that they be allowed to take on the project as the data came from one of their assets. It was agreed that AFSPACECOM would have lead on the project, with the navy helping with the TRAP/ TRE Communications Link and the army with the interfaces at the PAC II Missile Minder communications van. I requested that Lieutenant General Kutyna complete the project prior to my retirement on April 1, 1990. It was important that this get done, as there were other missile engagement systems in development, and they would all benefit from space derived queuing! Regrettably, it didn't happen; and when Desert Storm kicked off on January 16, 1991, the DSP direct to Patriot Battery capability didn't exist. The commander USSPACECOM was relegated to using the SPOC to plot the DSP derived launch and projected impact points in GeoRef coordinates and telephone them by voice to CENTCOM's Command Center in Tampa, Florida, to be relayed by voice to CENTCOM Forward in Riyadh, Saudi Arabia. It is doubtful the data shipped by voice over a double relay would arrive at a PAC II uncorrupted and in time to be operationally useful.

Gen. Colin L. Powell was promoted to general and assigned as commander of Forces Command, an Army Specified Command located at Fort McPherson, Georgia. Forces Command was a lot like the Air Force's Tactical Air Command, responsible for ensuring the training and readiness of army corps, divisions, and brigades and serving as a "force provider" for the army components of geographical Unified Commands. General Powell and I met at least once as he passed through Peterson AFB on a refueling stop as he traveled across the United States to visit his subordinate commands. The mission we shared in common was drug interdiction, and we also shared the same passion to do as much as possible to reduce the flow of illegal drugs in the United States. I shared with him our successful reconnaissance of the southern border and the effectiveness of the NORAD Drug Interdiction Center (NORDIC). General Powell stayed at the helm of FORCECOM for six months when he was appointed by President Bush to replace Admiral Crowe as chairman of the Joint Chiefs of Staff.

Sec. Dick Cheney visited NORAD and USSPACECOM the day after General Powell's appointment was announced. The secretary and I went to visit the CMCC, where I planned to show him the Missile Warning Center, Command Center, and brief him on our ability to carry out the Unified Command Plan (UCP) direction to "prepare to deploy Ballistic Missile Defenses." First, we had breakfast in Cheyenne Mountain. The dining facility had been remodeled, and the food was excellent. It is imperative that healthy and appetizing food be served to all military personnel, but especially those who spend twelve hours deep inside a cavernous mountain fortress.

As we sat down to eat, I congratulated Secretary Cheney on selecting General Powell for the CJCS position and opined that even though he was the most junior of the serving four-stars, all of his contemporaries held him in the highest regard and would support him. With that said, the secretary turned toward me and offered, "Pete, he wasn't my choice! I had prepared a folder with my recommendation and sent it to President Bush. I received a note from the President's chief of staff, Mr. John S. Sununu, saying that the president wanted Colin Powell as the CJCS instead of the person I initially recommended." Secretary Cheney went on to say that he put another note on the folder, saying that his plan for General Powell was to send him to Korea as CINCUNK and commander Eighth Army where he could get Unified Command and Army Command experience for two years and then appoint him to the CJCS position.

Mr. Sununu sent the folder back, saying, "President Bush wants him now—why should he have to wait?"

Secretary Cheney then said, "I made another folder with General Powell's records in it and sent it to the White House."

I looked the secretary in the eye and said, "Mr. Secretary, you were absolutely right both times!" He laughed, and we had an enjoyable breakfast and morning. The secretary was pleased with the research we had done on the ICBM/SLBM threat from the Soviet Union. The data showed we would have sufficient data to recognize an attack without fail in sixty-five seconds and be able to engage the Soviet SS-18s, with Brilliant Pebbles, long before missile motors burned out and their multiple warheads deployed. The Soviet SS-18 was the primary target for BPs because they carried ten high-yield independently targeted RVs that could be spread across the half the United States from a single SS-18 Booster.

Shortly after Secretary Cheney's visit, an invitation arrived to attend a dinner at the White House honoring Admiral Crowe's service to the nation on the eve of his retirement. All serving four star generals and admirals along with senior members of OSD were in attendance. It was a grand affair and both Sheila and I enjoyed talking with President and Barbara Bush that evening. Evidently the President knew a lot about the private lives of his senior officers, as he sought my advice on how to rig a 6 weight fly rod he had just acquired.

Gen. Edwin H. Burba, a severely wounded and highly decorated veteran of the Vietnam War, succeeded General Powell at Forces Command. And shortly after, General Powell assumed his JCS duties, he put out a request for combatant commanders in the United States to volunteer to establish a Counter Drug Command Center. I responded with a reminder to the chairman JCS that NORAD already had an up and running NORDIC that was working 24/7 to reduce the flow of illegal drugs into the United States. In this regard, it was suggested that NORAD could easily expand its role to support other commands involved in drug interdiction. About a week later, we received notification that Forces Command was selected to stand up a Drug Interdiction Center that would be the lead for all combatant commands supporting DOD's Drug Interdiction Program. I suspected that General Powell was just trying to provide a real combat mission for his former command. That aside, I called General Burba, congratulated him on his new mission, and offered my full support for anything he might need from NORAD.

A few weeks later, at approximately 1400 hours, the NORDIC duty officer came to my office with an eyes-only message from a DEA officer operating in Mexico forwarded through Forces Command Drug Interdiction Center. The message warned of a large movement of cocaine from northern Mexico into Texas by aircraft expected to cross the border just prior to daylight, or approximately 0600 hours, at the crossing point. I looked at the date of the message, and it was from the previous evening with the flight expected to take place about eight hours ago. Why we were informed of the flight so late in the day puzzled me, angered me. A large shipment of cocaine was dumped in our lap, and somehow it was fumbled. I called General Burba to alert him of the delay coming out of his Drug Interdiction Center when I explained that we had received the drug flight alert eight hours after the fact and therefore missed the opportunity to put up an AWACS to detect and track the smuggler. The AWACS would have detected the border crossing and then put F-16s on the intruder until a Customs aircraft could join the pursuit, or alerted local law enforcement that an airborne shipment of drugs was landing at a set of coordinates in their jurisdiction. He said he would get back with me. When he called back, he informed me that their procedure was to *first* vet the data by fusing it with other information to determine its validity, and that fusing data sometimes caused delays. In turn, I related that my experience with the DEA is that their agents were infallible when it came to drug movement tip-offs. Moreover, I suggested that if Forces Command wanted to fuse data, that was fine with me, as long as they immediately forwarded the raw data to the NORDIC. If I deemed that air support was appropriate based on a single source of information, I would make that decision. It was noted that an AWACS would have been some 225 miles away from the border crossing point and thirty-five thousand feet above the ground. It was not like a cheap detective story stakeout where we had cars parked along the border that could alert the smugglers. From that moment going forward, NORAD received the DEA alerts without delay.

It was important to visit NORAD and USSPACECOM overseas locations at least twice a year, which meant a swing through Europe and the Pacific every six months. These were short visits lasting a week in Europe and ten days in the Pacific because of the greater distance between locations. My personal rule was that I conducted visits seven days a week, no Saturdays or Sundays playing golf or lying on a sandy beach. There was always a command post, radar site, or optical site that operated 24/7 that warranted a visit. It was always easy to tell those sites that had few or no visitors. On one such visit in November 1989, Sheila and I were in West Berlin. I was visiting intelligence collection sites alongside the Iron Curtain and behind the Berlin Wall. Sheila was meeting with military wives so she could help me understand their problems and suggest where I could better their situation. The night of our arrival, we relaxed in an opulent house converted into VIP visitors' lodging. It was previously lived in by Herman Goring, one of Hitler's henchmen during WW II. As we watched the news on TV, we learned that five thousand demonstrators assembled in the streets of Dresden, East Germany, and the Stasi Police only stood by and observed the people in the streets! It was obvious to me that this might be the beginning of the end to the Soviet hold on East Germany.

The next morning, the Berlin Garrison commander, a US Army major general, gave our team an intelligence briefing on the situation in Berlin and on their intelligence collection capabilities. I asked if he had a plan that detailed the steps his command would take in the reunification of Germany. He said there currently wasn't such a plan, but that they were thinking about writing one. I suggested he get his team together that night and write one because events were moving in that direction and moving fast! Actually, I was dumbfounded by the fact they did not have such a contingency plan that was written a decade or so ago and only needed to be updated. That night, fifty thousand demonstrators took to the streets in Dresden, and the Stasi didn't intervene. Within a matter of weeks, the wall came down! East and West Germany were being reunited—President Reagan won!

Every morning without fail, there was a stack of message traffic waiting to be read. The one on top got my immediate attention. Chairman Powell was informing me that Congressman Les Aspin had visited the Soviet Union for twelve days in August 1989 where he had to opportunity to climb down into a Soviet nuclear submarine and visit one of their ICBM sites among other things. As Congressman Aspin was departing the Soviet Union, he extended invitations to his hosts to visit military facilities in the United States. As chairman of the House Armed Services Committee, I suppose it was within his authority to extend the invitation. His offer was immediately accepted, and one of the top spots to visit on the Soviet list was NORAD's Command Center in Cheyenne Mountain. About a dozen Soviet military officers would arrive on February 7, 1990, for an eleven-day visit. There were no accompanying instructions with regard to what they could see or what I could or should tell them.

The next day, I was on the phone with General Herres, asking if he or the chairman had any guidance on the visit. The response was surprising:

"No guidance, just show them what you think is appropriate." That was strange and unexpected! If I was going to speak to the local chamber of commerce in Colorado Springs, I was required to submit the full text of my speech to OSD Public Affairs for approval thirty days in advance of the event. In due time, I would receive a copy of my speech red lined on things they didn't want me to say with suggestions for things to include that OSD wanted me to say. But when the "evil empire" or at least a dozen representatives thereof were coming to town, there's no guidance? I called Deputy Secretary of Defense Taft and asked if he had any guidance on what to show to and say to our Soviet guests. The response was pithy: "Whatever you think is appropriate is OK with me!" On the positive side, it was reassuring to have the confidence of your superiors.

It was time to put the feet up on the desk, lean back, and ponder about what might best serve the United States and that would give the Soviets pause. What seemed appropriate to me was to convince the Soviet delegation that the Soviet Union could not launch a ballistic missile from anywhere on the planet that we would not detect, identify, and track. And that we would know very quickly where the missile was launched from as well as it's intended impact point. I would also show them a compilation of the last year's launches to substantiate that our missile warning crews were assimilating a lot of real-world experience as a result of the Iran/Iraq War and missile testing in China, the Soviet Union, and third-world countries. I believed that would convince them they could not launch an attack without our immediate detection and recognition of the nature of the attack. Imparting this knowledge to our potential Soviet adversaries would most likely reduce adventurism on their part while improving our deterrent credibility.

In addition, the briefing charts would be in Russian, so they wouldn't miss a word, or more importantly, the meaning of a word. The Mission Impossible Team and I set about crafting the briefing, and the J-2 was tasked to find two fluent Russian writers and speakers. Once the briefing was committed to memory in English, all the words on the charts were converted to Russian, not English and Russian, just Russian. I would give the opening remarks in Russian, memorizing a few phrases. The briefing would be given in English, while pointing to the Russian words and phrases. We had one of the Russian speakers convert the briefing to Russian and brought in the second as a quality check. After they quibbled over a couple of phrases, we were ready to go. It was likely there would be at least one KGB agent fluent in English in the group that would keep me from providing false and misleading information by saying something in English that was different than the Russian words on the charts.

Our Soviet guests arrived in the late evening by air force jet, were met by Admiral Hernandez, the new vice commander USSPACECOM, and me, and then were taken to rooms on base for convenience. Four staff cars picked them up in the morning and brought them to the officers' club for breakfast hosted by me. By this moment in time, Motorola had developed a cell phone that the DOD authorized for senior commanders. It replaced the radiophone I had lugged around for years, affectionately referred to as the "brick" because it was about the same size, shape, and heft of a brick used in home construction. The cell phone was considerably smaller and lighter but still gigantic compared to the iPods and Droids available in 2012. As we were seated around the breakfast table, enjoying a robust breakfast by my standards, the command post called to let me know that everything was ready for the visit to the CMCC. When I put the phone down, one of the guests asked if it was a secret device for combat commanders. When I responded that it was a commercial phone that anyone with $4,500could buy, they seemed astounded. The same gentleman asked if he could make a phone call, so I wrote down my home phone number and handed him the phone. He dialed it, and my wife answered the phone. The conversation was interesting from our side; I'm sure Sheila was somewhat confused on the other end.

The easiest way to Cheyenne Mountain was to take Interstate 25 that ran alongside of a commercial enterprise called Motor City, where at that point in time, all the new car dealerships in Colorado Springs were located along about a two-mile stretch of side road. The senior Soviet guest asked how much a new car cost and how long it would take to get delivery. I related that my daughter had recently purchased a new car and that she made a $500 down payment and drove the car home as soon as the paperwork was completed, which took a couple of hours. The remainder of the cost would be paid in monthly installments over three years. After three clarifications of my answer to their car purchase question, our Soviet guests still didn't believe the answer and asked if they could stop at one of the dealerships. I took the next off ramp and drove through Motor City. As we approached the first two dealerships, one on either side of the street, I said, "I will drive to the other end and back. After I turn around at the other end, pick the dealership you would like to visit, and I'll stop there." I forgot what dealership they selected, but I think it was Red Nolan's Cadillac Store. I suspected they were familiar with the luxury cars of America. The conversation between the salesman and the general was instructive. It was clear that the general couldn't accept the fact that any one of a hundred or so cars on the lot could be purchased immediately for about $1,500 down and driven off the lot if the buyer had good credit and a current driver's license. They so disbelieved what they saw and heard that I offered to stop at another car dealership of their choice. It was a repeat performance. I should have taken them to a supermarket grocery store. It would have really blown their minds! I learned subsequently on a visit to Moscow in 1992 that a Soviet grocery store was about twenty feet long and ten feet wide and contained a few canned goods, a few pieces of meat, some potatoes and cabbage, a few fresh fish, and a little more!

When we arrived at the Cheyenne Mountain Visitors Briefing Center, it was show time. I welcomed them in Russian along with the first briefing slide in Russian. After two charts in the Russian language, with me speaking in English, one of the Russians asked, "Are you fluent in Russian?"

My response was a solid "No, but I know my responsibilities, and I'm fluent with this briefing!" Everything went along smoothly until I brought up the chart on DSP Satellite Performance, indicating that the DSP could detect a missile launch anywhere on the globe in approximately 29.9 seconds. Again, one of our Russian guests stood up and said I was wrong because an authoritative source in Washington DC told them the detection time took only ten seconds. Obviously, someone in Washington DC didn't know what he or she was talking about or wanted to make the Soviets believe that the DSP performed better than it actually could. Or perhaps the "authoritative source" just misspoke because there was a ten-second component to the correct answer. It may have been just a ruse, as I never checked on what the Soviet delegation was told in Washington. I paused a few seconds while considering that the Soviets most assuredly had observed the DSP in orbit and knew that it was a rotating satellite; this was easily apparent, as the sun glinted off of the solar panels extended normally to the satellite's large cylindrical main body. They would know the rotational velocity as well because it was easy to time the rotation when the satellite was in the "terminator" with an 80 power or better resolution telescope. Hence, I decided to give them a tutorial on the DSP so that they would know that I knew our US Space Systems and that what I said about NORAD's ability to absolutely detect their missile launches anytime and anywhere on the globe was based on solid science embodied in the DSP.

The tutorial went something like this. The DSP Missile Warning Satellite is a rotating satellite with an arm covered with thousands of IR sensors (pixels) that can detect very low levels of IR sources on the earth. The DSP and sensor arm rotates 360 degrees every ten seconds, or six times a minute. Thus, if it just misses a missile motor ignition, it would see the motor burning at just under ten seconds later on the next rotation. Perhaps that is where the ten-second number came from. However, as some of you will know, it takes three detections of the same IR source travelling in an absolutely straight line with increasing distances between the first, second, and third points to determine that a missile launch is taking place. The increasing separation between the three IR points indicates acceleration and the acceleration rate of the missile being tracked. The IR sensors on the rotating paddle will also collect the IR intensity of each detection point indicating the type of missile that is being tracked. Once a track is calculated, the trajectory is reversed back to the earth's surface to determine the launch point with considerable accuracy. Last, missile motor burnout is determined when the DSP IR detectors no longer see the missile motor's IR signature. Again, the ten-second rotational period causes some inaccuracy in the actual burnout velocity on the missile. Hence, there is some uncertainty in the predicted impact point; however, it is sufficiently accurate to determine whether the missile will impact in eastern Kamchatka or western Alaska. Moreover, our ground-based missile warning radar in Shemya, Western Alaska, Central US, Greenland, and England will provide precision impact points in approximately nine minutes from launch, or twenty minutes from impact. There were a few questions after my tutorial, but it was evident to the NORAD staff present at the briefing that we achieved our objective and that our Soviet guests were convinced we knew what we were talking about.

It was a routine trip to Canada in the winter of 1989 to visit with the chief of the Canadian Defense Staff and the commander of the Canadian Air Command. Since I was going to Ottawa, it seemed appropriate to advise the US ambassador to Canada, Ambassador Edward N. Ney, of my travels.

Ambassador Ney, in turn, invited me to have breakfast with him in his quarters prior to starting my official visits at the Canadian Defense Ministry. He seemed to be a very nice gentleman who immensely enjoyed his work in the Diplomatic Service. Wanting to put the ball in his court and get him to do all the talking, I asked him who would be the most influential member of Pres. George H. Walker Bush's cabinet. Would it be Secretary of State James Baker, Secretary of Defense Dick Cheney, or his chief of staff, Mr. John Sununu? The ambassador chuckled and said, "Pete, none of those you named are or will be the most influential advisors to President Bush."

"Well, if not them, who can it be?" I asked.

In response, Ambassador Ney said, "It is Brent Scowcroft, the president's National Security advisor! He has immediate unfettered access to the president with an office in the White House, always travels with the president, and is the most convenient person for the president to turn to for advice when a crisis erupts." When I heard that, I was glad that I had worked closely and responsively with Lieutenant General Scowcroft (ret.) on the F-111 problems associated with the El Dorado Canyon punitive raid on Libya. It would not be a good thing for him to have a poor image of the air force and its leadership in his current position.

It was February 1990 when two members of Secretary Cheney's inner staff visited to talk about how USSPACECOM was progressing toward deployment of a BMD capability. I assured them that the command was leaning forward and that we were up on the latest technical developments coming out of Lawrence Livermore Laboratory with regard to Brilliant Eyes and Brilliant Pebbles. Then I gave them a briefing on the time sequence of events from the detection of multiple land- or sea-based Soviet missiles to the release of Brilliant Pebbles to engage Soviet SS-18 missiles, each carrying ten independently targeted reentry vehicles. After some lengthy discussion, they asked me if I would agree to serve another year beyond my mandatory retirement of April 1, 1990. My answer was "Yes, but why?" Their response was flattering. It seemed that they thought I had great credibility with the Congress, that I was the only one that saw a credible path to defending the nation against ballistic missile attacks, and the coming year was critical in moving BMD Programs forward. I suggested that the air force had likely already picked my successor and that they underestimated the capabilities of my fellow general officers. Again, they asked if I would serve another year! Yes was the answer, but I added that General Welch, CSAF, will not be an easy sell because he has to carefully manage his general officers, and he's planning that I will retire on schedule at the end of thirty-five years commissioned service, the policy at that time. A week later, the call came that Secretary Cheney would not entertain the idea of a year extension. The secretary argued that the sitting Congress had passed a significant pay raise for them that also raised four-star pay about an additional $25,000 annually. This pay raise could not take effect until after the next Congress took their seats in early 1991. If extended one year, I would benefit from that pay raise, while others with retirements in 1990 would not. Secretary Cheney said that he would not choose among his generals, extending one but not the others. Secretary Cheney was exactly right on the issue with impeccable logic.

There was one thing that continued to perplex me, and that was the lack of guidance or direction from OSD, or anyone else for that matter, on the Counter Drug Mission. There was a need to do something at my level if no one above gave a damn. So I grabbed the ball and ran with it! I sent invitations to all the senior officers and civilians that should have been involved in the War on Drugs. This included

CINCPAC: Adm. Hunt Hardisty, USN
CINCSOUTH: Gen. Max Thurman, USA
CINCFORCECOM: Gen. Edwin Burba, USA
CINCLANT: Adm. Frank Kelso, USN
JCS-J3: Lt. Gen. Thomas W. Kelly, USA
Commandant US Coast Guard: Adm. Paul Yost Jr., USCG
Customs Department
Border Patrol
DEA

The director of every agency came except for the Border Patrol, who sent their deputy. The format for the meeting was very straightforward. Each attendee, including myself, would have twenty minutes to present a briefing on what they were doing in the War on Drugs and what assistance they needed from the others in attendance. I made sure the conference room had all the proper name tags and were placed according to protocol. The meeting was scheduled for Tuesday, allowing Monday for travel; breakfast would be served at 7:30 a.m. in the conference room and lunch at noon following the briefings. We would conclude not later than 3:00 p.m. to accommodate return travel arrangements.

At 6:00 a.m., on Tuesday, I went to the office to check the arrangements and dry run my briefing one last time. My executive officer and a couple of members of the Mission Impossible Team were already in place, getting ready to greet our guests. Only one problem: the conference room was locked, and no one had a key to get in. It appeared that one of the enlisted staff took a key with him when he left late the night prior, and someone left the other key in the conference room when the door was closed and locked automatically. It was a top secret code word—cleared conference room, so it wasn't easy to break into. I had the exec call the director of intelligence in to prepare his conference room as a backup and also call the headquarters first sergeant to hunt down the enlisted member of the support staff who took off with the backup key. Then I personally called the Fire Department and chief of civil engineers, as both those agencies were alleged to have master keys for every door on base. The Fire Department showed up in about fifteen minutes with a master key and opened the executive conference room door at about 6:45 a.m.—what a relief that was.

The meeting went extremely well. All the briefings revealed that each military command and federal agencies were really leaning forward in a mission we all believed in and were having some successes. When the briefings were finished, all of us in the military commands had a new appreciation of the impressive work being done by our Coast Guard, Customs, DEA, and local law agency counterparts. It was also clear to all that General Thurman at SOUTHCOM not only could make the biggest impact on the airborne and seaborne flow of illegal drugs but also had the least resources. As a result, CINCPAC agreed to "chop" an Aegis Destroyer to support coverage of both air and sea lanes of SOUTHCOM, and I agreed to put one of NORADs E-3As at his disposal at Howard AFB, in the Panama Canal Zone. We also learned that the civilian agencies were reluctant to ask for our help in the fear that their budgets would be cut if the media and Congress learned they were receiving routine support from the US military. As an aside, the dollars that NORAD (First Air Force) received for jet fuel for our fighter interceptor training and operations dwarfed the budgets of DEA and Border Patrol combined by a factor of ten or more. All of the military commands assured our civilian counterparts in the War on Drugs that our support to them would never get in the media; we would be willing and silent supporters!

It was a very productive meeting, and we all parted with a firm commitment to do more. Lieutenant General Kelly said it was the most productive day he'd spent in years and promised to sponsor a similar meeting every six months. Unfortunately, the Invasion of Kuwait on August 1, 1990, and the US focus on the Middle East for the next decade or so took precedence, and there was never a follow-on meeting in support of the War on Drugs. You will remember Lieutenant General Kelly as the gruff JCS briefer for forty-two days on how Desert Storm was progressing once the fighting started.

Before long, the time allotted for me to serve our country had run out. At that time, thirty-five years of commissioned service was all that was allowed by custom for the United States Army and the United States Air Force. The United States Navy operated under different rules established by the Congress. My enlisted service and commissioned service prior to age twenty-one didn't count against the cap, so I was able to serve thirty-seven years and eight months before mandatory retirement.

It was difficult to find a date when all the principals required for a binational and Unified Command change of command. Schedules finally got sorted out for CJCS Gen. Colin Powell, chief of the Canadian Defense Staff, Gen. John de Chastelain, and CSAF Gen. Larry Welch. It was a miserable day in March with a late winter covering the area in fog and drizzle. Fortunately, one of the aircraft hangars was suitable and could handle the large crowd of American and Canadian forces personnel and their families. Regrettably, the weather could not support a flyby for a fighter pilot of thirty-two years and over seven thousand flying hours in thirty-five different aircraft. Prior to retirement, I was still flying the F-106 and F-4 with Air Defense Squadrons, as well as the KC-135, C-21, and Gulfstream. My last flight was flying a C-21 roughly a week prior to retirement.

The USSPACECOM Colors were exchanged with General Powel and General Kutyna, then the NORAD Colors with General de Chastelain and General Kutyna. Gen. Larry Welch, a good friend, read the retirement order, and I was once again a civilian. My thoughts were mostly with and of my wife, Sheila, of twenty-nine years, with twenty-six moves, and living in three foreign countries while raising three children. She was always supportive, a gracious hostess, and a pillar of strength when I was sent on extended missions away from home, often without the ability to stay in touch. As the song goes, "She was the wind beneath my wings . . ." and still is after fifty-one years of marriage.

General Kutyna took the commands to new heights, and we remain friends!

Lesson Learned

Know the business of your business better than your competition. In NORAD and USSPACECOM, our competition was the Soviet Union.

If you're new to the business/mission, burn the midnight oil and immerse yourself in learning it, top to bottom and end to end. Learning is continuous!

The more you know about the business of your enterprise, the more your staff will be forced to learn!

No matter how large or small the enterprise, have a vision for taking it to the next level and beyond! Think boldly! Then motivate your personnel to that end!

Leadership makes the difference! Hands-on, walkabout, and motivational leadership is the key!

Pick your subordinates with care and appropriate review. It is at the lower levels of any organization where battles are fought or revenues are generated. You need great leaders at every level to prevail!

Go where your people are! No enterprise can be run from the executive suite! You'll be amazed at what you find and how many people say that you're the first senior officer/person to visit in years! If you hear this, it speaks volumes about lack of involvement on the part of your subordinates.

When you find a personnel problem in the higher echelons of your organization, you are likely the last to know. Take appropriate and swift action, your loyalty should be to all the others who are working hard to better the enterprise.

Set high standards for yourself and your organization; if you don't, the quality will slide all the way to the lowest level in the enterprise.

You can delegate authority, but you cannot delegate responsibility.

To effectively lead and manage any large and far-flung enterprise, you need to look at data that will reveal if there are problems that require your attention. You need to develop the instincts of what are the critical activities and what are the revealing indicators, and look at the trends weekly and monthly.

Always have the courage to do and stand for what is right!

Gen. Pete with Gen. Paul Manson Chief Canadian Defense Staff,
Canadian Prime Minister Mulroney, & Canadian Defense Minister
Perrin Beatty. Ottawa, Canada

Gen. Vono, Chief of Staff U.S. Army & Gen. Pete activate
Army Space Command. Colorado Springs, CO

Gen. Pete briefs Vice President Quayle on Missile Warning in
Cheyenne Mountain Command Center. Colorado Springs, CO

Gen. & Mrs. Pete arrive Thule AB, Greenland to host Her Majesty,
Queen Margretha II & HRH, Prince Henrik of Denmark.

Gen. & Mrs. Pete on the eve of his retirement Peterson AFB, CO

Gen. Pete retires. Officiating are Gen. DeChastalain Chief Canadian
Defense Staff, Gen. Colin Powell Chief Joint Staff, and Gen. Larry
Welch, Air Force Chief of Staff.

Furling Gen. Pete's flag, signifying the end of his military service.

Dinner at the White House honoring Admiral Crowe

LESSONS IN LEADERSHIP AND LIFE SUMMARY

(Learned over 38 years of service including 8 commands
and 15 years as a General)

The formal record of your life begins in kindergarten.

Upon graduation from High School, your only life record is your grades which speak to your ability, willingness to study, hard work, and commitment.

Life is a continuum of learning. Recognize this early in life, rather than later.

Higher education is essential in the professions. Avail yourself of every opportunity.

Never give up on your dreams.

When opportunity knocks, don't hesitate! Jump through that door with all your energy, grit, and determination. Keep driving until you succeed.

It is always hard work, not luck that carries the day and wins the prize. Original comment by Thomas Jefferson, "I'm a great believer in luck, and I find the harder I work the more I have of it."

Work assignments are often a team effort, be a team player.

Leaders support their team.

There is nothing so rewarding as creating a team effort in pursuing a worthy goal.

Always be willing to meet with subordinates to clarify tasking.

Always be true to your moral compass.

Have the courage to do what is right.

Don't be bullied or intimidated by higher ranking individuals from doing what is right.

Always do your best in everything you do, and try to be the best in your field.

Approach every task and assignment with enthusiasm, energy, and commitment.

Volunteer for the tough and unpopular jobs/assignments. It will be noticed and appreciated.

Long hours never hurt anyone, but rather helped them advance.

Learn all you can about the areas you are responsible for. Manage the critical aspects above all others.

Know the business of your business and you will earn the respect of your subordinates.

Go where the action is and learn firsthand what is going on in your enterprise.

Challenges are to be met not avoided.

Never pass up an opportunity to improve something that is easy to do.

Most people have more ability and grit than they know, until challenged.

The crucible of life and combat tempers our steel challenge upon challenge.

Higher headquarters exist to support subordinate units in the field where revenue is generated and battles are won

Promotions and advancements lead to new and bigger responsibilities. It takes really hard work to learn the new job quickly enough. Make a personal assessment to identify what you don't know and then learn the critical aspects of the new job.

When moving to a new organization, immediately calibrate your subordinates' abilities and mentor where necessary.

Never, ever speak poorly of your predecessor; it only makes you look small. Just set new goals and standards and move forward.

Have a vision for your organization and develop a plan for achieving it. Ensure that everyone in the enterprise understands the overall plan and the part they play. Then execute smartly.

Always organize around the strategic purpose of an enterprise.

Culture is the most difficult characteristic of an organization to change.

Set high standards for yourself and your organization—it becomes contagious.

Always reward creativity and speedy execution of difficult tasks

Seek the counsel of subordinates who've demonstrated the rare trait of telling you the truth as they perceive it, even though it may be painful.

Publically reward and applaud good ideas whenever and wherever you find them.

No enterprise of any size can be run from the CEO's office with memos and telephone calls. Hands-on walk-about leadership is the hallmark of successful organizations.

You will never know what is happening at the lower levels of your enterprise unless you go there unannounced and without an entourage.

It is leadership that carries the day and wins wars! People are led and things are managed in any successful organization or enterprise.

When you find a personnel problem in the higher echelons of your organization you are usually the last to know and others are wondering why you tolerate it. Take swift and appropriate action to resolve the problem. Your loyalty should be to all the others who are working hard to better the enterprise.

The ultimate responsibility of leaders is the preparation of subordinate organizations to prevail in combat or in the marketplace. If a subordinate leader is inept, he/she must be replaced for the good of the enterprise.

Take care of your people and you'll have a loyal, hardworking team looking out for you.

When a crisis erupts, immediately do something that has the appearance of resolving the issue. This will buy time to resolve the issue in a less stressful environment.

Tact and comity are often more productive than a direct approach.

Determine what your boss is uncomfortable with and cover those areas like a blanket.

Addendum

Thirty-Five Different Aircraft Flown

Type Aircraft	Moniker	Recip or Jet
T-34	Mentor	Recip
T-28	Trojan	Recip
T-29	Flying Classroom	Recip Twin Engine
T-33	Shooting Star	Jet
T-38	Talon	Jet, Twin Engine
T-39	Sabreliner	Jet, Twin Engine
T-45	Goshawk	Jet, single engine
AT-28/B/C/D	Trojan	Recip
A-7	Corsair II	Jet
A-37	Dragonfly	Jet, Twin Engine
C-21	Lear	Jet, Twin Engine
C-45	Expeditor	Recip, Twin Engine
C-46	Commando	Recip, Twin Engine
C-47	Skytrain	Recip, Twin Engine
C-54	Skymaster	Recip, Four Engine
C-119	Flying Boxcar	Recip, Twin Engine
C-131	Samaritan	Recip, Twin Engine
U-3A	Blue Canoe	Recip, Twin Engine

O-1E	Bird Dog	Recip
O-2	Skymaster (reused)	Recip, Twin Engine
OV-10	Bronco	Turboprop, Twin Engine
B-26	Invader	Recip, Twin Engine
RB-26	Invader	Recip, Twin Engine
F-86F	Sabre	Jet
F-4C/D	Phantom II & Rhino	Jet, Twin Engine
RF-4C	Phantom II & Rhino	Jet, Twin Engine
F-15	Eagle	Jet, Twin Engine
F-16	Falcon & Viper	Jet
F-100F	Super Sabre	Jet
F-106	Delta Dart	Jet
CFA-18	Hornet	Jet, Twin Engine
AV-8	Harrier	Jet, STOL
KC-135	Stratotanker	Jet, Four Engine
E-3A	Sentry	Jet, Four Engine
E-3A	Mission Crew Sentry	Jet Four Engine
G-3	Gulfstream	Jet, Twin Engine

Total Flying Hours: **7,500+**

High Time Aircraft Flying Hours

AT-28	1,000+
B-26/RB-26	900
T-33	1,000+
F-86	600
F-4	1,000+
F-16	600+
F-15	300
E-3A Pilot & Mission Crew	500+

Acronyms

AAA	Antiaircraft Artillery
AAC	Alaskan Air Command
AAD	Air Assault Division
AB	Afterburner
ABCCC	Airborne Command and Control Center
AC	Aircraft commander
AD	Air Division
ACW	Air Commando Wing
ADC	Air Defense Command
ADO	Assistant Director of Operations
ADVON	Advanced or forward location
AFB	Air Force Base
AFLC	Air Force Logistics Command
AFSC	Air Force Specialty Code or Air Force Systems Command
AGL	Above Ground Level, height above local terrain
AIM	Air Intercept Missile
ARVN	Army of Vietnam (South Vietnam)
ASAP	As soon as possible
ASAT	Antisatellite
ATC	Air Training Command
ATO	Air Tasking Order
ATOL	Soviet/Russian air-to-air missile
AWACS	Airborne Warning and Control System
AUX	Auxiliary
BLU	Bomb Live Unit
BOQ	Bachelor officer's quarters
CAG	Combat Applications Group
CBS	Columbia Broadcasting System
CBU	Cluster Bomb Unit
CENTCOM	Central Command, a regional combatant command

CEP	Circular Error Probable
CHICOM	Chinese Communist
CJCS	Chairman, Joint Chiefs of Staff
CNO	Chief of Naval Operations
COIN	Counterinsurgency
CRC	Combat Reporting Center, ground radar control center
CSA	Chief of Staff of the Army
DCSOPS	Deputy Chief of Staff for Operations
DCS/Plans	Deputy Chief of Staff for Plans
DEA	Drug Enforcement Agency
DepSecDef	Deputy Secretary of Defense
DFC	Distinguished Flying Cross
DIVARTY	Division Artillery
DO	Director of Operations
DOD	Department of Defense
DSP	Defense Support Program
DT&E	Development Test and Evaluation
EO	Electro-optical
EUCOM	European Command, a regional combatant command
FAC	Forward Air Controller
FEBA	Forward edge of the battle area
FLYTAF	Flying Training Air Force
FOD	Foreign object damage
Frag	Fragment of an Air Tasking Order, applicable to a unit
FWS	Fighter Weapons School
G or Gs	Force of gravity where 6 Gs = six times pull of gravity
GCA	Ground-controlled approach, a radar-controlled approach
GD	General Dynamics
GEO	Geosynchronous orbit
GI	Government issue
GIB	Guy in back (backseater in the F-4)
GUS	Guy in the other seat

HEO	Highly elliptical orbit
IAS	Indicated airspeed, uncorrected for temperature, etc.
ICBM	Intercontinental ballistic missile
ID	Identification
IOC	Initial operational capability
IP	Instructor pilot
IR	Infrared
IRBM	Intermediate-range ballistic missile
JCS	Joint Chiefs of Staff
JROC	Joint Requirements Oversight Council
JSTARS	Joint Surveillance and Target Attack Radar System
KIO	Knock it off
LEO	Low earth orbit
MAC	Military Airlift Command
MEO	Medium earth orbit
MiG	Russian fighter aircraft design bureau
MRBM	Medium-range ballistic missile
MRE	Meals, Ready-to-Eat
MSL	Mean Sea Level, height above the ocean
NAF	Numbered Air Force
NCO	Noncommissioned officer sergeant, four-plus stripes
NMCC	National Military Command Center
NORAD	North American Aerospace Command, binational
NRO	National Reconnaissance Office
NVN	North Vietnam
OCAMA	Oklahoma City Air Material Area
OSD	Office of the Secretary of Defense
OSI	Office of Special Investigation
PACAF	Pacific Air Forces, air component of PACOM
PACOM	Pacific Command, a regional combatant command
PCS	Permanent change of duty station
PIC	Pilot in command, the pilot responsible

POW	Prisoner of war
PTO	Power takeoff (shaft)
RAT	Ram Air Turbine, emergency electrical generator
REDCOM	Readiness Command, no longer exists
RFP	Request for Proposal
RISOP	Russian Integrated Strategic Operations Plan
RSAF	Royal Saudi Air Force
RSLF	Royal Saudi Land Force
RSNF	Royal Saudi Naval Force
SAAMA	San Antonio Air Material Area
SAM	Surface-to-air missile
SAWC	Special Air Warfare Center
SCIF	Secret Compartmented Intelligence Facility
SecDef	Secretary of Defense
SOF	Special Operations Forces
SOS	Squadron Officer's School
SPOC	Space Operations Center
SRBM	Short-range ballistic missile
STRATCOM	Strategic Command, a regional combatant command
TAC	Tactical Air Command
TALC	Tactical Airlift Center
TARC	Tactical Air Reconnaissance Center
TAS	True airspeed, corrected for temperature, pressure, etc.
TAWC	Tactical Air Warfare Center
TECHTAF	Technical Training Air Force
TDY	Temporary duty, usually at another location
TFS	Tactical Fighter Squadron
TI	Tactical instructor in basic training
TWX	DOD message by wire
USAF	United States Air Force
USAFE	US Air Forces Europe, air component of EUCOM
USMTM	United States Military Training Mission

VCJCS	Vice Chairman of the Joint Chiefs of Staff
USMC	United States Marine Corps
USN	United States Navy
VC	Viet Cong
VCNO	Vice Chief of Naval Operations
VCSA	Vice Chief of Staff, Army
VCSAF	Vice Chief of Staff, Air Force
VNAF	Vietnamese Air Force (South Vietnam)
VOQ	Visiting officers' quarters
WP	White phosphorous
WSO	Weapon system operator (backseater in F-4)
WW II	World War 2
WX	Weather